The Ten Great Birth Stories of the Buddha

Carmel G.

The Ten Great Birth Stories of the Buddha

The *Mahānipāta* of the *Jātakatthavaṇṇanā*

VOLUME ONE

Translated and introduced by

Naomi Appleton and Sarah Shaw

Foreword by

Peter Skilling

Chulalongkorn University Press

Silkworm Books

Cloth ISBN: 978-616-215-112-5
Paper ISBN: 978-616-215-113-2

First published in 2015 by
Silkworm Books
6 Sukkasem Road, T. Suthep
Chiang Mai 50200 Thailand
info@silkwormbooks.com
www.silkwormbooks.com

and

Chulalongkorn University Press
Phayathai Road, Pathumwan
Bangkok 10330 Thailand
ChulaPress@chula.ac.th
www.ChulaPress.com

Typeset in Gentium Book Basic 10.5 pt. by Silk Type

Printed and bound in China

5 4 3 2 1

This book is dedicated to Her Royal Highness Princess Maha Chakri Sirindhorn of Thailand in honour of her 60th birthday anniversary on 2 April 2558/2015, and in recognition of her contributions to and steadfast support of Pāli scholarship.

Contents

Acknowledgements
ix

Note on the Illustrations
xi

Abbreviations
xv

Note on the Abbreviations
xvii

Foreword
xix

Introduction
1

1. The Birth Story of Temiya, or of the Dumb Cripple
51

2. The (Great) Birth Story of Janaka
81

3. The Birth Story of Golden Sāma
117

4. The Birth Story of Nemi
145

5. The Birth Story of Mahosadha, or of the Great Tunnel
187

Illustrations follow page 144

In Volume II

6. The Birth Story of Bhūridatta
335

7. The Birth Story of Prince Canda, or of Khaṇḍahāla
395

8. The (Great) Birth Story of Nārada (Kassapa)
423

9. The Birth Story of (Wise) Vidhura
455

10. The Birth Story of Vessantara
507

Illustrations follow page 454

Glossary
641

Bibliography
645

Index of Illustrations
655

Index
657

Acknowledgements

This book has been many years in the making. We have worked together for some years on various aspects of *jātaka*s, and to translate the last ten, considered in Southeast and South Asia the most significant, seemed a natural outcome of this. Peter Skilling has, as always, been a great source of encouragement, as has Arthid Sheravanichkul. Sarah is deeply grateful to Richard Gombrich for his inspiring classes on the *Nemi-jātaka*, the *Bhūridatta-jātaka,* and the *Vessantara-jātaka*. We are also indebted to L. S. Cousins, who read the *Nārada-jātaka* with us in the summer of 2010, and whom we often consulted. He died as we went to press, and we miss him heartily, as a true friend and teacher to us both. We take full responsibility for not 'getting' anything they were trying to teach.

Sarah would particularly like to thank Dr Rajith Dissanayake for his close reading of the forest passage in the *Vessantara-jātaka* and his many helpful comments. She would also like to thank Dr Elizabeth Moore and U Win Maung for explaining temples and pictures in Pagan, Sagaing, and Mandalay on a visit hosted by Ven. Dr Ashin Nyanissara and arranged by Ven. Dr Dhammasāmi. Ven. Dr Maha Laow has led chanting tours around Thailand, which has enabled Sarah to see *jātaka*s in various settings. We both thank Bodleian Library Publishing, Ven. Dhammika, Dr Alexandra Green, Dr Lilian Handlin, Ven. Bhatsakorn Piyobhaso, Ian Rose, Lucy Shaw, Dr Arthid Shervanichkul, and Dr Sébastien Tayac for their generosity with pictures.

We are very grateful to Silkworm Books for taking on this publication, and in particular to Trasvin Jittidecharak for her support of the project over a number of years and for all she has done to bring the project to fruition. Our editor, Joel Akins, has worked through the text with care and helped us to iron out various inconsistencies and errors.

We are both very lucky in our husbands, Anas and Charles, so lastly we would like to acknowledge their great support in helping us. May this book bring happiness to our families.

Note on the Illustrations

We are grateful to several scholars and friends who have generously shared their images with us for this publication. This is not a comprehensive survey of all kinds of Great Ten art in all periods. The pictures we have used are mostly from Myanmar and Thailand, at certain historical periods; there are other regions and historical periods that are not represented, such as in Cambodia, Sri Lanka, and ancient India, which also show individual stories from the Great Ten.

Lilian Handlin generously provided scans of her slides of the Pagan tiles, which were taken in 2004. The selection included here show sequences cladding the great *stūpa* at the eleventh- to twelfth-century Ananda temple, where Great Ten depictions involve hundreds of tiles, as opposed to the single tile per story reserved for early *jātaka*s in the *Jātakatthavaṇṇanā*. Visitors cannot see the Great Ten tiles from the ground, as the sequence of *jātaka*s starts at the base of the Great pagoda, and moves up to the Great Ten at the top, as the Bodhisatta's crowning achievement. The terracotta tile had by this stage become the standard medium for *jātaka* depiction in the region, and such tiles are found throughout temples of Pagan and, later, Mandalay, providing also a square template pattern used in linear friezes of painted murals within Burmese temples. Small differentiations in pattern and design make the overall effect of a series of tiles particularly noteworthy, and set a tendency for Burmese temple art to treat stories in a fairly systematic fashion. Evenly distributed scenes for each story demonstrate the continuity of a textual tradition too: the tiles tend to follow the events of the Pāli *jātaka*s closely. Single tile depictions are also frequent, as in the *Janaka-jātaka* depiction at the eleventh-century Anouk Hpetleik Stūpa, shown in a photograph taken by Venerable Dhammika.

Mural painting flourished in Myanmar at various periods from the eleventh century onwards. Alexandra Green has photographed and studied numerous seventeenth- and eighteenth-century murals from central Myanmar. These painted linear friezes are in the rich and colourful style, with complex patterning as decoration, which developed in temples throughout the regions she has studied. She graciously offered us a selection of depictions, some with inscriptions (which she translated for us), of each tale in this book to encompass as wide a selection of temples as possible, including some that are lesser known. This material will also contribute to her forthcoming book *Felicity, Power, and Piety: Essays on Late Burmese Wall Paintings*. Tiles also continued to be popular in Myanmar; shown in these volumes are many that were installed around the base of the Shwedagon pagoda in Yangon around 1900. Several series of Great Ten depictions, with four glazed tiles per story, appear to have been sponsored by individual patrons. The tiles are the same for each story, suggesting a commercial template had been made for their manufacture. Lucy Shaw photographed the tiles we have selected here.

We are grateful to Bodleian Library Publishing for allowing us to reproduce the *jātaka* images from the manuscript BODL MS. Pali a. 27 (R), a stunning *samut khoi* from central Thailand. These images were first published in a book the two of us wrote with Toshiya Unebe, *Illuminating the Life of the Buddha: An Illustrated Chanting Book from Eighteenth-Century Siam* (Oxford: Bodleian Library Publishing, 2013). The manuscript, made in the concertina 'folding book' style of the Siamese manuscripts of the time, presents scenes from each of the Great Ten, as well as from a single extra-canonical *jātaka* and from the final life of the Buddha, alongside texts for chanting.[1]

Such manuscript art is closely related to temple art, and we have tried to provide here a good sampling of Thai temple murals. Sébastien Tayac provided photographs of modern temple murals from Chiang Mai Province, as found in his doctoral thesis *La commande des peintures bouddhiques dans les monastères de la province de Chiang Mai*, which was submitted to the Sorbonne in 2010. His work shows a still-living tradition of Great Ten depiction in Chiang Mai in the nineteenth and twentieth centuries, often with stock scenes representing each story. Within this general pattern, however, there is still scope for artistry and experimentation, and some artists even depart from depicting the conventional scenes. We are grateful to Louis Gabaude for informing us of Tayac's work. Thai temple art in the nineteenth and twentieth centuries is represented in photographs of painted murals. While

1. For more on the composition of eighteenth-century Siamese manuscripts, see section 2.2 of Huang 2006.

details of some specific scenes have been shown, we have also tried to show how Thai mural art places favourite scenes in a network arrangement, or with a downwards pendulum effect down the side of the wall. We have taken some photographs of Wat Kongkaram, Wat No, and Wat Saket, and Venerable Bhatsokorn Piyobhaso provided those of Wat Nak Prok. This central Bangkok temple, first built in 1748, was completely restored in the nineteenth century by a Chinese businessman, Phra Boribunthanakon, married to a Siamese wife. Recently restored again, its Great Ten series still shows the influence of Chinese art.

Leedom Lefferts and Sandra Cate kindly shared an image of a Vessantara scroll procession, first published in their *Buddhist Storytelling in Thailand and Laos* (Singapore: Asian Civilisations Museum, 2012). We are grateful to Ian Rose for donating pictures of the recitation of the twelfth section of the Vessantara story, and Arthid Sheravanichkul for an image of a Vessantara festival in Bangkok in 2009. These images together show the ongoing life of the *Vessantara-jātaka* in ritual and artistic culture.

Abbreviations

AN	*Aṅguttara Nikāya*
BHSD	*Buddhist Hybrid Sanskrit Dictionary*, ed. Edgerton
DN	*Dīgha Nikāya*
DP	*A Dictionary of Pāli*, ed. Cone
DPPN	*Dictionary of Pāli Proper Names*, ed. Malalasekera
F	Fausbøll's edition of the *Jātakatthavaṇṇanā*
J	*Jātakatthavaṇṇanā* stories by number, or volume and page as in the Cowell/Rouse translation.
Ja	*Jātakatthavaṇṇanā* references to F by volume and page number
MN	*Majjhima Nikāya*
PED	*Pāli-English Dictionary*, ed. Rhys-Davids and Stede
PGPV	*The Perfect Generosity of Prince Vessantara*, trans. Cone and Gombrich
PTS	Pāli Text Society
Pva	*Petavatthuattakathā*
SED	*Sanskrit English Dictionary*, ed. Monier-Williams
SN	*Saṃyutta Nikāya*
UJST	*Ummagga Jātaka: The Story of the Tunnel*, trans. (from Sinhalese) Karunaratne
Vsm	*Visuddhimagga*, referred to by section divisions as found in Ñāṇamoli's translation.
VRI	Vipassana Research Institute electronic edition of the Pāli scriptures

Note on the Abbreviations

As MN and DN *suttas* are numbered, for ease of reference they will be cited by number too. So 'DN 33, PTS edn III 215', means *Dīghanikāya*, *sutta* 33, which is found on page 215 of volume 3. Other texts are cited by the PTS page reference.

The Great Ten (*Mahānipāta*) form volume six of the *Jātakatthavaṇṇanā*, so where there are page references to the stories they are all within this volume. 'Ja VI 34', for instance, means page 34 of the sixth volume of the PTS Pāli text. As will be explained in our introduction, we have chosen a different order of tales from the one used there, so there is not the same sequence of page numbers (in brackets) through our collection as in that Pāli text. Individual stories in the larger collection of *jātakas* are cited by number—e.g. 'J 9'.

Some readers may wonder why 'F', for Fausbøll's edition, is sometimes cited differently in notes from 'Ja'. The reason for this is that a reader familiar with Pāli texts will immediately recognize a reference like 'Ja VI 34' and know where to find it. When commenting specifically on Fausbøll's own choice of reading of different manuscripts, we sometimes refer to his textual comments in the PTS edition as 'F'. This means that we are focusing on textual issues, where there may be a different reading in a different manuscript. 'F' will always refer to the page being translated in the main text. Different readings are found at the bottom of the page of the PTS text. These are referred to by the letters Fausbøll uses, such as 'Ck' (Ceylonese manuscript 'k') or 'Bd' (Burmese manuscript 'd'), for instance.

Foreword

Jātaka stories are the shared heritage of all Buddhists, and *jātaka* culture runs wide and deep in the broad stream of Buddhist civilisation. It has done so for well over two thousand years. *Jātaka*s are a meaningful and vital part of Buddhist, Indian, and Asian literary culture, and a meaningful and vital part of the cultural and ethical heritage of the world—of all human beings. Put simply, a *jātaka* is a story relating an episode in a past lifetime of Gotama the Buddha, when he was known as the Bodhisatta. Taken together, the *jātaka*s present the *longue durée* of the Bodhisatta's career, starting hundreds of thousands of aeons ago—the huge and unimaginable succession of births during which he cultivated spiritual practices and perfected virtues like charity and wisdom.

The Buddha's final life and career as Gotama, and his extraordinary deeds such as his conversion of his half-cousin Nanda, inspired the second-century poet Aśvaghoṣa to compose two works which live on as classics of Indian literature: the Deeds of the Buddha (*Buddha-carita*) and the Poem on Beautiful Nanda (*Saundara-nanda-kāvya*). Similarly, the exploits of the Buddha's past lives, the *jātaka*s, were an inexhaustible source for some of the greatest poetry of ancient India. In the fourth century CE, Āryaśūra initiated a new genre, the 'Garland of Birth Stories' (*Jātaka-mālā*); in this he was followed by Haribhaṭṭa in the fifth century and Gopadatta in the eleventh century. Other master poets like Mātṛceṭa (second century) drew liberally on the legacy of legends of Gotama's last life and previous lives as metaphors of his measureless good qualities. At the end of the seventh century, the Chinese scholar-pilgrim Yijing noted that 'in order to edify living beings, the birth stories are written in poetry for purpose of catering to the literary taste of those readers who take delight in perusing fine writings.'[1]

What drove these poets to tell and retell the stories of the Buddha's past lives? Āryaśūra opens his collection by expressing his intention:[2]

> Glorious are the deeds
> of the Sage in his past births.
> Fame resides in them,
> fine virtues filling them with auspice.
> Impossible to censure,
> they captivate the mind.
> With this handful of flowers of poetry,
> I devoutly honour his wondrous feats.
>
> These commendable acts
> offer clear signposts
> revealing the path
> to Buddhahood.
> May even the hard-hearted
> become softened!
> And may religious teachings
> hereby increase with charm!

Introducing his 'Garland of Birth Stories', Haribhaṭṭa, addresses his audience:[3]

> A preacher of the dharma, having first recited one of the sermons of the Buddha, afterwards illuminates it in detail by telling a *jātaka* of the Bodhisattva—in the same manner as one illuminates a picture-gallery by the light of a torch—and (thereby) creates utmost happiness in the mind of his audience'—keeping this in mind, the listeners should abandon torpor and drowsiness and attentively relish—in the same manner in which a thirsty person would relish nectar—when a deed of the Buddha is being told who had made the great vow of abolishing the endlessly repeating stream of afflictions of the beings born in the three states of existence so that the sorrow of innumerable rebirths comes to an end.

1. Li Rongxi (tr.), *Buddhist Monastic Traditions of Southern Asia: A Record of the Inner Law Sent Home from the South Seas by Śramaṇa Yijing* (Berkeley: Numata Center for Buddhist Translation and Research [BDK English Tripiṭaka], 2000), 143.

2. Translation by Justin Meiland, *Garland of the Buddha's Past Lives by Arya-shura*, Volume 1 (New York University Press and JJC Foundation, 2009), 3.

3. Translation by Michael Hahn, *Poetical Vision of the Buddha's Former Lives: Seventeen Legends from Haribhaṭṭa's Jātakamālā* (Delhi: Aditya Prakashan, 2011), 6.

The *jātakas* were popular in India. In his *Harṣacarita*, the mid-seventh-century master poet Bāṇa paints a vivid picture of a utopian ascetic retreat in the vastness of the Vindhya mountains. We learn that in the ashram

> Very well-disciplined monkeys, who had turned to the three refuges (the Buddha, the Dharma, and the Saṃgha), were performing the rite of making miniature stūpas;
>
> Parrots, who were adept in the Buddhist system and had become high-status lay followers, were explaining the Treasury of Abhidharma;
>
> Myna birds, who were versed in the restraint of faults through the instructions in the rules of training, were giving sermons on the Dharma;
>
> And even the owls, as a result of their uninterrupted listening (to the Dharma), had gained insight, and—having grown used to the daylight—they were reciting stories of the past lives of the Bodhisattva.[4]

Haribhaṭṭa's comparison with the illumination of a 'picture-gallery' (*citra-bhavana*) by the light of a torch or lamp immediately brings to mind another aspect of *jātaka* culture. Side by side with the life and deeds of Gotama Buddha, the *jātakas* inspired some of the finest plastic and visual art of India and Asia. Over two thousand years ago, the followers of the Buddha erected giant stone monuments known as *caityas* or *stūpas* to enshrine and honour the relics of the human Buddha. Some of the great *stūpas* of India—at Bharhut and Sanchi in central India, and at Amaravati and Kanaganahalli in the south—were adorned with birth stories carved in stone. The great *stūpa* of Borobudur on the island of Java in modern Indonesia is a giant 'storybook in stone', illustrating karma and its results, the life of the Buddha, birth stories, and Mahāyāna sutras, showing how different narrative genres work together in a holistic architectural and metaphysical composition.

The earliest surviving narrative painting of India (not counting the pre- and proto-historic cave and rock-shelter paintings), those in Caves 9 and 10 at Ajanta, are *jātakas* and episodes from the Buddha's life. From then on, we can follow continuous traditions of *jātaka* painting across South, Central, and Southeast Asia. Tibetan mural painting and cloth scrolls are often devoted to birth-stories. The mural paintings of Ajanta, Sri Lanka,

4. Here the poet indulges in a playful pun on *āloka* 'light'. It is a commonplace that owls shun *āloka* in the sense of daylight or sunlight, but *āloka* is also a metaphor for wisdom or knowledge.

Thailand, Laos, and Burma, and other forms like the terracotta panels around the base of *stūpas* at Pagan in Upper Burma, are all blossoms of *jātaka* art. Himalayan and Southeast Asian Buddhists continue to depict the *jātakas* to this day, both in traditional and in bold and innovative styles. The weaving of *jātakas* into garlands did not stop with the *Jātaka-mālās* of the great poets. Buddhist devotion wove festoons of *jātakas* in poetry, painting, and stone across Asia.

The Pali *Jātaka* Collection

As the Buddha's *dhamma* (dharma) spread throughout India, his followers preserved and transmitted his teachings as scriptures in several languages, all of which belonged to the same family, Middle Indo-Aryan or Middle Indic. Scriptures were preserved in several Prakrits, including Pali and Gandhari, in Buddhist Hybrid Sanskrit, and, eventually, in the cultivated and mainstream Sanskrit of the sophisticated urban culture. When the *dhamma* spread beyond borders of the subcontinent, it was translated into what we may now regard as the 'classical languages' of Asian Buddhism—Chinese, Tibetan, and the languages of Central Asia. The result was a multilingual canon, vast and vibrant, of Buddhist texts on narrative, philosophy, monasticism, ritual, and sundry other topics. The collections that make up this informal canon are autonomous, but at same time they are intricately intertextual. All of them contribute to the understanding of the *dhamma*, and to the promotion of human values grounded in wisdom.

The *jātaka* collection preserved in the Pali language and transmitted by the Theravādin monastic order of Sri Lanka is unique. Each of its 547 stories is built around a verse or several verses, and these stories are arranged by ascending number of verses. The first chapter or section contains altogether 150 *jātakas* with a single verse. It is followed by chapters with two up to thirteen verses, after which the number of verses in each story increases with each chapter. At the same time, the length and complexity of the narratives increase. The last or 'Great Chapter' with ten stories stands apart. Each of these 'Great Ten' stories, which are translated in this volume, is an independent and intricate 'epic' that weaves a complex cast of characters and various sub-plots into a master narrative. The plots and themes are all different. The *Vidhūra-jātaka* (Chapter 9 in this collection) is an outlandish romance: a *yakkha* or spirit deity with a magic horse courts a *nāginī* or serpent princess, in a tale that moves back and forth between the human, the spirit, and the serpent worlds. The fast-paced *Mahosatha-jātaka*

(Chapter 5) is replete with battles and subterfuges, with romance, trickery, and treachery.

In all of these stories, the leading character is, of course, the Bodhisatta, with a supporting cast of gods and goddesses, kings and queens, princes and princesses, bird and serpent deities, demons and spirits, warriors and ascetics, nobles and commoners, fools and sages. The Bodhisatta is the 'sprout' of the future Buddha Gotama; he interacts with the other characters and negotiates his moral path through involved and shifting situations. But these are not simple morality tales, and the Bodhisatta is far from being an unambiguous stereotype. In each story, he is a very different and thoroughly complex character who cannot easily be flattened into a single 'ideal' or 'perfection', as has been attempted, not always successfully, by scholastic tradition.

Out of these ten stories—the Great Ten—it is the last tale, the *Vessantara-jātaka*, that has captured the imagination of artists, preachers, writers, and their audiences for well over two millennia. There is no evidence for the Great Ten as a group in the Indian Buddhist traditions, although most are known in some form or other, and some are well represented in early art. The *Vidhura-jātaka*, for example, is prominent at the ancient Bharhut *stūpa*, as well as at the Amaravati and Kanaganahalli *stūpa*s and in the cave paintings at Ajanta. The *Vessantara-jātaka* is illustrated in loving detail on the broad panel of Eastern gate at the Sanchi *stūpa*, in what is surely one of the grandest masterpieces of early Indian narrative art. It is depicted in less detail at Bharhut, like Sanchi in central India. In the South, it is portrayed at Amaravati, Goli, and Kanaganahalli. In Central Asia, the mural paintings at Miran devoted several panels to the story, which, again, became part of the repertoire of the Dunhuang caves. The *Vessantara* is presented in numerous literary versions in Indian languages and in translation, and it certainly enjoyed immense popularity in the tradition of the Thera school (Theravaṃsa). Its thirteen chapters and one thousand verses were integrated into literature, art, and ritual in a manner that no other *jātaka* ever enjoyed.

The *Jātaka*s in Siam

Thai culture has enjoyed a special relationship with—a remarkable fascination for, a distinctive flair for—the *jātaka* as an ideology, as a genre, and as an inspiration for the arts and for ritual culture. Some of the earliest representations are carved on the massive, megalithic-like 'boundary stones' of the Northeast. The few surviving Ayutthaya-period mural paintings depict *jātakas* and other narratives, as does the rich panoply of paintings of the Bangkok period, from the late eighteenth century through the twentieth century and up to the present. During these periods, the Great Ten were accorded special favour. They adorn the walls of countless temples like tapestries, lavish in narrative detail and set in undulating landscapes. In the art of the Great Ten, the artists express their talents and wisdom for future generations to cherish.

Crossing Cultures: The *Jātakas* in Translation

The *jātakas* were translated into English 120 years ago and published by Cambridge University Press in six volumes.5 This pioneering translation has done its duty as a classic of Buddhist narrative in English, and was accepted in the UNESCO Collection of Representative Works of Burma, Cambodia, Ceylon, India, Laos, and Thailand. The original translation was cast in the archaising English that was all the rage up to the end of the nineteenth century. This was the age when Sir Edwin Arnold's *The Light of Asia*, first published in London in 1879, became a worldwide bestseller and was translated into many European and Asian languages. The author sought through his poem 'to depict the life and character and indicate the philosophy of that noble hero and reformer, Prince Gautama of India, the founder of Buddhism', 'by the medium of an imaginary Buddhist votary'. The opening lines read,

> The Scripture of the Saviour of the World,
> Lord Buddha—Prince Siddártha styled on earth
> In Earth and Heavens and Hells Incomparable,
> All-honored, Wisest, Best, most Pitiful;
> The Teacher of Nirvana and the Law.
>
> Thus came he to be born again for men.
>
> Below the highest sphere four Regents sit
> Who rule our world, and under them are zones
> Nearer, but high, where saintliest spirits dead
> Wait thrice ten thousand years, then live again;
> And on Lord Buddha, waiting in that sky,
> Came for our sakes the five sure signs of birth

5. E. B. Cowell (ed.), *The Jātaka, or Stories of the Buddha's Former Births* (6 vols., 1895–1907). There is also an early German translation by J. Dutoit, *Das Buch der Erzählungen aus den früheren Existenzen Buddhas* (7 vols. 1908–1921).

So that the Devas knew the signs, and said
'Buddha will go again to help the World.'
'Yea!' spake He, 'now I go to help the World.
This last of many times; for birth and death
End hence for me and those who learn my Law.
I will go down among the Sakyas,
Under the southward snows of Himalay,
Where pious people live and a just King.'

The lines are impressive in their own way. The Biblical and Victorian styles were intended to make the exotic 'other' of the Buddhist narratives seem familiar to the readers of the time, and to situate stories like the *jātaka*s within a growing corpus of Eastern narrative and poetry, a never-never land of faeries, goblins, and sprites. A century has passed, and the English language has changed. That fickle zeitgeist, stylistic fashion, has changed costume more than once, and today the Victorian style is more likely to alienate readers than to attract them. Pali studies have matured; new lexicographic tools, new studies, text editions, and translations, allow for deeper and more precise understandings of the ancient texts. And, for better or for worse, English is no longer *a* world language but *the* world language. It is certainly time for a new translation of the *jātaka*s, and the present publication of the Great Ten into English is a welcome step towards that end.

One hundred and twenty years ago, the Great Ten, 'translated from the Pāli by various hands' under the editorship of Professor E. B. Cowell and W. H. D. Rouse, took up Volume 6 'in 314 pages' of their collection of all 547 *jātaka* stories. After more than a century, we can enjoy a new translation in 663 pages, into an English that is fresh and contemporary but does not sacrifice beauty and feeling to the expediencies of linguistic fashion.

For years my own research has followed Buddhist narratives across Asia over two millennia of dynamism and creative wisdom. I find that *jātaka*s are multidimensional and multifunctional. Can I say that *jātaka*s are universal, that they are part of the great Buddhist heritage, and by part of the heritage of all humanity?

Indian poet and Renaissance man Rabindranath Tagore (1861–1941) wrote that

> Whatever we understand and enjoy in human products instantly becomes ours, wherever they might have their origin. . . . I am proud of my humanity when I can acknowledge the poets and artists of other

> countries as my own. Let me feel with unalloyed gladness that all the great glories of man are mine.[6]

Let us apply Tagore's insights to the *jātaka*s, because he points out how the transfer of culture takes place: *instantly*. Wherever people have encountered the *dhamma* of Gotama Buddha, they have understood and enjoyed Buddhist narratives—especially the grand narratives of the life of the Buddha and the *jātaka*s. And these narratives have instantly—let us note Tagore's term, *instantly*—become their own. Cultural encounter as human exchange is instantaneous; a series of mental instants constitute the processes of localisation, translocalisation, acculturation, or inculturation—whatever term, fashionable or unfashionable, one may choose. For this reason Gotama is depicted as Indo-Greek in the art of Gandhāra, as Chinese in the art of the Middle Kingdom, as Tibetan in the Land of Snows, or as Thai in the art of Siam—to name only a few examples. Otherwise he would be foreign. Otherwise, how could we establish a relationship with him? In the same way, when a translation is vigorous and clear, it engages, captivates, and even bewitches the readers. The story and its multiple meanings enter the heart, and instantly become the readers' own.

Chiang Mai has been a dynamic centre of *jātaka* culture for centuries, for as many as six hundred years. It is therefore especially fitting that this new expression of *jātaka* culture, this brand new translation of the Great Ten, has been published in the northern city. This proves that Chiang Mai, with its traffic jams, shopping centres, and mass tourism, still has room in its heart for *jātaka* culture, and that Thailand continues to see the timeless value of the Ten Great Birth Stories of the Buddha.

This brave new translation of the Great Ten brings the stories home in English, domesticates them in this international language that is current for all in the current age. This new telling of the Great Ten deserves to be understood, savoured, and enjoyed, and acknowledged as a representative work of all countries that share *jātaka* culture. May the stories speak to all humanity, and may they be read with unalloyed gladness.

Peter Skilling
French School of Asian Studies (EFEO), Bangkok

6. Citation from Amartya Sen, 'Poetry and Reason: Why Tagore still matters', *The New Republic* (30 June 2011).

Introduction

The *Jātakas* and the *Mahānipāta*

A *jātaka* story is a story relating events that took place during a previous life of the Buddha. The Buddha is said to have told *jātaka* stories to illustrate his own values or to explain the behaviour of people he encountered. While *jātakas* are found in many different texts and contexts throughout the Buddhist world, the largest and most famous collection is the great Pāli *Jātakatthavaṇṇanā*, which is preserved in what is now known as the Theravāda school of Buddhism.

The core of the *Jātakatthavaṇṇanā* is its verses, and these belong to the *Khuddaka Nikāya*, the fifth section of the *Sutta Piṭaka*, or 'Basket of Discourses'. Around these verses are layers of commentary explaining the meanings of the verses and the context in which they were spoken. This context always includes both a 'story of the past', in other words the tale told by the Buddha of his past life, and a 'story of the present', the situation that prompted the telling of the tale. For example, the Buddha may hear the monks discussing his great renunciation and tell them of how he also renounced under very difficult circumstances in the past; to a monk battling attachment to his former wife he may tell a story of all the past difficulties caused by that woman.

The *Jātakatthavaṇṇanā* is not ordered chronologically, either in terms of the past lifetimes or the 'stories of the present'. Instead the ordering principle is the number of verses contained in each story. Thus the first one hundred and fifty stories each contain a single verse, and so that section of the text is called the *Eka-nipāta*, or 'Section of the Ones'. The following one hundred make up the *Duka-nipāta* (Section of the Twos), the next fifty form the *Tika-nipāta*, and so on in increasing numbers of verses, as shown in Table 1. The total number of stories in the *Jātakatthavaṇṇanā* is said to be 550, though only 547 titles are preserved in the extant text, and some of the titles have no stories attached. It is the long, elaborate narratives of the *Mahānipāta*, the final ten stories of the *Jātakatthavaṇṇanā*, that are contained within this translation.

Table 1. Arrangement of *Jātakatthavaṇṇanā* stories by section

Section title	**Story numbers**
Eka (One) *nipāta*	1–150
Duka (Two) *nipāta*	151–250
Tika (Three) *nipāta*	251–300
Catukka (Four) *nipāta*	301–350
Pañca (Five) *nipāta*	351–375
Cha (Six) *nipāta*	376–395
Satta (Seven) *nipāta*	396–416
Aṭṭha (Eight) *nipāta*	417–426
Nava (Nine) *nipāta*	427–438
Dasa (Ten) *nipāta*	439–454
Ekādasa (Eleven) *nipāta*	455–463
Dvādasa (Twelve) *nipāta*	464–473
Terasa (Thirteen) *nipāta*	474–483
Pakiṇṇaka (Miscellaneous) *nipāta*	484–496
Vīsati (Twenty) *nipāta*	497–510
Tiṃsa (Thirty) *nipāta*	511–520
Cattālīsa (Forty) *nipāta*	521–525
Paṇṇāsa (Fifty) *nipāta*	526–528
Saṭṭhi (Sixty) *nipāta*	529–530
Sattati (Seventy) *nipāta*	531–532
Asīti (Eighty) *nipāta*	533–537
Mahā (Great) *nipāta*	538–547

The ten stories of the *Mahānipāta* are long and complex, and contain extensive verse passages. Their character is therefore rather different to the shorter stories of the *Jātakatthavaṇṇanā*, in which verses are usually pithy moral summaries, dialogue, or descriptions of narrative. Presumably because of their position at the end of the collection, as well as due to their complexity and charm, a tradition has evolved that these ten stories relate the final ten births of the Buddha and illustrate his acquisition of the ten perfections required for Buddhahood. This idea has led to the stories having a central place in Southeast Asian art and culture.

In the printed edition of the *Jātakatthavaṇṇanā*, which was produced primarily from Sri Lankan manuscripts by V. Fausbøll in the late 19th century, the *Mahānipāta* stories are as follows:

538. *Mūgapakkha-jātaka*
539. *Mahājanaka-jātaka*
540. *Sāma-jātaka*
541. *Nimi-jātaka*
542. *Khaṇḍahāla-jātaka*
543. *Bhūridatta-jātaka*
544. *Mahānāradakassapa-jātaka*
545. *Vidhurapaṇḍita-jātaka*
546. *Mahā-Ummagga-jātaka*
547. *Vessantara-jātaka*

In the Southeast Asian manuscript and artistic traditions the order varies from Fausbøll's edition, with *Vidhura* appearing just before *Vessantara*, and *Mahā-Ummagga* being placed earlier in the list. This variation may be to do with the expansion of the *Mahā-Ummagga-jātaka* to include a number of earlier *jātaka*s associated with the hero Mahosadha, resulting in two different lengths for the story (with and without the extra verses) and thus two possible places for it in the list.[1] In addition, the names of the stories in Southeast Asia are in some cases different from the Sri Lankan tradition, betraying a desire to name each of the stories after the character of the Bodhisatta. So the *Mūgapakkha* ('Dumb Cripple') becomes *Temiya*, the *Mahāummagga* ('Great Tunnel') becomes *Mahosadha*, and the *Khaṇḍahāla*, named after Devadatta's character, becomes *Candakumāra*, after the Bodhisatta. Over time the order of the stories was fixed and became the subject of a Thai mnemonic made up of the first syllables of the story titles: Te-Ja-Su-Ne-Ma-Bhu-Ca-Na-Vi-Ve.[2]

The idea that *jātaka* stories illustrate the long path to Buddhahood is not found in the earliest layers of the text. However, the association between

1. For a fuller discussion see the introduction to the *Mahosadha-jātaka*.

2. Rendered here using the Pāli spellings, these abbreviations will also sometimes be used in this text.

the *Mahānipāta* stories and the Bodhisatta clearly became a key factor in their rising popularity. The stories demonstrate the greatness of the Buddha and the extraordinary qualities he acquired over many lifetimes. As such the stories are not just a part of a long sacred biography; they are also symbolic of Buddhahood itself.

The Perfections

Each of the *Mahānipāta* stories is traditionally associated with one of the ten perfections that the Bodhisatta must cultivate on his path to Buddhahood. However, the associations are difficult to trace, as several different lists exist both in the textual sources and later texts and traditions. Specific perfections are not often mentioned within the stories themselves, for the association between *jātaka* stories and the perfections came relatively late in the compositional history of the *Jātakatthavaṇṇanā*.[3] Even when stories do mention a perfection, it may not be the one that becomes associated with it; for example both Bhūridatta and Vidhura are said to 'put the perfection of resolve (*adhiṭṭhāna*) before everything else', but neither story is traditionally associated with that quality.

Two Pāli scriptures mention associations between some of the Great Ten *jātaka*s and particular perfections. In the *Jātaka-nidāna*, the preface to the *Jātakatthavaṇṇanā* that outlines the Buddha's life story in a chronological form, eight of the Great Ten are included in a list of stories that demonstrate perfections, but the perfections with which they are associated are not the same as those that developed in the Southeast Asian tradition. After mentioning *jātaka* stories for each of the perfections the *Jātaka-nidāna* refers the reader to another *jātaka* collection, the *Cariyāpiṭaka*, for a fuller account. This short text from the *Khuddaka Nikāya* contains thirty-five stories (including six from the *Mahānipāta*) retold in concise verse summaries in the first person. The stories are arranged according to the perfection that they are said to demonstrate, but once again the associations are somewhat different to the Thai tradition.

The perfections associated with *Mahānipāta* stories by the *Jātaka-nidāna* and the *Cariyāpiṭaka* are listed in Table 2, alongside the most common

3. For a full discussion of the history of the *Jātakatthavaṇṇanā* and the Theravāda *jātaka* genre more broadly see Appleton 2010a, especially Chapters 3 and 4.

traditional Thai association[4] and the reason that the Buddha is said to have told the story as given in the *Jātakatthavaṇṇanā.*

Table 2. The *Mahānipāta* and associated perfections in three traditions

Story	**Prompt for story in *Jātakatthavaṇṇanā***	***Jātaka-nidāna***	***Cariyāpiṭaka***	**Thai tradition**
Temiya	Discussion of the great renunciation	resolve	resolve	renunciation
Janaka	Discussion of the great renunciation	vigour	[none]	vigour
Suvaṇṇasāma	Debate about supporting one's parents	[none]	loving-kindness	loving-kindness
Nemi	A smile (ref. also to renunciation)	generosity	generosity	resolve
Mahosadha	Discussion about the perfection of wisdom	wisdom	[none]	wisdom
Bhūridatta	Discussion about keeping the *uposatha*	morality	morality	morality
Candakumāra	Discussion about Devadatta's attempts to kill	generosity	generosity	forbearance
Nārada	Discussion about the Buddha's ability to destroy wrong views	[none]	[none]	equanimity
Vidhura	Discussion about the perfection of wisdom	wisdom	[none]	truthfulness
Vessantara	A miraculous shower of lotuses and rain	generosity	generosity	generosity

4. In his Thai translation of the *Mahānipāta*, Prince Jinavarasiriwadhna, the Supreme Patriarch in the reigns of Kings Rama VI–VII, mentions two different lists. One of these is similar to that given in Gerini's 1892 study of the *thet maha chat*, for which no source

As is clear from Table 2, the tradition of associating a particular perfection with each story is found in both the *Cariyāpiṭaka* and the *Jātaka-nidāna*, but the identifications of these ten stories were not fixed at the time of these texts. In the *Cariyāpiṭaka*, which contains versions of six of the *Mahānipāta* stories, the difference in associated perfections is clearly linked to the different ways in which the stories are told. Thus, for example, the story of Candakumāra is merely a short account of how, after escaping from being sacrificed, Prince Canda gave great gifts. Similarly the account of King Nemi is simply of his great generosity, with no mention of his subsequent renunciation:

> And again, when in the superb city of Mithilā I was a great king
> named Nimi,[5] learned, desiring good,
> I had then four halls built (each) with four entrances. There I
> conferred gifts on beasts, birds, men and so forth,
> Clothing and beds and food and drink and (a variety of other)
> victuals—I conferred great gifts, making them continual.
> Just as a servant, going to the master for the sake of wealth, seeks
> for satisfaction by gesture, speech, thought,
> So will I seek in every becoming for what is produced for Awakening,
> refreshing creatures with gifts; I long for supreme Awakening.
> (*Cariyāpiṭaka* I 6 vv. 1–5, Horner 2000: 6)

The list of stories and their associated perfections in the *Jātaka-nidāna* would appear to be based upon a version of the *Cariyāpiṭaka*, though the identifications and stories do not match exactly.[6]

Because the tradition that aligns each *Mahānipāta* story with a single perfection developed somewhat later than the stories themselves, sometimes it can be hard to see how the given perfection is being demonstrated. Some associations are clear and obvious, namely Temiya

---

(other than the explanation of 'a prominent Siamese Prince and accomplished scholar') is given (Gerini 1976 [1892]: 18). The second of the two lists of Jinavara is the one reproduced in Table 2, as it is this one that has gained most currency within Thailand. We are grateful to Arthid Sheravanichkul for information on the rather obscure history of these associations in Thailand and for his comments on Jinavara's attempts to associate each story with one, two, or even all ten perfections.

5. This spelling is found in the *Cariyapiṭaka*. See Chapter 4, note 1 for discussion of the name.

6. For a discussion of how the perfections in the *Cariyāpiṭaka* relate to other lists and texts see Appleton 2010a: 98–103.

with resolve, Janaka with vigour, Sāma with loving-kindness, Mahosadha with wisdom, Bhūridatta with morality (here, as often in the *jātakas*, equated with keeping the *uposatha*), and Vessantara with generosity. Others, however, are more complex. Canda's demonstration of forbearance presumably applies to his willingness to look after his father despite the latter's attempt to kill him, but this is rather tangential to the story as a whole. Likewise Vidhura's honesty plays a small role in his story, in which an association with wisdom would seem more natural. The story of Nārada as a demonstration of equanimity is also less clear, although as Brahmā the Bodhisatta was perhaps felt to embody this fourth divine abiding.

The association between the *Mahānipāta* stories and the ten perfections has doubtless contributed towards their popularity and endurance, and on a symbolic level it adds potency and sacredness to the collection. However, the stories do much more than demonstrate the Bodhisatta's perfections, not least because they also contain a wealth of colourful characters that interact with and respond to the Bodhisatta. Their great length also permits detailed explorations of situations and problems that arise in the world and provide ground for the cultivation of the perfections. Indeed with their subtly argued, dramatic debates, their often harrowingly repetitive lyric outpourings of intense feeling on the part of principal players, and their extended descriptive verses of armies, palaces, and scenes in the epic style, the Great Ten assume a grandeur that places them in the forefront of the literature of the ancient world, justifying their continued appeal both as stories and, especially in South and Southeast Asia, as religiously moving texts. The character and mettle of the Bodhisatta and his followers are tested in relationship to one another to highlight his strength. In this way he, and sometimes his companions, becomes a truly epic hero, with all the majesty such an epithet implies.

The Bodhisatta and His Friends and Family

So while the presence of the Bodhisatta is what makes a story a *jātaka*, many *jātaka* stories actually place as much emphasis, if not more, on the actions and experiences of other characters in the unfolding events. In the *Mahānipāta* we find one example of a *jātaka* in which the Bodhisatta only appears towards the end of the story—the *Nārada-jātaka*. In the other nine stories he is undeniably the main focus yet not always the central actor. By making him a player in an unfolding drama, his search for the perfections is seen in the world of human interaction and exchange. The

Great Ten exploit features we associate with genres such as tragic and comic drama, lyric poetry, epic, and even, in some instances, the modern novel; so, with all the freedom for the Bodhisatta to relate to others this confers, they are not only heroic but also profoundly human and realistic in their psychological exploration.

Table 3. Identifications of characters that appear more than once in the *Mahānipāta*

Character in Present	Character(s) in Past
Uppalavaṇṇā (nun)	goddess (Te, Ja, Su), female ascetic (Ma), Bodhisatta's sister (Bhu, Ca), Bodhisatta's daughter (Ve)
Ānanda (monk and attendant)	fletcher (Ja), king (Su), Mātali (Ne), parrot (Ma), son of a hunter (Bhu), princess (Na), King Dhanañjaya (Vi)
Sāriputta (chief monk)	charioteer (Te), Nārada (Ja), enemy king (Ma), Bodhisatta's brother (Bhu, Ca), courtier (Na), nāga king (Vi), ascetic (Ve)
Moggallāna (chief monk)	Migājina (Ja), Bodhisatta's brother (Bhu, Ca), king of supaṇṇas (Vi)
Anuruddha (monk)	Sakka (Su, Ne, Vi, Ve)
Buddha's parents	Bodhisatta's parents (Te, Ja, Ma, Bhu, Ca [mother only], Vi, Ve)
Buddha's wife Bimbā	Bodhisatta's wife (Ja, Ma, Ca, Vi, Ve)
Buddha's son Rāhula	Bodhisatta's son (Ja, Ca, Vi, Ve)
Devadatta (murderous and schismatic monk)	evil brahmin (Bhu), Kevaṭṭa (Ma), Khaṇḍahāla (Ca), Alāta (Na), Jūjaka (Ve)
Sunakkhatta (Licchavi prince and ex-monk)	Bodhisatta's brother (Bhu), fatalist teacher (Na)

The drama of these interchanges is heightened by the association of so many of the cast of characters with those in the 'present' of the life of the Buddha—a feature of all *jātaka* stories. Minimally this means that the Buddha is identified with one of the actors in the *jātaka* story itself. However, in many cases the identifications are more numerous, with key members of the Buddha's family or monastic entourage featuring in the stories: not just a future Buddha, but also his *saṅgha*, are represented. The identifications for characters that appear more than once in the *Mahānipāta* stories are listed in Table 3.

The *jātakas* of the *Mahānipāta* have plenty to tell us about the characters and past relationships of the Buddha's family and close followers. The Buddha's parents are consistently identified as the Bodhisatta's parents, except in two cases: In the *Candakumāra-jātaka* the Bodhisatta's father is a bad character and so cannot easily be identified with King Suddhodana. In the *Suvaṇṇasāma-jātaka* Sāma's parents are said to have been past births of Kassapa and Bhaddakāpilānī, a husband and wife who never consummated their marriage but instead renounced together and eventually became a senior monk and nun in the Buddha's retinue. Since their story bears so much resemblance to that of Sāma's parents the identification is an obvious choice, but where no narrative features hint towards an alternative, the default position is for the stability of the Bodhisatta's family unit. This extends also to his relationship with his wife (usually called 'Rāhula's mother' or 'Bimbā' in the *jātakas*), whom he marries in half of the *Mahānipāta* stories. Similarly where he has a son, this character is inevitably identified with Rāhula. It would seem that family bonds remain impressively stable over multiple lifetimes.

Senior monks and nuns also feature in the *Mahānipāta* stories. Anuruddha is identified as king of the gods Sakka in four stories (a role which he occupies a total of fourteen times in the *Jātakatthavaṇṇanā*), perhaps because of his legendary supernormal powers (*iddhi*). Uppalavaṇṇā too is famous for *iddhi* and has three divine births in these stories—as goddess of the royal parasol, of the sea, and of a tree. In two of these stories (*Temiya* and *Suvaṇṇasāma*) she is said to have been the Bodhisatta's mother in a previous birth, and in other stories she features as his sister or daughter. Although often shown in close proximity to the Bodhisatta, she retains a certain independence, most clearly shown by her role as the female ascetic Bherī in the *Mahosadha/Ummagga-jātaka*.

The Buddha's two chief disciples, Sāriputta and Moggallāna, also feature heavily in these stories, usually in supportive roles. Thus Sāriputta is converted by the Bodhisatta, encourages his religious practices, or protects and supports him. Moggallāna seems less individual, appearing only as another brother, friend, or adviser when Sāriputta is also present in such a role. The characters identified as Ānanda, the Buddha's loyal attendant, are rather more colourful. He seems always to be an ambiguous character, with some positive virtues but also some flaws. Thus he is an impetuous king who is later converted, or he is prone to gambling, or comes from a family of hunters. Presumably in reference to his inability to attain arhatship during the Buddha's life due to his attachment, Ānanda's characters are all tied to the world in some way. Even when he is a divinity he is only a supportive one, driving the chariot for Sakka. Worst of all he is even born as a woman; the karmic backstory for this is given in the *Nārada-jātaka.*[7] It is very rare for characters to change gender across lifetimes in Buddhist narrative, so this portrayal of a feminine Ānanda is significant, and presumably refers to his emotional character and his reputed closeness to the nuns' community.[8]

It is not only the Buddha's supporters and allies that are bound to him in multiple births; two key enemies of the Buddha also feature in the *Mahānipāta.* Devadatta is the Buddha's cousin and is famous for his attempts to kill the Buddha and split the *saṅgha.* Unsurprisingly he always plays a villainous role in the *jātakas*. In the *Mahānipāta* he is identified as a nefarious brahmin four times and once more as a heretical army general. He captures the Bodhisatta, attempts to have him killed, goes into battle against him, leads him to false teachers, or requests his children for slaves and then beats them mercilessly. Another of the Buddha's adversaries is Sunakkhatta, a Licchavi prince who left the Buddhist monastic life under the influence of rival teachers and proceeded to badmouth the Buddha and his community. In the *Mahānipāta* he appears twice, both times as a heretical teacher: In the *Bhūridatta-jātaka* he is brother to the Bodhisatta and gives a long speech in support of the Vedic religion. In the *Nārada-jātaka* he is identified as the naked ascetic Guṇa who leads the king into the fatalist viewpoint that plunges his realm into disarray.

Thus, the Buddha's companions—good and bad—appear to have been bound together with him during his long path. Relationships such as parent and child or husband and wife remain stable, emphasising both

7. It is possible that one other character changes sex in the *Mahānipata* from that in the life of the Buddha. The verses at the end of *Mahosadha/Ummagga-jātaka* say that the nun Uppalavaṇṇā is Bherī, the sage who features in this tale. In the F edition this is a female renunciate, but the Sri Lankan tradition has made her male. This translation prefers the greater textual authority for a female attribution. She also remains a female character in later Southeast Asia textual and artistic traditions.

8. For a discussion of Ānanda's past life as a woman see Appleton 2011.

the multi-life adhesive affect of love and the magnitude of the Buddha's eventual renunciation of family ties.[9] That the Buddha's adversaries have also remained the same suggests that they are even more deluded than their contemporary actions convey. However, this message comes at the cost of suggesting that their evil character is so embedded that it would be impossible for them to change.

The presence of the Buddha's community in the *jātaka*s also helps the stories to convey the correct attitude to take towards the Bodhisatta, and by implication towards the Buddha. The best example of this is the *Candakumāra-jātaka*, in which the Bodhisatta is due to be sacrificed in order to help his father obtain heaven. Many other characters, including his brothers and sisters, are also lined up for sacrifice, yet it is the imminent death of Prince Canda himself that causes the people's lamentation. Verse after verse praises the Bodhisatta's great character and handsome charm, and the adoration shown towards him seems to implicitly support the honour paid to the Buddha. Similarly the long laments of Sāma's parents when they believe the Bodhisatta to be dead, or of Temiya's parents in seeing their son sitting immobile and mute, suggest great affection for the Buddha even in his past lives. Yet however positive this affection and devotion may seem, even positive bonds must eventually be overcome, as Janaka's attempts to leave his wife or Vessantara's determination to give away his family members remind us.

Kingship and Renunciation

At the beginning of the first tale in the Great Ten, the Bodhisatta, born as a prince who will inherit the kingship, recollects the terrible karmic consequences of being a king in the past, when the tortures and punishments he inflicted on others led him to rebirth in lower hells. This remembrance leads him, and the entire court, on a path of renunciation, in which both kingship and life under a king are roundly rejected by the end of the tale. The last story, *Vessantara*, however, shows him as a hero returning to the court after a period of exile, welcomed as a just monarch whose rule brings prosperity and happiness to all. At the end of the tale, this auspicious and triumphant embracing of kingship brings to a conclusion his search for the perfections, in his last complete worldly life as Bodhisatta. Tradition

9. For a discussion of the stability of multi-life relationships in Buddhist narrative see Appleton 2014, chapter 5.

holds that on his death there, he goes to the Tusita heaven realm, where he will wait to take his final rebirth as a human, destined to become the Buddha. The evocation of the hells in the first tale, and the anticipation of the heavens at the end of the last, provide a reminder of the 'all worlds' the Bodhisatta needs to come to know to be a fully awakened Buddha; extended examination of the whole notion of kingship, and life in the centre of the 'world' of the court in the Great Ten, shows this to be an essential part of this path through the world of *saṃsāra.*

The relationship between kingship and renunciation is therefore a key theme of the *Mahānipāta.*[10] The *jātaka* stories are well known as sources of worldly guidance as well as Buddhist teachings about the need to escape the world, and the *Mahānipāta* is no exception. While some stories laud good kingship or wise service to kings, others insist upon a life of quiet reflection in the forest. The multidimensional portrayals in these ten stories paint a complex picture in which no single perspective prevails. Each character must make his own choice about how he should engage in worldly duties, using the example provided by a variety of Bodhisatta kings and advisers.

Within the *Mahānipāta* the Bodhisatta displays a variety of attitudes towards kingship, becoming king four times and renouncing the kingship on two of those occasions. As already noted, the opening tale (*Temiya-jātaka*) shows the lengths to which the Bodhisatta went to avoid inheriting the kingship. Yet in the very next story, the *Janaka-jātaka*, we find the Bodhisatta doing everything he can to regain a lost kingdom, and his determination and persistence are implicitly praised within the story. Here, however, the importance of renouncing the kingdom is still highlighted when Janaka displays even more determination in leaving kingdom and wife and pursuing the solitary life of a renouncer. Similarly, the *Nemi-jātaka* shows the potential for good kingship as well as the importance of ultimately giving it up, while the *Candakumāra-jātaka* has the Bodhisatta becoming king and showing no inclination for renunciation at all. And the collection comes to a climax with the *Vessantara-jātaka*, in which the Bodhisatta is exiled from his kingship yet later is welcomed back as a popular and just ruler.

While the Bodhisatta does sometimes demonstrate the potential for positive kingship, in other stories kings show just how foolish and

10. For a fuller discussion of this and other aspects of Buddhist narrative, see Collins 1998.

dangerous they can be. Twice the Bodhisatta features as a wise adviser to the king, and in such stories his wit and wisdom are contrasted with the folly and lust of his royal patron. Thus in the *Mahosadha-jātaka* it is the Bodhisatta-as-adviser who protects his king from defeat both in war and in the face of more underhand strategies. The king himself is weak, especially when he becomes infatuated with the princess of a neighbouring kingdom. Similarly the *Vidhura-jātaka* presents us with a king who is so fond of gambling that he manages to lose his most treasured possession—his adviser Vidhura—to a demonic adversary. The kings in these stories are in great need of guidance and advice from the wise Bodhisatta, who remains, in both cases, in royal service until the end of the story.

The slightly witless kings who benefit from the guidance of Mahosadha and Vidhura cannot compare with the idiotic and villainous kings of the *Candakumāra-jātaka* and *Nārada-jātaka*, however. In these stories we see how dangerous bad kingship can be; in the former, the king is prepared to kill his own family and several key citizens in order to reach heaven, while in the latter he is so convinced by the fatalist teachings of a visiting ascetic that he neglects his duties and spends his time dallying with the wives of his subjects. Just as the wise rule of King Nemi brings great benefits to his whole realm, the unwise and selfish rule of these two bad kings causes disaster to befall their kingdoms. Even bad kings have the potential to reform, however, as we see with King Aṅgati in the *Nārada-jātaka* or the hunter-king who injures Sāma in the *Suvaṇṇasāma-jātaka*. Certainly one key message of the *Mahānipāta* would appear to be how to take the correct approach to kingship, with plenty of conflicting models to reflect upon.

In the *Mahānipāta* we often find kingship presented in direct contrast to a life of renunciation, and this tension between kingship and renunciation is played out in the physical spaces of city and forest. A life of simple fare and meditation is lauded in the stories of Temiya, Janaka, and Nemi. The wilderness is made comfortable thanks to the provision of hermitages (provided by the god Sakka) and the taming of wild animals by the peaceful living of the humans. Temporary retreat into the forest, such as in the *Bhūridatta-jātaka* and *Vidhura-jātaka*, allows for a time of reflection and precept-observance away from the pressures and temptations of the city. The peace and harmony of the forest is perhaps most vividly contrasted with kingship in the *Suvaṇṇasāma-jātaka*, in which a king invades the forest in pursuit of deer. As Sāma lies wounded by the king's arrow he wonders why anyone would wish to harm him given that he has no enemies in the forest. While the Bodhisatta, as Sāma, spends his entire life in the forest, his influence extends into the realm of this king when he offers him some advice on how to rule appropriately. The violent and impetuous king leaves the forest and returns to his city transformed by his experiences.

Thus the *Mahānipāta* stories provide us with a multitude of views on the correct attitude to kingship and deliberately leave some questions unanswered. Should we do all we can to avoid becoming king, or embrace kingship temporarily but then renounce it? Should we remain in service to royal patrons despite their folly, or offer teachings to kings from the safety and comfort of the forest? Or should we leave city life altogether and embrace a life of forest meditation? There is no definitive answer to any of these questions, and so the audience must assess the options for themselves. As for the Bodhisatta, he experiences a whole variety of situations, beginning with determined avoidance of kingship but ending with a joyous return to the throne after a period of enforced forest-dwelling.

Underlying this dynamic, we need to remember that for the Bodhisatta path to be fully accomplished, kingship is not just a necessary evil: the Bodhisatta *has* to be a king sometimes and to live in a world, of city and court, where there are kings. In the Great Ten his path is inextricably bound with finding and knowing its perils, responsibilities, dangers, and blessings so that he can be a fitting leader and teacher of humans and gods in his final life. For the ancient Indian, kingship represents the highest worldly ideal of happiness and responsibility in the lay life, and potentially, an opportunity for the great generosity, benevolence, and leadership qualities needed to become a Buddha. This is challenged in the *Temiya*, and it is noteworthy that in this first story the very institution of kingship is also rejected. But despite the often renunciatory ideals expressed in other stories, and often by appallingly childish kings, this active repudiation does not occur in the rest: it is a starting point in the Great Ten, which despite different orderings always starts with Temiya and ends with Vessantara. Vessantara, in the culmination of his path in the *jātakas*, finishes his life as a layman and a king who brings happiness to many. Where the Bodhisatta is not a king, he never challenges kingship itself, nor does he attempt any takeover bid, despite being treated very capriciously by his own. On several occasions he berates his own king roundly:

> For a king, not following the advice of one's wise adviser, seeking only for his benefit, is like being a deer caught in a trap. (Ja VI 437 v. 63)

He is also as Mahosadha often asked why he does not supplant his king or an enemy one. He replies to one such question:

> Great King, if I wished it, I could today seize the entire continent of India, killing all its kings. But it is not the way of wise men to kill others and gain glory from it. (Ja VI 460)

In all the stories the court and kings feature as major players, and the Bodhisatta either takes on the role of monarch or advises one, even though sometimes living outside the confines of the court, in a rural setting (Sāma) or the heaven world of Brahmā (Nārada). These perspectives remind us of the renunciate path too.

At this point it is worth remembering another *jātaka*, not in the main collection, that the Buddha tells immediately before the *Parinibbāna Sutta*, when, close to death, he arrives at his final destination as a human being, Kusinārā. Rebuking Ānanda for saying that such a run down place is not fit for a Buddha, he describes a birth there in which he was Mahāsudassana, a Universal Monarch, the other possible destiny open to Gotama/Siddhattha in his final life. As such a king, he practises as a layman the four *jhānas* of the divine abidings in the innermost part of his palace: the palace, its environs, and the city outside become a mandala of the awakening mind.[11] If we take the city and the palace (at centre stage in all the Great Ten except where actively renounced as in *Sāma* and *Temiya*) as metaphors for the human mind in its interactions with others, the four *jhānas* or divine abidings of loving-kindness, compassion, sympathetic joy, and equanimity can be seen as lying at the heart of a just kingship, where a benevolent leader exercises power for the benefit of others. The parallels between the Universal Monarch and the Buddha are emphasized in the *suttas*. For example, the *Aṅguttara Nikāya* states:

> There are these two people who arise in the world for the benefit of many people, for the happiness of many people, for the good, benefit, and happiness of devas and humans: What two? The Tathāgata, the *arahat*, the Perfectly Enlightened One and the Universal Monarch.[12] (AN I 76)

11. For the citadel used as a metaphor for the awakening mind, see AN IV 106–13.
12. For some discussion of this, see Jones 1979: 118 ff.

For a Bodhisatta, rebirth as a Universal Monarch is surpassed only by Buddhahood, and all the seers examining the baby Gotama at birth except one, Kondañña, who saw only a single destiny, considered such kingship a possibility even in his final life. In the Great Ten, interestingly, none of the kings involved are described as such Universal Monarchs, though Nemi has the long lifespan associated with them.

In fact, most kings in the starkly realist world of the *Mahānipāta* are notably deficient in all sorts of ways. But some, such as the one in *Sāma*, won over by the power of the Bodhisatta's loving-kindness in his rural enclave, return from their encounters reformed. Others, such as the one in *Nārada* and both kings in *Mahosadha*, also learn under his tutelage. In the final tale, the Bodhisatta also returns as king, when as Vessantara he assumes his rightful place at the centre of the court. He is interestingly not a Universal Monarch here: it is as if he is already preparing himself for the work of his final life, which is very much in the commonplace human world.

So in the Great Ten, kings may be greatly deficient and kingship itself sometimes questioned, but monarchy as an institution is not challenged, except in the first; rather, it is seen to represent leadership and good action in the world. For the Bodhisatta, contacts with monarchic rule and the assumption of that role are integral to his path. Historically, many kings in South and Southeast Asia have seen their role in this way too. The king of Siam was always considered a Bodhisatta: Rāma I made a public statement of truth to this effect, in an assertion that would be felt to be usual for Southeast Asian kings:

> I, a devotee of the Buddha, make an assertion of truth (*saccādiṭhāna*), announcing the dedication of the fruits of these wholesome deeds to all of the deities, in front of Buddha images and the holy physical relics—that in performing the holy perfections (*phra pāramī*) from past lives up until this life, I have not sought to achieve any worldly benefits (*lokiya-sampati*) whatsoever: I have set my mind to seek the supramundane benefit of the paramount consecration of the insight of awakening (*phra paramābhiśeka-sambodhiñāṇa-lokutara-sampati*), in order to save all beings to be guided (*venaiya-satva*), to free them from the suffering of Saṃsāra. This is my perfection of truth (*sacca-pāramī*).[13]

13. In Skilling 2012: 300–1.

This orientation appears to continue to some degree: in the twentieth century King Bhumibol of Thailand actually commissioned a rewriting and redepiction of the *Mahājanaka* to accord with modern ideals of ecology, action in the world, and benevolence. In Myanmar, kings traditionally were held to be working with the Buddha: as Lilian Handlin points out, their *bhagavā* was inextricably linked to the path of Buddhahood in eleventh- to thirteenth-century century Pagan.[14] Indeed from ancient times the association between good kingship and the inspiration of Buddhist teachings is attested: Buddhaghosa cites King Aśoka as an example of this in his description of the Recollection of the Buddha (*Buddhānussati*) as his twenty-first meditation object leading to *samatha*, or calm (Vsm VII 23).

While it is sometimes thought that there is a distinction in Southern Buddhism between salvific activities and those that are enmeshed in good behaviour leading to fortunate rebirths in the world, such a split has for the most part been created by Western anthropologists in the mid-twentieth century, perhaps puzzled by the complex interconnectedness of goals that seemed so different to them. Buddhists in South and Southeast Asia tend not to see things in this way. There certainly is an important dynamic between kingship and renunciation, but it is not just a case of 'either/or': the word for renunciation (*nekkhamma*), sometimes translated as 'freedom from desire', is also expressly equated with meditation and *jhāna* in early texts, and a just king may practise this too.[15]

This axis of renunciation and kingship is explored in more pragmatic ways in the Great Ten, however: The *jātaka*s as a whole, and the Great Ten in particular, place the renunciate life as the higher one. But they also validate all lay roles, meditative attainments, and even small acts of kindness as integral parts of a larger path that may take many lifetimes to fulfil and which many can follow (Handlin 2012: 200 ff.). In this regard it is

14. See Handlin 2012.

15. See Dhammapāla's fifth-century commentary to the perfections in Bodhi 1978: 244–8. This says that *nekkhamma* follows *sīla* in the list (a) because it perfects *sīla*; (b) because it refers to good conduct of mind, as opposed to good conduct of body denoted by *sīla*; (c) because it is easy to practise *jhāna* after *sīla*; (d) to show the purification of the mind after the purification of bodily action; and (e) to put the abandoning of mental defilements after the abandoning of bodily transgressions (245–6). See also the entries for *nekkhamma* in DP II 638–9 and, for instance, DN 33, PTS edn III 215, where the mind is described as subject to three kinds of unwholesome thoughts, for sense desires, hatred, and cruelty, contrasted with three wholesome: for renunciation, non-hatred, and the absence of cruelty.

important to note that for Southern Buddhists, the 'last' ten lives are felt to precede, chronologically, two others: the Bodhisatta's sojourn in the Tusita heaven, and his final life as Gotama/Siddhatta, where he is both royal and married, and then renunciate. As Appleton and others have noted, many stories take the events and circumstances of an earlier life as metaphoric of difficulties and auspiciousness in the present (Appleton 2010a: 38–9). So while great kings have some or all of the seven treasures—wheel, elephant, horse, jewel, woman, treasurer, and adviser—which feature in many and varied ways in many of the stories in this collection, Buddhas have the seven treasures of the factors of awakening—mindfulness, investigation, vigour, joy, tranquillity, concentration, and equanimity (SN V 99)—all metaphorically anticipated in these earlier lives. It is with these 'treasures' that they teach others. The Buddha, as the leader of gods and men, needs a full life in *saṃsāra*, represented by the Great Ten, including contact with kings and the power of the state and city, as a preliminary and anticipation of his final work in finding liberation and leading others to it.

Women

In a footnote to his influential article on women in early Buddhism, Alan Sponberg declared, 'The most blatantly misogynous texts of the Pali literature are found in the *jātaka* stories' (Sponberg 1992: 35). He is not wrong, for many of the stories in the *Jātakatthavaṇṇanā* fit well into his category 'ascetic misogyny', meaning negative portrayals of women as dangerous, lustful, and violent, most likely aimed at preserving the celibate life of a monk or male ascetic. Stories abound of women seducing sages, trying to kill their lovers, lying, and manipulating their husbands. However, the collection also contains many positive portrayals of women, most often acting bravely and kindly in support of the Bodhisatta's path. The *Mahānipāta* contains a particularly high concentration of these positive portrayals, and indeed there is practically no negative female character in sight. Taken as a unit, these ten stories paint women in an overwhelmingly good light: women are good and loving wives and mothers, equally able to renounce and pursue the religious life, and sometimes of superior wisdom to their male companions.

The role of mother is very prominent in the Great Ten. In the *Temiya-jātaka* the Bodhisatta's mother tries her hardest to save his life and laments his apparent death. The mother of Janaka is brave enough to escape a war-ravaged city in disguise and set up a new home to raise her son in secret. She wishes only for his welfare, even when he causes her pain. Sāma's mother is the first to realise that her son is not yet dead, and her Act of Truth is the first in the sequence that revives him. In each of these three stories another maternal character—a protective goddess—is also present. In the stories of Temiya and Sāma this goddess is said to have been the Bodhisatta's mother in a past life, and is thus motivated to look after him in his present circumstances. In Janaka's case the goddess who saves him is Maṇimekhalā, a popular goddess of the ocean and saviour of seafaring merchants. Motherhood is also particularly emphasized in the *Vessantara*: the crucial first verse, and the entire first section of the tale, is devoted to Vessantara's mother and to her auspiciousness, which allows the Bodhisatta to take this important rebirth in her womb. The positive contributions of these maternal figures should not be overlooked.

As well as being sometimes maternal figures, the local goddesses who assist in several of the Great Ten stories also demonstrate the power of female divinities. Many stories are completely turned around through the actions of benign goddesses. These local goddesses, so Indian in character for their protection of those in their domain, are able to act as such free agents and have so much power precisely because they are so deeply linked to their environs—the parasol, the sea, and the locality—not kings and states. In *Temiya* and *Mahosadha*, the goddesses change the course of the action entirely, in the first case by suggesting an escape route, and in the second by threatening the king with death unless Mahosadha is returned to his position of adviser in the court. No happy outcome would have been possible in *Sāma* or *Janaka* without the saving actions of the local goddess, the dea ex machina.

Positive examples of wifehood are also prominent in the *Mahānipāta*. Janaka must win over a princess who has robustly tested and rejected several weak suitors in order to gain the kingship. Mahosadha's wife also has a strong character and wisdom to rival her husband's, and so she is a perfect match for him. Canda's wife saves her husband by calling on the gods to disrupt the sacrifice in which he is soon to be slaughtered. But it is Vessantara's wife Maddī, who rejoices in and supports her husband in his great generosity even when his deeds lead to banishment and the loss of her beloved children, that is the paragon of devoted wifehood. Despite her natural feelings of loss when she learns her children have been given away, she praises her husband and willingly allows him to give her away to a stranger. Her support of the Bodhisatta's path is matchless. In all of these stories the Bodhisatta's wife is of course a past birth of the Buddha's wife, and thus the stories demonstrate her multi-life support of the Buddha's path. That she is, in her final life, rewarded with arhatship herself perhaps eases the distress of any reader that is uncomfortable with the hardships she has undergone, for these hardships would be seen as a part of her vow to accompany her spouse in so many lives.

The problematic side of women is not glossed over entirely in these ten stories, however. Women are temptresses used to torture the adolescent Temiya, albeit to no avail. Janaka's wise and strong wife, Sīvalī, must in the end be abandoned if he is to pursue the path of a renouncer. She follows him and tries her best to tempt him back, but in the end she is forced to accept the end of her marriage and turns her own attentions to secluded meditation. A renunciate path is also taken by the Bodhisatta's wife in another *jātaka* (*Kumbhakāra-jātaka*, J 408), when it is adopted by Bimbā's 'self' there, a potter's wife. Only in the *Janaka-jātaka*, however, however, is the Bodhisatta's wife explicitly described as practising *samatha* meditation and attaining a specific meditative state. Attachment to women is clearly an obstacle to the Bodhisatta's path, yet no real blame is attached to the women themselves. In contrast to the usual Indian expectations of the time, women are shown as having equal capacity for renunciation and spiritual practices, and they win heaven alongside their husbands or independently.

One of the most accomplished female characters in the *Mahānipāta* is Princess Rucā in the *Nārada-jātaka*, who gives a long and eloquent teaching about karma to her father, including extensive recollection of her past and future lives. However, Rucā amply demonstrates the broader context of women's achievements in the *jātaka*s, for she also explains her own negative karmic past—as a man going after other men's wives—as the cause of her female birth. Being merely a girl, she is unable to convince her father of the error of his fatalist beliefs and in the end must call upon the intervention of a deity. The story highlights the fact that as beings bearing a negative karmic load, women have limited capabilities and may need to rely upon ruses or the assistance of other beings. Thus Candā in the *Candakumāra-jātaka*, like Princess Rucā, is reliant upon the gods to save her husband. In the *Vidhura-jātaka* female *nāga*s play upon stereotypical female powers: Queen Vimalā pretends to be suffering from an insatiable craving, and her daughter Irandatī lures a potential suitor to carry out her desires. Thus, we learn, women have some power, but they may also have certain limitations at least in terms of their social standing.

That women's social limitations do not stop them exercising considerable personal initiative and courage is amply demonstrated by the *Mahosadha-jātaka*. Mahosadha's wife is truly his equal in nobility, ingenuity, and resource. She understands fully his non-verbal language of gestures when they first meet and challenges him with some of her own. She then describes a 'secret way' for him to follow to find her home, an anticipation of the 'secret way' of the tunnel he builds later in the tale. She also resourcefully safeguards his good name by carefully recording dates and names when people deliver 'gifts' to her house, so that when the Bodhisatta is accused of stealing them she can prove they were not taken by him. Her husband later uses a comparable ploy when he marks messages on the clothes and gifts he gives to the conquered kings, thus providing subsequent 'proof' of their lack of loyalty to their leader when messages from Mahosadha are found on their person. But perhaps the female character who is most independent is the ascetic Bherī, also in the *Mahosadha-jātaka*, who demonstrates the extreme alternative to the careful social negotiation of the other women in the stories. She, like the Bodhisatta's spouse, understands his 'secret' language of gestures; her 'water spirit' question, which asks the king to list his order of preference of whom to save in an emergency, is the last and perhaps the most skilled of all the many riddles posed in this story: it tests the king, ensures that the status of Mahosadha is recognized and safeguarded, and allows Mahosadha's often secretly exercised skills to be seen and made known to the general public.

Thus in many stories of the Great Ten, women are supportive, creatively resourceful, and truly active heroines in their own right. The few negative portrayals involve minor characters, and they do little to counteract the wealth of positive examples. Humour is very difficult to assess in ancient cultures, but there is perhaps an element of fun in some negative depictions: the brahmin's wife who berates him all the time in the *Vessantara* is, for instance, far more likely to raise a laugh than be taken as a serious criticism of women as a whole. Given the ways in which the female figures in the Great Ten predominantly display courage and wisdom, these stories go some way towards rebalancing perceptions of the *jātaka*s as misogynous.

Realms of Rebirth

The *jātaka*s are not only concerned with human protagonists; indeed many of the early stories of the *Jātakatthavaṇṇanā* are delightful animal fables that transport us to the world of deer, lions, monkeys, or other colourful characters. While animals do not feature heavily in the Great Ten, we do find a variety of other beings from different rebirth realms, including gods and spirit deities of various kinds. According to the Buddhist worldview, humans share the realm of rebirth (*saṃsāra*) with gods, animals, ghosts, and hell beings. Humans may be reborn in any of these realms as a result of karma, and although rebirth in some realms—particularly the heavens and hells—may be for a long time, any rebirth is ultimately temporary. Thus even the gods, powerful and happy though they may be, are inferior to those human beings who have achieved *nibbāna* and thus liberation from the cycle of rebirth altogether.

One way the gods are shown to be inferior to spiritually advanced human beings is through stories in which certain deities serve the Buddha or Bodhisatta. In *jātaka*s the deity is usually Sakka (Sanskrit Śakra, or Indra), king of the gods and overlord of the Heaven of the Thirty-Three (Tāvatiṃsa), which is so-named because it is home to the thirty-three gods of the Vedic pantheon. An Indian deity who is shared with Hindu and Jain mythology, Sakka is associated with a peculiar motif in which the great virtue of a human being causes his throne to heat up or to tremble. This is sometimes explained as being because such virtue might lead the human being to oust Sakka from his throne, for his position as king of the gods is temporary. After his attention has been drawn to the virtuous human being by the movement of his throne, Sakka usually pays a visit to test the human or to offer assistance. Thus in the *Janaka-jātaka* he guides the Bodhisatta's mother to safety, and in the *Candakumāra-jātaka* he disrupts a human sacrifice and thereby saves the Bodhisatta's life. One of his most significant contributions comes in the *Vessantara-jātaka*, when he requests Vessantara's wife as a gift in order to enable Vessantara's fulfilment of the perfection of giving without undue danger to him or his wife.

As king of the Tāvatiṃsa heaven Sakka has several other gods under his command. The divine architect Vissakamma (Sanskrit Viśvakarman), who is also taken over from wider Indian mythology, is several times ordered to build a suitable hermitage for the Bodhisatta or other renouncers (as in the stories of Temiya, Sāma and Vessantara) or to provide divine ornaments. Sakka's charioteer Mātali also features in the stories, driving the chariot that fetches King Nemi to heaven, and explaining to the king the different hells and heavens and the reasons for rebirth in them. Sakka's kingship is also demonstrated when he convinces fellow *deva*s to take birth in the realm of men; in *jātaka* stories the fellow *deva* is usually the Bodhisatta, and

Sakka invites him to take birth for the benefit of humankind and in order to fulfil the perfections, as in the stories of Temiya, Sāma, and Vessantara.

The other major Indian god to feature in Buddhist narrative is Brahmā, who in many Hindu sources is said to be the creator of the world and grandfather of all the other gods. In Buddhist terms Brahmā becomes a category of god rather than an individual, and in the *Mahānipāta* we encounter only one Brahmā, Nārada Brahmā of the *Nārada-jātaka*, who also shares his name with the great divine sage Nārada of wider Indian fame. The Brahmā heavens are higher than Tāvatiṃsa, and are the usual rebirth realm for the Bodhisatta when he has been practising *jhāna* meditation in the forest. Indeed, the Brahmā realms are closely associated with the different *jhāna* states, even sharing some of their names (see Table 4). In contrast, the heavens of the *deva* gods, such as Tāvatiṃsa, are associated more with generosity (*dāna*) and morality (*sīla*).

Table 4. Realms of rebirth according to Theravāda tradition

Formless (*arūpa*) Realm Equivalent to *jhānas* 5–8	Neither perception nor non-perception Nothingness Consciousness only Infinite space
Realm of Pure Form (*rūpa*) Equivalent to *jhānas* 1–4	Sixteen heavens of the Brahmās, the top five of which are the 'Pure Abodes' for non-returners
Realm of Sense Desires (*kāma*)	Six lowest heavens, including Tāvatiṃsa and Tusita Humans Animals Ghosts (*petas*) Hell realms (usually eight, with Avīci at the bottom)

In addition to gods of the heavens, several other deities play a role in the *Mahānipāta*. As we have already noted, localised goddesses often have a protective role: the goddess of the parasol in the *Temiya-jātaka*, for example, advises Temiya how to escape the kingship, while a forest goddess saves the Bodhisatta's life in the story of Sāma. The goddess of the ocean, Maṇimekhalā, who is famous from a Tamil epic that bears her name, rescues Janaka from the sea. These goddesses are very much tied to the earth, though they may also spend time in heaven realms, and indeed may neglect their protective duties as a result.

Also tied more to the earth than to the heavens are certain categories of being that might be labeled 'spirit deities' (following DeCaroli 2004). Such beings include *nāgas*, who are snake deities associated with opulent underwater palaces and the guardianship of valuable jewels. The Bodhisatta is born as a *nāga* in the *Bhūridatta-jātaka*, and while he is rich and powerful he realises the limits of his rebirth and has to enter the human realm in order to observe the *uposatha* holy day. The traditional enemies of the *nāgas* are the eagle-like *garuḍas* or *supaṇṇas*, who also appear in the Great Ten. In the *Vidhura-jātaka* four kings—of the *nāgas*, *supaṇṇas*, men, and gods (Sakka)—assemble in a park to observe the *uposatha* and compare their virtues. The *nāga* king is subsequently involved in a plot to kill the Bodhisatta, though only due to a misunderstanding of his wife's wishes. Also in the *Vidhura-jātaka* we encounter one of the more frightening of the spirit deities, a *yakkha*. These beings are sometimes violent and so can be a threat to humans, though they are also able to take on a protective role. A female *yakkha*, or *yakkhinī*, features in the *Mahosadha-jātaka* as a threat to a human child, pacified in the end by the wise Mahosadha. Such ambivalent beings, with their capacity for moral action but tendency towards violence, provide narrative colour in the *Mahānipāta* and remind us to look around at the wider realms outside our own human existence.

Literary Features of the Great Ten

Cowell's comments in the preface to his translation of the *jātakas* sum up an assumption that still persists in some quarters today: 'Their foremost interest to us consists in their relation to folk-lore and the light which they often throw on those popular stories which illustrate so vividly the ideas and superstitions of the early times of civilisation' (Cowell 1895–1907: I ix). It is always, however, risky to underestimate any folk composition: ballads, tales, songs, and poems of such a type are often imbued with their own rhythms, conventions, and literary styles. These are often far more sophisticated than they first appear, as Valerie Roebuck (2010: xlv–lvii) has indicated in her excellent introduction to the *Dhammapada* verses, which compares the verse form there to European ballads. Even if the term 'folk' is accepted for some of the short stories near the beginning of the collection, the Great Ten triumphantly exhibit the *jātaka* form at its most expressive, poetic, and heroic, often exploiting the genre to produce a literature with its own styles, tropes, and literary patterns. *Jātaka*s have evolved with their own conventions, not shared by any other form of Pāli Buddhist composition. Based in style on the ancient mix of prose and verse found in Vedic prose/verse commentaries, all *jātaka*s have their own distinctive template. There is the story in the present, the story in the past, verses, and final connections made at the end. This provides a flexible yet stable literary form allowing for a variety of types of tale to be incorporated within a standard pattern. The Great Ten, however, see the development of this form to create almost a new genre with affinities with the great works of Western and Indian epic and drama but demonstrating its own particular excellences. The Great Ten are quite different in tone, style, and structure from, for instance, the *Dhammapada* commentarial stories, perhaps their nearest relative in early Pāli literature, where a comparable mix of verse and prose is employed, however, to emphasise the long karmic journeys of individuals over several lifetimes and the means by which various *arahat*s attain awakening in their final lives (Burlingame 1990). The literary style and composition of the Great Ten require much more work and scholarly attention, but some reference to one feature, that of repetition, will help to demonstrate the artistic consideration that has gone into making this genre so distinctive.

The repetition of formulae is a key feature of oral literature, but for the Great Ten there is a risk we just leave it at that and do not explore the way it is used in specific stories of the Great Ten. Here, Parry's comments on Homeric epic are apt:

> These lines could be shown, by an examination of parallel passages, to be almost entirely made up of formulaic elements. That they are so amazingly beautiful is of course the consequence of Homer's art in arranging these formulae. (Parry 1964: 49)

Where repetition is used in the Great Ten, often of quite simple and unremarkable phrases, it is also often and indeed usually associated with a specific emotional or dramatic effect, allowing the refrain-like music of the verses to operate in accordance with the specific atmosphere or world each tale evokes. In the *Janaka-jātaka* (Chapter 2), for instance, simple formulae, repeated in each line, characterise all the *pada*s in both the verse eulogy made to Mithilā before the Bodhisatta renounces (vv. 48–77) whereas the pleasures of the holy life are described in an antithetical set of verses immediately afterwards that follow an identical structure (vv. 79–108).[16] These are in the standard sixteen-syllable *vatta* form, so the second line, of sixteen syllables, is repeated.[17] In this way the split in the tale between the quest for the royal life in the first part and the desire for renunciation in the second is powerfully reinforced and given lyrical expression through verse, simple repetition building up the weight of the Bodhisatta's decision to leave all the pleasures of the lay life behind. In the *Sāma-jātaka* (Chapter 3), a quite different type of tale, verse lines are repeated, sometimes unknowingly, by the few central characters in the tale, thus demonstrating their underlying affinity to one another, a major preoccupation in this tale dedicated to extolling the importance of loving-kindness. Sāma's parents often immediately echo each other's sentiments, while the same verses are used by Sāma and his parents at different times, in different situations (see, for instance, vv. 46–8 and 107–9). The king, who disrupts their idyll, importantly does not share this linguistic affinity with other players: he likes to introduce himself with a regurgitation of the same repeated boast of his own merits and grandeur.[18] In *Nemi*, with its descriptions of the heavens and the hells, repetition is used quite differently, yet is also central to the tale's effect, by evoking the apparently endless time schemes of both heavenly and hellish realms. In this story a sense of the apparently endless experiential time of hellish and heavenly states is also, importantly, balanced by sudden changes of events that take place in one moment. In *Vessantara*, as the introduction to the tale notes, refrain-like verse lines or half-lines constantly echo one another, repeated by several characters, producing an intricate and constantly moving network of speech repetitions and affinities between the many characters, circumstances, and events. In this story all characters seem interrelated; all play their part, and many mirror one another's speech patterns, as they contribute to the culmination of the Bodhisatta's great work in his search for the perfections. Much more work needs to be undertaken on this one feature of the long tales; but as these examples suggest, repetition in these stories is just one part of setting the linguistic pattern and tone of a particular tale. There is certainly a *jātaka* style for these very long stories.

16. For discussion of this see Shaw 2006a: 270 n. 41.

17. This is the usual metre for *jātakas*, though sometimes the archaic eleven- or twelve-syllable form is found, in portions that are possibly from an older layer of the text.

18. For discussion of this see Shaw 2006a: 278–9 and 309 nn. 30–1.

Elements it includes are simple tropes played in different ways for different exploratory effects; a love of ballad-like examinations of great feeling, sorrow and rejoicing, often, as in the *Janaka* lines quoted above, with a repeated eight- or sixteen-syllable formula; magnificent epic descriptions of armies and court processions; impassioned extended debate on points of *dhamma* and kingship; and a simple delight in the evocation of many different realms and kinds of beings. Character and details of personal interchange are explored with far greater depth and precision than is allowed in shorter tales: these are very human dramas. In the Great Ten these features are amplified to suggest heroic journeys of quite different kinds, not just for the Bodhisatta, but for other key players too.

Indeed there are many such 'felicities', to borrow a term so skilfully given by Steven Collins, for the benefits described as attendant on the Buddhist path, in the poetry, narrative, and content in the Great Ten (Collins 1998). Imagery and symbolic language are particularly memorable, with the great length of the stories allowing for a single trope or image to be explored for all its salvific and metaphoric implications (Meiland 2004). The extended swim of Janaka against all odds provides the underlying struggle for the tale devoted to vigour (*viriya*); the tunnel that can lead to safety but can be a hell if cut off from light, in *Mahosadha*, anticipates the power of the great wisdom said to be needed by the Bodhisatta to teach as a Buddha. In the Great Ten, kingship is explored, the possibilities of the householder's and the warrior's lifestyles examined (*Vidhura*), and the opportunities for wisdom in all walks of life tested and enacted (*Mahosadha*). Great grief and lamentation are given lyrical outlet, voicing the suffering underlying existence in *saṃsāra*. Perhaps most creatively symbolic of the panoramic vision of the Great Ten as a collection, however, is the image of the clear jewel that is the object of the gamble in *Vidhura*, the penultimate tale. This is so pure it can reveal an entire universe, with many different kinds of beings, all inhabiting their own worlds (Chapter 9, vv. 48–88). The even-mindedness and wide-ranging breadth of vision arising from equanimity, the last perfection, is suggested here and is characteristic of the fourth, and to some extent the third, *jhāna* (meditation) of the Buddha's own system (Vsm IV 153–202). It is this quality needed by the Buddha when he attains enlightenment to recollect all his past lives, see those of others, and encompass a whole universe of *saṃsāra* in his scope of understanding. Present as the great depth of feeling that arises in meditation when it is untroubled even by joy or pain, the jewel seems also like the perspective offered by the Great Ten as a whole. This capaciousness, and the generosity of the first perfection, manifest in the Bodhisatta vow and expressed in the last great story of the collection, have made the Great Ten historically so direct and accessible. Sometimes this is achieved simply through communicating how the ordinary can yet be heroic, such an important feature of *jātaka* expression, even when there is no metaphor involved (e.g. *Temiya*, vv. 12–21). As Roebuck (2010: lvii) says of *Dhammapada* verses, 'with no similes or ornaments and the plainest of vocabulary these verses leave the translator with nowhere to hide. In the original they are capable of bringing a tear to the eye; but it would be too much to expect a translation to do the same.'

The *Jātakas* and Other Indian Literature

The *jātakas* are the product of a broader Indian narrative scene, and the *Mahānipāta* stories in particular appear to have a strong relationship with Indian epic sources. The Indian epics, namely the *Mahābhārata* and *Rāmāyaṇa*, were composed during the same period as the *Jātakatthavaṇṇanā* and, like *jātakas*, drew on common themes and characters that were most likely already familiar to their audiences. Some of these common characters also appear in later Hindu sources as well as in the narrative literature of Jainism, an Indian religion that emerged during the same period as Buddhism under many of the same influences.

One character who is equally at home in the *jātakas* and the epics is the king of the gods, Indra, also known as Śakra, or in the Pāli of the *jātakas*, Sakka. We have already discussed how this divine monarch provides assistance to the Bodhisatta at various points in the *Mahānipāta* stories, often by commanding other deities to carry out their duties, and the two most significant of these deities—Mātali and Viśvakarman (Pāli Vissakamma)—are in the service of Indra in Hindu sources as well. In other cases Sakka intervenes more directly, answering questions of doctrine (*Nemi-jātaka*), preventing acts of violence (*Candakumāra-jātaka*), or granting sons (as in the *Temiya-jātaka* and *Suvaṇṇasāma-jātaka*); the latter motif speaks to a broader association between Indra and fertility. Sakka seems particularly associated with protecting women, for he is shown guiding the Bodhisatta's mother to safety (*Janaka-jātaka*) and responding to the pleas of the Bodhisatta's wife to save him (*Candakumāra-jātaka*).[19] He also tests

19. For further discussion of Indra's interactions with women see Söhnen 1991. In

the generosity of the Bodhisatta, or rather allows him to demonstrate his generosity, as he does in many other stories both within the *jātaka*s and in the epics.[20]

Another divine figure that is familiar from wider Indian narrative is the sage Nārada, who features in the epics and in several *Purāṇas*, as well as in Jain sources.[21] He is a divine sage (*deva-ṛṣi*) and is often portrayed as a messenger figure or a character that interferes in the affairs of both humans and gods. In the *Nārada-jātaka* he is further identified as a god of the Brahmā realm, thus playing also with the familiarity of the god Brahmā. The identification of the *Nārada-jātaka*'s Brahmā god as the divine sage Nārada suggests an awareness amongst the original audiences of the *Mahānipāta* of this pan-Indian character and his associations. Notably in the *Jātakamālā* version of the story the god is simply said to be from one of the higher heavens, and is not identified as Nārada.[22]

It is not only gods that appear in both epic and *jātaka* contexts. King Janaka is a prominent figure in wider Indian narrative, and in many cases he is associated with determined renunciation. The verses that he speaks in the *Janaka-jātaka* about his lack of concern for the burning city of Mithilā are found in the *Mahābhārata* as well as in a Jain context. Other Janakas, such as the father of Sītā, heroine of the *Rāmāyaṇa*, have little interest in renunciation. Vidhura too has a life in the *Mahābhārata*, where he features as the wise uncle of the two sets of warring cousins. The presence of a dicing match at the centre of the *Vidhura-jātaka*, as also at the centre of the *Mahābhārata*, suggests many layers of interaction.[23]

Hindu sources he is often characterised as a seducer of women, but as Söhnen argues, he also has a clear role as granter of children and preserver of women's virtue. In Buddhist sources it is this positive interaction with women that is most prominent. See Appleton (forthcoming).

20. Indra, as king of the gods, lives in constant fear of losing his position to a rival, and his role as tester of virtue is often linked to this fear. Thus, for example, he tries to disrupt ascetic practice or other activities that might lead to a human ousting him from his throne. However, this aspect of his character is not found in the *Mahānipāta* stories. Instead, in the *Vessantara-jātaka* we see him approach Vessantara in order to assist him and protect his wife from harm. For further discussion of this motif see Appleton (forthcoming).

21. For a discussion of Nārada's role in Hindu and Jain sources see Geen (forthcoming).

22. The story features as number twenty-nine in the collection. See Khoroche 1989: 205–12.

23. Connections such as this one are discussed in the introductions to the individual stories.

Many other stories in the *Jātakatthavaṇṇanā* also feature Indian gods or other familiar characters, yet there is a particularly high concentration of links to common Indian narrative heritage within the Great Ten. That is not to say that these stories are sympathetic to non-Buddhist *ideas*, however, only that they drew on a range of influences from a wider Indian tradition. The forceful critique of Vedic religion at the end of the *Bhūridatta-jātaka* and the common presence of brahmin villains (most prominently in the *Candakumāra* and *Vessantara*) leave no doubt about how the Brahmanical Hindu values of the Indian epics would have been viewed by our stories' composers. That these stories weave together so many different themes, characters and motifs only adds to their richness and endurance as products of a period of intense narrative activity in South Asia.

Jātakas in Buddhist Life and Practice

From early days *jātakas* were called one of the nine limbs (*aṅgas*) of the teaching, so they have always been central to Southern Buddhist practice: the Pāli version is our only complete extant collection of a type of tale found in many Buddhisms. Indeed at the end of most of the shorter stories, in the assigned connections (*samodhāna*), the assembled company are given teachings on the four noble truths, and many attain one of the four stages of the path to awakening on the basis of this instruction. The implications of this are interesting, for listening to *jātakas*, presumably with great mindfulness, can itself then be considered a salvific activity, aligned with *samādhi* and the last three factors of the eightfold path.

But how does this work in practice? The role of the tales must have varied in different places and times. Certainly their depiction in early temples and reports by the Chinese pilgrims of processions and portrayals representing the stories suggest that they were a central part of festive and imaginative culture from the earliest days (Legge 1886: 106; Skilling 2008: 59–68). In eleventh- to thirteenth-century Pagan, in Myanmar, they become core, shared narratives, translated into vernaculars, and offered images and well-known scenes that linked travellers, locals, and different linguistic groups and tribes through promotion of a Bodhisatta ideal and a Buddhist path that transcended culture, ethnicity, and caste (Handlin 2012: 210). There they constituted the major part of all visual cultures in temples from that period and formed the very ground of the imaginative life and Buddhist understanding of both lay and monastic visitors. In other places and times their status may have been more fluid, but they feature constantly in temple art from the earliest days. As Skilling (2012: 334) writes, 'the *jātakas* spill out of the baskets of the *Tripiṭaka* with an exuberance that cannot be stifled'.

Their most popular expression today, and perhaps also in ancient times, is on festive days, when they might be recited, dramatized, or sung, in various mixtures of Pāli and local vernaculars, and occasionally accompanied by music. Throughout early *jātaka* stories the injunction is given to practise generosity, morality and to observe the *uposatha*. It seems likely that historically, as is the case now, *jātakas* were told when the assembled company of laity are observing extra precepts, wearing white and observing the *uposatha* in a way that all activities would be part of a purificatory, collective *bhāvanā*, shared by all present. Being in temples where *jātakas* are depicted would enhance a sense of auspiciousness by placing practitioners in the presence of the Buddha's 'history', which has long been so central to Buddhist practice (Appleton 2010a: 128–32; Brown 1997; Swearer 2004: 232). During such festival days, known as *poya* days in Sri Lanka, the listeners make offerings of flowers, incense, lights, and food to the shrine, offer food to the monks, and share food with other practitioners. A *jātaka* recitation is part of an ongoing field of goodwill and festivity, and part of defining what people are and feel. The *Mahānipāta* is particularly important for such occasions. A yearly national competition in Myanmar gives an award and special performance of one of the last ten, which varies from year to year: there are songs, probably dating back to the nineteenth century, associated with the Great Ten.[24] The stories' influence is felt throughout the culture, in all sorts of ways (Pannavamsa 2007a and 2007b, Obeyesekere 2009: 20–1). They constantly interweave with popular anecdote, story, and song. Peter Skilling (2012: 336) writes, 'Vernacular literature is in constant conversation with Pali and Sanskrit, with *nīti* and narrative, with deities and protectors, with rote and recitation, with rhythm and metre, with brush and trowel.'

The stories permeate lay and monastic understanding of the Buddhist path as part of a larger life of the Buddha (Appleton 2010a: 41–64, 135). In Sri Lanka, Vesākha, the celebration of the birth, death, and final awakening of the Buddha, is a particularly important time for *jātakas*, with decorated lamps, processions, and pictures all introducing *jātaka* themes; some of

24. I am grateful to participants at the Buddhist Culture Conference at Sitagu Academy, Yangon, December 2012, for describing and singing a couple of these.

the songs are more recent innovations, showing the continued creativity the stories arouse, while others are perhaps more ancient customs (Appleton 2010a: 150–7). *Vessantara-jātaka* often has its own festival though is sometimes also performed, recited, or sung in Pāli or vernaculars at the Vesakha celebration. This story, so popular since ancient times, now has days of songs, rituals, offerings, and customs associated with its performance as a village and communal event, which will be discussed in its introduction later in this book.

One canonical passage says that there is 'hearing *dhamma* at the right time, discussing *dhamma* at the right time, calm (*samatha*) at the right time, insight (*vipassanā*) at the right time' (AN II 141). In societies in which reading was not the norm, listening to stories would not be just a diversion, albeit an auspicious one, or even simply a means of obtaining a 'didactic' service, in communicating principles by which to live. If we take the model of the earliest texts, and one suspects, the role they performed in many traditional rural societies, the extended narratives of the Great Ten are also themselves a way of arousing calm (*samatha*) and concentration (*samādhi*) by encouraging attentiveness and interest under conditions of mindfulness. The *Saṅgītī Sutta* (DN 33) lists five spheres of freedom (*vimuttāyatana*): hearing the teaching from one who knows, hearing it from one who has heard it, chanting the texts (*sajjhāyaṃ*), investigating them carefully (*dhammaṃ cetasā anuvitakketi anuvicāreti manasā'nupekkhati*), and grasping the sign of calm meditation,[25] leading to wisdom. In each case this process leads to gladdening of the mind, and then to joy. This joy makes the body tranquil, and the tranquil body becomes happy, and the happy mind goes to concentration, *samādhi* (DN III 241–2).[26] The stories are not specifically mentioned in this passage, but the role of *jātaka*s as a practice (*bhāvanā*) arousing sustained attention places them in the perspective of limbs of the teaching. The early commentator on meditation, Upatissa, certainly perceives them in that way: he incorporates them into his account

25. The 'sign' is the *nimitta*, the mental image that arises in some calm meditations.

26. The series, such as at MN 7, PTS edn I 38, is frequent in Pāli texts: *Tassa atthapaṭisaṃvedino dhammapaṭisaṃvedino pāmojjam jāyati, pamuditassa pīti jāyati, pītimanassa kāyo passambhati, passaddhakāyo sukhaṃ vedeti, sukhino cittaṃ samādhiyati.* 'He finds delight in the goal, finds inspiration from the teaching, and finds gladness associated with the teaching. And in the one who is glad, joy arises. In one of joyful mind, the body becomes tranquil. In the one whose body is tranquil, happiness arises. In one who feels happiness, the mind becomes concentrated.'

of the recollection of the Buddha (*Buddhānussati*), a meditation leading to calm, saying the Buddha 'revealed the birth stories of the time when he was Bodhisatta, in order to encourage others to gain the light' (Ehara et al. 1977: 144).[27] For many, they are a way of demonstrating and enjoying the happy lay life as well as the monastic, and a means of investigating the perfections in a way that can be understood at all levels of practice, to be developed by anyone. When these very long stories are recounted or chanted, sometimes in vernaculars or mixed with Pāli, many secular interests are accommodated, explained, and perhaps transformed by a Buddhist understanding, thereby contributing to a form of collective *bhāvanā*. But the heroes are taken as models for investigative insight and private meditation too: Janaka for instance is given sometimes in *dhamma* talks as a model for not giving up when things seem to go badly, and Sāma as an example of the power of loving-kindness.[28]

The history of *jātaka*s is one of chant, recitation, drama, song, and music, expressed in all kinds of vernaculars. Ranjini Obeyesekere (2012: xxxix) describes them still being chanted in Sri Lanka in village halls. But they are also included and eulogized amongst chants by the laity, often in daily practice. In Southeast Asia, two particularly popular chants, whose origins and dates are not clear, relate to the Great Ten. These may be seen as an extension of the recollection of the Buddha practice, a meditation producing calm and happiness that is frequently evoked in modern chanting as a preliminary to meditation, in group chanting, and as private homage in the morning and evening during visits to temples and *stūpas*.

The first is a general chant with a songlike melody, found with regional variations in style, rhythm, and arrangement of lines, about the ten perfections and the thirty-three variations therein (three levels for each of the ten perfections and the ten as a whole). The chant follows the usual sequence of the perfections when they are used as a list on their own: *dāna* (generosity), *sīla* (morality), *nekkhamma* (renunciation), *paññā* (wisdom), *viriya* (vigour), *khanti* (forebearance), *sacca* (truthfulness), *adhiṭṭhāna* (resolve), *mettā* (loving kindness) and *upekkhā* (equanimity).

27. The meditator reflects on such excellences of the Buddha in order to arouse cheerfulness, calm, and confidence in the path. For the recollection of the Buddha as a meditation practice, see also Buddhaghosa's instructions at Vism 197 VII 1–67 and for explanation, Shaw 2006b: 109–18.

28. Ven. Dhammasāmi at Oxford Buddha Vihāra, in a meditation class in 2012.

Sampanno iti pi so Bhagavā	This is how the Blessed One is endowed:
Dāna pāramī sampanno	Endowed with perfection of generosity
Dāna upapāramī sampanno	Endowed with the higher perfection of generosity
Dāna paramatthapāramī sampanno	Endowed with the highest perfection of generosity,
Mettā maitrī karuṇā muditā upekkhā pāramī sampanno	With friendliness, loving-kindness, compassion, sympathetic joy, and equanimity:
Iti pi so Bhagavā	This is how the Blessed One is endowed.

This is repeated, with *sīla*, *nekkhamma*, *paññā*, *viriya*, *khantī*, *sacca*, *adhiṭṭhāna*, *mettā*, *upekkhā*, and finally *dasa* (the ten perfections and then finally all ten together) in place of *dāna*; the chant then concludes:

Iti pi so Bhagavā	This is how the Blessed One is endowed.
Buddhaṃ saraṇaṃ gacchāmi	I go to the Buddha as my refuge
Namāmi'haṃ	

(Samatha Trust 2008: 34)

Another variation on the chant is much longer and says that the perfections are practised for personal enlightenment, for the sake of one's relatives and family, and for the whole world (Oxford Buddha Vihāra c. 2010: 11–14).

Even the names of the Bodhisatta in the *Mahānipāta* are associated with protection and good fortune, as in the Thai mnemonic to the first syllables of his names in each (Appleton 2010a: 139 ff.). Another popular chant takes the heroes of each of these 'last' ten lives and adds another, his life as Siddhattha, in a measure that integrates the final life with the ten that are popularly supposed to precede it (the Bodhisatta's unnamed sojourn in the Tusita realm before his final birth not being included).

> *Ayantu bhoto idha dāna sīla nekkhamma paññā viriya khanti sacca adhiṭṭhāna mettā upekkhā yuddhāya vo gaṇhatha āvudhāniti*
> *Iti pi so Bhagavā Temiyo nāma bhagavā seṭṭhaṃ vattahaṃ ārammaṇam dhuvaṃ sohaṃ buddho bhavissati kusalattā dhammā sammāsaṃbuddho*

This is repeated with *Mahājanako*, *Suvaṇṇasāmo*, *Nemiro*, *Mahosadho*,

Bhuridatto, *Candakumāro*, *Nārado*, *Vidhurapaṇḍito*, *Vessantaro*, and *Siddhattho* in place of *Temiyo*; the chant then concludes:

> *Iti pi so Bhagavā Buddho anantādiguṇo*
> *Iti pi so Bhāgavā iti pi so*
> (Oxford Buddha Vihāra: 9–10)

Here the perfections are extolled as 'weapons' for the 'struggle' of life, to be aroused by everyone: the 'heroes' all contribute to the great skilfulness of the Buddha in his final life and his immeasurable (*anantādiguṇo*) excellencies.[29] Both these chants add an eleventh component to the ten suggested by the *Mahānipāta*: in the first, the ten as a collection; in the second, the final life of the Bodhisatta as Siddhattha. As indicated earlier, a sense that the Bodhisatta is bringing together the ten perfections in his final life is reinforced.

*Jātaka*s in general, and the *Mahānipāta* in particular, may have assumed different roles within the teaching at various times. At certain times in Buddhist history, such as from the eleventh century onwards in Myanmar, they were central, and at others they provided more of an imaginative background, mixed with local legends, myths, anecdotes, marvels, and stories, percolating through into daily language and life. Their presence amongst the daily chants of practitioners in South and Southeast Asia shows that the *Mahānipāta* stories, and the associated heroes and perfections, are still very much part of Southern Buddhist life and practice.

The *Mahānipāta* and the Arts

Throughout Southern Buddhist history the relationship between text, practice and visual image is complex and interesting. We do know that stories from the Great Ten are amongst the earliest portrayals in Indian temple art. In different periods they functioned as offerings, exempla, didactic aids, means of acquiring great merit, and even showcases for the best artists, sculptors, and craftsmen. All of these functions perhaps

29. A full translation is not given as the Pāli is unclear and links together a number of epithets and homages from other chants that do not translate well. Chants and mantras often pose this problem, as the effect is not intended to be literal; in this case it is rather a gathering of formulae associated with auspiciousness. An analogy could be made to the sometimes non-grammatical and even unintelligible song-like refrains in ballads and folk songs in the West.

have come into play to varying degrees, with, at one end of the spectrum, *jātaka* pictures (though not the Great Ten) hidden from view in a tunnel beneath Wat Si Chum in Sukothai, Thailand, and at the other end, the full-size murals, painted by superbly trained artists, in the splendidly regal Cave 1 at Ajanta or the cheerful folk art of banners and lanterns paraded in South and Southeast Asian festivals. To depict a life of the Bodhisatta is itself an act of great merit; for those present where they are shown, the lives celebrate the Bodhisatta ideal and act as reminders of the Buddha's great compassion, with examples others can follow. The *jātaka*s, including the *Mahānipāta*, are recited for new Buddha images so that they 'know' their history (Swearer 2004). In recent times, depictions can be simply decorative as well as auspicious, with Great Ten scenes adorning tables, water bowls, table mats, and wall hangings for the house.[30]

From the time of the earliest depictions, individual stories have always been popular and not necessarily shown together (see Ahir 2000). At Bharhut a named roundel shows Temiya sitting on his father's lap, standing by the grave digger, and delivering a discourse at the end of the story: as happens at various periods in *jātaka* depiction history, key events are picked out in a network or rounded arrangement. A fifth-century terracotta plaque found at Thayekittaya (Sriksetra) in Myanmar also shows Temiya. Janaka appears at Bharhut, on a named coping stone, with Sīvalī and the Bodhisatta standing together with the fletcher, a rare depiction of the two as an equal couple and with an emphasis on the renunciation not usually found in later portrayals of the story.[31] At Ajanta most of the Great Ten heroes are shown, though not together: Janaka (Cave 1), Sāma (Cave 10), Mahosadha (Cave 1), Bhūridatta (Cave 2), Vidhura (Cave 2), and Vessantara

30. Tourist shops throughout Pagan and Mandalay in Myanmar show such artefacts, with designs often based on twelfth- to thirteenth-century tile portrayals, but often with modern folk-art interpretations of the scenes too. A great deal of *jātaka* art, either copied by British Victorian artists, or commissioned or bought from Southeast Asian craftsmen, can be seen on the Victoria and Albert Museum website, http://collections.vam.ac.uk. For instance, an ornamental lacquered water bowl made at the beginning of the twentieth century by Saya Saing, from Pagan, shows *Mahosadha-jātaka* scenes. (Search the collections for 'Saya Saing'.)

31. A photograph of this taken in 1874 by Joseph Beglar is in the online British Library catalogue. For detail and definition, nineteenth-century black-and-white photographs can be invaluable in looking at *jātaka* art, as much has been defaced or eroded by climate since excavation. See http://www.bl.uk/onlinegallery and enter '10031499' in the search box.

(Cave 16 and 17) (Schlingloff 1987, vol. III).[32] Other sites where individual stories are shown are Nagarjunakonda, Sanchi and Amaravati (Ahir 2000). The heroes Sāma and Vessantara are shown in Gandhāran art (Skilling 2008: 63).

Single stories of course get picked out for different reasons. It would be interesting to go through each one of the Great Ten and see the art and the reception of the story at different historical periods and in different locations, though there has been little work undertaken on this. Mary Brockington has written a comprehensive account of early Indian Sāma/Śyāma depictions (Brockington 2010); this *jātaka* was singly depicted as a series of plaster tableaux in the twentieth century in the Mon Kaw Gun caves at Hpa An, a rural setting to which it is perfectly suited. Lilian Handlin has explored varied depictions of *Vidhura-jātaka* in Myanmar (Handlin 2010). Sarah Shaw has examined some different representations of the *Janaka-jātaka*, from Ajanta to Myanmar and Siam from the twelfth century onwards (Shaw 2012a). Gombrich's study of Vessantara has included much historical consideration of the artistic depiction of that tale, in Sri Lanka particularly, along with literary examination of other versions of Vessantara in non-Southern Buddhist regions, which as he shows, is key to appreciating the way the story was understood (PGPV: xii ff.). Through such exercises we see what has appealed about a particular story at different times: the *Janaka-jātaka*, for instance, is depicted at Bharhut showing the Bodhisatta and his wife with the fletcher, thus emphasising the *paccekabuddha* aspects and renunciation. The Ajanta Cave 1 depiction of Janaka, sponsored by King Hariṣena, focuses on the beautiful women and the court of a splendid kingship, while the thoughtful hero considers his renunciation. From twelfth-century Mon depictions onwards, Southern Buddhist portrayals focus primarily, however, on his rescue at sea—a nautical image suitable for cultures based so strongly on the ocean and river—and Janaka being recognized as king (Shaw 2012a). In the twentieth century, King Bhumibol of Thailand commissioned a number of artists to illustrate a new retelling of the *Janaka-jātaka*, suited to modern times (Bhumibol Adulyadej 1996).

It is also difficult to assess the literary and artistic effect of each of the stories. Some themes can be cross-cultural and can be linked to many

32. The Huntington Archive (http://www.huntingtonarchive.osu.edu) is the best online resource for Indian temple art.

Indian narratives and local legends, though their treatment may differ in important detail; however, it is often not really possible to say which came first (Skilling 2006a; Skilling 2009). But amongst South and Southeast Asian *Paññāsa-jātaka*s, *Mahājanaka-jātaka* is clearly the most influential of the Great Ten, and many tropes from that tale are found in these stories and in their frequent depiction in temple mural and tableau art. The rescuing goddess Maṇimekhalā features in many, though her interventions are frequently on flooded rivers too (see Shaw 2012b and Jaini 1981–3). *Nemi-jātaka* must have been a great influence on the greatly popular Phra Malai stories, about an *arahat*'s visit to the heavens and hells (Ginsburg 1989: 72–88); there is no stated evidence connecting them. The impact of the *nāga*–human intermarriage content of *Bhūridatta-jātaka* on art, myth, and vernacular legend is less tangible, but the many legends and chronicles of *nāga*s marrying royalty seem to be a central part of Myanmar and its coastal culture—legend-based art in temples in Pegu in particular shows such themes—though whether this was influenced by this story is hard to say (see Stadtner 2011: 80–4). The cultural background and the reception of other single stories are discussed a little in the chapters devoted to them in this book.

At what point the Great Ten become associated specifically with each of the perfections is hard to say. Commentarial material makes no assignation of the ten perfections to each one of the *Mahānipāta*, so it is not surprising that we do not have early evidence of them being depicted as a grouping. The ten perfections were certainly perceived as central to early Buddhists: Acariya Dhammapāla's treatise on the ten *pāramī*s and the Bodhisatta path was composed around the time that Buddhaghosa was writing, in fifth-century Anuradhapura. At this stage however, they do not seem associated with *jātaka*s, which, oddly, he never mentions (Bodhi 1978).

The first evidence for the Great Ten having a symbolic, sequential role seems to start in their depiction as a series on ordination stones (*sīmā*) and tiles at Thaton, in what is now Southern Myanmar, in the eleventh century. Here, where scenes mark the boundary of an ordination space, they interestingly appear to offer an auspicious protective role: although the Bodhisatta renounces in several of the Great Ten, in these, as Bodhisatta he is primarily a layman dedicated to fulfilling his vow. Presumably such protective injunctions ensure the purity of the laity that enter into the sacred space they denote, where the *uposatha* would also be observed. Evidence is scanty for this period, and we simply do not know how the stories were viewed then, but the frequently lay figure of the Bodhisatta in the Great Ten, as well as the Buddha, perhaps was felt to offer a mediation between the world outside the temple and that within. At any rate, from this point onward the Great Ten, together or singly, find the prominence they are accorded in later art, and they are depicted on a number of *sīmā* stones in Thailand and Myanmar (Murphy 2010; Carbine 2012). We also see already a tendency for the emblematic encapsulation of a cluster of events to denote each of the Great Ten: from this time onwards, specific scenes are used to describe the whole story too, with a symbology that becomes quite stable, as if one memorable scene is a 'key-in' to the story as a whole (Appleton, Shaw, and Unebe 2013; Skilling 2008: 70 ff.).

In Myanmar the Great Ten, though still very much amongst other *jātaka*s, were particularly important from the twelfth century, as demonstrated in the temple art sites around Pagan such as the Ananda temple and the Lokahteikpan, when *jātaka*s seem to have become the main shared narrative for all the cultures brought together there; they have been richly explored and described by a number of scholars (Shin 1962; Luce 1969; Strachan 1989; Bautze-Picron and Bautze 2003; Handlin 2012). At this time, Mon, Burmese, and Pāli were employed fluidly to describe such depictions, suggesting that *jātakas* in this period acted as 'transregional and transcultural' systems of communicating Buddhist teaching (Skilling 2008: 68 ff.). Through validating the Bodhisatta path within a lay context, their cross-cultural appeal works across social groups to include monks, laity, visitors, and royal, aristocratic, merchant, and labouring classes. Handlin points out a strong sense of the societal, the injunctional, and the responsibilities of householders (*gahapati*s) in Buddhist emphasis during this period, with the king acting as a radiating focus for Buddhist principle (Handlin 2012: 199 ff.). We can sense the heritage of this *bhagavā* and the presence of a highly social and perhaps even grandiose patron, fulfilling his *cakkavattin* duties and gaining merit in funding temples but unable to resist guiding the hands of his artists in an exuberant display of regal and martial power. Throughout these temples, terracotta tiles, glazed and unglazed, in tiers outside temples are echoed by boxed pictures in continuous linear painted friezes inside; no space is filled without a *jātaka* story. In this role, *jātaka* depiction generally is didactic, and certainly decorative, but it seems also here celebratory and geared to societal concerns, providing a shared pool of narratives whose morals and codes are applicable to everyone. This was a fertile period of *stūpa* building and temple construction, with donative tiles, paintings, and a love of textual inscription in vernacular and Pāli. Commissioning patrons were the king or aristocratic Buddhists, but all seem to have felt the narratives applied to them (Handlin 2012: 210).

It was the custom to show all 547 stories on terracotta plaques surrounding the sides of *stūpas* in Pagan, such as at the Ananda temple (Maung 2012). So inevitably, though not seen on the ground, the Great Ten are near the peak and finial, the summation of the Bodhisatta path, often with more than one plaque per story. Later, with the influence of rich mercantile classes loyal to the institution of kingship, the last ten become increasingly prominent, with depictions as a group dominating temples, and their function seems to be illuminatory, meritorious, and as a general bringer of auspiciousness.

By the seventeenth century in Myanmar, for reasons that are not clear, the Great Ten assumed prime importance, superseding others as subjects for temple art. In central Myanmar, the rise of the merchant classes seems to accompany this trend. It is possible that the primarily royal and court preoccupations of the Great Ten, combined with a strong mercantile bias in tales such as *Mahosadha* and *Vessantara*, contributed to this appeal, and there is a strong advocacy of royal enjoyment and power in Burmese depictions of the Great Ten. In a forthcoming book, Alexandra Green describes the gradual changes affecting *jātaka* depictions over the next few centuries throughout Upper Burma. As she demonstrates, depictions of the Great Ten flourish in painted strip mural friezes that exhibit a burgeoning interest in background, landscape, natural environment, details of birds and animals, and jewels, as well as textiles and clothes; the latter two items would finance the murals. Textile designs inform the aesthetic of frieze surrounds, background, and boundary lines between pictures, suggesting that the paintings themselves were regarded as material objects and offerings to the Buddha (see Green forthcoming).[33] As Green notes elsewhere, from the fifteenth to the nineteenth century, a sense of process and continuity accompanies sequential and continuous narrative depictions of the Bodhisatta's quest. This sense of the path being ongoing and lasting many lifetimes—lay as well as monastic—is contrasted with depictions of the awakening in the final life as Gotama becomes Buddha; such moments are communicated in monoscenic mode, as if suspended in

33. It is significant that the first *jātaka*, the *Apaṇṇaka-jātaka* (Ja I 95–106), involves the Bodhisatta as a canny but responsible caravan merchant who protects his fellow traders from disaster and ruin; indeed the first four all involve traders, with the *Cullaka-seṭṭi-jātaka* (J 4; Ja I 114–23) constituting a celebration of mercantile values.

time (Green 2002: 67 ff.). The Great Ten describe the process of preparing for awakening: these are the stories, enacted through time and depicted as friezes that culminate in the full awakening of the final life and are of special appeal to a laity concerned with affairs in the world.

An inscription from 1380 at Sukothai describing the 'Dharma of the Ten Lives, extremely melodious to hear' suggests that in Siam the *Mahānipāta* were already being singled out from the rest of the collection from relatively early times (Skilling 2008: 70). From the seventeenth century onwards, throughout Southeast Asia, the sequence features as a series in its own right, a kind of background to the Buddhist path, and succession of stories where the Buddha, then a layman, has the usual dealings, debates, and meetings with others as Bodhisatta, not as a fully enlightened being. As Peter Skilling (2008: 72) notes, 'the *Jātaka* pictures are not illustrations: they exist in their own right, as amplifications and perfections of the Buddha.' Indeed for the last two or three hundred years the Great Ten have assumed in art the status of a kind of visual register of different kinds of Buddhist auspiciousness, with key images known to everyone.

By the end of the eighteenth century the pre-eminence of the Great Ten was emphasized in Myanmar, in King Bindon's royal orders, which stressed their importance as repositories of legal principle (Tun 1983). In art they still persisted as the main focus, a trend which has continued into the present day. At the Shwedagon pagoda in Yangon, there is a twentieth-century replica of the Mahābodhi temple in India, with large Great Ten depictions (Moore and Mayer 1999). Along the base of the great *stūpa*, a series of commercially produced glazed terracotta tiles from the first decade of the twentieth century, clearly all made from a template, show the Great Ten in sequences, with four tile scenes per story; these sequences are interspersed with tiles naming donors too, suggesting they were all privately commissioned as series (Shaw 2012a).

In Siam/Thailand, scenes from the last ten *jātakas* (*thotsachat* or *sip chat*) have been one of the most popular painted themes on temple mural walls since the Ayutthaya period, as the most popular expression of lay Buddhist devotion (Wray et al. 1996; Leksukhum and Mermet 2001: 136–59). There are some extant Great Ten depictions that seem to date from the Ayutthaya period in Siam, but unfortunately many of these simply and delicately coloured representations have been lost. Wat Chong Nonsi, Bangkok, from the late seventeenth century, is a notable exception to this (Leksukhum and Mermet 2001: 138, 154). From this time, always with the exception of the Vessantara, which seems always to have received particular attention as a 'one-off', outside the parameters of the Great Ten, the stories are most commonly seen as part of a sequence, representing the ten perfections, or at any rate the ten lives most associated with the completion of the work that is fulfilled in Buddhahood (Wray et al. 1996).

A new flowering occurred from the inception of a new monarchic line with the accession of Rama I in 1782, to the reign of King Mongkut, Rama IV (1851–68). This new capital, Bangkok, and a new monarchy, in a region already acting as a cosmopolitan hub of interchange, realigned the court and administration of Siam into a prime position for trade routes with China, India, and the West. The influx of contacts and increased mobility produced far greater interaction with people from other cultures, such as the Chinese, Dutch, Portuguese, and English, in an already internationally oriented society, and we often see depictions of them in Great Ten murals as part of the world observed by the Thai artists around them, as well as telescopes, guns, and contemporary clippers and sloops (Shaw 2014). Within the temple space, new features are absorbed as part of an ongoing delight in *Mahānipāta* portrayal: the stories feel as fresh as if they were happening in the 'present' of the artist. Temples where the series can be seen include Wat Yai Intharam, Wat Kongkaram, Wat Bang Yikhan and Wat Suwannaram (Leksukhum and Mermet 2001: 136 ff.; Wray et al 1996). The scenes often glow like jewelled visions on a dark background of Thai forest, making an emotionally organic, network movement that keeps each story separate but defies a sense of chronological time and place.

On a practical level, artistic curiosity and a desire for experimentation extended to new imported techniques and materials as well as outside subject matter for observation in figurative art. New matte paints and pigments of a far deeper and stronger shade, and by the middle of the nineteenth century, synthetic dyes introduced from China and the West as well as gold leaf from China, made the palette and appearance of Great Ten depiction more deeply colourful and highly contrasted, if occasionally a little less translucent and light than in the Ayutthaya period (Appleton, Shaw, and Unebe 2013: 101–9). Sometimes older murals were painted over with deeper, imported colours. The development of perspective and realist human depiction can all be seen entering the art during the nineteenth century. Subject matter, themes within that choice, and positioning of the murals, as well as a principle of integration that the narratives themselves suggest, seem to remain much the same: the Great Ten seem the natural adornments of the temple space (Shaw 2014). Great Ten depictions have continued in the twentieth and twenty-first centuries, though some Thai temples now favour *Vessantara* portrayals, usually with stock designs and styles for each of the thirteen chapters. From the late nineteenth century, sometimes the *Vessantara* is depicted along the wall behind the shrine, while the other nine are on the side walls, as in many temples restored or built in the twentieth century on the main market roads in Chiang Mai. In some ways scenes from the thirteen chapters are becoming a series like main scenes from the *Mahānipāta*, each evoking the whole of the chapter in which it occurs.

Sri Lanka is less well represented in modern art books and discussions of the subject. Gombrich's excellent slides of the *Vessantara-jātaka* frieze murals, mostly dating from the eighteenth century, are unfortunately only in the 1977 edition of PGPV and not in the 2011 one. They give a glimpse of this rich artistic tradition that still has some survivors, though many of the temples photographed by him are now in disrepair.[34] From early times, single stories, particularly *Vessantara*, were depicted, but there is no sense of the *Mahānipāta* as a distinct grouping. *Temiya* appears on the twelfth-century vestibule of the Tivanka shrine, Polonnuruwa. Holt (1996: 47–9, 65–6, 71–5) describes the depiction of *jātaka*s in general in the twelfth century. Coomaraswamy (1979: 11), quoting contemporary descriptions, says that in the Temple of the Tooth in the early eighteenth century, the 'thirty-two *jātaka*s' were painted superbly; this series included heroes Vidhura and Mahosadha. The great Kandyan period of frieze art, sometimes fresco and sometimes secco, dates from this period, with bright red colours and simple and striking ornamental motifs. Sometimes one or two of the Great Ten are shown, but there does not seem to be a sense of their distinctness as a collection: others such as *Kusa-jātaka* (J 531) and *Sattubhasta-jātaka* (J 402) are equally popular. Temples where such art has existed are Doḍantale, Danagirigala, Degaldoruva, and Laṅkatilaka. *Vessantara* of course is often depicted (Holt 1996: 70–2; PGPV: xii ff.). There is plenty of *jātaka* art going on: transient pictorial depictions include the 'made for the occasion' lanterns and *toraṇas*, towers with *jātaka* depictions that are lit from inside (Appleton 2010a: 154 ff.). Indeed more published work on Sri Lankan *jātaka* art would be most welcome.

34. Discussion involving Richard Gombrich SAALG conference, Taplow Court, conversation 2012.

Modern Cambodian art, with a strong folk element, continues an interest in the Great Ten. In Cambodia, an ethos that sees merit in creating rather than restoring Buddhist art and artefacts has meant there is now an emphasis on painting new works rather than preserving the old, so now much has been lost. But modern depictions of the *Mahānipāta* flourish. The sequence of the ten lives is greatly popular and usually includes many modern elements: there are often twentieth-century soldiers and costumes, extending the sense, throughout South and Southeast Asia, that *jātaka*s somehow exist in a kind of ongoing present, as living expressions of Buddhist principle.[35] Roveda and Yem contrast one scene from the *Vidhura-jātaka* with an older mural panel to demonstrate the highly distinct styles (Roveda and Yem 2009: 106–7). Again, there is a risk that more art will be lost through deterioration and disrepair in this region.

Another medium in which the stories are frequently depicted, and which may have contributed to the great wave of interest in portraying the Great Ten, is the *samut khoi*. This is a folding book which adheres to the same shape as the palm-leaf manuscript on which Buddhist teachings and chanted formulae were usually retained but whose pages, one long folded concertina strip, open like a Western book. Increasingly popular throughout the eighteenth century and into the nineteenth, the local *khoi* paper afforded artistic opportunities that the old palm-leaf books, requiring a stylus to inscribe the letters, had not, and Great Ten depictions started to become popular as freely painted pictures in addition to the simple flowers or decorative symbols. Amongst these, the Great Ten are a favourite theme, even where the text itself, usually chants and ordination material, is of quite different subject matter (see Ginsburg 1989: 44–71; Appleton, Shaw, and Unebe 2013: 6–9). In Western art, an emblem was the distillation of a quality portrayed through a visual symbol in which that quality is enacted in a particular context and which starts to be used as a means of communicating a particular story, quality, or series of events. This seems analogous to the way the stories are described through single memorable scenes. We can see this happening in eighteenth-century art and manuscripts, with one Great Ten scene often taken as the usual representation of one of the heroes. It provides a visual 'link' and reference

35. All of the *Mahānipāta* are represented, often as a series. Roveda and Yem show portrayals of all of the Great Ten. On *Bhūridatta*, for instance, see Roveda and Yem 2009: 63; Vessantara is always prominent: see pp. 10, 21, 64, 110–13, and 250–3.

to the entire contents of the story through an image that everyone recognizes: Sāma in the forest with the hunter, for instance, or Bhūridatta winding himself round his mound as a *nāga*, or Vessantara giving away his children or his elephant.

In Myanmar, folding books (*parabaik*) start from an earlier period to give pre-eminence to image, with only a little or sometimes no text at all, and images covering the whole surface. These sometimes show all of the Great Ten or singly depicted long Great Ten *jātakas*.[36] Alongside these are more ephemeral depictions such as banners (Thai *phra bot*), less able to survive the tropical climate, but in some regions essential to festivals. The Great Ten feature prominently and are sometimes depicted on the same banner; an early nineteenth-century example is in the San Francisco Art Museum (see Skilling 2008: 72, plate 3.18). The *Vessantara-jātaka* is, however, by far the most popular (Lefferts and Cate 2013).

From mediaeval times, monasticism created immense social mobility, so that by the eighteenth century there were frequent contacts between all Southern Buddhist countries and between classes operating within them, presumably with some effect on art and material culture too (Skilling 2012: 345). With such a system of multiple intellectual centres (in Southeast Asia, and in an earlier period, in South Asia), monastic hubs could be highly dispersed, through maritime, riverine, and overland networks. So *jātaka* art would never be entirely isolated: the Great Ten are recounted throughout South and Southeast Asia, and there must have been much transmission of symbol and text between these regions from early times. Local differentiation in the popularity of certain trends does operate, however. It is possible that the *Mahānipāta*'s association with the ten perfections, and the great popularity of the sequence as a series in Thailand, Cambodia, and Myanmar, arose in part from the simple fact that in those countries temporary ordination of all men is routine, rather than for life as in Sri Lanka. So many commissioning donors of temple murals would be ex-monks and favour a series that promoted a lay as well as a renunciate ideal: this can only be speculation however, and the Great Ten are certainly greatly admired in Sri Lanka too.

36. See for instance the *Vidhura-jātaka* on the online V and A collection website, from Mandalay, dating from around 1880. Such books were often commissioned by the British, and other travelling Europeans as well as locals: http://collections.vam.ac.uk/item/O63684/manuscript-unknown/

Assessing the formal literary effect of the Great Ten would require a separate study. In Sinhalese writing, there is a tradition of literary, ornate composition known as *kāvyaya*, often based on *jātaka* themes—single works include *Vidhura-jātaka Kāvyaya*, *Mahājanaka-jātaka Kāvyaya*, *Vessantara-jātaka Kāvyaya* and the *Mahosadha-jātaka Kāvyaya*, and many other kinds of narrative and dramatic adaptations; these were linked to portrayals too.[37] Such compositions were particularly favoured from the eleventh to the thirteenth century, receiving considerable support from the monarchy and the court. Historically, drama has also been particularly influenced by *jātaka* stories: John de Silva (1857–1938) composed a six-act *Vessantara*, considered to be the best of his extensive dramatic compositions (Pannavamsa 2007b: 53–5).

In Myanmar the Great Ten have attracted great literary and commentarial interest. A commentary on the Great Ten was compiled in the eighteenth century by Dan Daing Sayadaw; popular vernacular translations of eight of the Great Ten were compiled by Sayadaw U Obhasa (Pannavamsa 2007b: 69 ff.). From at least the seventeenth century, court and, subsequently, street-theatre and privately funded performances favoured the Great Ten for *Zāt Pwe* dramas, all-night *jātaka* enactments.[38] With an increasing emphasis on dance and music, such performances enjoyed immense popularity well into the twentieth century; *Nemi* and *Bhūridatta* were favoured in street theatre for their depiction of regions beneath the earth (See for instance, Bode 1909: 76ff and Yoe 1989 [1882]: 286–309). Even the names of the heroes of the Great Ten have percolated through to figures of speech in Myanmar, with a greedy person being known as Jujaka, a generous one as Vessantara, and a silent one as Temiya (Pannavamsa 2007b: 71).

In Thailand, Buntuan Siwaraphot has composed 'The Ten Lives in Chan Verse.' (Skilling 2008: 76). Somtow Sucharitkul's opera *The Silent Prince*, an adaptation of *Temiya*, premiered in Houston in 2010 and was then performed by Opera Siam in 2012 in Bangkok in honour of His Majesty the King's birthday. An opera-ballet based on *Mahājanaka* by Somtow was performed in Bangkok in July 2014 with the Siam Philharmonic Orchestra and the Orpheus Choir of Bangkok in honour of His Royal Highness the

37. See Obeyesekere 2013, and, for instance, Holt 1996: 130 n. 1; Appleton 2010a: 78–83; PGPV xxxvi–vii; and UJST.

38. I am grateful to discussions with Venerable Pannavamsa about this in connection with his doctoral work. See also, for *Vessantara-jātaka*, Pannavamsa 2007a and 2007b.

Crown Prince's birthday. As we go to press, Somtow has just announced his intention to compose an opera cycle based on all ten stories.

In Sri Lanka, plays, dances, and songs describe *jātaka*s, including the Great Ten; the most popular of the *Mahānipāta* stories for these are for the heroes Mahosadha, Vidhura, and Vessantara (Appleton 2010a: 154).

It is perhaps too early to understand fully perceptions of the *jātaka*s in diaspora communities in non-Buddhist countries and amongst Buddhists who were not brought up as such. Certainly in the UK, Sri Lankan, Burmese, and Thai parents like their children to hear all *jātaka*s, including the Great Ten, and they are often shown in comics and children's stories. The Thai temple in Wimbledon, UK, has a full *Mahānipāta* representation in the murals in its *ubosot* (Cate 2003: 71–8).

Our Text and Translations

We take Fausbøll's edition (F) as our base text, but we have also used his variant readings and of the Chaṭṭha Saṅgāyana edition published by the Vipassana Research Institute (VRI) on CD-ROM and online at tipitaka.org. We have included page numbers for Fausbøll's edition in square brackets within the translation, and also number the verses according to his edition. However, we number the verses per story, rather than continuously throughout the Great Ten, since we have the stories in a different order to Fausbøll's edition.[39] We have decided to present the stories in their standard Southeast Asian ordering, rather than the Sri Lankan ordering used by Fausbøll, since this order seems to have played an important part in ritual and artistic traditions.

In the introduction to the final volume of his edition of the *Jātakatthavaṇṇanā* (the volume in which we find the *Mahānipāta*) Fausbøll notes that he has not been able to take full account of the readings found in manuscript Bd, his only Burmese manuscript, since

> the text, in this part of the book, has been very much enlarged throughout, so as to make it in many places quite different from C[eylonese manuscripts]. The aim of the Burmese redactor seems to have been, to make the tale more lucid and intelligible, but as the difference in

39. Fausbøll provides both the verse number within the story and continuous numbering for the Mahanipata verses as a whole. We only note the former, in parentheses after each verse.

> many particulars consequently is so great I should advise some other scholar to give a separate edition of the Mahānipāta according to the Burmese redaction that we may judge of its exact relation to C. (Ja VI, 'Preliminary Remarks')

Now that we have the VRI edition it is easy to see that the Burmese recension of the *Mahānipāta* is substantially longer than that preserved in Sri Lankan manuscripts. Although it is not clear where the *Jātakatthavaṇṇanā* was composed, it seems likely that the Burmese *Mahānipāta* is an expansion of the text preserved in Sri Lanka or of some underlying source, since it tends to simplify archaic language, avoid the more difficult reading, and incorporate glosses into the text. The additional length in the prose is usually the result of adding more detail to the narrative, which rarely alters the story significantly. The difference may be a matter of stylistic preference, but for no better reason than the limits of time and resources, it is expedient to translate the shorter version. In some places where a detail of the narrative is enhanced or the meaning made different, the VRI reading has been noted in the footnotes. Occasionally the VRI reading is preferred; these cases too are noted. In the majority of instances, however, the VRI readings are not noted or included. In the verses the differences are more minor, usually restricted to the use of a more common linguistic form in the VRI edition. This suggests a more stable transmission process for the verses, which is no surprise given the restraints of metre and the traditional belief that the verses were spoken by the Buddha himself.

As is well known, Fausbøll's edition uses different font sizes to indicate different layers in the text. In particular he distinguishes between linguistic commentary on the verses, which is printed in small type, and the narrative commentary that forms the bulk of each story. We have omitted the linguistic verse commentary from our translation. However, we do occasionally disagree with Fausbøll's decision over what parts should be included in the linguistic commentary, and where portions of this commentary add value to the narrative we have translated them in the story.

We have tried to strike a balance by producing a translation that is both readable and reasonably loyal to the Pāli. These two aims of fidelity and elegance, which are often in tension with one another, have had various consequences. Because of the difficulty of verse renderings that bear any true relation to the original Pāli, we have not attempted a verse translation.

We have, however, indicated the verse form by preserving line breaks and distinctive formatting. We have generally not translated names, although where the meaning of the name appears relevant to the characterisation this is noted either in parentheses or in a footnote. Words are occasionally added or removed to improve clarity, for example when long strings of pronouns cause confusion over who is speaking to whom. Taking into account the oral tradition in which these stories originated, and aiming to reproduce an authentic text, we have decided to preserve the many passages of repeated verses or formulae that occur throughout many of the stories. If this seems too dry for the reader sitting in an armchair in silence, we recommend the text be read aloud.

Our philosophy of translation takes us fairly far away from the Victorian rendering of Cowell and Rouse, who chose to omit repeated passages, and to prioritise rhyme over meaning in their verse translations. We are nonetheless indebted to these pioneering translators for opening up the text to us and many other readers the world over. In addition to the Cowell and Rouse translation we have made some use of Dutoit's German translation and, in Appleton's translation of the first three stories, of Shaw's rendering of these for Penguin Classics. Sri Lankan retellings of the tales have also been helpful, in particular when translating the *Mahosadha-jātaka*. We greatly admire and have been inspired by Margaret Cone's translation of the *Vessantara-jātaka*, which we have also consulted, and we hope that Shaw's version here provides an alternative perspective on a wonderfully rich and multifaceted story.

TEMIYA

1

The Birth Story of Temiya, or of the Dumb Cripple

(*Temiya-jātaka* or *Mūgapakkha-jātaka*)

INTRODUCTION

In this, the opening story of the *Mahānipāta*, the Bodhisatta is born as a prince and pretends to be deaf, mute, and crippled in order to avoid inheriting the kingship. The two names by which the story is known reflect the name (Temiya) and feigned characteristics (*mūgapakkha* 'dumb cripple') of the Bodhisatta. The story is divided into two sections; the first in the palace and the second in the forest. With this simple setting and a very limited number of key characters, the focus of the story is on the psychology of the leading players, particularly Temiya's extraordinary resolve in the face of temptation and pain, and his mother's grief at her son's apparent disability and death. Tension is built up by the description of Temiya's childhood and the various tests to which he is subjected. Temiya's persistent determination to remain motionless is finally broken after sixteen years, when he stretches out his limbs, picks up his chariot, and swings it over his head like a toy. This climactic moment of the narrative—the motion of the chariot and the strength of the Bodhisatta contrasting so dramatically with his childhood 'paralysis'—is often illustrated in manuscripts and temple murals. It also forms the climactic moment in the recent opera production *The Silent Prince*, for it is the first time that the prince makes a sound.[1] The

Introduced and translated by Naomi Appleton.

1. The opera is the creation of Thai-American composer Somtow Sucharitkul and

story then moves to the forest, a peaceful juxtaposition to the busy life of the city and a place in which real spiritual progress can be made.

Friends and Family

This story hinges on the actions of four main characters: the Bodhisatta, his father, his mother, and the charioteer ordered to kill him. That the central figures of the narrative are so few allows the development of deep personal interactions. Temiya's parents are shown as essentially loving and concerned, but increasingly frustrated and upset by his lack of movement and sound. Temiya's mother demonstrates her affection by begging Temiya to change his ways and her husband to spare his life. The bitter questions she asks of the charioteer she believes has killed her son create a truly poignant interchange. Temiya's father also has affection for his son, but additionally he feels the influence of his brahmin advisers and the responsibility of providing for his kingdom. In the character of the charioteer, tasked with getting rid of the useless prince, we find a more neutral backdrop for Temiya's words and actions. Initially willing to carry out the king's command, the charioteer soon takes the advice of the prince and acts as intermediary between son and father. With a down-to-earth concern for his own welfare, he is careful to ensure that he is not going to be unduly punished by the royal couple, such that, in Shaw's (2006a: 184) words, his 'sense of diplomacy and pragmatism gives a non-heroic counterpoint to the unfolding drama'.

One of the interchanges between Temiya and the charioteer is considered to be a *paritta* text and is therefore chanted for its protective benefits. These verses concern friendship and the many rewards that come from loyalty towards and care of one's friends. Although delightful and popular verses in their own right, these sit rather oddly in the narrative, for Temiya and the charioteer are not friends: the latter is merely the employee of Temiya's father. In fact Temiya's rationale for speaking the verses is that he (Temiya) is like a branch of a tree (the king) under which the charioteer has been enjoying the shade. Just as one wouldn't cut off the branch of a tree that had been of service, so the charioteer should not kill Temiya. The background is therefore a discussion of service and reward. However, the inclusion of an extended sermon on the benefits of friendship works well

---

stars an international cast. It previewed in Bangkok in December 2012. I am grateful to Jak Cholvijarn, who starred in the role of Temiya, for sending me a DVD of the opera.

in a story that serves to deconstruct the hierarchies of city life by moving everybody—the royal family, the citizens, and even the charioteer—into the forest hermitage. All become friends and equals, and even the forest animals, by having friendly thoughts, attain a heavenly rebirth.

Renunciation

In the introduction to the story we hear that it was told by the Buddha after his monks sat discussing his great renunciation. Indeed, the perfection of renunciation (*nekkhamma*) is the one associated with the story by the Thai tradition, and it is a clear focus of the story. However, the story is also closely linked to another perfection, that of determination or resolve (*adhiṭṭhāna*), and it is this perfection with which the story is associated in the *Jātaka-nidāna* (the preface to the *Jātakatthavaṇṇanā*) as well as in the *Cariyāpiṭaka*. It is the great resolve of the Bodhisatta as the child Temiya, subjected to a whole host of difficult tests, that allows him to renounce as he wishes, and thus both perfections play a key role.

More perhaps than any other *jātaka* story, the *Temiya-jātaka* extols the benefits of renouncing for *everyone*. It is not only that the Bodhisatta wishes to escape his particular fate (as future king) and practise meditation. He then goes on to extol the general benefits of forest-dwelling such that first the charioteer, then the royal family, the citizens at large, and even enemy kings all wish to renounce too. Renunciation is explicitly presented as something suitable for everyone, not only to be left to older people: Temiya's verses to his father about the perils of youth and the unstoppable nature of death reinforce the urgency of renouncing even for the young. This serves as a counterpoint to other *jātaka*s, such as the *Nemi-jātaka* (Chapter 4), in which the Bodhisatta renounces only after seeing his first grey hair.

The forest life itself is appealing in its simplicity, and fits into a wider South Asian tradition of renunciation: the bark robe, the leaf hut, and the subsistence on fallen fruit are all pan-Indian ascetic ideals. Indeed, since this is a time without Buddhism, we do not see the characters becoming monks or studying the scriptures, though meditation is on the programme as are *dhamma* talks by Temiya. The renouncers appear to live a blissful unhurried life in which they are free to practise meditation and attain the higher knowledges. Since the gods kindly provide the hermitage, complete with a well and fruiting trees, the hardships that might be expected from an ascetic life are restricted to Temiya's decision to eat unseasoned boiled leaves, and even this apparently improves his complexion! The long-term benefits of the renunciate lifestyle are made clear by the declaration that all of the renouncers attain rebirth in the Brahmā heavens, and even the animals make it to the lower heavens.

Kingship

Although this story has much to say about the benefits of renunciation in general, the initial part of the story focuses on a more specific aim: Temiya's desire to avoid inheriting the kingship. Many *jātaka* stories portray the Bodhisatta as a just king. In the *Nemi-jātaka* (Chapter 4), for example, the Bodhisatta-as-king ensures the welfare of his subjects by setting an example with his moral and generous life. He does eventually renounce, but only after fulfilling his duties as ruler and beginning to grow old, at which point he passes the kingdom to his son. Similarly, in the *Janaka-jātaka* (Chapter 2) the Bodhisatta rules for many years before eventually deciding to leave his wife and kingdom and enter the forest as a renouncer. In other stories, such as the *Mahosadha-jātaka* (Chapter 5), the Bodhisatta is an adviser to a king and serves to preserve and support the kingdom. In none of these stories is kingship so heavily criticised as in the *Temiya-jātaka*. Rather, it seems that a distinction is made between good and bad kingship.

In the *Temiya-jātaka* we find a very different message. It is not the case that Temiya's father is a bad king, for keeping order by punishing criminals is shown as an important part of ruling a kingdom. Neither is there any indication that the Bodhisatta himself was a bad king in his past life, but his twenty years of rule still led to eighty thousand years in a hell realm. The necessary duties of kingship are thus shown as inevitably leading to bad karma and much suffering in future lives. Being a 'good king' like King Nemi is not an option: one must do everything in one's power to escape such a terrible fate.

Past Lives

It is Temiya's ability to see his past lives that prompts his resolve to escape the kingship. In Buddhist stories it is unusual for baby humans to be able to see their own past lives, for this attainment (one of the higher knowledges) comes with extended meditative practice. In Temiya's case we are told that he had recently been a god, who willingly took birth as Temiya after being requested to do so by another god. The birth is therefore intentional in a way that is not usually the case for the Bodhisatta in the *Jātakatthavaṇṇanā*.

Since gods are naturally able to see their past lives, one could assume that Temiya's supernormal memory was inherited, so to speak, from his former self. (Similar justifications are given for some modern cases of young children being able to remember their past lives as monks, since the monks could have been advanced practitioners of meditation.) Whatever the cause of the memory, the result is a potent one: terrible fear of repeating that experience of 'cooking in hell', fear that is strong enough to prevent the prince from moving or uttering a sound for sixteen years.

Temiya's past life memory raises a question of chronology, for it suggests that the Bodhisatta was at the time of his birth as Temiya both very advanced (able to choose his birth at will, able to see past lives, able to attain the higher knowledges and teach others to do so) and yet also only recently released from a long sojourn in a hell realm. It is rare to find evidence that the Bodhisatta experienced a hellish rebirth, for generally he is considered to be on the long path to Buddhahood, cultivating the perfections in a variety of human, animal, and divine rebirths. This story, coming as it does at the beginning of what are later believed to be the final ten rebirths of the Bodhisatta, reminds us to take such chronological impositions with a pinch of salt. The involvement of the goddess of the parasol, said to have been his mother in an unspecified past life, makes the timescale even more indeterminate. Where exactly the Bodhisatta sits on his long path in this story is less important than the narrative juxtapositions that his past life memory prompts: of hell torments compared with the torments of the tests endured by Temiya, and of one mother who wishes for his long-term welfare while the other laments his short-term suffering. That these tensions are so satisfyingly resolved during the course of the story is testament to its enduring qualities.

'Don't reveal your wisdom . . .'

[1] The Teacher related this story concerning the Great Renunciation while he was living in the Jeta Grove. For one day the monks were sitting together in the *dhamma* hall discussing the quality of the Blessed One's perfection of renunciation. The Teacher came and asked, 'Monks, what are you talking of as you sit here together?' and hearing their reply he said, 'Monks, rejecting the kingship and renouncing now, when my perfection is fulfilled, is not really a marvel, for when my knowledge was undeveloped and I was still

fulfilling the perfections, even then I rejected kingship and renounced.' Entreated by them he spoke of the past.

In times past, in Vārāṇasī a king called Kāsi ruled the kingdom righteously. He had sixteen thousand women, but did not have even a single son or daughter. The citizens, as happened in the *Kusa-jātaka*,[2] assembled saying, 'We have not even a single son to preserve the king's lineage!' and they said to the king, 'Pray for a son!' The king enjoined his sixteen thousand women to pray for a son. They worshipped the moon and so on, yet despite praying in this way they gained nothing. But his chief queen, who was the daughter of King Madda and called Queen Candā, was endowed with morality, and he told her to pray for a son. She observed the *uposatha* on the day of the full moon and, reclining on a small couch, reflected upon her morality. She made this Act of Truth: 'If I am one of unbroken morality, then by this truth [2] may a son be born to me!'

By the strength of her virtue Sakka's dwelling became hot. Sakka reflected and realised the cause: 'Queen Candā is requesting a son! I will give her a son!' Looking for a suitable son for her he saw the Bodhisatta, for the Bodhisatta at the time, after twenty years ruling the kingdom of Vārāṇasī, and having fallen from there and roasted in a hell[3] for eighty thousand years, had been reborn in the Heaven of the Thirty-Three (Tāvatiṃsa). And having been established there for the length of his lifetime, he wanted to go to a higher heaven realm after death. Sakka approached him and said, 'Friend, if you take birth in the world of men the perfections will be fulfilled and the people will prosper. Candā, the chief queen of the king of Kāsi, requests a son. Take birth in her womb!' He assented, and with five hundred gods he passed away. He himself took rebirth in her womb, and the other gods took rebirth in the wombs of the wives of courtiers.

2. In the *Kusa-jātaka* (J 531) the lack of an heir is greatly concerning to the populace and they urge drastic action. Eventually the queen is made available to other men in order that she might conceive a child. In order to save her from this indignity, Sakka in disguise as an old man takes her away to heaven, then grants her two sons.

3. He is said to have been in an *ussada* hell, which are the supplementary hells that protrude from the great hells.

The queen's womb was filled as if by diamonds.[4] Knowing that she had conceived, she told the king. The king ensured that good care was taken of the foetus, and when her pregnancy was complete she gave birth to a son who was endowed with auspicious marks. On that same day five hundred sons were born in the families of the courtiers. At that moment the king was seated on the terrace surrounded by his courtiers, and they announced to him, 'Your Majesty, a son has been born to you!' Hearing their words affection for his son arose, cut into his skin and so on, penetrated to the marrow of his bones, and abided in him. Joy arose within him and his heart became tranquil. He asked his courtiers, 'Are you pleased at the birth of my son?'

'What do you say, Your Majesty?' they responded. 'Previously we had no protector, but now our protector has been born. We have gained a lord!'

The king addressed his chief general: 'We should acquire a retinue for my son. See how many sons were born today in the families of my courtiers.' Having seen the five hundred boys, he returned and reported this to the king. The king sent princely ornaments for the five hundred boys and had five hundred wet nurses employed for them. And the Great Being [3] was given sixty-four wet nurses who were not defective in the sense of being too tall and so on, and had sweet maternal milk and breasts that did not droop. For having drunk milk while sat on the hip[5] of one who is too tall a child's neck becomes long, and if he drinks while seated on the hip of one who is too short his backbone becomes compressed. A child who sits on the hip of one who is too thin gets painful thighs, whilst one who sits on the hip of someone too fat becomes bow-legged.[6] The body of someone overly dark is too cold, whilst somebody too white is too hot.[7] A child that drinks from someone with drooping breasts gets a squashed nose. And furthermore some women's milk is sour, and the milk of others is bitter, and so on.[8] Thus having given him sixty-four wet nurses who were

4. *Vajira* could also be translated as '[Indra's] thunderbolt', and given the intimate involvement of Sakka (Indra) in ensuring the queen becomes pregnant, this is certainly a tempting option. However, I have not been able to find any suggestion that such a motif is known to other Indian mythological sources, and so I follow the translation 'diamonds' as chosen by Cowell, Dutoit, and Shaw.

5. Literally on the side or flank, in other words the child is breastfed while sitting upright on the woman's hip.

6. F *khalaṃkapādā* is obscure, but VRI reads *pakkhapādo* 'side-footed'.

7. VRI instead says the *milk* of one who is too dark is very cold, and the milk of one who is overly white is too hot.

8. VRI has: 'the milk of women who have a cough is too sour, and the milk of

devoid of all these defects, were not too tall and so on, and who did not have drooping breasts and had sweet milk, the king paid homage to the great one, and gave Queen Candā a boon. She accepted it and set it aside for later.

On the naming day the king paid homage to brahmins who were experts in the marks, and asked them if he had any obstacles. Having seen the magnificence of his marks they said, 'Great King, this boy has the marks of good fortune and merit! Leave aside this one continent—he is able to rule over the four great continents. We perceive no impediments in him.' The king was delighted, and named the prince. Because on the day of his birth the god rained on the whole of the country of Kāsi, and thus the birth was moistening (*temiyamāno*), he named him Prince Temiya.

Now when he was one month old they adorned him and took him into the presence of the king. Seeing his dear son, the king embraced him, seated him on his lap, and he sat playing with him. At that moment four thieves were brought in. He ordered that one of them be given a thousand lashes with a whip of thorns, one be chained up at the entrance to the prison, another one have his body struck with a sword, and the other be impaled on a stake. The Great Being, hearing his father's words, became frightened, thinking, 'Alas my father for the sake of the kingdom makes grave *kamma* that leads to hell!'

And the next day they lay him down on an ornamented royal couch underneath a white sunshade. Having slept a little he woke up, opened his eyes, and looking at the white parasol he saw the great royal splendour. And he, already afraid, became even more frightened. He reflected, [4] 'From where have I come to this palace?' and by remembering his past births he realised that he had come from a heaven realm. Then looking further back he saw that he had cooked in a hell, and looking beyond that he knew that he had been a king in this very city. He reflected, 'For twenty years I ruled this kingdom, and for eighty thousand years I cooked in hell, and now I have arisen in this very same prison! Yesterday my father, regarding four thieves that had been led in, spoke very harsh words that are conducive to hell. If I too am to rule the kingdom, then I will be reborn in hell again and experience great suffering!' He was terrified, and his golden body became discoloured like a withered lotus crushed in the hands. He lay there thinking, 'Oh how can I be freed from this prison?'

---

asthmatic women is too bitter and so on.'

Now a certain individual who had been his mother in former times was a goddess living in the sunshade. She comforted him saying, 'My dear Temiya, don't be afraid. If you wish to be freed from here then though you are not a cripple, be like a cripple, and though you are not deaf, become like a deaf person, and though you are not dumb, behave as if you are. Resolving on these three things, do not make your intelligence known.' And she spoke the first verse:

> 'Don't reveal your wisdom. Become a fool to all beings.
> Let all the people disregard you! This will be for your benefit.' (1)

Gaining comfort from her words, he said:

> 'I will do as you say, god that speaks to me.
> You desire my well-being, Mother. You desire my welfare, Goddess.' (2)

Having spoken this verse he resolved upon these three things.

The king for the sake of his contentment placed the five hundred young boys in his presence, and those children cried out in want of milk. But the Great Being, filled with the fear of hell, thought, 'Dying of thirst is preferable to the kingship!' and did not cry out. His wet nurses [5] reported this to Queen Candā, and she in turn told the king. The king summoned astrologer-brahmins and asked them about it. The brahmins said, 'Your Majesty, you should give the boy milk only after his ordinary time. Then he will cry and firmly seize the breast and drink of his own accord.' From then onwards they gave him milk only after going past the usual time, and sometimes they went past it just once, and sometimes they didn't give him milk for the whole day. He, fearful of hell, though he was very thirsty, did not cry out for milk. But although he was not crying, his mother thought, 'My son is hungry!' and made him drink, or the wet nurses did. The other children cried when they did not get milk, but he neither cried, nor slept, nor moved his hands and feet, nor responded to any noise.[9]

Then his wet nurses thought, 'Cripples do not have hands and feet of this sort, and mutes do not have such a perfect jaw as this, and deaf people don't have ears like this. There must be a reason for this, so we will investigate him.' Saying, 'We will test him with milk!' they did not give him milk the whole day. But although he was parched he did not make a sound for the sake of milk. Then his mother made them give it to him, saying, 'My son

9. *Saddaṃ suṇāti* literally means 'heard a noise' but since it is clear from the context that Temiya is not actually deaf, but is pretending to be so, 'responded to' seems more appropriate. VRI has *saddaṃ karoti* 'made a noise'.

is thirsty! Give him milk!' Giving him milk in this way time after time for one year they tested him but did not see any weakness.

Then they said, 'Little boys are fond of sweets and cakes. Therefore we will test him with those.' They seated the five hundred boys close to him, brought in various foods and placed them nearby, and saying, 'Take these foods according to your liking!' they stood hidden. The other boys, quarrelling and hitting one another, took them and ate. But the Great Being, thinking, 'Temiya, desiring hell desire cakes!' out of fear of the hells did not look at the food. Testing him in this way with cakes, for a year they did not see any weakness in him.

Then they said, 'Children are fond of all kinds of fruit!' and having brought fruits they tested him. [6] The other children, fighting, ate, but he did not even look. They tested him in this way with various fruits for a year.[10] Then they said, 'Children are fond of toys!' They placed various horses and so on fashioned out of gold and the like near to him. The other children, snatching, took them, but the Great Being did not even look. They tested him in this way with toys for a year. Then they said, 'Four-year-old children like food, so we will test him with that!' They served him with various foods. The other children made the food into little balls and ate, but the Great Being thought, 'Temiya, there is no reckoning the number of your existences in which you lacked food.' Out of the fear of hell he did not look. Then his mother, unable to endure it as if her heart was breaking, fed him with her own hands.[11]

Then they said, 'Five-year-old children are afraid of fire, so we will test him with that!' They had a large house with several doors constructed, and covered it with palm leaves. They sat him in the middle of it, surrounded by the other children, and set it on fire. The other children cried out and fled. But the Great Being thought, 'This is much better than cooking in hell!'[12] and he remained motionless as if he had attained cessation.[13] When the fire approached him they removed him.

10. For this and all successive descriptions of the tests, the VRI edition has a much longer description, in parallel to the description of the first test, with variations. VRI also specifies the age at which each test was carried out, by indicating, 'two-year-old children like fruits,' and so on.

11. Following VRI as well as F's Burmese manuscript. F is hard to decipher here.

12. VRI: 'The heat of this fire is a hundred, a thousand, a hundred thousand times better than the burning of the hell-fires!'

13. *Nirodha* is often used as a synonym for *nibbāna.*

Then, saying, 'Six-year-old children are afraid of elephants in rut!' they prepared a certain well-trained elephant, and sitting the Bodhisatta in the royal courtyard surrounded by the other children they set that elephant free. Trumpeting and beating the earth with its trunk it came and frightened them. The other children were terrified with the fear of death and ran off in the various directions. But the Great Being, terrified by the fear of hell, sat right there. The well-trained elephant picked him up and waved him to and fro, and without causing him any distress he left.

Then, when he was seven years old, they sat him amongst the other children and released snakes whose fangs had been removed and mouths bound. The other children cried out and ran away, but the Great Being reflected on the fear of hell: 'Even destruction at the mouth of a fierce snake is much better!' He remained motionless. Then the snakes wrapped themselves around his whole body and placed their hoods over his head, but even then he remained still. Even by testing him again and again they could not find any weak point in him. [7]

Then, saying, 'Children like performances!' they seated him in the royal courtyard along with the five hundred children and had a dance company perform. The other children saw the performance, and saying 'Bravo!' they laughed heartily. But the Great Being, thinking, 'There is no laughter or joy, not even the smallest amount, for a person when they are reborn in hell,' reflected on the fear of hell and was motionless—he did not even look. Testing him in this way at intervals they did not see any weakness in him.

Then, saying, 'We will test him with a sword!' they placed him in the royal courtyard with the other children. While the children were playing, a man wielding a sword with the appearance of crystal ran around, jumping about and roaring, 'They say the king of Kāsi's only son is black-eared (ill-omened)! Where is he? I will cut off his head!' Seeing him the others were frightened and ran off crying. But the Bodhisatta reflected on the fear of hell and remained seated as if unaware. Then that man touched his sword to Temiya's head and threatened him saying, 'I will cut off your head!' but being unable to frighten him, he left. Testing him in this way periodically they did not see any weak spot in him.

When he was ten years old, in order to test the state of his deafness, they surrounded his bed with a screen and made holes on four sides. Without allowing him to see they seated conch blowers underneath the bed and had them play the conches all at once, so there was a single sound. The courtiers waited on the four sides looking through the holes in the screen, but during the whole day they did not see any disturbance of the Great Being's mindfulness, or movement in his hands or feet, not even one tremble. When that year was past, for a further year they tested him in the same way with the sound of drums, but they did not see any weakness.

Then they said, 'We will test him with a lamp! Surely when it is dark he will twitch his hand or foot!' At night-time they kindled some lamps in bowls and blew out the other lamps and sat him there when it was a little dark. They raised up the lamps from the bowls and made it light all at once, looking out for movement. But even testing him in this way, a year went by and they did not see the slightest movement.

Then [8] they said, 'We will test him with sugar cane!' They smeared his whole body with sugar cane and laid him down in a place where there were lots of flies and agitated the flies. They covered his entire body and ate as if piercing him with needles, but he remained motionless as if he had attained cessation. Testing him in this way for another year they did not see any weakness.

Then when he was fourteen years old they thought, 'Now at this venerable age a child loves pure things and dislikes what is unclean. We will test him with filth!' From that point onwards they did not bathe him or wash him. He made faeces and urine, then fell over and lay there. From the stench of that bad smell it seemed as if his intestines had ruptured.[14] As flies ate at him, they stood around him and scolded and abused him: 'Oh Temiya! You are a grown man now! Who will look after you? Aren't you ashamed? Why are you lying there? Get up and look after your body!' But despite being immersed in a pile of faeces that was very disagreeable, he reflected on the stench of the hell of filth, which is strong enough to afflict the hearts even of those stood at a distance of a hundred *yojanas* from the bad smell, and remained impassive. Testing him in this way another year went by and they did not see any weakness.

Next they placed pans of embers under his bed, saying, 'Hurt by the heat, unable to endure the pain he will move, even if only a little.' It was as if blisters were appearing on his body, but the Great Being reflected, 'The heat of the Avīci hell penetrates a hundred *yojanas*! This suffering is better than that suffering by a hundred times, a thousand times!' He

14. *Antaruddhīnaṃ nikkhamanakālo viya* is obscure. Cone (PED) suggests *antaruddhi* equates to Sanskrit *antravṛddhi* which refers to an inguinal hernia or rupture of the intestines. Shaw follows Cone, translating 'as if he had had a ruptured hernia'. Cowell says that Temiya 'looked like a released prisoner'.

endured it and remained motionless. Then his mother and father, feeling as if their hearts were breaking, sent the men away and removed him from that burning fire. They begged him, 'Dear Prince Temiya, we know you are not a cripple and so on, for your feet, face, and ears do not have that appearance. You are the son that was received after great longing on our part. Don't ruin us! Free us from the reproach of the kings of all Jambudīpa!' But even begged in this way he lay there motionless as if he did not hear. Then his parents went away crying. [9] And another time his father approached him alone and begged, and another time his mother, but even testing him periodically like this, another year went by and they did not see any weakness in him.

Then when he was sixteen years old they reflected, 'Let him be a cripple or deaf and dumb! When of a mature age, is it not the case that one finds pleasure in enticements and displeasure in what is offensive? This is the proper way of things, like a flower bursting into bloom at the right time. We will arrange for dancing girls and test him with that!' Then they summoned women who were endowed with beauty as if they were daughters of the gods bearing the finest forms. They said, 'Whoever is able to make the prince laugh, or provoke lust, she will become his chief queen!' They bathed the prince in perfumed water and decked him out like a son of the gods, and placed him on the appointed royal couch in a bedroom that resembled a divine mansion. They made the interior chamber a single fragrance with perfumed garlands and flower garlands, incense, and perfumed powder and so on, then left. Then those women surrounded him and endeavoured to please him with various songs, dances, sweet speech, and so on. He, endowed with wisdom, looked at[15] those women, and thinking, 'Don't let them touch my body!' he restrained his in-breath and out-breath so his body became rigid. Without coming into contact with his body they announced to his parents, 'His body is rigid! This is not a man—he must be a *yakkha*!' Testing him in this way periodically his mother and father did not see any weakness in him. Thus even though they tested him with various little tests and sixteen serious tests for sixteen years they were unable to catch him out.

Then the king became remorseful and had the experts in the marks summoned. He said, 'When the prince was born you told me, "He has the

15. VRI says that Temiya did *not* look at them.

marks of merit and good fortune! There are no impediments in him!" yet he has turned out to be a deaf and dumb cripple. How did you not know this?'

'Great King, there is nothing that is not seen by the teachers. We did not tell you this because if we had said, "the son obtained through the requests of the royal courtiers [10] is ill-omened," you would have been upset.'

'But now what is to be done?'

'Great King, while this prince is dwelling in this house there are three dangers: to your life, to the parasol (the kingship), and to the queen. Therefore, some inauspicious horses should be yoked to an unlucky carriage, and having deposited him in there and driven him through the western gate, he should be buried in the cremation ground.' The king was frightened by hearing of the dangers and assented.

Queen Candā, having heard the news, approached the king and said, 'Your Majesty, you granted me a boon, and having accepted it I set it aside. Grant it to me now!'

'Take it, O Queen!'

'Give me the kingship for my son.'

'That is not possible, O Queen, for your son is ill-omened.'

'Why then, Your Majesty, if you won't give it for as long as he lives, grant it for seven years!'

'That is not possible, O Queen.'

'Then grant it for six years . . . five . . . four . . . three . . . two . . . one year . . . seven months . . . six . . . five . . . four . . . three . . . two . . . one month . . . half a month!'[16]

'That is not possible, O Queen.'

'Then grant it for seven days, Your Majesty!'

When he said 'Okay, take that!' she had her son adorned and made the drummers go around the city proclaiming, 'This is the kingdom of Prince Temiya!' She had the city adorned and had her son mount the back of an elephant and had the white parasol placed at the head. He circumambulated the city and returned. Then she laid him down on a royal couch and begged him all night, 'Dear Prince Temiya, because of you I have not slept for sixteen years and my eyes are swollen from crying! It is as though my heart is breaking from grief! I know that you are not a cripple and so on, so stop

16. VRI separates out each of these requests in full, with the king responding in the negative to each one.

making me helpless!' She entreated him in this manner the next day and the next, for five days.

On the sixth day the king summoned a charioteer named Sunanda and commanded him, 'My good sir, early tomorrow you must harness some inauspicious horses to an inauspicious chariot, place the prince in there and drive him through the western gate. Dig a four-walled pit in the charnel ground and throw him in there. Split his head with the side of a spade, and having deprived him of his life, cover him with soil, [11] smooth over the ground, wash yourself, and return.' On the sixth night the queen having begged the prince said, 'My dear, the King of Kāsi has ordered that you be buried in the charnel ground! You are going to die, son.' Hearing this the Great Being thought, 'Temiya, sixteen years of great effort has reached a head!' and joy arose within him. Even though his mother's heart appeared to be broken, he did not speak to her, thinking, 'Let not my wish be unfulfilled!'

Then at the end of that night, very early in the morning, Sunanda the charioteer yoked the chariot,[17] parked it at the door and entered the royal sleeping quarters. Saying, 'Your highness, don't be angry with me—it is the order of the king!' he removed the queen, who was lying with her arms around her son, with the back of his hand. He picked up the prince as if he were a bunch of flowers and descended from the palace. Queen Candā beat her breast and cried out a loud wail, left behind on the terrace. The Great Being saw her and thought, 'Unless I speak she will die from a broken heart!' He wanted to talk to her, but he endured it, reflecting, 'If I were to speak, then sixteen years of striving would be useless to me. Not speaking, I will become a support for myself and my parents.'[18]

Then the charioteer ascended the chariot and though he thought to send the chariot towards the western gate, he directed it towards the eastern gate.[19] The wheel of the chariot struck on the threshold stone, and the Great Being, having heard this noise, thought, 'My wish has reached the summit!' and was still more pleased of mind. The chariot, having left the city, by

17. VRI notes that by means of the goddess's power and the power of the perfections of the Great Being the charioteer unintentionally yoked auspicious horses to an auspicious cart.

18. VRI has 'and the people at large'.

19. VRI explains that although the charioteer directed the chariot towards the west, 'by the power of the Great Being's perfections he was taken over by the gods and having turned the chariot around he directed the chariot towards to eastern gate.'

the power of the gods went to a place three *yojanas* away. There a forest clearing appeared to the charioteer like a charnel ground. Considering it to be a convenient place, he drove the chariot aside and parked on the side of the road. Descending from the chariot he unfastened the Great Being's jewels and ornaments and placed them into a heap. He took the spade and began to dig a pit nearby.

Then the Bodhisatta thought, 'This is the time for me to exert myself. For I have not moved my hands or feet for sixteen years! But are they in my control or not?' He got up and massaged his right hand with his left, [12] and his left hand with his right, and rubbed his feet with both his hands, and thought about leaving the chariot. At the very place where his feet fell the great earth rose up like the skin of bellows that are full of air and touched the back of the chariot. Having got down he wandered to and fro a few times, and realised that even now in this way he had the strength to go a hundred *yojanas* in one day. In order to ascertain whether he would have enough strength to quarrel with the charioteer were the latter to be obstructive, he seized the back of the chariot, picked it up as if it was a toy vehicle belonging to princes, and held it there![20] Then he reflected, 'I have the strength to quarrel with him,' and began to think about his ornaments.

At that very moment Sakka's abode became hot. Sakka comprehended the reason: 'Prince Temiya's wish has reached a head! He is thinking about his ornaments. How can this one have human ornaments?' Having taken divine ornaments he ordered Vissakamma, 'Go and adorn the son of the king of Kāsi!'

'Very good.' Vissakamma went and enveloped him with ten thousand cloths, and adorned him so that he was like Sakka with human and divine ornaments. Temiya, with the grace of the king of the gods, went to the hole that was being dug by the charioteer, and standing on the other side of the pit he questioned him, speaking the third verse:

> 'Charioteer, why are you digging a pit in such haste?
> Asked this, friend, tell me: what will you do with the hole?' (3)

Hearing that, the charioteer, without looking up from digging the hole, spoke the fourth verse:

> 'The king's son was born a mindless dumb cripple.
> Under the order of the king I will bury his son in the forest!' (4)

20. VRI also has 'spinning it around'. This expressive movement is often suggested by Southeast Asian murals.

Then the Great Being said:

'I am neither deaf nor dumb, nor am I a cripple or lame!
Charioteer, if you bury me in the forest you will do a wrong deed. (5)
[13] Look at my arms and my thighs, and listen to my speech.
Charioteer, if you bury me in the forest you will do a wrong deed.' (6)

Then the charioteer thought, 'Now who is this? From the time he arrived he has praised himself.'[21] He abandoned the digging of the hole, looked up, and seeing his wonderful form he thought, 'Is he a man or a god?' He spoke this verse:

'Are you a god or a celestial musician? Or indeed Sakka the former giver?[22]
Who are you? Whose son are you? How should I know you?' (7)

Then the Great Being explained himself and taught the *dhamma* to him, saying:

'I am neither god nor celestial musician, nor indeed Sakka the former giver.
I am the son of the king of Kāsi, whom you would slay in a hole! (8)
I am the son of that king, whom you are dependent upon.
Charioteer, if you bury me in the forest you will do a wrong deed. (9)
If you were to sit or lie down in the shade of some tree
You would not break off its branch, for the betrayal of friends is evil. (10)
The king is like the tree, and I am like its branch,
It is as if you are the man in the shadow, charioteer.
Charioteer, if you bury me in the forest you will do a wrong deed.' (11)

[14] But even after the Bodhisatta had said this he still did not believe him. Then the Great Being, thinking 'I will convince him!' made the dense forest resound with his voice and with the applause of the gods and undertook ten verses in praise of friendship:

'He has plenty to eat when he is away from home;
Many depend on him, he who does not harm his friends. (12)
Whichever country he goes to, in market towns and royal cities,
Everywhere he is respected, he who does not harm his friends. (13)

21. It is not totally clear what is meant by *āgatakālo paṭṭhāya attānameva vaṇṇeti.* Shaw has 'Has he been speaking for himself since he came?' while Cowell has 'It is only since I came here that he has become as he describes himself.' My translation is closer to Dutoit: 'Seitdem er gekommen ist, preist er nur sich selbst.'

22. Purindada can mean 'breaker of fortresses' and is used in this way as an epithet of Indra (Sakka) in many Sanskrit texts. However, the creative etymology of Pāli commentators gives the meaning 'former giver'. The commentators point out that Sakka became a god precisely because of his past acts of charity.

Thieves do not overcome him, the ruler does not neglect him,
He overcomes all enemies, he who does not harm his friends. (14)
Without anger he goes to his house, and he is welcomed in the assembly hall,
He is the greatest amongst his relations, he who does not harm his friends. (15)
He gives honour and is honoured, respects and is respected,
He is praised and supported, he who does not harm his friends. (16)
He that honours obtains honour, the reverer is revered,
And he receives fame and renown, he who does not harm his friends. (17)
He blazes like a fire and shines like the gods,
He does not lose his splendour, he who does not harm his friends. (18)
His cows reproduce, what is sown in his field grows,
He eats the fruit of that which was sown, he who does not harm his friends. (19)
When falling from a cave, a mountain, or a tree,
He is protected from death, he who does not harm his friends. (20)
Like the wind in a banyan tree with its spread of growing roots,
Enemies cannot overcome him, he who does not harm his friends.[23] (21)

[15] But Sunanda didn't recognise him even after he had taught the *dhamma* in all these verses, and thinking, 'Who is this?' he went to the place where the chariot was. Failing to see either him or his ornaments there, he returned again, and looking at him he recognised him. Falling at his feet he saluted him respectfully, and spoke this verse of entreaty:

'Come, Prince, I will lead you back to your own home.
Rule the kingdom, sir! What would you do in the forest?' (22)

The Great Being replied:

'I've had enough of that kingdom, my relatives, and wealth,
Since I would obtain that kingship through unrighteous conduct, charioteer!' (23)

The charioteer said:

'Prince, you will receive a full cup when you are gone from here,
And your mother and father will give to me, when you go there, prince. (24)
The concubines and princes, the brahmins and traders,[24]

23. These verses form a *paritta* text, a text that is chanted for its protective benefits. The commentary makes various suggestions for stories that should be narrated to illuminate the sentiment.

24. *Vesiyāna* is equivalent to *vessa*, or Sanskrit *vaiśya*, and thus refers to the class of people below the warriors and brahmins. *Vaiśyas* appear to have been largely traders and agriculturalists, and the former play a particularly prominent role in *jātaka* stories.

Delighted they too will give, prince, when you go there. (25)
The elephant riders, army, charioteers, and infantry,
Delighted they too will give to me, prince, when you go there. (26)
And many others, country and city dwellers assembled,
Will give me presents, prince, when you go there.' (27)

[16] The Great Being replied:

'I am given up by father and mother, and by the kingdom[25] and citizens,
And by all the princes. I have no home of my own. (28)
I am given leave by my mother, given up by my father.
Having gone forth alone in this forest, I don't wish for sense pleasures!' (29)

Thus when calling to mind his own qualities the Great Being became joyful, and because of the force of his joy he uttered this exclamation:

'Desire for fruit succeeds for those who are unhurried!
I am on the fully ripe holy path—know this charioteer! (30)
A proper cause bears fruit for those who are unhurried!
I am on the fully ripe holy path, renouncing, with no reason to fear!' (31)

The charioteer said:

'This lovely speech is true, and you are of well-enunciated words.
Why did you not speak then in the presence of your mother and father?' (32)

Then the Great Being said:

'I am not an unjointed cripple; nor deaf, lacking ears;
I am not a tongueless mute—don't understand me to be dumb! (33)
I remember a previous birth, in which I ruled a kingdom.
Having ruled that kingdom, I suffered much in hell. (34)
Having ruled that kingdom for twenty years,
I cooked in hell for eighty thousand years! (35)
[17] I am afraid of the kingship, so don't crown me!
That is why I did not speak in the presence of mother and father. (36)
Having sat me on his lap, my father passed judgement:
"Kill one, bind one, torture one,
And impale one on a stake!"—thus he instructed. (37)
Having heard the harsh words uttered by him,
Not dumb yet appearing dumb, uncrippled but considered a cripple,
I sat immersed in my own excrement. (38)
Who would come to this life, short and miserable,
Bound with suffering, and who would do this evil? (39)

25. Shaw's emendation of F's *rathassa* 'of the chariot' to *raṭṭhassa* 'of the kingdom' is supported by the VRI edition.

And without wisdom, unheeding of the *dhamma*,
Who would come to this life, and who would do this evil? (40)
Desire for fruit succeeds for those who are unhurried!
I am on the fully ripe holy path—know this charioteer! (41)
A proper cause bears fruit for those who are unhurried!
I am on the fully ripe holy path, renouncing, with no reason to fear!' (42)

[18] Having heard that Sunanda thought, 'This prince rejects the kingship as if it were a corpse! Not breaking his resolve, saying, "I will go forth!" he enters the forest! What is the point of my useless life now? I will also go forth with him!' He spoke a verse:

'I too will go forth with you, prince!
Sir, summon me! Renunciation delights me.' (43)

But even though entreated in this way, the Great Being thought, 'If I allow him to renounce now, my mother and father will not come here and so they will lose out, and these horses and the chariot and the ornaments will be destroyed. Thinking, "He is a demon! Surely the charioteer has been eaten by him!" they will blame me.' So for the sake of being free from censure himself, and considering his parents' welfare, making the horses, chariot, and ornaments his debt, he spoke a verse of explanation:

'Having returned the chariot, free from debt, come charioteer;
For the renunciation of a debtless person, this is praised by the sages!' (44)

Hearing that the charioteer thought, 'If when I go to the city he were to go elsewhere, and hearing about this incident his father, saying, "Show me my son!" were to come and not see him, he would have me punished. So having spoken of his qualities I will obtain a promise that he will not go away.' He spoke two verses:

'May you be fortunate! As I have done what you said,
Entreated by me you should do what I say. (45)
Stay right here until I have brought the king:
Seeing you even a little your father would be pleased and happy.' (46)

[19] Then the Great Being said:

'I will do what you have told me to do, charioteer.
I too would like to see my father come here. (47)
Come, friend, you should return and speak skilfully to my relatives,
And speak words of salutation to my mother and father.' (48)

He bent down like a golden plantain, and facing the city of Vārāṇasī he honoured his parents with fivefold array, and gave a message to the charioteer.[26] He accepted the message.

> Having seized his feet and made his circumambulation,
> The charioteer ascended the chariot and approached the royal gate. (49)

At that very moment Queen Candā had opened a window and was wondering, 'What news of my son?' when she saw the charioteer coming up the road. Seeing him arrive alone she lamented. Explaining the matter the Teacher said:

> His mother, seeing the empty chariot, and the charioteer coming alone,
> With eyes full of tears, crying, looked at him: (50)
> 'This charioteer comes having slain my own child.
> Surely my son is dead, increasing the soil in the earth. (51)
> Enemies indeed rejoice, and the vengeful are delighted,
> Seeing the charioteer arrive having slain my child!' (52)
> His mother, seeing the empty chariot and the charioteer coming alone,
> With eyes full of tears, crying, asked him: (53)
> 'Oh was he dumb? And was he crippled? Then did he cry
> Being slain on the earth? Tell me that, charioteer! (54)
> How could a dumb cripple push you away[27] with hands or feet
> Being slain on the earth? Questioned, answer me!' (55)

[20] The charioteer said:

> 'Madam, if you would grant me freedom from fear, I would tell you
> What I saw and heard in the prince's presence.' (56)

Then Queen Candā said to him:

> 'I will grant you freedom from fear, friend charioteer—speak fearlessly
> Of what you saw and heard in the presence of the prince!' (57)

Then the charioteer said:

> 'He is neither dumb nor crippled, and he is well enunciated.
> He says he was afraid of the kingship, and so made many pretences. (58)
> He remembers a former life, in which he ruled a kingdom,
> And having ruled that kingdom suffered greatly in hell. (59)
> For twenty years he ruled that kingdom,

26. Or perhaps gave him an order. F relegates this sentence to the commentary. In VRI it is supplemented by 'He, having accepted the message [or order], respectfully circumambulated the prince, climbed onto the chariot and set off in the direction of the city. Explaining the matter the Teacher said:'. This is a more standard introduction to a verse.

27. *Vivajjati* usually means to avoid or abandon, but here it must have the meaning 'shun', as is suggested by the commentary, which equates it with *apanudati*, to remove or push away.

And for eighty thousand years he cooked in hell. (60)
Afraid of the kingship he thought, 'Don't consecrate me as king!'
Thus he did not speak in the presence of his mother or father. (61)
Endowed with limbs great and small, possessing length and girth,
Wise and with resonating voice, he stands on the path to heaven. (62)
If you wish to see the prince, who is born from you,
Come, I will bring you to the place where Temiya is dwelling. (63)

[21] But the prince, having sent the charioteer away, became desirous of renouncing. Sakka knew his mind and ordered the god Vissakamma, 'Friend, Prince Temiya wishes to renounce. Create a hut of leaves for him and the other requisites for renouncers, and then return!'

'Very good!' he assented. He went quickly and created a hermitage in a clearing in the forest three *yojana*s wide, complete with night-time and daytime abodes, a lotus pool, a well, and fruiting trees.[28] Having created all the requisites for renouncing he returned to his own abode. The Great Being saw it and knew it to be a present from Sakka. Having entered the leaf hut he removed his clothes and put on the robe of red bark. Covering himself with this one, he placed a black antelope skin over his shoulder. He bound his hair into a circular braid and put a carrying pole on one shoulder, and taking his staff he left the leaf hut. Wandering to and fro displaying his renouncer's splendour, he uttered 'Oh, happiness! Oh, happiness!' Having entered the leaf hut he sat on the wooden matting and generated the five higher knowledges. At evening he left and took some leaves from a *kāra* tree[29] and steamed them in unscented water, without salt or buttermilk, in a bowl that had been given by Sakka. He ate this as if it was ambrosia. He made his abode there, cultivating the four divine abidings.

The king of Kāsi, having heard Sunanda's words, summoned his chief general to make preparations for a journey. He said:

'Let them yoke the horses and chariots; bind girdles on the elephants!
Proclaim with conch and tambour, beat the drums! (64)
Sound the well-fastened kettle drums, play the beautiful timpani!
And let them follow me from the city—I will go to counsel my son. (65)

28. VRI is much more elaborate in its description, and includes: 'Close to the hermitage he created a walkway measuring eighty cubits, and he sprinkled the walkway with sand that had the beautiful appearance of crystal. Having created all the requirements for renouncers, he wrote these words on the wall: "Those who wish to renounce, they should take these and renounce." And he drove out all the fierce animals who make unpleasant noises, and the wild birds.'

29. Cowell notes that this is the tree *Canthium parviflorum*.

Concubines and princes, traders and brahmins,
Let them yoke their vehicles quickly—I will go to counsel my son. (66)
Elephant drivers, the army, charioteers, infantry,
Let them yoke their vehicles quickly—I will go to counsel my son. (67)
The country folk assembled, the city folk come together,
Let them yoke their vehicles quickly—I will go to counsel my son.' (68)

[22] Ordered by the king in this way the charioteer yoked the horses, placed the chariot at the palace entrance, and announced that to the king. Explaining the matter the Teacher said:

The charioteer harnessed the swift Sindh horses,
And approached the palace entrance: 'The horses are yoked, Your Majesty!' (69)

Then the king said:[30]

'The large sacrifice speed, and the lean are deficient in strength.' (70a)

So they told the charioteer; 'Do not take horses of that kind!'[31]

Having avoided the bulky and the lean, together the horses were yoked. (70b)

The king, going to meet his son, called together all the army of four ranks and eighteen guilds, and whilst he assembled all the army three days passed. Then on the fourth day he left and, taking what needed to be taken, went to the hermitage. Greeted by his son, he was warmly received. Explaining the matter the Teacher said:

Then the king quickly climbed onto his prepared chariot,
And addressed his womenfolk: 'Follow me all!' (71)
He mounted his chariot, ornamented with gold, with its apparel:
Yak-tail fan, turban, sword, and white parasol. (72)
Then the king set out, his charioteer in front,
And very quickly approached where Temiya was staying. (73)
[23] And seeing him approach, as if shining with radiance,
Surrounded by attendants, Temiya said this: (74)
'I hope, Father that you are skilful. I hope, Father, you are in good health,
And that the royal women, my mothers, are free from illness.' (75)
'I am indeed skilful, son, and also in good health,
And all the royal women, your mothers, are well.' (76)
'I hope, Father, that you are not a drunkard, that you are not fond of liquor,

30. VRI has 'Then hearing the charioteer's words the king spoke this half verse:'
31. VRI has 'Hearing that the charioteer also spoke a half verse:'

And I hope that you think of and delight in *dhamma*, truth, and generosity.' (77)
'Son, I am not a drunkard, and I am not fond of liquor,
And I think of and delight in *dhamma*, truth, and generosity.' (78)
'I hope your yoked animals are healthy and that your steeds bear you well.
I hope that you are not unwell, that your body is untroubled.' (79)
'My yoked animals are healthy and my steeds bear me well.
I am not unwell, and my body is untroubled.' (80)
'I hope that your borders are well populated, and your middle lands are dense;
I hope that your treasury and granary are well stocked.[32] (81)
Great King, you are welcome, not unwelcome.
Let them prepare a couch, where the king may sit.' (82)

But the king, out of respect for the Great Being, did not sit on the couch.[33] [24] Then the Great Being said, 'If he will not sit on the couch, spread out a covering of leaves!' and when it was spread out he spoke this verse:

'May you be seated here, on this prepared covering of leaves.
They will take water from here and wash your feet.' (83)

But the king, out of respect, did not sit on the covering of leaves—he sat on the ground. And the Great Being entered the leaf hut and took out the *kāra* leaves, and inviting the king he spoke a verse:

'These indeed are my greens, cooked without salt, O King.
Eat, Great King, you are my guest that has come.' (84)

Then the King said to him:

'I will not eat leaves, for this food is not for me.
I should eat fine rice and a pure meat sauce.' (85)

Having explained his own type of food, out of respect for his son, who said 'Father, you should eat this kind of food,' he took a little of the greens in the palm of his hand and sat conversing with him in sweet words.[34] At that moment Queen Candā, surrounded by the royal women, arrived, seized the feet of her dear son and paid him honour. With her eyes full of tears

32. VRI includes a verse in reply: 'My borders are well populated and my middle lands are dense / And my granary and treasury are all well stocked.' At this point the verse numbering in F and VRI diverges.

33. F includes this sentence in the word commentary, but it belongs to the narrative. F also has *pallaṅkena* 'cross-legged', but I concur with Cowell and VRI in reading *pallaṅke na* 'not on the couch'.

34. F includes this sentence in the word commentary.

she sat to one side.[35] Then the king said to her, 'My dear, see the food of our son!' and placed a little of the vegetables in her hand. He also gave each of the other women a little, and they all took it and said, 'Sir, do you really eat food of this kind? Sir, you do what is excessively difficult to do!' then sat down. And the king said, 'Son, this appears to me to be a great marvel!' and he spoke this verse:

'Wonder occurs to me: alone and secluded,
While eating such food, how is your appearance bright?' (86)
[25] Explaining, the Great Being said:
'King, I lie down alone, on the fixed spread of leaves;
Because of that solitary bed of mine, King, my appearance is bright. (87)
No royal guards stand over me, brandishing swords;
Because of that happy sleep, King, my appearance is bright. (88)
I do not mourn the past, I do not yearn for the future,
I live in the present, therefore my appearance is bright. (89)
By yearning for the future and mourning the past,
Fools wither like a freshly cut reed.' (90)

The king thought, 'Having consecrated him here, I will take him and go!' Inviting him to the kingship he said:

'My elephants and chariots, cavalry and infantry clad in armour,[36]
And delightful palaces, I give these to you, son! (91)
I will give you the women's apartments, all adorned and beautified;
Take them, son, for you will be our king! (92)
Skilled in song and dance, trained in the four female arts,[37]
They will delight you with sense pleasures. Why would you live in the forest? (93)
I will bring you adorned girls from enemy kings,
And after they have produced sons, then you will renounce. (94)
You are young and delicate, a boy in the first flush of youth,
So rule the kingdom, sir! Why would you live in the forest?' (95)

Following that the Bodhisatta gave a *dhamma* talk:

35. The VRI description is much more elaborate: 'At that moment Queen Candā, surrounded by the royal ladies, came along a path and alighted at the hermitage of the Bodhisatta. Seeing her dear son she fell down right there in a faint. Having got up from the place where she had fallen, she came and clutched hard at the Bodhisatta's feet, worshipping him and crying with eyes full of tears. After getting up from this worship she sat to one side.'

36. This is the traditional South Asian fourfold army.

37. *Cāturitthiyo* could mean there are four women, but given the previous statement this seems unlikely. The commentary states, '*Cāturitthiyo* means women of the four arts, or else women from four cities, or else four kinds of dancing women.'

'The young should follow a holy life, the young should be religious,
For the renunciation of the young is praised by the sages. (96)
[26] The young should follow a holy life, the young should be religious.
I will follow the holy life, and not covet the kingship. (97)
I see the young boy saying "mummy" and "daddy",
A dear son that was difficult to obtain, dead before growing old. (98)
I see the young girl, a beautiful princess,
Dying, crushed like a sprout of a reed or bamboo.[38] (99)
Men and women both, however young, will die,
So what person would think "I am young!" and trust in life? (100)
If at the end of the night one has a very small lifespan,
Like that of fish in little water, what use is youth there? (101)
The world is constantly attacked, and eternally surrounded;
The "unfailing ones" pass by:[39] why would you crown me?' (102)
'What attacks the world, and what surrounds it?
What are the "unfailing ones" that pass by? Questioned, explain to me.' (103)
'The world is attacked by death, and surrounded by old age;
Nights pass by unfailingly; know this, warrior. (104)
King, just as when thread is stretched out and woven,
What is left to weave decreases, in the same way are the lives of mortals. (105)
Just as a full river goes and does not return,
In the same way the lifespan of men goes and does not return. (106)
Just as a full river carries away trees on the riverside,
In the same way living beings are carried away by old age and death.' (107)

[27] The king, having heard the Great Being's *dhamma* talk, became dissatisfied with the household life and wished to renounce. He thought, 'I will not even go to the city, but I will renounce right now! Yet if my son would go to the city I would give him the white parasol of state!' In order to investigate this further, he invited him with the kingship and said:

'My elephants and chariots, cavalry and infantry clad in armour,
And delightful palaces, I give these to you, son! (108)
I will give you the women's apartments, all adorned and beautified;
Take them, son, for you will be our king! (109)
Skilled in song and dance, trained in the four female arts,
They will delight you with sense pleasures. Why would you live in the forest? (110)
I will bring you adorned girls from enemy kings,

38. VRI has 'like the newest sprout of bamboo'.

39. *Amoghāsu vajantīsu*—in Sanskrit *amogha* can be used as a poetic name for the nights that unfailing pass by, which must be the meaning intended here.

And after they have produced sons, then you will renounce.[40] (111)
The granary and the treasury, the army and its vehicles,
And delightful palaces, I give these to you, son! (112)
Surrounded by herds of cows[41] and honoured by slaves,
Rule the kingdom, sir! What will you do in the forest?' (113)

Then the Great Being, explaining his lack of desire for the kingdom, said:

'Why seek wealth that does not last? Why have a wife who will die?
What is the point of youth that decays,[42] when old age conquers all? (114)
What pleasure is there in that? What amusement, delight, or desire for wealth?
What would I do with sons and daughters? King, I am freed from bondage. (115)
I am one who understands this: death does not neglect me.
What delight or desire for wealth is there when seized by the end-maker? (116)
[28] Like ripe fruits in constant fear of falling,
In the same way mortals, born, have a constant fear of death. (117)
Many people who were seen in the morning are not seen in the evening,
And many people seen at night are no longer seen in the morning. (118)
Effort should be made today, for who knows if he might die tomorrow;
There is no fight with General Death. (119)
Thieves long for wealth, but I, King, am free from bondage.
Come, King, turn back! I have no desire for the kingship.' (120)

In this way the Great Being's *dhamma* teaching, together with its application, reached an end. Having heard it, the king and the sixteen thousand royal women with Queen Candā at their head became desirous of renouncing. The king had the drum sounded in the city: 'Whoever wishes to renounce with my son, let them renounce!' [29] And he had the doors of all the stores of gold opened, and had a golden plate on which was inscribed, 'There is in a certain place a great treasure trove: take as desired!' bound onto a big bamboo pillar. But the citizens abandoned their houses with doors wide open, as if they were shops open for business, and gathered around the king. The king, with the populace, renounced before the Great Being. The hermitage that was a present from Sakka was three

40. VRI also repeats v. 95 here, bringing the total number of verses in that edition of the *jātaka* to 122.

41. Following the commentary's explanation, Cowell and Dutoit both translate *gomaṇḍalaparivyūḷho* as surrounded by a circle of women or girls, rather than cows.

42. Following VRI *jiṇṇena* in place of *ciṇṇena*.

yojanas wide, and the Great Being distributed the leaf huts. He gave the leaf huts in the middle to the women, because they were fearful, and he gave the outer leaf huts to the men. And on every *uposatha* day amongst the fruit-laden trees created by Vissakamma they gathered fallen fruits and enjoyed them, observing the proper conduct of the renouncer.[43] And those who reflected on the thought of sense pleasures, or thoughts of ill will, or harmful thoughts, knowing their mind the Great Being sat in the sky and taught them the *dhamma*. Hearing that, they quickly attained the higher knowledges and meditative attainments.

Then a neighbouring king heard, 'The king of Kāsi has renounced!' Thinking, 'I will take the kingdom of Vārāṇasī!' he entered the city. He saw the city adorned, and ascended the throne and surveyed the sevenfold splendid jewels, and thought, 'Because of this wealth a certain fear has arisen.' He summoned some drunkards and asked, 'By which gate did the king leave?'[44] When they replied 'From the eastern gate,' he left by that same gate and set off along the river bank. And the Great Being, knowing that he was coming, came there, sat in the sky, and taught the *dhamma*. He, along with his retinue, renounced in his presence. In the same way three kings renounced.[45] And the elephants gave birth to wild elephants, and the horses to wild horses, and the chariots were destroyed by the forest, and they made the coins in the warehouses into sand and spread it around the hermitage. And they all produced the eight attainments[46] and when their lives were ended they were reborn in the Brahmā heavens. Even the animals that had gone there, the elephants and horses, inclined their hearts towards[47] the community of sages and were reborn in the six heavens of sense desires.

43. This is probably a reference to the idea that ascetics are not supposed to pick the fruits, but only to eat them after they have fallen naturally.

44. VRI has: '"Has your king now become afraid of the city?" "It is not so, Your Majesty." "Then what is the reason?" They replied, "Prince Temiya, our king's son, thinking, 'I will not reign over the kingdom of Vārāṇasī!' became like a mute, though he was not dumb, and left this city to enter the forest as a renouncer sage. For that reason our king, along with the populace, has left the city and gone to renounce in the presence of Prince Temiya." The neighbouring king, hearing their words, became happy. Thinking, "I too will renounce!" he asked, "Friend, by which gate did your king leave?"'

45. VRI says there were seven kings!

46. The eight *jhānas*, or stages of meditative absorption.

47. *Cittaṃ pasādetvā*—This is a reference to the importance of *pasāda*, sometimes translated as 'faith', in allowing a lower being to escape to a better rebirth, thanks to

The Teacher, having spoken this *dhamma* teaching, said, 'Not only now, monks, but also in the past did I give up the kingdom and renounce.' He connected the birth: 'At that time Uppallavaṇṇā was the goddess living in the parasol, [30] Sāriputta was the charioteer, the king's family were my parents, the Buddhist assembly was the remaining assembly, and I myself was the wise dumb cripple!'[48]

---

the calming or inspiring presence of a spiritually advanced human.

48. F has an additional paragraph here which attempts to link the arrival of various senior monks in Sīhaladīpa (Sri Lanka) with this *jātaka* story and two others. This paragraph is not attested in his Burmese manuscript, nor in VRI, and since it seems likely to be specific to the Sri Lankan recension and sits uneasily in the story I have chosen to omit it. For a translation and discussion of this passage see Shaw 2006a: 217 and 221.

2

JANAKA

The (Great) Birth Story of Janaka

(Janaka-jātaka or *Mahājanaka-jātaka)*

INTRODUCTION

The second story of the Great Ten continues the focus on renunciation started in the *Temiya-jātaka*. However, before the benefits and challenges of pursuing the religious life are discussed, the first part of the story has a more worldly focus: Janaka, the Bodhisatta, is brought up in exile and seeks to regain the kingdom that was taken from his father. In order to gain enough money to raise an army, Janaka goes to sea with a shipload of merchants. However, the ship sinks and his fellow mariners all die. Only Janaka, through his extraordinary effort, survives long enough to be rescued and taken to his kingdom. The graphic description of Janaka's plan to stay alive—clinging onto the mast until the last moment, leaping over the bodies of his fellow sailors, and swimming for seven days without any rest—is a lesson in what it really means to be determined. And since the ocean is a popular metaphor for *saṃsāra*, the cycle of rebirth and redeath, Janaka's efforts to reach the shore (*nibbāna*) are doubly praiseworthy.

The *Janaka-jātaka*[1] celebrates the perfection of *viriya* 'vigour, effort'. This term, along with the similar term *vāyāma* 'striving, exertion', occurs several

Introduced and translated by Naomi Appleton.

1. In F it is called *Mahājanaka-jātaka*, to distinguish it the *Cūḷa-* (small) *Janaka-jātaka* (which in fact is just a short reference to one episode of our story). However, in the Southeast Asian tradition the story is usually just referred to as *Janaka*, and the leading character is usually called Janaka.

times in relation to the Bodhisatta's response to being shipwrecked. His determination in this moment of peril is referred to again in the *Cūḷa-Janaka-jātaka* (J 52) in order to inspire a backsliding monk. However, there is some irony in the association between the story and the quality of exertion: Mahājanaka exerts himself for seven days getting nowhere, but his persistence impresses a goddess who then rescues him. He sleeps through his arrival in Mithilā and choice as king, and his very non-responsiveness is seen as proof that he is worthy of ruling. He further earns his right to rule by ignoring the princess and refusing to run around doing her bidding. And finally, after all the effort of regaining his father's kingdom he goes on to renounce it all. This story is therefore not a simple tale of effort; rather it explores the relationship between personal effort and assistance, physical and intellectual effort, and worldly and world-renouncing effort. The ultimate demonstration of Mahājanaka's effort is, after all, not his survival of the shipwreck, but his determination to shake off his wife and pursue the life of a solitary renouncer, though the former episode can be seen as foreshadowing the latter.

The solitary nature of Janaka's renunciation is emphasized very clearly in the story. Unlike Temiya, who renounces with his entire family and kingdom and teaches them the way to heaven, Janaka refuses to allow his wife or citizens to follow him into the dense forest. Even his earlier actions are solitary: he refuses to take all of his mother's wealth and instead insists on going to sea, where he alone escapes the sea monsters and lives to reclaim his kingdom. The emphasis on Janaka's solitary path links to the *paccekabuddha*s that are mentioned several times as being supported by the king of Mithilā. These *paccekabuddha*s are awakened beings that differ from full *buddha*s (such as Janaka will eventually become) in that they do not found a Buddhist community or teach extensively. When Janaka decides to renounce he wants to live like a *paccekabuddha*, and he resembles one so closely as he leaves the palace that his own wife does not recognize him. The *Janaka-jātaka* thus suggests that each person must take individual responsibility for their actions, whether they are working towards liberation or towards worldly success.

Shipwrecks and the Ocean of *Saṃsāra*

The first half of the *Janaka-jātaka* reaches its climax when the hero is shipwrecked in the middle of the ocean.[2] Refusing to give up hope despite not even being able to see the shore, Janaka keeps trying his best to stay alive and reach his destination. Eventually he is rewarded for his fortitude by the goddess of the sea, Maṇimekhalā, who rescues him from the ocean. This scene is commonly depicted in temple and manuscript art, and artists have freely played around with concepts of time and place by showing European-style vessels staffed by foreign sailors. The dramatic depictions of such scenes lead us to assume that this is the high point of Janaka's *viriya*, and indeed this episode becomes symbolic of all struggles in Buddhists' lives.

The motif of the shipwreck plays into the wider metaphorical language of early Buddhism. For Buddhists, as for all early religions of South Asia, the world of rebirth and redeath—*saṃsāra*—is like an ocean constantly sweeping us around from one existence to the next. To cross that ocean and reach the further shore—*nibbāna* or liberation—is the ultimate aim. The Buddha's teaching is sometimes compared to a raft that enables his followers to cross over the ocean of rebirth, while the teachers of Jainism are referred to as 'ford-makers' (*tīrthaṅkaras*) because they too have shown a safe route across to the further shore. By depicting the Bodhisatta surviving a shipwreck and demonstrating his unshakeable determination to reach the shore, this story hints at his later role in carrying Buddhists across the ocean of *saṃsāra* to the safety of *nibbāna*.[3] Janaka's ambition to eventually become a Buddha is later helped by another act of determination, that of renouncing everything he has won and retreating into the wilderness to practice solitary meditation.

Janaka and Renunciation outside the *Janaka-jātaka*

While some artists and audiences tend to focus their attention on Janaka's first demonstration of vigour (his survival of the shipwreck) others pay more attention to his second demonstration—his determination to renounce.[4] These two halves of the story seem at first glance to sit somewhat uneasily next to one another. However, the presence of Janaka and other great renouncers outside of the *jātaka*s helps to shed light on why the worldly and world-rejecting actions are juxtaposed.

2. See Shaw 2013 for a discussion of the shipwreck motif in Buddhist texts.
3. For further discussion about the use of boats in Buddhist narrative imagery see Shaw 2012b.
4. For a discussion of the artistic life of the *Janaka-jātaka* see Shaw 2012a.

The great renunciation of King Janaka is mentioned in the great Hindu epic *Mahābhārata*. The setting is the 'Book of Peace' (Śānti Parvan), in which King Yudhiṣṭhira, victor of the great war between two sets of cousins, reflects upon the destruction he has witnessed and caused. At one point he insists that he is going to renounce and practice a life of asceticism in order to atone for the killing of so many warriors, including members of his own family. His brothers and other fellow survivors attempt to talk him out of it. At one stage in the discussion Yudhiṣṭhira mentions King Janaka as a role model, for he was so set on renunciation that he was unmoved even by the vision of Mithilā on fire; he quotes the same verse as that which forms verse 125 in this *jātaka*.[5] Although the full story of King Janaka is not given, the parallel is instructive. Like Janaka, Yudhiṣṭhira had his rightful kingdom stolen by a relation (in his case a cousin) and had to go to huge lengths to get it back (including an exile of twelve years and a horrendous battle). Like Janaka, having finally obtained his kingdom Yudhiṣṭhira decides to give it all up. Like Janaka, Yudhiṣṭhira faces opposition from his family. However, unlike the Buddhist context, we are left in no doubt by the ensuing argument that renunciation is the *wrong* choice for Yudhiṣṭhira, as it was also for Janaka: Arjuna, Yudhiṣṭhira's brother, cites the arguments of Janaka's wife *against* renunciation, and the conversation moves on.

The parallels between Yudhiṣṭhira and Janaka, both of whom are exploring the propriety of renouncing a kingdom that has been very hard to win, help us to understand how the two parts of this *jātaka* fit together. The demonstration of great energy and determination in the first half of the *Janaka-jātaka* provide a necessary backdrop to Janaka's determined renunciation. If Janaka had won back his kingdom with ease, his renunciation would have been less impressive. And by contrasting the two examples of his great energy—the shipwreck and the renunciation—we see which one we should be emulating. There is an implicit lesson that we should not strive too hard to win worldly goals, for we may later wish they would just go away and leave us alone.

The *Mahābhārata* parallel is not the only example of intertextuality in this *jātaka*. The verse about Mithilā burning is also found in a Jain text, the *Uttarādhyayana*, during the story of the determined renunciation of

5. The verse, with slight variations, is found three times in the *Mahābhārata*, all in the Śānti Parvan. The Critical Edition references are 12.17.18, 12.171.56, and 12.268.4. It is the first occurrence that is discussed here.

a king called Nami.[6] In addition, the divine sage Nārada, who converses with the Bodhisatta, is famous from Brahmanical Hindu narratives and also appears—this time as the Bodhisatta—in the *Nārada-jātaka* (Chapter 8).[7] The lessons provided by the mango trees, the little girl's bracelets, and the fletcher are also found in other tales of renunciation in South Asian religious texts.[8] An earlier *jātaka* story, the *Kumbhakāra-jātaka* (J 408), contains the first two amongst four prompts for renunciation that enable four kings to become *paccekabuddhas*. The third king in this story is King Nimi, who rules in Mithilā, and who is prompted to renounce and become a *paccekabuddha* by the vision of hawks fighting over meat (another motif also found elsewhere in Indian narrative). This name and location call to mind King Nimi/Nemi of the *Nemi-jātaka* (Chapter 4), though in that story the king is the Bodhisatta and therefore cannot also be a *paccekabuddha*. The story of the four kings and the four signs that prompt their awakening is also found in *Uttarādhyayana* 18, though the association of king with sign is different in that text.[9] The name and location also resonate with the Jain story of the renouncing King Nami in the same text, who is unmoved by the sight of Mithilā on fire. Thus we can see that there are several intertwined stories of a king leaving Mithilā behind in order to pursue a renouncer's life. There are also stories of a King Janaka of Videha in which he shows no signs of renouncing at all,[10] suggesting a very open-ended series of motifs and identifications.

6. *Uttarādhyayana* IX v. 14; Jacobi 1895: 35-41. It is spoken by King Nami in reply to Indra (disguised as a brahmin), who is questioning him about his recent renunciation.

7. I cannot find any references in other texts to Migājina ('Deerskin'), the other sage that visits the Bodhisatta in this story. For more discussion of Nārada see the *Nārada-jātaka* (Chapter 8).

8. As just one example, the lesson of the noisy bangles and a fletcher story (though here emphasizing the one-pointed concentration of a fletcher rather than his decision to look through one eye) feature in the list of the twenty-four teachers of Dattatreya, one of the *avatāras* (incarnations) of the god Viṣṇu, as found in *Bhagavata Purāṇa* 11. Another of his teachers is the hawk, who fights over meat, as mentioned in relation to the *Kumbhakāra-jātaka* below. That Dattatreya learns from nature rather than from a human guru is paralleled by Janaka's declaration that his teachers are the mango trees.

9. For an interesting discussion of what these stories say about the nature of a *paccekabuddha* in each tradition see Norman 1991: 233–49. Norman argues that both Buddhists and Jains borrowed the term from some other tradition, and that it had an early association with the idea of being awakened by external signs or prompts.

10. For example King Janaka is one of the interlocutors in the *Upaniṣads*, where he gives gifts and sponsors sacrifice, and various King Janakas are found receiving teachings in the Śānti Parvan of the *Mahābhārata*.

The presence of several independent motifs relating to the benefits of renunciation, many of which would have been familiar from other stories, as well as the presence of a well-known renouncer-king, makes the *Janaka-jātaka* feel like a grand repository of teachings on the subject. Rather than showing the Bodhisatta renouncing quietly as in the stories of Temiya or Nemi (Chapters 1 and 4), the *Janaka-jātaka* ensures that we properly appreciate the motivations for renunciation as well as the difficulties experienced by those who choose to leave home and family behind.

'Who is this in the middle of the ocean . . .'

[30] The Teacher related this, while living in the Jeta Grove, about the Great Renunciation. For one day the monks were seated in the *dhamma* hall praising the great renunciation of the Tathāgata. The Teacher arrived and asked, 'What are you talking about as you sit together here, monks?' They told him, and saying, 'Not only now, monks, but also in former times, has the Tathāgata performed a Great Renunciation,' he spoke of the past.

In times past, a king named Mahājanaka ruled in Mithilā in the country of Videha. He had two sons, Ariṭṭhajanaka and Polajanaka, and to the eldest of these he gave viceroyalty and the youngest he made general. Later on, when Mahājanaka had passed away, Ariṭṭhajanaka became king and gave his brother viceroyalty. But then a certain foot servant approached the king and said, 'Your Majesty, the viceroy wishes to kill you!' Having heard this said again and again he was divided from his younger brother[11] and had Polajanaka bound in chains. He appointed guards and detained him in a certain dwelling not far from the royal residence. The prince made an Act of Truth: 'If I am my brother's enemy then may these chains not free me and may the door not open! But if I am no enemy then may the chains release me and the door open!' [31] Right away the chains were broken into bits and the door opened. Leaving, he went to a village on the borders and

11. Following the interpretation of VRI, which has *kaniṭṭhassa sinehaṃ bhinditvā* 'having broken off affection for his younger brother' where F has only *bhijjitvā* 'having been broken'.

made his home there. Those who lived in the borders recognized him and looked after him, so the king was unable to seize him.

In the course of time he took possession of the borderlands and gained a great entourage. Thinking, 'I was not my brother's enemy before, but now I am!' he arrived at Mithilā with a great retinue of people and established his army outside the city. When the inhabitants of the city heard, 'Prince Polajanaka has come!' most of them took elephant mounts and so on and approached him, while others came out of the city. He sent a message to his brother: 'I was not your enemy before, but now I am your enemy! Give me your royal parasol or else give battle!' The king left to go and give battle, telling his chief wife, 'My dear, it is impossible to know whether I will meet with victory or defeat in battle. If I should meet with danger, take care of our unborn child.' Then in that battle Polajanaka's soldiers put an end to his life.

There was a single uproar in the whole city: 'The king is dead!' Thus knowing of his death the queen very quickly placed valuable gold and so on into a basket, stretched a rag over the top, and poured rice on top of that. She dressed herself in dirty rags and made her body look ugly. Placing the basket on her head she set out at sunrise, and nobody recognized her. She left by the northern gate, but not having been anywhere before she did not know the way and was unable to work out the directions. She had only heard that there was a city called Kāḷa Campā, and so she sat there asking, 'Is anyone going to Kāḷa Campā city?'

Now in her womb was not just any old being, but the Great Being reborn, filled with the perfections. On account of his glory Sakka's abode shook. Sakka reflected and knew the cause. Thinking, 'The being arisen in her womb has great merit. It is right that I go!' he created a covered wagon and spread out a couch, and like an old man he drove the wagon and stopped it at the entrance to the hut where she was sitting. 'Is anyone going to Kāḷa Campā city?' he asked.

'I would like to go there, father.'

[32] 'Then climb up on the wagon and sit, mother.'

'Father, I am with child, and not able to ride in a wagon. I will follow behind. But please make room for this basket of mine.'

'What are you saying, mother? There is nobody equal to me in skill and ability when it comes to driving a wagon. Do not be afraid; climb up and sit.' When it was time for her to climb up, by his power the earth rose and touched the back of the wagon. Having climbed up and lain down on the couch she knew this was a god. As soon as she lay down on the divine couch she fell asleep.

After thirty *yojanas* Sakka arrived at a river. He woke her up: 'Mother, get down and bathe in the river. There is a cloak on the pillow—dress yourself in that. Then there is a rice cake in the wagon—eat it.' She did so and then lay down once more. In the evening they arrived at Campā and saw the gates, watchtowers, and ramparts.

'Father, what is this city?' she asked.

'It is the city of Campā, mother.'

'What are you saying, father? Surely from our city to Campā city is a distance of sixty *yojanas*!'

'That is so, mother, but I know a shortcut.' Then having let her alight near the southern gate he said, 'Mother, our village is over there. You enter the city.' Having gone before her, Sakka disappeared and went to his own abode.

The queen sat down in a certain hut, and at that very moment a resident of Campā, a brahmin who was a scholar of mantras, surrounded by five hundred young men, was going to a bathing place. Looking from afar he saw this beautiful and perfect form sitting there, and because of this sight—but also through the power of the one in her womb—he became affectionate towards her as towards a younger sister. He left the young men and alone went into the hut. 'Which village are you from, sister?' he asked.

'I am the chief wife of King Ariṭṭhajanaka of Mithilā.'

'Why have you come here?'

'The king has been killed by Polajanaka, and so I am frightened and come here wishing to protect my unborn child.'

'But do you have any relatives in this city?'

'None, father.'

'Well, do not worry. I am a high-born brahmin with a big house, famed in the world as a teacher. I will establish you in the place of a sister and look after you. Now calling me brother grasp my feet and cry.' She made a great noise [33] and fell at his feet, and then they both lamented at each other.

His pupils ran up and asked, 'Teacher, what is going on?'

'This is my younger sister, who was separated from me some time ago.'

'But now that you have seen her, do not worry, teacher.'

He had a large covered wagon fetched and seated her in it, then sent her to his house, saying, 'Friend, you should tell the lady brahmin that this is my sister, and have her do all that is needed.' Then the lady brahmin had her bathe in hot water, assigned her a bed, and invited her to lie down. After he had bathed, the brahmin came home at dinner time and asked for his sister to be summoned. Then having eaten together with her, he looked after her inside his house.

A short time later she gave birth to a son and named him Prince Mahājanaka after his grandfather. When he was growing up he played with other children who annoyed him. He hit them hard because they were full of pride and very strong, being born in unmixed warrior families. They cried out making a huge noise, and when asked, 'Who has hit you?' they replied, 'The son of the widow.' The boy thought, 'They always call me "the widow's son". I will ask my mother about this.' So one day he asked, 'Mummy, who is my father?' And she deceived him, replying, 'My dear, your father is a brahmin.' The next day, when he was hitting them and they were calling him the widow's son he said, 'My father is a brahmin!' but they said, 'What is a brahmin to you?' He thought, 'They say, "What is a brahmin to you?" My mother did not explain this matter, and out of pride she will not explain it to me herself. I will have to make her speak.' While he was drinking his mother's milk he bit her on the breast and said, 'Tell me of my father! If you will not speak I will cut off your breast!' Unable to deceive him, she explained, 'My dear, you are the son of King Ariṭṭhajanaka of Mithilā. Your father was killed by Polajanaka, and in order to protect you I came to this city. The brahmin established me in the place of a sister and looks after me.' From then on he was no longer angry when they called him the son of the widow.

Within sixteen years he learned all the arts of the three Vedas, [34] and when he was sixteen he had the most impressive appearance. Thinking, 'I will seize the kingdom that belongs to my father!' he asked his mother, 'Mother, do you have any possessions, for if not I will go into business, make money, and then seize the kingdom that belongs to my father.'

'My dear, I did not come here empty handed. There are these valuable pearls, precious jewels, and excellent diamonds, each one appropriate for seizing a kingdom. So take them and seize the kingdom! Do not go into business.'

'Mother, give me that wealth, and taking half I will go to Suvaṇṇabhūmi to get more wealth, and then seize the kingdom.' So he had half fetched, and taking goods he loaded the stock into a boat with merchants who were going to Suvaṇṇabhūmi. He went to his mother and honoured her, saying, 'Mother, I am going to Suvaṇṇabhūmi.'

'My dear, the ocean is dangerous and full of obstacles. Don't go. You have plenty of wealth for getting the kingdom.'

Saying, 'I am going, Mother!' he honoured his mother, left, and boarded the boat. That very day Polajanaka became ill and took to his bed, unable to get up.

Seven hundred men[12] boarded, and in seven days the boat went seven hundred *yojanas*. But then she entered very violent waters and was unable to carry them. The boards broke, and by and by the water came in until the boat plunged into the middle of the ocean. The people cried out and lamented and paid homage to various deities, but the Great Being neither cried nor lamented nor venerated a deity. Realising that the boat was sinking, he crushed some grain with ghee and ate until his belly was full. Then he smeared his two tunics with sesamum oil, dressed himself firmly, and stood near the mast. When the boat sunk down he got on the mast. The many beings became food for the fish and turtles, such that the water all around was red with blood, but the Great Being stood on the top of the mast. He worked out the directions—'Mithilā must be this way!'—and leaping off the top of the mast he passed beyond the fish and turtles and through his great strength he fell at a distance of 140 cubits.[13] That day Polajanaka passed away.

From there the Great Being set off in the crystal-clear waves, like a mass of gold [35] crossing the ocean. And just as on the first day he crossed for seven days, then looking for the shore he washed his face with the salty water[14] and became an observer of the *uposatha*. Now at that time the Four World Guardians[15] had appointed a daughter of the gods named Maṇimekhalā[16] as protector of the ocean, saying, 'Beings that are of suitable quality in terms of honouring of their mothers and so on should not fall in the ocean—you should rescue[17] them!' She had not been looking at the

12. *Jaṃgha* is obscure but must, by association with *jaṃghā* (the lower leg, used also to refer to walking) mean walking (able-bodied?) beings.

13. Translating *usabha* as 140 cubits. An *usabha* 'bull' is said to be equivalent to 20 *yaṭṭhis* 'sticks', which are each 7 *ratanas* 'elbows', a measurement from the elbow to fingers, in other words a cubit.

14. Following VRI *loṇodakena* rather than F *leṇodakena*.

15. These are the deities of the four directions.

16. Maṇimekhalā is a goddess of the sea known most famously from the Tamil epic *Maṇimekhalai*.

17. Following VRI *uddhārehi* rather than F *upadhāreti*, which could be an instruction to the goddess to look out for such worthy beings.

sea for seven days, because she was experiencing divine bliss. Or some say she had become forgetful, having gone to an assembly of the gods. Thinking, 'Today is my seventh day of not looking at the ocean, so what has happened?' she looked and saw the Great Being. 'If Prince Mahājanaka were to perish in the ocean, I would not be allowed in to the assembly of the gods.' She stood in the sky not far from the Great Being with her body adorned, and testing the Great Being she spoke the first verse:

> 'Who is this in the middle of the ocean, straining though he cannot see the shore?
> What purpose do you perceive in exerting yourself so strongly in this way?' (1)

Then the Great Being said, 'Today is my seventh day crossing the ocean, and I have not yet seen another being. Who on earth is this speaking to me?' He looked in the sky and saw her, and spoke the second verse:

> 'I am careful of my duty to exert myself in the world, goddess;
> That is why I am in the middle of the ocean, straining though unable to see the shore.' (2)

Wanting to hear a *dhamma* teaching from him she spoke another verse:

> 'In the deep and boundless ocean in which one cannot see the shore,
> You, fool, though a man of effort, will die without reaching it.' (3)

Then the Great Being, saying, 'Why do you say this? Dying while making an effort I will be free from blame!' spoke a verse:

> [36] 'He is free from debt towards his relatives, the gods, and ancestors,
> He who does what should be done without subsequent regret.' (4)

The goddess spoke a verse:

> 'That action which is unattainable is fruitless and results only in exhaustion.
> So what is the point of striving, when the result[18] of it is death?' (5)

When she had said this the Great Being bewildered her by speaking further verses:

> 'He who considers that something is completely unattainable, goddess,
> Does not protect his own life. He realizes this if he gives up. (6)
> There are some in this world, goddess, who undertake actions
> Wishing for results, and they may prosper or not. (7)
> You can see the visible fruits of actions, goddess,

18. For interpretation of *abhinippatan* as 'result' see DP I 201.

For the others are sunk while I am crossing and see you nearby. (8)
So I will keep striving to the best of my ability and with all my strength,
Heading for the ocean's shore; I will do what men should do. (9)

[37] The goddess, having heard his resolute words, spoke a verse praising him:

'You who carry on in the flood, the boundless great ocean,
Endowed with dutiful exertion, not giving up on the deed,
You should go wherever your heart desires.' (10)

And having said this she asked, 'Wise one of great endeavour, where should I take you?' When he replied, 'The city of Mithilā,' she picked up the Great Being as if he were a bunch of flowers and held him in both arms, lying him against her chest. Going along as if she were carrying her dear little child, she sprung forward through the sky. The Great Being's body, shriveled from seven days in salty water, was thrilled by the divine touch and he fell asleep. So she took him to Mithilā and lay him down on his right side, on an auspicious stone slab in a mango grove. Ensuring that the park deities took over his protection, she went to her own abode.

Now Polajanaka had no son, but he had one daughter, called Princess Sīvalī, and she was wise and accomplished. When he was lying on his deathbed they asked him, 'Great King, when you have gone to the divine state, to whom should we give the kingdom?'

'Give it to whoever is able to please my daughter Princess Sīvalī, or who knows the head of a square bed, or who can string the thousand-strong bow, or who is able to take the sixteen treasures.'

'Your Majesty, explain to us a summary[19] of the treasures.'

The king said:

'There is treasure at the sunrise and treasure at its setting,
There is treasure inside, treasure outside, and treasure that is neither inside nor outside. (11)
[38] There is treasure ascending and treasure descending,
And treasure at the four great *sāl* trees[20] and for a *yojana* all around. (12)
There is great treasure on the tip of the tooth, and on the tip of the hair, and in the 'kebuka',
And there is great treasure in the tops of the trees. These are the sixteen great treasures,

19. Following VRI *uddāna* for F *udāna* 'inspired utterance'.

20. It is possible that a pun is meant here, for *sālā* could mean 'halls' or '*sāl* trees'. The former meaning might be more likely, but we discover later on that *sāl* trees are meant.

And the thousand-strong bow and the bed, and by satisfying Sīvalī.' (13)

He gave a summary of other treasures along with these.

After the death of the king, the courtiers performed his death rites and gathered together on the seventh day to consult: 'The king said that the kingdom should be given to someone able to please his own daughter. Who will be able to please her?'

'The favourite general,' they said, and sent him a message, to which he assented.

He came to the palace gates seeking the kingship and had his presence announced to the king's daughter. She understood why he had come and wondered, 'Does he have the firmness to bear the royal parasol?' In order to test him she said, 'He may come!' Hearing that message and desirous of pleasing her, setting off from the bottom of the steps he went quickly and stood in her presence. Then testing him she said, 'Run quickly to the roof terrace!' Saying, 'I will please the daughter of the king!' he sprung forward fast. Then she said, 'Come!' and he came back speedily. Realising that he was not of firm character[21] she said, 'Come here and massage my feet!' He sat down and massaged her feet, in order to please her. Then she hit his chest with her foot and made him fall on his back, and giving a sign to her female servants she said, 'Beat this blind fool of a man who is lacking in resolve. Take him by the throat and throw him out!' They did so. When he was asked, 'Well, general?' he said, 'Don't ask. She is not a human woman!'[22] Next the royal treasurer went, but he was shamed in the same way. Similarly a guildsman, the holder of the parasol, and a sword-bearer were all shamed in this way.

Then the people consulted: 'There is nobody able to please the king's daughter. Give the kingdom[23] to the one able to string the thousand-strong bow!' But there was nobody able to string it. 'Give it to the one able to tell the head of a square bed,' they said. But nobody knew that. Then they said, 'Give it to the one able to extract the sixteen great treasures. But nobody

21. The term translated here as 'firm character' and elsewhere as 'resolve' is *dhiti* 'holding', which has a range of meanings surrounding the idea of firmness or constancy. Clearly the princess is testing for a man's ability to stand firm against her unreasonable demands, seeking somebody with sufficient resolve to run a kingdom.

22. VRI clarifies that he calls her a *yakkhinī*—a demoness!

23. Following VRI. It is not clear from F whether the object to be given is the kingdom or the princess, but given the king's earlier instructions the former seems more likely, and this is made explicit in the VRI version.

[39] was able to find them. Then they took counsel: 'It is not possible to protect a kingdom that is without a king! What on earth should be done?' The royal chaplain said, 'Do not worry. The state chariot[24] should be let loose, for with the state chariot a king will be found who is able to rule over the whole of Jambudīpa.'

'Very well,' they assented. They had the city decorated, and yoked four horses the colour of the white lotus to the auspicious chariot. They spread out an upper cover on it and prepared the five emblems of royalty,[25] and had it surrounded with the four-limbed army.[26] Musical instruments are played in front of a chariot with a driver, but behind one that has no driver, so the chaplain said, 'Sound the instruments behind!' Then having sprinkled the goad and the yoke[27] from a golden vase he said, 'Go and approach one who has the merit to rule the kingdom!'

The chariot circumambulated the royal residence and then climbed the road of the drum.[28] The general and so on thought, 'Let the state chariot come towards me!' but it passed by all their houses, and having made a complete circuit of the city it left through the eastern gate and set out towards the park. Seeing it going so fast they said, 'Bring it back!' but the chaplain prevented them, saying, 'Don't bring it back. If it wishes to, let it go as far as a hundred *yojanas*.' The chariot entered the park, and having circumambulated the auspicious stone slab it remained there ready to be mounted. The chaplain saw the Great Being lying there, and consulting with the courtiers he said, 'Look here, see this one lying on the stone slab. We do not know whether or not he is steadfast and fit for the white royal parasol. If he has sufficient merit he will not look at us, but if he is black-eared (ill-omened) he will jump up in fear and look at us, shaking. Quickly take up all the musical instruments!' Right then they took up several hundred musical instruments and it was like the roar of the ocean. The Great Being was awoken by that noise, and uncovering his head he looked and saw the crowd of people. Thinking, 'It must be that they have come for me with the white parasol,' he covered his head again and turned

24. In the *jātakas* a *phussaratha* is a state chariot that runs of its own accord, seeking out its appropriate rider.

25. As explained earlier in the *Jātakatthavaṇṇanā*, these are the fan, diadem, sword, parasol, and slippers.

26. Namely cavalry, elephants, chariots, and infantry.

27. Following VRI *rathadhūrañ* rather than F *rathanandiñ.*

28. Perhaps this is the road along which proclamations are made.

over to lie on his left side. The chaplain uncovered his feet and saw the auspicious marks: 'Never mind this one continent; he is able to rule over all four continents!' He had them take up the musical instruments again. [40] The Great Being uncovered his face, turned over, and lay back down on his right side, looking at the people. The chaplain calmed the assembled people, and saluting him, he bowed down and said, 'Arise, Your Majesty! Attain to the kingship!'

'Where is the king?'

'His time was done.'

'Had he no son or brother?'

'He did not, Your Majesty.'

'Very good, then I will rule the kingdom.' He got up and sat cross-legged on the stone slab, and they consecrated him right there, naming him King Mahājanaka. Having mounted the excellent chariot he entered the city with great pomp and splendour and went into his residence. Having done some administration—'Let them be in the position of general and so on!'—he went up onto the terrace.

The king's daughter, wanting to test him because of her previous notion, ordered a certain man: 'Go approach the king and say, "Princess Sīvalī summons you—go quickly."' But the wise king, as if he had not heard his words, spoke of the appearance of the palace, saying 'Oh, splendid.' Unable to make him listen, he returned and said to the king's daughter, 'My lady, the king heard your words but, describing the palace, he took as little notice as of a blade of grass.' Thinking, 'This must be a man of great character,' she ordered him a second and third time, but the king, walking as he pleased and yawning like a lion, went into the palace. When he approached, the daughter of the king was unable to stay composed due to his own nature and splendour, and she approached offering him her hand as a support. Resting on her hand he climbed up to the terrace, sat down on the royal couch under the elevated white parasol, and addressing the courtiers he asked, 'Look here, was there not some command given to you by the king when he was dying?'

'Yes, Your Majesty.'

'Tell it.'

'He said that whoever could please Princess Sīvalī should be given the kingdom.'

'When I came Sīvalī gave me her hand as a support, so surely she is pleased. Speak of another.'

'Your Majesty, he said that whoever was able to know the head of a square bed should be given the kingdom.'

The king thought, 'That is difficult to ascertain, but by this means it is possible to know,' and having extracted a golden hairpin from his head he placed it in Princess Sīvalī's hand and said, [41] 'Place it.' She took it and put it at the head end of the bed.[29] By that means he knew this was the head end, and as if he hadn't heard their speech he said, 'What did you say?' and when they said it again he responded, 'It is no wonder to know this. This is the head end.' He asked, 'What else?'

'Your Majesty, he commanded that whoever could string the thousand-strong bow should be given the kingdom.' Saying, 'Bring it here,' he had it fetched, and even as he sat there on the couch he strung that bow as if it was a women's bow for preparing cotton.[30] Then he asked, 'Tell me of another,' and they replied, 'He said the kingdom should be given to the one who is able to find the sixteen great treasures.'

'Is there some sort of summary?'[31]

Saying, 'Yes there is,' they related the summary, beginning, 'There is treasure at the sunrise'. Even as he listened the meaning became clear like the moon in the expanse of the sky. He said to them, 'Today there is certainly not time. Tomorrow we will seize the treasure.'

The next day he assembled the courtiers and asked, 'Did your king feed *paccekabuddhas*?'

'Yes, Your Majesty.'

He thought, '"The sun" does not mean the actual sun, but *paccekabuddhas* are called "sun" because they are like a sun. The treasure must be where they were met.' Then the king asked, 'When the *paccekabuddhas* came, where did he meet them?' When they replied, 'Such and such a place,' he ordered, 'Dig in that place and you will find treasure.' Then he asked, 'And after their arrival, where did he place them and take leave?'

'In such and such a place.'

29. Here I have omitted *khaggaṃ adāsīti pi vadanti yeva* 'and just as they say she gave him the sword' as this is obscure and interrupts the flow of the narrative. Cowell and Rouse explain it with reference to the story of a snake-maiden giving the hero a sword in the *Kathāsaritsāgara.*

30. F *poṭhana* and VRI *phoṭana* are both obscure, but the reference must be to the Indian method of preparing cotton for spinning using a small bow. Cowell & Rouse and Shaw translate as 'carding cotton', which is an equivalent process, though the Indian method does not use cards.

31. Once again following VRI in reading *uddāna* rather than *udāna.*

'Then extract treasure from there,' he ordered. The people produced a thousand shouts and wandered back and forth digging in the region of the sunrise, according to what he had said was the sunrise. And they wandered around digging in the place of the sunset, according to what he said the sunset was. They declared their joy and satisfaction: 'Oh, that this wealth is right here is a real wonder!' Then for the 'treasure inside' he had them extract treasure from inside the threshold of the great gates to the royal house, and for the 'treasure outside' he had them extract treasure from outside the threshold, and for 'neither inside nor outside' he had them extract treasure from underneath the threshold. [42] For 'ascending' he had them extract it from the carpet on the golden staircase used when climbing onto the auspicious elephant, and for 'descending' he had them extract it from the place for getting down from the back of the elephant. For the 'four great *sāl* trees' he had them extract four pots of treasure from the ground underneath the four feet—made of *sāl* wood—of the royal couch in the place where ministering is done. For 'a *yojana* all around', since a *yojana* is a yoke of a chariot, he had them extract pots of treasure from the measure of a yoke all around the royal bed.[32] For 'great treasure on the tip of the tooth', in the place of the auspicious elephant he had them extract two treasures from the area facing his two tusks.[33] For 'on the tip of the hair', in the place of the auspicious horse he had them extract it from the place facing its tail.[34] For 'kebuka', explaining that *kebuka* is water, he had them extract water from the auspicious lotus pool, and the treasure was revealed. For 'great treasure at the top of the tree', in that same park at the root of the great *sāl* tree he had them extract pots of treasure from within the circular shadow at the moment of midday. In this way he had them extract the sixteen treasures. 'Is there anything else?' he said.

'There is not, Your Majesty.'

The people were pleased and delighted. The king said, 'I will scatter this wealth in the mouth of generosity!' and had five alms halls built, at the four gates and in the middle of the city, and gave great gifts. He had his mother and the brahmin fetched from the city of Kāḷa Campā and established them in great honour.

32. A *yojana* is a large measure of distance, said to be the distance one can travel on a single yoke of an ox, but it also refers to the yoke itself, which is the meaning deduced by the king here.

33. Following VRI *dvinnaṃ* 'two' rather than F *dinnaṃ* 'given'.

34. VRI has this treasure at the tail of the elephant, rather than the horse.

They say that when his reign was young the son of King Ariṭṭhajanaka, called Mahājanaka, ruled the whole kingdom of Videha. The whole city was stirred up and wished to see him: 'They say the king is wise! Let us go and see him.' They came one after the other bringing great presents, and they prepared a great festival in the city. They spread elephant rugs and so on in the royal residence, and arranged wreaths of flowers and scented wreaths, and made it dark by strewing it all over with *lāja* flowers,[35] perfumes, and incense. They had him served with food and drink of various flavours. Taking hard and soft food, drinks, and fruits and so on of various flavours, in bowls made of silver and gold and so on, in order to present them to the king, [43] they attended on him one after the other and remained there. On one side sat a circle of courtiers, on another side a group of brahmins, on another side the wealthy merchants and so on, and on the other side dancing women bearing the finest forms. Brahmins that were utterers of blessings, auspicious-mouthed, skilled in auspicious chants and so on, produced chants of various kinds, and several hundred musical instruments were played. The whole royal residence sounded in unison like the middle of the Yugandhara ocean, and it trembled wherever you looked. The Great Being sat on the royal throne beneath the white parasol and looked at the great splendour and beauty that was like the splendour of Sakka. He remembered the great effort he made in the middle of the ocean and thinking, 'Surely effort had to be made, for if I had not made an effort in the middle of the ocean, I would not have attained this success.' While he was remembering his effort he became joyful and impelled by the joy he breathed forth an utterance, saying:

'You should take heart. A wise person should not give up:
I see how I myself got what I wanted. (14)
You should take heart. A wise person should not give up:
I see how I myself was pulled out of the water and placed on dry land. (15)
You should exert yourselves. A wise person should not give up:
I see how I myself got what I wanted. (16)
You should exert yourselves. A wise person should not give up:
I see how I myself was pulled out of the water and placed on dry land. (17)
Though made to suffer, a man with wisdom
Should not cut off hope in the pursuit of happiness.
For there are many contacts, beneficial and harmful;

35. PED identifies this as *Dalbergia arborea*, which has dark purple flowers.

Those that are not reflected upon approach death.[36] (18)
That which is not thought comes to be, and that which is thought is destroyed;[37]
For there is no such property as pure thought, either for woman or man.' (19)

[44] Then he ruled the kingdom righteously without transgressing the ten royal duties, and attended on the *paccekabuddhas*. In the course of time Queen Sīvalī gave birth to a son with all the marks of merit and fortune, and they gave him the name Prince Dīghāvu. When he was grown, the king gave him viceroyalty.

One day the king saw the various flowers and fruits that had been brought by the head gardener, and, pleased, he honoured him. 'Good head gardener, I would like to see the park. Have it adorned,' he said.

'Very good,' he replied, and having done so he announced this to the king.

Riding on the back of an excellent elephant, with a great retinue he reached the gate of the park. There there were two mango trees, lush and green, one lacking in fruit and the other bearing extremely sweet fruit. Because the king had not eaten a mango nobody dared to take the fruit. Even as he sat on the back of his elephant the king took a fruit and ate it, and as he placed it on the end of his tongue it was heavenly. He thought, 'I will eat more on my way back.' But seeing that the king had eaten the first fruit, everyone beginning with the viceroy and even the elephant keepers took and ate, and those who did not get fruit broke the branches with sticks and left it bare. The tree was all broken up, while the other stood there as beautiful as a jewelled mountain. When the king was leaving the park he saw this and asked his courtiers, 'What is this?'

'Sire, the people stripped it after Your Majesty had eaten the first fruit.'

'But neither the leaves nor the lustre of this one have been destroyed.'

'It is because it had no fruit it was not destroyed, Your Majesty.'

The king experienced a sense of urgency:[38] 'This tree [45] because it had

36. See Shaw's (2006a: 269 n. 34) note on this verse, which explains it according to the abhidhammic idea that the 'contacts' (*phassā*) that make up our experience need to be investigated mindfully. Contacts that are left unreflected upon (*avitakkitā*) would appear to result in death—and presumably repeated rebirth.

37. The commentary provides examples, such as that although Janaka thought to fetch wealth from Suvaṇṇabhūmi in order to wage war, this did not happen yet he still obtained the kingdom.

38. *Saṃvega* refers to an intense feeling of shock or urgency, and is often a prompt for renunciation.

no fruit stands green and lush, while the tree that had fruit is broken and split. This kingship is like the fruiting tree, while renouncing is like the tree without fruit. It is those with belongings, rather than those without, that have fear. I will stop being like a fruiting tree and become like the fruitless tree. Abandoning my splendour and going forth I will renounce.'

Having made this strong mental resolve, he entered the city and, standing at the palace gates, he sent for the general: 'Chief general, from this day forth, apart from one servant who will bring food, water for rinsing the mouth, and a toothpick, don't let anyone else see me. Take the elders and discerning courtiers and govern the kingdom. From now on I will practice the *dhamma* of a renouncer on the roof terrace.' Having said this he climbed onto the palace and practised the *dhamma* of a renouncer alone. When he had gone, the populace assembled in the royal court and not seeing the Great Being they said, 'This is not like our king of old,' and spoke two verses:

> 'Surely this is not our king of before, lord of the directions, all the earth.
> Today he does not observe dancing, nor does his mind turn to songs. (20)
> He does not look at deer, nor the parks, nor even the geese.
> He sits silent as a mute, and does not attend to his business.'[39] (21)

With his mind unattached to sense pleasures and bent upon solitude, the king remembered the *paccekabuddhas* who were dependent on his family. 'O who will point out to me the dwelling place of those without possessions who are engaged in morality and other qualities?' he said, and uttered three inspired verses:

> 'Desiring happiness, modest about their morality,[40] ceasing killing and bondage,
> In whose park do they, young and old, stay today? (22)
> [46] Homage to those great sages: the wise ones who have passed beyond the thicket of desire,
> Who live quietly in the world of activity. (23)
> Having cut the net of death and the strong string of deceit,

39. F has a line here that seems rather to belong in the verse commentary, explaining why they said the king sits in silence: 'They asked the servant and the one who took the food, "Does the king talk to you?" They replied, "He does not talk." That is why they said this.' In VRI this is included in the word commentary.

40. *Rahosīlā* should mean something like 'secret morality'. The commentary glosses with *paṭicchannasīlā* 'concealed morality' and *na attano guṇapakāsanā* 'not publicising one's own qualities'.

With desires cut off they go. Who would bring me to where they are going?' (24)

While he was practising the life of a renouncer in that very palace, four months went past, and then his thoughts turned strongly to the homeless life. Being a householder seemed like the Lokantarika hell,[41] and the three states of existence[42] appeared to be on fire. With his mind turned towards the homeless life he thought, 'When indeed will it be time for me to abandon Mithilā with its adornments like the abode of Sakka, enter the Himalayas, and take on the guise of an ascetic?' He began to praise Mithilā:

'When will I give up prosperous Mithilā, broad and radiant all around,
And go forth into homelessness? When indeed will this be? (25)
When will I give up prosperous Mithilā, evenly laid out and partitioned,
And go forth into homelessness? When indeed will this be? (26)
When will I give up prosperous Mithilā, replete with ramparts and towers,
And go forth into homelessness? When indeed will this be? (27)
When will I give up prosperous Mithilā, with its strong watchtowers and gatehouses,
And go forth into homelessness? When indeed will this be? (28)
When will I give up prosperous Mithilā, with its large and well-portioned roads,
And go forth into homelessness? When indeed will this be? (29)
When will I give up prosperous Mithilā, with its well-laid-out market places,
And go forth into homelessness? When indeed will this be? (30)
When will I give up prosperous Mithilā, overrun with cows and horses and carts,
And go forth into homelessness? When indeed will this be? (31)
[47] When will I give up prosperous Mithilā, garlanded with gardens and woods,
And go forth into homelessness? When indeed will this be? (32)
When will I give up prosperous Mithilā, garlanded with parks and forests,
And go forth into homelessness? When indeed will this be? (33)
When will I give up prosperous Mithilā, garlanded with palaces and groves,

41. The 'hell between the worlds', said to be a place of darkness and despair.

42. The entire realm of rebirth—these are (1) the realm of sense desires (*kāma*), which includes the human, animal, and heavenly and hellish realms, (2) the realm of pure form (*rūpa*), and (3) the formless realm (*arūpa*), which consists of higher heavens of various kinds of abstraction.

And go forth into homelessness? When indeed will this be? (34)
When will I give up prosperous Mithilā, its three fortresses filled with the king's relations,
Built by Somanassa that famous Videhan,
And go forth into homelessness? When indeed will this be? (35)
When will I forsake the prosperous Videhans, filled with protectors of the *dhamma*,
And go forth into homelessness? When indeed will this be? (36)
When will I forsake the prosperous Videhans, unending in their protection of the *dhamma*,
And go forth into homelessness? When indeed will this be? (37)
When will I give up my lovely inner quarters, evenly laid out and partitioned,
And go forth into homelessness? When indeed will this be? (38)
When will I give up my lovely inner quarters, smeared with whitewashed clay,
And go forth into homelessness? When indeed will this be? (39)
When will I give up my lovely inner quarters, sweet smelling and delightful,
And go forth into homelessness? When indeed will this be? (40)
When will I give up the belvedere, evenly laid out and partitioned,
And go forth into homelessness? When indeed will this be? (41)
When will I give up the belvedere, smeared with whitewashed clay,
And go forth into homelessness? When indeed will this be? (42)
When will I give up the belvedere, sweet smelling and delightful
And go forth into homelessness? When indeed will this be? (43)
When will I give up the belvedere, smeared and sprinkled with sandalwood,
And go forth into homelessness? When indeed will this be? (44)
When will I give up the golden couch, covered with various fleeces,
And go forth into homelessness? When indeed will this be? (45)
When will I give up the cotton and silk and linen and Koṭumbara cloth,[43]
And go forth into homelessness? When indeed will this be? (46)
When will I give up the delightful lotus pools, resounding with the call of *cakkavāka* birds,[44]
Covered with all kinds of lotuses and water lilies,
And go forth into homelessness? When indeed will this be? (47)
When will I give up my multitude of elephants, all adorned and decorated,
Elephants wearing gold harnesses and gold ornaments, (48)

43. The commentary explains that this is a type of fine cloth that comes from the kingdom of Koṭumbara.

44. PED suggests the ruddy sheldrake.

Mounted by village headmen, lance and goad in hand,
And go forth into homelessness? When indeed will this be? (49)
When will I give up my multitude of horses, all adorned and decorated—
Sindhs, thoroughbreds of good birth, swift vehicles, (50)
Mounted by village headmen bearing bows and short-swords—
And go forth into homelessness? When indeed will this be? (51)
[48] When will I give up my chariot division, armed and with flags aloft,
Covered in tiger skins and all adorned and decorated, (52)
Mounted by village headmen, armoured and with bows in hand,
And go forth into homelessness? When indeed will this be? (53)
When will I give up my golden chariots, armed and with flags aloft,
Covered in tiger skins and all adorned and decorated, (54)
Mounted by village headmen, armoured and with bows in hand,
And go forth into homelessness? When indeed will this be? (55)
When will I give up my silver chariots, armed and with flags aloft,
Covered in tiger skins and all adorned and decorated, (56)
Mounted by village headmen, armoured and with bows in hand,
And go forth into homelessness? When indeed will this be? (57)
When will I give up my horse chariots, armed and with flags aloft,
Covered in tiger skins and all adorned and decorated, (58)
Mounted by village headmen, armoured and with bows in hand,
And go forth into homelessness? When indeed will this be? (59)
When will I give up my bison chariots, armed and with flags aloft,
Covered in tiger skins and all adorned and decorated, (60)
Mounted by village headmen, armoured and with bows in hand,
And go forth into homelessness? When indeed will this be? (61)
When will I give up my bullock chariots, armed and with flags aloft,
Covered in tiger skins and all adorned and decorated, (62)
Mounted by village headmen, armoured and with bows in hand,
And go forth into homelessness? When indeed will this be? (63)
When will I give up my goat chariots, armed and with flags aloft,
Covered in tiger skins and all adorned and decorated, (64)
Mounted by village headmen, armoured and with bows in hand,
And go forth into homelessness? When indeed will this be? (65)
When will I give up my ram chariots, armed and with flags aloft,
Covered in tiger skins and all adorned and decorated, (66)
Mounted by village headmen, armoured and with bows in hand,
And go forth into homelessness? When indeed will this be? (67)
When will I give up my antelope chariots, armed and with flags aloft,
Covered in tiger skins and all adorned and decorated, (68)
Mounted by village headmen, armoured and with bows in hand,
And go forth into homelessness? When indeed will this be? (69)
When will I give up my elephant riders, all adorned and decorated,
Heroes bearing blue armour and with lance and goad in hand,

And go forth into homelessness? When indeed will this be? (70)
When will I give up my horse riders, all adorned and decorated,
Heroes bearing blue armour and carrying short-swords and bows,
And go forth into homelessness? When indeed will this be? (71)
[49] When will I give up my archers, all adorned and decorated,
Heroes bearing blue armour, with quivers and bows in their hands,
And go forth into homelessness? When indeed will this be? (72)
When will I give up my royal sons, all adorned and decorated,
Heroes bearing beautiful armour and garlanded in gold,
And go forth into homelessness? When indeed will this be? (73)
When will I give up my worthy congregations, all done up in their garments,[45]
Their limbs smeared with yellow sandalwood and wearing superior Kāsi cloth,
And go forth into homelessness? When indeed will this be? (74)
When will I give up my seven hundred wives, all adorned and decorated,
And go forth into homelessness? When indeed will this be? (75)
When will I give up my seven hundred wives, skilled[46] and slender-waisted,
And go forth into homelessness? When indeed will this be? (76)
When will I give up my seven hundred wives, loyal and pleasant in their speech,
And go forth into homelessness? When indeed will this be? (77)
When will I give up my hundredweight of bronze and my hundredweight of gold,[47]
And go forth into homelessness? When indeed will this be? (78)
O when will the multitude of elephants, all adorned and decorated,
Elephants wearing gold harnesses and gold ornaments, (79)
Mounted by village headmen, lance and goad in hand,
Not pursue me as I go? When indeed will this be? (80)
O when will the multitude of horses, all adorned and decorated—
Sindhs, thoroughbreds of good birth, swift vehicles, (81)
Mounted by village headmen bearing bows and short-swords—
Not pursue me as I go? When indeed will this be? (82)

45. For *vatthavante alaṃkate*. VRI has *vatavante* 'devout'.

46. It might be better to read *susoññā* 'of beautiful hips' for *susaññā* 'skilled, intelligent' as Shaw does. However, both F and VRI read *susaññā* and the commentary glosses *susaññātā* 'well-skilled'.

47. *Sataphalaṃ kaṃsaṃ sovaṇṇaṃ satarājikaṃ*—both *phala* (usually spelled *pala*, as in VRI) and *rājikā* are measurements of weight, and *sovaṇṇa* and *kaṃsa* mean gold and bronze respectively. The commentary seems unfamiliar with these terms, glossing *kaṃsaṃ* as *pātiṃ* 'dish, bowl', and *satarājikaṃ* as *piṭṭhipasse rājisatena samannāgataṃ* 'with a hundred stripes on the back'.

O when will my chariot division, armed and with flags aloft,
Covered in tiger skins and all adorned and decorated, (83)
Mounted by village headmen, armoured and with bows in hand,
Not pursue me as I go? When indeed will this be? (84)
O when will my golden chariots, armed and with flags aloft,
Covered in tiger skins and all adorned and decorated, (85)
Mounted by village headmen, armoured and with bows in hand,
Not pursue me as I go? When indeed will this be? (86)
[50] O when will my silver chariots, armed and with flags aloft,
Covered in tiger skins and all adorned and decorated, (87)
Mounted by village headmen, armoured and with bows in hand,
Not pursue me as I go? When indeed will this be? (88)
O when will my horse chariots, armed and with flags aloft,
Covered in tiger skins and all adorned and decorated, (89)
Mounted by village headmen, armoured and with bows in hand,
Not pursue me as I go? When indeed will this be? (90)
O when will my bison chariots, armed and with flags aloft,
Covered in tiger skins and all adorned and decorated, (91)
Mounted by village headmen, armoured and with bows in hand,
Not pursue me as I go? When indeed will this be? (92)
O when will my bullock chariots, armed and with flags aloft,
Covered in tiger skins and all adorned and decorated, (93)
Mounted by village headmen, armoured and with bows in hand,
Not pursue me as I go? When indeed will this be? (94)
O when will my goat chariots, armed and with flags aloft,
Covered in tiger skins and all adorned and decorated, (95)
Mounted by village headmen, armoured and with bows in hand,
Not pursue me as I go? When indeed will this be? (96)
O when will my ram chariots, armed and with flags aloft,
Covered in tiger skins and all adorned and decorated, (97)
Mounted by village headmen, armoured and with bows in hand,
Not pursue me as I go? When indeed will this be? (98)
O when will my gazelle chariots, armed and with flags aloft,
Covered in tiger skins and all adorned and decorated, (99)
Mounted by village headmen, armoured and with bows in hand,
Not pursue me as I go? When indeed will this be? (100)
O when will my elephant riders, all adorned and decorated,
Heroes bearing blue armour and with lance and goad in hand,
Not pursue me as I go? When indeed will that be? (101)
O when will my horse riders, all adorned and decorated,
Heroes bearing blue armour and carrying short-swords and bows,
Not pursue me as I go? When indeed will that be? (102)
O when will my archers, all adorned and decorated,
Heroes bearing blue armour and with quivers and bows in their hands,

Not pursue me as I go? When indeed will that be? (103)
O when will my royal sons, all adorned and decorated,
Heroes bearing beautiful armour and garlanded in gold,
Not pursue me as I go? When indeed will that be? (104)
O when will my worthy congregations, all done up in their garments,
Their limbs smeared with yellow sandalwood and wearing superior
Kāsi cloth,
Not pursue me as I go? When indeed will this be? (105)
O when will my seven hundred wives, all adorned and decorated,
Not pursue me as I go? When indeed will this be? (106)
[51] O when will my seven hundred wives, skilled and slender-waisted,
Not pursue me as I go? When indeed will this be? (107)
O when will my seven hundred wives, loyal and pleasant in their speech,
Not pursue me as I go? When indeed will this be? (108)
When will I take my bowl and, shaven-headed and dressed in a robe,[48]
Wander for alms? When indeed will this be? (109)
When will I wear for a robe some rags
That have been cast out on the road? When indeed will this be? (110)
When will I, rained upon by a week's rain and in a wet robe,
Wander for alms? When indeed will this be? (111)
When will I, staying everyday at a tree or not, in a forest or not,
Dwell indifferent? When indeed will this be?[49] (112)
When will I, abandoning fear and terror on difficult mountain roads,
Dwell without companion? When indeed will this be? (113)
When will I, like the lute player his delightful seven-stringed lute,
Make my mind straight? When indeed will this be? (114)
When will I, like a chariot maker the edges of sandals,[50]
Cut off the bonds of sense desire, whether divine or human?'[51](115)

[52] It is said that he was reborn at the time when lifespans were ten thousand years. Having ruled the kingdom for seven thousand years he renounced when he had three thousand years remaining. But after renouncing he lived at home for four months from the time he saw the

48. Specifically a *saṃghāṭī* robe, which is the waist cloth, and one of three robes of a Buddhist monk.

49. VRI has 'When will I, having gone everywhere—from tree to tree and forest to forest—go indifferently?'

50. A *rathakāra* is considered a very low profession, but quite why he is here said to be cutting sandals is not clear. Following the PED entry for *parikanta* I have read it as *pariyantaṃ* 'boundary, edge'.

51. VRI has a slightly longer series of verses, owing to several repeated variations not found in F: after v. 45 there is a repeat about a jewelled couch, after vv. 71 and 102 a repeat about chariot riders, and after vv. 74 and 105 a repeat about the group of courtiers.

mango tree at the park gates and then thought, 'The guise of a renouncer is much better than this appearance. I will go forth!' He commanded his servant in secret, 'Friend, without letting anyone know, bring me yellow cloth from the marketplace and a clay bowl.' He did so. The king sent for his barber, and had his hair and beard shaved off before dismissing him again. He dressed himself in a single yellow robe, covered himself with another, and put another over his shoulder. He placed the clay bowl in a bag and hung it over his shoulder. Then, taking a walking stick he wandered to and fro a few times on the terrace with the grace of a *paccekabuddha*. On that day he remained there, but at sunrise the next day he began to descend from the palace.

Then Queen Sīvalī summoned seven hundred concubines and said, 'We have not seen the king for a long time—four months have passed! But today we will see him. All of you adorn yourselves, and displaying your charming nature and womanly wiles according to your own means, try to catch him in the bonds of sensuality.' With them all adorned and dressed up, she said, 'I will see the king!' [53] While she was ascending the palace she saw him coming down, but she did not recognise him. 'Here is a *paccekabuddha* come to offer advice to the king,' she thought, and having honoured him she stood to one side. The Great Being continued descending from the palace, and the other climbed up onto the palace and saw the king's hair, the colour of bees, on top of the royal couch, along with his ornaments and belongings. 'That was no *paccekabuddha*, that was my dear husband! I will entreat him to return.' She descended from the terrace and reached the royal courtyard, where she and all the others released their hair, letting it fall down their backs, and beat at their hearts with their hands. Lamenting pitifully—'Why would you do such a deed, Great King?'—she followed the king. The whole city was stirred up: 'They say the king has renounced! How will we get another king so righteous as this?' Lamenting, they too followed the king.

Explaining the lamentation of the women there, and how the king abandoned them even as they were lamenting, the Teacher said:

> Those seven hundred wives, all adorned and decorated,
> Lamented with outstretched arms: 'Why do you forsake us?' (116)
> Those seven hundred wives, skilled and slender-waisted,
> Lamented with outstretched arms: 'Why do you forsake us?' (117)
> Those seven hundred wives, loyal and pleasant in their speech,
> Lamented with outstretched arms: 'Why do you forsake us?' (118)

Those seven hundred wives, all adorned and decorated, said:
'The king has renounced and run off! The honoured one has gone forth!' (119)
Those seven hundred wives, skilled and slender-waisted, said:
'The king has renounced and run off! The honoured one has gone forth!' (120)
Those seven hundred wives, loyal and pleasant in their speech, said:
'The king has renounced and run off! The honoured one has gone forth!' (121)
[54] Having given up his hundredweight of bronze and hundredweight of gold,
He took up a clay bowl for his second consecration.[52] (122)

Despite her lamentations, Queen Sīvalī was unable to make the king turn back. Thinking, 'Here is a stratagem!' she summoned the chief general and commanded him, 'Sir, going ahead in the direction the king is walking make a fire in some old houses and old halls. Gather together grass and leaves; make them smoke in places here and there.' When he had done this she approached the king, fell at his feet and, announcing that Mithilā was on fire, spoke two verses:

'A terrible fire is blazing! The treasuries are being consumed bit by bit:
Great quantities of silver and gold, pearls and beryl, (123)
Jewels, mother-of-pearl, cloths, and yellow sandal,
Antelope hide, ivory goods, much bronze, and black iron.
Come, King, turn back. Do not let your wealth be destroyed!' (124)

Then the Great Being, explained: 'What are you saying, Queen? For those who have something it may burn, but I have nothing.' He spoke a verse:

'Surely we live in great happiness, we who have no possessions.
Though Mithilā may be on fire, nothing of mine is burning!'[53] (125)

[55] And having said that the Great Being left by the northern gate, and his wives left too. Queen Sīvalī thought of another stratagem: 'Make it look as if the villages have been destroyed and the kingdom plundered,' she ordered. At that very moment they showed the king men from here and there with weapons in their hands chasing and plundering. They sprinkled

52. The commentary explains that the second consecration is the going forth. Since this final verse is separated from the preceding ones by their commentary, and since the commentary for this verse begins with *bhikkhave* 'O monks', I take this verse as being in the mouth of the narrator, the Buddha, rather than forming part of the women's lament.

53. As noted in the introduction, this verse is also found in the *Mahābhārata* and the Jain *Uttarādhyayana*.

red lac dye on their bodies to make them look as if they had been wounded, and carried them away on planks as if they were dead. The people scolded, 'Great King, even while you live, they are plundering the kingdom and killing the people!' Then the queen honoured the king and spoke a verse in order to get him to turn back:

> 'The wild men have risen up and are destroying the kingdom!
> Come, King, turn back. Do not let this kingdom be destroyed!' (126)

But the king, thinking, 'It is surely not the case that thieves have risen up even as I live and are destroying the kingdom,' subdued her and said:

> 'Surely we live in great happiness, we who have no possessions.
> While the kingdom is being destroyed, nothing of mine is harmed. (127)
> Surely we live in great happiness, we who have no possessions,
> And we will feed on joy like the Radiant Gods.'[54] (128)

But even after he had said this, the people followed the king. It occurred to him, 'These people do not wish to turn back. I will make them turn back.' When he had gone half a league he turned around, stood on the great road, and asked his courtiers, 'Whose is this kingdom?'

[56] 'Yours, Your Majesty.'

'Then make a royal decree not to cross this line!' The king drew a horizontal line using his walking stick, and because of the power of his observances nobody was able to cross the line he had made. The people placed their heads on the line and wailed with great lamentation. The queen too was unable to cross that line, and seeing the king going away with his back to her she could not contain her grief. Beating at her chest she fell down across the great road, thereby proceeding over the line. The people said, 'The line has been broken by the line's masters!' and went on the road on which the queen had gone. The Great Being approached the upper Himalayas, but the queen and everyone including the armed forces went with him. Unable to make the people turn back the king travelled sixty *yojanas* on the road.

At that time an ascetic called Nārada, who was possessed of the five higher knowledges, was living in a golden cave in the Himalayas. While he was experiencing the bliss of meditation seven days passed, and then he got up from that meditation and exclaimed, 'Oh the joy! Oh the joy!' Thinking, 'Is there anyone on the surface of Jambudīpa who is seeking this happiness?' he looked with his divine eye and saw Mahājanaka, the nascent

54. *Devā ābhassarā*—a class of Brahmā gods.

Buddha. 'This king is making a great renunciation but is unable to make the people, headed by Queen Sīvalī, turn back. They will make an obstacle for him. I will give a sermon in order to strengthen his resolve still further.' Through the strength of his psychic power he went and stood in the sky before the king and in order to produce exertion he said:

'What is this great noise? What is it, like games in a village?
We ask the renouncer: why do these people gather around?' (129)

The king said:

'These people gather here as I have gone forth and renounced;
I have gone across the boundary to obtain the wisdom of the sages.
My going is mixed with pleasure. Knowing this, why do you ask?' (130)

[57] Then in order to strengthen his resolve he spoke another verse:

'Surely you do not imagine you have crossed over, bearing this body?
This action may not lead to the far shore, for there are many obstacles.' (131)

Then the Great Being said:

'Who is an obstacle to me, to one who lives in the way I do?
One who does not wish for sense pleasures either seen or unseen?'[55] (132)

Then, explaining the obstacles to him Nārada spoke a verse:

'Sleep, sloth, and drowsiness, discontent and lethargy after eating:
There are many obstacles for those living in a body.' (133)

[58] Then the Great Being praised him with a verse:

'Brahmin, you have surely instructed me in the good life.
I ask the brahmin: Who are you, sir?' (134)

Nārada replied:

'Nārada is my name, and they know me as Kassapa.
I have come to see you, sir, for it is good to meet with good men. (135)
May all the bliss of your way of life come to pass.
May you supplement what is deficient with calmness and forbearance. (136)
May you give up debasement but also give up pride,
And having paid honour to *kamma*, wisdom, and *dhamma*, go forth!' (137)

Having advised the Great Being in this way he went through the sky to his own abode. After he had gone, another ascetic called Migājina emerged from meditation, looked around, saw the Great Being, and thought, 'I will

55. The commentary explains that the 'seen' pleasures are those in the world of men, while the 'unseen' are in the world of the gods.

give a teaching for the purpose of making the people turn back.' Having gone there, revealing himself in the sky he said:

[59] 'Having given up many elephants and horses, cities and provinces,
Janaka, the renouncer has found pleasure in an alms bowl. (138)
Perhaps these friends, courtiers, relations, and country folk
Have committed some treachery, Janaka, for why else would you take pleasure in this?' (139)

The Great Being said:

'No Migājina, I have never wrongly overpowered any of my kinsmen,
And nor have my kinsmen overpowered me.' (140)

Then having rejected his question in this way he next explained his reason for going forth, saying:

'Having seen the world turning, being devoured and defiled,
And worldly folk being beaten and bound here where they have sunk,
I compared myself to them and became a mendicant, Migājina.' (141)

[60] The ascetic wanted to hear his reasons in greater detail, so he spoke this verse:

'Who is your exalted teacher? Whose is this pure speech?
Bull among charioteers, they call a renouncer one who lives having abandoned
Neither precepts nor learning, such that he has overcome suffering.' (142)

Then the Great Being said:

'No, Migājina, surely I did not enter upon this,
After at any time honouring any brahmin or renouncer.' (143)

And having said this, in order to explain the reasons for his renunciation from the beginning he said:

'Going along with great power and splendour I burned,
While songs were being sung and sweet words spoken,
And while it resounded with the beating of musical instruments and striking of cymbals. (144)
Migājina, I saw outside the hedge a mango tree in fruit,
Being struck by the people—a crowd desiring the fruit. (145)
So I gave up my majesty and climbed down, Migājina,
And I approached the root of the mango tree, the fruiting and fruitless. (146)
I saw the fruiting tree destroyed, shattered and leafless,
And this other mango a splendid dark green, delightful. (147)
[61] Thus surely the many thorns of our enemies destroy us kings,
Just like the fruiting mango tree was destroyed. (148)
Tigers are killed for their skin, elephants for their tusks,

The wealthy kill the homeless and friendless for wealth.[56]
The fruiting mango and the fruitless are both teachers for me.' (149)

Having heard this Migājina said, 'May you be diligent!' and having given that teaching to the king he went to his own abode. When he was gone, Queen Sīvalī fell at the king's feet and said:

'Elephant riders, cavalry, charioteers, and infantry:
All the people are afraid, saying, "The king has gone forth!" (150)
Having comforted them appoint a protector for the people:
You should renounce after having established your son on the throne.' (151)

Then the Bodhisatta said:

'I have given up the country folk, friends, courtiers, and relatives,
[62] but there are sons of the Videhans—Dīghāvu will further the realm.
They will look after the kingdom of Mithilā, Queen. (152)

The queen said, 'Your Majesty, what can I do when you have gone forth?' He replied, 'I will teach you—do as I say,' and he said:

'Come, I will teach you, with a speech pleasing to me:
Ruling the kingdom you would do much bad action and evil,
With body, speech, and mind, because of which you would go to a bad realm. (153a)
So keep yourself going through almsfood given by others
And prepared by others: That is the *dhamma* of the wise.' (153b)

The Great Being taught her in this way, and while they were going along talking with one another the sun set. The queen set up camp in a suitable place, and the Great Being approached the foot of a certain tree and dwelled there. The next day, having taken care of his bodily needs, he set off on the road. The queen said, 'Let the army follow close behind,' and so they followed behind him. When it was time to beg for alms they entered a city called Thūṇā. At that moment inside the city a man had bought a piece of meat and had it cooked on a spit over charcoal. Having extinguished the fire he placed the meat on the edge of a board and remained there. But while he was engaged in something else a dog took it and ran off. Realising this, he pursued it up to the outside of the southern gate, where, tired out,

56. The commentarial understanding of this verse is somewhat different to what the grammar suggests. The commentator argues that the active *hanti* 'kill' should be read as a passive *haññate* 'be killed' as in the first line, meaning 'the wealthy are killed for their wealth'. This would leave 'homeless and friendless' without any context in the sentence; the commentator suggests this refers to a renouncer who has no reason to be killed.

he lost sight of it. The king and queen were coming along in front of that dog, in two parties, [63] and in fear he spat out the meat and ran off.

Seeing this the Great Being thought, 'He has abandoned this and run away without a second thought, and I cannot see any other owner. Surely there is no rag-wearer's almsfood as blameless as this. We will eat it.' Having taken out his clay bowl he picked up the piece of meat, wiped it, and placed it in the bowl; then he went to a pleasant watery spot and ate it. Then the queen thought, 'If he was suitable for the kingship he would not eat something so disgusting, smeared with dirt and rejected by a dog! He is no longer ours.' She said, 'Great King, are you eating such a disgusting thing?'

'Queen, in your blind folly you do not recognize the quality of this almsfood.' Having contemplated the place where it had fallen he ate it as if it was ambrosia, then rinsed his mouth and washed his hands and feet. At that moment the queen censured him and said:

> 'He who would not eat even at the fourth mealtime,
> Would die of hunger—death by starvation.
> Yet a good man of a good family would not resort to
> Almsfood that is contaminated and ignoble.
> This is not good, this is not appropriate,
> That you should eat what has been abandoned by a dog.' (154)

The Great Being said:

> 'It is not the case, Sīvalī, that I should not eat
> That which is abandoned by a householder or a dog.
> [64] Whatever possessions are obtained justly here,
> All are said to be edible and blameless.' (155)

While they were speaking with one another in this way they reached the city gate. There were some children playing there, and one of them, a little girl, was striking the sand with a small basket. On one of her wrists she had a single bracelet and on the other she had two, and they knocked against one another, while the one remained silent. The king understood the reason and thought, 'Sīvalī follows behind me, yet a woman is surely a stain for a renouncer. They will censure me, saying, "Even after going forth this one is unable to abandon his wife." If this little girl is wise, she will tell Queen Sīvalī the reason for letting go, and after she has heard that, I will send her away.' He said:

> 'Dear little girl, always adorned with bracelets,
> Why does one arm make a sound and the other arm not?' (156)

The young girl said:

'Renouncer, on this hand are fastened two bracelets,
And coming together they produce sound: this is the effect of the second. (157)
On this hand, renouncer, a single bracelet is fastened,
And not having a second it makes no sound, but remains silent as a sage. (158)
The second makes a dispute—for with whom would *one* quarrel?
Solitude is pleasing for those who wish for heaven.' (159)

[65] Having heard the young girl's speech, he gained confidence and speaking to the queen said:

'Hear, Sīvalī, the verses declared by this little girl!
This servant girl censures me: "This is the effect of the second." (160)
Good woman, there is a fork in the path that is pursued by travellers;
You should take one of them, and I the other one;[57] (161)
And no longer say "You are my husband!" or "I am your wife!"' (162a)

Hearing his words she honoured him, saying, 'Your Majesty, take the most splendid path to the right, and I will take the left.' But after having gone a little way she could no longer contain her grief, and returning once again she entered the city behind the king. Explaining the matter, the Teacher spoke this half verse:

Speaking these words they entered the city of Thūṇā. (162b)

[66] And having entered, the Great Being wandered for alms and reached the door to a fletcher's house. Sīvalī too stood to one side. At that time the fletcher was making an arrow—he had heated the arrow in a pan over charcoal, moistened it with sour rice gruel, and was scrutinising it with one eye shut. Seeing that the Great Being approached, thinking, 'If he is wise he will explain this task to me. I will question him.' Explaining the matter the Teacher said:

In the storeroom, when the fletcher's mealtime had come,
There that fletcher closed one eye, and observed the crookedness with the other. (163)

Then the Great Being said to him:

'Hear me, fletcher: it is good that you look in this way,
That having shut one eye you observe the crookedness with the other.' (164)

Then explaining to him the fletcher said:

57. F has a three-line verse here, but since the next is clearly a half verse, it would seem that we have one and a half verses here, as in VRI.

'With two eyes, renouncer, it appears too wide.
You cannot see the features of the other side or make it straight. (165)
Shutting one eye and regarding the crookedness with the other,
Seeing the features of the other side it is made straight.[58] (166)
The second makes a dispute—for with whom would *one* quarrel?
Solitude is pleasing for those who wish for heaven.' (167)

[67] And having given that teaching he became silent. Continuing on his alms round the Great Being collected a mixture of food and then left the city and sat down in a pleasant spot by some water. Having done the needful he placed his bowl back in his bag and addressing Sīvalī said:

'Hear, Sīvalī, the verses declared by this fletcher!
This servant censures me—"This is the effect of the second." (168)
Good woman, there is a fork in the path that is pursued by travellers;
You should take one of them, and I the other one;[59] (169)
And no longer say "You are my husband!" or "I am your wife!"' (170a)

Yet even when he said this she still followed the Great Being, and unable to make the king turn back the people pursued him. But there was a forest not far away, and when the Great Being saw the dark rows of trees he wished to send them back. As he was going along he saw some *muñja* grass close to the road and picked a reed. Saying, 'Look, Sīvalī, it is not possible to put this back together again, and neither is it possible to rejoin me and you in intimacy,' he spoke this half verse:

'Like a *muñja* reed pulled out, I will live alone, Sīvalī.' (170b)

Having heard this she said, 'From this moment on there is no intimacy for me with Mahājanaka the king of men,' and she was unable to bear her grief. She beat at her chest with both hands, and becoming unconscious, she fell in the road. [68] The Great Being, realizing that she was unconscious, entered the forest covering his tracks. The courtiers came and sprinkled her body with water and rubbed her hands and feet, making her regain consciousness. 'Friends, where is the king?' she asked.

'Do you not know?'

'Look for him, friends.'

Though they ran here and there they could not see him. So lamenting loudly she had a shrine (*cetiya*) built at the place where the king had stood,

58. Following the commentarial explanation, which glosses *paraṃ* as *parato* 'behind', and *sampatvā* as *disvā* 'having seen'.

59. I am again assuming one and a half verses here, following VRI, rather than the three-line verse of F.

and having honoured it with fragrant garlands and so on, she turned back. The Great Being entered the Himalayas, and within a week he had produced the higher knowledges and the attainments and never again crossed the path of men. And the queen had shrines erected everywhere, namely where he had spoken with the fletcher, where he had spoken with the little girl, where he had enjoyed the meat, where he had conversed with Migājina, and where he had talked with Nārada. Having honoured them all with fragrant garlands and so on, she reached Mithilā surrounded by the army. She arranged the consecration of her son in the mango park and sent him into the city surrounded by the army. She herself took the going forth of a seer and lived in that park. Having undertaken the preparations for *kasiṇa* meditation she attained meditative absorption and met her end in the Brahmā world. And the Great Being, having become complete in his meditation, met his end in the Brahmā world.[60]

The Teacher, having spoken this *dhamma* teaching, said, 'Not only now, monks, but also in former times has the Tathāgata gone forth in a great renunciation.' Having said this he connected the births: 'The goddess of the ocean at that time was Uppalavaṇṇā, Sāriputta was Nārada, Moggallāna was Migājina, the nun Khemā was the little girl, Ānanda was the fletcher, the mother of Rāhula was Sīvalī, Rāhula was Prince Dīghāvu, the royal family was the mother and father, and I myself was Mahājanaka, the king of men.'

3

The Birth Story of Golden Sāma

(*Suvaṇṇasāma-jātaka*)

INTRODUCTION

The third story of the *Mahānipāta* is known as the *Sāma-jātaka* or, particularly in Southeast Asia, *Suvaṇṇasāma-jātaka*—the Birth Story of Golden Sāma. The story tells of the Bodhisatta taking birth as Sāma, the son of ascetic parents who live a simple life in the forest. When his parents go blind, Sāma looks after them admirably, until he is shot by a misguided king who is out hunting. Much of the story is taken up with describing Sāma's calm and kind response to being attacked, and his great pain at the thought of the suffering it will bring his parents. Sāma's compassion, along with that of his parents, is contrasted dramatically with the king's rash and selfish actions. More broadly the world of the king—weapons, meat, and thoughtless action—is contrasted with the world of the hermitage—living at peace with all the animals and cultivating loving-kindness. And at the heart of the story is the message that is explicitly drawn out by the frame narrative: the importance of looking after one's parents, and the benefits this brings.

Several versions of the story of Sāma are found in other Indian texts, and the differences between them help to reveal the concerns of the authors of the *Mahānipāta*. In the version in the *Mahāvastu*, an early Indian Buddhist text, the story is different in subtle but important ways.[1] For a

Introduced and translated by Naomi Appleton.

1. Jones 1949–56: II 199–218.

start the child is not provided by Sakka in order to look after his parents but conceived in the normal way. His parents do not become blind as a result of past karmic accrual but simply because of old age. The king shoots Sāma (here called Śyāmaka) thinking he is a deer, and when he realises the truth he is terrified that this wounded sage might reduce him to ashes with his ascetic power. On hearing of their son's death Śyāmaka's parents wish to see him in order that they may be able to bring him back to life. There is no assistance from a goddess, no sermon given to the king about living virtuously, and the story is told not to demonstrate the importance of looking after one's parents but to provide an example of a past time when the Buddha's father (Śyāmaka's father in the story) refused to believe his son was dead. The emphasis of this story, therefore, is on the power of seers to pacify the forest creatures and defeat poison and injury. The king is not such a bad character, shooting Śyāmaka by accident and immediately offering to make reparations, even if this is motivated by fear.

The *Mahāvastu* version has quite a lot in common with another important occurrence of the story, in the Indian epic *Rāmāyaṇa*. In this text, the story occurs to explain why King Daśaratha was cursed to die lamenting the absence of his son Rāma, who has been exiled into the forest. King Daśaratha recalls the story as he lies dying: in his youth he had been out hunting and shot an arrow towards a noise he thought was an elephant drinking, but was actually the sound of a young ascetic filling his water pitcher. The dying ascetic had lamented the inevitable death of his aged and blind parents, and insisted the king should go to them and appease them. Again motivated by fear of the ascetics' power, as well as by regret, the king had gone to the hermitage and led the old couple to their son. In a crucial departure from both Buddhist versions, in the *Rāmāyaṇa* the young ascetic actually died, though he did reappear to assure his parents that he had been admitted to a heaven realm. Not appeased by the young ascetic's happy ending, his father cursed King Daśaratha to die lamenting for his son.[2]

Both the *Mahāvastu* and *Rāmāyaṇa* versions of the story depict a king accidentally killing a human and then fearing the vengeance of ascetics. Both the son and his parents are frightening and powerful characters with the potential to destroy the king as a result of his deed. While in the *Rāmāyaṇa* ascetic power does result in a curse, in the *Mahāvastu* it is

2. The story is found in *Ayodhyākāṇḍa* 57–8. See Pollock 1986: 204–11.

instead used to cure the dying boy. In contrast to both of these versions, the *Suvaṇṇasāma-jātaka* places its emphasis on loving-kindness: not only is Sāma not angry, but neither are his parents, and none of them would dream of doing violence to the king despite his potentially murderous actions. This emphasis on loving-kindness is echoed by a three-verse reference to the story in another Pāli text, the *Cariyāpiṭaka*. Here the story is summed up as simply the ability of Sāma to bring loving-kindness to all the wild animals and live in peace with them.[3]

Loving-kindness

In the Pāli tradition this story is associated with the perfection of *mettā*, or loving-kindness. It is this quality that is cultivated by both Sāma and his parents while they live in their forest retreat. We are told that loving-kindness keeps the peace, ensuring the wild beasts do no harm to the humans, or vice versa. However, the protective power of *mettā* becomes a contentious issue, for in two places in the narrative we see *mettā*-filled individuals nonetheless being harmed. First, Sāma's parents are blinded by an angry snake, and later Sāma himself is shot and apparently killed by a reckless king. In both cases we see attempts to explain the suffering experienced without compromising on the idea that *mettā* is a protective. In the case of Sāma's parents we find a karmic backstory which explains the bad deeds done in a past life that led to being blinded in this life.[4] In the case of Sāma himself, the commentary tells us that Sāma momentarily lapsed in his mindfulness as he fetched the water, and that this allowed the arrow to hit him. This explanation is also taken up by the *Milindapañha* during a discussion about the protective benefits of loving-kindness.[5]

Another aspect of loving-kindness is also emphasised in this story, though it is not explicitly called *mettā*. As the frame story tells us, the tale is really about the importance of looking after one's parents, even after one has decided to renounce the life of a householder. Such care and attention for one's parents comes not only from a sense of filial duty but from a compassionate and loving attitude. Sāma is able to care for his parents' practical needs while still cultivating meditative attainments, and so too

3. *Cariyāpiṭaka* III 13, Horner 2000: 46.

4. One could say that the parents demonstrated a lack of *mettā* in the past and that their current *mettā* cannot protect them from these prior acts of harm.

5. *Milindapañha* IV 6, *Mettāya ānisaṃsā*. See Trenckner 1997: 198–9.

the monk in the frame story is able to care for his parents without disrobing. This frame narrative contributes to the story's wider message about the interlinking ideals of compassion, love, and duty. Loving-kindness is not an abstract quality perfected through meditation; it is enacted every day by those who care for one another.

Who Cured Sāma?

Alongside the association with loving-kindness, the story of Sāma has a strong focus on another perfection, that of truthfulness. It is one of many stories in the *Jātakatthavaṇṇanā* that demonstrate the great power of declarations of truth—or Acts of Truth (*saccakiriya*). Such declarations have the power to turn back fire (J 35, *Vaṭṭaka-jātaka*), affect the fall of dice (J 62, *Aṇḍabhūta-jātaka*), or, as here, bring someone back from the brink of death. It is the Acts of Truth performed by Sāma's mother, father, and the goddess who has been his mother in past lives that expel the poison from Sāma's blood and allow him to recover.

While the truth appears to rouse Sāma, another thread of the narrative suggests that his recovery is really down to the goddess alone. The motif of a helpful maternal goddess is also found in the *Temiya-jātaka* (Chapter 1), in which a goddess of the royal parasol advises Temiya how to avoid the kingship. In both cases the goddess is said to have been the hero's mother in a past life, thereby showing how bonds of love and affection can last multiple lifetimes. Although this goddess is a little careless allowing her divine enjoyments to interrupt her care of Sāma (rather like the goddess of the ocean in the *Janaka-jātaka* in Chapter 2), she is also very powerful. She is said to use her power to cure Sāma as well as to allow his parents to regain their sight. This explanation is consistent with Sāma's later statement that the gods look after those people who care for their parents. And if further proof were required of her great power, she also brings about the dawn.

These interlocking ideals work on the audience because of the huge dramatic tension in the narrative. The audience, represented by the king and later Sāma's parents, believes that Sāma is dead. His resurrection is therefore nothing short of a miracle, brought about by the power of the truth and of a benevolent deity. Yet alongside this drama, the story is careful to point out that Sāma was never *really* dead. His mother realises this when she touches him and feels his warmth.[6] The goddess knows this

6. This relies upon my translation of the passage in which Sāma's mother places her

all along, as she encourages events to unfold in such a way as to cure him. Only the king remains truly overawed by the events, so much so that he completely reforms his character. His response is presumably the one hoped for in the story's audience.

Kingly Concerns

Throughout the events of this story the king provides an excellent contrast to the admirable life lived by the forest ascetics. It is surely no coincidence that Sāma's parents are said to have been born in hunter families but deliberately turned away from such a life. Their encounter with someone who is at the top of the social hierarchy and yet engaged in the immoral practice of hunting is thus very pointed. The king is shown as concerned only with satisfying his own desires. His lust for venison leads him to abandon his kingdom and wander the forest alone, armed with his weapons, including poisoned arrows. He is also deeply concerned with preserving his reputation, and it seems to be this that leads him to shoot Sāma in the first place, in order to make sure he has a good story to tell when he gets home. After he realises the horror of what he has done he still contemplates shirking his responsibilities and hiding in the forest where nobody will be able to tell him off or remind him of his actions. Encouraged by the goddess and by his fear of hell, he stomps into the hermitage and announces his royal status to Sāma's parents *before* telling them he has killed their son, so they will be too afraid to get angry with him. Overall he comes across as a selfish, impetuous, and cowardly man.

As in the *Temiya-jātaka*, kingship is derided in this story, yet the focus is not upon persuading the king to give up his kingdom. Rather the king is instructed in how to be a better ruler, and he is said to become just and generous and go after death to heaven. It is therefore shown as possible for a king to get to heaven—even a king that is as bad as this one; this message is quite a contrast to that of the *Temiya-jātaka*, in which renunciation is the only way to avoid hell. The world of the forest ascetics remains clearly superior, however, and Sāma and his parents live in peace and happiness, cultivate various meditative states and go to a higher heaven after their deaths.

---

hand on his chest and feels the heat: *ure hatthaṃ ṭhapetvā santāpaṃ upadhārentī*. Cowell & Rouse and Shaw take the passage as referring to the mother beating her hand on her own chest and realising her torment. VRI adds *tassa* 'his' to the beginning of the passage, consistent with my reading. In the earlier description of the parents beating their chests in despair, the phrase *hatthehi ure patipiṃsantā* is used.

'Who has pierced me with this arrow . . . ?'

[68] The Teacher related this story while living in the Jeta Grove, about a monk who looked after his parents. Now in Sāvatthi there was an only son in a certain treasurer's family that had eighteen crores of wealth, and he was pleasing and dear to his parents. One day he went to the roof terrace, unfastened a window, and looked out at the street. He saw that a great many people were going to the Jeta Grove with flowers and perfumes and so on in their hands in order to hear the *dhamma*. [69] 'I too will go!' he thought, and taking perfumes and flowers and so on he went to the monastery. He had cloths, medicines, and drinks given to the community of monks, worshipped the Blessed One with the flowers, scents, and so on, and sat to one side. Having heard the *dhamma* he realised the danger of sense pleasures and understood the benefits of renunciation. When the assembly got up he entreated the Blessed One for renunciation, but hearing, 'Tathāgatas do not allow renunciation without parental permission,' he went away. Having gained permission from his parents by not eating for seven days he returned and asked for ordination.[7] The Teacher instructed a monk and he ordained him. Having gone forth he acquired great fame and achievements. He pleased his teacher and preceptor, and five years after receiving ordination he was proficient in the *dhamma*. Thinking, 'I live in this crowded place, which is not suitable for me,' he became desirous of practising insight meditation dwelling in the forest. In the presence of

7. VRI explains in more detail: 'He bowed to the Blessed One and went back home. He respectfully honoured his parents and spoke thus: "Mother and father, I will go forth in the presence of the Tathāgata!" But hearing his words his parents, because they had only one son, trembled with affection as though their hearts were split into seven pieces. They said, "Dear darling son, tender shoot of the family, leader, dear heart, like our own breath, how would we live without you? Our life is dependent on you. For we are aged and old, of many years, and we will attain death today, tomorrow, or the next day. So don't leave us and go! Dear son, renunciation is very painful, whereas at home when it is cold there is heat, and when it is hot there is cold. So, my dear, don't go forth!" Hearing that, the young man was distressed and sat down with a heavy heart and a head bent in disappointment. For seven days he refused to eat. Then his parents thought, "If our son is not given leave to ordain surely he will die! We will not see that happen—we will see him live and ordain!" Having considered this they granted him permission saying, "Darling sweet son, we permit you to go forth. You may ordain!" Hearing that, the young man was delighted and bowed his whole body down to worship his parents. He went to the monastery and entreated the Blessed One to ordain him.'

his preceptor he took a meditation object and then settled in the forest near to a neighbouring village. There he developed his insight, but despite striving and exerting himself for twelve years, he was not able to attain any distinction.

Meanwhile, as time went on his parents became worse and worse off. For those who worked the fields or engaged in trade thought, 'Now there is no son or brother in the family to call in the debt and take it back!' They each took what they could carry and ran off to wherever they wished. Even the household servants and so on took gold and money and ran off. In time the two of them became beggars, and not receiving even a sprinkle of water in their hands they sold their house and became homeless. Having become pitiable, dressed in rags, bowl in hand, they wandered in search of alms.

At that time a certain monk had left the Jeta Grove and come in time to the monk's residence. He did what was customary for greeting a guest, and when the monk was seated happily he asked, 'Where have you come from?'

'I have come from the Jeta Grove.'

Hearing this he inquired after the health of the Teacher and his great disciples and so on, and then asked for news of his mother and father: 'Bhante, is the treasurer family of a certain name in Sāvatthi in good health?'

'Brother, do not ask for news of that family.'

'Why, Bhante?'

'Brother, it is said that there was only one son in that family, and he became ordained in the teaching, and from the time he renounced this family has declined. Now the two of them wander for food, greatly pitiable.' Hearing his words the monk was unable to control himself and with eyes full of tears he began to cry.

'Friend, why do you cry?'

'Bhante, they are my parents, and I am their son.'

'Friend, because of you your parents have reached ruin. Go and take care of them!'

He thought, 'Despite striving and exerting myself for twelve years I have not been able to bring forth the path or the fruit. [70] I will be incapable of doing so. What is renunciation to me? I will become a householder and look after my parents. Having practised generosity I will be destined for heaven.'

Having given over his forest dwelling to that Elder, the next day he set out and in due course arrived behind the Jeta Grove not far from Sāvatthi. There there were two paths: one to the Jeta Grove and the other to Sāvatthi. Standing there he thought, 'Should I see my parents first, or the Ten-Powered One? I have not seen my parents for a long time, but after this time it will be difficult for me to see the Buddha. So today I will see the Fully Awakened One and hear the *dhamma*, and tomorrow morning I will see my parents.' And so he abandoned the road to Sāvatthi and at evening he entered the Jeta Grove. But that day the Teacher, surveying the world at dawn, saw this young man's potential. When he came to him, he explained the quality of parents with the *Mātiposaka Sutta*.[8] The monk was standing in the congregation and listening to the *dhamma* talk. He thought, 'Having become a householder I would be able to look after my parents. But the Teacher has said, "Even a son who is a renouncer can be a support." If I had gone without seeing the Teacher I would have abandoned my renunciate status.[9] But now I will not become a householder but will support my parents while being a renouncer.'

He took some tickets—tickets for food and tickets for rice milk—and after living in the forest for twelve years he felt as if he had severely transgressed the rules.[10] Early in the morning he reached Sāvatthi. 'Should I get rice milk first,' he thought, 'or go and see my parents? It is not appropriate to visit beggars empty-handed.' So he got some rice milk and went to the door of their former house. His parents, having wandered in search of alms, were by the opposite wall. Approaching, he saw them seated there and became very upset. Tears welled up in his eyes as he stood a little way off. They saw him but they did not recognise him. Then his mother reasoned, 'He will be stood there for the sake of alms,' and said, 'Bhante, there is nothing suitable to be given to you. Please go on.' Hearing her words his heart was filled with grief and he stood there in tears. A second and third time she said this but he stayed there. Then his father said to his mother, 'Go and see, could this be our own son?' She got up and approached, and recognising

8. This is found in the *Brāhmaṇasaṃyutta* of SN I 182 (Bodhi 2000: 277), and relates how a brahmin who used almsfood to support his parents was praised by the Buddha.

9. Following VRI *sacāhaṃ* 'if I' rather than F *svāhaṃ* (*so aham* 'that me'). Cowell & Rouse and Shaw follow F and thus consider the sentence to refer to the monk's earlier departure to the forest and his failure in his renunciate practice.

10. Presumably the monk is feeling as if he does not deserve his alms given his failed practice in the forest, or perhaps he still has misgivings about taking the alms for his parents. The term used, *bhikkhupārājika*, refers to the transgressions of monastic rules severe enough to result in expulsion from the community, namely sexual relations, stealing, killing, and falsely claiming supernormal powers. Perhaps he is worried that in taking food from the *saṅgha* for his parents he is essentially stealing.

him she fell at his feet sobbing. And then his father also came there and lamented greatly.

Seeing his parents he was unable to control himself and began to sob. He gave himself up to grief, and saying, 'Do not worry—I am going to look after you!' [71] he comforted his parents. He gave them rice milk to drink and sat to one side of them. Then he fetched almsfood and made them eat, and then sought out food for himself before returning to them. After he had asked after their food, he had his meal and then set up a dwelling to one side. From that time onwards he looked after his parents in this way: he gave them the food that he had obtained for himself, even the fortnightly food and so on,[11] and then wandered for alms for himself. If he got some, he ate. Whatever he received, whether food for the rains retreat or something else, he gave to them. He put patches on the worn-out rags they were using, and after dyeing them he used them himself. But the days of receiving little or nothing were more frequent than those of getting food, and his undergarment and outer robe were meagre. Thus, as he nourished his parents, in due course he became thin and pale.

Then his friends and companions asked him, 'Friend, your body used to be a beautiful colour, but now you are very pale. Surely you are ill?' Saying, 'I am not ill, friend, but I do have an obstacle,' he explained what had happened. Then those monks said, 'The Teacher does not allow that gifts of faith be destroyed, but you have taken gifts of faith and given them to householders. You have done what is unsuitable.' Hearing their words he was ashamed and hung his head. They, being unhappy with this, went and addressed the Teacher: 'Bhante, a monk of a certain name destroys the gifts of the faithful and supports householders!' The Teacher had that young man summoned and asked, 'Is it true, as they say, that you take gifts of faith and use them to nourish householders?' When he answered 'It is true, Bhante!' the Teacher wanted to explain that action of his. Desirous of illustrating his own former conduct, he asked, 'Monk, in supporting householders whom do you support?'

11. *Pakkhika-bhatta* is food associated with the lunar fortnight. It is included in lists of four or five special provisions of food. Another type, food by ticket (*salākabhattha*), has already been mentioned, and later we also hear of rains retreat food (*vassāvasika*). The implication would appear to be that he used his institutionally-protected alms for his parents, and subjected himself to the more difficult process of direct begging.

'My mother and father, Bhante.'

The Teacher, wishing to bring forth fortitude, gave approval three times: 'Good, good. You are stood on the path on which I have gone, for I too when living a former life supported my parents.' The monk gained fortitude, and entreated by the monks the Teacher spoke of the past in order to explain his former conduct.

In times past, not far from Vārāṇasī, there was a village of hunters on the near side of the riverbank and another on the further shore. In each lived five hundred families. The two chief hunters of the two villages were friends, and they made an agreement when they were young: 'If one of us has a daughter and the other a son, then they will be married.' Now a son was born in the house of the chief hunter who lived in the near-shore village, [72] and because at the moment of his birth they obtained *dukūla* cloth they called him Dukūlaka. And in the other's house a daughter was born, and because she was born on the far shore (*paratīra*) they called her Pārikā.[12] Both of them were handsome and golden coloured, and though born into a family of hunters they did not destroy life.

In due course, when the boy Dukūla was sixteen years old, his parents said, 'Son, we will bring you a young woman.' But he had come from the Brahmā realm and was a pure being, so he covered both his ears and said, 'I have no use for a household life. Don't speak in this way!' Although they said this as many as three times he did not want it. And the young woman Pārikā's parents also said to her, 'My dear, there is a son of a friend of ours who is golden coloured and handsome. We will give him to you!' But she covered her ears and said the same, for she too had come from the Brahmā realm. The young man Dukūla secretly sent a message to her, saying, 'If you wish for sexual intercourse, go to the house of another, for I have no desire for sexual relations.' She too sent the same message to him. Then, even though they knew that they did not desire it, they performed the wedding. Neither of them descended into the ocean of the defilements, but they lived together as if they were two great Brahmās.[13]

12. She is also called Pārī at various points in the story in F, but I have retained the single form of her name for simplicity's sake, as does VRI.

13. In other words disinterested in sexual relations. *Mahābrahmā* gods do not experience lust.

The young man Dukūla would not kill fish or deer, and would not even sell meat that had been brought. So his parents said to him, 'Son, although you have been born into a family of hunters, you do not wish for the household life and will not destroy living beings, so what will you do?'

'Mother, Father, with your permission I will renounce this very day.' His parents told the two of them to go, so having honoured their parents they left. They entered the Himalayas along the shore of the Ganges, and in the place where there was a river called Migasammatā which descended from the Himalayas and joined the Ganges, they abandoned the Ganges and climbed up following the Migasammatā.

At that moment Sakka's abode became hot. Sakka understood the reason, summoned Vissakamma and said, 'Friend Vissakamma, two great beings have gone forth and entered the Himalayas. It is appropriate that they should have a dwelling place. In a place half a mile[14] from the river Migasammatā [73] create a leaf hut for them, with all the requisites for renunciants, then return.'

Saying, 'Very good!' he agreed, and he arranged it all as happened in the *Mūgapakkha-jātaka* (*Temiya-jātaka*). He drove out the animals that made unpleasant sounds, created a little footpath, and then went back to Sakka's dwelling. And when they saw that path they followed it to the hermitage. The wise Dukūla entered the leaf hut and saw the requisites for renunciants, and thinking, 'These are given by Sakka,' he knew that they were Sakka's gifts. He took off his cloak and dressed himself in a red bark robe, and having covered himself, he arranged an antelope skin on his shoulder, bound his hair into a circular braid, and took on the appearance of a sage. He gave ordination to Pārikā, and the two of them lived there having cultivated friendliness with regard to the realm of sensual pleasures.[15] By cultivating loving-kindness they obtained friendly thoughts towards one another as well as all the wild animals, and nobody hurt anybody. Pārikā fetched water for drinking and washing, swept the hermitage floor, and did all that needed to be done. They both collected various fruits and ate

14. *Aḍḍhakosa* means half a *kosa*, a *kosa* being reckoned as 500 bow lengths.

15. *Kāmāvacaramettaṃ bhāvetvā*. This could perhaps mean that they maintained a friendliness towards one another without any sensual desire or sexual activity. More likely is that they cultivated loving-kindness that is appropriate to this realm (the realm of sense desires thus contrasted with the Brahmā realm in which they previously resided), or towards all the beings of this realm.

them, then entered their own leaf huts and, acting according to the correct conduct of renouncers, they made their abode there.

Sakka came to attend upon them. One day he was looking around and saw an obstacle: 'Their eyes are going to deteriorate!' He approached the wise Dukūla, honoured him, sat to one side, and said this: 'Bhante, an obstacle has appeared for you. It is appropriate to obtain a son to look after you. Practise worldly conduct.'

'Sakka, why do you speak thus? Even in the midst of houses we shunned this worldly conduct as if it were a mass of maggot-ridden excrement. So now, having entered the forest and gone forth into the renunciation of a sage, how could we behave in this way?'

'Bhante, if you will not do that, you must touch the sage Pārikā's navel with your hand at the time of her menstruation.'

The wise Dukūla[16] assented, saying, 'It is possible to do this.' Sakka paid him honour and returned to his own abode.

And Dukūla the wise explained to Pārikā and touched her navel at the time of her menstruation. Then the Bodhisatta fell from the *deva* world and took rebirth in her womb. [74] After ten months had elapsed she gave birth to a son who was golden, and so they named him Golden Sāma. The *kinnarīs* in the mountain became wet nurses for Pārikā.[17] The two of them bathed the Bodhisatta, lay him down in the leaf hut and went out to gather fruit, and at that moment the *kinnaras*[18] seized the child, bathed him in the mountain caves and so on, took him to the top of the mountain, adorned him with various flowers, and made a mark on his forehead with red and yellow paste. Then they took him back and lay him down in the leaf hut, and Pārikā came back and gave him milk. In due course he grew up, and at

16. Following VRI here and in the next sentence. F has *M*, his abbreviation for Mahāsatto, but the character speaking is not in fact the Great Being.

17. This sentence is unclear. Both Cowell & Rouse and Shaw translate it as saying that the *kinnarīs* of another mountain had suckled Pārikā, but this makes no sense to me. Both resort to putting the sentence in parentheses, and Shaw also moves it slightly later in the passage. It may be better to follow the meaning of VRI, which has: 'When it was time for Pārikā to go to the forest in search of various fruits, the *kinnarīs* inside the mountain suckled him.' In the *Mahāvastu* version the child is said to be suckled by wild animals.

18. *Kinnara* is the masculine term for this type of spirit-deity, literally a 'what-man', that dwells in the forest. Although the term is masculine, it can include reference to both male and female *kinnaras*, while *kinnarī* refers specifically to female *kinnaras*.

the age of sixteen years they still looked after him. His parents seated him in the leaf hut and they themselves went in search of various forest fruits and roots. The Great Being, thinking, 'At some point they will encounter danger,' observed the path that they went by.

Then one day they had fetched fruits and roots, and in the afternoon, while they were returning and not far from the hermitage, a thunderstorm arose. They sheltered in the roots of a certain tree, but they stood on top of an anthill which had a snake in the middle of it. The water, mixed with the smell of sweat from their bodies, descended and entered his nostrils. He became angry, and struck them with the wind of his nostrils, and the two of them became blind and were unable to see one another. Dukūla the wise called out to Pārikā, 'Pārikā, my eyes are destroyed, and I cannot see you!' and she said the same. Unable to see the path they wandered around, lamenting, 'There is no livelihood for us now!' And what was their former *kamma*? It is said that formerly he had been in a medical family. He was a doctor who treated an eye disease in a particular man of great wealth, but the man did not pay him anything. The doctor got angry and said to his wife, 'What should we do?' She too became angry, and said, 'There is no point in getting his money. Having given him medicine and spoken a charm,[19] make his eyes blind!' He agreed and did this.[20] And because of this action the eyes of the two of them became blind.

Then the Great Being thought, [75] 'On other days my parents came back at this time, but now I do not see their return. I will go on the path they went by.' Going on that path he made a noise. They recognised the noise and made a noise in reply. With affection for their son they said, 'Dear Sāma, there is danger here—don't come!' So he said, 'Taking hold of this, come to me!' and he gave them a long stick. They took the end of the stick and came to him. Then he asked them, 'For what reason are your eyes destroyed?'

'My dear, when the gods were raining on us, we stood on the top of this anthill at the foot of the tree here; that is the reason.'

19. *Bhesajjaṃ tassa vatvā ekayogaṃ datvā*. I follow the suggestion in PED (under *yoga*) that *datvā* and *vatvā* should be exchanged in this line. Cowell & Rouse and Shaw prefer to translate as him giving the man a remedy and calling it his medicine. VRI omits *vatvā* altogether, which would mean something like 'having given him medicine as a remedy'.

20. VRI clarifies that the man did go blind as a result.

Hearing his parents' words he understood, 'There must be a snake there, and because of his anger he will have let loose air from his nose.' Looking at his parents he cried and laughed. They asked him, 'Why, son, do you both cry and laugh?'

'Mother and father, because your eyes have been destroyed in this way at such a young age I lament, but now I will be able to look after you, so I laugh. Do not worry! I am going to take good care of you.'

He led his parents back to the hermitage, and prepared ropes between all of the places, namely their daytime and night-time shelters, the walkway, the leaf hut, and the toilets.[21] From that time onwards he left them in the hermitage and went to fetch forest roots and fruits himself. In the early morning he would sweep their dwelling, then go to the river Migasammatā and fetch water for drinking and washing. Having given[22] them water for their faces and sticks for their teeth and so on, he would give them sweet fruits. After they had rinsed their mouths he would himself eat. After eating he would honour his parents, and in the company of the deer he would enter the forest to find fruits. Along with a group of *kinnaras* from within the mountain, he would collect fruits and return in the afternoon. He would fetch water in a pitcher, and with hot water he either bathed them or washed their feet, according to their liking. Having brought the ash pan he would warm their limbs and give them various fruits whilst they were seated. When they had finished, he himself ate, and then stored what was left. In this way he looked after his mother and father.

At that time a king called Pīḷiyakkha ruled in Vārāṇasī. Desiring deer meat he entrusted the kingdom to his mother and entered the Himalayas armed with five weapons. There he killed some deer and ate the meat, [76] and in due course he arrived at the river Migasammatā at the place where Sāma fetched water. Seeing the tracks of the deer, he made a hut with branches the colour of crystal, then took out his bow, and armed with a poisoned arrow he lay there in wait, hidden. Meanwhile the Great Being in the afternoon fetched various fruits and placed them in the hermitage, honoured his parents, and said, 'Having bathed I will fetch drinking water.' He took the pitcher, and surrounded by a herd of deer he gathered two deer together and placed the water pitcher on their back. Holding onto it

21. There are said to be two toilets—*vaccaṭṭhāna* for solid waste and *passāvaṭṭhāna* for liquid.

22. Following VRI *datvā* rather than F *katvā*.

with his hands, he came to the bank of the river. The king, stood in his hut, saw them coming in this manner and thought, 'I have wandered for such a long time and never before seen a man. Is he a god, or a *nāga*? Well, if I approach him I will ask. But if he is a god, he will fly up in the air, and if he is a *nāga* he will enter the earth. I will not stay all this time in the Himalayas and return to Vārāṇasī to be asked by my courtiers, "Your Majesty, did you indeed see any wonder not seen before when wandering in the Himalayas?" Then I will say, "I saw a being of this form," and they will say, "What is it called?" and I will say, "I don't know," and they will censure me. So I will strike this being, and weakening him I will question him.'

After those deer had first gone down and drunk the water and then come back out, the Bodhisatta, like a Great Elder who has taken up the vows, descended slowly to the water, delighting in the tranquillity, and came back up again. He clothed himself in bark robes, and placed a deerskin over one shoulder. He took up the water pitcher, wiped off the water[23] and placed it on his left shoulder. At that moment the king thought, 'Now is the time to strike!' and he fired a poisoned arrow which struck the Great Being on his right side and exited by his left side. Knowing that he had been hit, the herd of deer ran off in fear. But the wise Suvaṇṇasāma, though he had been hit, did not knock over the water pitcher just like that,[24] but recovered his mindfulness and gradually lowered it. Having heaped up some sand he placed it there. Getting his bearings, he placed his head in the direction of his parents' dwelling place and lay down like a golden statue on the silver-coloured tablet of sand. [77] Keeping his mind composed, he thought, 'In this region of Himalayas I have no enemies, and neither do I have any enemy elsewhere!'[25] He vomited blood from his mouth, and, not seeing the king, he spoke a verse:

> 'Who has pierced me with this arrow, careless as I fetch water?[26]
> Warrior, brahmin or merchant, who is my hidden assailant?' (1)

23. F *udakaṃ puñjitvā*; VRI *udakaṃ puñchitvā*. Both Cowell & Rouse and Shaw translate 'filled it with water' but I cannot find any record of this meaning in Pāli or the Sanskrit equivalent *proñch*.

24. Following VRI *anavasumbhitvā* 'not overturning' rather than F *anusumbhutvā*, which is not an attested form and thus probably an error.

25. VRI has 'and neither do my mother and father have any enemy'.

26. The term I have translated as 'careless' is *pamatta*, which might also be rendered 'not mindful'. As the commentary explains, this is a reference to the lapse in *mettā* (loving-kindness) that made the attack possible.

And having said this he spoke a verse in order to show that the meat on his body was not considered edible:

'My meat is not edible, there is no use for my skin,
So what reason do you have to strike me?' (2)

Having spoken the second verse, he asked about his name and so on:

'Who are you, or whose son are you? How should we know you?
Asked by me, friend, tell why having struck me you remain hidden?' (3)

Hearing him the king thought, 'Having been hit by my poisoned arrow, though he has fallen down he neither scolds nor censures me. He addresses me with sweet words as if massaging my heart. I will go into his presence.' He went and stood near him and said:

'I am the king of Kāsī. They know me as Pīḷiyakkha.
Having abandoned the country out of greed, I wandered seeking deer. (4)
And I am skilled in archery, famous as a proficient!
Even a *nāga* could not escape me[27] when I come to let fly an arrow!' (5)

[78] Having praised his own strength in this way, he asked about his name and clan:

'Who are you, or whose son are you? How should we know you?
Explain the name and clan of yourself and your father.' (6)

Hearing that the Great Being thought, 'If I were to say I am a certain god, *nāga*, *kinnara*, warrior, or so on, he would believe me, but it is appropriate to speak the truth.' He said:

'Sir, I am the son of hunters. They named me Sāma.
They addressed me thus when I lived, but today I am gone, I sleep. (7)
I am struck, like a deer, by a single poisoned arrow.
See, O King, I lie here drenched in my own blood. (8)
The arrow has gone right through me.[28] Look—I am spitting up blood.
Ailing, I ask you, why did you strike me and hide? (9)
A tiger is killed for its skin, an elephant on account of its tusks,
But why do you think I should be killed?' (10)

27. Here *nāga* may mean 'elephant', but given the presence of spirit deities in this story the other meaning, 'serpent deity', is equally possible.

28. F has *paṭicammagataṃ* which PED notes Kern suggests may be short for *paṭibhinna-camma-gataṃ* meaning piercing the skin so as to go all the way to the other side. VRI has *paṭivāmagataṃ*, which could mean 'expelled', though the inclusion of *vāma* 'left' in the commentarial explanation (that the arrow entered his right side and exited his left) suggests some confusion here.

The king, having heard his words, did not explain the true situation. Speaking falsely he said:

'A deer was standing there, come to destruction,
Seeing you, Sāma, it was frightened off, and so I was flooded with rage.'[29] (11)

[79] But the Great Being said, 'What are you saying, Great King? In this Himalaya region there is no deer that runs away having seen me.' He said:

'For as long as I can remember, since I reached the age of discretion,
Deer have not been frightened of me, nor have the predators of the forest. (12)
Since I guarded this treasure,[30] since I became a young man,
Deer have not been frightened of me, nor have the predators of the forest. (13)
King, the timid *kinnaras*[31] on this Gandhamādana Mountain,
I proceed on friendly terms with them, in the mountains and forests.
So for what reason would that deer be afraid of me?'[32] (14)

Hearing that the king thought, 'I have attacked this innocent, and spoken lies! I must now speak the truth.' He said:

'Sāma, the deer was not frightened of you. Why did I lie to you?
Overpowered by anger and greed, I let loose that arrow at you.' (15)

And having said this he thought, 'This Golden Sāma must not live alone in this forest—he must have relatives. I will ask him.' He spoke another verse:

'Friend, where have you come from? Sent by whom,
Saying, "Go fetch water from the river," have you come to Migasammatā?' (16)

[80] Having heard his words, enduring great pain, he spat forth blood from his mouth and spoke a verse:

29. Reading *tena* as in VRI and two of F's three manuscripts. F nonetheless has *na te*, meaning the king tells Sāma that he felt no anger towards him, hence the translation in Cowell & Rouse and Shaw.

30. The commentary explains that he is referring to his bark robe, symbolic of the forest dweller's life.

31. The text actually gives *kiṃpuruṣas*, which is metrically different to *kinnaras* but otherwise hard to distinguish. I have kept to *kinnaras* for the sake of consistency.

32. Instead of a three-line verse, VRI repeats the line 'Deer have not been frightened of me, neither the predators of the forest,' thus making two two-line verses.

'My mother and father are blind, and I support them in the forest.
I fetch water for them, having come to Migasammatā.' (17)

And having said that he lamented about his parents, saying:

'They have enough food to live six days,[33]
But without any drinking water, surely the blind ones will die! (18)
This pain is not painful for me, for it is to be expected of men;
My greater suffering is that I will no longer see my mother. (19)
This pain is not painful for me, for it is to be expected of men;
My greater suffering is that I will no longer see my father. (20)
Surely my wretched mother will mourn for a long time,
And at midnight or early morning[34] she will dry up like a river. (21)
Surely my wretched father will mourn for a long time
And at midnight or early morning he will dry up like a river. (22)
Lamenting for their dear Sāma, who tirelessly attended to them
And massaged their limbs, they will wander about in the wild forest. (23)
This is the second arrow that makes my heart tremble:
I will not see the blind ones, and I will not live.' (24)

[81] The king heard his lament and thought, 'This thoroughly pious one, established in *dhamma*, supports his parents. Even now, when he suffers much pain, he laments about them. Since he is endowed with such qualities I have done a great sin. But how can this be relieved?' He resolved, 'What will I do with a kingdom when I have gone to hell? By nourishing them I will look after his parents. In this way his death will be like no death at all.' He said:

'Do not lament so much, Sāma, beautiful to behold!
Becoming a servant I will support them in the wild forest. (25)
I am skilled in archery, famed for my proficiency.
Becoming a servant I will support them in the wild forest. (26)
Searching for scraps amongst the deer and fruits and roots of the forest,
Becoming a servant I will support them in the wild forest. (27)
In which part of the forest, Sāma, do your parents live?
I will support them in the same way as you supported them.' (28)

33. For the rather obscure term *usā* the commentary offers two glosses: food (*bhojana*) and heat (*usmā*). I have followed the former explanation, since it appears to be the preference of the commentator, and it makes good sense within the story. Cowell & Rouse incorporate both meanings into their translation, while Shaw follows the latter meaning.

34. Following the commentary, which glosses *ratte* as *pacchimaratte*.

Then the Great Being said, 'It is good, Great King, for you to support my parents!' Indicating the path he said:

> 'This is the footpath, King, in which direction my head lies.
> Having gone half a mile from here, there is their small house.
> There my parents are. Gone from here support them.' (29)

Having indicated the path in this way, [82] with great affection for his parents he endured that pain, and stretching forth his hands respectfully he entreated him further to support them, saying:

> 'Homage to you, King of Kāsi! Homage to you, prosperity of Kāsi!
> May you support my blind parents in the wild forest. (30)
> I salute you; may there be homage to you, King of Kāsi.
> Please deliver what is said in homage to my mother and father.' (31)

The king agreed, and the Great Being, having sent his regards to his parents, fell unconscious. Explaining the matter the Teacher said:

> Having said this, that Sāma, youthful and beautiful to behold,
> Fainting because of the strength of the poison, became unconscious. (32)

For before, when he was saying all that, he spoke as if out of breath. But now his speech was cut short, as his body, heart, and the continuity of his conscious and subconscious life force were overcome by that swift poison. His mouth was closed, his eyes shut, his hands and feet became rigid, and his whole body was wet with blood. The king thought, 'Even now he spoke with me! How can this be?' and looked for the in-breath and out-breath, but it had ceased and his body had become rigid. He thought, 'Now Sāma is dead,' and unable to bear the grief he clasped his head with both hands and lamented loudly. Explaining the matter the Teacher said:

> The king lamented wretchedly:
> 'Before today I thought I was not subject to decay and death; (33)
> Seeing Sāma fulfil his time, there is no stopping the arrival of death.
> He that discoursed with me, affected by the poison, (34)
> [83] He today has gone to his time, and says nothing.
> Surely I will go to hell, of this I have no doubt,
> For the evil I have done will be demerit for a long time. (35)
> In a village people will speak about a wrongdoer;
> In the forest devoid of men, who is able to speak? (36)
> Men come together in the village and remind one of one's actions;
> In the forest devoid of men, who will make me remember?' (37)

Now a goddess named Bahusundarī (Very Beautiful) who was a resident of Gandhamādana, and who had been the Great Being's mother seven lifetimes before this one, out of affection for her son reflected frequently on the Bodhisatta. But on that day, experiencing heavenly bliss, she did not observe him. Or some say that she had gone to an assembly of the gods. At the time that he fell unconscious she reflected, 'How indeed fares my son?' and saw, 'King Pīḷiyakkha has struck down my son with a poison arrow, and having brought him down on the sandy bank of the Migasammatā he laments loudly. If I do not go, my son Golden Sāma will die right there, the king's heart will burst, and Sāma's parents, not having food or drinking water, will wither and die! But if I go, the king will take the water pitcher and go to his parents and speak to them, and having heard their words [84] he will lead them to their son, and then I will perform an Act of Truth and the poison in Sāma will be destroyed. In this way my son will regain his life and his parents their sight, and this king, having heard a *dhamma* sermon from Sāma, will go and give great gifts and become destined for heaven. Therefore I must go there.' She went to the bank of the river Migasammatā, stood invisible in the sky, and spoke to the king. Explaining the matter the Teacher said:

> That goddess invisible on the Gandhamādana Mountain,
> Out of compassion for the king, spoke these verses: (38)
> 'It is indeed an offence, Great King, a very bad deed done.
> These innocent parents and son, three are slain with one arrow! (39)
> Come, I will teach you how you may get to heaven.
> Properly nourish the blind ones in the forest, and I am sure you will
> reach a good realm!' (40)

Hearing the goddess' words he had faith, thinking, 'Surely if I nourish his parents then I will go to heaven!' He made a strong resolve: 'What is the kingship to me? I will look after them!' Having lamented loudly, he supressed his grief, and thinking Golden Sāma to be dead he honoured his body with various flowers, sprinkled it with water, circumambulated it three times, and worshipped the four directions. Then he took the water pitcher which he had filled, and grieving he set out towards the south. Explaining the matter the Teacher said:

> Having lamented loudly, the king, feeling really wretched,
> Took the water pot and set out facing south. (41)

[85] Now the king was naturally very strong, and so carrying the water pitcher he entered the hermitage as if he was pounding on the ground. He arrived at the entrance to wise Dukūla's hut. Wise Dukūla,[35] seated

35. Here and in several places hereafter, Dukūla is referred to simply as *paṇḍito* 'the

inside, heard his footsteps and wondering, 'This is not the sound of Sāma's feet. Whose can it be?' he spoke two verses:

'What man's arrival makes this sound of footsteps?
It is not the noise of Sāma, so who are you, sir? (42)
For Sāma proceeds quietly, and places his feet gently.
So this is not the sound of Sāma. Who are you sir?' (43)

Hearing that the king thought, 'If I, without saying that I am a king, say "I have killed your son!" they will be angry and will speak harshly to me. Then I will get angry at them and become hostile, and that will be unskilful for me. But there is nobody who is unafraid when they hear "the king", therefore I will speak to them of my royal status.' He placed the water pitcher on the water stand, and standing in the doorway of the leaf hut he said:

'I am the king of Kāsī. They know me as Pīḷiyakkha.
Having abandoned the country out of greed, I wandered seeking deer. (44)
And I am skilled in archery, famous as a proficient!
Even a *nāga* could not escape me when I come to let fly an arrow!' (45)

Wise Dukūla, making him welcome, said:

'You are welcome, Great King, and not unwelcome.
You have attained lordship, as has been declared here. (46)
Eat as you wish, King, fruits as sweet as honey,
From *tinduka* and *piyāla* trees, *madhuka* and *kāsumārī* trees.[36] (47)
And this cold drinking water has been fetched from the gorge,
Therefore drink, Great King, if you wish to.' (48)

[86] Then the king, having been cordially received by him, thought: 'It is not suitable to mention straight away, "I have killed your son." I will speak as if I do not know, in order to raise the subject.' He said:

'Surely the blind cannot see in the forest. Who fetched these fruits for you?
This store of food must have come from a non-blind person.' (49)

Hearing that wise Dukūla said, 'Great King, we did not fetch these various fruits, but we have a son who fetched them for us,' and spoke these two verses to explain:

---

wise one' in F, but I have followed VRI *dukūlapaṇḍito* (Dukūla the Wise) as this is easier for the reader.

36. *Tinduka* (*Diospyros embryopteris*) is a type of ebony, *piyāla* (*Buchanania latifolia*) is also known as the chauli nut tree, *madhuka* (*Bassia latifolia*) is known as the honey tree, and *kāsumārī* (*Gmelina arborea*) is a type of beechwood or teak.

'A young man, a youth, not that tall, Sāma who is beautiful to behold,
His hair long and black and curly,[37] (50)
He indeed, having fetched fruit, took the water pot from here,
And went to the river to fetch water. Surely he has not gone far.' (51)

Having heard that the king said:

'I have killed that Sāma, who attends on you,
The young man of whom you speak, Sāma who is beautiful to behold. (52)
His hair is long and black and curly,
And smeared with blood! The great Sāma lies slain.' (53)

Now Pārikā's leaf hut was not far from wise Dukūla's, and she heard the king's words while she was sitting there. [87] Wanting to know more of this incident she came out, followed the rope, and approached Dukūla. She said:

'Dukūla, what speaker has declared "Sāma is slain"?
Hearing "Sāma is slain", my heart trembles. (54)
Like a young branch of the fig tree moved by the wind,
Hearing "Sāma is slain", my heart trembles.' (55)

And the wise one gave the following advice:

'Pārikā, this is the king of Kāsī. He, angry, struck Sāma
With an arrow at Migasammatā. Do not desire evil of him.' (56)

Pārikā replied:

'With difficulty our dear son was obtained, who supported us in the blinding forest.
When our only son is killed, how can the mind not be disturbed?' (57)

Dukūla the wise said:

'With difficulty our dear son was obtained, who supported us in the blinding forest.
When an only son is killed, the wise speak kindly.' (58)

And having said that, they both beat their hands on their breasts, and having extolled the qualities of the Great Being they lamented greatly. Then the king, comforting them, said:

'Don't lament so strongly at the words "Sāma is slain".
Becoming a servant I will support you in the wild forest. (59)
I am skilled in archery, famed for my proficiency.
Becoming a servant I will support you in the wild forest. (60)
Searching for scraps amongst the deer and fruits and roots of the forest,
Becoming a servant I will support you in the wild forest.' (61)

37. The term *sunaggavellitā* (VRI *sūnaggavellitā*), literally 'dog-hairtip-curled', is not totally clear to me, so I have chosen to simply translate 'curly'.

[88] They, talking with him, said:

'Great King, this is not fitting. This is not seemly for us.
You are our king, and we honour your feet.' (62)

Hearing that, the king was greatly pleased, thinking, 'Oh wonderful! In this way even when my action is so faulty, they do not speak unkindly to me, but they greet me kindly.' He spoke the verse:

'You hunters speak the *dhamma* and behave with honour.
You are our father, and you, Pārikā, are our mother.' (63)

But holding forth their hands they entreated him, 'Great King, it is not proper for you to become our servant. But make us hold on to the end of a stick and lead us to see Sāma.' They spoke two verses:

'Homage to you, King of Kāsi! Homage to you, prosperity of Kāsi!
We raise our hands to you, that you may lead us to Sāma. (64)
Stroking[38] his feet and his face beautiful to behold,
Beating ourselves, we will stay by the deceased.'[39] (65)

[89] Whilst they were speaking in this way the sun went down. The king thought, 'If I lead them there right now, having seen him their hearts will break, and then I will have killed three of them, and surely I will go to hell. So I will not allow them to go there.' He addressed them in four verses:

'Predatory animals are seen covering the lofty sky
Where Sāma lies slain, like the moon fallen on the ground. (66)
Predatory animals are seen covering the lofty sky
Where Sāma lies slain, like the sun fallen on the earth. (67)
Predatory animals are seen covering the lofty sky
Where Sāma lies slain, surrounded by dust. (68)
Predatory animals are seen covering the lofty sky
Where Sāma lies slain. Stay here in the hermitage!' (69)

But they, to show they had no fear of the wild beasts, spoke the verse:

'Even if there were a hundred, a thousand, a myriad there,
We would have no fear of the beasts of the forest.' (70)

The king, unable to refuse them, took their hands and led them there. Explaining the matter the Teacher said:

Then, leading the blind ones, the king of Kāsi in the vast forest
Took their hands and set out to where Sāma was slain. (71)

38. Following VRI *samajjantā* 'rubbing, stroking, cleaning' rather than F *pavaṭṭantā*, which is difficult to render.

39. Alternatively this could mean 'until death'.

[90] And after leading them there he placed them near Sāma, and showed them: 'This is your son.' The father placed Sāma's head in his lap and the mother his feet, and then they sat there and lamented. Explaining the matter the Teacher said:

Having seen the fallen Sāma, their little boy covered in dust,
Discarded in the vast forest, like the moon fallen to the earth; (72)
Having seen the fallen Sāma, their little boy covered in dust,
Discarded in the vast forest, like the sun fallen to the earth; (73)
Having seen the fallen Sāma, their little boy covered in dust,
Discarded in the vast forest, they cried out piteously! (74)
Having seen the fallen Sāma, their little boy covered in dust,
They lamented with outstretched arms, 'My dear, this is wrong! (75)
Surely you sleep too much, beautiful Sāma,
Who met your death today. You say nothing. (76)
Surely you are completely intoxicated, beautiful Sāma,
Who met your death today. You say nothing. (77)
Surely you are too slothful, beautiful Sāma,
Who met your death today. You say nothing. (78)
Surely you are very angry, beautiful Sāma,
Who met your death today. You say nothing. (79)
Surely you are being insolent, beautiful Sāma,
Who met your death today. You say nothing. (80)
Surely you are distracted, beautiful Sāma,
Who met your death today. You say nothing. (81)
Now who will adjust our matted hair when it is dirty?
Sāma, attendant to the blind, is dead! (82)
Who will take up the broom and sweep the hermitage?
Sāma, attendant to the blind, is dead! (83)
Who now will bathe us with hot and cold water?
Sāma, attendant to the blind, is dead! (84)
[91] Who will feed us with forest fruits of roots?
Sāma, attendant to the blind, is dead!' (85)

Then his mother, having lamented greatly, placed her hand on his chest and realised he was hot. She thought, 'There is still warmth in my son. It must be that he is unconscious as a result of the poison. In order to expel the poison I will make an Act of Truth.' And she made an Act of Truth. Explaining the matter the Teacher said:

Having seen the fallen Sāma, her little boy covered in dust,
Pained by grief at her son, his mother spoke the truth: (86)
'By this truth—this Sāma was formerly virtuous—
By this truth spoken, may Sāma's poison be destroyed. (87)
By this truth—this Sāma was formerly chaste—

By this truth spoken, may Sāma's poison be destroyed. (88)
By this truth—this Sāma was formerly honest—
By this truth spoken, may Sāma's poison be destroyed. (89)
By this truth—this Sāma was a supporter of his parents—
By this truth spoken, may Sāma's poison be destroyed. (90)
By this truth—this Sāma was respectful of his family elders—
By this truth spoken, may Sāma's poison be destroyed. (91)
By this truth—this Sāma was dearer to me than life—
By this truth spoken, may Sāma's poison be destroyed. (92)
Whatever good has been done by me and his father,
By this virtuous truth may Sāma's poison be destroyed.' (93)

[92] On account of these truth acts, these seven verses spoken by his mother, Sāma moved, then lay still. Then his father thought, 'My son lives! I too will make an Act of Truth!' and in the same way he made an Act of Truth. Explaining the matter the Teacher said:

Having seen the fallen Sāma, his little boy covered in dust,
Pained by grief at his son, his father spoke the truth: (94)
'By this truth—this Sāma was formerly virtuous—
By this truth spoken, may Sāma's poison be destroyed. (95)
By this truth—this Sāma was formerly chaste—
By this truth spoken, may Sāma's poison be destroyed. (96)
By this truth—this Sāma was formerly honest—
By this truth spoken, may Sāma's poison be destroyed. (97)
By this truth—this Sāma was a supporter of his parents—
By this truth spoken, may Sāma's poison be destroyed. (98)
By this truth—this Sāma was respectful of his family elders—
By this truth spoken, may Sāma's poison be destroyed. (99)
By this truth—this Sāma was dearer to me than life—
By this truth spoken, may Sāma's poison be destroyed. (100)
Whatever good has been done by me and his mother,
By this virtuous truth may Sāma's poison be destroyed.' (101)

While he was making this Act of Truth the Great Being stirred, and lay down on his other side. Then the goddess made an Act of Truth. Explaining the matter the Teacher said:

The goddess, unseen in the Gandhamādana Mountain,
Out of compassion for Sāma spoke this truth: (102)
'I have lived for a long time on Mount Gandhamādana.
Nobody else exists that is dearer to me than Sāma.
By this truth declared may Sāma's poison be destroyed. (103)
All the forests on Mount Gandhamādana are fragrant.
By this truth declared may Sāma's poison be destroyed.' (104)
And while they wept in great wretchedness,

Sāma got up quickly, the youth who is beautiful to behold. (105)

Then four things were made manifest in the hermitage in the same instant by the power of the goddess: Sāma's recovery, the restoration of the sight of his mother and father, and the onset of dawn. [93] The mother and father were extremely joyful, saying, 'We can see! And Sāma is well!' And the wise Sāma spoke the verse:

'I am Sāma. Hail to you! I am safe!
Do not lament too much: speak sweetly to me.' (106)
Then, seeing the king, he paid him honour and said:
'You are welcome, Great King, and not unwelcome.
You have attained lordship, as has been declared here. (107)
Eat as you wish, King, fruits as sweet as honey,
From *tinduka* and *piyāla* trees, *madhuka* and *kāsumārī* trees. (108)
And this cold drinking water has been fetched from the gorge,
Therefore drink, Great King, if you wish to.' (109)

And the king, seeing that wonder, said:

'I am bewildered! I am mystified! All that I have seen confounds me!
I saw Sāma dead, so how can you, Sāma, be alive?' (110)

Sāma thought, 'This king thought I was dead! I will explain my resurrection to him.' He said:

'Great king, even alive a person of strong feeling
Rendered unconscious,[40] though living, is considered dead. (111)
Great king, even alive a person of strong feeling
Being gone to extinction,[41] though living, is considered dead.' (112)

And after saying, 'The world thinks me dead though I am living,' the Great Being wanted to set the purposes of the king in order, and so teaching the *dhamma* he spoke two more verses:

[94] 'Whichever man properly looks after his mother or father,
The gods indeed cure him, the person who supports his parents. (113)
Whichever man properly looks after his mother or father,
They praise him in this world, and after death he enjoys heaven.' (114)

Having heard that the king said, 'Oh it is indeed marvellous, sir, that the gods cure the diseases that have arisen in a person who supports his parents, and likewise that this Sāma is so resplendent.' Honouring him he said:

40. Following DP I 460. The term is *upanītamanasa(ṅ)kappaṃ*, which the commentary glosses as *bhavaṅgaṃ otiṇṇacittācāraṃ*.

41. This presumably refers to somebody who has attained *nibbāna* and thus become an *arahat* but not yet passed away.

'I am bewildered further! All the directions confuse me!
Sāma, I go to you for refuge, and you must be my refuge.' (115)

Then the Great Being said to him, 'If, Great King, you wish to go to the world of gods, and you wish to enjoy great divine bliss, establish yourself in these ten forms of righteous conduct.' He spoke the ten verses of righteous conduct:

'Great King, warrior, act properly with regard to your mother and father,
And having acted properly in this, King, you will go to heaven. (116)
Great King, warrior, act properly with regard to your sons and daughters,
And having acted properly in this, King, you will go to heaven. (117)
Great King, warrior, act properly with regard to your friends and courtiers,
And having acted properly in this, King, you will go to heaven. (118)
Great King, act properly with regard to your army and elephants,
And having acted properly in this, King, you will go to heaven. (119)
Great King, act properly with regard to your towns and villages,
And having acted properly in this, King, you will go to heaven. (120)
Great King, act properly with regard to your kingdom and country,
And having acted properly in this, King, you will go to heaven. (121)
Great King, act properly with regard to recluses and brahmins,
And having acted properly in this, King, you will go to heaven. (122)
Great King, warrior, act properly with regard to animals and birds,
And having acted properly in this, King, you will go to heaven. (123)
Great King, act properly, for good done is conducive to happiness,
And having acted properly here, King, you will go to heaven. (124)
Great King, act properly, for the gods including Indras and Brahmās
Attained heaven by well-done deeds. Do not neglect the *dhamma*, King.' (125)

[95] The Great Being, having explained the ten kingly duties to him in this way, and having instructed him further, gave him the five precepts. He accepted the teaching with head bowed and, having paid his respects, he went to Vārāṇasī and made merit by giving and so on, and, along with his court, became destined for heaven. And the Bodhisatta along with his parents cultivated the higher knowledges and the attainments, and reached the Brahmā realm.

The Teacher, having given this *dhamma* teaching, said, 'Monks, the tradition of the wise is the nourishment of parents.' He revealed the Truths and connected the birth, and at the end of the Truths the monk who looked after his mother attained the fruit of stream entry. 'At that time Ānanda was the king, Uppalavaṇṇā was the daughter of the gods, Anuruddha was Sakka, Kassapa was the father, Bhaddakāpilānī was the mother, and I myself was the wise Golden Sāma.'[42]

42. Once again Ānanda, the Buddha's attendant, plays an ambiguous role, and Uppalavaṇṇā is a maternal goddess, as in the *Temiya-jātaka*. (Mahā) Kassapa and Bhaddakāpilānī were husband and wife before entering the *saṅgha*, but are said to have had a chaste and ascetic marriage similar to that described here. Mahākassapa was famous for his solitary ascetic practices. Anuruddha was another senior monk in the Buddha's community.

A

Depictions of Multiple *Jātakas*

Fig. A In this impressive *uposatha* hall from the Rattanakosin period, 538 painted panels depict the majority of the *jātakas* of the *Jātakatthavaṇṇanā*. Although the images have been restored several times through to the present day, the hall remains a striking example of the popularity of *jātakas* in the period. It is a rare example of the depiction of all (or nearly all) the *jātakas*, rather than just the Great Ten, as is more common. Painted mural, Wat Khrua Wan, Bangkok, Thailand, first half of the 19th century. Photograph copyright Naomi Appleton.

B

Fig. B The twentieth-century Mahā Bodhi shrine on the north-east part of the Golden Shwedagon Pagoda platform in Yangon, Myanmar, honours the original Mahā Bodhi shrine at Bodh Gaya but does not replicate it. This face shows the Great Ten with key scenes, also depicted in the twentieth-century tiles series that surround the base of the Pagoda itself. Glazed terracotta tile. Photograph copyright Sarah Shaw.

c

Fig. c The West (Anauk) and East (Ashe) remains of the twin eleventh-century Hpetleik Paya, excavated in 1905, show all the *jātaka*s, mostly with one scene per tile, in vaulted corridors filled with large tiles in linear friezes. Terracotta tile, Anauk Hpetleik Stūpa, Myanmar, 11th century. Photograph copyright Ven. Dhammika.

1.1

1.2

1. The Birth Story of Temiya

Fig. 1.1 The king, with his baby son Temiya on his lap, passes judgement on some thieves. **Fig. 1.2** Young prince Temiya's resolve is tested by dancing girls.

Temiya-jātaka, terracotta tile, Ananda Temple, Pagan, Myanmar, 11th–12th century. Photographs copyright Lilian Handlin, 2004.

1.3

1.4

Fig. 1.3 Temiya tries his strength by lifting the chariot. **Fig. 1.4** Temiya teaches the three kings who have come to visit him in his forest hermitage.

Temiya-jātaka, terracotta tile, Ananda Temple, Pagan, Myanmar, 11th–12th century. Photograph copyright Lilian Handlin, 2004.

1.5

1.6

Fig. 1.5 The central row of this mural shows the trials undergone by the child Temiya. *Temiya-jātaka*, cave 478 at Powindaung, Myanmar, mid-18th century. Photograph copyright Alexandra Green. **Fig. 1.6** Temiya interrupts the charioteer, who is digging a grave for him. *Temiya-jātaka*, glazed terracotta tile, Shwedagon Pagoda, Yangon, Myanmar, c. 1900. Photograph copyright Lucy Shaw.

1.7

Fig. 1.7 In this scene, located on the right side of the original manuscript folio, Temiya remains motionless as beautiful women dance around him. **Fig. 1.8** Here (on the left side of the original manuscript), he swings a chariot overhead in what has become the most iconic representation of the story.

Temiya-jātaka, painted *khoi* manuscript, MS. Pali a. 27 (R), fol. 6, mid-18th century, Central Thailand. Copyright Bodleian Library, University of Oxford, 2013. Taken from Appleton, Shaw, and Unebe, *Illuminating the Life of the Buddha* (Oxford Bodleian Library Publishing, 2013).

1.8

1.9 

Fig. 1.9 Temiya sits motionless while an elephant and a man wielding a dagger attempt to provoke movement or sound. *Temiya-jātaka*, painted mural, Wat Nak Prok, Bangkok, Thailand. Photograph copyright Ven. Bhatsakorn Piyobhaso.

1.10 

Fig. 1.10 The charioteer is startled by Temiya swinging the chariot over his head. *Temiya-jātaka*, painted mural, Wat Nak Prok, Bangkok, Thailand. Photograph copyright Ven. Bhatsakorn Piyobhaso.

1.11

1.12

Fig. 1.11 Temiya swings the chariot over his head to the amazement of onlookers. Although painted in the 1960s, this mural retains the earlier focus on this pivotal moment in the story, and Temiya's posture resembles murals from a hundred or more years previously. *Temiya-jātaka*, painted mural, Wat Chang Khong, Chiang Mai Province, Thailand, 1967. Photograph copyright Sébastien Tayac. **Fig. 1.12** In this modern temple mural (dated to 2006), Temiya watches calmly as the charioteer digs his grave. *Temiya-jātaka*, Wat Ubosot, Chiang Mai Province, Thailand, 2006. Photograph copyright Sébastien Tayac.

2.1

2.2

2. The Birth Story of Janaka

Fig. 2.1 Janaka's boat founders in the ocean, and the mariners are swallowed by fish. **Fig. 2.2** Janaka descends from his house to begin life as a renunciant. His wife, mistaking him for a *paccekabuddha*, honours him as he passes.

Janaka-jātaka, terracotta tile, Ananda Temple, Pagan, Myanmar, late 11th or early 12th century. Photographs copyright Lilian Handlin, 2004.

2.3

2.4

Fig. 2.3 Janaka and his wife see a fletcher making an arrow straight. *Janaka-jātaka*, terracotta tile, Ananda Temple, Pagan, Myanmar, late 11th or early 12th century. Photograph copyright Lilian Handlin, 2004.
Fig. 2.4 Janaka perches on the top of the mast as the ship sinks and his fellow mariners struggle in the water. *Janaka-jātaka*, terracotta tile, West Hpetleik Stūpa, Myanmar, second half of 11th century. Photograph copyright Ven. Dhammika.

2.5

2.6

Fig. 2.5 Janaka, dressed as a renouncer, descends from his palace. *Janaka-jātaka*, glazed terracotta tile, Shwedagon Pagoda, Yangon, Myanmar, c. 1900. Photograph copyright Lucy Shaw. **Fig. 2.6** Janaka's ship sinks into the sea as he perches on the mast, determined to survive. *Janaka-jātaka*, painted mural, Laung U Hmaw monastery, Ywathitgyi Village, Myanamar, late 18th century. The writing reads 'Mahajanaka Jataka. A depiction of . . . ill . . . to a place . . . boat blown off course [?] . . . the son of King Mahajanaka was in the sea for seven full days . . .' Photograph and translation copyright Alexandra Green.

2.7

2.8

2.9

Fig. 2.9 In this nineteenth-century mural painting, Janaka is seen surviving his shipwreck and being rescued by the goddess of the ocean. While the scene chosen for illustration is rather timeless, the detail of the magnificent clipper ship and its foreign mariners betrays the time of its painting. *Janaka-jātaka*, painted mural, Wat No Phutthangkun / Wat Makham No, Suphanburi Province, Thailand, 1848. Photograph copyright Naomi Appleton.

Previous page
Fig. 2.7 The most iconic scene of the *Janaka-jātaka*: Janaka rescued from the shipwreck. **Fig. 2.8** Brahmins check Janaka's feet for auspicious signs as he lies on a stone slab in a park; the chariot stands ready to take him to the palace.

Janaka-jātaka, painted *khoi* manuscript, MS. Pali a. 27 (R), fol. 7, mid-18th century, Central Thailand. Copyright Bodleian Library, University of Oxford, 2013. Taken from Appleton, Shaw, and Unebe, *Illuminating the Life of the Buddha* (Oxford Bodleian Library Publishing, 2013).

2.10

2.11

Fig. 2.10 Janaka is shipwrecked and rescued. **Fig. 2.11** Janaka is led into the city of Mithilā on the chariot that has magically identified him as the true king. *Janaka-jātaka*, painted mural, Wat Nak Prok, Bangkok, Thailand. Photographs copyright Ven. Bhatsakorn Piyobhaso.

2.12

Fig. 2.12 This magnificent temple mural painted in the early twenty-first century depicts the opening of the *Janaka-jātaka* Janaka's mother escapes on a cart driven by Sakka disguised as an old man, while the city of Mithilā is captured by Janaka's uncle. *Janaka-jātaka*, painted mural, Wat Phra That Doi Kham, Chiang Mai Province, Thailand, 2009. Photograph copyright Sébastien Tayac.

3.1

3.2

3. The Birth Story of Golden Sāma

Fig. 3.1 The baby Sāma is bathed by *kinnaras* or *supaṇṇas*. **Fig. 3.2** Sāma uses a stick to lead his parents out of their shelter after they have been blinded during a storm.

Sāma-jātaka, terracotta tile, Ananda Temple, Pagan, Myanmar, late 11th or early 12th century. Photographs copyright Lilian Handlin, 2004.

3.3

3.4

Fig. 3.3 Sāma fetches water for his parents, placing his pitcher on the back of two deer. **Fig. 3.4** The king brings Sāma's parents to their son, who is lying prostrate on the ground.

Sāma-jātaka, terracotta tile, Ananda Temple, Pagan, Myanmar, late 11th or early 12th century. Photographs copyright Lilian Handlin, 2004.

3.5

Fig. 3.5 Sāma's parents cry over his body and make their statements of truth to revive him. *Sāma-jātaka*, painted mural, Pokala temple, Shwezayan Village, Myanmar, mid-19th century. Photograph copyright Alexandra Green.

3.6

3.7

Fig. 3.6 In this unusual image we see Sāma's parents being blinded by a snake as they seek shelter from a storm. **Fig 3.7** Sāma fetches water in the company of some deer.

Sāma-jātaka, glazed terracotta tile, Shwedagon Pagoda, Yangon, Myanmar, c. 1900. Photographs copyright Lucy Shaw.

3.8

Fig. 3.8 The king informs Sāma's parents of their son's death. **Fig. 3.9** The parents, the king, and the goddess all lament beside Sāma's prostrate body. Sakka appears from the sky, carrying a conch shell; this motif would appear to have been imported from another story.

Sāma-jātaka, painted *khoi* manuscript, MS. Pali a. 27 (R), fol. 10, mid-18th century, Central Thailand. Copyright Bodleian Library, University of Oxford, 2013. Taken from Appleton, Shaw, and Unebe, *Illuminating the Life of the Buddha* (Oxford Bodleian Library Publishing, 2013).

3.9

3.10

3.11

Fig. 3.10 The whole of the Sāma story is shown on this nineteenth-century temple mural, in separate but unbounded scenes. At the bottom we see the king shooting Sāma. Above right the king visits Sāma's parents in their hermitage, and in the top left Sāma lies on the ground while his parents and the goddess lament. *Sāma-jātaka*, painted mural, Wat No Phutthangkun / Wat Makham No, Suphanburi Province, Thailand, 1848. Photograph copyright Naomi Appleton.

Fig. 3.11 While Sāma fetches water in the company of some deer, he is struck by the king's arrow. **Fig. 3.12** The king fires his arrow at Sāma.

Sāma-jātaka, painted mural, Wat Saket, Bangkok, Thailand. Photographs copyright Sarah Shaw.

3.12

3.13

3.14

Fig. 3.13 In the foreground of this 1967 mural Sāma is struck by the king's arrow as he fetches water. Behind, the king brings Sāma's parents to their son's side. The king is depicted as a *yakkha*, reflecting his name Pīḷiyakkha. *Sāma-jātaka*, painted mural, Wat Thung Yu, Chiang Mai Province, Thailand. Photograph copyright Sébastien Tayac. **Fig. 3.14** In this distinctive image, Sāma carries his aged and blind parents through the forest. This method of transport is not mentioned in the story, though this type of ascetic's pole is fairly common in the *jātakas*. *Sāma-jātaka*, painted mural, Wat Rong San, Chiang Mai Province, Thailand. Photograph copyright Sébastien Tayac.

4.1

4.2

4. The Birth Story of Nemi

Fig. 4.1 The lower register of this mural shows Nemi in his palace, while the carriage waits for him outside. The inscription is not clear. *Nemi-jātaka*, painted mural, Ywagyigone complex, central Myanmar, late 18th century. Photograph copyright Alexandra Green. **Fig. 4.2** The barber shows a grey hair to Nemi. On the left is his renunciation, or that of his predecessor, Makhādeva. *Nemi-jātaka*, glazed terracotta tile, Shwedagon Pagoda, Yangon, Myanmar, c. 1900. Photograph copyright Lucy Shaw.

4.3

4.4

Fig. 4.3 Mātali, sitting in his carriage, invites Nemi to join him.
Fig. 4.4 Nemi watches a guardian of hell beating an unfortunate person who has been reborn there; the concerned carriage driver seems to be turning back to speak to Nemi.

Nemi-jātaka, terracotta tile, Ananda Temple, Pagan, Myanmar, late 11th or early 12th century. Photographs copyright Lilian Handlin, 2004.

4.5

4.6

Fig. 4.5 Nemi looks at a heavenly mansion and meets a female reborn here as a *deva* both his hands are thrown up in delight, and the facial expression and bearing of both driver and Nemi have changed from their appearance on the previous tile. **Fig. 4.6** Nemi giving his teachings in the Heaven of the Thirty-Three, represented by the *pārichattaka* tree, behind the listening figures.

Nemi-jātaka, terracotta tile, Ananda Temple, Pagan, Myanmar, late 11th or early 12th century. Photographs copyright Lilian Handlin, 2004.

4.7

Fig. 4.7 Nemi's carriage flies right up to the zigzag line (*sintao*) that separates stories and themes in Thai murals and here provides a boundary between the journey and the scene of the Heaven of the Thirty-Three shown at the top of the wall. The painting betrays nineteenth-century Western influence in the use of some perspective, and in the soft, impressionistic effect of greenery and cloud, which emphasises the sharp lines of the figures and carriage. *Nemi-jātaka*, painted mural, Wat Saket, Bangkok, Thailand, 19th century. Photograph copyright Sarah Shaw.

4.8

Fig. 4.8 On the left in the manuscript, we see the gruesome detail of various hells that seem to proliferate in Siamese temple art out of their Pāli textual base. **Fig. 4.9** Nemi in his chariot, pointing downwards, as if to the hells, while Mātali turns back to explain the reasons for beings' rebirths there.

Nemi-jātaka, painted *khoi* manuscript, MS. Pali a. 27 (R), fol. 11, mid-18th century, Central Thailand. Copyright Bodleian Library, University of Oxford, 2013. Taken from Appleton, Shaw, and Unebe, *Illuminating the Life of the Buddha* (Oxford Bodleian Library Publishing, 2013).

4.9

4.10 

Fig. 4.10 This mural, painted in 2001, places the story as a kind of pictorial network, with all events appearing to take place at the same time. Below, Nemi's chariot visits the hells; all beings in hell realms have grotesque and painfully constricted or misproportioned bodies. Above, celestial nymphs enjoy music and dance. In the centre Nemi teaches his people in the palace. Such images are far more popular in Thailand, where the monarchy has been felt so important, than that of Nemi renouncing. *Nemi-jātaka*, painted mural, Wat Saen Luang, Chiang Mai Province, Thailand, 2001. Photograph copyright Sébastien Tayac.

4.11

Fig. 4.11 Nemi visits the hells. Sakka, flying easily down, with the green body that always marks him in Siamese iconography, contrasts with the skeletal figure, partially seen here, whose whole body has become a face racked by pain. *Nemi-jātaka,* painted mural, Wat Nak Prok, Bangkok, Thailand. Photograph copyright Ven. Bhatsakorn Piyobhaso.

4.12

Fig. 4.12 This full mural shows how an artist can exploit physical features such as doors and windows for impressive effect, in this case allowing a superbly executed visit to the hells on the lower right of the mural, with the chariot seeming to gallop down along the line of the door frame. *Nemi-jātaka,* painted mural, Wat Buak Khrok Luang, Chiang Mai Province, Thailand, 19th century. Photograph copyright Sarah Shaw.

4.13

Fig. 4.13 This detail of a hell visited by Nemi shows the sense of constriction and oppression through its boxed-in arrangement of struggling unfortunates. The hells in Nemi depictions do not always correspond to those in the Pāli version, perhaps being derived from vernacular retellings, or simply the artist's imagination. *Nemi-jātaka*, painted mural, Wat Saket, Bangkok, Thailand, 19th century. Photograph copyright Sarah Shaw.

4.14

Fig. 4.14 This 1933 interpretation of Nemi's visit to the heavens makes swirling clouds and skies key to the mystery of the journey. *Nemi-jātaka*, painted mural, Wat Upakhut, Chiang Mai Province, Thailand, 1933. Photograph copyright Sébastien Tayac.

5.1

5.2

5. The Birth Story of Mahosadha

Fig. 5.1 All the depictions in the Ananda temple tile series of the Great Ten (with the exception, for unclear reasons, of *Nemi*) begin with the conception of the Bodhisatta, shown in a comparable image for each, that reinforces a sense of their completion as a unit within the *jātaka* sequence. Here the conception of the Bodhisatta as Mahosadha is shown, with him seated above in the heaven realm awaiting rebirth. **Fig. 5.2** King Sakka gives Mahosadha the healing herb as he is born; his mother is sitting.

Mahosadha-jātaka, terracotta tile, Ananda Temple, Pagan, Myanmar, late 11th or early 12th century. Photographs copyright Lilian Handlin, 2004.

5.3

5.4

Fig. 5.3 The Question of the Piece of Meat. The playfulness of the boys trying to get the hawk to drop the meat has made this historically one of the most popular scenes from the story. **Fig. 5.4** The Bodhisatta decides the case of the wife (the Question of the Dark Lump).

Mahosadha-jātaka, terracotta tile, Ananda Temple, Pagan, Myanmar, late 11th or early 12th century. Photographs copyright Lilian Handlin, 2004.

5.5

5.6

Fig. 5.5 The depiction here of the Question of the Chameleon accords less prominence to its subject than it does to the splendid elephant being ridden by the king. **Fig. 5.6** The Bodhisatta planting a flower before the war of words (*dhammayuddha*). This incident is not described in the Pāli version of the story.

Mahosadha-jātaka, terracotta tile, Ananda Temple, Pagan, Myanmar, late 11th or early 12th century. Photographs copyright Lilian Handlin, 2004.

5.7

5.8

Fig. 5.7 Mahosadha directs the digging of the tunnel. **Fig. 5.8** The shipwrights make their ships over to Mahosadha, after the tunnel has been dug.

Mahosadha-jātaka, terracotta tile, Ananda Temple, Pagan, Myanmar, late 11th or early 12th century. Photographs copyright Lilian Handlin, 2004.

5.9

5.10

Fig. 5.9 The birth of Mahosadha. **Fig 5.10** The story of the piece of meat.
Mahosadha-jātaka, glazed terracotta tile, Shwedagon Pagoda, Yangon, Myanmar, c. 1900. Photographs copyright Lucy Shaw.

5.11

5.12

Fig. 5.11 The case of the oxen. **Fig. 5.12** Mahosadha is honoured by the king, perhaps when he is given a necklace of pearls after the nineteen questions.

Mahosadha-jātaka, glazed terracotta tile, Shwedagon Pagoda, Yangon, Myanmar, c. 1900. Photographs copyright Lucy Shaw.

5.13

Fig. 5.13 One of the most popular images from the story is the defeating of Kevaṭṭa, whose scramblings on the ground after missing the jewel in the first picture make him appear to be the loser in his war of words with Mahosadha. Iconography is shared in Siamese temple and manuscript art. *Mahosadha-jātaka*, painted *khoi* manuscript, MS. Pali a. 27 (R), fol. 12, mid-18th century, Central Thailand. Copyright Bodleian Library, University of Oxford, 2013. Taken from Appleton, Shaw, and Unebe, *Illuminating the Life of the Buddha* (Oxford Bodleian Library Publishing, 2013).

5.14

Fig. 5.14 Mahosadha and Bherī conduct their private conversation of gestures. Siamese interpretations regard the ascetic as female, unlike some other readings of the tale. *Mahosadha-jātaka*, painted *khoi* manuscript, MS. Pali a. 27 (R), fol. 12, mid-18th century, Central Thailand. Copyright Bodleian Library, University of Oxford, 2013. Taken from Appleton, Shaw, and Unebe, *Illuminating the Life of the Buddha* (Oxford Bodleian Library Publishing, 2013).

5.15

Fig. 5.15 The Bodhisatta is shown here in his own residence, with the parrot perched in the upper right-hand corner. *Mahosadha-jātaka*, painted mural, Wat No Phutthangkun / Wat Makham No, Suphanburi Province, Thailand. Photograph copyright Naomi Appleton.

5.16

5.17

Fig. 5.16 The great army march with elephants. *Mahosadha-jātaka*, painted mural, Wat Saket, Bangkok, Thailand, 19th century. Photograph copyright Sarah Shaw. **Fig. 5.17** The building of the lattice that hides any view of Mithilā from Kevaṭṭa, emissary for the enemy king, is here shown with an almost modernist vigour. The construction work is being undertaken by Chinese workmen; in the nineteenth century Thailand was experiencing an influx of Chinese immigration, while Chiang Mai had extensive contacts with Yunnan traders from the north. *Mahosadha-jātaka*, painted mural, Wat Buak Khrok Luang, Chiang Mai Province, Thailand, 19th century. Photograph copyright Sarah Shaw.

5.18

Fig. 5.18 The Bodhisatta rides an elephant as he goes to the enemy city. *Mahosadha-jātaka,* painted mural, Wat Nak Prok, Bangkok, Thailand. Photograph copyright Ven. Bhatsakorn Piyobhaso.

5.19

Fig. 5.19 This mural shows the downwards pendulum style often used in temple art to show the story sequence. The four wise men are at the court at the top and the city is below, where the Bodhisatta stands confidently on the rampart to await the enemy king; at the bottom the Bodhisatta shows his dominance as Kevaṭṭa scrambles on the ground for the jewel. The military has a decidedly modern air Western guns were frequently introduced into *jātaka* pictures in the nineteenth century. *Mahosadha-jātaka,* painted mural, Wat Nak Prok, Bangkok, Thailand. Photograph copyright Ven. Bhatsakorn Piyobhaso.

Fig. 5.20 This painted mural shows the Pañcalan king, Brahmadatta, and his adviser, Kevaṭṭa, plotting how to invade Mithilā and the kingdom of Videha. The discussion takes place in the court; soldiers and guards are shown arrayed on the rest of the panel. Those on the lower register are wearing Western-style hats. The inscription reads 'The four parts of the army were surrounded by soldiers holding swords, spears, and guns. In Pancalarit country, King Brahmadatta discussing with Kevata the brahmin how to attack Videharit country.' *Mahosadha-jātaka*, painted mural, Lokamangin Temple, Monywe Town, Myanmar, 1782. Photograph and translation copyright Alexandra Green.

5.21

Fig. 5.21 In Thai art each of the tales tends to have stock images that become emblematic over a long period; one such scene for *Mahosadha* is the Bodhisatta brandishing a sword over the terrified soldiers who have been trapped in the tunnel. *Mahosadha-jātaka*, painted mural, Wat Phra Chao Lueam, Chiang Mai Province, Thailand. Photograph copyright Sébastien Tayac.

5.22

Fig. 5.22 This is another twentieth-century representation of the Bodhisatta threatening the soldiers in the tunnel. *Mahosadha-jātaka*, painted mural, Wat Suan Dok, Chiang Mai Province, Thailand, 1976. Photograph copyright Sébastien Tayac.

4

The Birth Story of Nemi

(*Nemi-jātaka* or *Nimi-jātaka*)

INTRODUCTION

This famous story creates the perfect hoop that echoes the name of its hero: Nimi/Nemi 'the Wheel'.[1] It opens with a 'story in the present' in which the Buddha recollects that he had been reborn in the time of Makhādeva and delighted in meditation (the incidents recounted in J 9).[2] The events of this tale concern however another Bodhisatta-king, Nemi: through a narrative nicety only possible in a story involving rebirth, many aeons have passed since Makhādeva's time and the Bodhisatta is born as his own descendent. The family lineage of monarchs who take the renunciation late in life has endured for hundreds and thousands of years until the character who initiated it, the Bodhisatta/Makhādeva, sees from the heaven realm in

Introduced and translated by Sarah Shaw.

1. The F edition only gives 'Nemi' instead of 'Nimi' once: when the association of the wheel is made. Because that is how he is known generally, however, Nemi is used here throughout. There are many Buddhist and Indic associations with King Nimi/Nemi and the path of *paccekabuddhas*. Although in this story he could not follow this route to enlightenment, as he is the Bodhisatta, the character of his experiences here clearly aligns him with that path (see the introduction to Chapter 2; also Norman 1983, Norman 1991, and Shaw 2006a: 222–6).

2. See Shaw 2006a: 26–36 (Ja I 137–9). The *Nemi-jātaka* is in some ways only fully appreciated by knowing this famous, short *jātaka* which forms its precursor. Peter Skilling (2008: 136–8) discusses the story, some of its associated art, its relationship with the *Nemi-jātaka*, and some variations to the tale. For discussion of Nemi see also pp. 72 and 77. For the *sutta* on this subject see the *Makhādeva Sutta* (MN 83).

which he has taken rebirth during these aeons that the time has come for the lineage to reach its natural conclusion. When he takes rebirth again in the line as King Nemi, he too follows the tradition he has established. He enjoys the 'play' of youth for 84,000 years, acts as viceroy for 84,000, is a just and generous king in the Mahāsudassana mould of the Universal Monarch for another 84,000, and at the appearance of a grey hair, takes the going forth to enjoy the 'play' of meditation. But he is the last of the line to so do, for his son does not continue this tradition of renunciation. At the end of his life, Nemi enjoys, like all his predecessors, meditation, and is reborn in a Brahmā heaven, the rebirth of those that practice *jhāna*. So the tale comes full circle, with the progenitor of this line of renouncing kings also acting as its last. It is the memory of his happiness in meditation as Makhādeva—aeons and aeons of leisured time away—that elicits the Bodhisatta's smile.[3]

Within this framework however are set the incidents that occupy the bulk of the story and which have rendered it, with others of the *Mahānipāta*, such a popular subject for temple art. After making his monumental act of generosity in establishing the five halls within the city for the dispensation of alms, a defining act of all just kings within the *jātaka* worldview, King Nemi, at the height of his career, asks one question which excites the attention of Sakka, the lord of the Heaven of the Thirty-Three: 'Which is of the higher fruit: the holy life or the practice of generosity?' The lord of the heaven realm that is both attained and characterised by great acts of generosity descends to the human realm and appears in all his magnificence to visit Nemi. He listens to the question and gives an unequivocal reply. He cites great kings and warriors in the past who, despite continued donations, were reborn as ghosts, unable to rise even to a human rebirth. The fruit of the holy life, and all its attendant meditative skill, is far higher than that of generosity. He then sends Mātali, his charioteer, to escort Nemi in his carriage and act as his guide through a Dantesque vision of the hells and heavens, before entertaining him in his own heaven and

3. The ability to smile is an important aspect of the Buddhist path, and is here associated with the Buddha's recollection of his earlier life and joy within it. Wisdom is described sometimes as 'smile-producing' (Chapter 5; Ja VI 329). In one *sutta* the Buddha smiles for instance when some *devatās* come to apologise for their bad behaviour in SN I 24 (Bodhi 2000: 113). One short *sutta* warns against monks laughing out loud, or excessively, but says: 'When you smile rejoicing in the *dhamma*, you may simply show a smile.' See AN I 261, *Alaṃ vo dhammappamoditānaṃ sataṃ sitaṃ sitamattāya* (Bodhi 2012: 342). According to the *Avadānaśataka* the smile of a Buddha makes hot hells cool, and cold hells warm.

returning him back to the safety of Mithilā. The main portion of the tale describes his visits to the realms above and those below, where he is told the karma of those that have attained each state. The underlying message of the tale at first seems simple: those in the hells have behaved with various transgressions of the precepts and must face their karma there; those in the heavens enjoy great happiness and luxury through acts of generosity, supported by *sīla*, restraint, and observance of the *uposatha* days. The king's question at the beginning, however, presents even the good fortune of the sense-sphere heavens in a larger cosmological and psychological perspective, for the practice of generosity needs the balance of virtue, *sīla,* for the attainment of sense-sphere heavens. And even those realms, delightful and important though they be, are not the Bodhisatta's goal and are, within the terms of this narrative at any rate, seen as less useful either than the lay life spent working for others or the meditative life: they are rejected by Nemi when he returns to what he claims as the greater happiness of helping others from Sakka's heaven, and they do not entirely allow the far greater 'play' (*kīli*) and pleasures of the holy life, with a particular emphasis on the divine abidings of loving-kindness, compassion, sympathetic joy, and equanimity. These are all required for the Bodhisatta to have access to the vast meditative reserves necessary for the teaching of a full path in his final life, but they also seem associated with the ideal of a Universal Monarch, as radiating out naturally from the mind that turns to others—both to their sufferings, and to their happiness; as Sudassana, in the *suttas*, he practises the *jhānas* of the divine abidings too (DN 17).[4] The story reads, and must have seemed to those who listened to it, like a prolonged guided imaginative exercise. From the mandalic construction of the five alms halls, one at each of the gates of the four directions and one in the middle of the city, to the magnificently flashy and glamorous arrival of Sakka in his spectacular carriage, with his charioteer's neat line-in-reverse parking, to the stark visions of desperation and the sparkling palaces of paradisical contentment, all seen conjured up and then dissolved, to the final renunciation, the story seems almost cinematic in its unfolding, impelled by the momentum provided by Nemi's question. As an

4. These are objects 31–4 in Buddhaghosa's system of meditation. The divine abidings can be practised in daily life, or can be used as objects leading to meditation (*jhāna*). One of these four is supposed in the *Abhidhamma* to be present in all skilful consciousness (*Dhammasaṅgaṇī* 9 ff.; reading, for instance, *mettā* for *avyāpādo*, according to that text's method).

exploration of various dramatically different modes of existence, resolved by the final decision to adopt the meditative and homeless life, a number of issues are raised by this deceptively straightforward tale. A few of these are discussed here.

Which Is the Higher: Generosity or the Holy Life?

Of the stories so far, *Nemi-jātaka* is the first of the Great Ten that explores the active possibilities of kingship with strongly argued deliberation. *Jātakas* present monarchy and the role of authorised power within the state politic in a highly varied light. As was discussed in brief in the Introduction, in different stories a number of different types of kingship are explored and, as Steven Collins has demonstrated, various models of social coexistence and monarchy are posited through different imaginary realms and states.[5] In the last ten, where the Bodhisatta is so often in a courtly or regal rebirth, issues concerning the reconciliation of the exercise of secular power and Buddhist principle are dramatically embodied and debated, often in the older, verse portion of the narratives, suggesting that preoccupation with these themes dates from the earliest strata of the texts. In the *Temiya-jātaka* (Chapter 1) for instance, the Bodhisatta cannot perceive a means of reconciling kingship with an ethical code that that avoids karmic misfortune, and the story's finale involves a kind of *serio ludere* that enacts a Buddhist utopian and Arcadian state, with all the inhabitants living outside the city state, freed from all institutions involving the exercise of power and externally imposed law. Other stories where the benevolent aspects of monarchy are stressed, with the Bodhisatta reborn as a Universal Monarch who rules by *dhamma*, not force (J 9 and J 95), employ the notion of extended lifespans, idealised palaces, and a benign, just kingship as a means of depicting the possibilities of secular power within a thoroughly Buddhist framework. These models, which perhaps provided a paradigm for King Aśoka's radical reforms, integrate within their role as kings the exercise of secular authority with the possibility of the meditative practices more usually associated with the pursuit of the holy life, thus ensuring for the Bodhisatta in these tales rebirth not in a sense-sphere heaven, but in the restorative Brahmā realms of meditative peace. As was noted in the Introduction, the concept of the 'Universal Monarch' and his royalty-based politic indicate that the exercise of secular

5. See Collins 1998: 433 ff.

power can, according to the larger *jātaka* narrative, be reconciled with Buddhist principles for state and king.[6] Indeed in some stories, such as the *Mahāsudassana-jātaka* (J 95), this is not only possible but actively desirable, a paradigm for the beneficent exercise of power in any worldly pursuit and indeed in the operation of the mind itself.[7] For it is through the exercise of a leadership dedicated to service that the monarch completes his duties within the householder's life—the second stage of life in the traditional Indian system—and is then ready to pursue the last stages of such a life in meditative preparation, in line with the traditional last stages of the ideal existence, the forest dweller and then, finally, the *sannyāsin*.[8] The *Nemi-jātaka*, in which kingship is presented according to such a model, deepens an examination of the role in the last ten *jātakas* by its questioning of the status even of the traditional donations of the Universal Monarch and other acts of generosity, where they are unsupported by restraint and ethical behaviour. Although attributed to generosity in the *Jātaka-nidāna* and the *Cariyapiṭaka*, it is really offering a sharp critique of generosity where it occurs without the support of moral integrity and good action in the world.[9] It also however stresses that in the world of lay life it is possible to prepare for the practice of 'renunciation'. *Nekkhamma* is perceived here not just as taking the going forth, but as the freedom from sense desires, which allows a different kind of 'play'—that of the four *jhānas*, and an emotional purification that may ensue through meditation as the culmination of ethically pursued and generous secular authority.[10]

During the course of the story there are a number of indicators that the first perfection, generosity, while unchallenged as the foundation of Buddhist practice, is considered insufficient without balancing factors associated with the practice of *sīla*. The first shadow of doubt occurs in Nemi's question. At the height of his reign, after constructing the donation halls that identify him as a just king, an act employed in other *jātakas* as an emblem of a just monarch's rule (e.g. J 276), he experiences an intimation

6. See Introduction 11–18.

7. For this story (Ja I 391–3) and discussion see Shaw 2006a: 75–9.

8. A *sannyāsin* completely renounces all worldly and family ties. For a discussion of the *āśrama* system of life stages see Olivelle 1993.

9. For attributions, see Introduction, Table 2.

10. The words *jhānakīḷaṃ kīlanto*—playing with the play of meditation—are found in later works, referring to the lightness of touch needed to move flexibly from one meditation (*jhāna*) to another with ease (Shaw 2006a: 26 ff.).

that generosity is not enough, a problem that prompts him to ask the question. The second is the announcement by Sakka that there are generous warrior kings who take rebirth as ghosts (*petas*), and whose actions do not lead to a heavenly existence. That this declaration comes from Sakka, the king of the Heaven of the Thirty-Three, where beings are reborn on the basis of generosity as well as virtue, reinforces this sense of equivocation in this story about the status of this realm. Sakka, 'the giver of gifts in the past' (*purindado*), is an interesting figure in this regard. Despite his association with abundant donations, he also embodies a kind of common sense too: a characteristic feature of the Pāli *jātaka* collection is his skilled *prevention* of wildly unsuitable acts of generosity in the *jātakas*. In the *Sāsa-jātaka* he stops the hare from fulfilling a reckless wish to offer his own life to feed a wandering ascetic, keeping the animal unharmed by the fire it jumps into (J 316). In the *Vessantara-jātaka* he protects Maddī and Vessantara by asking for her, ensuring that the Bodhisatta's enthusiasm for giving does not allow his wife to fall into dishonour, should she be given to someone with other intentions (J 547). He also sometimes ensures the restoration within a being's lifespan of any destructive elements they might incur, as in returning King Sibi's sight for instance in the *jātaka* of that name (J 499).[11] This rather commonsensical perspective on offering provides a striking contrast to acts of generosity described in Sanskrit and Chinese versions of such stories, or in stories such as the famous hungry tigress *jātaka*, which, significantly, does not feature in the Pāli collection.[12] Conversely, when Temiya is reluctant to take rebirth in a royal family, because of the potentially hellish karmic consequences, it is Sakka who chivvies him along, so that he can benefit others and exercise the perfections fully (Chapter 1: 56). In Pāli tales a kind of benign protective force, enacted through Sakka, runs like a thread through the stories. So Sakka occupies an important and often unrecognized role in *jātaka* causality, as a protector of lay and ascetic happiness and a reminder of innate balance and *sīla*, interceding not only to save the Bodhisatta on a number of occasions from his own passionate commitment to giving but also to remind him of his path.[13]

11. See Ja III 51–6; Shaw 2006a: 114–21; and Khoroche 1989: 37–45. Treatments of Sibi/Śibi display more similarities between the two versions: see J 499, Ja IV 401–12 and Khoroche 1989: story 2.

12. See Khoroche 1989: xviii.

13. The Bodhisatta is actually born as Sakka in one *jātaka* (J 450) on the basis of his great generosity as a merchant.

As we shall see in the visits to the heavens, the various divine habitations are filled with the generous, though it is pointed out they are all virtuous too. When Nemi visits the heaven realm himself, he enjoys the discussion and sense pleasures but is anxious to return 'home' to his proper domain, the human realm; he does not want to stay in the heaven realm, though invited to do so, as he will be dependent on the gods' generosity, separated from his proper realm and unable to fulfil his particular duties.[14] Generosity and hospitality, though essential as a basis of a practitioner's life, are in this instance limiting for the recipient too if they prevent freedom of movement and autonomy within one's rightful domain. Giving is undoubtedly being presented as the foundation of the lay and the holy life. It leads—along with virtue, faith, and investigation of *dhamma*—to heavenly rebirths in sense-sphere heavens. In this story, however, its potential shortcomings where there is not a corresponding restraint of body and mind are examined with some care; as with so many of the narratives in the last ten stories, modifying factors necessary to fulfil particular perfections are dramatically and painstakingly explored.

Association with Perfections

The story is associated with different perfections by the various traditions. The *Cariyāpiṭaka* and the *Jātaka-nidāna*, the introduction to the *jātaka*s, link it to the perfection of generosity; the *Cariyāpiṭaka* cites the construction of the almshouses as an instance.[15] While not unjustified, this association is rather puzzling, perhaps missing some of the subtlety and point of the tale. As an attribution, however, it does highlight the fact that the practice of giving, while subjected to much scrutiny within the narrative, is nonetheless depicted as the foundation both of the king's duty and of the Buddhist path in general: Nemi is not only generous himself but also encourages his people in the finale to be so too. The answer to his question, however, of whether generosity or the holy life is better, is that the holy life is superior, and that, by implication, the perfection of *nekkhamma* is celebrated in the tale. This would certainly accord with the later commentarial tradition that

14. In the *Campeyya-jātaka* a comparable wish is expressed by the king who visits the Bodhisatta in a *nāga* realm, for 'only in the realm of humans is restraint possible' (see J 506; Ja IV 467; Shaw 2006a: 174). While the Heaven of the Thirty-Three Gods does offer the possibility of restraint, as always in the *jātaka* literature the realm of humans is perceived as the most fertile place for its continued practice.

15. See Introduction 4–6 and *Cariyāpiṭaka* I 6.

perceives each perfection as superior, in ascending order, to those that precede it: equanimity is described as the highest perfection for instance and generosity a necessary, but lesser, basis for the others.[16] Indeed the theme of renunciation informs the tale: the motif of the barber who finds the grey hair, the renunciate background of the kings, and the comments in the concluding lines of the tale describing it as an example of the Great Renunciation, align it as well with the *Makhādeva-jātaka* (J 9), an earlier story usually linked by most traditions, and by its own story in the present, to *nekkhamma.* The conclusion supports this: at the end of the tale Nemi rejects the lay path of generosity for the higher path of the holy life. It is worth noting in this context that the word *nekkhamma* operates, like many other Buddhist terms, on a literal and a metaphoric level. It refers literally to the 'letting go' of leaving the household life. It is also frequently associated with the renunciation of sense pleasures (*kāmā*) for the practice of meditation.[17] Meditation, associated with the Brahmā realms, encloses the lives of the great kings of which Nemi is the last: within the tale, Brahmā heavens are described as constituting the precursor of some of these kings' rebirths, and their destination after practising the *samatha* meditations as a culmination of their lives. In a nice circular movement that echoes his name, Nemi takes the course of action favoured by his forefathers, and Makhādeva, his earlier incarnation and the first of this royal house. Thus the theme of renunciation, and the repetitive way it wheels through this succession of just kings, provides an underlying background to the tale. That even such auspiciousness may indeed be impermanent, however, is emphasised by the final breaking of the familial line of renunciates by the son.

Yet another dimension to the tale is supplied by the usual Southeast Asian attribution of the tales to the perfection of resolve (*adhiṭṭhāna*). Presumably this is a reference to Nemi's decision to act as a just king, his decisiveness in returning to the human realm to teach his subjects after his visit to the heavens, and his determination to forfeit the monarchy for the renunciate life as a culmination of his reign and line. Multiple attributions, of course, do not necessarily denote confusion; rather, they indicate the many levels of meaning that distinguish this complex tale.

16. See Dhammapāla's commentary on the ten perfections in Bodhi 1978: 244–8. While generosity is certainly the theme of the last story of the Great Ten, the commentary on the perfections, as opposed to the stories, sees them as working in ascending order to the last as highest.

17. See Bodhi 1978: 245 and Introduction 17, and note 16.

They also, perhaps, provide some sense of the inextricably linked nature of the perfections when enacted within a dramatic narrative and in a practitioner's personal path.

Hells

When Nemi addresses his subjects he encourages them with the promise of heaven and frightens them with the threat of hell. For many from non-Buddhist cultures, these descriptions inevitably raise associations with the depictions of the underworlds, shades, nether regions, and hells of primary and secondary epic literature within a Western context. It is worth exploring these resemblances a little as a means of highlighting both affinities and differences between the early Buddhist worldview and classical Graeco-Roman and Christian depictions of comparable realms.[18]

Like Dante in *The Divine Comedy* (*Divina Commedia*, 1308–21) it is the hells that we visit first. Indeed from the variety of Western models of the underworlds, it is the hells of Dante's late mediaeval Christian adaptation of classical material, in the *Inferno*, which seem to have the most notable affinities with the realms of early Buddhism. These, though in texts composed at least fifteen hundred years before, perhaps also in part represent an attempt to reconcile pre-existing notions of lower rebirths with a new emergent cosmology arising from the integration of a number of systems. In the case of Dante's time, this integration would be shaped by his awareness of the need to include Graeco-Roman, early Middle Eastern, and various Christian elements, and indeed appropriate historical characters, in descriptions of the various levels. Composers of early Buddhist texts would also be exploring the cosmological implications of the Buddhist position on the nature of volition (*cetanā*), for instance, in the light of traditional Indian soteriology, and allowing this perspective to inform the character and style of subsequent rebirths. In the *Nemi-jātaka*, mention too is made of supposedly 'historical' and mythical characters, whose famous actions

18. A more obviously structured array of hells than in this story is presented in the perhaps rather late *Devadūta Sutta* (MN 130). See, for discussion of this, Silabhadra 2000: 73–81. For some analogous visits to heavens and hells, see the underworld of book VI in Virgil's *Aeneid* and book XI of Homer's *Odyssey*, as well as Dante's *Inferno* and *Paradiso*. See also for British secondary epic 'underworlds', Spenser's *Faerie Queene* (1590–6), book II, canto VII, and the hell scenes in Book I of Milton's *Paradise Lost* (1667). Milton's paradise before the fall is shown in book IV (Williams 1946: 113–60, 181–206). For another *jātaka* account of the hells, see Nārada's warnings in Chapter 8, vv. 153–72.

have brought them to a lower realm; so the collective 'history' and identity of early Buddhists is ordered and reinterpreted according to the terms of a new cosmological ranking.

Both realms are highly systematised: Dante's by the circles of hell and the early Buddhist by various descriptions of the length, extent, and lifespans of the beings they contain. Both appear to have a geographical location. When Dante visits the nether regions with his guide, Virgil, he finds a number of circles of hell precisely and vividly explained as geographically defined areas, with the punishments aptly fitting the crimes of those that he finds there. The space, architectured by a creator god, is carefully organised into a hierarchy of crime and corresponding result. Nemi's vision, like the *Inferno* and other Western visions of a dark underworld such as *Paradise Lost* (1667) and the underworld of the *Aeneid*, is located 'beneath' or 'down below'. It is also, like Dante's infernal regions a lonely realm, devoid of light, loud with screams and full of pain. The arrangement of the Buddhist lower realms within an organised and hierarchical space is also comparable to subsequent Christian models (though little sense of this is communicated in the *Nemi-jātaka*), in which each hell appears dissociated and remote, a world within itself. The realms in early Buddhism are not the product of design: they appear to inhere as a byproduct of and a symptom of the 'beginningless' round of existence. Yet while Nemi does not find such interconnected spatial precision in the ordering of the sections of hell in this tale, the similarities are striking. Beings are condemned to hells for crimes comparable to those found in the *Inferno*; these also involve transgressions of basic human courtesy and respect for other beings that in most Buddhist and Christian contexts would be acknowledged as wrong. They also often have the unhappy aptness of the punishments of Dante's circles of hell.

As in the *Inferno*, Milton's *Paradise Lost* (1667), and the classical underworlds of Homer and Virgil, entrance to the realms beneath are designated by a river, perhaps symbolic of the process of death, or of the endless flow of suffering involved in the kinds of behaviour which lead in this instance to a descent and an unfortunate rebirth. Vetaraṇī however has attributes that it shares not so much with Acheron, the Classical river that leads to the underworld, but with Phlegethon, the steaming hot river of Greek mythology and Dante's hells, reserved for those who are enraged. Its depiction is also reminiscent of Milton's description of this terrible torrent: it too is hot, caustic, and without stillness or flow, like 'fierce Phlegethon, / Whose waves of torrent fire inflame with rage' (*Paradise Lost* II, line 580).

Odysseus takes his ship and fulfils special rituals to engage with beings from the underworld; Nemi makes his tour protected in his heavenly carriage or chariot. Like Dante, or the narrator of the *Inferno*, he is accompanied by a guide, a *psychopomp*, who explains, leads, and crucially, ensures his safe return. Unlike Dante, who speaks to some of the beings of lower realms, Nemi has no contact with the inhabitants of the hells or heavens until he reaches the Heaven of the Thirty-Three Gods, where he receives an appreciative welcome, steps out of the protective vehicle, and is able to converse freely with the gods on their own terms.

There are other crucial differences from Christian and classical counterparts. Nemi, protected in his divine carriage, has no interaction at all with the beings that inhabit the hells: Mātali 'shows' heaven and hells, but can also 'make them disappear' (Ja VI 106, *antaradhāpetvā*). They seem like nightmarish visions, which frighten but do not have any direct relationship with the visitor. In this important regard it is unlike the *Inferno* where Dante, with Virgil's intercession, does interact with beings of the lesser hells. Despite this Nemi is filled with fear and dread at each vision. Repetition, a feature of oral literature in general and Buddhist texts in particular that so often troubles translators, is here used to devastating effect: there is an almost incantatory quality to Nemi's repeated, grammatically simple refrain of horror at what he sees, and his desperate questioning of his guide about the actions of those that suffer such torments. This reinforces the sense of time as excruciatingly long. Nemi, it is said, would die before he could see all the hells, and finally, needs to be shown them at a stroke so that he can leave; their fascination and gravitational pull is here implicit in their endless time scheme and their apparently infinite diversity and extent.

Some affinities with Western underworld visions are worth noting. Sin is sometimes defined in a Christian context as separation, both from the union with God and from other beings.[19] Separation from happiness and contentment and any communion with others are also features of the hells of the Buddhist *jātaka*. There is not even a Dis or Pandemonium to function as a city of the dead; these hells seem deprived even of that sense of company. There are also, interestingly, no cold hells, as in Dante's third circle, though they feature in other Buddhist texts. There are no hells

19. I am grateful to Professor Keith Ward, sometime Canon of Christ Church, Oxford, for seminars I attended about this and some other resonances between Buddhism and Christianity.

specifically for gluttons, or the vain. The main culprits, as in Dante's vision, are those that practise fraud, deceit, disloyalty, or who are arrogant: crimes that are particularly reprehensible as they cause unhappiness to others. Considerable emphasis is also placed on straightforward physical cruelty: those that harm and maim animals are themselves harmed and maimed, in a peculiarly apt fashion.

While the realms are considered ontologically extant, there is an implication, in the way they are evoked for Nemi, that they are mind-made too, extrapolations of mental states that have brought such vitiated and unfortunate karma. As for Dante's *Inferno*, Milton's *Paradise Lost*, or, to some extent, other underworld voyages, it is perhaps in this sense, as a mirror of the mind, that the modern reader will understand these regions, reflecting Satan's sentiment in *Paradise Lost*: 'Which way I fly is Hell; myself am Hell' (*Paradise Lost*, IV, line 75). The experience of what one drinks turning to chaff or to excrement sums up the sense of the hells as a wrong apprehension or way of viewing the world and other beings: wrong view, the transgression that leads to the last hell shown to Nemi, distorts through being associated not just with an insistence on eternalism or annihilationism but with a lack of loving-kindness and compassion, important accompaniments to right intention (*sammāsaṇkappo*; see *Dhammasaṅgaṇī* 12).[20] In traditional classical and Christian depictions of various realms and, in a modern context, in visions of utopias and dystopian worlds, a repertoire of demonic and paradisical imagery suggests different modes of existence.[21] Buddhist depictions of realms seem to act not only as warnings and admonitions, or inspiring forms of encouragement, but as ways of understanding the present moment. With wrong view, perception is said to become tainted; there is darkness, regret, pain, and lamentation, and in this life no joy in what is tasted can be found. One important feature, however, distinguishes

20. See *Atthasālinī* 142–3. According to traditional *abhidhamma*, the first two path factors of right view and right intention only arise in skilful consciousness, accompanied by one of the divine abidings of loving-kindness, compassion, sympathetic joy, or equanimity.

21. For a late canonical work on the Heavens of the Thirty-Three, see Masefield 1989. The heavens feature *topoi* found in Western depictions of paradise as well as in recent utopian fiction. See Thompson 1955–8: 'other world journeys' (F0–199), including, 'Objects of crystal in other world' (F162.0.1); 'house of gold and crystal in other world' (F163.3.1); 'Golden castle in other world' (F163.1.2); 'Pillars of silver and glass in other world' (F169.1); 'walls of crystal in other world' (F169.2); and related entries.

the hells of the West and those of Buddhism: even a rebirth in one of the lowest realms, with its apparently limitless lifespans, is impermanent.

Heavenly Cities

The heavens form something of a relief after the hells, and they present us with a picture of the kind of circumstances that would seem ideal to an ancient Indian. While again Nemi has no interchange with the inhabitants, it is clear that they are thoroughly enjoying the circumstances and interactions with each other. These rebirths are not isolated or in any way uncomfortable; beings have their own personal space yet are surrounded by other heavenly beings with whom they can happily communicate. All the enjoyment of the senses is suggested: the sounds of bells and musical instruments, the smell of perfumed flowers and bushes, the sight of bright shining colours that includes too a sense of light, and even tastes in the endless supply of delicious food and drink. An underlying sense of ease, physical comfort, and flow animates each realm. The heavens employ both paradisical imagery of the kind found within Buddhism in the *Mahāsudassana Sutta* (DN 17), the *Sukhāvativyūha-sūtra*, and the variations of the Pure Land, involving gold, silver, crystal bells of many kinds, and magical trees, as well as images suggestive of the abundance and beauty of the natural world, such as the fountains, verdant bushes, simple and common yet beautiful flowers, and food.[22] The whole invites the visualising area of the mind, with movement and change not bound and confined within a painful repetitiveness but enacted through also repetitive but fluidly enjoyable images of delight that suggest the continuity of airiness, freedom, and space. While any sign of impermanence is, unfortunately, stiflingly lacking in evidence in the apparently endless and constantly renewed sufferings of the hells, in the heaven realms it seems joyfully evident, animating both the natural and the paradisical, crystalline imagery with movement, refreshment, and a restorative sense of repetitive peacefulness, as an enactment, or skilful result (*kusala vipāka*), of the skilful consciousness (*kusala citta*) which prompted each inhabitant.

> 'He reveals to me this celestial mansion, beautifully constructed
>   from crystal,
> Brilliant with turrets and crowded with excellent nymphs. (115)

22. See Gomez 1996 and Müller and Nanjio 1883.

It is furnished with food and drinks, and filled with both dance and song.
Rivers endowed with many flowers and trees encircle it. (116)
A royal realm of abundant mango trees, rose-apple, *tinduka* trees,
Piyāla, and trees that perpetually bear fruit: (117)
I am possessed by happiness, charioteer, to see this.
I ask you, Mātali, charioteer of the gods:
What good has this mortal done,
Who rejoices on reaching heaven in a flying palace?' (118)
Asked, Mātali, charioteer of the gods, knowing,
Explained to one who did not know, the fruit of meritorious deeds. (119)
'This man was a householder who was a generous host in his house in Mithilā,
Who respectfully provided groves, wells, drinking places, and canals. (120)
He was virtuous, a lay disciple, and respectfully provided groves, wells,
Drinking places, and canals to *arahats*, whose minds had become cooled; (121)
And gave with clear mind robes, food, support [in sickness]
And beds to those who lived in straightness;
On the fourteenth, the fifteenth, the eighth day of the fortnight,
And on special holidays too, he was good at keeping the eight precepts: (122)
He kept the *uposatha* and always restrained in behaviour:
Through his discernment and generosity he takes delight in a palace.' (123)

The beings who inhabit these realms have, within the worldview of early Buddhism, in effect created them for themselves. Rebirth in these heavens is on the basis of skilful volition (*cetanā*) translated into generous actions performed on the basis of a life of restraint: according to the doctrines of early Buddhism such activities, by their nature, create in time resultant realms around the practitioners that accord with such behaviour. Despite this, the world of humans is still, from Nemi's point of view, pre-eminent:

I'll go amongst men and I'll do a great deal of good,

By generosity, living calmly with restraint and control.
The one who does this is happy; he has no regrets. (165)

Time and Repetition

The time schemes in this, as in every story that involves a heaven realm or the human realm at a mythical time when human beings had very long lifespans, are vast.[23] Time schemes in ancient India are spectacularly long. According to the introduction to the *jātakas*, human beings live only for quite a short period of time—between 100 and 84,000 years. King Nemi however is said to have lived to four times eighty-four thousand years: as a youth, as a king, and in the practice of the meditations. If we multiply this by 84,000, the total number of kings involved, we get a number in the region of seven billion years.[24] This is quite a good line of kings! A *kalpa*, or aeon, the length of time this world system is said to last, is the lifespan of those born in the highest realm of the first meditation, that of Great Brahmā: the other two heavens in that level have lifespans of one-third and half an aeon. Buddhist scholars, and indeed many practitioners, now generally accept that there is an equivalence operating between meditational state and cosmological description: just as those in the sense-sphere heavens experience a rebirth in accordance with the practitioner's mind and inclinations, so the deeply peaceful Brahmā heavens, where beings have 'bodies' that fill a universe and experience only the senses of sight and sound, seem enactments of mental states produced by *jhāna* (meditation).[25] Indeed the idea that one is actually *in* a Brahmā realm when practising the meditation on loving-kindness can be found in the *Mettā Sutta*: concerning *brahmam etam vihāram idha-m-ahu* Norman (1995: 177) writes, 'it would be possible to translate as "They say this realm is Brahmā"'. The sense of aeons of time passing in such realms is also an expression of this sense of extended meditative bliss.

Repetition is constantly exploited within this tale, emphasising a sense of cycles within cycles. The endless sorry varieties of hell are sustained by the terrible repetition of Nemi's alarm at each stage. Similarly heavens go on forever; the fruits of happiness seem to involve lengthy experiences of time, with the variety of pleasant rebirths unified by the repetitive

23. For the physical extents and lifespans of some heaven realms see Vsm VII 40–4 and XIII 29–65; and *Abhidhammattha Saṅgaha* 22–4. See also table 2 in Gethin 1998: 116–7.

24. Jones 1979: 190 puts it at 7,056,000,000 years.

25. See for instance Collins 1998: 297–309; Gethin 1998: 118–24; Harvey 2013: 350.

structural template of the description of a character, his environment, and his fortunate karma that has produced that rebirth. But through the offices of Sakka and Mātali, impermanence is built into the story too: it is said that the hells are draining Nemi's life away; there is no end of viewing them, so he views them all 'in an instant' before being taken to the heavens. Nimi's stay in the heavens is also completed with comparable rapidity, and again when he simply expresses the wish to return to his own domain and is returned quickly to his own palace. The culmination of the story is the end of the family line of renunciates, the law of impermanence severing even the auspiciously repetitive cycle that underlies the whole of the plot. This wheel-like structure is constantly reflected in the story, for the Buddha starts his recollection with the assertion that the tale is about the great renunciation, undertaken first by Makhādeva, but not until the end of the tale by Nemi. This story constitutes a sustained exploration of the nature of cycles within cycles and experiential time: it seems to exist enclosed within the time schemes of the Brahmā heavens, embodying the aeons of meditative bliss. The very short story in the present, in which a smile is evoked by recollections of events 84,000 times 84,000 years ago, gives us in this instance a key to the tale: it is the play of meditation which is higher even than the heavens described as the destinations of the generous. It is as a householder, or layman, that Nemi sees the heavens and experiences the sense pleasures there; at the end it is as a recluse that he takes the decision to prepare in meditation for his final life.

Ritual

In reading this and other stories involving beings taking rebirth and inhabiting other realms, it is important to consider the ritual context in which the stories were probably told at the time, and where, in Southeast Asia, they are often recounted now. This would be at an *uposatha* day festival at a temple or within some other festive context, in either a private residence or a public space. A story exploring the merits of such activities and describing the heavens that will result from such offerings, combined with restraint, would then be particularly powerful. Equally effective would be the caveat that generosity without accompanying self-restraint does *not* necessarily produce a heavenly rebirth, and the various injunctions concerning the 'higher' perfection of *nekkhamma,* associated with the practice of meditation. Whether the tale is interpreted as a *psychomachia* or a literal 'visit' to other realms, investigation of these themes would be occurring in a context where they would be particularly resonant. Another important background element would also be the ritual acknowledgement and associated attitude such festivals promote towards other beings, both 'seen and unseen, those dwelling far and near', in the words of the *Mettā Sutta* (*Suttanipāta*, v. 147). In this *sutta* the suffusion of loving-kindness is enjoined to all beings, in all of the compass directions, as well as above and below, as the practitioner then extends this quality to fill both heavens and hells. The verses of *anumodanā*, the transference of merit, formally transfer the merit of such festive undertakings to all beings around, including *devas* (the happy beings described in this *sutta*), the more generalised 'living beings', and finally *bhūta*, or ghosts (of the kind described at the beginning of this narrative by Sakka), who might have practised generosity but have not exercised restraint and so take a form where they are unhappy and lacking in solid substance. Water that has been blessed by the chanting is poured into a bowl as the merit is transferred to the dead and other beings through the chanting of these verses. Some festive days are explicitly dedicated to the transference of merit to deceased family members who may have taken unhappy rebirths. Such rituals place those listening to this narrative, and hence participating in a larger ritual, in a particularly active and potentially compassionate relationship to the beings inhabiting lower and higher realms—maybe those described in the story. The tale is recited in a performative context, where help is offered and blessings invoked and shared with the highly various universe both 'above' and 'below' that surrounds any one human being. According to Buddhist doctrine all can be aided, and receive merit for future rebirths, by the ritual the practitioner is conducting.

Art

Wat Suwannaram (north wall, 1830) in Thonburi, Thailand, contains several scenes from this story. In the Heaven of the Thirty-Three, Sakka's heaven, some gods listen to *dhamma* discussion; others just have fun, in accordance with the spirit of this gregarious and fun-loving realm. Other temples where the *Nemi-jātaka* is depicted are those where all the last ten are shown, such as Wat Chong Nonsi in Bangkok, Wat Yai Intharam in Chonburi, and Wat Pumin in Nan. In Sri Lanka it features amongst the last ten at the Northern Temple in Polonnaruwa, which dates from the twelfth century, and at the eighteenth-century Medawela temple in Kandy. Gory details abound in the visions of the hells depicted in Buddhist temples. Not necessarily associated specifically with the *Nemi-jātaka*, they can be grotesque in the extreme, with the bodies shown bound and cramped, with a sense of distortion and sexual perversion; those beings who have practised restraint and kept the precepts (*sīla*) experience a kind of ease of body and mind suggested by the grace and relaxed beauty of the *devas* in temple art.[26] The literary and artistic heritage of Nemi may be seen in the fourteenth-century Siamese work by King Lithai of Sukothai, *Traiphum Phra Ruang* (Three Worlds). The story has also exercised influence in the popularly depicted legend of Phra Malai, an *arahat* whom Sakka also shows the heavens and hells, perhaps the most popular figure in Siamese nineteenth-century temple and manuscript art. While these works do not supersede the *Nemi-jātaka* they incorporate many elements that are found in it.[27]

'It is a wonderful thing that in the world...'

[95] The Teacher told this story while living in Makhādeva's mango grove next to Mithilā, taking as a starting point the making of a smile. One day the Teacher was taking a walk with a large number of monks in the mango grove when he saw a delightful piece of ground. Wishing to recount an earlier life of his, he let a smile appear. Asked by the Venerable Ānanda the reason for this, he said, 'Ānanda, this piece of ground was once somewhere I used to live, in the time of King Makhādeva, where I used to delight in the play of the meditations.' When invited, he sat down in a seat that had been laid out and narrated a story of long ago.[28]

In times past, in the city of Mithilā in the kingdom of Videha, there was a king called Makhādeva. For eighty-four thousand years he delighted in youthful play, for eighty-four thousand years he held the viceroyship, and for eighty-four thousand years the kingdom. Then he said, 'Good barber,

26. For a generic depiction of those suffering in the deepest hells, see for instance Van Beek and Tettoni 1991: 186 (Wat Suthat, Bangkok).

27. For visual representations connected to these, see Ginsburg 1989: 13–21 (*Traiphum*) and 72–88 (Phra Malai); Leksukhum and Mermet 2001: 128–31 (*Traiphum*).

28. This story was translated by Rouse, according to his preface to the translation, after Cowell's death. It was also translated in part by Caroline Rhys Davids, who omits most of the verses (Rhys Davids 1929: 221–39).

when you see some grey hairs on my head, then let me know.' Some time later the barber did see some grey hairs and the king was informed. He had him pull them out with tweezers, got him to put them in his hand and considered them. It was as if he were looking at death sticking on to his forehead. [96] 'It is time for me to become an ascetic,' he said. He gave the boon of a village to the barber, and had his eldest son summoned. 'Son, accept my kingdom. I am going to become an ascetic.'

'What is the reason for this, sire?' he asked.

> 'These messengers from the gods have appeared and grown on my head.
> Taking away the prime of my life: It is the time for me to become an ascetic.'

After he had said this he anointed him in the kingship and, giving him advice, told him, 'You should proceed in this and that way.' Then he left the city and became an ascetic as a mendicant, cultivated the four divine abidings for eighty-four thousand years, and took rebirth in the Brahmā world. His son also became an ascetic in the same way and was one who was bound for the Brahmā sphere. And then his son, and so there were eighty-four thousand, less two, warriors who saw a grey hair on the head, went forth into this mango grove, cultivated the four divine abidings and took rebirth in the Brahmā world. The first of all of them who took rebirth in the Brahmā realm, King Makhādeva, remained there, took a look at his own lineage and saw that eighty-four thousand, minus two, had gone forth. He was delighted in his heart. 'Will it continue or will it not?' When he looked he saw that it was not going to continue. 'It is I who will make my lineage fixed.' So falling away from there he took rebirth in the womb of the chief wife of the king of the city of Mithilā.[29] On his naming day the seers read the marks on his body and said, 'Great King, this prince has been born to consolidate your lineage. Your family, which is a line of renunciation, will not go beyond this one.' When he heard this the king said, 'This child will consolidate the family like the felly on the wheel of a carriage.' So he gave him the name Prince Nemi (Hoop).[30] From the time of his youth he took

29. The word *cavitvā*, literally 'falling away', is the term used to describe death in a heavenly realm. The gods get little notice that their heavenly sojourn is about to finish.

30. This is the one place in the F edition where the word Nemi, or the rim of the wheel, occurs for Nimi. It appears sometimes with the words old age and death (*jarāmaraṇa*) to denote the rim of the wheel of existence (Vsm 198; *Dhammapada-aṭṭhakathā* II 124; *Vimānavatthu-aṭṭhakathā* 277; see PED 377) .

great pleasure in generosity, in virtue, and in observing the *uposatha* days. Then his father in the same way as before saw a grey hair, gave the boon of a village to his barber and handed on the kingdom to his son. He then went forth into the mango grove and was destined for a Brahmā realm. King Nemi, in his devotion to generosity, had five halls for giving food set up at the four gates of the city, with one in the middle, and [97] performed a great act of generosity. In each hall he distributed a hundred thousand coins—five hundred on each day. He guarded his virtue continually, kept the *uposatha* day each fortnight, and saw that the people practised generosity and suchlike and did auspicious things. He taught the *dhamma* to them by showing them the path to heaven and frightening them with fear of hell. On his instructions they were established in acts of generosity and suchlike and auspicious deeds, and as each in turn died they were reborn in a heaven realm, so that heaven was full and hell was virtually empty. At that time in the Heaven of the Thirty-Three an assembly of gods met together in Sudhammā, the gods' meeting place. 'Ah! Our teacher King Nemi! Because of him we experience a divine happiness that is boundless!' So saying they praised the excellencies of the Great Being. In the world of men also their paean of his virtues spread, like oil poured over the surface of the ocean.

The Teacher explained the meaning and said this to the monks:

It is a wonderful thing that in the world arose attentive people
At the time of King Nemi, the wise one, the one who wishes for
goodness![31] (1)
The king of all the Videhans, the conqueror of his enemies,
Made a great act of generosity.
And when he had given the donation the thought arose in him:
'Which has the greater fruit—generosity or the holy life?' (2)

At that moment Sakka's dwelling appeared hot, and Sakka reflected upon the reason for this.[32] He saw Nemi there, pondering, and said, 'I'll cut through his doubt.' [98] Alone, he quickly descended and filled the

31. As Caroline Rhys Davids observed, 'good is a stodgy word' (Rhys Davids 1929: xxiii), but 'good' has to be the translation here. As Damien Keown points out, no boy scout ever tried to do a 'skilful' or a 'healthy' deed. For this and other considerations of the word *kusala* and its associations with health, skilfulness, and wisdom, see Keown 1992: 119–20; Harvey 2000: 42 ff.; and Cousins 1996.

32. Sakka discovering the kindness or generosity of humans and animals by the curious device that his throne becomes hot when some great act of worth is about to happen is a frequent occurrence in *jātaka* literature. In verses, he is sometimes addressed as Maghavā or Vāsava (see DPPN).

entire dwelling with a single light. Then he entered the royal chamber and, standing in the air, suffused radiance. When asked, he explained this.

The Teacher made the meaning of this clear:

Maghavā, with a thousand eyes, the elephant king, perceived Nemi's thought and
Appeared before him in his glory, dispelling darkness. (3)

With his hair standing on end, Nemi, the king of men, spoke to Vāsava:

'Is this a god, a divine being indeed, Sakka, a giver of gifts in the past?
I have never seen anyone of such an appearance, nor heard such a being!' (4)

Vāsava, seeing Nemi with his hair standing on end, spoke:

'I am Sakka, lord of the gods; I have come to you.
Do not be frightened, lord of men, and put to me any question you wish.' (5)

Nemi, at this invitation, spoke to Vāsava:

'Lord of all beings, most powerful, I ask this:
Which is of the greater fruit—generosity or the holy life?' (6)
As he was asked by a god amongst men, Vāsava spoke to Nemi.
He, knowing, told the fruit of the holy life to one who did not know: (7)
'By the practice of the holy life in the lesser way, he is reborn as a warrior;
In the middling, the state of a shining god, a *deva*,
And in the highest, he is purified. (8)
These bodies are not easy to obtain by generosity alone:
The bodies in which homeless ascetics are reborn.'[33] (9)

[99] With this verse he made clear that the greater fruit was indeed for the one who lived the holy life, for there were those in the past who made great acts of generosity and could not pass beyond the sense sphere. He explained this to the king by saying:

'Dudīpa, Sāgara, Sela, Mucalinda, Bhagīrasa,
Usīnara, Aṭṭhaka, Assaka, and Puthujjana: (10)
These are the warrior and priest kings who have made sacrifices

33. The commentary explains that abstaining from the pleasures of sexual intercourse is the lesser, proximity to the meditation the middling, and the eight meditations themselves the higher; some mistakenly call these last states *nibbāna*. For a Buddhist—which Sakka at this time probably was not, for there is usually no Buddha in the 'time' of the *jātakas*—the lesser way is the holy life, the middling the eight meditations, and the attainment of arahatship, enlightenment, the highest. The point being made is that arahatship is only possible when there is a Buddha's teaching.

And could not rise above the Realm of Ghosts.'[34] (11)

Showing in this way that the fruit of the holy life was greater than that of generosity, he cited those ascetics who, by living the holy life, did pass beyond the Realm of Ghosts and were headed for the Brahmā sphere:

'These homeless ascetics certainly went beyond:
The seven sages Yāmahanu, Somayāga, Manojava, (12)
Samudda, Māgha, Bharata, and the seer Kālikarakkhiya,
As well as Aṅgīrasa, Kassapa, Kisavaccha, and Akitti.' (13)

[100] In this way, going by what he had heard in the tradition, he extolled the great fruit of the holy life and then went on to relate what he had seen for himself in the past:

'In the north the river Sink is deep and hard to cross;
Golden mountains shine continually with the appearance of a fire of reeds. (14)
There are long-grown grasses, fragrant *tagara* shrubs, and forests of tall bulrushes,
And in the past there were ten thousand sages there. (15)
I am noble, by generosity, by restraint, and by training, having made the highest vow;
I gave up society and dwelt supporting those with concentrated minds.[35] (16)
I will pay homage to the man who is upright, whether of high or low birth:
For every mortal is the kinsman of his *kamma*. (17)
All castes who do not follow *dhamma* fall to hell below.
All castes who practise the highest *dhamma* are purified.'[36] (18)

[102] When Sakka had said this, he added, 'Great King, although the holy life is of greater fruit than generosity, they are both the intentions of

34. The *Peta* realm, of ghosts, is one of the four descents, lower than the world of humans; it is surprising that beings are said to be reborn in these even though they have been generous. The commentary explains that this is because of the matter of their defilements (*kilesavatthussa*). In this and in following verses so many lists of proper names are featured that it is not possible to explore their background; it would require a complete critical edition. Some appear in other texts but many are of people or beings not described elsewhere. Dante, or the narrator of the *Inferno*, is also surprised to find people he did not think of as particularly bad in the unhappy regions (*Inferno*, canto III).

35. The text here seems corrupt, as if there is a lacuna, with a few lines missed out altogether.

36. Ja VI 100–1 gives an explanation of vv. 14–18, and a long commentarial story.

a great man.[37] So be careful in both; be generous and guard your virtue.' With this advice, he went back to his own realm. The Teacher then spoke explaining the matter:

> Saying this, Maghavā, king of the gods, Sujampati,[38]
> Gave instruction to the Videhan and went off in a divine body. (19)

And then the assembly of shining gods said, 'Great King, we have not seen you! Where have you been?'

'Sirs, a doubt arose for King Nemi in Mithilā. I went to free him from doubt after he had told me his question.' When he had said this he explained the reason for this in verse:

> 'Sirs, as many as are assembled here, attend to the eulogy,
> Various and abundant, of men who are just! (20)
> As this King Nemi, king of all the Videhans, conqueror of enemies,
> Was wise and wishing for goodness, he made an act of generosity. (21)
> And as he gave his gifts this thought arose:
> "Which has the greater fruit—generosity or the holy life?"' (22)

[103] He gave a paean about the king, without leaving anything out. When they heard this the gods were anxious to see the king and spoke, 'Great King, King Nemi is our teacher. By following his advice and through his support we have obtained this divine bliss. We want to see him! Send for him and show him to us, Great King!' Sakka agreed and ordered Mātali to come. 'Good Mātali, have the chariot Vejayanta made ready. Go to Mithilā and get King Nemi to ascend on to the divine vehicle!'[39] He agreed, had the carriage prepared, and set out. And while Sakka was talking with the gods, giving orders to Mātali, and having the chariot prepared, a month, according to human reckoning, had passed. It was the day of the full moon, and King Nemi had opened the eastern window and was sitting on the upper floor, surrounded by his courtiers and reviewing his own virtue.[40]

37. A great man (*mahāpurisa*), is one who will become either a Universal Monarch or a Buddha; see *Lakkhaṇa Sutta* (DN 30).

38. This is an alternative name for Sakka, and comes from his marriage to a woman named Sujā (DPPN, 'Sakka').

39. Mātali is Sakka's charioteer and companion; Vejayanta is the name of Sakka's chariot, drawn by a thousand horses (see DPPN).

40. When he reviews (*paccavekkhati*) no complacency is suggested. As a technical term it refers to the recollection of one's own meditation practice (see *Paṭisambhidāmagga* I 459). For explanation of this practice, see Shaw 2006b: 123–5. Here it means that the king is recollecting his own virtue, also a meditative practice (*sīlānussati*), intended to arouse confidence and contentment (AN V 330–1 and Bodhi 2012: 1566–7). Every month Buddhist monks also review their adherence to their monastic rules, the *Pāṭimokkha*.

Just as the moon's disc appeared in the eastern direction the chariot became visible. People had eaten their evening meal and were sitting in the doors of their houses, talking comfortably. 'Today two moons have appeared!' they exclaimed. As they were chatting the carriage appeared. 'It is not a moon—it is a chariot!' In due course the thousand thoroughbred horses and Mātali the charioteer became clear. 'For whom has this divine carriage come?' they wondered. 'Who else but our just king? The chariot Vejayanta must have been sent by Sakka. It is suitable for our king!' Delighted, they spoke this verse:

> 'A wonderful thing has arisen in the world, to make the hair stand on end.
> The divine chariot has appeared, for the glorious Videhan.' (23)

As the people talked and talked Mātali came as swift as the wind, and having reversed the carriage, set it down out of the way by the window sill. He made it ready for mounting and invited the king to ascend.

[104] The Teacher spoke, elucidating the matter:

> Mātali, the son of the gods, of great power, the divine charioteer,
> Has invited the Videhan king and householder of Mithilā. (24)
> 'Come and mount the carriage, noble king and lord of the directions!
> The gods, those around Sakka, those of the Heaven of the Thirty-Three, wish to see you.
> The gods remember you and are sitting in the Sudhammā hall.' (25)

The king thought, 'I'll see a heaven realm, which I have never seen before—and I'll have done Mātali a favour! So I'll go.' So he said to the household, 'I will not be gone long. Be careful and be generous and suchlike things, and perform auspicious actions.' He then alighted onto the carriage.

The Teacher spoke, making the matter clear:

> The Videhan king, who was a householder in Mithilā,
> quickly rose from his seat and alighted onto the carriage in front of him. (26)
> When he had got onto the divine carriage, Mātali said this:
> 'By which route should I take you, noble king and lord of the directions?
> Through the place where there are those who have performed evil actions,
> Or where there are those who have made merit?' (27)

At this the king said, 'There are two places I have never seen before. I will see both.'

> 'Mātali, charioteer of the gods, lead me even by both!

Through the place where there are those who have performed evil actions
And where there are those who have made merit.' (28)

Then Mātali said, 'It is not possible to see two at one go; I'll ask him.' Inquiring again, he spoke this verse:

'Noble king, lord of the directions, by which route should I lead you first?
Through the place where there are those who have performed evil actions,
Or where there are those who have made merit?' (29)

THE SECTION ON THE HELLS

[105] The king thought about it. 'I am certainly going to be going to a heavenly realm, so I'll see then a hell.' He recited the next verse:

'I'll see then a hell, dwelling place of those who have performed evil deeds,
The abodes and destinies of those who have behaved badly and have evil *kamma.*' (30)

And then Mātali showed him Vetaraṇī, the river of hell. Explaining the matter the Teacher said:

Mātali showed the wretched river Vetaraṇī to the king,
which is steaming, mixed with caustic soda, glowing like the flames of the fire. (31)

Then the king saw beings experiencing terrible suffering and was frightened. 'What evil have these beings done?' he asked Mātali and he explained. As clarification the Teacher said:

Nemi, indeed, addressed Mātali
When he had seen beings that had fallen into terrible straits:
[106] 'Charioteer, seeing this, fear has taken possession of me!
I ask this, Mātali, charioteer of the gods:
What evil have these people done,
The people who have fallen into Vetaraṇī?' (32)
Mātali, the charioteer of the gods, when asked by him,
Knowing, explained to one who did not know the fruit of evil *kamma.* (33)
'Those who are powerful in their life in the world, but corrupt,
And harm and harass the weak:
Vicious practices and cruel deeds bring forth evil,
And these people fall into Vetaraṇī.' (34)

In this way Mātali answered the question, and when the king had seen the hell of Vetaraṇī, he made the place disappear and drove the chariot on ahead, showing the place where they are eaten by dogs and suchlike. When he saw this the king in terror asked questions, and he answered them.

In explanation the Teacher said:

'Brown dogs and many-coloured vultures, terrible flocks of crows that prey!
Fear has taken possession of me, charioteer, when I see this.
I ask this, Mātali, charioteer of the gods:
What evil have these mortals done that crows should eat them?' (35)
Asked by him, Mātali, charioteer of the gods, explained.
Knowing, he told to one who did not know the result of evil deeds. (36)
'There are those who are envious, mean-spirited,
Speaking contemptuously to ascetics and brahmins,
Who harm and harass:
Vicious practices and cruel deeds bring forth evil,
And the crows eat these people.'[41] (37)

The other questions are answered according to the same method.

[107] 'Those who travel the earth with their bodies ablaze,
And are beaten with hot lumps:
Charioteer, seeing this, fear has taken possession of me!
I ask this, Mātali, charioteer of the gods:
What evil have these mortals done,
Those who lie pelted by lumps?' (38)
Mātali, the charioteer of the gods, when asked by him, knowing,
Explained to one who did not know the fruit of evil *kamma*. (39)
'Those who are in the world of life really sinful
To man and woman who are innocent;
Those who harm and harass:
Vicious practices and cruel deeds bring forth evil,
And these people lie pelted with lumps.' (40)
'Others sift in a pit of embers;
Men grieving with their bodies burnt all over:
[108] Charioteer, seeing this, fear has taken possession of me!
I ask this, Mātali, charioteer of the gods:
What evil have these mortals done, who sift in embers?' (41)
Mātali, the charioteer of the gods, asked by him,
Explained to one who did not know the fruit of evil *kamma*. (42)
'Whoever bears witness for the sake of a guild, and makes the money disappear,
Lord of the people, they deceive people:

41. The contemptuous live on the borders of Acheron in the *Inferno* (canto III).

These vicious practices and cruel deeds bring forth evil,
And these people sift in a pit of embers.'[42] (43)
'With their bodies blazing, set on fire; a great copper cauldron is seen.
Charioteer, seeing this, fear has taken possession of me!
I ask this, Mātali, charioteer of the gods: What evil have these mortals done,
That they fall head first into a cauldron?' (44)
Mātali, the charioteer of the gods, asked by him,
Explained to one who did not know the fruit of evil *kamma*. (45)
'Whoever harms and harasses a virtuous man, an ascetic, or a brahmin:
These vicious practices and cruel deeds bring forth evil,
And these people fall headfirst into a cauldron.' (46)
[109] 'They pluck them and then wring them by the neck,
And fling them into boiling water.[43]
Charioteer, seeing this, fear has taken possession of me!
I ask this, Mātali, charioteer of the gods: What evil have these mortals done,
That they lie with their heads broken?'[44] (47)
Mātali, the charioteer of the gods, asked by him,
Explained to one who did not know the fruit of evil deeds. (48)
'Those who in the world of life are vicious,
Seizing birds and tormenting them, lord of men,
Having harmed living beings:
The cruel actions bring forth evil
And these beings lie with necks broken.' (49)
'There flows a river, with deep water and shallow banks,
That is easily approachable.[45]
Overpowered by heat, men drink there,
But as they drink, the water turns to chaff. (50)
Charioteer, seeing this, fear has taken possession of me!
I ask this, Mātali, charioteer of the gods:
What evil have these mortals done,

42. The commentary explains that these people have collected money for a guild and misappropriated it. They mistakenly sprinkle hot embers over their heads. Dante's fraudsters, tyrants, and oppressors suffer grievously in the seventh circle of hell (*Inferno*, canto XII).

43. The beings who administer the punishments are the guardians of hell. Here the punishment mirrors precisely the seizing and killing of animals to cook them.

44. The commentary explains that the heads reappear again, so that the suffering is perpetuated.

45. In otherwise unleavened descriptions of hell these two *padas* (comprising one line in translation) employ the ironic technique of introducing an apparently pleasant place.

That as they drink the water turns to chaff?' (51)
[110] Mātali, the charioteer of the gods, asked by him,
Explained to one who did not know the fruit of evil deeds. (52)
'They are those who mixed with good grain chaff;
These malpractitioners sold it to the buyer.
They are overpowered by heat and parched with thirst,
So that while they drink, water turns to chaff.' (53)
'With spikes and spears and arrows,
They pierce weeping beings on both sides,
Charioteer, seeing this, fear has taken possession of me!
I ask this, Mātali, charioteer of the gods:
What evil have these mortals done,
That they lie injured with spears?' (54)
Mātali, the charioteer of the gods, asked by him,
Knowing, explained to one who did not know the fruit of evil deeds. (55)
'Whoever in the world of life are malpractitioners,
Taking what is not given as they ply their livelihood:
Grain, bread, money, coins, goats, cattle, and buffalo.
These cruel practices give rise to evil and they lie wounded with spears.' (56)
[111] 'Why are there some beings tied by the neck, others cut and others torn?[46]
Charioteer, seeing this, fear has taken possession of me!
I ask this, Mātali, charioteer of the gods,
What evil have these mortals done,
That they lie torn to pieces?' (57)
Mātali, the charioteer of the gods, asked by him,
Explained to one who did not know the fruit of evil deeds. (58)
'Butchers, pig merchants, and fishermen who kill cattle, buffaloes, and goats,
They also are laid out in slaughterhouses:
These cruel practices bring forth evil and those people lie cut into bits.' (59)
'There is a lake filled with urine and faeces,
With a terrible stench, impure, emitting a putrid odour;
Overcome by hunger men imbibe there.
Charioteer, seeing this, fear has taken possession of me!
I ask this, Mātali, charioteer of the gods,
What evil have these mortals done, that they eat urine and faeces?'[47] (60)
Mātali, the charioteer of the gods, asked by him,

46. They are tied like animals for the slaughter, in accordance with the actions that have created rebirth in this hell.

47. Dante describes the 'horrible excess of stench thrown up by the profound abyss' (*Inferno*, canto XI, line 145). The arrogant are thrown into the mire in canto VIII.

Knowing, explained to one who did not know the fruit of evil action. (61)
'Whoever, whilst discharging responsibilities
Are continuously devoted to harming others:
[112] these cruel practices give rise to evil.
Foolish, they that injure friends, drink urine.' (62)
'There is a lake filled with blood and pus:
Foul smelling, impure, and with a putrid smell;
Overpowered with heat men drink there.
Charioteer, seeing this, fear has taken possession of me!
I ask this, Mātali, charioteer of the gods:
What evil have these mortals done,
That they drink from blood and pus?' (63)
Mātali, the charioteer of the gods, asked by him,
Explained to one who did not know the fruit of evil action. (64)
'Whoever in the world kills mother, father,
Or in a profound offence, an *arahat*,
These cruel practices give rise to evil:
These are the people who drink blood and pus.' (65)
'See! A tongue pierced by a hook,
Like a shield hit by a hundred spikes.
[113] Why, [like] fish wriggling when thrown on the ground,
Do these beings dribble spit and cry out? (66)
Charioteer, seeing this, fear has taken possession of me!
I ask this, Mātali, charioteer of the gods:
What evil have these mortals done,
That they lie, having swallowed a hook?' (67)
Mātali, the charioteer of the gods, asked by him,
Knowing, explained to one who did not know the fruit of evil action. (68)
'Those men who in marketplaces lower the price, bit by bit,
And from greed for wealth, through crooked practice
Keep their crooked practice hidden, as for the killing of a fish.[48] (69)
There are no shelters for the one who follows crooked practices.
They are brought face to face with their own deeds, and cruel deeds give rise to evil;
These are the beings who lie having swallowed the hook.' (70)
'These women have limbs which are broken,
Stretching out [their arms] and weeping,
Smeared and stained with blood and pus,
Like cattle cut in a slaughterhouse:
They are dug all the time into a portion of the ground,
Their bodies ablaze while massy weights pass over them. (71)
[114] Charioteer, seeing this, fear has taken possession of me!

48. In the *Inferno* (canto VII), the fourth circle of hell is reserved for the avaricious.

I ask this, Mātali, charioteer of the gods:
What evil have these women done,
That they are continuously dug into a portion of the ground
And, bodies ablaze, massy weights pass over them?' (72)
Mātali, the charioteer of the gods, when asked by him,
Knowing, explained to one who did not know the fruit of evil action. (73)
'Those who in the world of life were of good family
And did evil with impure actions;
They who in the world of life were arrogant and proud
And abandoned their husband,
For the sake of lust and play giving pleasure to another:
Massy weights pass over them while they are ablaze.' (74)
'Grabbing them and dragging them by the feet,
They make them go head first into the Niraya.[49]
Charioteer, seeing this, fear has taken possession of me!
I ask this, Mātali, charioteer of the gods:
[115] What evil have these mortals done,
That they are plunged into the Niraya?' (75)
Mātali, the charioteer of the gods, when asked by him,
Knowing, explained to one who did not know the fruit of evil *kamma*. (76)
'Whoever in the world of life acts badly
And seduces the wife of another,
His most precious possession:
They are plunged headfirst into a Niraya hell. (77)
They experience painful feeling for heaps of years in hell.
There are no refuges for the one who does evil:
They are brought face to face with their own deeds.
These cruel practices give rise to evil
And these people fall into the Niraya hell.'[50] (78)

As he said this Mātali the charioteer caused the Niraya hell to disappear and pushed the chariot forwards and showed him the hell where those who are of wrong view stew. When asked, he said this:

'Various and many methods of torture,
With much wailing, are shown in the hells.[51]
Charioteer, seeing this, fear has taken possession of me!
I ask this, Mātali, charioteer of the gods:
What evil have these mortals done,

49. Again it is the guardians of hell enforcing the punishments. The Niraya is the lowest hell, where beings may exist for many aeons, though no rebirth is permanent.

50. Considered the deepest hell; these transgressions also lead to the deepest hell in the *Inferno*.

51. Dante describes the deafening roar of human misery in *Inferno*, canto XVI.

That they experience such sharp, keen, harsh, and painful feelings?' (79)
Mātali, the charioteer of the gods, asked by him,
Explained to one who did not know the fruit of evil *kamma*. (80)
'Whoever in the world of life has an extreme wrong view,
Does ignorant actions and causes another to follow his views:
[116] They, with their wrong views, bring forth evil.
These beings experience such sharp, keen, harsh, and painful feelings.'[52] (81)

In the world of *devas*, the shining gods, waiting for the king's arrival, sat in the Sudhammā hall. Sakka, reflecting on the reason for Mātali's delay, saw the reason. 'Mātali, to show that he was a very special kind of messenger, travels revealing the hells, explaining, "Great King, they cook in this and that hell for this and that reason'. But the lifespan of Nemi might run out, as he would never come to the end of viewing hells!' So he ordered a particularly swift messenger: 'Go and tell Mātali to come quickly and bring the king.' He obeyed and went with speed. Mātali listened to the instruction and thought there should be no delay. In one stroke he showed the deep hells in the four directions and spoke this verse.

'Great King, you know the dwelling of those of evil *kamma*:
The places of those who are cruel and the destination of those who behave badly.
Now, seer king, go into the presence of the king of the gods.' (82)

THE SECTION ON THE HEAVENS[53]

As he said this Mātali drove the carriage to the entrance of the realm of the gods. The king went into the *deva* realm and saw a flying palace in the air.[54] It was twelve yojanas long, with golden cupolas made of jewels. It was decorated and adorned in every way, [117] possessed a park with lotus ponds, and was surrounded by wishing trees. It belonged to the goddess Bīranī. He caught sight of her, sitting on a couch within her turreted dwelling, surrounded by a thousand beautiful nymphs and looking out of a jewelled window she had opened. The king asked Mātali about her, and he explained:

52. Heretics suffer torments in the sixth circle of hell in *Inferno*, canto IX.

53. This is the arrangement of sections given in VRI.

54. A *vimāna* is a floating feature of heaven realms of the sense sphere, a kind of happy multi-sensory environment that sails in the sky, equipped with boundless food, drink, and music and entertainment; see Masefield 1989 for extensive examination of the term in the *Vimānavatthu*.

'See this flying palace with five cupolas: in the middle of a couch
There sits a lady adorned with garlands,
Of great majesty, gracious in speech, of great power,
And able to transform herself by magic! (83)
Charioteer, happiness takes possession of me as I see this.
I ask you, Mātali, charioteer of the gods:
What good has this lady done,
Who rejoices on reaching heaven in a floating palace?' (84)
Asked, Mātali, charioteer of the gods, knowing,
Explained to one who did not know the fruit of meritorious deeds. (85)
'Now then, in the world of the living,
Bīranī was the daughter born of a slave in the household of a brahmin.
She received a guest at the right moment, and welcomed him
As a mother would her child.
Restrained and bountiful, she delights in this flying palace.'[55] (86)

[118] When he had said this Mātali drove the chariot forward and showed him the seven gold flying palaces of the god Soṇadinna. He saw these and that man's glory and asked about the *kamma* that he had performed, and Mātali explained it to him:

'Seven resplendent flying palaces have been created, which shine out.
There a *yakkha* of great magical power, adorned with all kinds of embellishments,
Is honoured by a crowd of nymphs who surround him on all sides. (87)
Charioteer, happiness takes possession of me as I see this.
I ask you, Mātali, charioteer of the gods:
What good has this mortal done,
Who rejoices on reaching heaven in a flying palace?' (88)
Asked, Mātali, charioteer of the gods, knowing,
Explained to one who did not know the fruit of meritorious deeds. (89)
'The householder Soṇadinna was a generous host
Who built seven temples for recluses. (90)
He attended respectfully the monks who lived there;
With a clear mind he gave coverings, food, lodgings, and lights
To those who lived in straightness. (91)
On the fourteenth, the fifteenth, the eighth day of the fortnight,
And on special holidays too,[56] he was good at keeping the eight precepts; (92)

55. The commentary goes on to say that in the time of the Kassapa Buddha, Bīranī was born a slave into a brahmin household. When the brahmin wanted to give food to eight monks daily the wife refused, as did his daughter, but Bīranī carried it out with great devotion, and so was reborn in heaven (see DPPN).

56. PED 451 gives *pāṭihāriyapakkha* as an extra holiday, not now kept.

He kept the *uposatha* and was always self-controlled in behaviour;
Through his restraint and generosity he takes delight in a flying palace.'[57] (93)

[119] In this way he explained what Soṇadinna had done and sent the chariot forward and showed him a flying crystal palace, twenty-five *yojana*s high. It was endowed with hundreds of different columns made of the seven kinds of jewels and hundreds of turrets. It was encircled with nets of tinkling bells, and a banner made of gold and silver was raised. It was decorated with many different kinds of flowers in the park and wood, had a delightful lotus pond, and was filled with water nymphs skilled in songs, music, and suchlike. When he saw them the king asked about what the water nymphs had done previously, and he explained it:

'He reveals this mansion, well-constructed with crystals,
Shining with peaked roofs and covered with a company of the best of nymphs;
It is furnished with both food and drink, and with dances and songs. (94)
Charioteer, happiness takes possession of me as I see this.
I ask you, Mātali, charioteer of the gods:
What good have these women done,
Who rejoice on reaching heaven in a flying palace?' (95)
Asked, Mātali, the charioteer, knowing,
Explained to one who did not know the fruit of meritorious deeds. (96)
'Whatever women who in the world of life were virtuous lay disciples,
Delighting in generosity, with minds always full of faith:
They abide in truth, are careful of the *uposatha,*
And, from their restraint and generosity, they delight in their flying palace.' (97)

And then he drove the chariot forward and revealed a single palace of jewels. It was set on a level piece of ground, was of a great height, and stood shining like a jewelled mountain. It was filled with the sound of heavenly songs and music from many gods and goddesses. Seeing this the king asked about the *kamma* performed by the gods, and he explained it to him:

[120] 'He revealed this palace, constructed from lapis lazuli,
Well proportioned and set out, and furnished with pleasant plots of land. (98)
Drums, tabors, and beautifully musical dances and songs:
Divine sounds emanate, melodious and pleasing to the mind. (99)
I have never before been aware of such a beautiful sight

57. The commentary says that Soṇadinna gave food to monks in the time of the Kassapa Buddha. See also DPPN.

Or heard such divine sound! (100)
Charioteer, happiness takes possession of me as I see this.
I ask you, Mātali, charioteer of the gods:
What good have these mortals done,
Who rejoice on reaching heaven in a palace?' (101)
Asked, Mātali explained to one who
Did not know the fruit of meritorious deeds. (102)
'Those mortals who, in the world of life
Were virtuous lay disciples, and respectfully provided groves,
Wells, drinking places, and canals to *arahats*,
Whose minds had become cooled; (103–4)
And gave with clear minds robes, food, support [in sickness],
And beds to those who lived in straightness;
On the fourteenth, the fifteenth, the eighth day of the fortnight,
And on special holidays too, they were good at keeping the eight precepts: (105)
They kept the *uposatha* and were always restrained in behaviour;
Through their discernment and generosity they take delight in a palace.' (106)

When he had described what they had done, he sent the chariot forward and showed another crystal palace, encircled with various turrets, covered with all kinds of flowers and surrounded by trees. On the opposite bank of a river of stainless water, filled with many kinds of birdsong, there was the enclosed dwelling of a [121] certain virtuous man, surrounded by water nymphs. When he saw this the king asked what this man had done, and Mātali explained it to him in this way:

'He shows this celestial mansion, beautifully constructed with crystals,
Delightful gables, crowded with a troop of delightful nymphs. (107)
It is furnished with food and drinks, and filled with both dance and song;
Rivers endowed with many flowers and trees encircle it. (108)
I am possessed by happiness, charioteer, to see this.
I ask you, Mātali, charioteer of the gods:
What good has this mortal done,
Who rejoices on reaching heaven in a palace?' (109)
Asked, Mātali, the charioteer, knowing,
Explained to one who did not know the fruit of meritorious deeds. (110)
'This man is a householder who was a generous lord of his house in Kimbilāya,
Who respectfully provided groves, wells, drinking places, and canals. (111)
He was virtuous, a lay disciple, and respectfully provided groves, wells,

Drinking places, and canals to *arahat*s, whose minds had become
cooled;[58] (112)
And gave with clear mind robes, food, support [in sickness],
And beds to those who lived in straightness;
On the fourteenth, the fifteenth, the eighth day of the fortnight,
And on special holidays too, he was good at keeping the eight
precepts: (113)
He kept the *uposatha* and was always restrained in behaviour;
Through his discernment and generosity he takes delight in
a palace.' (114)

When he had reflected upon what had been done by this man he sent the carriage forward and showed him another crystal palace, even better than the one before, covered in various kinds of flowers and fruit, endowed with a grove of trees. When he saw this the king asked what the god possessed of such good fortune had done and reflected upon this next one:

'He reveals to me this celestial mansion, beautifully constructed from
crystal,
Brilliant with turrets and crowded with excellent nymphs. (115)
[122] It is furnished with food and drinks, and filled with both dance
and song.
Rivers endowed with many flowers and trees encircle it. (116)
A royal realm of abundant mango trees, rose apple, *tinduka* trees,
Piyāla, and trees that perpetually bear fruit: (117)
I am possessed by happiness, charioteer, to see this.
I ask you, Mātali, charioteer of the gods:
What good has this mortal done,
Who rejoices on reaching heaven in a flying palace?' (118)
Asked, Mātali, charioteer of the gods, knowing,
Explained to one who did not know the fruit of meritorious deeds. (119)
'This man was a householder who was a generous host in his house in
Mithilā,
Who respectfully provided groves, wells, drinking places,
and canals. (120)
He was virtuous, a lay disciple, and respectfully provided groves, wells,
Drinking places, and canals to *arahat*s, whose minds had become
cooled; (121)
And gave with clear mind robes, food, support [in sickness],
And beds to those who lived in straightness;
On the the fourteenth, the fifteenth, the eighth day of the fortnight,

58. The formula in these three verses (as vv. 104–6) is repeated throughout the heaven realm exposition, emphasizing a different kind of repetition, based on skilfulness.

And on special holidays too, he was good at keeping the
eight precepts: (122)
He kept the *uposatha* and was always restrained in behaviour;
Through his discernment and generosity he takes delight in a palace.' (123)

When he had described the *kamma* performed by this man he drove the carriage on and showed him another palace, equal to the one before, yet made of lapis lazuli. When asked, he explained the *kamma* of this man of great splendour:

He described this palace, well constructed from lapis lazuli,
Well proportioned and set out, furnished with pleasant plots of land. (124)
'Drums, tabors, beautifully musical dances and songs:
Divine sounds emanate, pleasant to hear and delighting the mind. (125)
To be sure, I do not recollect hearing such a wonderful sound before
Or seeing such divine things. (126)
Charioteer, joy takes possession of me seeing this.
I ask you, Mātali, charioteer of the gods,
What good has this mortal done,
[123] Who rejoices on reaching heaven in a palace?' (127)
Asked, Mātali, charioteer of the gods, knowing,
Explained to one who did not know the fruit of meritorious deeds. (128)
'This man was a householder who was a generous host in Vārāṇasi,
Who respectfully provided groves, wells, drinking places, and canals; (129)
He was virtuous, a lay disciple, and respectfully provided groves, wells,
Drinking places, and canals to *arahats*, whose minds had become
cooled; (130)
And gave with clear mind robes, food, support [in sickness],
And beds to those who lived in straightness;
On the fourteenth, the fifteenth, the eighth day of the fortnight,
And on special holidays too, he was good at keeping the eight precepts;
He kept the *uposatha* and was always restrained in behaviour;
Through his discernment and generosity he takes delight
in a palace.' (131–2)

And then he ordered the chariot on further and showed a golden palace, resembling the splendour of the sun. When asked, he explained the good fortune of the god who dwelt in that:

'Just as is the magnificent red rising of the sun,
So is the example of this celestial mansion, made of gold. (133)
Charioteer, happiness takes possession of me seeing this.
I ask you, Mātali, charioteer of the gods,
What good this mortal did,
Who rejoices at the attainment of heaven in a palace?' (134)

Asked, Mātali, charioteer of the gods, knowing,
Explained to one who did not know the fruit of meritorious deeds. (135)
'This man was a householder who was a generous lord in Sāvatthi,
Who respectfully provided groves, wells, drinking places, and canals; (136)
He was virtuous, a lay disciple, and respectfully provided groves, wells,
Drinking places, and canals to *arahat*s, whose minds had become cooled; (137)
And gave with clear mind robes, food, support [in sickness],
And beds to those who lived in straightness;
He observed the fourteenth, the fifteenth, the eighth day of the fortnight,
And was good at keeping the eight precepts, always restrained in behaviour:
Through his discernment and generosity he takes delight in a palace.' (138–9)

[124] Thus when the description of these eight palaces had been completed, Sakka, king of the gods, thinking, 'Mātali has taken too long!' sent out another swift son of the gods. Mātali, hearing the message, decided not to delay any more. In one stroke he showed him many palaces, and when asked he explained the *kamma* of the good fortune of those who were there:

'Abundant heavenly mansions made of gold,
Blazing forth, shine brilliantly like lightning in the midst of the clouds. (140)
Charioteer, happiness takes possession of me seeing this!
I ask you, Mātali, charioteer of the gods,
What good these mortals did,
Who rejoice on reaching heaven in a palace.' (141)
Asked, Mātali explained to one
Who did not know the fruit of meritorious deeds. (142)
'You see, King, these are the dwellings for those
Who through faith and virtue are instilled with justice and well taught:
They have acted in accordance with the *dhamma* of the teacher,
As in the dispensation of the Fully Awakened Buddha.' (143)

When he had shown him the heavenly mansions, he spoke, making a resolution to go to the presence of Sakka.

'You have seen, Great King, the abodes of those who have performed evil;
The dwellings of those who have performed lovely deeds are also known by you.
Now go, seer king, into the presence of the king of the gods!' (144)

[125] When he had said this he sent the chariot on further and showed

him the seven mountains that make a ring surrounding Mount Sineru. To explain how the king questioned Mātali about this the Teacher said:

The Great King, standing upon the divine chariot yoked with a thousand horses,
Drove on and saw the mountains on the edges of Sīdantara, the Sea of Sink.
Seeing them he asked the charioteer: 'And what are the names of these mountains?' (145)

Asked by Nemi, Mātali, the son of the gods, replied in this way:

'Sudassana, Karavīka, Isadhara, Yugandhara,
Nemidhara, Vinataka, Assakanna: they are vast mountains.
These peaks arise in ascending order;
You, a king, are looking at the dwelling places of the Great Kings.' (147)

When he had shown him the heaven realm of the Four Great Kings he drove the chariot on and showed him the images of Sakka that surround Cittakūṭa, or Multicoloured Point, the gateway of the Heaven of the Thirty-Three. And when he saw this the king asked about it and Mātali explained it to him:

'This gateway is of diverse form, brilliant, with various colours,
Filled with images of Sakka, as if protected by tigers.
Tell me, what is its name? (148)
[126] Charioteer, joy takes possession of me seeing this.
I ask you, Mātali, charioteer of the gods: what is the name of this gateway?' (149)
Asked, Mātali, charioteer of the gods, explained to one
Who did not know the fruit of meritorious deeds. (150)
'This is Cittakūṭa: the entrance for the heavenly kings
And gateway to Sudassana (Beautiful Sight), the beautiful mountain, appears. (151)
This gateway is of diverse form, brilliant, with various colours,
Surrounded by images of Sakka, as if protected by tigers.
Enter by it, seer king, and tread upon spotless ground.' (152)

As he said this Mātali led the king into the heavenly city, and, as it is said:

Standing upon the divine chariot yoked with a thousand horses,
The great king drives on and sees the meeting place of the gods. (153)

Standing in the divine carriage, he went to the meeting place of the gods, Sudhammā, and as he saw it he enquired about it to Mātali, who replied:

'Just as in autumn the sky appears deep blue,
So is the example of this mansion, made from lapis lazuli! (154)
Charioteer, happiness takes possession of me seeing this!

I ask you, Mātali, charioteer of the gods:
Tell me, what is the name of this mansion?' (155)
Asked, Mātali, charioteer of the gods, knowing,
Explained to one who did not know the fruit of meritorious deeds. (156)
[127] 'This is Sudhammā,' he said. 'See this hall that has appeared,
Beautifully constructed, bright, of shining lapis lazuli! (157)
Eight well-constructed columns, all made of lapis lazuli, act as supports.
And there are all the Thirty-Three Gods, with Sakka placed in front, (158)
All gathered together, considering the happiness of gods and men.
Enter by this way, wise king, to the appreciation of the gods.' (159)

The gods were sitting watching for his arrival and when they heard that the king had come went out to meet him with heavenly scents and flowers in their hands, as far as the gates of Cittakūṭa. They paid homage to the Great Being with their perfumes and the rest and led him into the Sudhammā hall. The king came down from his chariot and entered the divine assembly, and there the gods welcomed him with a seat, and Sakka too, and plied them both with the pleasures of the senses:

In explanation the Teacher said:

The gods are delighted to see the arrival of the king!
'We hope you are well, Great King; we hope you are in health.
Sit down, wise king, in the company of the heavenly king.' (160)
Sakka gladly welcomed the Videhan, a layman of Mithilā;
Vāsava invited him with all the pleasures of the senses and asked him to take a seat. (161)
'It is really wonderful that you have come to the dwelling place of those that have power.
Stay amongst the gods, seer king, amongst the prosperity of all the pleasures of the sense.
Enjoy with the Thirty-Three Gods the pleasures of the realm above humans!' (162)

Thus Sakka welcomed him with divine sense pleasures. The king, declining, answered him:

'Just as when a chariot is given when it is demanded,
Or as wealth is given when it is demanded:
Of such a kind is the generosity that depends upon another. (163)
[128] And I have no wish for the generosity that depends upon another;
Things which are brought about by my own efforts and meritorious actions:
This is unmixed wealth for me. (164)
I'll go amongst men and I'll do a great deal of good,
By generosity, living calmly with restraint and control.

The one who does this is happy; he has no regrets.' (165)

Thus the Great Being, with a sweet voice, taught *dhamma* to the gods, and when he had done this he had stayed, by the counting of humans, seven days and delighted the assembly of the gods. Standing in the midst of the divine assembly he spoke of the excellence of Mātali:

'Mātali, charioteer of the gods, is venerable, and most helpful.
He has shown me the abodes of the good, and of those that do evil.' (166)

Then the king addressed Sakka, 'Great King, I would like to return to the world of men.' Sakka gave the command: 'Good Mātali, lead King Nemi to Mithilā.' He agreed and fetched the chariot. The king exchanged greetings with the gods, and, taking leave of them, alighted onto the chariot. Mātali drove the chariot in the eastern direction until he reached Mithilā. The people saw the divine chariot and were delighted that their king had returned. Mātali made a circle around the city and deposited the Great Being by the same window ledge. Mātali took his leave of the king and returned to his own abode. Everyone surrounded the king: 'What is the realm of the gods like?' they asked him. The king praised the glory of the gods, and Sakka, king of the gods. 'And now practise generosity, and suchlike things, and you will be reborn in that heaven realm.' And he taught them the *dhamma*. In due course his barber found a grey hair and informed him of it, and he had the barber put it aside and [129] gave him the boon of a village. Wishing to go forth he handed his kingdom over to his son. When he was questioned, 'But why are you going forth?' he replied, 'The hairs of my head.' And he said this verse, going forth just like the earlier kings. And he stayed in the same mango grove, cultivated the four divine abidings, and arrived at a Brahmā heaven.

The Teacher explained his going forth and pronounced this final verse:

As he said this King Nemi, the Videhan, the layman of Mithilā,
Made the great sacrifice and entered into restraint. (167)

And his son was called Kaḷārajanaka and severed the lineage when he did not take the going forth.[59]

59. F's Burmese manuscript, Bd, omits the initial 'a' in *apabbaji*, which would mean the verb is not a negative and that he did take the going forth, severing the secular 'lineage' by, presumably, leaving no heir. But according to F, Nemi's son severs the lineage by *not* taking the going forth and so ending the line of renunciates. In the *Suttanta* version of the tale, his son also severs it by not going forth in the manner of all his predecessors: in that version, the lineage is clearly perceived as being defined

The Teacher related this story. 'Monks, not only now, but in the past too, I made the great renunciation.' After he had said this he gave the key to the births: 'At that time Sakka was Anuruddha, Mātali was Ānanda, the eighty-four kings were the followers of the Buddha, and I was King Nemi.'

by the renunciation of all these kings, not their monarchic rule (see MN 83, PTS edn II 77–82; Ñāṇamoli and Bodhi 1995: 695–7). The Buddha takes his example in the *sutta* as a negative example, exhorting the monks not to break the line by being 'the last man' and so keep the lineage of the noble Aryan path going. It is noteworthy that the *jātaka* version does not hint at any pejoration in the ending of the line; rather it emphasises the simple fact of impermanence operating in even the most lengthy and auspicious family lines.

MAHOSADHA

5

The Birth Story of Mahosadha, or of the Great Tunnel

(*Mahosadha-jātaka* or *Mahā-Ummagga-jātaka*)

INTRODUCTION

The *Mahosadha-jātaka*, or, as it is commonly known in Sri Lanka, the *Ummagga-jātaka*, (the Tunnel Story), is singled out as one of only three lives in which the Bodhisatta speaks at birth. On each occasion of this extraordinary occurrence, the other two are also cited, emphasising the way they have historically been linked to one another. In the *Jātaka-nidāna,* the Bodhisatta in his final life is said to have spoken and announced his pre-eminence in the world, foreshadowing his Buddhahood. In the *Vessantara-jātaka* he expresses his wish to his mother to be generous. In this story, as he is being born, King Sakka slips a healing herb, *osadhī*, into the Bodhisatta's hand. He immediately gives it to his mother and asks that it be used to cure people's sickness, which it does, with miraculous effect.

The story is attributed to the perfection of wisdom, and it is this quality that pervades the style and content of the tale, making it one for which no other attribution seems possible, though it makes clear that wisdom needs to be rightly placed, and not used for one's own gain.[1] Through riddles, questions, answers to apparently insoluble problems, advice to kings, intelligence gathering, planning, and forethought the Bodhisatta brings his great wisdom, or perhaps more accurately in the situations

Introduced and translated by Sarah Shaw.

1. For attributions, see Introduction, Table 2.

described, his extraordinary ingenuity, to sort out the immense difficulties, challenges, and dangers that face him and the other characters. 'Wisdom'—and even that term is scrutinized—is, when skilful in the *Abhidhamma* sense (associated with skilful and wholesome consciousness and right intention), an agent for healing people's mundane problems and a means of extricating the Bodhisatta and, crucially, others from difficult situations. Such wisdom animates each episode in which the Bodhisatta finds himself; words associated with wisdom—*bhūri* or *paṇḍito*—are explicitly mentioned throughout, both applied to the Bodhisatta, and, challengingly, to other characters, some good and some bad, in a way that forces us to confront what is meant by this essential, but difficult, perfection. The story constitutes a sustained exploration of wisdom in the world, examining its manifestations in different situations, and positing, in a method characteristic of long *jātakas*, all kinds of scenarios where it is also vitiated, used to wrong intent, and misapplied, to which the only antidote is true wisdom, to be understood through the way the Bodhisatta confronts and challenges those who misuse wisdom's near enemies: deceit, spiteful ingenuity, and self-seeking craft.

The other striking thing about the story is that it is very long, and in modern terms something we would class a great and absorbing read, with all the skilfully suggested elements of suspense, danger, and uncertainty we associate now with literary genres including folk, popular, court, and now globally marketed bestseller novels designed to grip, entertain, and mystify. It even includes a 'high-tech' element, in the various contraptions that guard the city from attack and which allow the tunnel to be lit throughout. So there are plentiful tropes and storylines that fit very well, for instance, the often strictly conventionalised demands of nineteenth- and twentieth-century Anglophone genre novels, including detective 'whodunnits', mysteries, spy thrillers, and sensation fiction of various kinds. Winternitz has noted how the story exploits elements in Indian fictions, ancient and modern. The various forms of *Vetāla*, or ghost, stories, with their varied puzzles, show many affinities with the tales in this *jātaka*; no doubt many other similarities to South and Southeast Asian forms could be found. From a theatrical point of view, its appeal also has many affinities with other global dramas, including elements of the highly complicated intrigue and misunderstanding that animate the energetic and fast-moving machinations of Jacobean melodrama, the farce, and some Sanskrit drama. It even, in some of its paradoxical components, echoes the tragic drama of ancient Greece. It has, in the grandeur of its hero and some female characters, an occasional sense of the heroic that aligns it with Homeric and Indian epic: though perhaps lacking the complex stature of Greek and Sanskrit poetic language and style, some verse sections are truly epic in their magnificence and richly leisured and complex appeal (see for instance vv. 123–35). From the point of view of the verse and prose composition as a whole, it deploys elements we can recognize from Romance ballads, mediaeval riddles from the east and west, and folkloric puzzles and rhymes, common to many cultures but beloved particularly, perhaps as an outcome of the popularity of the tale on the island, in Sri Lankan folklore, medicine, and story. Rhys Davids (1925: xlii–xliii), tracing related elements in the mediaeval and ancient cultures of other Asian and European nations, estimated that *Mahosadha* contains about a hundred and fifty varied stories. Winternitz, admitting its undoubted attractions, is left, however, somewhat bemused by its apparently inchoate and discursive series of puzzles and dramas, so reminiscent of the *Thousand Nights and a Night* (Winternitz 1977: 137 ff.), but says also 'there is nothing buddhistic in the whole of the long Romance' (138).

In some ways the plot is not excessively complicated. The Bodhisatta is born in a wealthy family and by the age of seven is known as a 'wise man' (*paṇḍito*). The king tests him with puzzles and questions, finally bringing him to court as a wise man to join four others, all brahmin, led by their chief, Senaka. More problems are solved by the Bodhisatta, and the king finds a new queen, Udumbarā. On her encouragement the Bodhisatta finds a fellow in wisdom, the resourceful Amarādevī, as his wife. After Mahosadha solves more problems the major conflict of the story ensues, when he has to save his somewhat witless king from attack. An enemy, Cūḷani Brahmadatta, influenced by his own *paṇḍito*, lays siege to the city, and the Bodhisatta, through forethought, planning, clever spying, and intelligence work, ensures his defeat. Cūḷani invites the king of Mithilā to his own city under the pretext of marrying him to his daughter, Caṇḍī, while really planning his execution. The canny Mahosadha goes on ahead, builds a town and an enormous tunnel as an escape route out of the city, and gets his king and army to safety through a mixture of guile, careful planning, and creative deployment of his highly skilled labour force. When the king dies, the Bodhisatta, fulfilling an earlier promise, returns to the court of Cūḷani Brahmadatta and is vindicated and celebrated as the female ascetic Bherī questions the king, and the Bodhisatta's wisdom is known to all.

The story is full of twists of plot and asides, but it is in the many stories and sub-stories that punctuate this tale that its complexity lies. While connections between the tales sometimes appear tenuous, these are not just adjuncts without bearing on the plot. In its many internal relationships between imagery, in the complexity of the categories of its problems, and in its recurrent themes, such as the correct understanding of secrecy and trust, or the nature of true wisdom, the story not only subjects the manifold ways of solving questions and enigmas to a close investigative analysis in terms of Buddhist morality and doctrine. It also, in the outcomes of the plot and its exploration of rightly placed motive, carefully deploys a completely Buddhist understanding of the notions of karma and intent. Despite Winternitz's objections, this makes it thoroughly deserving of a place in the *Mahānipāta*, and indeed makes it one of the greatest works of this collection. The world of Mahosadha is not a gracious or polite one: the Bodhisatta, like others in the tale, and true to the genres of thrillers and detective fiction with which the tale often now seems aligned, is sometimes ruthless and downright rude, particularly in his brusque denunciations of the other 'wise' men and his own king. His extraordinary canniness and boldly imaginative analysis, are, however, always loyal, and clear in their intent to help and not cause harm, and he is constantly mindful of the well-being of the court, city, and countryside. He is compassionate and forgiving to his enemies. His 'skill' is often a pragmatic one, but in this regard, it reflects the practicality and nous of his teaching in his final life, for which this one is both a metaphoric and realistic anticipation.

The Text

But crucial to understanding the tale is consideration of the nature of the composition, language, and style of the story, which themselves pose some of this tale's most curious puzzles. These question the very nature of *jātaka*s as a genre and offer intriguing hints as to how it may have developed, not as a subspecies of epic with Buddhist elements, as writers such as Winternitz have suggested, but as a distinct oral literary form which for its very performative nature is ongoing, evolutionary in style, and highly dependent upon the personal initiative and tastes of the storyteller, responding to the audience and sensing their needs. *Jātaka*s are not subspecies of anything, but their own genre. They are told to an audience as one of the limbs of the teaching, and their very methods and style, drawing heavily on other forms and transforming them at the root with Buddhist intent, engage our attention through their appeal to so many genres and kinds of attentiveness. The story's own role in delivering, reinterpreting, and questioning events through a Buddhist understanding is explored throughout this tale.

Structure

This can be seen in the structure of the tale, characterized by elements so unlike others of the *Mahānipāta*. Many of the *Mahānipāta* include lines or verses found in other *jātakas*. The *Janaka-jātaka* has a counterpart in the *Cūḷajanaka-jātaka* (J 52), which does not tell the story but refers us to the later version. This story, however, has a full twelve tales that are found elsewhere in the collection, outlined by Oskar von Hinüber (1998: 110 ff.):

1. *Sabbasaṃhāraka-jātaka* (J 110) 'The Question of the Threaded Necklace'
2. *Gadrabhapañha-jātaka* (J 111) 'The Question of the Ass'
3. *Amarādevī-jātaka* (J 112) 'The Secret Way (Amarādevī)'
4. *Kakaṇṭaka-jātaka* (J 170) 'The Chameleon Question'
5. *Sirikālikaṇṇi-jātaka* (J 192) 'The Question about Good and Bad Luck'
6. *Devatāpañha-jātaka* (J 350) ' The Riddles of the Goddess'
7. *Khajjopanaka-jātaka* (J 364) 'The Question of the Firefly'
8. *Bhuripañha-jātaka* (J 452) 'The Wisdom (*bhūri*) Question'
9. *Meṇḍaka-jātaka* (J 471) 'The Question about the Goat'
10. *Sirimanda-jātaka* (J 500) 'The Question of the Rich and the Poor'
11. *Pañcapaṇḍita-jātaka* (J 508) 'The Questions of the Five Wise Men'
12. *Dakarakkhasaja-jātaka* (J 517) 'The Question of the Water Spirit'

These stories are cited in Fausbøll's edition with a simple reference to the *Mahosadha-jātaka* (or *Ummagga* as it is termed there) and no other description. What appears to have happened is that there were originally a number of stories associated with Mahosadha that occurred throughout the collection of 547 *jātakas*.[2] Seeing these as imports to the story also makes more sense of the way it is split into episodes. Most of the very long tales in the *Mahānipāta* are divided into sections (*khaṇḍa*), sometimes termed episode (*pabba*) or description (*vaṇṇanā* or *kathā*). These each

2. This kind of duplication of hero occurs throughout the collection; there is a sequence of stories, for instance, all loosely related, about Mittavinda, which do not make literal sense as a sequence and show simple variations on a theme (see Shaw 2012b).

comprise several pages of text and would usually take from thirty to fifty minutes to chant. So there are natural divides at appropriate moments for the person chanting or telling to take a break, stretch his legs, have a glass of water or, in the case of the *Vessantara-jātaka*, allow another monk to come and recite or chant a particular section. The *Mahosadha-jātaka*, however, has no sense of this. Splits occur after quite short stories, as in the nineteen questions, and after very long ones. Divisions seem to have very little to do with natural pacing, and there are numerous sections in the tale. It certainly seems likely that at some point all the stories were brought together under the umbrella of the *Mahosadha-jātaka*, and placed to form a sequence. This does introduce some difficulties in the plot. For example, Queen Udumbarā, so central a character in several of the 'imported' stories as the Mithilan king's chief wife, somehow just disappears after the first sections of the story, where most of these imports occur. While the king might, like that of Kālidāsa's drama *Śakuntalā*, have taken a second chief wife, Udumbarā is not mentioned in any way again, and her occurrence seems confined to those parts of the story imported from other tales.

Another problem is solved if the stories are seen as new additions. The verse tag that starts each story is usually the same as the first few words of the first verse in the jātaka and is presumably a mnemonic for the reciter. A notable exception to this is here in *Mahosadha*, where the first verse tag refers to a verse which occurs on page 396 in the original text. All eighty-three verses before this, which were inserted at a later time and are termed by von Hinüber (1998: 110 ff.) *paribhindaka*,[3] occur in the sections derived from other *jātakas*. This feature Fausbøll clearly noted by having two sets of numbering in his edition. In this translation, the inserted verses are numbered in italics. But this does not solve all of the problems of this story, as most of the riddles and questions of the nineteen are not imports and are clearly part of the story itself. But they have no verses, and we face the likelihood that the sections with all of the nineteen questions, and much of the extensive prose at the outset of the story, are late.[4] Fausbøll

3. This term, derived from the word *paribhindati* 'to split or break', refers to the 'split' sections of a tale.

4. The older sections, if they are to be ascertained by the presence of the archaic 11/12 metre, are mainly in 'imported' tales in the early part of the story that mostly occur after the nineteen questions but before the first verse 'tag'. This again suggests an early sequence of Mahosadha stories later integrated under one tale, as well as existing independently. These are vv. *3*, *8–41*, *48–52*, *55–6*, *62–78*, *83*; 12, 13 (mixed?),

clearly felt this to be the case for the nineteen and placed most of them as commentarial backstory in over ten pages of tiny, unbroken prose, undistinguished even by the insertion of one change of paragraph.

Narrative Style

While most of the nineteen stories are probably later incorporations (except for numbers three and eighteen) and lack the early verse content, they have historically formed much of the most loved material in this story. The Sinhalese version, attributed to a thirteenth-century scholar monk from Tanjore, who apparently composed it during the reign of Parakrama Bahu IV (1308–47), makes a great deal of each one of the stories, and the text has been one of the most popular *jātaka* compositions in Sri Lanka for centuries.[5] It is easy to see why: the tests give us a fascinating glimpse into ancient legal cases (*aṭṭā*) and moral wisdom, and their longstanding appeal is well deserved. But there is also an inordinate amount of prose before the first verse. Are we to dismiss that? How do you tell commentary from prose story? In his introduction to *Vessantara-jātaka*, Gombrich discusses these issues in relationship to that story and makes a loose distinction between what is actual story, if a later evolution, and commentary, with its analysis of terms and the occasional backstory—a mix of forms found in Indian prose as early as the first commentaries on the *Ṛg Veda.* As he notes, this stratification may be unjustified in terms of authorship anyway (PGPV: xxiv). Indeed in *Mahosadha-jātaka* however, we seem to have a major problem even with this distinction. Clearly monks who 'read' the story for retelling are aware that few of their listeners are going to be interested in the breakdown of words and their explanations. But how should all the copious 'backstories' that accompany each stage of the tale be handled? Sometimes they are entirely necessary, as in the wonderfully funny verse courtship between the parrot and the mynah bird, as explanations of verses involving characters many would have known in the story's early days in India but who would have become strange as the stories moved to a new geographical location (vv. 22–43). Sometimes they are not, as in the extensive stories at the end surrounding the water spirit questions, which

---

14–16, 20, 45? (mixed?), 46–48, 67–70, 90.

5. There have been two single translations into English in recent times. One was translated from the Sinhala by the Japanese scholar T. B. Yatawara and published in London in 1898. The other, used because of its availability, is that of David Karunaratne (1962; referred to here as UJST).

are clearly disjuncts (and have not been translated); if we take them out, the 'actual' prose, story, and verses flow much better. Perhaps all these tales occupy a kind of hinterland between the prose story and the commentary. They offer a storehouse of narratives, to be told at the discretion of the storyteller. Many of them are ancient, and many probably later; all can be drawn on as and how the raconteur wishes.

This makes the 'real' text of the story fluid and, because of its performative context, a fund of anecdotes and backstories, presumably told as wished. This *jātaka* seems to know it is a *jātaka*, and is as full of narrative interventions, questions, and anticipated complaints as a novel such as Thackeray's *Vanity Fair*, composed also at a time (1847–8) when much 'reading' would actually be listening to someone read it aloud. Many of the *Mahānipāta* have distinguishing features which permeate the whole story, such as the constant greetings and courtesies of the *Vessantara-jātaka* that highlight its strong social basis in mutual generosity and goodwill, or the repeated speech affinities between characters in the *Sāma-jātaka* that seem to embody that story's association with the perfection of loving-kindness. This story is marked by a narrator always inviting the listener, or perhaps more precisely its reader, to think. We are being made conscious that this is actually *jātaka*, a story which we are hearing or reading.

Where a new element on an old variation is introduced, its points of similarity are stressed:

> This is to be understood for all the cases, and we'll give each in the sequence that it occurs in on the list. (Ja VI 335)

Sometimes this sort of instruction is given to the reader or listener:

> And do not wonder, 'How did she leave in the night?' For this boon had been given to the queen first by the king, and so no one obstructed her. (Ja VI 385)

Sometimes more standard commentarial advice to the storyteller is given:

> All of this is to be told according to the method described before. (Ja VI 336)

Perhaps most tellingly, the following comment is made by the narrator about Senaka's silence after the Bodhisatta has demonstrated the superiority of wisdom over wealth and good fortune:

> Even if he could bring another argument, even with a thousand verses, it would not have finished this *jātaka* story. (Ja VI 363)

We are being invited, it seems, to remember that this is a story, and it needs to be ended at some point. The tale is full of interrogatives on the part of the narrator: the word *kiṃkāraṇā*, usually translated as, 'And why is this?' often precedes explanations of an odd development in the plot. It appears thirteen times in the story, but not at all in, for instance, the *Vessantara-jātaka,* so authoritative in its telling and assumptions. Even the simple interrogative *kiṃ*, again often on the part of the narrator, is copious compared to its incidence in other tales.[6] The finale does indeed again remind us that the tale needs, at some point, to come to an end:

> In this way this *jātaka* has moved along to its conclusion. (Ja VI 477)

One feels the storyteller is almost surprised!

The prose in this story seems really a capacious catch-all of stories, anecdotes, and pieces of advice to teller and audience. The tales within tales are usually linked together by the theme of wisdom, but with their constant references to the story as a story, to be told and thought about, they seem to blur the lines between what is 'real' story and what is not.

These oddities seem to have affected its placing in the ten too. In some lists of the *Mahānipāta*, where positions depend on the number of verses in the tale, its length places it before the *Vessantara-jātaka*. Indeed this would be justified by the fact that the Bodhisatta speaks at birth, as he does as Vessantara and Siddhattha. More usually, it is now placed where we have it, as number five, according to the Thai and Burmese placement.[7] This would accord with the fact that the story has 234 verses (*gāthā*) in its old form, 83 added by incorporating others from other *jātaka*s, and one or two verses on the list of nineteen questions, making 317 only after this process has occurred, with minor additions. *Vidhura-jātaka*, the ninth in the Burmese and Thai placement, has 312.

6. For both of these see Yamazaki and Ousaka 2003: 188–9.
7. See Appleton 2010a: 76 n. 20.

Riddles, Questions, and Tests

The various tests and questions to the Bodhisatta fit no easy categorisation. Early tests are for the most part like legal cases (*aṭṭā*), in which Mahosadha, Solomon-like, has to deliver judgement: indeed one, involving a stolen child, gives us a counterpart to Solomon's judgement in the Biblical book of 1 Kings, in which the true mother refuses to participate in a trial that involves the suffering of her child, thereby proving her true status. A similar story is found in China too.[8] Others are like detective stories: a mystery is posed that is solved by the clever questioning of the Bodhisatta, such as in his tracing of the perfume worn by two women, which reveals the true owner of a stolen necklace. It is worthy of note that he always recognizes the culprit where there is a wrong doer, and shows that he is someone with skill in means (*upayakusalo*) not just in knowing this, which no one else can, but in finding a way of 'proving' it satisfactorily to those that are present and allowing the innocent party the restoration of their happiness: surely a fitting anticipation of his role as a teaching Buddha. Some are word games, as in the play on the words 'horse treasure' when Mahosadha is admitted to court (Ja VI 342). Others fall into the category of 'impossible questions', a favourite of traditional folklore, in which a demand, such as one to make a rope of sand, is met by a counter-question—in this case, a request to see the old one which it is replacing—in order to satisfy the king.[9]

Once in the royal court, the tests he faces become more complex and involve extensive storylines and political intrigue. The puzzle of the friendship between goat and dog, whom the king notices become friends when they bring each other food, involves the Bodhisatta working out what the king had been doing beforehand that made him ask the question in the first place: it is a psychological observation, not one arising from the question itself. In this way he finds out the truth. But again, the fact that his wisdom is primarily oriented to others means he does not stop there. Despite the intrigues of the other four advisers against him, he also ensures that they are 'let off the hook', by making them learn riddles, to be told to the king, to suggest they too know the answer and so can avoid banishment by the king. Other riddles are more human in orientation, such as those of 'the riddles of the goddess'. Presiding over the royal parasol,

8. Rhys Davids 1925: xliv.

9. For this story, Grey's *Concordance* is particularly helpful, giving folk-motif index references for many of the incidents and demonstrating affinities with tropes in other Indian and worldwide folk story and literature (see Grey 2000).

this sphinxlike being lifts the quality of the questioning considerably, to questions about the nature of human life and temperament. So her riddles elicit superbly observed answers from the Bodhisatta. That it is the beloved child with whom one is angry, but loves dearly despite misbehavior, for instance, is explained in terms of the child who runs away from his mother in annoyance; it is one of the most finely observed and poignant stories of everyday childhood life in the whole of the *jātaka* collection.

At the court, the Bodhisatta's character, as befits the mode of interchange in this story, is not soft: he is hard-hitting in speech, and counters with his own tough ripostes, for instance, Senaka's criticisms of 'What does the householder's son know?' This gibe, an allusion to the Bodhisatta's birth in a mercantile class, and hence the third Indian caste, is echoed by the king. It would have reinforced the Bodhisatta's appeal to the newly emergent trader classes, sponsors and donors of so much early Buddhist temple architecture and art, and themselves great practitioners of craft, initiative, and resourcefulness. Resourcefulness in this story pays. Thinking in advance and technological skills, deployed in the play hall and the tunnel, are mobilized and used. Even new technologies such as writing are endlessly exploited. Writing had not really existed at the time of the composition of early verses; by the time this story was written down, it was full of the uses of this new means of communication. This has more written messages than any other story in the collection; nearly all are used to further the Bodhisatta's aims and to ensure the safekeeping of his king or his family.

Indeed the art of secret communication is central to this story, expressed through its constant sending and deciphering of messages and puzzles. Riddles and wordplays are imbued with meaning in Indic cultures, and feature throughout Hindu and Jain religious and lay poetry, narrative, and discourse, often intended for very specific effects. We tend to smile or groan with amused exasperation at a pun; perhaps the ancients smiled too, though they treated them with far greater respect. *Nirukti*, or encoded puns, are central to Indian religious commentary, for their betrayal of surprising affinities between apparently unconnected phenomena; they thus momentarily reveal the interrelatedness of the created universe. Verbal communication through hidden understanding is regarded as the mark of a cultivated person (*vidagdha*), revealing the hidden and even secret world beneath the familiar outer surface of things (McHugh 2012: 124ff). Riddles of all kinds are also considered specially appropriate between lovers or those who are closest friends (Balbir 1991–2). It is this incessant revelation of what is hidden and the ability to communicate it to others, in an ever-changing ground of new problems, puzzles and difficulties, that give unity to the apparently disparate plots of *Mahosadha*. Indeed these features render the story both truly Indic as well as Buddhist. Unravelling riddles, puzzles, and wordplays, an activity beloved in Indian culture generally, becomes here, in a Buddhist context, the ongoing work of 'the light of wisdom, shining wisdom, the lamp of wisdom, the jewel of wisdom' (*Dhammasaṅgani* 11), that always has to deal with odd situations, new problems, and the ever-fresh present. By revealing truths that are often subterranean and need to be found, the Bodhisatta shows himself not only as a truly cultivated hero, despite his background, but a wise one too.

Wisdom as a Faculty—and a Power

Throughout the story, 'knowing' is power, and central issues involve the keeping of secrets, the nature of wisdom, and its application in maintaining the safety of the state. Messages, counter-intelligence, false news, and wrong reports punctuate the Bodhisatta's sophisticated gathering of intelligence and its dissemination in the story, from the skilled eliciting of information from the mynah bird by the parrot to the systematic spying network carefully planned by the Bodhisatta to ensure his receipt of information from all over India; this system saves his king, his people, and the whole of India from a ruthlessly dictatorial king. But silence and other forms of bodily communication also transmit information: the parrot gives a sign to the Bodhisatta when he wants to see him privately, the Bodhisatta sends his silence as a message (*mantapadaṃ*) more eloquent than any other to his king via his enemy. Wisdom based on virtue is also the safeguard of the Bodhisatta. Returning from exile to Mithilā, his lack of regality and humble, carefully unwashed clothes send a clear message of reassurance to his king that he is loyal to him and will not usurp the throne.

It is in the language of gestures, however, that the Bodhisatta finds his true equals, both women. In line with Indian expectations that lovers will have a private language (Balbir 1991–2), he communicates with his future wife in signs that she understands and answers. Then she plays her own game of secret intelligence by explaining a 'secret way'—an anticipation of his great work in the tunnel—back to her house. After proving himself by bringing in money with his dexterity as a tailor, the Bodhisatta plays a tough courtship game on his prospective wife, in his ruthless testing of her virtue, that echoes the harshness of her earlier rebirth, Sīvalī, facing her prospective suitors in the *Mahājanaka-jātaka*. But she proves herself through her simple friendliness and acquiescence: it is this, even above her beauty and cleverness, that proves her ability to 'speak the same language' as her potential husband and ensures her safety in incidents to come. They live together, after this episode, in happy accord. She also writes down the names and addresses of those that have delivered the stolen goods on the part of the other wise men: an interesting indication not only that a brahmin's daughter at this time could read and write, but also that she can use these new technologies to good use, to protect her household. This device is again an anticipation of one the Bodhisatta's plots, in marking the gifts given to the hundred and one kings so they can be used as 'proofs' of their disloyalty to Cūḷani. The other female figure who speaks with gestures is Bherī, the independent female ascetic who thinks up 'The Question of the Water Spirit' and ensures that the great wisdom and loyalty of the Bodhisatta is known to all. When this is interpreted wrongly by the ladies who watch their interchange, she and the Bodhisatta protect themselves from charges of disloyalty by simply speaking the truth: their secrecy has not been used for plotting, but simply for communication among equals.

These two female characters seem far more intelligent than other characters in the story, using the same hidden communication system as the Bodhisatta—that of gesture—and protecting him from harm. Indeed it is the female characters in this story who are the most ingenious, basing their skill not on the desire to gain power, but to ensure the safety of the kingdom and the Bodhisatta as the adviser, who becomes 'the white parasol' of the state itself to the king. The goddess of the parasol threatens the king with death if he does not reinstate Mahosadha after his banishment, and poses riddles, testing the Bodhisatta's human understanding as well as his cleverness, that she knows only he can answer. Queen Udumbarā, also a good writer, his protector and adviser in the early part of the tale, sends messages to him secretly that protect him from execution on the advice of the king's other wise men. Indeed if we look at most of the *Mahānipāta*, we see that women are quite crucial in ensuring the Bodhisatta's safety and wellbeing. Perhaps Nemi is the only one so far where a female interceder does *not* at some stage act as protector and saviour. Goddesses come to his aid as Temiya, Janaka, Sāma, as if their very apartness from affairs of state confers a freedom to intervene and act on behalf of the environment, vehicles for his earlier good karma and actions in the kingdom. The

Mahosadha-jātaka gives a tough world, and the story's women are all equal to it: where wisdom is based on virtue, it gives an ingenuity that far exceeds that of others.

In this *jātaka* the Bodhisatta, and indeed the central female characters, are learning and using the intangibles of wisdom with, as Hallisey points out, a 'moral creativity' that ensures that not only is the truth recognized, but a solution found to make it clear to others, a far more difficult and often highly subtle task (see Hallisey 2010). In the endlessly resourceful creativity applied to all sorts of ends in the tale, their wisdom is not just the ability to know something—it is how to second-guess disaster, how to protect others, and how to keep king and city safe. This *jātaka* represents the hard world of *realpolitik*: from the outset of his time at court the Bodhisatta, occasionally supported but never challenged by these female characters, has to participate in all kinds of debates, challenges, counter-challenges, and underhand plots which all involve the testing of various aspects of his ingenuity, statecraft, and ability to work out problems that seems utterly insuperable to others. In this he has appeared to some Machiavellian, and in one sense he is, but the misunderstood term *accusata/escusata* derived from *The Prince* (1513) does not just mean the 'ends justify the means'. In this story the means have to work, and the work has to be for the good.

Many people are called 'wise' or *paṇḍito* in this tale: the people of the East Market Town are reputedly wise; so are the wise men, as is Kevaṭṭa, the adviser to the enemy king. But being a 'wise man' for the Bodhisatta involves many other features that place his ingenuity out of the class of the puzzle solver, as one who looks, observes, and does what is necessary and apt for the people concerned, in a way that is appropriate to the situation and times. In this he really is *upayakusalo*, possessing the ability to think up an *upaya*, a stratagem or a trick, a trait that is shared by many characters with an often febrile inventiveness that characterises the good, and the bad, such as Kevaṭṭa and the other advisers of the king. Although the mores and standard of courtesy in this tale, often including the Bodhisatta in his ruthless interchanges and intelligence work, stretch our definition of what is healthy or *kusala*, his intention and orientation is both healthy and 'good' in that it brings happiness to others too. The *Abhidhamma* text *Dhammasaṅgaṇī* notes that *paññā* only arises in skilful consciousness, and is only true wisdom, not cunning, when accompanied by one of the divine abidings of loving-kindness, compassion, sympathetic joy, and equanimity (see, for instance, *Dhammasaṅgaṇī* 11).[10] Wisdom is a faculty and power in the *Abhidhamma*, present in all correct *jhāna* and potentially active in dealings with the world, for ordinary people, those who have attained stages of the path, and *arahats*. We see nothing of its meditative application in the world of this story; some nature of its correct placing and motivation, even in the midst of war and intrigue, is never entirely lost. It is sometimes thought that *jātakas* do not show 'real' wisdom, but a lowly counterpart. But perhaps we need to see this the other way around: that from a *jātaka* and *abhidhamma* point of view the mental factor (*cetasika*) of wisdom can be present in all kinds of activities in daily life, including the many crafts, such as pottery, tailoring, and statecraft, as practised in this story.

Imagery

The rich language of imagery and metaphor in this story can rest in the mind as applying to wisdom too. There is much in the tale that uses the language of hunting and catching: the deer on the path or the fish on the hook, for instance (vv. 16, 19, 66). But the most memorable images are those that in some way suggest the intuition of the wisdom that gets answers, and the way the Bodhisatta teaches in his final life as the Buddha. From the nineteen questions, the unraveling of a ball of thread to find what is underneath, the ability to see the true jewel and not its reflection, the question that makes people reveal the truth themselves, and the capacity to 'smell' the true perfume are all effective ways of describing not just the Bodhisatta's skill in means, but the abilities of the Buddha too in dealing with practitioners on the path.

Merlin Peris has explored the image of the curious jewel, or 'curved jewel cluster' (*maṇikhaṇḍho aṭṭhāsu ṭhānesu vaṃko*) described in 'The Question of the Jewel', that the Bodhisatta sees needs to be threaded by ants. It perhaps has eight curves or is octagonal, with eight faces; the descriptive word is *vaṃko*, variously translated as 'crooked', 'bent', or 'curved' (PED 591). Given to the Bodhisatta when he is king in the *Kusa-jātaka*, it is still in the royal

10. For discussion of *kusala* and *akusala* consciousness, see Cousins 1996. Wisdom is not always present in skilful consciousness, which may arise with two roots of non-greed (generosity) and non-hatred (loving-kindness). Actions that are kind and generous, for instance, may be skilful but lack understanding. According to the *Abhidhamma*, interestingly, it *never* occurs, however, in unskilful consciousness: cleverness and ingenuity, without a basis in *kusala citta*, which is always accompanied by an underlying motive of non-harm, are not considered to be true wisdom.

coffers and is later secretly stolen by Devinda, the king's jewel valuer (v. 77). Whenever he carries it, its auspiciousness brings him wealth, reckoned in multiples of eight coins, and popularity in the king's own court. It is called a jewel treasure by the Bodhisatta, an image that aligns it with the seven treasures of a Universal Monarch, and is requested by him for his great challenge with the enemy king's adviser, Kevaṭṭa.[11] But when the jewel is tossed to him, Kevaṭṭa, unskilful in intention, cannot catch it and it slips to the ground, so he is left greedily scrambling around at the others' feet, thereby inadvertently showing his own inferiority, and that of his state, to the king of Mithilā. This incident is one of the most popular images in Southeast Asian temple art. As Peris points out, there is something about this jewel, connected to the eight curves, that means it cannot be threaded. In the 'Question of the Jewel' it needs to be done by ants, who are led on by the honey smeared on its side. Usually shown in Sri Lankan temple art as a kind of square, with curves around the side, the jewel was clearly intended to be more unusual in some way. Peris makes a comparison with the ancient Greek story of Daedalus ('clever worker'), the great inventor and designer of the labyrinth. He used ants to take a thread through a spiral shell, tempting them also by honey. Peris points out that maybe the 'crookedness' is a kind of spiral effect in the jewel—it is a present from Sakka, after all, and need not be a 'real' type of stone (Peris 1978). While Peris carefully avoids discussion of the tales' origins, his analysis of the affinities between the jewel and the shell, and the tunnel and the labyrinth, is a good one. Something has to be done that is hidden, involving work in secret, away from sight.

Amarā's 'Secret Way', the lattice that hides from Kevaṭṭa the fact the city has been decorated for a wedding (Ja VI 412), and indeed the threading of this curious jewel all anticipate the climactic image of the story: the tunnel, an escape route for the King of Mithilā and his men, a means of ensuring the safe departure of King Cūḷani's family, and a restorative resting place for the hundred and one kings, their armies, and their attendants. Here we see a powerful metaphor for the Bodhisatta's final life. It is built to his recommendations by craftsmen, including members of an army 'released from prison'. These followers of the Bodhisatta, like his *saṅgha* in his final life, construct a whole world in which liberation is made possible.

11. Here the jewel is called, *aṭṭhavaṃkamaṇiratanaṃ*, a treasure with 'eight curves' or 'eight crooked features' (Ja VI 403 ff.)

Sun, moon, Meru and the four continents, and the six sense heavens are skilfully painted on its walls. New gadgets are employed: the lights can all be revealed or not, in one stroke of a switch. Fully lit, it is like the meeting place of the gods, Sudhammā. But the enemy army is subjected to great terror inside it when the Bodhisatta extinguishes the lights to ensure they are mindful of his power. Unlit, and closed off, it is a hell. In a self-conscious nod to the way so many *jātaka*s begin, he points out when he releases the army, and the tunnel is again filled with light, that once before they had been delivered by him: when Cūḷani's plan to poison them all is foiled by the Bodhisatta's spies. This finally cures them of enmity and is a good description of the way the Bodhisatta, if sometimes hard, actually uses wisdom in the stories. In some ways the incident is an encapsulation of the *jātaka* form and function. Wisdom is compared throughout the *sutta*s to a lamp, restored to place, that fills what has been dark with light. In this last great episode of the *Mahosadha-jātaka*, the puzzle that lies behind existence, which is dark without the light of wisdom, is demonstrated. It reminds us of the wisdom of the Buddha's final life and his very exposition of the *jātaka*s themselves that illuminate the past and the lives of those that listen to them.

Art and Literature

The tale has always been amongst the most popular of the last ten, particularly in Sri Lanka, where the Sinhalese version expands on the story greatly. It has also prompted new texts, such as the *Lokaneyyapakaraṇa,* roughly contemporaneous with the *Paññāsajātaka* collection.[12] In Sri Lanka it seems to have influenced architectural planning: the fourteenth- and fifteenth-century fortress at Kotte is reputedly modeled on the Bodhisatta's plans for defence for his own city. *Mahosadha-jātaka* often features as a single tale in Sinhala and Burmese manuscripts.[13] In the twentieth century, anecdotes derived from the story frequently feature in children's tales and retellings, such as Perera's *The Sage of India* (1976).[14] There is also a

12. See Appleton 2010a: 76 n. 22.

13. See, in the Bodleian collection, the Pāli-Burmese *nissaya* on the story, purchased in 1898, MS. Pali b.11. There are various single translations into Southeast Asian languages listed under 'Mahosadha' in the British Library's online catalogue, along with a Siamese palm-leaf manuscript (1845). The story is linked to the establishing of legal precedent in Myanmar and Thailand (see Huxley 1997).

14. For discussion of this see Appleton 2010a: 80 ff.

Tibetan version, perhaps unfairly described as 'enlarged and deteriorated' by Winternitz (1977: 139 n. 3).[15]

In art it is depicted along with the others of the Great Ten. Oddly enough, tunnels, secret places, and caves often do feature in Buddhist places of worship, though without any apparent connections with this story. The thirteenth- and fourteenth-century temple complex at Wat Umong in Chiang Mai, Thailand, has extensive manmade tunnels, now painted with woodland life. At Hpa An in Myanmar, dark caves with carvings and paintings, such as at Kawgun and Yathaypyan, were used by early Mon culture, as now, as places of worship, and lead through to Buddhist shrines. At Wat Si Chum, in Thailand, a tunnel of *jātaka* stories appears to have been intended to be sequestered, a hidden treasure beneath the temple. Keeping *jātaka* stories in a dark place is also a feature of the twelfth-century Gubyaukgyi temple in Pagan, where tiny Mon windows mean the richly painted murals in its tiny corridors can only be seen by the light of a torch or a candle: here too, some light from elsewhere is needed to bring these vivid images to life.

'The Pañcālan has come with his entire army...'

[329] The Teacher told this story while staying in the Jeta Grove about the perfection of wisdom.[16] One day the monks were in the *dhamma* hall extolling the great wisdom of the Tathāgata. 'The lord of great wisdom is the Tathāgata—of wide wisdom, of smiling wisdom, of quick wisdom, of sharp wisdom, crushing contrary teachings, by the power of his own wisdom making gentle and subduing the brahmins Kūṭadanta[17] and the

15. See Schiefner 1876: 673 ff.

16. This first chapter of the Sri Lankan version and translation (UJST) demonstrates its imaginative elaboration of the Pāli, in that an extensive 'story of the present' describes in lively and expressive terms the city of Sāvatthi. In a paean to the Buddha, this describes in detail his miraculous presence, including his emission of brightly coloured rays as well as his great compassion, loving-kindness, and wisdom (UJST 1–4).

17. Kūṭadanta challenges the Bodhisatta in the *Kūṭadanta Sutta* (DN 5) about the nature of sacrifice; the Buddha routs him in argument and persuades him of the importance of generosity and suchlike instead, whereupon his opponent asks to join the *saṅgha* as a monk.

rest, the ascetics Sabhiya[18] and the rest, the thieves Aṅgulimāla[19] and the rest, the *yakkhas* Āḷavaka and the rest, the gods Sakka and the rest, and the Great Brahmās Baka and the rest.[20] He gave the going forth to a vast multitude and established them in the path and its fruits. It is in this way that the Teacher is of great wisdom.' When the Teacher sat down they explained this to him. When he had approached he asked, 'What, monks, were you discussing?' and they told him. [330] He said, 'It is not only now that the Tathāgata is wise in this way. Once long ago, he was full of wisdom, before his wisdom had become ripe, as he practised wandering, for the sake of awakening wisdom.' And he told this story about the past.

In times past in Mithilā there ruled a Videhan king, and he had four wise men who instructed him in the rule of the kingdom: Senaka, Pukkusa, Kāvinda, and Devinda. At that time, at dawn on the day when the Bodhisatta took rebirth in his mother's womb, the king saw the following dream: four columns of fire blazed upwards in the four corners of the royal court up to the height of the great wall. In the middle of them rose up a flame the size of a firefly and at that moment it went far higher than the pillars of fire, and rose right up to the Brahmā heaven, and remained there, shedding a radiance over the entire world, so that even a grain the size of a mustard seed on the ground could be discerned. The world with all its *devas* worshipped it with garlands and incense. Many people wandered through this flame, but not even a hair on their skin was singed. The king saw this dream and rose up terrified: 'What is going to happen?' And he stayed up till dawn, sitting and mulling it over. Now the four teachers went to him and approached him, asking whether he had had a comfortable sleep: 'How did you sleep, sire?'

'How could I sleep well after I had such a dream!' he exclaimed.

18. Sabhiya wandered from teacher to teacher until he found and was convinced by the Buddha (see *Sutta Nipāta* III 6 and DPPN).

19. Aṅgulimāla is one of the most famous of the Buddha's followers. A serial killer, he had undertaken to take the little fingers of five hundred victims and make a necklace from them, until he was converted by the Buddha and attained arahatship (see his entry in DPPN). His *paritta* blessing (see *Aṅgulimāla Sutta*, MN 86), given to a woman unable to deliver her baby, is used to this day for women in labour.

20. Baka had strong eternalist beliefs that were dissolved by the Buddha (SN I 142–144; Bodhi 2000: 237; and DPPN). A variant reading to *brahmāno* (F) has been taken, *mahābrahme* (Bd).

Then the teacher Senaka said, 'Don't be frightened by this, Great King, it is an auspicious dream, and there will be prosperity.'

'How?' asked the king, and he explained, 'Great King, a fifth wise man will be born who will surpass us four; we four are like the columns of fire, but in the midst of us there will be as if a fifth column of fire has come into being. And he will be without equal, and take on a responsibility that has no parallel in the world of gods and men.'

'And where is he at the moment?'

'Great King, today he must have either taken rebirth at conception, or he has come out from his mother's womb.' So he explained through the power of his craft what he had seen, as if by divine vision. From that time the king remembered his words.

Now at the four gates of Mithilā there were four market towns, called East Market Town, South Market Town, West Market Town, and North Market Town. [331] And in these, in the middle of East Market Town, lived a merchant called Sirivaḍḍha (Auspicious Wealth) and his wife was called Sumanādevī (Queen of Jasmines). On the day at the same time the king saw his visionary dream the Great Being fell away from the Heaven of the Thirty-Three and took rebirth in the womb of Sumanādevī, and at the same time a thousand others also took rebirth in various merchant families. At the end of the tenth month she gave birth to a child the colour of gold. At that moment Sakka, looking down on the world of men, recognized the birth of the Great Being, and said, 'It is fitting to make known to gods and men this shoot of the Buddha.' And in one moment he entered, without being seen by men, and placed a healing herb (*osadhī*)[21] in the child's hand as he was being born; and then he slipped back to his own abode.

The Great Being grasped the herb firmly in his fist, and at the moment he emerged from his mother's womb she felt no pain, but rather he came out as easily as water from a pot. When his mother saw the herb branch in her son's hands she asked, 'What have you got there?'

'A medicinal herb,' he said. He placed the divine herb in his mother's hands and said, 'Dear mother, please give this to anyone who is suffering from a sickness.' She was filled with joy, and took it to the merchant Sirivaḍḍhaka, who had suffered for seven years with a headache. He was also filled with joy and said, 'This child emerged from his mother's womb

21. *Osadhī* refers generally to a medicinal plant, and is also the name for the morning star (see DP I 593).

holding this herb, and from the moment of his birth he conversed with his mother. A medicine given by a being of such auspicious merit must be full of potency.' So he took the herb and rubbed it on a grindstone and then smeared just a little on his forehead. The seven-year old headache just disappeared, like water off a lotus leaf. Filled with happiness, he exclaimed, 'This is a potent medicine!' And he made known everywhere the arrival of the Great Being clutching the herb in his hand. And those who were ill all came to the merchant's house and asked for the herb. After rubbing it on the grindstone and mixing it with water, they gave a tiny bit to everyone who came.

Through the divine herb smeared on the body, people allayed all kinds of illnesses, and were happy. 'Sirivaḍḍha the businessman has the potency of the herb in his house,' they said as they left extolling his virtues. [332] And on his name-taking day the great businessman said, 'There can be no other name for him than this: let it be Osadha.' So he gave the name Prince Osadha to his son, and then he thought, 'My son has great wisdom. He will not remain alone; young men born on the same day should be with him.' So he got people to look around, and hearing that there were a thousand young men born on the same day, he gave them all ornaments and sent them wet nurses, saying, 'These will be my son's attendants.' And he arranged a blessings festival for them with the Bodhisatta. He adorned the young men, and on that very day let them into the service of the Bodhisatta.

The Great Being grew up playing with them, and by the time he was seven years old he was as beautiful as a golden statue. As he was playing with them in the town, elephants and other animals used to pass by and disrupt their games, and sometimes the children became upset by the rain and the heat. Now one day as they played, an out-of-season rainstorm rose up. When the Great Being, who was as strong as an elephant, saw it, he ran for cover into a house and as the other children ran after him they fell over each other's feet and got bruises and sprains on their knees and other limbs. So the Bodhisatta thought to himself, 'There ought to be a hall for playing here so we will not play in this way.' And he said to the boys, 'Let's build a hall here, where we can stand, sit, or lie in time of wind, heat, or rain. So each one bring a bit of cash.' The thousand boys all did so, and the Great Being sent for a distinguished housebuilder and said, 'Please build a hall at this spot,' and he gave him the thousand coins. The housebuilder took the thousand coins and agreed.

He levelled the ground, got the ground ready for a floor by getting rid of tree stumps and suchlike, and stretched out a measuring thread, but he just did not get what the Great Being had in mind. The Great Being described how to arrange the stretched-out thread in the way he had in mind, saying, 'Stretch it out in this way and you'll be doing it right.'

The housebuilder replied, 'Sir, I have stretched it out in the way that accords with my own training. I don't know any other way.'

'If you do not know, then why have you taken so much of our money? I will do a plan for the hall; bring the thread and stretch it out as I show you.' He had him bring the thread and he laid it out himself, as if the job had been done by Vissakamma.[22] [333] Then he said to the housebuilder, 'Would you be able to mark out the plan in this way?'

The carpenter replied that he would not.

'But will you be able to do it from my calculations?'

The carpenter replied that he could.

The Great Being made arrangements for the hall so that there was one place for all other guests who visited, one place for living accommodation for those who were poor, another place for the lying-in of destitute women, another place for visiting ascetics and brahmins, another for all other kinds of visitors, and another for visiting merchants to store their goods; and all these places had doors to the outside. And he organized here a sports and playground, here a court of justice, and here a *dhamma* hall. And when the work was finished he got together some artists and arranged for them to do delightful paintwork, so that it was just like the hall of the *devas*, Sudhammā (Good Teaching/Justice). Then he said, 'This hall is not yet completely beautiful. It would be good to have some water features.' So he had the ground for a water feature dug out for an architect, and after discussing it with him and giving him the money, he arranged for him to construct a water feature with a thousand bends and a hundred bathing places. The water was covered with the five kinds of lotuses and was as

22. Vissakamma, the architect of the gods, appears in a number of places in the Great Ten, always acting on the request of King Sakka. He prepares a place to stay in *Temiya* for the Bodhisatta and his family and friends, with fruit bearing trees to sustain them, and a pool. In *Sāma*, he creates a leaf hut and a single-track path for the arrival of the parents of the Bodhisatta in their pastoral wilderness. In *Vessantara* he also prepares a hermitage for the Bodhisatta and his family when they are sent in exile. See Chapter 1: 72; Chapter 3: 127; Chapter 10: 574; and DPPN.

beautiful as the lake in the heavenly garden, Nandana.[23] On its banks he had planted various trees and made a pleasure garden just like Nandana. And close by he set up a public distribution point of food and drink to holy men, whether brahmin or those following a good doctrine,[24] and for visitors and people from the neighbouring villages. These actions became famous everywhere, and crowds of people flocked to the place, and the Great Being used to sit in the hall, discussing the rights and wrongs of the good or bad situations of all the people who came, and gave a judgement on each one. It became like a happy time when a Buddha comes to arise in the world.

Now at that time, after a gap of seven years, the Videhan king remembered, 'The four wise men advised me that a fifth wise man would be born who would surpass them. Find out where he lives now.' And he sent his four ministers to the four gates of the city. They went out by three of the gates, but did not see the Great Being. But leaving by the eastern gate they saw the hall and its various attractions, and thought to themselves, 'This hall must have been built, or caused to be built, by a wise man.' [334] They asked people who the architect of the hall was, and received this reply: 'This hall was not built by the power of any architect on his own: it was made with designs by the son of the merchant Sirivaḍḍha, the wise man Osadha.'

'And how old is he?'

'He has just completed his seventh year.'

The minister calculated what had happened since the king had had his dream and thought, 'This is just as the king saw in his dream.' He sent a messenger to the king, with this message: 'Sire, Mahosadha, the son of the businessman Sirivaḍḍha, is now seven years old, but has masterminded a hall as if he were an ascetic of a hundred years. He has arranged a water feature and a pleasure garden. Shall I get him and take him to you, or not?' The king heard this and was delighted, and summoned Senaka to inform him of the matter, and asked him, 'Should I send for him?' But Senaka was jealous of his reputation, and replied, 'Great King, a man is not to be called a wise man just because he has created a hall and suchlike. Anyone can do this: it is just a trifling matter.' When the king heard his comment, he thought, 'There must be a reason for this.' And he kept silent. Then he sent

23. Nandanavana is the name of the pleasure garden in the Tāvatiṃsa heaven, and Nandana the lake that adorns it.

24. *Dhammikasamaṇabrāhmaṇāñ ca* 'ascetics and brahmins who are just', or who follow a just or good doctrine or way of life.

back the messenger with instructions that the minister should remain for a while in the place, and examine the wise man carefully.

So when the minister heard this, he did stay for a while, and did conduct an investigation. Here is a list of the series of tests that took place:

The piece of meat, the oxen, the threaded necklace, the cotton thread,
the son, the lump, and the carriage;
The stick, the skull, the snake, the cock, the jewel, the calving;
The rice, the sand, the pool, and the ass, and the jewel.[25] *(1)*

1. THE QUESTION OF THE PIECE OF MEAT

One day, when the Bodhisatta was going to the play area, a certain hawk carried off a piece of meat from the slab at a slaughterhouse and flew up into the sky. Some young boys saw this and thought, 'Hey, let's make him drop it.' And they followed the hawk. The hawk flew here, there, and everywhere, and they looked up and were going backwards and forwards and all over the place, throwing stones and suchlike, falling over each other and tiring themselves out. Then the wise man said to them, 'I'll get him to drop it.'

'Then get him to drop it, sir.'

25. This little verse is the first of a series that come at the beginning of the story. It is really a memory device (omitted from the Cowell and Rouse translation). The text probably refers here to a further jewel test, which takes place later, after the boy has been installed in the palace. The entire section that follows, up to the beginning of 344, is in small type in F; indeed laid out without even paragraph divisions, it was clearly not regarded by him as worthy of inclusion in the story as a whole. There is some justification in this: there are no verses, and the tales have no obvious connection with the rest of the story beyond being an extensive means of testing the Bodhisatta further. One suspects they were added as a kind of grouping of folk tales associated with legal 'cases' (*aṭṭā*) popular amongst early Buddhists. They certainly give us a delightful picture of village life, with an authentic feel: the *timbaru* seed in the cotton, the necklace perfumed with panic grass, and the funny story of the man pretending the river is shallow are all suggestive of longstanding folktales being collected together under the umbrella of Bodhisatta rulings. The section also contains the famous story that has its counterpart in the rulings of Solomon: the disputed baby. (See also Grey 2000: 218–26 for extensive reference to folk motifs and tropes found in other Indic and world literary traditions.) VRI and the Sinhalese version include all this section as part of the main text. For those interested in comparisons between translations, it is also worth noting that the editor of the six-volume translation of the *jātakas*, Cowell, died while he had not completed this section or the remaining text of the sixth volume (his manuscript ends, Rouse's preface notes, on p. 338).

He said to them, 'Just look.' Then, without looking up, he ran after the hawk as quickly as the wind and entered into the hawk's shadow. He clapped his hands and gave a loud shout. The power of the shout seemed to penetrate through to the bird's innards, and he, terrified, dropped the meat. The Great Being, watching the shadow of the bird, knew where the meat would be dropped, [335] and caught it in the air before it fell to the ground. The people, seeing this wonder, made a great roar, shouting and clapping their hands. The minister heard of this, and sent an account to the king, telling how the wise man had by this means made the bird drop the piece of meat. The king heard about this and asked Senaka, 'Shall I bring him to the palace?' But Senaka thought, 'From the moment he comes here, my glory will diminish, and the king will forget that I am around. He cannot be allowed to be brought here.' Coloured by envy, he said, 'Great King, no, not for such a trifling matter.' So the king, being even-handed, sent a minister to test him where he was.

2. THE QUESTION OF THE OXEN

A certain man, living in the village of Yavamajjhaka (Village-in-the-Corn)[26] bought some oxen from another village, thinking, 'I'll plough when the rains have been.' The next day he led them to some grassland and sat on the back of one of the oxen, but he was so tired that he got down and fell asleep, and just at that moment, a rustler came and drove the oxen away. When the man woke up he could not see his oxen, but as he looked all around he saw the oxen rustler running away. So he jumped up and shouted, 'Hey, where are you going with my oxen!'

'They are mine, and I'll take them wherever I want.'

A large group of people collected around. The noise of the argument reached the wise man as he was standing by the door of the hall. He called both of them, and saw the culprit: he realized that one was the thief and one was the owner. But he asked them, 'Why are you arguing?'

The oxen owner said, 'After buying them I was moving them from one place to another with my own hands, and brought them to graze on my land on a grassy patch. Then I was negligent, and saw someone had taken my oxen and run away. I looked all around, saw him, and tried to follow him. The villagers know that he took them from me to sell them.'

26. See PED 551, 'lying in the middle of the cornfield', on the four market places at the cardinal points outside Mithilā. Mithilā features in *Janaka* and *Nemi* too.

The thief said, 'He is lying; they are mine and were born in my household.'

So then the wise man said, 'I will examine this legal question justly. Shall we sort it out with a thorough examination?'

'Yes, let's sort it out,' they replied. Thinking he needed to get the hearts of the people on his side, he questioned the thief first. 'Regarding these three oxen: what have they been fed and given to drink?'

He replied, 'This one has been fed rice gruel, this one crushed sesame seeds, and this one beans.'

Then he asked the oxen owner, who said, 'Sir, where would someone as poor as me get rice gruel and suchlike! They have been given grass to feed on.'

Then he asked a man to fetch some panic seeds[27] and had them beaten in a mortar and mashed in water and then fed to the oxen. The oxen vomited grass. He showed this to the people, and questioned the thief. 'Are you or are you not the thief?'

'I am,' admitted the thief.

'Then do not do anything like this again.'

But the Bodhisatta's retinue took him away and chopped off his hands and feet and rendered him powerless. Then the wise man spoke to him, admonishing him. 'This suffering has come to you in your present life. But in future you will suffer terrible torment in the Niraya hells. So from now on abandon this behavior.' And he gave him the five precepts.

The minister sent news of this exactly as it had occurred, and he consulted Senaka. But he said, 'This is only a case about oxen; anyone could decide it.' The king, being even-handed, sent the same instructions as before. This is to be understood for all the cases, and we'll give each in the sequence that it occurs in on the list.[28]

3. THE QUESTION OF THE THREADED NECKLACE

A certain poor lady wove together various threads in different colours and made them into a necklace. When she went to bathe in the pool constructed by the wise man, she took it off her neck and put it on her clothes. A young woman saw it and conceived a great desire for it. So she picked it up and

27. Foxtail millet (*Setaria italica*, formerly known as *Panicum italicum*) was used as an emetic when mixed with water (Ja I 419). It has a long history in Asia, and has been grown in China since the sixth millennium BCE. It is primarily used as cattle fodder.

28. *Ito paraṃ pana uddānamattam eva vibhjitvā dassessāma.* This sentence perhaps suggests instructions to a storyteller.

went up to the woman and said, 'This necklace is *so* beautiful! How much did it cost to make? [336] I am going to make one myself. Could I put it on to get the measurements of it?'

The other woman, being of a straightforward disposition, said, 'Please, try it on.'

The woman put it on her neck and then went away. The other woman quickly got out of the water, put on her clothes, and ran after her and grabbed her clothes. 'You're running off wearing the necklace I made!'

The young woman said, 'I haven't taken anything of yours. This is the necklace I wear around my neck.' A large group of people collected around as they heard this. The wise man was playing with some lads when noise from the commotion they were making came through the door of the hall. He asked what the noise was, and when he heard he called both arguing women together. He immediately recognized the thief by her bearing. But he asked them, 'Will you abide by my ruling?'

They said, 'Yes, sir.'

He questioned the thief first. 'What perfume did you anoint the necklace with?'

She said, 'I always use "All-Flower Bouquet".'[29] 'All-Flower Bouquet' is the name for a combination of various perfumes. And then he asked the other woman.

She said, 'Where would a poor woman like me get "All-Flower Bouquet"? I always just use panic-grass flowers to scent my necklace.'

The wise man had a bowl of water brought, put the necklace in it and asked for a parfumier to come and smell it. He did and recognized the smell of panic-grass flowers. He recited a verse, found also in the first book of the *jātakas*:[30]

> 'This is not "All-Flower Bouquet"; only pure panic-grass flower
> pervades!
> This deceiver has told a lie; the older lady the truth.' *(2)*

The Great Being explained to the people what had happened, and asked the woman, 'Are you or are you not the thief?' And he made her deceitful

29. The word *sabbasaṃhāraka*, 'collector of all things' seems to refer to a known collection of perfumes, presumably bought from a shop, and so an expensive choice.

30. See J I 424 for *jātaka* 110, *Sabbasaṃhāraka-jātaka*, which recounts this incident with the verse as its single verse. *Gadrabha-pañha-jātaka* (J 111) gives the question of the ass, and *Amarādevī-pañha-jātaka* (J 112) is Queen Amarā's question. See the introduction to this story for a full list of associated *jātakas*.

nature known. From that time the wise nature of the Great Being was revealed to people at large.

4. THE QUESTION OF THE THREAD

A certain woman who used to guard cotton fields was watching over the fields and she picked up some pure cotton, spun it into fine thread, then wound it up into a ball and placed it on her knees.[31] Then she thought, 'I think I'll bathe in the wise man's pool.' She placed the ball on her clothes and went into the pool to bathe. Now another woman saw her and with a covetous mind picked it up and said, 'Ah, lady, what a pleasing ball of thread! Did you make it?' She snapped her fingers and put it on her knees as if to examine it—and then went off. All of this is to be told according to the method described before.[32]

The wise man asked the thief, 'What did you put inside the ball when you made it?'

She replied, 'A cotton seed, sir.'

Then he asked the other lady, and she said, 'A *timbaru* seed, sir.'[33]

He informed the people around what both women had said, unwound the ball of cotton, and found a *timbaru* seed. He got the thief to admit her theft, and people around were delighted at the way the case had been investigated, and gave great rounds of applause.

5. THE QUESTION OF THE CHILD

A certain woman took her baby and went to the wise man's pool to wash her face. She bathed her child and sat him down on her clothes while she went to wash her face and bathe. At that moment, a certain *yakkhinī* saw the child and wished to eat him up. She took hold of the dress and said, 'This is a lovely child; is he yours?'

She said, 'Yes, lady.'

'May I give him something to drink?' she asked.

31. She would be guarding the field from crows and birds, usually a woman's job. Cotton was usually mangled to free it from seeds, dried and then spun from tufts into thread. For this later Sri Lankan way of spinning thread on a spindle, held against the thigh and usually undertaken by women, see Coomaraswamy 1956: 235 and plate VI on p. 3.

32. Again, this sentence possibly gives instructions to the storyteller.

33. *Timbarukkha* is possibly *Diospyros embryopteris* or *malabarica* (DP II 328), the pale-moon ebony tree or gaub. See Ja VI 529, v. 334.

'Yes, do feed him.'

So she took him and played with him for a little while, and then started to run away with him. When the other woman saw this she rushed after her and grabbed her saying, 'Where are you taking my baby?'

The *yakkhinī* said, 'Where did you get this baby? It's mine!' As they were having this argument they passed the door of the hall, and the wise man heard the commotion. He called the women and asked them, 'What is it?' When he heard the case, although he saw at once that one was a *yakkhinī*, by her having red eyes that did not blink, [337] he said, 'Will you abide by my judgement?'

'Yes, we will,' they both agreed.

So he drew a line and placed the baby in the middle of it. He told the *yakkhinī* to take the child by the hands, and the mother to take him by the feet. Then he said, 'Now, pull the child: the one who can pull it to her keeps him.' So they both pulled. The child, pulled in both directions, cried out in great pain. The mother let go of the child as if her heart were being broken, and stood there in tears. The wise man asked the assembly, 'Is it the heart of the mother that is tender towards the child, or her who is not the mother?'

'It is the heart of the mother, wise man,' they replied.

'Is the one who held on to the child the mother, or the one who released him?'

'The one who released him,' they replied.

'Do you know who it is who took the child?'

'We do not know her,' they replied.

'She is a *yakkhinī*, and took the child to eat him.'

'How do you know that, wise man?' 'Because her eyes are red and do not blink, and she leaves no shadow, and she has neither fear nor compassion.'

Then he asked, 'Are you or are you not a *yakkhinī*?'

'I am.'

'And why did you take the child?'

'To eat him, sir.'

He admonished her: 'You are a blind fool. Because you did wrong in an earlier life, you were born a *yakkhinī*. Now you are also doing wrong, and are a blind fool.' He established her in the five precepts, and sent her on her way. The child's mother, said, 'May you live for a long time, wise man!' She sang his praises, and went away with her child.[34]

34. See Grey 2000: 218 ff. for various scholars who have discussed the parallel with

6. THE QUESTION OF THE DARK LUMP

Now there was a certain man called Goḷakāḷa (Dark Lump). He got the name 'lump' because he was very small, and the name 'dark' because that was his colour. He worked in a certain house for seven years and obtained a wife called Dīghatālā (Long Palm Tree).[35] One day he addressed her, 'Dear lady, cook some pancakes and food, and we will go and see your parents.' At first she opposed the plan, arguing, 'What's the use of parents?' But after asking her three times, he got her to cook some pancakes for the journey, and taking some provisions and a present, he set out on the road with her. While on the road he came to a river that was not very deep, but they were both terrified of water. So they dared not cross it, and stood on the bank. Now a certain poor man named Dīghapiṭṭhi (Long Back) was wandering up and down on the bank and arrived at that spot. When they saw him, they asked him, 'Sir, is the river deep or shallow?'

Seeing that they were terrified of water, he told them it was very deep, and filled with hungry fish.

'Sir, how will you get across it then?' they asked.

'I have made a friendship with the crocodiles and *makaras* that live here; because of this they do not harm me.'

'Take us with you,' they said.

When he agreed, they gave him some meat and drink. When he had finished his meal he asked them, 'Which one of you should I carry over first?'

'Take your sister first,[36] and then take me,' said Goḷakāḷa. So the man picked her up on his shoulders and took the provisions and the present and went down into the river. When he had gone a little way, he bent down and walked crouched in a sitting posture. Goḷakāḷa, standing on the bank, thought, 'This river must be very deep. It is so hard for even such a man as Dīghapiṭṭhi. It will be impassable for me.' When the other had carried the woman to the middle of the river, he said to her, 'Lady, I will look after you, and you shall live dressed in fine clothes and ornaments, and have menservants and female attendants. What will this crooked little fellow do for you? Please do what I say.' She listened to his words, and broke her

Solomon's judgement in the Bible (1 Kings 3:16–28).

35. Her name suggests she was very tall, like perhaps the man the couple meet.

36. All three manuscripts give *tava* 'your' instead of the *mama* 'mine' one would expect (Ja VI 337 n. 5). Is he implying that the word 'long' in both their names makes them kin? On the other hand, it could simply be a usual honorific for a lady.

affection for her husband. Now in love with the stranger, she agreed and said, 'If you do not leave me, I will do as you say.' So when they reached the other bank, they flirted with one another and left Goḷakāḷa, telling him to stay where he was. Even though he was standing and looking on, they ate the meat and drink and went on their way.

When he had seen this, he exclaimed, 'They are now together, and have just left me here behind!' [338] As he ran up and down he went a little way into the river and recoiled with fear. Then, furious at their behaviour, he made a reckless leap, saying, 'So—let me live or let me die!' When he was well into the water, he realized how shallow the water was. So he crossed over, and pursued the man, shouting, 'You terrible thief! Where are you going with my wife?'

'In what way is she your wife? She is mine.' And he seized him by the throat and threw him around, and then down to the ground.

The other man seized Dīghatālā's hand and cried, 'Stop! Where are you going? You are my wife. I got you after working for seven years in one house.' As he was making such a commotion in this way he came near the hall, and a large crowd of people had gathered. The Great Being asked what the noise was. He summoned them, listened to their arguments, and asked them if they would keep to his decision. They both agreed to do this, and he sent for Dīghapiṭṭhi and asked him his name. Then he asked his wife's name. As he did not know what it was, he gave another name. Then he asked for the names of his parents, and he said these, 'Such-and-such'. But when he asked him the names of his wife's parents, as he did not know, he gave other names. The Great Being put the story together and had him taken away. Then he asked for the other man, and asked him all the names, using the same method as before. As he knew things as they really were, he did not make any mistakes. Then he had him sent away, and sent for Dīghatālā. He asked her her name and she gave it. Then he asked her her husband's name, and she, not knowing, gave a wrong name. Then he asked her her parents' names, and she said, 'Such-and-such'. But when he asked her husband's parents' names, she started babbling, and gave the wrong names. Then the wise man sent for the other two and asked the large crowd of people. 'Does the woman's story agree with Dīghapiṭṭhi or Goḷakāla?' They said, 'With Goḷakāla.' So then he gave his judgement. 'This man is her husband; the other is the thief.' And when he asked him, he admitted that he had been the thief.

7. THE QUESTION OF THE CARRIAGE

Now there was a certain man sitting in a carriage[37] and he dismounted from it to wash his face. At that moment Sakka was looking around and as he saw the wise man he decided, 'I will make clear the power of the wisdom in Mahosadha, the embryo Buddha.' So he came down assuming the guise of a man and followed the carriage, holding onto it behind. The man who was sitting in the carriage asked, 'Why have you come?' He replied, 'To help you out.' The man agreed and got out of the carriage to see to his bodily needs. Immediately, Sakka alighted onto the carriage and rode off with it at great speed. The owner of the carriage, having done what he needed to do, came back and when he saw Sakka hastening away in the carriage, he ran after him behind, crying, 'Stop, stop, where are you taking my carriage?' Sakka replied, 'Your carriage must be another one. This one is mine.' Arguing in this way, they came to the gate of the hall. The wise man asked, 'What is this?' and sent for him. As he came, by his lack of fear and unblinking eyes, the wise man recognized that this was Sakka, and the other was the owner. Despite this he asked the reason for the dispute, and asked them, 'Will you abide by my judgement?' They said, 'Yes.' He continued, 'I will have the carriage driven and you must hold on to it behind. The owner went a little way, then being unable to run further, he let go, but Sakka carried on running with the carriage. When he had called the carriage back, the wise man said to the crowd, 'This man ran a little way [339] but then let go. The other ran with the carriage and came back with it. But there is not even a drop of sweat on his body, no huffing and puffing,[38] he is without fear and he does not blink. This is Sakka, king of the gods.' Then he asked, 'Are you king of the gods?'

'Yes.'

'Why did you come here?'

'To make your wisdom clear, wise man.'

So he told him off: 'Then do not do anything like that again.' Now Sakka revealed the power of Sakka by standing in the sky, and gave his praise of the wise man, saying, 'This is a good judgement!' So he went back to his own abode. Then the minister went of his own accord to the king and said,

37. The Sinhalese version gives *ratha* as a cart (UJST 24).

38. The text says *assāsapassāso*, literally no 'in and out breath'. But as a god of a lower heaven realm, he would breathe like a human: according to the commentaries the physical breath is only suspended after the fourth *jhāna*. Excessive exertion would not however be a problem for him as it would for humans.

'Great King, the case of the carriage has been decided. Even Sakka was defeated by him! Why do you not recognize the great distinction of this man?' The king asked Senaka, 'Senaka, shall we bring the wise man here?' But Senaka replied, 'That is not enough to make him a wise man. Wait and I will test him and find out more.'

8. THE QUESTION OF THE STICK

Now one day, he said, 'Let's test the wise man.' So he had an acacia stick brought, and taking it back by about twelve finger-breadths, had it beautifully worked by a turner and had a message written on it and sent to the people of the East Market Town:

They say that the inhabitants of this town know a thing or two.[39]
So which is the tip and which the root of this stick?
Let them work it out. And if no one knows,
there will be a fine of a thousand coins.

The people of the town met together and could not work out which was the tip or the root, so they said to an elder, 'Maybe the wise man Mahosadha will know.' So they called him and asked him, and the elder had him summoned from his playground. He told him about the problem. 'Dear one, we just cannot work it out. Surely you will be able to?' When he heard this, the wise man thought to himself that there would be no profit for the king in making a distinction between root and tip, and that the message must have been sent to test him. 'Bring it to me, and I will work it out,' he said. So he took it in his hand and recognised which was the tip and which was the root. In order to capture the hearts of the people at large, however, he had a bowl of water brought, and tied a string around the middle of the stick. Then he held it suspended in the water, and the root of the branch, being heavier, sunk first into the water. Then he asked the populace at large, 'Which is heavier—the root or the tip of a tree?'

'The root is, wise man.'

He explained then that the root of the tree had sunk first, being heavier. The people sent the stick back to the king, explaining to him which was the root and which was the tip. The king was pleased, and asked, 'Who worked this out?'

39. The word is *paṇḍito*, used for wise men. See the introduction to this story.

'Mahosadha, son of our elder, Sirivaḍḍha.'

When the king heard this he asked Senaka, 'So—should we bring him here?' And Senaka said, 'Wait sire. Let's test him with another trick.'

9. THE QUESTION OF THE SKULLS

One day, two skulls were brought in, one from a woman, and one from a man. These were sent to be distinguished, with a fine of a thousand coins if no one could tell the difference. The people in the town did not know, and asked the Great Being. He saw at once the head of the man: they say that the sutures of the skull in a man are straight. Those in a woman, however, are curved. By this advanced knowledge, he could say, 'This the skull of a woman and this is the skull of a man.' The people of the town informed the king. And the rest is just the same as before.

10. THE QUESTION OF THE SNAKE

One day he had a male snake and a female snake brought in. He asked them to decide and say, 'This is the male and this is the female.' They asked the wise man, and he realised at once when he saw them. The tail of the male snake is thick and that of the female snake, thin. The head of the male is thick, while the head of the female is long. The eyes of the male are large, the eyes of the female are less so. The slough of the male is well formed, with sexual organs, and that of the female is damaged.[40] By these tokens[41] [340] he could say, 'This is the male and this is the female.' And the rest is as before.

11. THE QUESTION OF THE COCK

One day a message was sent to the people of East Market Town:

Send us a bull that is completely white, with horns on his legs, and a hump on his head, who gives his call at three times, without fail. Otherwise there is a fine of a thousand coins.

40. 'Slough' is an uncertain translation for *paribhaṇḍa* (see PED 430); taking the Burmese reading of *savatthika* for *sovatthika*, it would perhaps mean 'with sexual organs.' It is unclear. The Sinhalese version gives 'The hood of the male is perfect all round, while that of the female is imperfect as if a portion on a side has been chopped off.' (UJST 29).

41. For *abhiññāṇa* see DP I 196.

They did not know one, so they consulted the wise man. He said, 'The king means you to send him a cock. This animal has horns on his legs, the spurs; a hump on his head, the crest; and he makes his crow three times a day. Then send him a cock as he describes it.' They sent one.

12. THE QUESTION OF THE JEWEL

The jewel that King Sakka gave to Kusa was a curved jewel cluster with eight sides.[42]

Its thread was broken, and no one could get the old thread out and put a new one in. One day they sent the jewel cluster, with instructions to take out the old and put in the new. The villagers were quite unable to do either, and in their perplexity they sent it to the wise man. He told them not to be frightened, but asked for a blob of honey to be brought to him. He smeared the jewel cluster with the honey on both sides of the hole, and twisting a thread of wool, he smeared the end of this with honey too. Then he inserted it a little way into the hole of the jewel and put it in a place where ants were passing. The ants smelled the honey and came out of their hole. They ate away the old thread, and biting the new thread pulled it through the hole and came out the other end. When the wise man saw that it had passed through, he told them to give it to the king. He was pleased when he heard how the thread had been passed through.

13. THE QUESTION OF THE CALVING

Now they say that one day, when the auspicious bull had been fed for many months, so that his stomach was very large, his horns were washed, he was rubbed down with sesame oil, and, after being bathed in turmeric, he was sent to the East Market Town, with this message:

They say that the inhabitants of this town know a thing or two.
Here is the king's auspicious bull, in calf.
Deliver him and send him back with the calf,
or there is a fine of thousand coins.

The townspeople did not know what to do, and asked the wise man, 'What

42. See *Kusa-jātaka* (J 531; J V 310–11). The jewel is given to the Bodhisatta, Kusa in that story, triumphant at the end and in possession again of his wife. It is called there Verocana. This jewel raises interesting issues, discussed in the introduction to this story (and see Peris 1978). The Pāli here is *maṇikhaṇdho aṭṭhāsu ṭhānesu vaṃko.*

shall we do?' He thought that it would be best to meet the question with a counter-question.

'Can you find a brave man capable of speaking to the king?'

'That is not difficult,' they replied.

So they summoned him, and the Great Being said, 'Go, sir, let your hair down over your shoulders, and go to the palace wailing and grieving. Answer no one except for the king, and wail. If the king sends for you to ask you why you are wailing, say, "My son has been in labour for seven days, and cannot give birth. Help me! Tell me how I can help him to deliver." Then the king will say, "What madness. This is impossible. Men cannot give birth to babies." Then you must say, "If this is true, then how can the people of East Market Town deliver a calf from the auspicious bull?"' And he did as he was instructed. The king asked who had thought of the counter-question, and when he heard that it was the wise man Mahosadha he was very pleased.

14. THE QUESTION OF THE RICE

Another day, to test the wise man, this message was sent:

The people of East Market Town must send us some
boiled rice. It is to be cooked with eight conditions.
These are: [341] *without rice, without a pot, without an oven,*
without fire, without firewood, without being sent on a road,
and by neither a man nor a woman. If they cannot do it,
there will be a fine of a thousand coins.

The people, worried, consulted the wise man. He said, 'Do not worry about this. Take some broken rice, for that is not rice. Snow, for that is not water. An earthen bowl, as that is not a pot. Chop up some logs, for that is not an oven. Kindle fire by rubbing, for that is not proper fire. Take leaves instead of firewood. Cook your sour rice, put it in a new vessel. Press it down well, and put it on the head of a eunuch, who is neither man nor woman. Leave the main road and go along a footpath, and take it to the king.' They did this. And the king was pleased when he heard who had solved the question.

15. THE QUESTION OF THE SAND

Another day, to test the wise man, they sent this message to the townspeople:

The king wishes to have fun on a swing, but the old rope is broken.
You are to make a rope of sand, or else there will be
a fine of a thousand coins.

They did not know what to do, and consulted the wise man. He saw that the best thing was for a counter-question. He reassured the people and sent for two or three skilled in speaking, and told them to say this to the king: '"Sire, the townspeople do not know if the rope should be thick or thin. Send them a piece of the old rope, a length of about four or five fingerbreadths. They will examine this and twist a rope of the same size." If the king replies, "There never was a rope of sand in this palace," they should reply, "If Your Majesty cannot make a rope of sand, then how can the townspeople do so?"' They did this, and the king was pleased when he heard the wise man had thought of this counter-question.

16. THE QUESTION OF THE POOL

On another day, a message was sent:

The king wishes to indulge in some water sports.
You must send him a new pool, covered with water lilies of all five kinds.
Otherwise there is a fine of a thousand coins.

They informed the wise man, who realized that a counter-question was needed. He sent for several men who were skilled in speaking, and said to them, 'Go and play in the water until your eyes are red. Go to the palace door with wet hair and wet clothes and your bodies covered in mud, holding in your hands ropes, sticks, and clods of earth. Send a message to the king that you have arrived, and when you are admitted, say to him, "Sire, as Your Majesty had ordered us to send a pool, we brought a great pool to suit your liking. But she was used to living in the forest, and when she had seen the city with its walls, moats, and lookout towers, she became frightened and broke the ropes and went off into the forest. We pelted her with clods of earth and beat her with sticks, but could not get her to come back. Give us then the old pool which they say your majesty brought back from the forest, and we will yoke them together and bring the other one back." The king will say, "But I have never had a pool brought in from the forest! [342] And I have never sent a pool there to be yoked to any other either!" Then you will say, "If that is so, then how can the townspeople send you a pool?"' They did this, and the king was pleased to hear the wise man had thought of this.

17. THE QUESTION OF THE GARDEN

Then, on another day, the king sent a message:

I wish to have fun in the garden, and my garden is old.
The people of East Market Town must send me a new garden,
Filled with trees in blossom and flowers.

The wise man reassured them in the same way as before and sent men to speak in the same way as before. Then the king was delighted, and said to Senaka, 'Well, Senaka, shall we bring the wise man here?' But he was envious of his attainments, and said, 'This is not enough to make a man wise.'

18. THE QUESTION OF THE ASS

When he heard this, the king thought: 'Mahosadha the wise man has been wise even though a child and has captured my imagination. In all these secret tests and counter-questions he has given his replies as if he were a Buddha. Yet a wise man of such a kind will not give me leave to bring him here with me. What is Senaka to me? I will bring him anyway.' So with a great retinue he set out for the town, mounted on the auspicious royal horse. But as he was going along his horse got his foot stuck in a hole that had cracked open in the ground, and broke it, so the king turned back for the city from that place. Then Senaka approached the king and asked, 'Sire, they say that you went to the East Market Town to bring the wise man back.'

'Yes, I did, wise man,' said the king.

'Great King, you went against all my advice just to wait and see. But you dashed off and the auspicious horse broke his foot just as you were first setting out!' The king listened to this statement and was silent.

On another day he asked Senaka, 'Shall we send for the wise man, Senaka?' Senaka replied, 'If so, sire, don't go yourself, but send a messenger, saying, "Wise man, as I was on my way to get you my horse broke his foot; he should send us a horse treasure, or a more excellent one."[43] And if he

43. DP I 268 says that *assataram* (a kind of horse, PED 90) is wrong and reads *assaratanam*. Rouse (who takes the translation work over from Cowell after his death,

sends the horse treasure, he will come himself, but if he sends the more excellent one, he will send his father. This will be a question for him.' The king agreed and sent a messenger to say this. The wise man heard what the messenger had to say and reflected that the king wished to see both him and his father. So he went to his father and paid his respects to him, and said, 'Dear one, the king wishes to see both you and me. You should go on ahead with a great retinue of a thousand merchants; and do not go empty-handed. Take a sandalwood casket filled with fresh ghee, and the king will make you welcome and will say, "Please sit down on a seat suitable for householders." When you are seated, I will come in. The king will extend his greetings to me and say, "Sit on another seat." When I give you a glance, you should get up from your seat and say, "Dear Mahosadha the wise man, please sit here." Then the question will be ready for its resolution.' He agreed, and went in the way described above and stood by the door until the king asked him to come in. When asked, he entered into the king's presence and paid homage to him, and then stood to one side. The king made him welcome, and asked, 'Householder, where is your son Mahosadha, the wise man?'

The man replied, 'He is just coming, sire.' The king was delighted in his heart and asked the man to sit down in a seat that was suitable, and he saw one that was, and sat down to one side. [343]

The Great Being adorned himself finely, and sitting in a decorated carriage with a retinue of a thousand young men, entered the city, whereupon he saw an ass just beside a ditch. He got some of his tougher young men to have it brought to him: 'Follow this ass and take him, and so that he does not make any noise, make a gag for his mouth, and then put him in a bag, and bring him on your shoulders.' They did this, and the Bodhisatta entered the city with his magnificent retinue. And all the crowds gazed at the Great Being and just could not get enough of singing his praises: 'They say that this Mahosadha, the merchant Sirivaḍḍha's son, is a wise man: he was born holding a healing herb in his hand! And they say that he was able to answer all those questions posed to test him!' He went to the gate of the palace and sent a message saying that he had arrived. The king heard this and was very glad at heart. 'Let my son, Mahosadha the wise

---

and so is the translator from Ja VI 338, or in his translation, from J VI 164), notes the play on words here: *assataran no pesetu seṭṭhataraṅ ca. Assataram* means 'mule' or 'calf' (J VI 169 n. 1). *Seṭṭhi* is 'merchant'; *seṭṭho* is 'better' or 'excellent' (see PED 722).

man, come in!' So he entered into the palace with his retinue of a thousand young men and paid homage to the king before standing to one side. The king was overjoyed to see him and gave him the warmest welcome, saying, 'Wise man, take a suitable seat and be seated.' The wise man looked at his father. At this sign from him, his father rose from his seat and said, 'Sit in this seat, wise man.' He did sit there, and when they saw this, Senaka, Pukkusa, Kāvinda and Devinda, all as foolish as each other, clapped their hands and roared with laughter. 'They say this is a wise man, but he is a blind fool! He gets his father to get up from his seat and then sits there himself! It is not right to call him a wise man.' The king was disconcerted by this, but the Great Being said, 'Why, sire, are you shocked?'

'Yes, wise man. I was glad to hear about you, but seeing you I am not so glad.'

'Why is this?'

'At your sitting down when you got your father to rise from his seat.'

'So, sire, do you think that in all situations the father is better than the son?'

'I do indeed, wise man.'

'Then did you not send a message to me to bring a horse treasure, or an excellent one?' Saying this, he rose and looked at his young men: 'Bring in the ass that you have caught.' And he had it laid down at the king's feet, and posed him a question. 'Great King, what is the worth of this ass?'

The king said, 'If it is good for work, then eight *kahāpanas*.'

'But if he sires a colt with a thoroughbred Sindh mare, what will he be worth then?'

'He will be beyond price!'

'Why do you say that, sire? Did you not just say that in all situations the father is worth more than the son? So is the colt then worth more than its father, the ass? Now your wise men did not understand this, and clapped their hands and roared with laughter. What kind of attainment of wisdom is this? Where did you get them from?' And berating the four, he addressed the king in this stanza from the first book of the *jātakas*:

'Do you think that in this case the father is always better than the king,
your majesty?
Then is that colt better than his father?'[44] *(3)*

44. *Haṃsi* is an odd word in this verse, where the metre is odd, as Rouse points out (J VI 171 n. 2). PED 727, citing this passage alone, suggests it means 'if, in case

Speaking in this way [344], he continued: 'Great King, if the father is better than the son, then take my father, and if the son is better than the father, take me instead.' The king was delighted, and all the court applauded and gave a thousand praises, and a thousand snaps of their fingers, a thousand waving of scarves: 'The wise man has solved the question well!' The four wise men were deeply annoyed. No one recognizes the great virtue of one's parents more than the Bodhisatta. 'Why did he do this?' one could ask. It was not to show disrespect to his father, but when the king sent the message 'Send a horse treasure—or a more excellent one', he acted in this way in order to give a good explanation of the question and to make his wisdom clear to those around—and to get the better of the four wise men.

The question about the ass is finished.[45]

19. THE QUESTION OF THE JEWEL

[344] The king was delighted, and, taking a golden vase filled with perfumed water, poured water onto his hands, and said, 'Enjoy the East Market Town as a boon from the king. And let the other businessmen and traders honour this.' When he had done this, he sent all kinds of ornaments to the Bodhisatta's mother, and full of confidence after the Ass Question, he wished to install the Bodhisatta as his own son. So he said to his father, 'Householder, give me the Great Being to be my own son.' The father replied, 'But he is young—even his mouth smells of milk. When he is older, he will be with you.' The king persisted. 'Sir, from this time on be without attachment: from this day onwards he will be my son. I am able to take good care of him, so now go on your way.' So the man paid homage to the king, embraced his son, and, throwing his arms around the boy, kissed him on the head and gave him encouragement and advice. The boy paid his respects to his father, saying, 'Please don't worry about me,' and sent him on his way.

Now the king asked the boy: 'Will you eat inside the palace walls, or outside?' The boy thought to himself, 'I am going to have a big entourage,

---

that'. The story from which the verse is taken is the *Gadrabha-jātaka* (J 111; Ja I 424), which is the same as this section of the story. The way the story refers to another is a characteristic of this *jātaka*, which has so many of its incidents distributed as single stories throughout the collection.

45. All of these questions up to here are in small type in F. The only section omitted here is the brief commentarial discussion of the terminology of the verse given regarding the horse.

so it's better for me to eat outside the palace,' and so said this in his reply. The king gave him a fitting house, and provided for the upkeep of the thousand boys as well, and gave him what was needed. From that time the boy attended upon the king.

The king now wished to test the wise man. At that time there was a precious jewel in a crow's nest in a palm tree that stood on the bank of a lake by the southern gate. The image of the jewel could be seen reflected in the lake. People informed the king that there was a jewel in the lake, and he sent for [345] Senaka and asked him, 'They say that a jewel can be seen in the lake. How are we to get it?'

'It is necessary to drain the water to find it,' he replied.

'Then do that!' replied the king.

And he did this big job, collecting together a crowd of men and getting them to drain the water and mud, and dig up the ground at the bottom. But they did not see the jewel. But when the lake was full again, the reflection of the jewel could be seen again. Again Senaka did the same thing, but the jewel could not be found. Then the king sent for the boy, 'A jewel can be seen in the lake. Senaka has had the lake drained of water and mud, and has dug up the ground underneath, but did not see it. Then the lake filled up again, and the jewel could be seen again. Will you be able to find it?' The boy replied, 'That is not difficult, Great King, I'll get it for you.' The king was very pleased, and thought, 'I'll see today the power of knowledge in this boy!' Going with a large retinue to the banks of the lake, the Great Being stood on the banks looking at the jewel. 'This jewel is not in the lake, it is to be found in the palm tree,' he decided. So he said, 'Sire, the jewel is not in the lake.'

'But it can be seen in the water!'

So the boy had a pitcher of water brought, and said, 'Now take a look, sire. This jewel is neither in the lake, nor is it in the pitcher.' 'Then where can the jewel be?'

'Sire, the jewel is not in the water, nor is it in the pitcher; it is in the crow's nest in the palm tree. Just send a man to get it down.' So then the king had the jewel brought down, and the boy took it and placed it in the king's hand. Everyone applauded the boy and made fun of Senaka. 'The jewel was in the crow's nest in the palm tree, and Senaka makes strong men dig it up out of a lake! He ought to be more like Mahosadha!' In this way they praised the Great Being, and the king, very pleased indeed, gave him a pearl necklace from his own neck, and strings of pearls for the thousand boys too. And he granted to him, and his entourage, the right to wait upon him without ceremony.

The nineteen questions are finished.

THE CHAMELEON QUESTION

Now one day, the king went with the boy to his pleasure garden. [346] There, a certain chameleon who lived at the top of the arched gateway saw the king arriving and came down and lay flat on the ground. The king saw this and asked, 'What is he doing?'

'He is paying respects to you, Great King.'

'If so, then don't let his respect go without benefit. Give him a reward.'

'Sire, there is no point in a reward. Something to eat will be enough for him.'

'But what does he eat?'

'Meat, sire.'

'How much should he have?'

'As much as a very small coin's worth.'

'A very small coin's worth is not enough for a king's gift.' He gave a man an instruction, 'Go and bring regularly half a rupee's worth of meat.' The man agreed, and from that time he did this. But on an *uposatha* day, when there is no killing, the man could not find any meat. So he made a hole in a half-rupee piece and strung it on a thread and tied it around the chameleon's neck. Because of this the chameleon became very conceited. That day the king again visited the park but the chameleon, seeing the king coming, felt great conceit because of his wealth, thinking, 'You may be rich, Videha, but so am I!' Making himself an equal of the king, he did not come down but remained lying on the archway, shaking his head. The king, noticing this, said, 'Wise man, usually he comes down but today he does not. What is the reason for this?' And he recited the first verse:

> 'Your chameleon did not use to climb up an archway.
> Explain why the chameleon has become so obdurate, Mahosadha!' *(4)*

The wise man saw that the man must have been unable to obtain any meat on the *uposatha* day when there was no killing and that the chameleon must have become conceited because of the coin strung around his neck, and he said this verse:

> 'Never before has the chameleon had a half-rupee coin.
> Now he looks down his nose at the Videhan king, the lord of Mithilā.' *(5)*

[347] The king summoned the man and questioned him, and he recounted

it all as it had happened. The king exclaimed, 'Without even asking, the wise man understood the disposition of the chameleon as if he were a completely awakened Buddha!' And he felt even more confidence in him. He had the tolls from all four gates given to him. Angry with the chameleon, he was going to stop the gifts to him, but the wise man told him it would be unfitting to do this, so he did not.

The chameleon question is finished.

THE QUESTION ABOUT GOOD AND BAD LUCK

Now a young man called Piṅguttara (Very Yellow), from Mithilā, went to Taxila and studied under a teacher renowned in all directions, and soon completed his training. After passing his examination, he told his teacher that he would be leaving. It was a custom in that family that if there was a daughter of marriageable age she should be given to the most senior student. This teacher had a daughter who was as beautiful as a nymph from a heaven realm, and so he told him, 'I give you my daughter, and when you leave, you can take her with you.' But the young man was unfortunate and unlucky, while the girl was full of auspiciousness and virtues. When he saw her, he did not feel anything for her, and not wanting to go against the contract of the teacher, he agreed without enthusiasm.[46] The brahmin gave him the daughter. When night came he lay upon the bed, which had been decorated and prepared, but when she came on the bed he threw himself off the bed moaning and, climbing down, lay on the ground. Although he had crossed over her, she also went and lay beside him, and he then went up and lay on the bed again, but she also got up and went again on the bed. When she came into the bed he again got out, for they say the unlucky is not equal to the one who is auspicious. So the lady stayed in the bed and he stayed on the ground. They passed seven days in this way, and with her accompanying him he took his leave of his teacher and left. And in the road there was not a word of conversation between them. So they both unwillingly reached Mithilā, and Piṅguttara, not far from the town, saw a fig tree covered with fruit. As he was hungry he climbed up and ate some figs. The lady, gnawed by hunger, went to the roots of the tree and called out to him. 'Throw me down some fruit too!' He replied, 'You've got hands and feet too! You climb up and get some yourself.'

46. Reading *arocento* for *ārocento* in F.

She climbed up and ate some, and he, seeing that she was climbing up, quickly climbed down and piled up thorns around the roots of the tree, [348] saying, 'Now I am free of this unlucky woman!' He escaped, but she could not get down, so sat there. And then the king, having fun in his pleasure garden, was coming back to town on his elephant and saw her there. He fell in love with her. So he sent to ask if she had a husband or not. She answered, 'Yes, I do have a husband to whom my family gave me. But he has run away and left me sitting here.' The minister informed the king about this, and the king announced, 'This treasure, who is without a husband, now comes to the king!' He had her brought down and placed on his elephant, and taken to the palace, where she was given the ceremonial sprinkling as his chief queen. She was very dear and pleasing to him, and the name Queen Udumbarā, the queen of the figs, was given to her, because he saw her first on a fig tree.

One day those who lived by the city gate had to clear the road so that the king could go to his pleasure garden. Piṅguttara was now earning his living and was repairing the road with a spade. Before the road had been finished, the king came by with Queen Udumbarā in their carriage. The queen saw the unlucky man repairing the road and could not contain her good fortune, and smiled when she saw him, thinking, 'What a miserable fellow.' The king, seeing her smiling, was angry. 'Why are you smiling?' he asked. She replied, 'Sire, this man mending the road used to be my husband. He left me in the fig tree after making me climb up it, and leaving thorns around. I was looking at him and could not contain my good fortune, thinking, "What a miserable fellow."'

'You are lying,' the king replied. 'You saw someone else and were smiling at him. I'll kill you!' He drew his sword, and his queen, terrified, said, 'Sire, please consult the wise men.'

So the king asked Senaka, 'Do you believe what she says?' He replied, 'No, I don't believe it, sire. Who would abandon such a beautiful woman?' She heard this and was frightened even more. But then the king thought, 'What does Senaka know? I'll ask the wise man.' Thinking this, he asked him, and repeated this verse:

> 'Can a woman be beautiful and still virtuous?[47]
> And a man not desire her? Tell me, Mahosadha!' *(6)*

47. This story and verse occur as *jātaka* 192, *Sirikālakiṇṇi-jātaka* (Ja II 115).

[349] When he had listened to him, the wise man replied with this verse:

> 'I do believe her, Great King. This man could just be very unlucky.
> Good fortune and bad luck can never be equals, at any time.' *(7)*

The king lost his anger when he heard these words, and his heart was pacified. Delighted, he said, 'Well, wise man, if you had not been here, I would have trusted the say-so of that fool Senaka, and would have lost this treasure of a woman; now I have her, all because of you.' And he paid homage to the wise man with a boon of a hundred thousand coins. The queen then paid homage to the king, and said, 'Sire, because of this wise man I have kept my life. Please grant me the boon that from this day he is established in the position of my youngest brother.'

'Very well, lady, I grant this.'

And she said, 'Then, sire, from this day I will only eat sweet foods when he is there; from this day, I will make sure my door is open to him, to send him sweet foods, in season or out of season: I ask for this boon.'

'Yes, lady, you may have this boon too,' said the king.

The question about good and bad luck is finished.

THE QUESTION ABOUT THE GOAT

On another day, the king was strolling on his long walkway after breakfast, when he saw through a window in the gateway[48] a goat and a dog exchanging friendly greetings with one another. Now they say that the goat had used to eat the grass thrown to the elephants in front of their elephant stable before they got to it. But the mahouts had beaten him and driven him away. Bleating, he had scampered off, but a man had quickly chased him and struck him on the back with a stick. He, with his back bent over with so much pain, had gone and lain down on a bench by the walls of the royal household. On the same day, a dog who used to eat all the skin, bones, and leftovers of the royal kitchen had been quite unable to hold back at the smell of the fish and the meat. As the cook had finished preparing the food and was wiping the sweat from his body, the dog entered the kitchen, pushed off the cover, and ate the meat. [350] But the cook had heard the clattering of the dishes, gone back in, seen the dog, slammed the door shut, and then beat him with sticks and stones. The dog had dropped the meat from his mouth and had run off yelping. The cook, seeing him escape, had

48. PED 332 and DP II 449 read *dvāravātapānantarena* for *dvārapānantarena.*

chased after him and hit him right across the back with a stick. So the dog, with back bent over and limping, had also come to the place where the goat was lying. The goat had said, 'Friend, why is your back bent over? Are you suffering from indigestion?' The dog had replied, 'But you are lying down with your back bent too. Have you got indigestion then?' He told him everything that had happened, and then the goat had asked, 'So will you be able to go back to the kitchen?'

'No I can't! My life would be over then. And you can't go back to the elephant stable either.'

'Absolutely not. My life would be over then.'

'So how are we going to survive now?' they had asked each other. They had mulled over the problem for a solution (*upaya*), and then the goat had said, 'If we can live together peacefully, there is a way.'

'What do you mean?'

'From now on, friend, you go to the elephant stable. The mahouts will not have any suspicions, as they'll think, "This animal does not eat grass." So you can take the grass. Meanwhile, I'll go to the kitchen, where the cook will not have any suspicions either, thinking, "This animal does not eat meat." And I can take the meat.' They had both agreed on this stratagem (*upaya*). So the dog had gone to the elephant stable and fetched a bundle of grass, holding it in his mouth, and laid it beside the great wall of the palace. The goat had gone to the kitchen and brought a good chunk of meat and had taken it there too. So the dog ate meat and the goat ate grass. With this stratagem, they lived together in great harmony and accord by the great wall.

When the king saw their great friendship, he thought, 'I've never seen this happen before. These two enemies are living together in harmony. I'll take this question and ask the wise men, and the one who cannot find out the answer I'll drive from the kingdom, and the other I'll call the sage without equal and accord great honour to him. [351] Today there is no time, but tomorrow I'll ask them to come and pay me attendance.'

So the next day he asked the wise men to attend him, and as they were sitting there, he posed them his question with this verse:

> 'There are two enemies who never in this world go within seven paces of each other,
>
> Who live now in accord, the greatest of friends. What is the reason?' *(8)*

After this, he set out another verse:

> 'And if you cannot solve this question for me before noon today,
> I'll banish you all!

Foolish men are no use to me at all.' *(9)*

Senaka was sitting in the highest seat; the wise man, in the last, thought to himself that the king would not have worked out a solution to such a question. 'This king is a little foolish, and would not be able to work out this question: he must have seen something. I'll get out of this for one day, and then I'll have a chance to come up with a solution.' Senaka thought, 'It's important to get him to wait for one day by some means or another.' The four could not see anything, being like people who had walked into a darkened room. Senaka looked at the Bodhisatta. 'I wonder what Mahosadha is going to do.' He looked at him. By the way the Bodhisatta was looking at him, Senaka discerned his wish, and that he would not be able to answer it today, but would like to think it over, and wished for the chance of a day to do so. So he thought he would fulfil this wish and laughed a great roar of laughter, to reassure the king. 'Why, Great King, are you going to banish us all if we are unable to give the answer?'

'Oh yes, wise man,' replied the king.

'You know it is a tangled question and that we cannot answer it. So hold on a little. A tangled question cannot be worked out in the middle of a large group of people. We'll think it over, to one side, and then tell you; [352] just give us the chance.' So he spoke, relying on the Great Being, and uttered these two verses:

> 'In a large group of people, in the din of a big gathering, our minds are at odds and distracted;
> We cannot bring our minds to bear on the question. *(10)*
> But with a single mind, after going away alone, they will consider the question.
> Firmly, in seclusion, they will master this, and explain the matter for everyone.' *(11)*

The king was not pleased when he heard him, and indeed threatened them: 'Very well. Think about it before explaining it. I will banish the one who cannot explain it.' The four left the palace, and Senaka said to the others, 'Friends, the king asks a very subtle question. There is great danger for us if we cannot answer it. So go away and eat a good meal, and think it over.'

The wise man rose and went up to Queen Udumbarā and asked her, 'Your highness, where did the king pass the time most, today and yesterday?' She replied, 'Sir, he was looking out of the window on the long walkway.' Then the Bodhisatta thought, 'It will be something the king saw as he was looking around.' So he went there and saw what was happening with the dog and the goat. 'The king's question has been solved,' he realized. He went home with the job done.

Now the other three could not see anything, and went up to Senaka and he asked them, 'Have you seen the question?' They replied they had not. 'So what if the king banishes you? What will you do?'

'So you have seen it.'

'No, I have not.'

'But if you cannot see it, how can we? We roared like a lion before the king and said we'd think about it, and now the king will be angry without an explanation. What are we going to do?'

'This question is not for us to see. [353] The wise man will have worked it out in a hundred ways.'

'Let's go and see him.' And the four went to the gate of the Bodhisatta's house and had him informed they were there. They then entered the house and greeted him. Standing to one side they asked the Great Being, 'Have you worked the question out?'

He replied, 'If it's not worked out be me, will anyone else do it? Yes, I have worked it out.'

'Then please tell us.'

The wise man reflected, 'If I do not tell them, the king will banish them and will honour me with the seven kinds of treasure.[49] I'll tell them and let the fools not perish.' So he got the four to sit down on low seats, and got them to raise their hands in *añjalis*. He did not let them know what the king had seen, but told them, 'Reply at the time of the king's question in the following way.' And he composed four verses, and taught one to each of them to memorise in order to recite when the king asked them.[50] Then he dismissed them.

On the second day, they went to attend upon the king and sat in their appointed seats. The king asked Senaka, 'Do you know the answer, Senaka?'

49. This could be a reference to the seven treasures of the Universal Monarch (see, for example *Ambaṭṭha Sutta*, DN 3, PTS edn I 89, and *Mahāsudassana Sutta*, DN 17, PTS edn II 173–7), the wheel, the elephant, the horse, the jewel, the woman, the treasurer and the adviser. It could possibly refer to seven kinds of jewel: the stairways in the palace of the Universal Monarch are decorated with seven kinds of jewel, but the last is the category of 'many varieties'.

50. For the very few references in *jātaka*s to the word *pāli*, used here to denote not the language but rather a recited text, see Yamazaki and Ousaka's index (2003: 453).

'Great King, if I do not know it, who will?'

'Then tell me.'

'Listen, sire.' And he recited the verse he had been taught:

> 'The sons of beggars and the sons of kings
> Find the meat of the ram delightful and pleasing.
> But they do not eat the meat of the dog.
> And yet . . . there may be friendship between a dog and a ram.'[51] *(12)*

Although Senaka had recited the verse, he did not understand the meaning; but the king did because he had seen this made clear for himself. Therefore he said, 'Senaka knows the answer. Now I'll ask Pukkusa.' And he asked Pukkusa, and he said, 'So, am I not a wise man?' And he recited the verse that he had been taught:

> 'They take the fleece of a goat to cover the back of the horse;
> But they do not use the skin of a dog as a covering.
> And yet . . . there may be friendship between a dog and a ram.' *(13)*

[354] Although he did not have a clue about the meaning, the king, who had seen it happen, thought he did. So he asked Kāvinda, who recited his verse:

> 'The ram has horns that are twisted; the dog has none.
> The one eats grass; the other eats meat.
> And yet . . . there may be friendship between a dog and a ram.' *(14)*

The king thought that he knew the answer too, so asked Devinda, who recited his verse in the way explained:

> 'The ram eats grass and leaves; the dog does not eat grass and leaves.
> The dog would eat a hare or a cat.
> And yet . . . there may be friendship between a dog and a ram.' *(15)*

And then the king asked the wise man. 'Do you know the answer to this question?'

'Great King, who else, from the Avīci hell to the highest heaven, would know the answer?'

'Then explain it.'

'Great King, listen.' He explained his understanding with this couplet of verses:

> 'The ram, with eight pads on his four feet, and eight hooves,
> Unobserved, brings meat for one, and he brings grass for him. *(16)*

51. See PED 540 for reference to this story and the word *meṇḍa* 'ram', which here perhaps became a goat in the commentarial prose story. See also Rouse's comment at J VI 177 n. 1.

In his own palace the Videhan lord saw, it seems,
The exchange of food between one another,
Between the one who goes "baa-baa" and the one who goes "woof-woof"!' *(17)*

[355] The king did not know that the others' apparent knowledge had been dependent on the Bodhisatta, and so was delighted: 'Each of the five has discerned the solution through the power of wisdom.' And he recited this verse:

'It's no small gain for me that there are such wise men amongst my people.
A deep and tricky matter, they all worked out, with good strong speech!' *(18)*

And then he added, 'The one who brings delight deserves it too!' And he spoke this verse:

'A carriage with a she-mule I give to each,
A prosperous village is the boon for each of you.
These I give to all the wise men,
Delighted at their splendid speeches!' *(19)*

And saying this he made all these gifts.

The question of the goat, in the twelfth book, is ended.

THE QUESTION OF THE RICH AND THE POOR

Now Queen Udumbarā, of course, knew that the knowledge of the others had been derived from the Bodhisatta. She thought, 'The king has been even-handed in according honour to each one of them, like one giving the same honour to peas and beans. Surely he ought to give greater distinction to my brother!' So she went and asked the king, 'Sire, who explained the riddle to you?'

'The five wise men, my lady.'

'But from whom did four of them derive their knowledge?'

'I do not know, my lady.'

'Great King, what do people know! It was the wise man, who, wishing that these fools should not perish, taught them the question. [356] You have made them all equal in honour and it just is not fair, as you should be singling out the wise man.'

The king was pleased, and thought, 'He did not tell me that the others did not get their knowledge on their own.' He wanted to make a special reward for him. 'What I'll do is make the boy a great reward when he gives me the answer to another question.' Reflecting on this, he came up with the question of the rich and the poor.

After mulling it over, one day he called together the five men and while they were attending him, all sitting comfortably, he said, 'Senaka, I am going to ask you a question.'

'Ask away, sire.'

And the king recited the first verse [of this question]:

> 'Having wisdom, but no wealth; or being wealthy, and having no wisdom.
> I ask you, Senaka, a question.
> Which of these do wise men call the better?' *(20)*

Now this question had been passed down through the generations as a family question, and quickly he gave his answer:

> 'Sagacious men and fools, those endowed with skills and those who are untrained,
> Are servants of the rich, whether high or low born.
> Seeing this, I declare: the one with wisdom is the inferior,
> The one who is rich the superior.' *(21)*

The king listened to the answer. Then, without consulting the other three, he consulted Mahosadha, sitting nearby.

> 'Now I ask you, Mahosadha, the one supreme in wisdom, who knows all the law;
> The fool with money, or the wise man with none.
> Which do those that are good say is better?' *(22)*

[357] And then the Great Being said, 'Listen, Great King,' and gave his explanation:

> 'The foolish man does evil things,
> Thinking that he is better in this world here.
> He looks at this world, and not at the next,
> And, getting the unlucky dice, is a fool in both.
> Seeing this, I declare:
> The one with wisdom is the superior, the one who is rich is lesser.' *(23)*

When he had heard this the king considered Senaka, 'Mahosadha says that the wise man is surely the best.' And Senaka replied, 'Great King, Mahosadha is young; even now his mouth smells of milk. What does he know?' And he recited this verse:

> 'Skill does not provide wealth, nor does family or bodily beauty.
> Look at that stupid sheep Gorimanda, happily prospering.
> Good fortune favours the lesser. Seeing this I declare:

The one with wisdom is inferior, and the one who is rich the better.' *(24)*

[358] When he heard this the king said, 'So what about this, dear Mahosadha?' The wise man said, 'Sire, what does Senaka know? He is like a crow whose rice is scattered, like a dog attempting to lick up milk, who sees himself and does not see the stick about to fall on his head. Listen, sire.' And he delivered this verse:

'The one who has little wisdom becomes intoxicated with comfort.
Touched by suffering, he becomes confused.
Touched by good or bad experiences that come by chance,
He wriggles around like a fish in the dry heat.
Seeing him, I declare:
The one with wisdom is better than the fool in his success.' *(25)*

When he heard this the king said, 'What about this, teacher?'

Senaka said, 'But sire, what does he know? Leaving aside human beings, the tree that is abundant and full of fruit is the one the birds eat from.' And he said this verse:

'Just as in a forest, where birds flock from all around
To the tree that is full of fruit,
So in this way crowds flock around the one who is wealthy
And has plenty of money, for the sake of gain.
Seeing this, I declare:
The one with wisdom is lesser than the one with good fortune.' *(26)*

The king heard this and said, 'So what about this, dear one?' And the wise man replied, 'What does this fatty know? Listen to this, sire.' And he recited this verse:

'It is not good that the powerful fool obtains wealth by violence.
For they drag this stupid fellow off to hell, wailing.
[359] Seeing this I declare:
The one with wisdom is better than the fool in his success.' *(27)*

Then Senaka, replying to the king's 'Well then, Senaka?' gave this verse:

'Whatever rivers pour into the Ganges, they all lose name and family.
The Ganges, tumbling into the sea, is not identifiable.
So with the wealth of this world. Seeing this, I declare:
The one with wisdom is inferior to the one with good fortune.' *(28)*

Then the king said, 'Well, wise one?'

He replied, 'Listen, Great King.' And he gave this couplet of verses:

'That magnificent container of waters he describes,
Where all rivers, measureless, flow:

This powerful sea, perpetually tossing and turning, with such great urgency,
The ocean, cannot pass over the boundaries of the shore. *(29)*
It is the same with the chattering of the fool.
Even if he is fortunate, he cannot pass over to wisdom.
Seeing this, I declare:
The one with wisdom is superior to the fool in his success.' *(30)*

[360] Hearing this, the king said, 'Well, Senaka?' And he replied, 'Listen sire,' and spoke this verse:

'A man of position may be lacking in sense,
But what he says in the courthouse[52] is important to others
And carries weight in the midst of his relatives.
Even wisdom does not have this effect for the one who lacks fortune.
Seeing this, I declare:
The one with wisdom is inferior to the one with good fortune.' *(31)*

Again the king asked, 'Well, dear one?' And he replied, 'Listen sire; what does that foolish Senaka know?' And he spoke this verse:

'The fool, with little wisdom, speaks falsely, for his own or for another's sake.
He is blamed in the midst of the assembly,
And he goes then to an unhappy rebirth.
Seeing this, I declare:
The one with wisdom is superior to the fool in his success.' *(32)*

And then Senaka said this verse:

'The one full of wisdom speaks with worth,
But if he is without a measure of rice,[53] with little wealth, and impoverished,
It carries no weight in his assembly of relatives.
[361] Prosperity does not come to someone because of his wisdom.
Seeing this, I declare:
The one with wisdom is inferior to the one with good fortune.' *(33)*

The king again asked the wise man: 'Well, dear one?' And he replied: 'What does Senaka know? He looks only at this world, and not the next.' And he said this verse:

'The wise one, for his own or for another's sake, does not speak a lie.
He is honoured in the midst of the assembly,
And goes then to a happy rebirth.
Seeing this, I declare:

52. See PED 671 for *saṇṭhānagata*.
53. See Rouse's comment, J VI 181 n. 1.

The one with wisdom is superior to the fool in his success.' *(34)*

Then Senaka uttered this verse:

'Elephants, oxen, horses, jewelled earrings, and women
Are found in successful families.
They are all for the enjoyment of the successful man,
Without successful mental powers.
Seeing this, I declare:
The one with wisdom is inferior to the one with good fortune.' *(35)*

Then the wise man said, 'What does he know?' And he continued his explanation of the matter with this verse:

'But good fortune abandons the fool,
Who commits thoughtless actions and makes foolish statements,
Like a snake discards its skin.
Seeing this, I declare:
The one with wisdom is superior to the fool in his success.' *(36)*

[362] And then Senaka, when the king had asked him, 'Well, Senaka?' replied, 'Sire, what does such a little boy know? Listen to this.' Thinking, 'I will make the sage quite speechless,' he spoke this verse:

'We are five sages, revered one.
We all attend you and offer *añjali*s up to you.
You are our lord and ruler,
Just as Sakka, the heavenly king, is the lord of beings in his realm.
Seeing this, I declare:
The one with wisdom is inferior to the one with good fortune.' *(37)*

When he heard this the king thought, 'That was so well expressed by Senaka. Now, will my son be able to rebut his argument and say something else?' And he said, 'Well, wise one?' There was no one except for the Bodhisatta who was able to rebut his argument, and because of this, through the power of his knowledge, he did so, saying, 'Great King, what does this fool know? He considers only himself, and he does not see the great excellency of wisdom. So listen, Great King.' And he said this verse:

'A slave of the wise man is the wealthy fool,
When matters of this kind come up.
Whatever the wise man penetrates clearly,
The fool just falls right into in muddledness.
Seeing this, I declare:
The one with wisdom is superior to the fool in his success.' *(38)*

As if bringing up golden-coloured sand from the foothills of Sineru, as though he brought the full moon into the sky, he set out his argument. In this way the Great Being demonstrated the power and glory of his wisdom. And the king said, 'Well, Senaka, what about this? Put a better argument if you can!' But like someone who has exhausted all the corn in the granary, he sat without speaking at all, deeply troubled. [363] Even if he could bring another argument, even with a thousand verses, it would not have finished this *jātaka* story.[54] As he remained there, not speaking at all, the Great Being continued with praise of wisdom, as though pouring out a deep flood:

'Wisdom is valued particularly by the awake;
The mass of people take delight in good fortune and wealth.
The knowledge of the Buddhas is unsurpassable:
So good fortune and wealth can never surpass wisdom.' *(39)*

When he heard this, the king was delighted with his exposition of the question and showered him with wealth as if with a great rain, and paid homage to him with this verse:

'Whatever question was asked by me: that he answered.
Mahosadha, the explainer of a complete teaching.
A thousand oxen, a bull, an elephant,
And ten carriages drawn by thoroughbreds,
And sixteen of the best villages: these, I bestow on you,
And I am delighted with your explanation of the question!' *(40)*

The question of the rich and the poor is finished.

THE SECRET WAY

From this time the Bodhisatta had a great reputation and Queen Udumbarā managed everything for him. When he had reached sixteen years of age, she thought 'My brother is now a grown up; his reputation is great: it is time to find a wife for him.' So she told the king about her thoughts, and when he had listened to her he was very pleased: 'Very good. Let him know.' [364] She informed him, and he agreed, and she said, 'Then let us find you a lovely girl.'

The Bodhisatta thought, 'I would not be happy with a wife that I had not chosen; I'll find one for myself.' So he said, 'Your majesty, please don't speak to the king about it for a few days, and I will find a wife that will make me happy at heart, and then I'll let you know.'

54. I have made this a negative by supplying *na*, as does Rouse (J VI 182). Otherwise it could just be translated perhaps as 'this *jātaka* would come to a standstill'; this seems odd, though not impossible, but the negative is preferred. For discussion of this self-reflexive tendency in this story, see the introduction to this story.

She said, 'Then do this, dear one.'

He paid his respects to the queen and went to his house, and told his companions about it. Then, by hook or by crook, he obtained the clothes of a tailor, and left alone by the northern gate into the town to the north. Now in this town there was a very old family, who had fallen on hard times. The daughter in this family was called Amarādevī (Deathless Queen), and she was very beautiful and endowed with all kinds of auspicious marks and virtues. Early that morning, thinking that she would go to where her father was ploughing, she had set out with some rice gruel for him she had cooked. And so she came upon the same road as the Great Being. He thought, 'This woman is endowed with all kinds of auspicious marks. If she does not have a husband then she must be my wife.' And she too, when she saw him, thought, 'If I could live in the same household as that man, then it would restore my family's fortunes.' The Great Being reflected, 'I do not know if this girl is married or unmarried. I'll ask her by hand gestures, and if she is wise, she will understand.' So, standing far away, he made a clenched fist with his hand. She realized, 'He is asking me if I have a husband.' And she spread her hand out open. He understood the meaning, and went up to her and asked her her name. She said, 'My name is something that exists not in the past, nor in the future, nor in the present.' He said, 'Lady, there is nothing in this world that is immortal. You must be Amarā.'

'Yes, sir.'

'Lady, to whom are you taking the rice gruel?'

'For a lord, the god of the past.'

'The gods of the past are parents; I think you are taking it to your father.'

She said, 'That must be so, sir.'

'What does your father do?'

'He makes two things from one,' she replied. Ploughing divides one thing into two, so he said, 'So he ploughs then, lady.' [365]

'Yes, sir,' she replied.

'And where is the place where your father ploughs?'

'Where those go who will not return.'

'The place where those go who do not return is a charnel ground. So he ploughs near a charnel ground.'

'Yes, sir.'

'And lady, will you go there again today?'[55]

55. Reading *essasīti* with Bd. See Geiger 1943: 185 for extensive discussion of this

'If something comes, then I will not go; and if something does not come, I will go.'[56]

'I think, lady, that your father ploughs by the riverbank. And if the water comes, you will not come, and if the water does not, you will.'

'Yes, sir.' Making such conversation, Amarādevī asked him, 'Would you like some rice gruel, sir?' The Great Being thought, 'It would be unlucky to refuse!' So he said, 'Yes, I'll drink some.' She then put down the jar of rice gruel. The Great Being thought, 'If she offers it to me without washing her hands, and the bowl too, then I'll leave and go.' She brought up water with the bowl and offered it to him to wash his hands. Then she placed it empty upon the ground, not in his hands, stirred up the rice gruel in the jar, and filled the bowl with it. Now there was not very much rice in it, so the Great Being said, 'But lady, there is not much rice here!'

'We have no water, sir.'

'I think you mean that when the paddy fields were growing, there was not much water there?'

'Exactly, sir.' She gave the rice gruel to the Bodhisatta, except for the portion for her father. He drank, and rinsed his mouth.

'Lady, I will go now to your house. Please point out to me the way.' She did, and recited a verse that is to be found in the first book of the *jātakas*:[57]

> 'By the path of rice cakes and sour gruel,
> The two-virtued tree is in flower.
> By this, with which I eat, I say go;
> Do not go by this, with which I do not eat.
> This is the way to Yavamajjha;
> This is the secret way you must find.'[58] *(41)*

[366] He went by the route she had explained to her house, and there Amarādevī's mother saw him and gave him a seat. 'I'll arrange some food for you, sir.'

'Young sister Amarādevī has given me a little already.'

She realized that he must have come for Amarādevī. The Great Being,

---

verb here. It has been translated as both 'come' and 'go' for better English here.

56. There are two futures here, and so some riddle is implied. See Rouse's note in J VI 183 n. 3.

57. See *Amarādevī-pañha-jātaka* (J 112; Ja I 424), which is the same as this section.

58. The commentary explains he must go to where there is a rice-cake shop and a gruel shop, then pass a *koviḷāra* tree (*Bauhinia variegata*; see DP I 739), and then take a path on the right: in Asian countries the right hand is used for eating and the left for the toilet.

knowing their straitened circumstances, said, 'Lady, I am a tailor, and I can mend anything.'

'Yes, sir, but there is no money to pay.'

'Lady, there is no need to pay: just bring me things and I will mend them.' She brought him some old clothes, and he mended each as she brought it, for the trade of a wise man always succeeds. And then he said, 'Let everyone on the street know about this.' She told the entire town. The Great Being did his stitching, and in one day he earned a thousand coins. The old lady cooked him a midday meal, and in the evening asked him, 'How much should I cook?'

'Enough, lady, for everyone in the house,' he replied.

So she cooked a large amount of rice, with all kinds of accompaniments. Amarādevī came back from the forest in the evening, carrying a log of wood on her head and leaves on her hip. She left the wood by the front door and entered the house by the back door. Her father came home later in the evening. The Bodhisatta ate a richly varied meal. Then, she served her parents their food before serving herself, and washed her parents' feet, and washed the Great Being's feet. And he remained there for several days, making his assessment of her.

Then, one day, he tested her. 'Dear Amarādevī, please take half a measure of rice and with it make me some rice gruel, a cake, and boiled rice.' She agreed, saying, 'Certainly.' She beat the rice, and made rice gruel with big grains, and with the middling grains she made boiled rice and with the little grains she made a cake, adding accompaniments. She gave the rice gruel and accompaniments to the Great Being. [367] As soon as he put it in his mouth he could feel the special tastes pervading through him. But to test her he said, 'Dear one, if you do not know how to cook something, why do you spoil the rice?' He then spat it out onto the ground. She did not become angry, but gave him the cake, saying, 'If the rice gruel is not pleasing, then eat the cake.' He did the same with that, and then rejected the boiled rice too, saying, 'If you don't know how to cook then why do you spoil what belongs to me?' As if he were angry, he mixed the three together into one and smeared it over her entire body, from the head downwards and told her to sit by the door. Not angry at all she replied, 'Certainly, sir,' and did so. Realising that she had no pride in her, he asked her to come back. And at his first word she did so.

When the Great Being had arrived, he had brought with him a thousand coins and a dress in his betel-nut bag. Now he took out this dress and placed it in her hands, saying, 'Lady, bathe with your friends and put on this dress, and then come back.' She did so, and the wise man gave her parents all the money he had brought with him, or earned, and gave them words of reassurance, and took her back to the town with him. There, to test her, he got her to sit down in the gatekeeper's dwelling and, explaining things to the gatekeeper's wife, went to his own house. Then he sent for some of his men. 'I have left a woman in such-and-such a house. Take a thousand coins with you and put her to the test.' He gave them the money and sent them on their way. They did this. She wanted none of it, thinking, 'That is not worth the dust on our guest's feet.' They went back and informed the wise man of this. He sent them there again, and a third time. On the fourth time, he told them, 'Just grab her hands and drag her here.' They did so. She did not look at the Great Being and his great magnificence, but started to smile and to cry at the same time.[59] He asked her why she was doing both. She said, 'Sir, I am smiling looking at your magnificence, thinking, "This greatness is not there without a cause. You must have done something good in a past life. So this is the result of great merits!" And I smiled. But I started crying as I thought, "But now he is going to sin against someone who has been protected and looked after by another, and will surely go to a Niraya hell." [368] And then I cried, through compassion.' After this test he recognized her great purity, and said, 'And now then, just take her back.' Putting on his tailor disguise, he went back to her, and there spent the night with her.

Next morning he entered the royal palace and told Queen Udumbarā all that had happened. She told the king, and adorned Amarādevī with all kinds of ornaments and sat her down on a great carriage. With great honour she led her to the Great Being's house, and she made a great festive day. The king sent the Bodhisatta a gift worth a thousand coins. The entire city, from the gatekeeper up, sent messages and presents too. Amarādevī split the gift from the king in two, and sent one half back to the king. In

59. UJST, which is not a translation from Pāli but perhaps indicates how the story was interpreted historically in Sri Lanka, says here: 'Amara Devi when brought before the Bosat could not recognise him, as he was dressed in his State attire (and not in the robes of a tailor) and she smiled and wept as she looked at him. The Pandit inquired of her the cause of her smiling and weeping.' (UJST 72). But this is not suggested in the Pāli. The use of the word *oloketvā* in the Pāli suggests 'looking' rather than 'recognising', and so when she says later that she looked and smiled, perhaps it means she did look momentarily, but not for long.

the same way she split the presents from the citizens back to them, and showed her goodwill to them too.

THE QUESTION OF THE FIREFLY

From that time the Great Being lived with her in happy accord and gave instruction to the king about his monarchy and the *dhamma*. But then one day Senaka said to the other three, who had come to visit him, 'Sirs, we are not good enough for this householder's son. And now he has brought back a wife cleverer than he is. Let's cause division between him and the king.'

'What do we know, teacher? You find a way.'

'So be it. Don't worry. There is a way—and I will take the jewel in the king's topknot; you, Pukkusa, take his golden necklace; you, Kāvinda, take his woollen shawl; and you, Devinda, take his golden sandal.' They all four found a way to take these. And then Senaka said, 'We must smuggle them into this householder's son without him realizing.' So he slipped the jewel into a buttermilk jar and put it in the hands of a servant girl, saying, 'Do not give this jar to any other people who want it, but give it only to the people in Mahosadha's household.' She went to the wise man's house, and wandered around saying, 'Do take this buttermilk!' Now Amarādevī was standing by the door and saw what the girl was doing. 'She does not go anywhere else; she has not come here without good reason.' So she made a sign to her servants to come near, and said to the servant girl, 'Hello, you. I'll take the buttermilk.' [369]

When she came up to her the lady summoned her servants, but not a sound came from them, so she sent the girl, 'Go and summon the servants.' When the girl was doing this Amarādevī stretched her hand into the jar and saw the jewel. When the girl came back she asked her, 'Whose servant are you?'

'I am the servant of the wise man Senaka,' she replied.

Then she asked her name, and that of her mother, and then said, 'Give me some buttermilk.'

'If you would like it, lady, then take it all, and there is no need for payment. Take it, with the jar.'

'Then you may go,' said the lady, and sent her on her way. Then she took some leaves and wrote on them:

In such-and-such a month, on such-and-such a day, the teacher Senaka sent the topknot jewel of the king in the hand of such-and-such a servant girl, of such-and-such a family, who had come on this errand.

Pukkusa sent the golden necklace hidden in a flat basket of jasmines, Kāvinda sent the woollen shawl in a basket for green-leaf vegetables, and Devinda sent the golden sandal in a bundle of straw. Amarādevī accepted them all, and wrote down names and details on a leaf for each of them, and put them away. She kept the Great Being informed about it all.

So then the four went to the royal residence and said, 'Why, sire, do you not wear your jewel on your topknot?' The king replied, 'I'll put it on! Bring it.' But they could not see the jewel, nor the other things. And then the four said, 'Sire, your ornaments are in Mahosadha's house, and he wears them. That householder's son is your enemy!' In this way they reviled him. And so then the wise man's friends went to tell him about this. He said, 'I'll see the king and find out about this.' He went to attend the king, and the king was very angry. 'I don't know him, nor what he is doing here!' And he did not grant him an audience. When the wise man found out about the king's rage, he returned home. The king gave orders for him to be seized. When the wise man heard from friends about this, he said, 'It is time to go.' He gave Amarādevī a signal, and left the city in disguise, to South Market Town. There, he worked as a potter in a potter's household, while the whole city was in uproar with the news that he had left.

Now Senaka and the other three heard of his escape. Each sent a message to Amarādevī saying, 'Don't worry—are we not wise men?' And did not tell each other about it. [370] She accepted the messages, and gave a reply to each of them, 'Please come at such-and-such a time.' When they came, she had them shaved bald with razors, flung them into a cesspit, and made them suffer greatly. Then she had them wrapped them in reed mats, and had the king informed. Taking them, and the four treasures, she went to the royal household and, standing there, paid homage to the king. She said, 'Sire, the wise man Mahosadha is not a thief. Senaka was the one who stole the topknot jewel, [Kāvinda was the one who stole the woollen shawl],[60] Pukkusa was the one who stole the golden necklace, and Devinda was the one who stole the golden sandal. In such-and-such a month, on such-and-such a day, in the hand of such-and-such a servant girl, they set up these errands. See this leaf record. Take your property, and get rid of these thieves, sire.' Denouncing them with vehemence, she paid respects to the king and went back home. But the king was at a loss at this, and in the

60. Kāvinda's theft is omitted from the text.

absence of the Bodhisatta and any other wise men, did not say anything to them, and gave the order, 'Just go home and wash yourselves.'

Now the goddess who lived in the royal parasol, not hearing any words of *dhamma* from the Bodhisatta, was puzzled. 'Why is this?' she asked herself. When she realized the reason she thought, 'I'll do something to bring the wise man back.' So that night she appeared in an opening in the in the side of the parasol and asked four riddles, which are to be found in 'The Riddles of the Goddess', in the verses beginning, 'He hits with his hands and with his feet.'[61] The king did not know the answer. 'I do not know; I will ask some other wise men.' And he asked for a day's consideration. The next day he sent a message asking them to come to him, but received the reply:

We are now bald. We are ashamed to go into the street.

So he sent four straw hats for them, with the message,

Let them wear these straw hats on their heads and come.[62]

That, they say, was the time when such straw hats came into being. The four came and sat down on the appointed seats. The king said, 'Today, Senaka, the goddess that lives in the royal parasol asked me four riddles, which I could not answer, but I said I would ask the wise men. Explain the answer to these questions to me.

'He hits with hands and feet, he strikes the face,
Yet, sire, he is dear, and dearer than a husband.' *(42)*

Senaka blurted out, 'How is it they hit, what's it that they hit?' [371] He just did not see the point; the others were just bewildered. The king was profoundly disturbed. When that night the goddess asked, 'Have you worked out the riddle?' The king replied, 'I asked the four wise men, and they did not know.' The goddess said, 'Well, what would they know? No one except the wise man Mahosadha is able to explain them. And if you do not summon him and get him to answer the riddles, then I will cut your head open with a fiery sword!' Having terrified the king, she said, 'Great King,

61. *Devatā-pañha-jātaka* (J 350; Ja III 152).

62. The word translated here as 'straw hats' is *nālipaṭṭe*, literally 'caps made from reeds'. See DP II 531.

it's no good blowing on a firefly to start a fire, or milking a white animal horn to get milk.' And she repeated the Firefly Question from the fifth book:

> 'When a lamp has gone out, who, wandering in search of a fire,
> Thinks a firefly is a fire, when he sees it at night? *(43)*
> It is just a contrary thing to think, and if he crushes the firefly
> And scatters cow dung and grasses over it, he will not be able to get a fire going. *(44)*
> In this way also, a wild animal will get no benefit with a stupid course of action,
> And he gets no result if he milks a cow by the horn, where no milk comes out. *(45)*
> By many varied means, young men do get benefit,
> By restraining their enemies and encouraging their friends. *(46)*
> By bringing on side the generals, and by the guidance of favoured friends,
> Those that guard the earth possess the earth,
> And all the wealth the earth can give.' *(47)*

[372] 'They are not like you, blowing on a firefly and thinking to get fire. No, you are like someone blowing on a firefly when there is already fire there. Or like someone throwing away the scales and weighing with his hand, or like someone who wants milk and milks an animal horn, when you pose a deep riddle to Senaka and the rest. What do they know? They are like fireflies, while Mahosadha is like a great bonfire, on fire with wisdom. Ask him to come back, and if you do not answer the riddle, there's no life left for you!' Having terrified the king, she disappeared.

The question of the firefly is finished.

THE WISDOM (BHŪRI) QUESTION

And then the king, terrified of death, summoned his ministers and gave them his orders. 'You four put yourselves in four carriages and leave by the four gates of the city. Wherever you see my son, Mahosadha the wise man, pay him homage and bring him back here quickly.' Three went by their gates, and did not find him. But the fourth, who went by the south gate, found the Great Being in South Market Town. After bringing clay and turning his teacher's wheel, he was sitting on a bale of straw, with his body smeared with mud, eating handfuls of barley rice dipped in a little curry sauce. And why was he behaving like this? He was acting in this way, as he thought, 'They say the king might think, "Wise Mahosadha is undoubtedly going to take the kingdom." But when he hears, "He is living as a potter," he will not have doubts about this.' When he saw the minister he realized he had come for him, 'My reputation will be restored. I'm going to be eating all kinds of choice food prepared by Amarādevī!' So he dropped the ball of rice on the ground, stood up, and rinsed his mouth. At that moment the minister, who was a supporter of Senaka, approached him. Because of this, the man spoke to him harshly. 'Wise teacher, Senaka's words about you sum it up: your reputation has gone, your wisdom could not do anything to help, and now, smeared with mud, you sit on a bale of straw eating a rice ball like that!' And he recited this verse from the *Bhūripañha*, or question about wisdom, in the tenth book:[63]

> [373] 'So is it true, as they say, that you are full of wisdom?
> But such good fortune, cleverness, and understanding
> Are no help to you, reduced to this,
> You who eats a little curry sauce for barley.' *(48)*

And then the Great Being said, 'Blind fool! When I want to restore that reputation, by the power of my wisdom, I'll do it.' And he said this couplet of verses:

> 'I bring my happiness to ripeness with suffering,
> I discriminate between the right and the wrong time, wishing to be hidden.
> I unlock the doors to my advantage: and I am even content with this rice. *(49)*
> When I see the moment for effort, I'll ripen my advantage with my plans.
> I will behave like a brave lion, and you will see me in my powerful glory again.' *(50)*

And then the minister said, 'Wise man, the goddess who lives in the royal parasol has asked the king a riddle, and the king has asked the four wise men. Not one was able to answer it, so the king sent me to you.'

[374] 'You just do not see the power in being wise. At such a time there is no support in pomp, but the one who is endowed with wisdom is a support.' The Great Being extolled the power of wisdom, and then the king's minister said, 'Take the wise man and make sure he is bathed and clothed so he can be seen, at once.' He handed over a thousand coins and a suit of clothes from the king. The potter was very frightened. 'They'll say the wise man Mahosadha has been doing service with me!' The Great Being reassured him, 'Do not be afraid, my teacher, you have been a great help to me.' He gave him the thousand pieces, and, still smeared with mud over his body,

63. See *Bhūripañha-jātaka* (J 452; Ja IV 72).

sat in the carriage and entered the city. The minister informed the king, who asked, 'Where did you find the wise man?'

'Sire, in South Market Town; he was making his living as a potter. When he was told that you were summoning him, without washing and with his body smeared with clay, he immediately came.'

The king thought, 'If he were an enemy, he would have come in pomp and glory. So he is not my enemy.' He said, 'Dear son, go back home and get yourself washed and dressed up, and come back in my robes of office.' He did this, and came back. At the command to enter he entered, made his greetings and stood to one side. The king gave him a warm welcome, and examined the wise man with this verse:

'Some do not do evil for happiness,
Others through fear of association with blame.
If you had a mind for great wealth, you could get it.
So why don't you do wrong?' *(51)*

The Bodhisatta said:

'Wise men do not do wrong things for the sake of their own happiness.
[375] The good, even when dislodged from their position,
Do not abandon the *dhamma*, either through willingness or through hatred.' *(52)*

Again the king spoke this verse, a warrior caste saying, as a test:

'The one who in any guise, weak or strong, raises himself up from poverty,
That one goes in justice.' *(53)*

The Great Being, explaining through the simile of the tree, spoke this verse:

'From the tree under whose shade he has sat and rested,
The man should not cut off the branch: a disloyal friend is despicable.'[64] *(54)*

'Great King, if it is only a disloyal friend who cuts off a branch from a tree where one has rested, then what about the murderer? You have given my father so much glory and wealth and I have been graced with so much kindness from you, how could I be a bad friend and bring you harm?' Having given an extensive account of his lack of disloyalty, he admonished the king for his lapse:

'A man who has discerned the teaching for someone

64. This verse is also found in the *Vidhura-jātaka*, Chapter 9 (Ja VI 310 v. 227).

Or those who purify the mind of doubt,
Such a person is like a lamp, and a support.
The wise man does not spoil this friendship.' *(55)*

Then he advised him with this couplet of verses:

'The lazy householder is no good, just following sense pleasures.
The one who goes forth mindlessly is no good either.
The king who does not make an effort is no good.
And the wise man who gets angry is also no good.[65] *(56)*
[376] 'The noble warrior acts when he has attended carefully, lord of the directions.
The king who makes a practice of this increases in his glory and repute.' *(57)*

The wisdom question is finished.

THE RIDDLES OF THE GODDESS

When he heard this, the king had the Great Being sit on the royal seat under the white parasol, spread out full, while he sat on a low seat. Then he said, 'Wise man, the goddess of the white parasol posed four riddles for me. I asked the wise men, and none of the four could solve them. So you explain them to me.'

'Great King, whether it is the goddess of the white parasol, or the Four Great Kings, or anyone at all, let them pose a riddle and I will solve it.'

The king posed the riddles in the same way as the goddess had, and recited the first verse:

'He hits with hands and feet, he strikes the face,
Yet, sire, he is dear, and dearer than a husband.' *(58)*

When the Great Being heard the riddle, the meaning was as clear to him as if the moon had risen in the sky. 'When a mother has a baby sitting on her lap playing and laughing, he hits out at his mother with his hands and feet, pulls her hair and strikes her face with his fist, and she exclaims, "You rascal! What are you hitting me for?" And through the power of her affection she cannot restrain her affection for the baby, and snuggles him close to her chest and kisses him. At such a time he is dearer to her than the child's father.'[66]

65. See Ja III 154.

66. This explanation has been put into small type in F, but is clearly here an integral part of the story.

In this way, as if making the sun rise in the middle of the sky, he explained the riddle. The goddess slipped from the opening in the parasol, and revealed just half of her body. She gave her support with a voice like honey, 'That was well solved!' She filled a jewelled casket with divine perfumes and flowers, and gave it to him as an offering; and then she disappeared. The king also paid his homage to the Great Being, [377] with flowers and suchlike, and then asked him the second question, saying this verse:

> 'She abuses him, yet wants him near.
> Yet, sire, he is dear, and dearer than a husband.' *(59)*

The Great Being explained. 'When a child is seven years old the mother sends her child on an errand he can now do. She says, "Go to the field; go to the market place." And he replies, "If you give me this or that nice food then I'll go." And she says, "Here you are then," and she gives a snack to him and he eats it up. But he says, "So, you get to sit in the shade and I get to go and do some hard errand!" And he pulls a rude face or makes a rude hand gesture and doesn't go. She is furious and gets a stick and says, "You eat what I give you and then you decide you don't want to go and do anything in the fields!" He is scared off and runs away at great speed. She cannot follow and shouts, "Off you go, and I hope the bad men chop you up limb from limb!" So she abuses him saying whatever she wants, but what she says with her mouth she does not wish at all, and really she wishes him to be near to her. He plays out the whole day, and does not dare to go home but goes to some relatives. Meanwhile, his mother looks out for his return on the road, and not seeing him, thinks, "I think he does not dare to come home!" With her heart full of grief and her eyes full of tears, she searches the houses of her relatives. When she finds him, she kisses him and hugs him with both arms and clutches him tight. "Oh my son, did you take my words seriously?" and she holds him in even deeper affection. In this way, Great King, at the time of her anger the child is dearer to her.' Mahosadha explained the second riddle, and the goddess paid homage to him. The king then also paid homage to him and asked him about the third riddle. 'Speak, Great King,' he said, and the king said this verse:

> 'She reproaches him without cause, she berates him with lies.
> Yet, sire, he is dear, and dearer than a husband.' *(60)*

The Great King said to him, 'When lovers are together in secret, [378] enjoying their love together, they say, "You don't really love me. Your heart is somewhere else." So they reproach one another in this way, without a cause, and berate each other with lies, and are angry, yet each is dearer to one another than before: now understand the answer to the riddle.' He explained the third riddle, and the goddess paid homage to him. The king then also paid homage to him and asked him about the fourth riddle. 'Speak, Great King,' he said, and the king said this fourth verse:

> 'He takes food and drink, clothes and places to stay.
> These good men follow another aim.
> Yet, sire, he is dear, and dearer than a husband.' *(61)*

He told him, 'This, Great King, refers to those who follow the *dhamma* as ascetics and brahmins. Faithful householders having faith, and other qualities, and feeling trust in this world and the next, give to them, and they wish to give. And when they watch these ascetics and brahmins eating and accepting their wealth, they say, "It is our wealth they are accepting! They are eating food, drink, and suchlike that is from us!" And so their affection for them grows even greater. In this way, they follow another aim, and they accept offerings, putting the robe over their shoulder, and so they become dear.' When he had explained the riddle the goddess right there made an offering to him and congratulated him. She laid a casket filled with the seven kinds of jewels at the Great Being's feet, 'Please accept this, wise man.' The king's heart was made peaceful, and he gave him the position of general of the army. And from that time his glory was magnificent.

The riddles of the goddess are finished.

THE QUESTIONS OF THE FIVE WISE MEN

Again the four met together. 'The householder's son now has yet greater glory; what are we to do?' They took counsel, and then Senaka said, 'Let it be. I've seen a plan. We'll ask the householder's son this question: "To whom is it right to reveal a secret?" He will say, "To no one." Then we say to the king, "Sire, the householder's son is your enemy." And we will cause a breach between them.' So the four went to the wise man's house and made their greetings. 'Wise man, we would like to ask you a question,' they said.

He said, 'Ask away.'

So Senaka asked him, 'Wise man, where is it that a wise man should be firmly established?'

'In truth,' he replied. [379]

'And once established in truth, what should be done?'

'He should make his fortune.'

'And once he has made his fortune, what should he do next?'

'He should learn good sense.'

'And when he has learned good sense, what should he do next?'

'He should not tell anyone else his secret.'

They said, 'That is very good, wise man.' And they were delighted: 'Now we'll see the back of the wise man!' So they went to the king, and said, 'Great King, the householder's son is your enemy.'

The king refused to accept this. 'I just do not believe you. He cannot be my enemy.'

'Truly, he is, Great King. Trust us, and do not trust him. Just ask him, "Wise man, to whom should you reveal your secret?" And if he is not your enemy, he will say, "To such-and-such a person." And if he is your enemy, he will say, "It should be revealed to no one. Only when your heart's desire has been fulfilled should you speak it out." Then, you will place your trust in us, and you will not have any doubts.'

The king said, 'Very well.' And one day, when they had called them all together, and they were sitting down, he spoke the first verse, from the Wise Man's Questions:[67]

> 'Five wise men are met together.
> A question has come up for me. So listen.
> To whom should any secret matter be revealed,
> Whether it is a matter deserving praise or blame?' *(62)*

When he heard this Senaka, thinking, 'We won't oppose the king in anything,' said this verse:

> 'You, protector of the earth, explain!
> You are our support, and carry our burdens. Tell us!
> The five wise men will apprehend your wish
> And your pleasure, and speak then.' *(63)*

And then the king, having defilements in him, recited this verse:

> 'Whatever lady is virtuous, does not go to another man,
> Does not go against her husband's wishes, and is pleasing:
> [380] to her, his wife, should be told the secret,
> Whether it deserves blame or praise.' *(64)*

Then Senaka was pleased, thinking, 'Now I can get the king over to our side.' And he repeated a verse explaining his own behaviour:

> 'Whoever is a refuge to one who has fallen on hard times,
> Who is in pain, and is his support:
> To him, the friend, should be told the secret,
> Whether it deserves blame or praise.' *(65)*

67. *Pañca-paṇḍita-jātaka* (J 508; Ja IV 473).

And then the king asked Pukkusa, 'How about you, Pukkusa, how do you see it? To whom should the secret be told?' And Pukkusa recited this verse:

'Whether old, young, or middle-aged,
The one who is reliable and controlled in his behaviour:
To him, the brother, should be told the secret,
Whether it deserves blame or praise.' *(66)*

And then the king asked Kāvinda, and he spoke this verse:

'Whoever follows his father's heart,
and takes after his parents, and has developed wisdom:
To him, the son, should be told the secret,
Whether it deserves blame or praise.' *(67)*

And then the king asked Devinda, and he recited this verse:

'The mother, the best of the lords of men,
Who nurtures a child with willingness and love:
To her, the mother, should be told the secret,
Whether it deserves blame or praise.' *(68)*

[381] Having asked them, the king asked the wise man. 'How do you see it, wise man?' And he delivered this verse:

'The secret of a secret is its good:
The telling of a secret is not to be praised.
The wise man keeps it to himself, when it has not been achieved,
And when it has happened, he may speak it whenever he likes.' *(69)*

When the wise man had spoken, the king was very unhappy. And then the king looked at Senaka. And Senaka looked at the king. The Bodhisatta saw this, and realized why. 'These four have slandered me to the king beforehand. This question must have been posed to test their accusations.' While they were talking, the sun had set and the lamps had been lit. The wise man thought, 'The deeds of a king are weighty. There is no knowing what he'll do. It's best just to leave as quickly as possible,' so he got up from his seat, paid his respects to the king, and left. He thought, 'One of these four said the friend, one the brother, one the son, and one the mother as the one to tell. They must have done something, or seen something, and I think that they have been told what one of them has seen. Let it be: I'll find out today.' When they had reached a conclusion in their proceedings on other days, the four used to leave the king's household and sit on a certain food trough chatting about their business before going home. Therefore, the wise man thought, 'If I go secretly behind the food trough, I'll find out what they are plotting.' So he had the trough lifted and had a rug laid down, giving a sign to his attendants: 'Come back and get me when these four wise men have finished their deliberations.' They said, 'Certainly,' and left.

Now Senaka said to the king, 'Great King, do you not have faith in us, [382] so what now?' He accepted the word of these troublemakers and without testing it, and, terrified, asked, 'Now what shall I do, wise man Senaka?'

'Great King, without making a fuss, and without telling anyone, the householder's son should be killed.'

'Senaka, except for you, no one else wishes for my prosperity. Take your friends. Position yourselves inside the entranceway, and in the morning, when he comes to wait on me, cut his head off with a sword.' He gave him his jewelled ceremonial sword.[68] They said, 'Very well, sire. Do not be afraid; we will kill him.' And then they left, saying, 'We've seen the back of our enemy.' They went to sit down on the food trough, and then Senaka said, 'So sirs, who is going to kill the householder's son?' The others said, 'You, teacher,' and gave the responsibility to him. Then Senaka asked, 'You, sirs, said that a secret should be told to such-and-such a person. Was this because of something you had seen or heard?'

'Leave it, teacher. When you said that a secret should be told to a friend, was that something you had done?'

'What is it to you?'

'Go on, tell us, teacher.'

He said, 'If the king ever gets to hear of this secret, my life will be over.'

'Don't be frightened, teacher, there'll be no breaking of a secret amongst us. Go on, tell us, teacher.'

He tapped the trough with his nail. 'What if that householder's son is under this!'

'Teacher, the householder's son, with all his power, would not get into this. He is too trumped up in his glory. Go on, tell us.'

So Senaka told them his own secret. 'Now, do you know such-and-such a prostitute in this city?'

'Yes, teacher.'

'Is she seen around now?'

'No, she is not seen around, teacher.'

'Well, I made love to her in the *sāl* grove, and then killed her out of desire for her ornaments. These I tied up in her clothes and took to my house.

68. Cone notes that *khagga* is often a ceremonial sword (DP I 742).

I hung them up on an elephant's tusk in such-and-such a room of such-and-such a floor. But I cannot wear them. [383] I am waiting for it to be long past. I have told this crime to one friend only, and he has not told anyone yet. Because of this I said, "A secret can be told to a friend."' The wise man paid close attention to this secret and mulled it over.

Then Pukkusa told his secret. 'On my thigh there is a skin disease. Every morning my young brother washes it, rubs ointment into it, and gives it a new bandage, without telling anyone. The king calls me when his heart is tender, 'Come here, Pukkusa,' and he lies down resting on my thigh. But if he knew, he would certainly have me killed. Except for my young brother, no one else knows about this. That was the reason I said a secret could be told to a brother.'

Kāvinda then explained his secret. 'On the *uposatha* day in each dark fortnight[69] a *yakkha* named Naradeva (Man-god) seizes hold of me. And I howl like a maddened dog, and I told this thing to my son. So, when he notices that I am possessed, he locks me into an inner room. He bolts the door so I cannot leave, and then he gets around a crowd of people and they drown out the noise from me. That is why I said that a son was someone that could be told a secret.

Then they asked the third, Devinda, and he related his secret. 'I am the king's jewel valuer. I stole the beautiful and lucky jewel that had been given to King Kusa by Sakka on his auspicious visit. I gave it to my mother. She has not told anyone, but gives it to me at the time of my visit to the king, and when I go into the king's dwelling I am filled with the great auspiciousness of the jewel. The king speaks to me first, before you, and gives me eight, sixteen, thirty-two, or sixty-four coins each day as my wages. If the king were to find out that I had concealed this jewel treasure, I would be dead. For that reason I say that a mother can be told a secret.'[70]

The Great Being, having found out for himself the secrets, noted them. [384] But they, as if bursting open the belly and letting the innards out, had told each other their secrets. They were careful. 'Come in the morning, and we'll kill the householder's son.' Saying this, they got up from their seat and left.

At the moment of their departure, the men came and let the Great Being out of the trough and went home with him. He washed and adorned

69. This refers to the time when the moon is on the wane.

70. The jewel has already been mentioned in this story, under the earlier questions.

himself, and ate a hearty meal. 'Today my sister Queen Udumbarā will give a command for me to go to the king's palace.' Realising this, he positioned a reliable man at the door, 'If anyone comes from the palace, send him to me quickly.' When he had said this, he went and lay down on his bed.

At that moment, the king was also lying on his bed, bringing to mind the virtues of the wise man. 'The wise man Mahosadha has served me since he was seven years old, and has never done any harm to me at all. When the goddess asked me the questions, I would not have remained alive. I have accepted the words of his enemies, who said, 'Kill the peerless wise man.' Even by giving my sword I did something that was unworthy. And after tomorrow, I will never see him again!' Grief welled up in him, and sweat poured down his body. Stricken by grief, his heart had no peace. Queen Udumbarā, who was sharing his bed with him, saw his state. 'Have I done anything wrong, or has anybody else caused such grief to arise in your majesty?' And she spoke this verse:

'Why are you distraught, sire?
We do not hear the voice of the lord of men.
Why are you worrying, with such sadness?
There is no offence from me, sire.' *(70)*

And the king spoke this verse:

'Wise Mahosadha must be killed, they said!
The one filled with wisdom is to be killed at my command.
That is why I am worrying, with such sadness.
There is no offence from you, good lady.' *(71)*

[385] When she heard the words of the king, grief for the Great Being,[71] like a mountain, arose in her. She thought, 'By means of a strategem, I'll bring comfort to the king. When he has fallen asleep I'll send a message to my brother.' And then she said, 'Great King, you have established the householder's son with such great glory, and you made him general. Now, they say that he has become your enemy. An enemy is not a trifling thing, and he must be killed. But do not worry about it.' And so she comforted the king. His grief was allayed, and he went to sleep. The queen got up and went into her chamber, and wrote on a leaf:

Mahosadha, the four wise men have denounced you.

71. The F text is emended here in accordance with Bd: *sā tassa vacanaṃ sutvā va mahāsatatassa atthāya soko uppajji*. VRI has *tassā tassa vacanaṃ sutvāva mahāsatte sinehena pabbatamatto soko uppajji*.

The king is angry and has ordered them to kill you in the entranceway.
You should not come to the palace tomorrow.
If you do come, do so able to hold the power of the city in your hand.

She put the letter inside an envelope and tied it up with thread, laid it in a new jar, sealed it, and gave it to one of her attendant women. 'Take this envelope and give it to my brother.' She did so. And do not wonder, 'How did she leave in the night?'[72] For this boon had been given to the queen first by the king, and so no one obstructed her. The Bodhisatta received the gift and sent the woman, and she reported back that she had given it. At that moment, the queen went to lie with the king, and the Bodhisatta broke open the envelope and read the leaf and understood its meaning. He went to bed pondering it over.

The next morning, the four stood inside the entranceway with swords in their hands. They were disappointed not to see the wise man and went to the king. 'Have you killed the householder's son?' he asked. They replied, 'We have not seen him, sire.' But the Great Being, at sunrise, had got the city under his sway.[73] Setting up a guard here and there, he alighted onto a carriage with a great crowd of people around, and went to the gates of the palace. The king stood looking at him from an open window, and the Great Being got down from his carriage and paid homage to him. The king thought, 'If this man is my enemy, [386] he would not pay homage to me.' And then the king called him and sat on his couch, while the Great Being came and sat to one side, and the four wise men sat down there too. Then the king, feigning ignorance, said, 'Dear one, you walked out yesterday and come now today; are you giving up on me?' And he recited this verse:

'Now you have come, who went away yesterday evening.
What did you hear? What has brought doubt to your mind?
Who has spoken to you, wise one?
Come, we are listening to what you have to say. Speak to me.' *(72)*

And then the Great Being said, 'Great King, you listened to the four wise men and gave a death sentence for me. But I have come,' and spoke this verse in reproach:

72. This narrator's address to the listener, or reader, is unusual but consistent with the literary style of this story, where an active narrative presence is so pervasive; such instructions are usually reserved for relating how the story should be told.

73. Reading *katvā* 'making' with Bd rather than F *datvā* 'giving'.

'"The wise man Mahosadha must die." If you said this secretly to your wife,
Your secret was revealed to me and I heard it.' *(73)*

The king listened to this. 'This command must have been revealed to him just in this moment!' He looked at his wife in anger. The Great Being understood this, however. 'Sire, why are you angry with your wife? I know it all: past, present, and future. Sire, let your secret be told to your wife! I know the secrets of the teacher Senaka, Pukkusa, and the rest. Oh yes, I know all their secrets.' And he told the secret of Senaka in this verse:

'Whatever evil deed it was
That Senaka did in the *sāl* grove in secret—
[387] A friend was told this secret,
And now this secret has been revealed to me.' *(74)*

The king considered Senaka. 'Is it true?' he asked. 'It is true, sire,' he said. The king ordered him to be sent to prison. Then the wise man revealed the secret of Pukkusa with this verse:

'A disease has arisen in the man Pukkusa,
That is not fitting to be near a king.
His brother was told this secret,
And now this secret has been revealed by me.' *(75)*

The king looked at him and asked him if this was true. He said, 'Yes, sire,' and the king ordered him to be sent to prison. Then the wise man spoke of Kāvinda's secret with this verse:

'This man, however, is diseased in his very nature:
Kāvinda is touched by Naradeva!
His son was told this secret,
And now this secret has been revealed by me.' *(76)*

[388] The king asked Kāvinda if this was true, and he said, 'It is true, sire.' The king ordered him to be sent to prison. Then the wise man revealed the secret of Devinda with this verse:

'An eight-curved jewel[74] of the highest water,
That Sakka gave to your father—
That is in Devinda's hand today.
His mother was told this secret,
And now this secret has been revealed by me.' *(77)*

The king asked if it was true, and he answered, 'It is true.' And he was sent to prison. In this way all those who had said, 'Let's kill the Bodhisatta,'

74. *Aṭṭhavaṃkaṃ maṇiratanaṃ*. See introduction to this story.

were in imprisonment together. The Bodhisatta said, 'For this reason I said that one should not reveal a secret to anyone. Those who said that one should tell it to someone have all come to ruin.' And saying this, he gave a talk on the higher teaching, in these verses:

'The secret of a secret is its good:[75]
The telling of a secret is not to be praised.
The wise man keeps it to himself, when it has not been achieved,
And when it has happened, he may speak it whenever he likes. *(78)*
One should not reveal the matter of a secret, but should guard it like a treasure.
A secret matter is not revealed by the discerning. *(79)*
A wise man does not tell a secret to a woman, nor to an enemy,
Nor to one motivated by self-interest, nor because of the inclination of the heart. *(80)*
The man who makes known a secret matter to someone who does not know
Becomes a slave to him, through fear of it being discussed. *(81)*
As many people that know a man's secret matter: just so many are his worries.
Therefore he should not tell a secret. *(82)*
Be secluded and tell a secret in the daytime;
Whisper it in quietness in the night.
[389] There are listeners who hear discussion,
And discussion quickly leads up to a split.' *(83)*

When the king had heard the Great Being's words he was angry and thought, 'These men were traitors to the king when they behaved treacherously to him.' He gave the order, 'Go and drive them out of the city. Impale them or cut off their heads.' So they bound their arms behind them, and gave them a hundred blows at every street corner. As they were being dragged off, the Great Being said, 'Sire, these men were your ministers for a long time, be forbearing in the punishment given to them.' The king agreed to this, and ordered that they be made his slaves. He set them free there and then. Then the king said, 'But they are not to live in my kingdom,' and he exiled them. The wise man said, 'Be forbearing with their blind folly, sire.' He managed to appease him and persuaded him to restore them to their positions. The king reflected on this: 'If his practice of loving-kindness is like this to his enemies, what must it be to others!' And he came to trust him deeply.

75. The Bodhisatta reiterates in this verse his earlier answer to the king (v. 69).

And from that time, the four wise men, like snakes with their teeth pulled out and poison gone, could not find anything to say—or that is what they say.

The questions of the five wise men, and the story of the betrayal, are finished.

THE SECTION ON THE GREAT TUNNEL

And from that time the wise man gave advice to the king on matters of state and matters of *dhamma*. He thought, 'I am the white parasol for the king, [390] as I deliberate for him. It is necessary for me to be diligent so that he arranges the affairs of state in the city.' He had a great rampart and a walkway built, with lookout posts at the gates, and between the lookout posts he had dug three channels: a water channel, a mud channel, and a dry channel. Within the city he had all the old houses renovated, and he had great water tanks made, and filled them with plenty of water. He had all the storehouses filled with corn. He got the practitioners of psychic powers to bring down mud and lotus seeds from the Himalayan foothills. He had the drainage systems cleaned out, and the old houses on the outskirts of the city were also renovated. And why was this? As a contingency to avert danger in the future. Merchants travelling from one place to another were asked to reveal where they had come from. And when they replied, 'From such-and-such a place,' they were then asked what policies were dear to their king. When people heard what was dear to their kings, they were treated with hospitality and sent on their way. Then he summoned one hundred and one soldiers and said to them, 'Men, take these presents to the hundred and one royal cities, and give them to their respective kings, to please them. Stay there and attend to them, and get to know their behaviour and their talk and send news of this to me here. I will care for your wives and your children.'

He sent some of them with golden slippers, and some with golden necklaces, and inscribed letters on them. 'Let these be made public when I give the word.' He sent them with these in their hands, and they went here and there, and gave their respective presents to the kings. 'We have come to live as your attendants,' they said. When asked where they had come from they gave the names of places different from those of the places they had come from. They were willingly accepted, and made themselves good and reliable attendants.

At that time, in Ekabala, was a king called Saṅkhapāla (Protector of the Conch), who was gathering weapons and bringing together an army. The man who was operating as a spy at his court sent a message to the wise man. 'This is the news, but what he is planning to do I do not know. You had better send someone to find out.' Then the Great Being addressed a parrot. 'Sir, go to the kingdom of Ekabala and find out what King Saṅkhapāla is planning to do. [391] Then travel across the entire continent of India (Jambudīpa) and tell me what he is planning.' Saying this, he fed him some honeyed grain and gave him some honey and water to drink. Then he anointed his wings and joints with oil, a thousand times refined, and stood by a window and released him. The parrot went to the man who was at that king's court, and found out what was going on from him. Then he travelled through India and reached the city of Uttarapañcāla in the kingdom of Kapilla.

There, a king ruled called Cūḷani Brahmadatta. A brahmin called Kevaṭṭa, who was wise and experienced, advised the king on matters of state and of *dhamma*. The brahmin woke up one morning and looked at the light of a lamp in his splendidly decorated room, and saw its great glory. 'To whom does this glory belong?' he reflected. 'To none other than Cūḷani Brahmadatta. A king of such glory should be the chief ruler of the whole of India. And I will be his high priest.' And so in the morning he had gone to the king and asked him if he had slept soundly. Then he said, 'Sire, there is a matter that should be discussed.'

'Speak, teacher!' the king had replied.

'Sire, it is not possible to keep something secret in this city, let's go to the garden.'

He said, 'Certainly, teacher.' So he went with him into the garden, left his entourage outside, had a guard set up, and sat down with the brahmin on the auspicious stone.[76] The parrot saw this and thought, 'Something must be going on. Today I'll hear something that ought to be relayed on to the wise man.' He entered the garden and alighted and sat amongst the leaves of the auspicious *sāl* tree. The king said, 'So tell me, teacher.'

'Great King, bend your ears to this; for it is a discussion that must be only for four ears. If, sire, you do what I advise, you will be king of the entire continent of India.'

76. The auspicious stone is a recurrent feature of *jātakas*: Janaka is found and accepted as the true king when lying on one (Chapter 2).

The king heard this statement with great thirst, and was delighted. 'Speak, teacher, for I will do it.'

'Sire, let us raise an army, and then lay siege to a small city. Then I will enter the city by a small side gate and speak to the king. "Great King, there is no point in struggling. Come over to our side. Your kingdom will remain yours; but if you fight in opposition to us, with our big army, you will be defeated." [392] If he does what I say,[77] we'll take him on board; if not, we'll kill him and then, taking two armies go to another city, and then another, and in this way we'll take the entire continent of India, and drink the wine of victory!' He went on: 'And then we will bring one hundred and one kings to our city, and have a pavilion for drinking set up, and have them all drink poisoned alcohol while they are sitting there. So we'll get them all dead, and we'll throw them into the Ganges, and have the kingdoms of a hundred and one kings under our power! You will be the highest king, of all of India.'

The king said, 'Certainly, teacher, I'll do this.'

'Great King, this is a discussion for four ears alone. No one else must know about this. Don't make any delay, and do this quickly.' The king was pleased, and agreed.

Now the parrot heard this, and let fall a lump of bird droppings, as though they had dropped from a branch, onto Kevaṭṭa's head. 'What is that?' He said, and looked upwards with his mouth wide open. The parrot let fall some more bird droppings into his mouth, and flew off the branch, crying, 'Kree! Kevaṭṭa, you think your discussion was just for four ears! But now it is for six! Soon it is going to be for eight, and then hundreds more!'

'Catch him, catch him!' they shouted. But he flew off as quickly as the wind and went to Mithilā, and flew into the wise man's house. Now this was the parrot's habit: If he had something to be told to the teacher, he flew onto his shoulder blade. If it was suitable for Amarādevī to hear as well, he flew onto his lap, and if it was suitable for everyone to hear, he alighted on the ground. He alighted this time on his shoulder blade. Seeing the signal that this was for private consumption, the attendants left. The teacher took him to the top storey and asked him, 'Well, dear one, what did you see and what did you hear?'

He replied, 'Sir,[78] I have seen a threat from no other king in India. But

77. The second-person verb has been amended to the third person (as in J VI 199).

78. His address here is *deva*, usually reserved for a king, but perhaps the parrot regards him in that light.

Kevaṭṭa, priest to King Cūḷani Brahmadatta in the city of Uttarapañcāla, took the king aside and led him to the garden for a conversation supposed to be for four ears alone. I sat on a branch and let drop some bird droppings into his mouth, and then came here!' And he told the wise man everything that he had seen and heard. [393]

'Did the king agree to this?' he asked.

'Yes, sir, he did.'

The wise man had the parrot given all the hospitality and homage he deserved, and put him to rest in a golden cage covered with soft mats. 'I think Kevaṭṭa does not know about Mahosadha's nature. I will not now let him bring his plan to fruition.' With this in mind, he got all the poor people in the city to leave, and had brought into the city instead all the wealthy and powerful families from the kingdom, the country areas, and the small towns, as well as a large supply of corn.

King Cūḷani Brahmadatta took Kevaṭṭa's advice. He went with a well-supported army and besieged one city. Then, following Kevaṭṭa's suggested method, he entered into another kingdom, and a second, and another, until he had brought all the kings of India under his power, except for King Videha. Now the men who had been working as spies at the orders of the Bodhisatta, constantly sent messages:

These cities have been taken by Brahmadatta: be vigilant.

To these he replied:

I am vigilant; you be watchful, without dropping your guard.

In seven years and seven months and seven days Brahmadatta had taken control of all of India, except for Videha. Then he said to Kevaṭṭa, 'Teacher, let's take control of Mithilā, in the kingdom of Videha.' But Kevaṭṭa replied, 'Great King, we will not be able to take the kingdom of Videha, as it is where Mahosadha lives. He is full of resourcefulness (*upayakusalo*), and endowed with great wisdom.' Then he explained the great qualities of Mahosadha, as if delineating them on the circle of the moon. Now he was also very resourceful, so he said, 'The kingdom of Mithilā is a little small. The entire India is quite sufficient for us, so there is no point.' In this way through his device he made him satisfied with the rest of India. But the other princes said, 'But let's seize the kingdom of Mithilā, and drink the wine of victory!' Kevaṭṭa, trying to prevent this, said, 'What is the point in taking the kingdom of Mithilā? The king is on our side anyway; turn back!' In this way he brought them to their senses, and they listened to him and did turn back. The Great Being's representatives sent this message:

Brahmadatta had been on his way, with a hundred and one kings, to Mithilā, but he has now gone back to his own city.

[394] The Great Being sent then this message:

Let me know anything that he does from now on.

Brahmadatta took counsel with Kevaṭṭa. 'Now what are we to do? Let's drink the wine of victory!' He had the garden decorated festively and gave orders to his servants, 'Put out strong drink, in thousands of jars, and bring on plenty of varieties of fish and meat!' The wise man's representatives kept him informed about these goings on. But they did not know that the king was planning to poison the kings; the wise man, however, had heard about it from the parrot. So he sent them a message asking them to inform him of the day for the festival of food and drink, and they did. When he heard this, the wise man thought, 'It is not right that so many kings should meet their end while the wise man survives, so I will be their refuge.' He called together the thousand warriors, who had been born at the same time as him. 'Friends,[79] they say Cūḷani Brahmadatta is having his garden decorated and wishes to partake of some strong drink with the hundred and one kings. So you go and sit on an empty seat amongst those set up, next to the king, and say, "This seat is for our king, next to Cūḷani Brahmadatta." And when people ask whose men you are, say that you are those of the King of Videha. They will make a big hulaballoo, and say, "For seven years, seven months, and seven days we have been taking control of kingdoms and not seen the Videhan king! What sort of a king is he? Go and find him a seat at right at the end." Then you will reply, "Except for Brahmadatta, there is no other king who is higher than ours!" Then kick up a commotion and say, "We cannot even get a seat for our king from you. So we'll make sure you won't be eating and drinking your booze, and fish and meat!" Then shout

79. All three manuscripts in F have *samma*, a form of greeting like 'hail' (PED 695). 'Friends' seems to carry this meaning in a colloquial way.

and leap about, and let them know about it with a loud din. Shatter the pots with large clubs, spill all the food, and make it inedible. Then charge at the army at speed, and create a loud commotion like *asuras* barging in on the city of the gods:[80] "We are the sage Mahosadha's men from the city of Mithilā! Catch us if you can!" Let them know you're there, and then come back.'

They consented to this instruction [395], paid their respects and, armed with five kinds of weapons, they went on their way.[81] When they entered the decorated garden, it appeared like Nandana's grove. White parasols were laid out, and the seats were arranged for a hundred and one kings. When they saw this great splendour, the men did everything in the way outlined by the Great Being, and after causing confusion amongst the general populace, they came back to Mithilā. The king's men informed Brahmadatta of what had taken place with regard to the kings, and he was furious. 'What a setback to my plans to poison them!' The kings were also furious. 'This has taken away our drinking of the wine of victory!' The soldiers were also furious. 'We won't be having our free drink!' So Brahmadatta said to the kings, 'Right. We'll go to Mithilā and cut of the king of Videha's head with a sword, and trample it with our feet. And then we'll sit down and drink the wine of victory! Go and tell the army to prepare themselves.' Then he went aside with Kevaṭṭa and explained things to him. 'Now look here. We are going to seize the enemy who has put up an obstacle to such a good plan. We'll go to the city, surrounded by a retinue of the hundred and one kings, and with eighteen armies. Come, teacher!' The brahmin, however, was by nature wise himself. He thought, 'They will not be able to overcome the wise man Mahosadha. We will be put to shame. I must change the king's mind.' So he said this: 'Great King, the king of Videha has no strength; his administration is in the hands of Mahosadha, the wise man, who has great personal power. Mithilā is guarded by him, as if it were a den guarded by a lion, and it will not be possible to capture it. We will all be put to shame, so don't go.' But the king was mad with military ardour and drunk with power. 'What will he do!' So he left, taking the hundred and one kings and the eighteen armies with him. Kevaṭṭa,

80. This refers to the legend that the *asuras*, born in a lower rebirth and inimical to the gods, attack the Heaven of the Thirty-Three (see DPPN).

81. See *Pañcāvudha-jātaka* (J 55) and, for story and discussion of five weapons, Shaw 2006a: 51–9.

unable to turn the king back, thought, 'It is no good trying to stand in the king's way.' So he went with him.

The soldiers reached Mithilā in one night, and told the wise man what had transpired, and the men who had been first sent as attendants continually sent him updates to his information:

Cūḷani Brahmadatta is coming to such-and-such a place.
[396] *Today he arrives in such-and-such a place.*
Today he will reach the city.

When he heard all of this the Great Being was particularly vigilant. But the Videhan king heard the wailing all around, 'They say that Brahmadatta is coming to capture the city.'

In the early evening Brahmadatta surrounded the entire city under the light of a thousand torches. He surrounded it with ramparts of elephants, ramparts of chariots, and ramparts of horses, and at regular intervals set up a powerful military force. Men stood there, shouting, snapping their fingers, roaring, dancing, and crying out loud. Under the light of the torches and the reflected shine of the armour, the entire city of Mithilā, seven leagues long, was one blaze of light, and the din of the elephants, horses, chariots, and men was as if the earth were cracking open. The four wise men heard the waves of sound and not knowing what it was, went to the king. 'Sire, there is a great uproar but we do not know what it is. We must find out, Great King!' The king listened to them and said, 'Brahmadatta must have arrived.' And he looked from a window and saw what had happened. He was terrified. 'We are finished. Tomorrow he will surely kill us all.' And they sat there in urgent discussion. But when the Great Being realized what had happened, like a lion, without fear, he set up a guard around the whole city, and thought, 'I will go and give comfort to the king.' Paying his respects, he stood to one side. The king saw him and took courage from that. He reflected, 'There is no one who can deliver us from this terrible suffering other than the wise man Mahosadha.' And he addressed him in this way:

'The Pañcālan has come with his entire army, Brahmadatta—
O Mahosadha, this Pañcālan army is without limits![82] (1)

82. The verse tag at the beginning of the story takes this verse as the first; all others preceding it, which have been numbered in italics here, must have been added later, or

Infantry soldiers with packs on their backs,
Foot soldiers, and warriors skilled in war,
Men who are destroyers, a great uproar,
And the noise of kettle drums and conches! (2)
All kinds of skill in weaponry, banners, soldiers in armour,
Highly trained and well established in all kinds of martial skills and
warcraft! (3)
Ten wise men there are, deep in wisdom and in secret stratagem;
And the eleventh, the mother of the king, encouraging the army of
Pañcāla. (4)
[397] Here are one hundred and one warriors, of great repute, all in
attendance.
Torn from their kingdoms, they are conquered men, under the
vassalship of the Pañcālas. (5)
Whatever they say, they do so on the king's behalf;
When they must speak kind words they speak them;
Unwillingly they come as vassals of Pañcāla, and act on his command. (6)
Mithilā, the royal city, is completely encircled
By this army with three sections,[83] dug in on all sides. (7)
It is surrounded as if by rising stars, on all sides.
Mahosadha, think. How can there be an escape from all of this?' (8)

[398] When he had heard this statement of the king's, the Great Being thought, 'This king is really terrified by the fear of death. But a doctor is a refuge for a sick man, [399] just as food is the refuge of the hungry man and drink is for the thirsty man. There is no other refuge for him other than me; so I will comfort him.' And then the Great Being, as a lion roars on the Manosilā region,[84] said, 'Do not take fear, Great King. Enjoy your kingship in safety. Like a crow picking up a clod of earth to throw, or a monkey the branch of a tree, I will drive these eighteen armies away without even a band for their waist in their possession!' Saying this, he spoke this verse:

'Stretch your feet out, sire, feast, and relax,
I will drive Brahmadatta and his Pañcāla army away!' (9)

The wise man cheered the king and left. He then had the kettle drums struck in the city and made an announcement:

---

the story fused with others. See introduction to this story.

83. Rouse suggests (Ja VI 203 n. 1) that *tisandhiparivāritā* means surrounded by sections between each of the encircling bands and the wall. The commentary says that it refers to the ramparts of elephants, chariots, and horses—supports for the army.

84. This is a region in the Himalayas, near Anotatta, supposedly a habitat for lions (see Ja II 65 and DPPN).

No cause for alarm. Have a seven-day festival and get flowers, perfumes and ointments, and all kinds of food and drink, and have a holiday. Let people drink here, there, and wherever they please, and let them make music, and shout and dance and whoop it up and snap their fingers, and it will all be on me! I am Mahosadha, the wise man: see my power.

In this way he cheered the citizens, and they did this. Those standing outside the city heard the noise of singing and dancing, and men entered in by the side gate. It was not the custom to arrest men on sight, so they broke through no barrier, and when they entered the city they saw people having a festival. Cūḷani Brahmadatta heard the rumpus in the city and said to his ministers, 'Now look here. You have surrounded the city with the eighteen armies, but there is no fear or worry in the citizens. They are full of joy and happiness, snapping their fingers, rejoicing, whooping it up, and singing! What is this?' Then the men who were attendants made up a story and said, 'Sire, we entered the city by the side gate and saw people involved in a festival, we asked, [400] "You are not bothered while all the kings of India have encircled your city. Why is this?" And they replied, "When our king was just a prince we had this wish: that when all the kings of India surrounded our city, we'd have a festival, and today our wish is fulfilled. Because of this he had a festival drum beaten and is drinking too himself in his great palace courtyard."' The king was furious when he heard this and had a section of the army sent. 'Quickly; spread yourselves around the city, break up the trenches, knock down the enclosure walls, demolish the gate towers, enter the city, and collect the heads of the people, just like gourds on carts. Bring me the head of the Videhan king.' The soldiers heard this and with various kinds of weapons in their hands went right up to the gate, helped by the wise men's representatives, with beams as missiles,[85] showers of mud, and stones thrown. 'We'll break down the ramparts!' they said, but when they had crossed into the trench, the men in the gate towers bombarded them with arrows, javelins, and spears. The wise men's soldiers made rude hand gestures at Brahmadatta's soldiers, and jeered them with taunts. 'You can't take us at all—so have a drink and some food!' They held out jugs of drink and fish and meat on skewers, and drank and ate as they

85. Rouse points out that so many variants suggest some corruption in the word *māḷa* (J VI 204 n. 1), but some sort of missile must be meant.

paraded around the ramparts. The others, unable to gain entry, returned to Brahmadatta. They said, 'Sire, no one, except for someone with psychic powers, could do this.'

The king remained for four or five days, but could not see a way of taking what he wanted to capture. So he asked Kevaṭṭa, 'Teacher, we cannot take the city. No one is able to get in. What is to be done?'

He said, 'Let it be, Great King. The city gets its water from outside. So we will stop the water supply and then take control. When people are exhausted with thirst, they'll open the gates.'

'This is a good plan,' he said.

And so from that time they let no water go in, and the wise man's representatives wrote a message on a leaf and fastened it onto an arrow, and so sent him the news. The wise man had given this instruction: 'If anyone sees a message on a leaf fastened to an arrow, [401] bring it to me.' Then one man did see it and showed it to the wise man. He worked out what had happened, and said, 'They do not know the mettle of me, the wise man Mahosadha.' And he split poles of sixty hands, had them stripped clean, and bound them together with leather hide and smeared with mud. Then he sent for the mud and lotus seeds brought by the practitioners of psychic powers from the Himalayan foothills, and planted the seeds in the mud by the side of a water tank, positioned the bamboo over it, and filled it with water. In one night it grew and blossomed, so that it rose a bamboo-length high, and then he picked it and sent it with his men, 'Give this to Brahmadatta.' They made a roll around the stalk, and threw it, saying, 'Here you are, Brahmadatta's lackeys! Don't die of starvation! Just pick the flower, and eat the stalk and fill your stomach.' One of the wise man's representatives picked it up and took it to the king. 'See, sire, the stalk of this flower. Such a long stalk has never been seen before!' The king said, 'Measure it.' And so the wise man's representatives did so and made it out to be eighty hands rather than sixty. The king asked, 'Where did that grow?' One of them made up a story and said, 'Sire, I was thirsty and thought I'd have a good strong drink. I went into the city by the side gate, and I saw great water tanks for people to splash and play in. There were people in a boat picking flowers. That was where this grew, by the side of the water tank. Those that grew in the deep water would be a good hundred hands long.' When the king heard this he said to Kevaṭṭa, 'Teacher, it will not be possible to stop the water supply. Take this advice.'

He replied, 'But sire, we can stop their grain. The city has only outside supplies.'

'So be it, teacher,' he replied.

When the wise man heard the plan by the same means as before, he thought, 'He does not know the mettle of me, the wise man Mahosadha.' He laid mud down along the rampart and had some rice planted. Now the wishes of a Bodhisatta are always successful. In one night the rice grew and could be seen bursting up above the rampart. [402] When Brahmadatta saw this he asked, 'Sir, what is that dark green thing you can see coming up above the rampart?' The wise man's representatives said, as if pulling the words right out of his mouth, 'Sire, they say the householder's son, Mahosadha, has anticipated future danger and had food collected from all over the kingdom and threw the surplus over the ramparts, and they say this rice was warmed by the heat and watered by the rain, and just grew right there into plants. And moreover, one day, I went into the city by the side gate on some business and picked a handful of rice from a heap on the ramparts and dropped it in the road. At this, people just laughed and said, 'Looks like you're hungry! Tie up some of it in the corner of your shirt, take it home and get it cooked and eat it.' Hearing this, the king said to Kevaṭṭa, 'Teacher, by cutting off the grain supply we won't be able to capture the city. This is no good as a plan.'

He replied, 'Then, sire, we will capture it by cutting off the supply of wood, as they get this from outside the city.'

He replied, 'Yes, teacher, so be it.'

Now when the wise man heard about this, by the same means as before, he had made a big pile of firewood that showed up, even above the rice, on the ramparts. And the people laughed at Brahmadatta's men. 'If you're hungry, then just cook your rice on this!' And they threw log upon log of wood down on the ground. The king said, 'What is this wood showing above the rampart?'

'They say that the householder's son, in anticipation of future danger, had wood collected and stored in outhouses and the surplus he had stacked against the ramparts.' When he heard this the king said to Kevaṭṭa, 'Teacher, we cannot capture the city by cutting off the supply of firewood. So you can take that plan.'

'Don't worry, Great King. There is another plan.'

He replied, 'Teacher, what is this plan? I can't see an end to your plans. We can't take Videha, so let's go back to our city.'

Kevaṭṭa replied, 'Sire, it's going to be shameful for us if it is said, "Cūḷani Brahmadatta could not capture Videha even with a hundred and one soldier kings." Mahosadha is not the only wise man, as I am one too. Let's try just one stratagem.'[86]

'And what is this stratagem?'

'We'll have a war of words (*dhammayuddha*).'[87]

[403] 'And what is a war of words?'

'Great King, the army will not fight. Two of the wise men of the kings will come to one spot, and whichever shall concede homage to the other will be defeated. Mahosadha has no inkling of this plan. I am older; he is younger. He will see me, and pay homage. And so it will be that Videha will be defeated. When we have subjected him to defeat, we will go back to our city. In this way there will be no shame. This is what a war of words will be.'

Again the wise man found out the secret by the method that he had used before. He thought about it. 'If I defeat Kevaṭṭa, I will not be a true wise man.' Now Brahmadatta said, 'This is a beautiful plan.' He had a message written on a leaf and sent by the side gate to Videha:[88]

Tomorrow there will be a war of words between the two wise men.
Victory and defeat will be under the same rules of engagement.
Whoever does not engage in the war of words will be adjudged the loser.

When Videha heard this he had the wise man summoned and explained the matter to him. The wise man responded, 'Certainly, sire. Send a message, sire, saying,

Let them prepare a court for the war of words tomorrow by the western gate, and let them go there.

He listened and had a messenger take the message on a leaf. The next day the wise man, thinking, 'May Kevaṭṭa be the loser,' prepared court for the war of words at the western gate. The hundred and one men went as a

86. The word is *lesa*, usually 'a pretext' (PED 586).

87. Translating this is difficult: it could also be termed a '*dhamma* contest'.

88. Unlike the writing of Amarādevī or Queen Udumbarā, earlier in the story, which they do themselves, the verb 'to write' for the king is in the causative: he has it written down for him. In *Vessantara-jātaka* the god Vissakamma does his own writing (Chapter 10: 574; Ja VI 520).

guard, surrounding Kevaṭṭa, thinking, 'Who knows what will happen?' They went to the place that had been prepared, and stood looking towards the east, and there stood the priest Kevaṭṭa too.

In the morning, the Bodhisatta bathed in perfumed water and dressed himself in a Kāsi cloth worth a hundred thousand coins. He adorned himself in every way, and after eating a variety of the choicest flavoured foods, he went with a magnificent retinue to the palace gate. When he heard the request, 'Let my son enter,' he went in to the king and paid homage, and then stood to one side.

'Well, dear Mahosadha?'

'I am going to the court for the war of words.'

'And what should I do?'

'Sire I wish to defeat Kevaṭṭa with a jewel. So please may I take the jewel treasure, with eight curves?'[89]

'Take it, dear one,' the king replied. And he paid his respects to the king and took it, and, surrounded by a retinue of the thousand warriors born at the same time as him, [404] he alighted upon the carriage drawn by a collection of white Sindh horses, worth ninety thousand coins, and came to the gate at the time for the meal. Meanwhile, Kevaṭṭa stood watching for his arrival and kept on saying, 'Here he comes; now here he comes.' The Great Being, with his magnificent retinue, like an overwhelming ocean, or like a lion, without fear and completely unruffled, had the gate opened. He left the city, and getting down from his carriage like a lion stirred to awakening, he prowled forward. The hundred and one kings saw his impressively auspicious appearance and acclaimed him with a thousand cries, 'So here is the wise man Mahosadha, child of Sirivaḍḍha, who has no rival in wisdom in the whole of India!' He, holding the jewel in his hand, stood in unparalleled glory face-to-face with Kevaṭṭa, like Sakka surrounded with a host of thundering gods.

Kevaṭṭa saw him in all his glory and could not go forward but said, 'Wise man Mahosadha, we are the two wise men, but although we have been staying beside you, you have never before sent so much as a gift in a message. Why do you do it now?' The Great Being replied, 'Wise man, I was looking out for a gift worthy of you, and now today I have brought the jewel

89. The jewel that has already featured in this story is described here as *aṭṭhavaṃkamaṇiratanaṃ:* the jewel treasure with eight curves. UJST just says 'eight-sided' (UJST 121).

treasure. Take it, for there is none other like it in the world.' Kevaṭṭa saw the jewel treasure, blazing with light, in his hand, and thought, 'He must be wishing to give it to me.'

'Give it to me then,' he said, stretching out his hand. The Great Being said, 'Take it.' And he tossed the jewel onto the fingertips of of Kevaṭṭa's outstretched hand. But the brahmin could not carry the weight of the jewel treasure on his fingers, and it fell down and rolled to the Great Being's feet.[90] The brahmin, through greed, wanting to possess it, bent himself right down at his feet. But the Great Being did not let him get up. He put one hand on his shoulder blade and one hand on his back by the armpit. 'Get up, teacher; get up teacher. I am so much younger than you, like a grandson. Do not pay homage to me!' Saying this, he rubbed his face and forehead in the ground, till it was bloody, and said, 'Fool! You thought that you would get a homage from me!' [405] He grabbed him by the throat, and threw him out of his way, and then, getting up, Kevaṭṭa fled.

The Great Being's men then picked up the jewel treasure, but the deep voice of the Bodhisatta's words, 'Get up, get up, do not pay homage to me!' resounded throughout the entire assembly. People made a great uproar, as one voice: 'Kevaṭṭa the brahmin has paid homage to the wise man's feet!' Indeed Brahmadatta and all the kings had seen him bent down at the Great Being's feet. 'Our wise man has paid homage to Mahosadha. We are vanquished. They will not spare us.' Each one got on his own horse and started to escape to Uttarapañcāla. Seeing them running away, the Bodhisatta's men made more of a clamour, shouting, 'Cūḷani Brahmadatta and his hundred and one men are making an escape!' Hearing this, the kings were so terrified and in fear of their lives that they hurried even more, splitting up the army. The Bodhisatta's men let out an even greater roar, shouting and crying out after them. The Great Being and his entourage returned to the city, and Brahmadatta's army fled for as much

90. The inability of the person with an unskilful mind to receive and hold an auspicious jewel is also seen in the *Bhūridatta-jātaka* when the cruel hunter brahmin cannot catch it (see Chapter 6: 370). This character is also attributed to Devadatta. Here, the failure has political implications, and the scene of Kevaṭṭa struggling on the ground, thereby acknowledging his king's defeat, is one of the most popular in Siamese mural and manuscript depictions. See for instance the early nineteenth-century painted mural at Wat Suwannaram, Thonburi (Wray, Rosenfield, and Bailey 1996: 60, plate 16), and the late eighteenth-century manuscript illustration in MS. Pali a. 27 (R), a folding book (*samut khoi*) held in the Bodleian library (Appleton, Shaw, and Unebe 2103: 33, illustration 2.18), reproduced in this volume as Fig. 5.13.

as three *yojanas*. Kevaṭṭa alighted on his horse, wiped the blood from his forehead, and, sitting on his horse's back, went after the army. 'Hey, don't be frightened. I didn't really pay homage to the householder's son. Just hold on! Stay!' But the army did not stop and called back at him, abusing him. 'Stupid, evildoing brahmin. Going on about how you'd make a war of words and then bowing before a boy young enough to be your grandson! This was not worthy of you.' They did not listen to him and went right on, but he went in all haste in pursuit of the army: 'Please believe me! I really did not pay homage to him. He just deceived me over the jewel treasure.' With all kinds of arguments he won the kings over and had them accept his defence, and he got the scattered army together again. So great was the army that if each man had picked up a handful of soil or a clod of earth and thrown it into the trench, they could have filled the trench and made a heap as high as the rampart. But the wishes of Bodhisattas are always successful. Not one person threw a handful of soil or a clod of earth at the city. They all returned to the same position at their camp. [406] The king consulted Kevaṭṭa: 'What shall we do, teacher?'

'Let no one leave by the side gate, and cut off all access. The people, unable to leave, will open the gates and we will be able to take our enemies.'

Yet again the Bodhisatta got the information by the usual method, and reflected, 'If they remain here for a long time, there will be no peace of mind for us. We must get them to go. I'll work out a plan to do this.' So he looked around for a skilled and clever minister and noticed one called Anukevaṭṭa and had him brought to him. 'Teacher, there is just one task I would like you to do.'

'What am I to do, wise man? Tell me.'

'Stand on the ramparts, and when you see our men off their guard, throw down cakes, fish, meat, and other foodstuffs to Brahmadatta's men. Say to them, "Eat this—or what about that? Don't be down in the dumps. Just hold out and stay another day. Soon the people of the city will be like hens in a cage, and they will open the gate themselves, and then you will be able to capture the city and that terrible householder's son too!" Our men will hear this and then, abusing you, will tie you up hand and foot within sight of Brahmadatta's army. Then they will make as if to beat you with bamboo canes and suchlike. They'll drag you down and tie your hair in five knots,[91] and smear you with ground up bricks and put a garland

91. See J VI 208 n. 1, and J V 125 n. 2.

of oleander[92] around you and shower you with blows until weals show on your back, and then they will let you down by a rope in the sight of Brahmadatta's men, shouting, "Clear off, traitor!" Then you will be taken to Brahmadatta, and he will ask you, "So what was your offence?" Then you should say to him, "Sire, formerly I had a great reputation. But the householder's son was jealous and called me a traitor. He took everything off me. I want to get the head off the householder's son and his reputation got by plunder! Scared, and in grief at the downheartedness of your men, I gave them food and drink. [407] Because of that and his old grudge in his heart, he has brought me to ruin. But your men know all about this, Great King." Gain his confidence with all kinds of tricks and then say this: "From the time you got me, sire, you have had no cause for alarm. Now there is no life left for Videha or the householder's son. I know the strong and weak points in the ramparts of the city. I know where there are crocodiles in the waterways and where there are not. I'm going to show you how to capture the city in no time." The king will trust you then, and give you due honour, and place the army under your control. Then bring the army down to cross the waterways where there are snakes and crocodiles and suchlike, and his army will not cross through fear of them. Then you say, "Sire, your army has been divided by the householder's son. There is not one of them—not even the teacher Kevaṭṭa—who has not been bribed. They wander around guarding you, but they are all really under the power of the householder's son. I am the only one who is your man. If you do not believe me, then ask all of the kings to present themselves to you in full dress. Then examine all the words on the clothes, adornments, and swords given to them by the householder's son, with inscriptions written on them with his own name. Draw your own conclusions." When he has done this he will indeed draw his own conclusions and, terrified, he will send the kings away. Then he will ask you about what can be done. You will reply, "Great King, the householder's son is full of deceit. If you stay a few days more the householder's son will capture your entire army and have you in his hands. Don't delay. This very day, in the middle watch of the night, we'll get on horseback, and let's make a getaway. Don't let death come to us at the hands of the enemy." He will listen to what you say and act accordingly. Then, you leave at the time of the escape and let my men know about it.'

92. Oleander is *kaṇavera/kaṇavīra* (DP I 617). *Nerium Oleander* is toxic in all its parts, presumably the reason for its use here.

When he had heard this, Anukevaṭṭa said, 'Very well. I will do just as you say.' The other said, 'And it will just have to be that you get a few blows.' Anukevaṭṭa replied, [408] 'Do what you wish with my body; but please leave my life, my hands, my feet, and my head.' Mahosadha paid his deepest respects to the people in Anukevaṭṭa's household, and in the way just described he had him treated badly, and handed him over to Brahmadatta's men. The king questioned him carefully, believed his story and entrusted the army with him. He brought them down to places where there were dangerous animals and crocodiles, and the men were terrified by the crocodiles, and those who had been pierced by the arrows shot by men on the lookout posts came to the end of their lives. And from that time they were not able to approach those places because of the danger there. Anukevaṭṭa came up to the king and said, 'Great King, none of your men will fight for you. They have all taken bribes. If you do not believe me, summon the kings and look at the signs on their clothes and garments.' The king did this and saw the signs on their clothes, and came to a conclusion: 'Surely they have accepted bribes.'

So he went to Anukevaṭṭa and asked, 'What is to be done now, teacher?' 'Sire, there is nothing else to be done. If you do more damage, the wise man will capture you. Great King, the teacher Kevaṭṭa wanders around with a wound on his forehead. But he has also accepted a bribe. When he took the jewel treasure you were routed for three *yojana*s and then he got you to have faith in him again and return. But he is a traitor. He would not please me for a single night. Even today, in the middle watch of the night, you should escape. Except for me, there is no one who wishes you well.' When he had said this the king replied, 'Then, teacher, get my horse and chariot ready yourself.' The brahmin realized that without a shadow of a doubt the king was intent on flight, and reassured him. 'Do not be frightened, Great King.' And he went outside and gave the attendants instructions: 'Today the king is going to flee. Do not go to sleep.' He bridled the reins in such a way that the more he pulled when he was fleeing, the quicker he would go. In the middle watch of the night he said, 'Sire, the horse is ready. Please understand that now is the time.' The king mounted his horse and fled. Then Anukevaṭṭa also mounted his horse, and went with him a little distance, and then went back. But the king's horse, because of the way he had been bridled, [409] went on, even though the king was pulling the reins. Anukevaṭṭa entered the middle of the army's ranks, and cried, 'Cūḷani Brahamadatta has fled!' And he made a big commotion. So the attendants and the men cried out too. When the rest of the kings heard the din, they were terrified. 'The wise man Mahosadha has opened the gate and will come out, and he will not spare our lives!' Not even glancing at all the various objects of enjoyment and equipment, they also fled. The men then called out all the more, 'The kings have fled too!' When they heard the noise all those positioned at the gate and on the lookout posts shouted out, and slapped and clapped their hands. At that moment, like the earth being broken up or the ocean stirring to its depths, a great roar went up through the entire city, inside and out, and the eighteen armies and all the men led by the conch, panic-stricken by the fear of death, without any refuge for themselves, threw down even their belts around their waist, and their cloaks, and then fled: 'They say that Brahamadatta and the hundred and one kings have been seized!' The camp was emptied. Then Cūḷani Brahmadatta, taking the hundred and one warriors, went back to his own city.

The next day the soldiers opened the gates and left the city with a great company. They saw the large quantities of plunder, informed the Great Being, and asked him what they should do. He said, 'Any wealth they have left behind belongs to us. Give everything to the king that belonged to the hundred and one kings, and bring everything belonging to Kevaṭṭa to me. Then let the citizens of the city have the rest.' It took half a month to remove all the various kinds of jewels and other precious booty, and four months all of the rest. The Great Being accorded Anukevaṭṭa great honour, and from that time, or so they say, the residents of Mithilā had large quantities of gold.

A year then went past, and Brahmadatta with the kings stayed in the city of Uttarapañcāla. Then one day Kevaṭṭa looked at this face in the mirror and saw the scar of the wound on his forehead. 'This is the work of the householder's son,' he thought. 'He put me to shame in front of all those kings.' And a terrible anger arose up in him: 'Why shouldn't I be capable of seeing the back of my enemy? Ah. Here is a plan (*upāya*). The king's daughter, Pañcālacaṇḍī, is very beautiful. [410] She is without an equal, like a heavenly nymph. I will show her to King Videha. He will be caught by lust, just as a fish is caught swallowing a hook. I will bring him and Mahosadha here, and kill them both, and drink deep of the wine of victory!' Having set his mind on this, he went to the king. 'Sire. There is a plan.'

'But teacher, your plan left me without even a cloak to cover myself with. What will you do now? Please just keep silent.'

'But, Great King, there is no plan that will ever be as good as this one.'

'Well, tell me it.'

'Sire, it must be just between us two.'

'Very well then,' the king agreed.

Then they went up to the upper storey of the palace, and then he spoke. 'Through his being overcome with the defilement of desire, Great King, I will bring the Videhan king here, with the householder's son, and we will kill them both.'

'Yes. This is a beautiful plan, teacher. How shall we bring him here and make him overcome with desire?'

'Great King, your daughter Pañcālacaṇḍī is without rival in her great beauty. We will have court poets and composers of songs capture her charm and grace, and have them sung throughout Mithilā! He will have contact through just hearing about her, and he will become infatuated with her: "If the great lord of Videha cannot have this treasure of a woman, then what is his kingdom to him!" I shall go there and settle a day with him. He will come like a fish that has swallowed the bait, and bringing the householder's son, will come here. Then we kill them.' The king heard what he had to say and was delighted. 'This is really a beautiful plan, teacher. We'll do it.' He agreed. But the guardian of the bed, a bird of flight, heard him, and kept it in her mind.

The king sent for skilled poets, and giving them a very large payment, he showed them his daughter, and said, 'Now make a poem[93] about her wonderful beauty!' And they composed songs of exceedingly beautiful sweetness, and the king listened to them and gave them a large amount of money. Musicians and poets heard these songs in the marketplace and learned them and sang them, and in this way they circulated. When they had been spread around, the king called the singers and said to them, 'Dear ones, at night-time, please climb trees and, sitting there, sing these songs to the great birds, then in the morning, [411] tie bells around their necks and let them go, and come down and then return.' He did this, they say, so that he would make everyone think, 'Even the *devas* sing about the daughter of the king of the Pañcālans!' Then the king called the poets again. 'Now dear ones, please make some more songs, capturing both the powerful strength of the king and the beauty of this girl, and saying, "The

93. *Kabba* refers to a poem, a piece of fiction, or any kind of poetical composition (DP I 637). The word for poet here is *kavi* and singer, *gāyaka*. All arts and sciences seem to be deployed for the art of spying and the calculated dissemination of intelligence in this story.

only match for such a beautiful princess is the King of Mithilā!"' They did so and informed the king. The king gave them great wealth, and gave this order. 'Dear ones, go to Mithilā and sing it just like that!' They went to Mithilā gradually, singing as they went, and sang them in the middle of the courtyard. People heard them and gave them a great reception, crying out their appreciation and paying them thousands of coins. Then at night they went into the trees and sang, and in the morning tied bells on to the birds before they came down. People heard the tinkling of bells in the sky, and all the city resounded with the news, 'The *devas* themselves are singing about the beauty of King Cūḷani's daughter!' There was a big commotion in the city, and the king hearing it had the poets summoned to him and set them up in the middle of his palace. 'They say that King Cūḷani wants to give the king his beautiful daughter,' was the buzz. He was delighted, and gave them a great deal of wealth too.

So they went back and informed Brahmadatta, and then Kevaṭṭa said, 'Now I will go, Great King, and get the day arranged.'

'Very well, teacher, what do you need to take with you?'

'Just a little present and letter,' he replied. And the king gave that to him and told him to take it. So with a large entourage he arrived at the Videhan kingdom, and when people heard of his arrival there was a commotion in the city. 'King Cūḷani, they say, and Videha are now making friends! Cūḷani is giving his daughter to the king, and Kevaṭṭa has come to arrange the day.' The Videhan king heard about this, and the Great Being heard about it too, but thought, 'His arrival does not please me. I'll find out some more about this.' And he sent a message to his men, who were spies at the court of Cūḷani. They sent a message back: 'We do not know anything about this plan. The king and Kevaṭṭa have been sitting and plotting this in his bedchamber. The bird that acts as the guardian of the bed will know what is going on.' When he heard this, the Great Being thought, 'So that there is no chance for our enemies [412] to see everything that is going on in detail, I will not let Kevaṭṭa see the city all decorated and ready.' And from the city gates to the palace, and from the palace to his own quarters, he had put up latticework, on both sides, and had it covered all over with mats, and had pictures put up, and flowers strewn all over the ground. He set jugs full of water around, and had banana leaves tied everywhere, and hung banners too. So Kevaṭṭa entered the city but could not see how everything had been arranged in it. Kevaṭṭa thought that the road had been so greatly decorated because of him, and did not realise that it had been done so that he would not catch sight of the city. He went to the king, handed him the present and the letter, and extended his greetings before sitting to one side. Then after honour had been extended, he informed the king of the reason for his visit, and recited two verses:

'A king who wishes for your friendship sends these treasures.
Allow messengers with friendly and dear words to come from there. (10)
Let them speak their tender speeches and words that bring delight,
Let Pañcāla and Videha both be as one!' (11)

When he had said this, he added, 'Great King, he would have sent another great minister in this place, but sent me, saying, "Another person just would not be able to make such a pleasing case to inform him! Go, teacher, and awaken the king to the great good of this, and bring him back with you." So, Great King, please go and you will receive this beautiful, excellent princess, and there will be great friendship between you and my king.' The king listened to what he had to say, and was very happy. 'I will receive a princess who, they say, is of the highest beauty.' And he fell in love just through contact with the reports of her. 'Teacher, they say that there was a conflict between you and Mahosadha in the war of words. Go to my son and see him, and then both wise men [413] can forgive one another and have a chat, and then come here.' When he heard this Kevaṭṭa agreed to see the wise man, and went to do so.

Now the Great Being that day drank a little ghee in the morning, thinking, 'Let there be no conversation between me and that evil man!' And he smeared the floor with wet cow dung, and the pillars with oil, and all chairs and stools were removed except the couch on which he lay. He gave this directive to his men: 'When the priest has started talking, say "Brahmin, don't have any conversation with the wise man today, as today he has drunk some bitter ghee." And when I start up a conversation with him, prevent me, saying, "Sire, you have drunk ghee that is too sharp, you are not allowed to talk."'[94] Then the Great Being covered himself up in a red blanket, and lay down on his couch, after positioning men at the seven doors leading to his room.[95] When Kevaṭṭa came to the first door, he asked where the wise man was. The man said, 'Brahmin, please do not make a noise, and if you go in be silent, as today the wise man has drunk some ghee

94. VRI gives *ajja tena tikhiṇasappi pivitanti* rather than F *ajja tena sappi pītan*, and so makes it sound as if it was too sharp, and disagreed with him because of that.

95. Rouse notes some confusion here (J VI 213 n. 1). *Sattamesu dvārakoṭṭhakesu* sounds like a room by a gate tower.

that was too sharp, and he cannot take any noise.' At the other entrances, they all said the same thing. When he came to the seventh gate, he went past the man and entered into the presence of the wise man. And the wise man gave a show of starting to speak, but the men restrained him. 'Sire, do not talk. You have drunk some ghee that was too sharp. Why are you talking with this bad brahmin?'

And then Kevaṭṭa came in, but he could not find anywhere to sit, nor a place to stand near the couch. He crossed over the wet cow dung and remained standing. And when one looked at him he rubbed his eyes; another raised an eyebrow; another scratched his elbow. When he saw their behaviour, he became annoyed. 'Wise man. I am leaving.' Another brahmin said, 'Don't make such a noise, wretched brahmin!' And another said, 'You are making too much noise. I'll break your bones.' So, terrified at their words, he left and looked back. And then another struck him on the back with a bamboo stick. Then another grabbed him by the throat and pushed him down, and another hit him in the back, until he left in terror, like a baby deer out of the mouth of a lion. Then he returned to the palace.

[414] 'Today my son will have heard the news and will be pleased. What *dhamma* discussion there will be between the two wise men! Today they will be reconciled and surely it will be a great gain for me.' So when he saw Kevaṭṭa he asked him how the conversation had gone, saying this verse:

> 'How did your meeting with Mahosadha go, Kevaṭṭa? Tell me about it.
> Was Mahosadha appeased? Was he content?' (12)

When he had heard this, Kevaṭṭa said, 'Sire, you think him a wise man, but there is no one less good than he is.' And he recited this verse:

> 'This fellow is not a true wise man, lord of men. He is not pleasant.
> Stubborn, vile of character, like a dumb or a deaf person, he said
> nothing at all.' (13)

The king was not happy with this statement but he made no criticism. He gave Kevaṭṭa and those who had come with him everything they needed and a house to stay in, and dismissed him saying, 'Now go, teacher, and have a good rest.' Then he reflected, 'My son is a wise man, and good at being hospitable, but he did not extend a welcome to him and did not want to see him. He must have seen some threat in him.' And he composed this verse himself:

> 'Certainly this secret advice[96] is hard to understand.

96. This is a loose translation of *mantapadam*. PED 523 cites for this word an

This is purified vision, in a man of great strength.
Because of this my body trembles;
Who will find personal harm, and go into the hands of an enemy?' (14)

[415] 'My son must have seen something blameworthy in the brahmin coming, and this man then will have come without a friendly intention. He must have wished to capture me by means of desire, and take me to his city, and there seize me. The wise man must have anticipated some grave danger.' As he was turning the problem over in his mind, in considerable fear, the four wise men came. The king consulted Senaka. 'Senaka, does it seem a good idea to you for me to go to the city of Uttarapañcāla and bring back King Cūḷani's daughter?'

'What are you saying, Great King? Great good fortune has come to you! Is it right to push it away with blows? If you go there and marry her, there will be no one else who is equal to you in the whole of India, except for King Cūḷani Brahmadatta. And why is this? Because you will have possession of the daughter of the senior king. The king knows that the other kings are his men and that only Videha is his equal. So it is natural that he wishes to give you his daughter, whose beauty is unrivalled. Do what he says, and we will also receive ornaments and finery.'

The king consulted the others too and they said the same. As they were talking, the brahmin Kevaṭṭa came to take his leave, and said, 'I go now, and ask your leave, sire, first.' The king paid his respects to him, and let him go on his way. The Great Being, realizing what had happened, went to bathe and adorn himself and came into the presence of the king, paying his respects and sitting to one side. The king thought, 'My son, Mahosadha the wise man, is of great knowledge, and has considerable understanding of texts.[97] He knows the past, present, and the future. He will know whether I should go or not.' But infatuated by desire, and confused, he did not stick to his first question, and instead consulted him with this verse:

'Whatever teachers who have found the highest knowledge:
Amongst the six, there is one opinion, which is the same.[98]

---

occurrence in the DN I 104, where there is discussion about mantras passed on from one generation to another (*mantapada* is glossed in the commentaries as *vedasankhāta*, suggesting a collection of the Vedas). The idea seems to be of encoded knowledge, passed on from one to the other.

97. *Mahāmantī* 'of great good counsel' and *mantapāragato* 'one who has mastered the Vedas'.

98. The commentary says that the six are the four wise men, Kevaṭṭa, and the king.

So tell me your opinion, Mahosadha,
Should I go, or not go and stay here?' (15)

[416] When he heard this the wise man thought, 'This king is sexually infatuated. Foolishly, he accepts the suggestions of these four. I will explain the problem and dissuade him from going.' And he recited four verses:

'Know this, O King. Cūḷani Brahmadatta is a
King of great strength and great power.
Yes, the king wants you, but for his purposes:
As a hunter a deer, with tame deer as his decoy. (16)
It is like a fish greedy for food, who is oblivious to the hook hidden in the bait,
A piece of meat, and like a man oblivious about his own death.[99] (17)
In just this way, O King, you, sexually infatuated with Cūḷani's daughter,
Are oblivious, like a man about his own death. (18)
If you go, you will destroy yourself in no time at all,
Just as a deer going on the road meets with terrible danger.' (19)

[417] The king was furious at such an extreme insult. 'This man thinks I am just his slave, and does not remember that I am a king. He knows that the offer, sent as a message, to give his daughter is made by the highest king, and does not even give suitable congratulations. Instead, he just calls me a foolish deer! And that I am like a fish caught by a hook or a deer captured on the road.' Enraged, he delivered a verse immediately.

'I was a complete fool, deaf and dumb,
To confide in such important matters to you.
Who are you, who grew up at the tip end of a plough,
To understand other matters, such as this?' (20)

So he berated him and spoke harshly. 'The householder's son is putting up obstacles to my good fortune. Take him away.' And he spoke this verse in dismissal:

'Take this man by the throat and get him out of my kingdom,
Who speaks making an obstruction to my obtaining a treasure.' (21)

He saw the king's furious mood, and thought, 'If anyone does what the king says and takes me by the hands or the throat it would be a humiliation for me as long as I live. So I'll just get out.' [418] So he paid homage to the king and went home. The king had just spoken under the power of

99. VRI and the F edition read *maccho va maranam attano*. This could be another fish, but some play on mortal, with *macco* or *maccu*, and so a kind of pun seems intended.

his anger, and, with respect for the Bodhisatta in his heart, did not give orders to carry out his threat. Then the Great Being thought, 'This king is powerful. He does not know what is for his own good. He is infatuated by desire to take this man's daughter, and has no sense of dangers to come. If he goes, he will come to ruin. But it is not right to carry his words in my heart. He has been a great patron for me and given me a magnificent reputation. Because of this reason, something must be done by me. But first I'll send the parrot, find out what is going on, and then go myself.' With this in mind, he sent for the parrot.

Explaining the matter the Teacher said:

Then he left the presence of Videha,
And spoke to his messenger Māṭhara, the wise and clever parrot. (22)
'Go, dear green and yellow bird, and do a job of service for me.
The king of Pañcāla has a mynah bird, the guardian of his bed.[100] (23)
Ask her for the full story, for she is clever in everything that goes on,
And she knows everything about the king and Kosiya.' (24)
Māṭhara,[101] the clever parrot, heard him and went,
A yellow and green bird paying court to a mynah bird. (25)
Then this clever Māṭhara spoke to the sweet-voiced mynah bird
In her splendid cage. (26)
'I hope you can put up with being in this splendid cage?
Is all well with you? And do you get sweetened corn?' (27)
'Yes, thank you. I am in good health, and all is well with me;
I do get sweetened corn, O wise and clever one. (28)
Where have you come from, sir, and who has sent you?
I have never seen you or heard of you before.' (29)

[419] He heard her words and thought, 'If I say that I have come from Mithilā, she will not have trust in me. On my way here I observed the town Ariṭṭhapura, in the kingdom of Sivi. I'll make up a story that I have been sent by the king of Sivi to come here and have a discussion.'

'I was the guardian of the bed in Sivi's palace.
Then that just king released those in chains from bondage.' (30)

[420] Then the mynah bird gave him some sweetened corn and honeyed water, standing ready for her in a golden dish, and asked him, 'Sir, you have come a long way. What was your reason for coming here?' He heard her words and, wishing to hear the secret, made up a story:

'Once I had a wife, a sweet-voiced mynah bird.

100. See PED 707, *sāḷiyā*.
101. F inexplicably gives Maṭṭharo once here. VRI and Bd read Mādharo throughout.

But a hawk killed her before my own eyes, in her golden cage.' (31)

And then she asked him, 'How did the hawk kill your wife?' He explained, 'Listen, dear lady. One day, our king went for some water sports and asked me to come too. I took my wife and joined in the sports with them. In the evening we returned to the palace with the king and entered the palace. So we could get dry, I left by a window with my wife and sat in a turret by a roof ridge. At that moment, as we were leaving the turret, a hawk came from the roof ridge and swept down to seize us. I, terrified of dying, flew away at speed, but she was heavy in pregnancy, and could not fly away. Even though I was looking on he killed her and carried her away. Seeing me weeping in my grief for her, the king asked me why I was crying. When he heard the reason, he said, "Do not grieve, dear one, but find another wife." "But why, sire, should I marry another, perhaps of bad habits and disposition? It is a good choice to live alone." He replied, "Dear one, I know of a certain bird, endowed with all virtues and good behaviour, who is quite equal to your wife. It is the beautiful guardian of the bed of King Cūḷani. Go and find out her mind about this, if she gives you leave. If she likes you, come and tell me. And then I or my queen will go with a great entourage and bring her for you." Saying this he sent me, and that is the reason I am here.' And he said:

'Full of love, I have come from him to you.
And if you give me leave, let's both live together!' (32)

[421] She heard his words and was delighted, but, not letting him know, she behaved unwillingly and said:

'A parrot should love a parrot, and a mynah bird a mynah bird.
What union can there be between a parrot and a mynah bird?' (33)

When he heard this, he thought, 'She is not turning me down. She is just maintaining her dignity. She will certainly want me. I'll gain her trust in various ways.' And he said:

'The one whom a lover loves, even an outcaste, is equal in all things:
In love there is no inequality.' (34)

Speaking in this way, he demonstrated the differences in the various kinds of birth and status amongst humans, and gave this verse to show this:

'The mother of the king of Sivi is called Jambāvatī,
And she was the beloved wife of Vāsudeva the Kaṇhan.'[102] (35)

102. This is the Pāli form of the name Vāsudeva Kṛṣna, famous from the Hindu Epics and believed to be an *avatāra* 'descent' of the god Viṣṇu.

Now the mother of the king of the Sivi was an outcaste, and was the dearly loved chief queen of Vāsudeva, of the Kaṇhagana clan and the eldest of ten brothers.[103] The story goes that he went out one day from Dvāravatī into the garden. He saw a very beautiful girl, standing at the entrance into the city. He fell in love with her, and had the question asked of her, 'What is your birth?' When he heard that she was an outcaste, he was very upset. He then had the question asked as to whether she was married. When he heard that she was not, he took her with him and went back home, and set her up with all kinds of jewels and made her his chief wife. She gave birth to a son named Sivi, and after his father he ruled the kingdom of Dvāravati. This was said as an illustration.

[422] Having given this example, he said, 'So even a warrior prince like him married an outcaste woman. So what is to be said about us, who are animals? The measure of the union between us is our own wish for it.' And saying this, he gave another verse as an illustration.

> 'Rathavatī, a *kiṇṇara*, also loved Vaccha, and the man loved the animal:
> In love there is no inequality.' (36)

Vaccha was an ascetic of that name.[104] And how did she come to love him? Once upon a time a certain brahmin, who had seen the danger of the sense pleasures, abandoned his great reputation and took the going forth as a seer. He made himself a leaf hut in the Himalayas and lived there. Now not far from the leaf hut a large group of *kinnaras* lived in a cave. A spider also lived there, who spun his web and cracked open the heads of these beings and drank their blood. The *kinnaras* were frail and born very timid. The spider however was large and very poisonous. They could not do anything to him, so they approached the ascetic and having greeted him, asked him the question that was the reason for their coming: 'Sire, a certain spider is threatening our lives and we can see no protection from him except for you. Please kill him and ensure our safety.' But the ascetic did not agree, saying that he had undertaken to refrain from killing. Amongst them there

103. This short paragraph is in small type in F. This *jātaka* in particular has many explanatory backstories of this type, and deciding whether they should go in the main body of the story is difficult; they seem to occupy a hinterland between story and commentary. This tale is however central to an understanding of the verses and seems intended to be at least summarized by the storyteller recounting the whole *jātaka*, as does the story that follows the next verse example.

104. This paragraph is given in small type in F, as commentary, though Rouse includes it in the main body of his translation.

was a *kiṇṇara* called Rathavatī, who did not have a husband. They adorned her and led her to the ascetic, saying, 'Let this lady be your wife, and kill our enemy for us.' When the ascetic saw her he fell in love with her and got her to stay with him. He stood at the opening to the cave and, when the spider came out for food, he killed him. He lived in harmony with the lady, and had sons and daughters with her, until he died. In this way she loved him.' The young parrot made his comparison, and continued, explaining the example of a human and a wild animal. 'Vaccha the ascetic, although a human, lived with a *kiṇṇara* and married her, despite her animal rebirth. So what of us? We are both birds, in an animal rebirth. In this way, just as a humans can live with animals, so there is no inequality in love: only the heart is the measure of it.'

She listened to his words; she said, 'Sir, the heart is not however the same at all times. I am frightened of separation from what is dear.' He, being wise to the ways of women, was skilful, and tested her with another verse:

> 'Ah so! I shall go away, dear, sweet-voiced mynah bird.
> This is a rejection. Obviously you only despise me.' (37)

[423] She listened to him and, as if her heart were breaking, and, as if desirous love was only just arising in her, burning ardently, she spoke a verse and a half.

> 'There is no luck for the one who is in a hurry, wise Māṭhara.
> Stay here, until you can see the king. You will hear the noise of the kettle drums,
> And encounter the glory of the king.' (38)

When evening came they made love, and they stayed together in union, and happiness, and delight. Then the parrot thought. 'She won't hide the secret from me now. Now is the time to question her.'

'Mynah bird!' he said.

'What is it, husband?' she replied.

'I wish to ask you about something. Shall I talk about it?'

'Talk away, husband,' she replied.

He said, 'Let's leave it; today is a day of festival. I'll find out another day.'

'But if it is suitable for a festival day, then speak out; or do not speak about it at all, husband.'

'Indeed this is something suitable for a festival day.'

'Then tell me.'

'If you wish to listen, I will tell you.' Saying this, he asked her about the secret in this verse and a half:

'Whatever is this sound so loud it is heard throughout the land!
The daughter of King Pañcāla, shining like the morning star:
He is going to give her to the Videhan, and this will be their wedding.' (39)

[424] 'Oh husband, on this festival day you have said something that is unlucky.'

'I say it is lucky, you say it is unlucky. What is this?'

'Let there not be such lucky goings on even for your enemies!'

'Tell me why, dear lady.'

'Husband, I cannot say.'

'But dear lady, from the time that you leave untold a secret that you know, then there is no more of our union.' She, urged by him, relented, and telling him to attend, said:

'O Māṭhara, let not such a wedding happen even for your enemies,
Such as the one between King Pañcāla and the Videhan.' (40)

When she had said this verse he replied, 'Dear one, why are you telling me this story?' She said, 'Just listen to this, and I will tell you the problem.' Saying this, she spoke another verse.

'The great lord of the Pañcālas is going to bring the Videhan.
Then he will kill him and he will not be his friend.' (41)

In this way she told her secret to the clever bird without leaving out anything. The clever parrot listened to her, and extolled his praises of Kevaṭṭa, 'This teacher is full of resourcefulness (*upāyakusalo*). What a wonderful plan to kill the king. But why is such a thing unlucky for us? Silence is best.' So he had reached his objective in his coming there, and spent the night with his wife. Then he said, 'Dear lady, I will go to Sivi's kingdom and inform King Sivi of my gain of a loving wife!' And he said his goodbye:

[425] 'Now, let me go, just for seven nights,
Until I have informed King Sivi of my wife,
And that I have found a mynah bird to be my companion.' (42)

When the mynah bird heard this she did not want him to go, but could not say anything against it, and spoke this verse.

'Now, I let you go, just for seven nights.
And if you do not come to me at the end of seven nights just remember:
I will have gone to the grave and will be dead when you come back.' (43)

Then he said, 'Dear lady, what are you saying? How could I live for an eighth day without seeing you?' So he spoke with his mouth. But he was thinking, 'Alive or dead, you are not in my heart. What are you to me?' So he flew off and, aiming for a short distance for the kingdom of Sivi, diverted and went to Mithilā. When the Great Being had taken him to the upper storey and asked his news, he alighted upon the wise man's shoulder and recounted all that had happened. The other paid him all due honours, in the way he had before.

Then the Teacher explained the matter:

> Then when he had gone, the wise parrot, Māṭhara,
> Related to Mahosadha the story of the mynah bird. (44)

Then the Great Being thought, 'My king, even though uncertain,[105] will go. And when he goes, he'll meet with disaster. Then, if I [426] harbour in my heart the words of the king who has given me so much glory and wealth, and do not act with friendliness towards him, there will be a cause for great reproach to me. How can he perish, with wise people like me around? So I'll go on ahead of the king and see Cūḷani. I'll organize things well, and I will have a city built for King Videha to live in. And I'll have built a secret passage a *gāvuta* long, and a big tunnel of half a *yojana*. And I will anoint King Cūḷani's daughter and make her our king's wife. And even when our city is surrounded by the hundred and one kings, with their army of eighteen armies, I will release the king, as the moon is released from the jaws of Rāhu,[106] and bring him back home. It's up to me now.' And great joy arose throughout his body as he thought of this. And through the urgency of this joy, he gave this inspired utterance:[107]

> 'In whose house someone earns and eats his food:
> That is the one for whom he should bring benefit.' (45)

And he spoke this half verse.

When he had bathed and adorned himself he went to the palace in great glory. Paying homage to the king, he stood to one side. He asked him, 'Sire, are you going to go to the city of Uttarapañcāla?'

'Yes, dear one. If I cannot take Pañcālacaṇḍī, then what's my kingdom to me? Don't give up on me; come too. By going there, there will be two

105. This is a bit odd, as *anicchāyāpi* suggests a lack of willingness. Perhaps 'against his better judgement' is the meaning here.

106. Rāhu is the god of the eclipse, who seizes the moon and the sun from time to time.

107. *Udāna,* the word translated as 'inspired utterance' is often used for the verse given by an *arahat* or Buddha on the attainment of awakening, as well as being used for the inspired teachings, expressed in poetry of the Buddha, found in the Pāli collection of that name. In the latter sense it is regarded as one of the nine limbs of the teaching. Its occurrence here adds emotional weight to his loyalty.

advantages for me. I will take possession of a woman treasure, and there will be friendship between me and the king.'

The wise man said, 'Then I will go on ahead and have some lodgings built, and you come when I send a message to you.' Saying this, he recited two verses:

> 'Yes, I'll go on ahead, lord of men, to the delightful city of the king of Pañcāla,
> And build lodging houses for the glorious Videha. (46)
> When I have had lodgings built for the glorious Videha,
> Then when I send the word, please come.' (47)

[427] The king listened to this and was pleased that he was not going to leave him. He said, 'My son, if you go on ahead, what do you want?'

'An army, your majesty.'

'Take whatever you wish, dear one.'

The other continued. 'Sire, have the four prisons opened, and break the chains binding the thieves that are in there, and send these also with me.'

'Do as you wish, dear one.'

So the Great Being had the prisons opened up, and so set free a magnificent army of valiant men, capable of doing what was needed, wherever it was needed. 'Be my attendants,' he said, and accorded them all kinds of honour. So he took with him eighteen armies: of builders, leather workers and painters of pictures, and those highly skilled in all kinds of trades, and had them bring their sharp knives, spades, trowels, and many kinds of tools. With this magnificent entourage, he left the city.

Explaining the matter the Teacher said:

> He went on ahead, Mahosadha, to the delightful city of the king of Pañcāla,
> And had built lodging houses for the glorious Videha. (48)

As he went, the Great Being had a village built at the end of each *yojana*, and left a royal minister positioned at each one, saying, 'When they return, you escort fierce Pañcāla and get elephants, horses, and chariots ready for this. These will keep his enemies at bay, and set up a guard for him so that you can quickly convey him to Mithilā.' Then he arrived at the Ganges bank, and he summoned a young man called Ānanda, and said, 'Ānanda, you take three hundred builders and go to the upper Ganges and obtain some of the best wood, and have three hundred boats built, get them to chop logs as a benefit of the city, and then have the boats filled with light wood, and then come quickly back.' And he himself crossed the Ganges in a boat, and from the place where he landed he counted out and reckoned, with this own feet. 'This is a half *yojana*. Here there will be a great tunnel. And on this spot there will be a city for the king to live in. And from this place to the palace is a *gāvuta* [428] and there will be a small passageway.' When he had made his division of the area, he entered the city.

King Cūḷani heard that the Bodhisatta was coming. 'Now my heart's desire will be fulfilled. I'll see the back of my enemy. If he is arriving, then it won't be long before Videha arrives too. And then I'll have them both killed, and I'll make the whole of India one kingdom.' He was delighted, and the whole city was in uproar. 'They say Mahosadha is here, who put to flight a hundred and one kings like a crow a clod of earth!' The Great Being went to the palace entrance while the people of the city marvelled at his handsome appearance. He alighted from his carriage, and sent greetings to the king. 'Let him come,' said the king. The king, after extending his welcomes, asked, 'When is the king coming, my friend?'

'When he is sent for by me, sire.'

'But what is your reason for coming?'

'I am here to have a lodging built for the king.'

'Very well, my friend.' Then he had provisions given for the army and had the Great Being given all due honour, and organised a house for him to stay in, then said, 'Friend, stay here until the king arrives, and do not be idle, but arrange everything that needs to be done.'

Now they say that when he had arrived at the palace, he had stood at the foot of the stairs and reflected, 'The door to the great tunnel will be here.' Then he had thought, 'The king has told me to arrange everything that needs to be done. I must take care that the staircase does not fall down while digging the tunnel.' Thinking about this, he said to the king, 'Sire, when I came here and stood at the foot of the stairs, I looked over some new work and saw a fault in it. If it pleases you, I will take some wood and make it look really good.'

'Certainly, please arrange this.'

He then looked it over carefully, and thought, 'Hmm . . . the door of the tunnel should not quite be here.'[108] So he moved the staircase, and where the door to the tunnel would be had a platform of planks put in so that the

108. Rouse omits *mā* in this sentence, included in the F edition, with VRI and Bd. I have tried to include it on the grounds it implies that he has modified his plans (see PED 527 for the occasional equivalence of *mā* with *na*).

earth would not cave in, and then fixed the staircase in this way so that it would be stable. The king did not know about his business, and thought, 'He is doing this out of affection to me.' The wise man spent the day [429] overseeing the new work, and the next day he said to the king, 'Sire, if I could find out where the king will be staying, I could take care of it and make it pleasing.' The king replied, 'Certainly, choose any place in the entire city for his lodgings, except for my palace, and take that.'

'Great King, we are newcomers and you have many favourites. The soldiers will be in a commotion with us if we take their houses. So what should we do?'

'Wise man, don't pay any attention to what they say. Just pick wherever you like.'

'But sire, they will keep on coming to you with complaints, and there will be no peace of mind for you. So if you are happy with this, let our men act as doorkeepers until such time as we take possession of the houses, and then people, unable to go through the door, will go away. With this scenario, there will be peace of mind for us and for you.'

'Very well,' the king agreed.

The Great Being positioned his own men at the foot of the stairs, at the top of the stairs, and at the great gate, and everywhere around, and gave instructions for no one to pass. Then he ordered the men to go to the queen mother's house, and ordered his men to look as if they were demolishing it. When they started to demolish bricks and mud from the gates and the walls, the queen mother heard the news and came out, saying, 'What are you doing destroying my house, sir?' They replied, 'The wise man Mahosadha has got us to demolish this as he wants to build a dwelling for his king.'

'But you can stay here if that is the case.'

'Our king has a very big entourage. This will not suffice, so we are building a large house.'

'You do not know me. I am the king's mother. I will go to my son and find our about this.'

'We are doing this demolition on the orders of the king. You can't stay here!'

She was furious, 'Now I'll find out what's to be done about you lot!' And she went to the palace gate. But there they would not let her go past. 'But I am the queen mother!'

'We know you, but the king has given the command for no one to pass. Now you can get going.' She, not seeing how to get in, stood looking at her house, and one of the men said to her, [430] 'What are you doing here? Get going.' And he grabbed her by the throat and threw her onto the ground. She thought, 'Well, surely this must be at the king's command, as they should not be able to do this. I will go to the wise man.'

She went to him and said, 'Dear Mahosadha, why are you having my house demolished?' He would not speak with her. Then a man standing there said, 'What are you saying, your majesty?' She replied, 'My good man, why is Mahosadha demolishing my house?'

'To build a house for King Videha.'

'Why, my good man? Does he think that in a city as great as this there is nowhere else to take as a dwelling? Take this bribe of a hundred thousand coins, and let him have it built somewhere else!'

'Certainly, your majesty. We will leave your house as it is, but please don't mention to anyone else that we have taken the bribe in case others wish to give us bribes to spare their houses too.'

'My good man, it would be a shameful embarrassment to me if it were said that the queen mother has been offering bribes! So I won't mention it to anyone.'

'Very well,' the man replied, and taking the hundred thousand coins from her, he left her house and went to Kevaṭṭa's house. Now he had gone to the gates of the palace, and had the skin of his back flayed with bamboo sticks. He could not gain access, and he too gave a hundred thousand coins. Through this stratagem, by taking possession of houses throughout the city, and receiving bribes, they got nine *koṭis* of money. The Great Being, after wandering around the whole city, came to the palace.

The king asked him, 'Wise man, have you managed to get a house?' He replied, 'Great King, people offer them, but when we have taken the house they are upset, and it is not right for us to cause a separation from what is dear to them. So we'll build a palace for our king outside the city, about a *gāvuta* away, between the Ganges and the city, at such-and-such a place. The king listened to him and thought, 'To fight with them within the city confines is a trouble, as it won't be possible to tell the difference between the friendly army and the enemy one. But a battle outside the city is easy. Therefore, outside the city [431] I will attack and kill them.' So he was very pleased, and said, 'Good, dear man. Build in the place that you have seen.'

The wise man replied, 'Great King, I will build there, but your men must not come to the place where the new build is going on, for firewood, leaves, or anything else. If they go, there will be a conflict, and with will not bring peace of mind to our men or yours.'

'Very good, wise man. Set a barrier on people going in.'

'Sire, our elephants delight in water and play in water there. If the water becomes muddy, the citizens will become angry and complain, "Since Mahosadha's arrival we have had no clean drinking water." This promise must be honoured.'[109] The king said, 'Let your elephants play.' And he had a drum beaten around the city: 'Whoever goes to the building site where Mahosadha's work is going on will pay a fine of a thousand coins.'

The Great Being paid his respects to the king, and, taking his own assembly, he left the city and started to build at the place that had been set aside for it. On one side of the Ganges he built a village called Gaggali, and he positioned there his elephants, horses and chariots, and his oxen and livestock. He put his mind to the construction of the city, 'Let these people do this; let these people do that.' When he had assigned all the various jobs, he set about work in making a great tunnel.

This great tunnel had an entrance on the banks of the Ganges. Sixty groups of a hundred soldiers dug the great tunnel. They removed the earth in leather sacks and deposited it in the Ganges. When each load was dropped on the ground the elephants trampled it, and the Ganges flowed with mud. The citizens complained, 'Since Mahosadha has come we have been unable to get clear drinking water. The Ganges now flows with mud. What are we to do?' The wise man's spies said, 'They say that his elephants are playing in the water and are making it muddy with their trampling, and now the river flows with mud.' Now the wishes of a Bodhisatta always meet with success. Because of this, in the tunnel, all the roots and stones sank down to the ground. The entrance to the smaller tunnel was in the city, and seven groups of a hundred men dug out the lesser tunnel. [432] They brought the earth out in leather sacks and dropped it in the city, and when they had dropped each load, they mixed it with water, and built a rampart, and used it for other jobs. The entrance to the great tunnel was in the city. It was fitted out with a door, eighteen hands high, and fitted out with mechanisms of various kinds. When one catch was pressed they all

109. See PED 701 for use of the term *sahitabbo* at Ja VI 525 v. 296, meaning 'keeping his vow' (Cone) or, in this translation, 'true to his word'.

shut down.[110] The great tunnel was worked on both sides with bricks and a whitewashed coating of cement.[111] It was roofed with planks, plastered, whitewashed, and covered with an awning of cloth.[112] There were eighty major doors and sixty-four minor doors, and all had contraptions whereby when one catch was pressed they closed completely; when one was pressed they opened. On both sides of the tunnel there were a hundred various niches for lamps. These also were fitted with mechanisms whereby if one was opened they all were, and if one was closed they all were too. On both sides there were bedrooms for one hundred and one soldiers, and for each bed there was laid a bedspread of many colours, and each magnificent bed was beautifully shaded by a white parasol, and there was a lion throne for each bed, and each had a statue of a very beautiful woman that you would not know was not a human being unless you touched it. In addition, on both sides of the tunnel highly skilled painters of pictures had made all kinds of murals: the splendour of Sakka, the regions of Mount Meru, the seas and the great ocean, the four continents, the Himalayas, Lake Anotatta, Manosilā, the sun, the moon, the Four Great Kings, with the six sense heavens, and all their regions. All of these were shown in the tunnel. The floor was strewn with sand as white as a silver plate, and on the roof there was an awning of lotus flowers. And on both sides were shop stalls of all kinds, and here and there hung wreaths of perfumes and wreaths of flowers. They decorated the tunnel so that it looked like the hall of the gods, Sudhammā.

Then the three hundred carpenters, who had built three hundred boats, loaded them with cargoes of artefacts that they had made, and brought them down the Ganges, and informed the wise man.[113] He found good use for them in the city, and got them to dock the boats in a secret moorings, saying, 'Bring them here on the day I give the order.' And in the city, the water channel, the eighteen-hand rampart, [433] the lookout tower,[114] the

110. Rouse (J VI 223 n. 1) notes the anomaly of one subject and a plural verb here, suggesting elements left out by a scribe.

111. See PED 719.

112. For *ulloka* see von Hinüber 1967, and DP I 512. But it is tricky here: the word is *ullokamattikā*, which suggests both plastering and a cloth.

113. On the peculiarly Buddhist literary interest in the nautical in *jātakas*, which contrasts with other contemporaneous Indic traditions, even including the Jains, see Shaw 2012b.

114. The meaning of *gopuraṭṭālako* is uncertain, but it seems to be a compound of watchtower, or lookout post, and some form of *gopeti* 'to guard'.

king's palace and all his apartments, and the houses, the elephant stables, and the lakes, were all completed. So the great tunnel, the smaller tunnel, and all the city were finished in four months. Then, after the four months had passed, the Great Being sent a messenger for the king to come.

Explaining the matter, the Teacher said:

> When he had built the dwelling places for Videha the glorious,
> Then he sent a messenger to him: 'Come now, Great King. Your palace is built.' (49)

The king listened to the messenger and was delighted in his heart. He set out with a magnificent entourage.

Explaining the matter the Teacher spoke this verse:

> Then the king set out with his four-flanked army
> To see the prosperous city of Kampilliyā, with its innumerable carriages. (50)

Eventually he reached the banks of the Ganges, and then the Great Being went to meet him, and then led him into the city he had built. He entered the palace and enjoyed a meal of fine and varied foods, and rested a little while. In the evening he sent a messenger to King Cūḷani to inform him of his arrival.

Giving further explanation, the Teacher said:

> When he had arrived he sent a message to Brahmadatta:
> 'I have come, Great King, and pay homage at your feet. (51)
> Now give me my wife, whose every limb is loveliness,
> Endowed with the finest beauty and surrounded by her retinue of ladies.' (52)

[434] Cūḷani heard the message from the messenger and was very pleased indeed. 'Now where will my enemy go? I'll chop the heads off both of their necks, and drink the wine of victory!' But he showed only innocent[115] joy to the messenger, and paying him his respects, he delivered the following verse:

> 'Welcome, Videha. It is a happy arrival!
> Just ask for the auspicious moment, and I will give you my daughter,
> Endowed with the finest beauty and surrounded by her retinue of ladies.' (53)

When the messenger heard this he went into the presence of Videha and announced, 'Sire, the king says, "Find the moment that is auspicious for

115. The word is *kevalaṃ*, which means 'pure, entire'.

this lucky event, and I will give you my daughter."' Videha replied, 'Today is the very lucky moment!' and sent the messenger back.

Explaining the matter the Teacher said,

> Then King Videha announced the lucky moment,
> And sent the messenger to announce this auspicious time. (54)
> 'Now give me my wife, whose every limb is loveliness,
> Endowed with the finest beauty and surrounded by her retinue of ladies.'[116] (55)

King Cūḷani said:

> 'Now I give you your wife, whose every limb is loveliness,
> Endowed with the finest beauty and surrounded by her retinue of ladies.' (56)

When he had spoken this verse, he told a lie: 'Now I will send her; now I will send her.' And he gave a sign to the hundred and one kings. 'Let all the soldiers mobilize for battle with the eighteen armies, and come out. I will chop off the heads of both of them and drink the wine of victory!' And he came out himself, and installed four people—the queen mother, Queen Talatā; his chief queen, Queen Nandā; his son Pañcālacaṇḍa; and his daughter Pañcālacaṇḍī—in the women's apartments of his own palace.

The Bodhisatta accorded the army that had arrived with King Videha great honour. [435] Some of the men drank strong drink and some ate fish and meat and suchlike, and some, as they had travelled a long way, just lay down exhausted. But the Videhan king, with Senaka and the other wise men, sat on a great platform, surrounded by ministers. King Cūḷani, with his eighteen armies and the army led by the conch shell, encircled the city in four lines with three spaces and lit many hundreds and thousands of torches, and stood on the ready waiting for the first rising of dawn. The Great Being sent three hundred of his army. 'You go into the smaller tunnel and bring through it the king's mother, and his chief queen, and his son and his daughter. Then take them to the great tunnel, but do not let them go out by the entrance. Guard them in the great tunnel until we arrive, and then lead them out and place them in the Great Enclosure.' They heard his command and went through the lesser tunnel, pushed up the platform at the foot of the stairs, and seized by the hands and feet the guards, humpbacks, and the rest at the foot of the stairs, at the top, and

116. This verse repeats v. 52. King Cūḷani echoes the verse in his own response, guilefully suggesting his affinity with his guest.

in the great courtyard, gagged their mouths, and concealed them here and there in secret places. Then they ate some food prepared for the king, destroyed all that was left, and went up into the palace.

Now there, Queen Talatā, wondering what was going to happen, had got Queen Nandā, the prince, and the princess to sleep with her in one bed. The soldiers called out, standing at the door of the bedroom. She came out and said, 'What is it, dear friends?'

'Your majesty, our king has killed the Videhan and Mahosadha, and with their deaths has made the entire continent of India one kingdom. And now he drinks the wine of victory, surrounded by the hundred and one kings, in great glory and splendour. He has sent us to bring you four there.' They came down from the palace and reached the bottom of the stairs, and when the men led them into the tunnel they exclaimed, 'We have lived here for all this time and have never seen this street before!'

They said, 'People do not often come to this street, for it is an auspicious one, and today, because it is an occasion for festivities, [436] the king has commanded us to escort you by this way.'

They believed him, and some of the men escorted these four; others returned to the palace, broke into the treasure house, and seized as many of the choicest of precious things as they wished. The four went ahead through the great tunnel, and seeing it decorated like the hall of the gods, made a sign, 'This is really fit for a king!' Then they were escorted to a place not far from the great Ganges, and were asked to be seated in a fully adorned room within the tunnel. Some of the men stayed to keep guard, while some others went to inform the Bodhisatta that they had arrived. He heard their news and thought, 'Today my heart's desire is to be fulfilled.'

Very happy indeed, he went into the presence of the king and stood to one side. The king was agitated with his lust. 'Now he will send his daughter to me; now he will send her to me.' Getting up from his palanquin he looked out of a lattice window. The city was one blaze of light from the hundreds and thousands of torches and he could see it surrounded by a vast army. In great doubt and fear he asked, 'What is this?' And he recited this verse to his wise men:

> 'Elephants, horses, chariots, foot soldiers:
> An army dressed for battle stand on the ready.
> Torches are aflame with light—what do you make of it, wise men?' (57)

When he heard this Senaka said, 'Don't be concerned. Large numbers of torches have come into view! The king is coming to give you his daughter, I think.'

Pukkusa said, 'He'll be coming to pay you great honour at your arrival, and has brought a large guard with him.' Whatever they happened to like, that is what they told him.

But the king heard the sounds of commands being given: 'Let the army position itself here, put up a guard there, and be careful!' And when he saw the army he was stricken with the fear of death. Longing to hear what the Great Being had to say, he delivered this verse:

> 'Elephants, horses, chariots, foot soldiers:
> An army dressed for battle stand on the ready.
> Torches are aflame with light—what will they do, wise man?' (58)

[437] When he heard this the Great Being thought, 'I will give some reassurance to this blind foolish man—when I have frightened him and shown him my power.' And he said:

> 'Great King, the great force of Cūḷani is putting you under guard.
> Brahmadatta is treacherous, and in the morning he will kill you.' (59)

When they heard this they were all terrified with the fear of death. The king's throat dried up, and the spit in his mouth stopped its flow, there was a burning in his body, and he wailed, terrified of death, speaking these two verses:

> 'My heart is pounding; my mouth has gone dry.
> I am burnt in the fire but I do not come to peace—only more heat. (60)
> Just as the fire of a smith burns inside and not out,
> So my heart burns inside, if not outside.' (61)

The Great Being heard his wailing and thought, 'This blind, foolish man would not do what I suggested at other times, so I'll torment him a bit more.' And he said:

> 'Warrior, you are careless, ignoring good counsel, wilful;
> At least now let your wise men give you advice. (62)
> For a king, not following the advice of one's wise adviser
> Seeking only for his benefit, is like being a deer caught in a trap. (63)
> Just as a fish, greedy for the bait, does not see the hook in the piece of
> meat that encloses it,
> So is the mortal who does not see his own death.[117] (64)
> In this way, sire, greedy with lust, you do not see Cūḷani's daughter

117. Fish caught on hooks, like hunted deer, feature throughout this story (e.g. Ja VI 417). The play on fish and mortal is used before, in v. 21 for instance.

As the mortal does not see his own death. (65)
And if you go to Pañcāla, you will quickly lose your life,
Like a deer going into danger on a road that shows ahead. (66)
Lord of men, a man that is ignoble will bite you when you go to his lap.
The wise man does not make a friendship with such a man;
Unhappy is association with such a man as that. (67)
[438] Whatever man, lord of men, one recognizes as virtuous, who has heard much,
Then happy is the association with such a man as that.' (68)

Then, telling him not to make a friendship with such a person, he rebuked him the more, and bringing up the words that the king had said before, continued:

'A fool you are, sire, and deaf and dumb, that did berate my good advice.
How could I know what was good, growing up at the tip of a plough,
As another man could?[118] (69)
"Take this rascal by the throat and get him out of my kingdom,
Who speaks making an obstruction to my obtaining my treasure!"' (70)

When he had said these two verses, he asked, 'Great King, how could I, "a householder's son", know as well as Senaka and the others what is of benefit? This is not my domain! I know only the householder's business, and what is of real benefit is known only by Senaka and the likes of him. So today let these noble sirs [439] be refuges while the city is encircled by the eighteen armies, and tell them to grab me by the throat and get rid of me! Why do you ask me now?' And he scolded him roundly. The king listened and thought, 'The wise man speaks of the faults that I have committed. In the past he recognized the danger that was to come. Now he rebukes me severely. But he will not have spent his time doing nothing. He will have done something to secure my safekeeping.' And he gave these two verses in reproach:

'Mahosadha, wise men do not hit out for things done in the past.
Why do you strike at me, as at a horse tied by the foot? (71)
If you see release or safety, but although you see it you do not tell me,
Then you are just hitting out for the past!' (72)

Then the Great Being thought, 'This king really is blindly foolish. He does not know the excellence of men. I am going to wear at him just a bit more, and then I will act as his refuge.' And he said:

'The time has gone for a man to act: it is now too hard—

118. This refers back to the king's insults earlier, in his own court.

There is too much to overcome.
I cannot free you, warrior, and you must realise this. (73)
There are elephants possessed of great power and glory, who fly in the sky:
For the king who has such as these, then they can escape, taking him too. (74)
There are horses possessed of great power and glory, who fly in the sky:
For the king who has such as these, then they can escape, taking him too. (75)
There are birds possessed of great power and glory, who fly in the sky:
For the king who has such as these, then they can escape, taking him too. (76)
There are *yakkha*s possessed of great power and glory, who fly in the sky:
For the king who has such as these, then they can escape, taking him too. (77)
The time has gone for a man to act: it is now too hard—
There is too much to overcome.
I cannot free you, warrior, by flying through the sky.' (78)

[440] The king heard this and sat down, cowed. Then Senaka thought, 'Now there is no other refuge for the king and for us except for the wise man. The king heard what he said and is now terrified, and cannot say anything to him. So I will ask the wise man.' And he recited these two verses:

'A man who cannot see the shore when in the great ocean,
Wherever he finds a landing place, there he takes great happiness. (79)
In this way, Mahosadha, you be a firm place for the king and for us.
You are the greatest of advisers: from our suffering set us free.' (80)

And then Mahosadha rebuked him with this verse:

'The time has gone for a man to act: it is now too hard—
There is too much to overcome.
I cannot free you, Senaka, and you must realise this.'[119] (81)

The king, unable to clutch at anything, was stricken with the fear of death and could not say anything to the Great Being. 'Perhaps Senaka will work out a stratagem: I'll ask him.' And he spoke this verse of request:

'Please listen to my words: you see this great fear,
So now I ask you, Senaka, what do you think is to be done?' (82)

119. Mahosadha's exact verbal echo of his earlier rebuke to the king shows his paramount position over king and wise men.

[441] When he heard this Senaka thought, 'The king is asking for a stratagem, so I'll tell him one, whether it be good or bad.' And he spoke this verse:

'Set fire to the entrance; let us take a knife.
And killing one another we will at least meet death quickly.
We should not let King Brahmadatta[120] kill us with a protracted death.' (83)

When he heard this the king was not happy at all, and thought, 'Well, make a funeral pyre for yourself and your children then.' And he asked Pukkusa and the others, and they just made foolish statements that were completely unfitting. This is what was said:

'Please listen to my words: you see this great danger,
So now I ask you, Pukkusa, what do you think is to be done?'[121] (84)
'We could take poison and then would at least die quickly.
We should not let King Brahmadatta kill us with a protracted death.' (85)
'Please listen to my words: you see this great danger,
So now I ask you, Kāvinda, what do you think is to be done?' (86)
'We could fasten a noose with a rope, and then would at least die quickly.
We should not let King Brahmadatta kill us with a protracted death.' (87)
'Please listen to my words: you see this great danger,
So now I ask you, Devinda, what do you think is to be done?' (88)
'Start a fire at the entrance; let us take a knife.
We should not let King Brahmadatta kill us with a protracted death.'
I cannot get you out of this, but Mahosadha can, with ease.' (89)

Then Devinda thought, 'What is the king doing? He is blowing at a firefly when there is a fire![122] Except for Mahosadha, there is no one else here capable of bringing about our safety. This man asks us, [442] but does not ask him. And what do we know?'[123] As he could not see any other plan, he suggested the one Senaka had made, and praised the Great Being in two verses:

120. The verse uses the name Brahmadatta for King Culāṇi here, probably to fit in with the metre.

121. The verbal repetitions of the king and his wise men emphasise their shared helplessness.

122. This is the image that was used by the goddess to compare Mahosadha's great worth to the others in the riddles of the goddess section; it also recollects the dream the king had at the outset of the story.

123. With their own mouths they now align themselves with the contemptuous statements made by the Bodhisatta in the debate about the wise man and the rich man near the beginning of the story: 'What does he know?' is the usual introduction to the defences of both Mahosadha and Senaka at that time.

'There is a refuge, Great King.
Let us all ask the wise man,
And if despite being asked Mahosadha cannot deliver us easily,
Then we can follow the plan suggested by Senaka.' (90)

When he heard this the king remembered the Bodhisatta's severe rebukes, and could not talk with him, but lamenting, so that he could hear, he said:

'Just as one searching cannot find sap in the plantain,
So we are asking our question and are not getting an answer. (91)
Just as one searching cannot find sap in the silk-cotton tree,
So we are asking our question and are not getting an answer. (92)
Like an elephant dwelling in a place without water,
We are amongst unkind men who are ignorant fools. (93)
My heart is pounding; my mouth has gone dry.
I am burnt in the fire but I do not come to peace—only more heat. (94)
Just as the fire of a smith burns inside and not out,
So my heart burns inside, if not outside.'[124] (95)

When he had listened to this the wise man thought, 'This king has now been tormented too much. If I do not give him some cheer he will die from a broken heart.' So he gave reassurance to him.

[443] Explaining the matter the Teacher said:

Then the wise man Mahosadha, seeing the situation,
Saw the Videhan suffering, and spoke these words: (96)
'Do not have fear, Great King; do not have fear, O lord of men.
I will deliver you, as the moon set free when in the grasp of Rāhu. (97)
Do not have fear, Great King; do not have fear, O lord of men.
I will deliver you, as the sun set free when in the grasp of Rāhu. (98)
Do not have fear, Great King; do not have fear, O lord of men.
I will deliver you, like an elephant set free when stuck in the mud. (99)
Do not have fear, Great King; do not have fear, O lord of men.
I will deliver you, like a snake set free after being kept in a basket. (100)
Do not have fear, Great King; do not have fear, O lord of men.
I will deliver you, like fishes set free when stuck in a net. (101)
Do not have fear, Great King; do not have fear, O lord of men.
I will deliver you, with your chariots and your strong army. (102)
Do not have fear, Great King; do not have fear, O lord of men.
I will drive away Pañcāla, like a crow with clods of earth. (103)
What kind of wisdom is it that a minister such as I cannot release you from
Terrible suffering when you are beset with difficulties?' (104)

124. The king repeats the verses he gave in vv. 60–1.

The king heard his words, and was deeply relieved. 'Now my life is saved.' Everyone was happy at the Bodhisatta and his lion's roar. And then Senaka asked, 'Wise man, with what sort of plan are you going to escape and save us all?'

'Through the decorated tunnel; be on the ready.' Saying this, he gave orders to the soldiers to open up the entrance to the tunnel, and spoke this verse:

> [444] 'Come—arise, young men. Clear the bolts at the entrance:
> Videha will go through the tunnel with his ministers!' (105)

So they got up and opened the entrance to the tunnel, and the entire tunnel shone, in one blaze of light, like the hall of the gods.

Explaining the matter the Teacher said:

> 'When they heard the words of advice from the wise man,
> They released the catches and the bolts and opened the entrance to the tunnel.' (106)

They informed the Great Being that they had opened the door to the tunnel, and he gave the sign to the king. 'It is time, sire; go into the palace.' The king went across and Senaka removed his straw hat from his head[125] and took off his outer garment. Then the Great Being saw him and asked, 'What are you doing?'

'Wise man, those going through tunnels need to take off their outer clothing and tie it up into a belt to pass through.'

He replied, 'Senaka, you do not have to think, "I am going into a tunnel, so I'll go in and crawl on all fours." If you wish to go on an elephant, then mount one. The tunnel has high ceilings, of eighteen hands, and a wide entranceway. You can go in front of the king, and deck yourself up as much as you like.' After reflection, the Bodhisatta arranged it so that Senaka went first, then the king in the middle, and himself behind. And why was this?[126] [Because Senaka would say] 'Do not dawdle, looking at the way the tunnel has been decorated.'[127] But in the tunnel there were quantities of rice gruel,

125. See DP II 530 and this story (Ja VI 370), for the time when the wise men adopted this headgear: Senaka has presumably been wearing this hat since his head was shaved by Amarādevī!

126. Rhetorical questions of this kind are a noteworthy feature of this story.

127. The Sinhalese version attributes this command not to go slowly (*saṇikaṃ*) to Senaka, who would be in great haste and would not encourage the king to look at the decorations. Rouse oddly changes the meaning, so that it is 'do not go quickly', a reading the Pāli does not support, and attributes this command to the men. Although it is not clearly supported either, the Sinhalese interpretation has been followed.

snacks, and various foods of different kinds for people, and the men did drink and look around as they went through the tunnel. The Great Being said, 'Now go, your majesty,' and urged him on from behind, while the king also looked around the tunnel, decorated as it was like the hall of the gods.

[445] Explaining the matter the Teacher said:

Senaka went on in front, Mahosadha behind;
And in the middle was the Videhan, surrounded by his retinue of
ministers. (107)

The men who were on guard, seeing that the king had come, brought the queen mother, the queen, the son, and the daughter from the other royal family and settled them in the great courtyard while the king came out of the tunnel with the Bodhisatta. When they saw the king and the Bodhisatta, they cried out in terror for their lives, 'Without a doubt we are in the hands of our enemies! It must be that the wise man's men have come to seize us!'

Now they say that King Cūḷani, fearing an escape by King Videha, had come to a spot about a *gāvuta* away from the Ganges. When night had settled deeply, he heard their cries, and wished to say, 'That is Queen Nandī's voice!' But he did not say anything, through fear of people's derision and of them asking where he could see her. Meanwhile, the Great Being placed the Pañcāla princess on a heap of jewels, and consecrated her with the ceremonial sprinkling with water at that very spot. 'Great King, you have come her for her hand: now let her be your chief queen.' They brought on the three hundred boats, and the king came out from the great courtyard and embarked on a richly adorned boat, and the four noble members of the royal family also embarked.

Explaining the matter the Teacher said:

Videha left the tunnel and embarked on a boat,
And when he had seen him aboard, Mahosadha gave him this advice: (108)
'Sire, this is now your father-in-law, and this your mother-in-law, lord
of men.[128]
Just as you would treat your mother, so you should this mother-in-law,
lord of men. (109)
Just as you would your own brother, born from the same womb and
having the same mother,
In this way Pañcālacaṇḍa is to be honoured too, lord of chariots.[129] (110)

128. The commentary says that the son is now the father-in-law; another reading might be that the mother-in-law fulfills both roles, as the mother is being discussed in this verse.

129. The commentary says that this is because he is now like an elder brother to

Here is the Pañcālan, Caṇḍī, a royal daughter, who has been desired by many,
Take your pleasure with her, as yours, and as your wife, O lord of men.' (111)

[446] The king spoke his agreement, 'Very good.' But the Great Being said nothing to the queen mother; and why was this? Because she was very old, and the Bodhisatta said all this while standing on the bank. And then the king wished to sail, freed from his great sufferings. 'Dear one, you are saying this but you are standing on the bank.' And he delivered this verse:

'We have boarded the boat, but why you do you stand on the bank?
We are released from our suffering, so let's go now, Mahosadha!' (112)

The Great Being replied, 'Sire, it is not right for me to go with you.' And he spoke in this way:

'Great King, it is not right that I, the leader of an army,
Should leave my army and come to freedom myself. (113)
Sire, the army that I left in dwellings here, I will lead away,
When Brahmadatta has granted his permission, lord of chariots. (114)

Some of the men are worn out after such a hard journey and are sleeping, some are eating, and some are drinking. They do not know about our leaving. Some are ill, as they have worked hard for four months, and I have many attendants. It is not possible for me to leave even one of them, but I will return and lead the army that I left when consent has been given by Brahmadatta. You, Great King, go now quickly, not lingering anywhere. I have posted elephants and vehicles and suchlike on your route back, so you can leave behind any that are tired and just get on your way as quickly as possible to return to Mithilā.' Then the king spoke this verse:

'But a small army against a big army! How will you get on?
We are weak against such great force, wise man!' (115)

[447] So then the Bodhisatta spoke this verse:

'A small army that is wise against a big army that is not is victorious:
The king will win against many, as the dawn conquers darkness.' (116)

When he had said this the Great Being paid his respects to the king. 'Now, please go,' he said, and sent them on their way.

---

the son. It also glosses the verse with the comment that the verse says they are both from the same father, with the word *niyako*, meaning 'one's own'. Although this is of course usually the case, except for half-brothers, the words *saudariyo* 'from the same womb' and *ekamātuko* 'from the same mother or origin' suggest that only the mother is specifically referenced here.

He exclaimed, 'I am freed from the hands of my enemy, and I have obtained my heart's desire.' With joy and gladness arising inside him, he extolled the virtues of the Bodhisatta to Senaka, and said this verse:

'Oh such happiness it is, Senaka, to live with wise men!
As a bird is freed from a cage or a fish from a net, so Mahosadha has delivered us, when we fell into the hands of our enemies!' (117)

When he heard this Senaka spoke this verse on the virtues of the wise man:

'Being with the wise is indeed happy,[130]
As a bird is freed from a cage or a fish from a net, so Mahosadha has delivered us when we fell into the hands of our enemies!' (118)

Then King Videha went up the river for about a *yojana* and reached the village built by the Great Being, and there the men positioned by the Bodhisatta gave him elephants, vehicles, and more food, drink, and provisions. He returned carriages, elephants, and horses when they were tired out, and took others with them and reached another village, and by this means he covered over a hundred *yojanas*, until he reached Mithilā early in the morning of the following day.

The Bodhisatta, however, [448] went to the entrance to the tunnel and drew his own sword, which was fastened onto him, took it away and placed it in some sand at the entrance to the tunnel. And when he had put it there he went into the tunnel, through it, and into the city. Then he washed in perfumed water and ate a meal of various choice flavours and went on his excellent couch. 'I have attained my heart's desire,' he reflected, and lay down. When the night had passed, King Cūḷani organized his army and came into the city.

Explaining the matter the Teacher said:

Keeping guard for the entire night, Cūḷani of great power,
At the rising of the dawn, came up to Upakārī. (119)
Mounting the most noble elephant, of great strength, of sixty years of age,
The Pañcālan king, Cūḷani, of great power, spoke out. (120)
Fully equipped, in jewelled armour, grasping an arrow in his hand,[131]
He addressed the great swarm of men, all gathered around. (121)

130. Senaka's verse echoes the king's, with the exception of the word *sukāvahaṃ* 'conducive to happiness' (PED 716) rather than *susukhaṃ* 'very happy'. The slight change would be because of the metre (*metri causa*), to make up sixteen syllables for the line.

131. Amending *gharaṃ* 'building' to *saraṃ* (here 'an arrow') with Cone (DP II 82) and also Rouse (J VI 231 n.1), on the basis of Burmese interpretations.

And now a description of their particular appearance:

Mahouts, bodyguards, charioteers, foot soldiers,
Those who have mastered skills in archery, archers who can hit a hair:[132]
All were gathered around, it was said. (122)

Now the king gave orders to them to take Videha alive, and said:

'Send the tusked elephants, powerful, of sixty years of age,
And let them trample the city so skilfully created by the Videhan. (123)
An army of calf-tooth arrows, with sharpened tips, bone-piercers—
Let them be released with a speedy bow, and let them fall, here, there, and everywhere! (124)
Young men in armour, valiant warriors, with brilliantly coloured staffs as weapons:
Let them come forward, great and powerful men on elephants. (125)
And swords washed in sesame oil, gleaming and shining:
Let them stand sparkling like constellations of stars!' (126)
[449] With such soldiers and their powerful weapons,
Carrying bows and wearing their regalia,[133]
Incapable of flight in battle, where will Videha escape? (127)
Thirty-nine thousand[134] men, all individually picked:
Travelling the whole world I do not see their equal. (128)
Elephants with mighty tusks, all equipped, of sixty years of age:
On their backs shine the noble young men, wonderful to behold. (129)
Golden ornaments, golden clothes, and golden cloaks:
How the princes shine on elephant backs, as if they were gods in Nandana. (130)
The swords[135] have the sheen of lanchi fish,[136] washed in sesame oil,
Radiant, well finished, held in an even line by the heroes, and finely sharpened. (131)

132. The Sinhalese version says that they can aim at and pierce through a black horsehair with a small *brinjal* berry suspended from it (UJST 181).

133. Cone suggests this as a possible translation for *guṇi* here (DP II 56); regalia is an alternative translation for arm-guard, which *kāyura* could also mean here (DP I 672).

134. Cone, noting that *nāvuti* is a number of indeterminate status, suggests that it is nine thousand here (DP II 531), as does the commentary and Rouse (J VI 231 n.4). Rouse puts 'thirty and nine thousand'. It could also possibly be thirty groups of nine thousand, in line with other numbering systems, possibly military, peculiar to this story. UJST 182 suggests 'thirty-nine thousand'.

135. In the absence of a good subject noun for all these epithets, I am following the commentary's interpretation of the word *nettiṃsā* here.

136. The word is *pāṭhīna*, thought to be *Silurus boalis*, a catfish called sheatfish, wallago, or lanchi. The fish is found throughout South and Southeast Asia, and has a silvery shine, with hints of purple and blue. UJST oddly omits the content of this verse completely.

Flashing, stainless, made of tempered steel, and strong,
They are held by mighty men, who make one blow and then another! (132)
Yes, they shine, equipped in wonderful gold, and with red sheaths and
scabbards,
Turning like lightning in a thick rain cloud, (133)
Heroes in armour, skilled in sword and shield,
Holding firmly the hilts of their swords,
Highly disciplined, on elephant backs they go for the kill![137] (134)
Surrounded by such as these, there just is no escape for you.
I cannot see the power for you to return to Mithilā.' (135)

[450] He voiced his threats for Videha, thinking that he would capture him now. And he urged on his elephant with his staff and gave his orders to his army, 'Seize, bind, and destroy!' King Cūḷani swept like a flood towards the city of Upakārī. Then the Great Being's spies, thinking, 'Who knows what's going to happen?' gathered their own attendants and surrounded him.

At that moment the Bodhisatta rose from his excellent couch, saw to the needs of his body, ate his breakfast, adorned and equipped himself, and put on his Kāsi cloak, worth a hundred thousand coins, slung a red woollen shawl over his shoulder, took his staff that had been given as a present and was brightly ornamented with the seven kinds of jewel, and put on his golden sandals. Then, as if he were a divine maiden, all adorned, being fanned with a yak-tail fan, he strolled onto the palace terrace, opened a window, and revealed himself to King Cūḷani, and then walked up and down with the easy playful grace of Sakka, lord of the gods.

King Cūḷani gazed on his magnificent appearance and could not find any confidence in his heart at all. But he drove his elephant urgently, [451] saying, 'Now I'll capture him!' The wise man reflected, 'So this king is hastening and giving the sign to take the Videhan for him. But he does not know that I have seized his young people, and that our king has gone. I will show him my face, like a golden mirror. Then I will speak.' So he stood at the window and spoke with him in a voice as sweet as honey:

'What are you driving your elephant for in such haste?
You have arrived with a jubilant expression; do you think you've got
me? (136)
Throw down this bow; throw down this sharp arrow,
Throw off your beautiful armour, studded with lapus lazuli
and jewels.' (137)

137. For *atipāti* 'transgressing, attacking' see DP I 65.

The king heard these words, and threatened him: 'The householder's son makes fun of me, but today I know what is going to be done to you.' And he spoke this verse:

'Your face is clear with confidence, you speak with traces of a smile at an earlier joke:
It is at the moment of death that there is such a face.' (138)

The soldiers also noticed the magnificent appearance of the Great Being while the interchange was going on, and said, 'Our king speaks with the wise man Mahosadha, what are they saying? Let's listen to them.' And they went close to the king. The wise man had listened to what the king had said, and thought, 'You do not know that I am Mahosadha the wise man. And I will not allow you to kill me. Your plan is [452] in shreds. What Kevaṭṭa and you conceived of in your hearts has not come to be. But what you said with your mouth has come to be.' And he explained this:

'Your thundering is in vain, sire. Your plan is in shreds, noble sir.
The king is as hard to get as a Sindh horse by an old nag. (139)
For the king has crossed over the Ganges, with ministers and entourage,
And you will be just as a crow, trying to fly after the king of the geese.' (140)

And now, like a full-maned lion, without any fear, he gave this example and said:

'Jackals in the night-time see a Judas tree[138] in full flower, and gather in packs,
Thinking that the flowers are really pieces of meat, wild beasts that they are. (141)
When the watches of the night have passed, and the sun is high,
They see the flowers on the Judas tree and are disappointed, wild beasts that they are. (142)
In just this way, sire, when you come to surround the Videhan,
You too will be disappointed, just as the jackals at the Judas tree are!' (143)

The king listened to his fearless declaration and thought, 'This householder's son is too full of his own pith! No doubt the Videhan will have fled.' In a great rage, he thought, 'In times past [453] I did not have so much as a cloak to cover me, just because of this householder's son. Now he has come here and by his hand my enemy has escaped. He has been the maker of great mischief for me, and for both of these reasons I'll get him in return.' And he gave orders of what to do, saying:

'Cut off his hands and feet and nose,

138. The Judas tree, *Butea frondosa* or thingumme tree (*kiṃsuka*).

The one who delivered my enemy from my hands. (144)
Let them cook his flesh, putting it on skewers:
The one who delivered my enemy from my hands. (145)
And just as the hide of a bull is stretched down on the ground,
Or of a lion, or a tiger, set with iron stakes, (146)
In just this way I will kill him and stake him down,
The one who delivered my enemy from my hands!' (147)

The Great Being heard this and smiled, thinking, 'This king does not know that his queen and his relatives have been sent by me to Mithilā, and he plots this punishment for me. But in his rage he might pierce me with an arrow, or do whatever he pleases. So I will tell him about it, and make such agony of feeling for him that he will fall down right on his elephant's back, unconscious.' So he said:

'If you cut off my hands, feet, and nose,
The Videhan will cut off Pañcālacaṇḍa's too. (148)
If you cut off my hands, feet, and nose,
The Videhan will cut off Pañcālacaṇḍī's too. (149)
If you cut off my hands, feet, and nose,
The Videhan will cut off Queen Nandā's too. (150)
If you cut off my hands, feet, and nose,
The Videhan will cut off your children's too. (151)
[454] If you cook my flesh and put it on skewers,
The Videhan will cook Pañcālacaṇḍa's too. (152)
If you cook my flesh and put it on skewers,
The Videhan will cook Pañcālacaṇḍī's too. (153)
If you cook my flesh and put it on skewers,
The Videhan will cook Queen Nandā's too. (154)
If you cook my flesh and put it on skewers,
The Videhan will cook your children's too. (155)
If you make me suffer, and stretch my flesh with stakes,
The Videhan will stake out Pañcālacaṇḍa's too. (156)
If you make me suffer, and stretch my flesh with stakes,
The Videhan will stake out Pañcālacaṇḍī's too. (157)
If you make me suffer, and stretch my flesh with stakes,
The Videhan will stake out Queen Nandā's too. (158)
If you make me suffer, and stretch my flesh with stakes,
The Videhan will stake out your children's too.
In this way, a secret agreement has been devised
Between us—the Videhan and me. (159)
Just as a hide worth a hundred golden bronze coins,
Finished off by leather-working tools, is a defence to keep off arrows, (160)
So I am able to repel your plans,

As a sword is by a shield worth a hundred golden coins!' (161)

[455] When he heard this the king thought, 'What is the householder's son saying? He says the Videhan king is going to inflict punishment on my children in return for what I do to him. He does not know that my children are under a very close guard, and now he will die. He only makes threats because he is terrified of dying. I don't believe him.'

The Great Being thought, 'He thinks I am speaking just through fear, I'll let him know how things stand.' And he said:

'Come and see, Great King, that your women's quarters are empty.
Your women, your children, and your mother, noble warrior,
Have been taken and escorted by the Videhan through the tunnel.' (162)

When he heard this the king thought, 'The wise man is making a powerful claim. Indeed I heard the scream of Queen Nandā in the night-time: what if the wise man in his great wisdom is correct?' A most terrible grief rose up in him. But, summoning up his courage, as if he were not grieving, he called a certain minister and ordered him to find out, and spoke another verse:

'Come, and go to my women's quarters and look around.
Find out if what he says is true, or if it is a lie.' (163)

Then, with his retinue, he went into the king's residence and opened the door, and saw the guards of the women's quarters and the various kinds of attendants tied up by the hands and feet with their mouths gagged, deposited in places all around. The debris of food and drink that had been for him was scattered around. The doors of the treasure house were also open and he saw the treasure looted, the open doors of the bedroom, and a gaggle of crows had flown in [456] through the windows. It was like a village that had been deserted, or a charnel ground. Seeing the palace in such an unfortunate mess, he informed the king and said:

'It is just as Mahosadha said, Great King.
The women's quarters are empty, like a town beset by crows.' (164)

The king was shaken to the core with a great grief at his separation from his four close ones. 'This suffering has come to me because of the householder's son!' And he was enraged at the Bodhisatta, like a snake hit with a stick. The Great Being saw his look, and thought, 'This king has great glory and reputation. He could in his fury say, 'What use is this fellow to me?'[139] and then he would harm me, through warrior instinct. Why don't I

139. See DP I 543 for *eta*.

sing the praises of the bodily form of Nandā, the queen, as if she has never been seen before. Then he would remember her and would realise that if he kills Mahosadha, he will never possess this jewel of a woman again. So I'll win him over through his affection for his wife.' So he stood on the upper level of the palace, to protect himself, took his golden-skinned hand from his red woollen shawl, and extolled her virtues, with a description of the way she had gone:

'So Great King, the lady, whose every limb is loveliness, has gone.
Her beautiful hips are like a piece of *kosambha* wood,[140]
Her speech is like that of a flock of geese. (165)
So, Great King, the lady, whose every limb is loveliness, has been led away.
She is dark, dressed in silk, with a girdle of purest gold. (166)
She is lovely: her feet have been beautifully stained with red,
And have girdles[141] of gold and jewels. Her eyes are like doves,
She has a beautifully slender body, red lips, and her waist is slim. (167)
She is nobly born, and her arms are like budding sprouts;
Her waist is like a golden rail.[142] Her hair is long and black,
And curls at the tips, like that of an antelope. (168)
She is nobly born, like a young doe, or a crest of fire in the snows,
Or a river flowing deep in inaccessible mountains, strewn with young water reeds. (169)
[457] Her thighs are lovely, like the trunks of elephants,[143]
And her breasts, like *timbaru* fruit, neither too long nor too short.' (170)

In this way the Great Being extolled her beauty, as if she had never been seen before, and a powerful affection for her arose in the king. The Great Being saw this feeling in him and spoke this verse:

'And do you now delight in the death of Nandā, the delightful one,[144]
For I, and Nandā, go to an accounting with Yama, the lord of death!' (171)

140. Cone suggests this tentative translation (DP I 740) for *kosumbhaphalakasussoṇī*. Rouse says 'her lips are like plates of gold', and UJST 190 'her lips and lions dazzle like plates of solid gold.'

141. The word *mekhalā* usually refers to a girdle for the waist, but with Rouse, I have taken it to mean adornments for the feet.

142. I am taking the commentarial explanation for *valli*; and see PED 650. Rouse suggests it to mean the sacrificial site (*vedi*), as the ground is raised and narrow in the middle.

143. See DP II 522. See also Ja V 155. Elephant-derived epithets are frequent in describing the beauty of women in ancient Indian literature, where the regal grace of these animals does not have our rather negative connotations!

144. The verb here, *nandati*, has the same root as Nandā's name (delight).

[458] So the Great Being extolled the praises of Nandā alone, and no one else. And why was this? Because people do not have the same affection for others as they do for their beloved wives, and he praised her alone as he thought he would also then remember his mother and children too. But he did not praise his mother, on account of her great age. As she was being praised with such sweetness by the Great Being, endowed as he was such knowledge, it was as if Queen Nandā had come in front of the king and was standing there. Then the king thought, 'Except for the Great Being there is no one who is able to bring my wife and give her to me.' And as he remembered her, grief arose in him. Then the Great Being said to him. 'Do not worry, Great King, the queen and your son and your mother, the three of them, will come back. But this depends on my return. So take comfort, lord of men.' He reassured the king, and then the king thought, 'I myself put this city under great protection and guard, and stood surrounding the city of Upakārī with such great might. But this wise man despite the city being so well guarded, has led my queen, my son, and my mother away and handed them over to the Videhan. Even as the city was being surrounded by me, and without anyone realizing, he has got the Videhan to go on his way, with his army and vehicles. Does he know some divine magical powers, or a way of deceiving my very eyes?' And then, asking him, he recited this verse:

'Have you studied some divine magic,
Or have you made some deception for my eyes,
That you can deliver my enemy the Videhan from from my hands?' (172)

When he heard this the Great Being said, 'Great King, I do know divine magic, for wise men have learned a truly divine magic, whereby when danger comes, they save themselves and others from suffering.' And he spoke this verse:

'Great King, wise men study divine magic, and in this wise men,
Being knowledgeable and full of good counsel, deliver themselves. (173)
I have some wise youths, skilful, who can break down barriers;
A route was made by them, through which the Videhan has gone to
Mithilā.' (174)

[459] Hearing this, he thought, 'He has gone through the decorated tunnel.' So the king wished to see the tunnel, and asked, 'What is this tunnel like?' Then the Great Being, realizing his hint, said, 'The great king wishes to see the tunnel. So I shall show him the tunnel.' And he said, offering this:

'Come and see, Great King, the tunnel that has been so wonderfully built,
For elephants, for horses, and for chariots, and foot soldiers,

It is there all lit up, beautiful in its completion!' (175)

In this way he spoke: 'Great King, see the beautifully adorned tunnel, constructed through my wisdom: it shines as though the sun and moon had arisen within it! It has eighty large doors and sixty-four smaller ones, a hundred and one bedrooms, and many hundreds of niches for lamps. Come with me, in peace and delight, and enter, sire, the city of Upakārī, with all your soldiers.' And he had the gate to the city opened, and the king entered the city surrounded with the hundred and one kings. The Great Being stepped up into the palace and paid homage to the king. Then, taking his retinue, he entered the tunnel. The king looked at the tunnel as at the beautifully adorned city of the gods. And he spoke this verse in praise of the Bodhisatta:

'It's no small gain for the Videhans that there are such wise men
As you, Mahosadha, who live in his house and his kingdom!'[145] (176)

[460] Then the Great Being showed him the one hundred and one bedrooms. And when the door to one was opened, they all opened, and when the door to one was closed, they all did too. The king gazed at the tunnel in the front, and the wise man went behind. Then all the army entered, and the king left the tunnel, and the wise man, seeing that he had gone, left also himself. Then he did not let the others leave but drew the bolt and shut them in, so the eighty major doors, the sixty-four minor doors, and the doors to each one of the bedrooms and the coverings to each one of the light niches all shut in one stroke. The whole tunnel became dark, as if it were the end of the world. The people there were terrified.

Then the Great Being, holding the sword he had placed there the day before[146] when entering the tunnel, leapt eighteen hands into the air and landed, taking the king's arm. He brandished his sword and threatened him, asking, 'So, Great King, to whom does the entire continent of India belong?' The king replied in terror, 'To you, wise man. Please grant me my safety!'

'Do not have fear, Great King, I do not take up the sword with the wish to kill you. I do it to demonstrate the power of my wisdom.' And he handed the sword over to the king, who took the sword as the wise man stood there. He said, 'If, Great King, you wish to kill with this sword right here and now, then do so. If you wish to spare me, then do so.'

145. This echoes v. *18* (Ja VI 355) of this story, as Rouse notes.
146. Reading *hiyyo* 'yesterday' for *bhiyyo* 'more' with Rouse.

The king replied, 'Wise man, your life is spared. Have no concerns about this.' He held the sword, and they both struck an agreement, with no pretence. Then the king addressed the Bodhisatta. 'Wise man, seeing that you are possessed with such wisdom as this, why do you not seize the kingdom?'

'Great King, if I wished it, I could today seize the entire continent of India, killing all its kings. But it is not the way of wise men to kill others and gain glory from it.'

'Wise man, people are crying in terror through not being able to get out. Please open the door and grant them their lives.'

So the Great Being opened the door and the entire tunnel became one blaze of light, and the people there were deeply relieved. All the kings, with their armies, left the tunnel and came up to the wise man, and he stood in the great courtyard with the king. [461] Then the kings said, 'Wise man, because of you our lives are saved. If the door to the tunnel had remained shut even for a moment more, we would all have died, right there.'

'Great kings, this time is not the first when your lives have been saved by me.'[147]

'When was that, wise man?'

'Do you remember, when all the kingdoms of India had been conquered, except for our city, that you went to the garden at Uttarapañcāla in order to drink the wine of victory?'

'Yes, wise man.'

'At that time this king, with Kevaṭṭa, through a malicious trick, had poisoned the wine, the meat, and the fish in order to kill you all. But I decided that it would not be right for you to die while I just looked on. So I ordered my men to destroy all the plates and bowls there and so spoiled their plan, and then I gave you the gift of your lives.'

Shaking with alarm, they all asked Cūḷani about this. 'Is this true, great king?'

'Yes, and I did this because I took the advice of Kevaṭṭa. The wise man is speaking the truth.'

147. This is the formula that prefaces many *jātaka* stories, when, in the story of the present, the Buddha speaks of the time when he was Bodhisatta. This story involves a highly 'realist' world, however, in which all events take place in a highly pragmatic and even rationalist framework; the past is one remembered from this lifetime. The echo would not be lost on an early audience, who would feel the Bodhisatta is preparing for his final life as a psychological 'refuge' in *saṃsāra*.

They all then embraced the wise man. 'Wise man, you are our refuge. Because of you we have survived.' And, with minds cleared by faith, they all paid the deepest respects to the Bodhisatta. Then the Bodhisatta spoke to the king. 'Great King, do not have worries about this. The fault was in the association with this evil friend. Ask these kings to forgive you.' The king said, 'Because of this bad man I did such a thing to you. This was my fault. Please forgive me. I will never do such a thing again.' He received their forgiveness, and then they taught one another further and were in good accord. Then the king had brought in a great spread of various foods, perfumes, and garlands and suchlike, and they all had fun in the tunnel for seven days, and then entered the city. They accorded great honour to the Great Being. Sitting in the great terrace surrounded by the hundred and one kings, the king, wanting the wise man to stay with him, said:

'I give you livelihood, protection, and a double dispensation of food,
And means of livelihood, and other rich presents.
Eat, enjoy yourself, and have a good time!
Do not go back to Videha—what will Videha do?'[148] (177)
[462] But the wise man declined, saying:
'Great King, he who gives up his livelihood for the sake of wealth
Is an enemy both to himself and to the other.
While Videha is alive, I could not be the man of another. (178)
He who gives up his livelihood for the sake of wealth
Is an enemy both to himself and to the other.
As long as Videha endures, I could not live in the kingdom of another.' (179)

Then the king said, 'Then, give me your promise to come back here when your king has attained the state of a *deva*.'

'If I am alive, I will come, Great King.'

And then the king gave him all honour and hospitality for seven days, and on the seventh, as he was about to leave, he spoke a stanza, promising him various things.

'I give you a thousand weights of gold,[149] eighty villages in Kāsi,
Four hundred female attendants, and a hundred wives.
Take your entire army, and go in safety, Mahosadha.' (180)

Then he said to the king, 'Great King, do not have fears for your family. I have told the king to treat Queen Nandā as his own mother, and

148. This verse echoes the insult that permeates this story, of 'What will so-and-so do?' or 'What does so-and-so know?'

149. See DP II 538 for *nikkha*, which is approximately five *suvaṇṇas*.

Pañcālacaṇḍa as his younger brother. I gave your daughter to the king with a ceremonial sprinkling and sent him on his way. Soon I will send back your mother, your queen, and your son.' The king said, 'That is very good, wise man.' And he gave a dowry for his daughter, of female and male attendants, dresses, ornaments, gold and precious metals, fully adorned and equipped elephants, horses, and carriages. 'I give you these for her.' He then made arrangements for things to be done by the army:

> [463] 'Let them give him elephants and horses, twice as much as they need.
> And let them satisfy the charioteers and the foot soldiers with food and drink!' (181)

Speaking in this way he sent the wise man on his journey and said:

> 'Elephants and horses and chariots and foot soldiers: go with them, wise man.
> And may King Videha see you with them as you go to Mithilā.' (182)

Speaking in this way, he then sent the wise man on his way. The hundred and one kings all accorded the Great Being great honour and gave him many letters and presents. His attendants who had been his spies surrounded him as his entourage. So he went with his great retinue, and at intervals on the journey he sent men to accept the revenue from the villages given to him by King Cūḷani.

And when he reached the kingdom of Videha, they say that Senaka had positioned a man on the route and said to him, 'Find out if King Cūḷani is coming or not, and if he is coming, then inform me of his time of arrival.' And three *yojanas* away he saw the Great Being arriving and informed him that the wise man was coming with his entourage. Hearing this Senaka went to the palace, and as the king stood within the palace he looked out of the window and saw the great army. Stricken with fear, he thought that as Mahosadha had only a small army, this great one must mean that Cūḷani had arrived. And he spoke this verse as a question about this:

> 'Elephants, horses, chariots, foot soldiers: a great army has come into sight.
> It has four flanks, and its appearance strikes terror. What do the wise men think?' (183)

Senaka informed him of what was going on, and said:

> 'Great King, the greatest joy is what you see!
> Mahosdaha has arrived in safety, and come with all his army.' (184)

Hearing this the king said, 'But Senaka, the wise man's army is only small. This one is very large.' [464] Senaka replied, 'Great King, King Cūḷani will have inclined his heart towards him, and he will have given this to him in good faith.' So the king had a drum beaten throughout the city:

Let the city be decked out for the return of the wise man!

And the citizens did this, and the wise man entered the city and went into the palace and paid his respects to the king. Then the king rose and embraced him, and, returning to his palanquin, made him most warmly welcome:

'Just as four men leave a ghost abandoned in a cemetery,
So you abandoned the kingdom of Kampilliyā but then returned and came back. (185)
So through what disguise, or by what means,
And with what cause, did you deliver yourself?' (186)

Then the Great Being said:

'One purpose by means of a purpose, Videha,
One plan by means of another, noble warrior.
So I encircled the king, just as the ocean circles the continent of India.' (187)

The king was delighted to hear this, and the wise man explained to him the gift and letters that the king had given him:

'A thousand weights of gold were given to me, and villages in Kāsi,
Four hundred female attendants, and a hundred wives were accorded to me.
So, bringing this entire army, I am now here, arriving safely.' (188)

At this the king was exceedingly joyful and indeed overjoyed. Extolling the excellency of the Great Being he gave this inspired utterance:

[465] 'Oh what happiness it is to live with wise men, Senaka:
Mahosadha has delivered us from the hands of the enemy,
Like a bird from a locked up cage, or a fish from a net!' (189)

Then Senaka, agreeing with his words, spoke this verse:

'Yes, there is great happiness in living with one wise man.[150]
Mahosadha has delivered us from the hands of the enemy,

150. These verses are much the same as the interchange between the two when they leave by boat, but with a difference. Although again echoing his king's words precisely in this verse, Senaka now demonstrates his newly won humility and rephrases the king's praise from the plural to the singular, and one wise man, not several.

Just as a bird from a locked up cage, or a fish from a net!' (190)

Then the king had the festival drum beaten throughout the city, saying:

Let there be a festival for seven days
and let all those who have affection for me celebrate
the wise man with due honour!

The Teacher, explaining the matter, said:

'Let them play all kinds of lutes, drums, and kettle drums!
Let the conches of Magadha resound, and may all kinds of drums be beaten!' (191)

The citizens and the country people all wanted to pay great honour to the wise man, and hearing the drum they all rejoiced in the festival.

Explaining the matter the Teacher said:

Wives, girls, merchant and brahmin women:
All brought plentiful food and drink for the wise man. (192)
Mahouts, bodyguards, charioteers, and foot soldiers:
All brought plentiful food and drink for the wise man. (193)
Country people, village people, all kinds of people came in:
All brought plentiful food and drink for the wise man. (194)
Everyone there, with minds cleared by faith, came to see the return of the wise man.
And cloths were thrown and waved in the air at his return. (195)

[466] When the festival had concluded, the Great Being went to the palace. 'Great King, it is best for the mother, the queen, and the son to be sent quickly home.'

'Very well, dear one,' replied the king. And he accorded the three of them great honour, and paid great honour also to the army that had come with them. Then he sent the three, surrounded with a great entourage, with his own men. With Queen Nandā he sent the hundred wives and the four hundred female attendants that King Cūḷani had sent, and the army that had come with him he also sent back. And so surrounded with a great retinue they returned to the city of Uttarapañcāla. Then the king asked his mother, 'Were you treated well by the King of Videha, my lady?' She replied, 'Dear one, what are you saying? He put me in the position of a goddess!' Then she recounted the way that Queen Nandā had also been treated as his mother, and Pañcālacaṇḍa as a younger brother. When he heard this the king was filled with great joy, and sent a large quantity of presents and letters, and from that time they lived in the greatest accord and delight.

The section on the great tunnel is finished.

THE QUESTION OF THE WATER SPIRIT

Pañcālacaṇḍī was very dear and pleasing to the king, and in the second year she bore him a son. When he was ten, King Videha died. The Bodhisatta raised the royal parasol for him, and asked him, 'Sire, I will go now to your grandfather, King Cūḷani. 'Wise man,' he replied, 'Do not go and leave me while I am just a young boy. I will treat you with honour, as a father.' And Pañcālacaṇḍī added her request, 'Wise man, there is no other refuge for us at your departure. Please do not go.' He said, 'But I made the king a promise, it is not possible for me not to go.' So despite the general populace grieving piteously,[151] he took his own attendants and left for the city of Uttarapañcāla. The king heard that he was coming and came to meet him, with great honour and with a large retinue, and led him into the city and gave him a house to live in. As well as the gifts he had made before, [467] of eighty villages, he gave more, and he then served in attendance on that king.

Now at that time, there was a female renunciate called Bherī, who always used to eat in the royal household. She was very wise and experienced and had never seen the Great Being before. She heard reports that Mahosadha the wise man was now serving the king. He had never seen her before either, and he also heard reports of her eating in the royal household. But Queen Nandā was not happy at all with the Bodhisatta, and said, 'You have caused me harm, and a separation between me and what I love.' So she gave orders to five of her women favourites, 'Be on the lookout for a fault in the Bodhisatta, and cause a breach between him and the king.' They looked out for any chink in him. One day, the female renunciate took her meal and, as she was leaving, saw the Bodhisatta in the courtyard, on his way to attend on the king. He stood and paid respects to her, and she thought, 'This must be the wise man that is talked about. I will find out if he really is wise, or if he is not, by asking him a question with a gesture of my hands.' And she looked at the Bodhisatta and opened her palm. And she asked the question in her mind: 'Does the king look after the wise man that he has brought in from elsewhere, or does he not?' The Bodhisatta realized that she was communicating to him and asking a question with her hand gesture, and

151. Reading *kalunam* rather than *karuṇā*, with Bd and Cone (DP I 466).

answered it with a closed fist. What he meant was, 'Venerable lady,[152] he called me here to keep a promise, and now the king keeps his fist tight closed, and gives me nothing.' And so he answered the question with his mind. She understood the communication, and lifting her hand, rubbed her head,[153] by which she meant, 'Wise man, if you are weary of this, then why do you not take the going forth, like me?' He understood this, and rubbed his own stomach, by which he meant, 'Venerable lady, there are many people that must be fed by me, and that is why I do not take the going forth.' After this questioning through hand gesture, she then returned to her own dwelling place. The Great Being paid his respects to her and went to attend on the king.

Now Queen Nandā's favourites stood at the window and had watched what had taken place. So they went to King Cūḷani and said, 'Sire, Mahosadha has been with the ascetic Bherī and wishes to take your kingdom: he is an enemy.' And so they slandered him. The king responded, 'Why? What have you seen or heard?' [468] They replied, 'Great King, when the ascetic was going after eating her meal she saw Mahosadha. She opened her hand, meaning, "Can you not make the king flat, and take him in hand, like my hand has gone flat, or like a circular threshing floor?" Mahosadha responded to her by closing his fist, as if taking his sword, meaning, "I will take him in hand, and in a few days I will cut off his head." She told

152. Bd gives *ayye* (f. voc.) here rather than the masculine *ayyo* (F), and I have amended it in line 23 too. F gives a female figure, with *paribbājikā*. According to Rouse the Burmese version has a male ascetic here, though he makes her female. UJST (210 ff.) makes the ascetic male; this would mean, however, that the *arahat* Uppalavaṇṇā had been a male in this lifetime. She is attributed as the later rebirth of the ascetic by the Buddha in the attributions at the end of the story in the *samodhāna*, which are in the rare verse form, the *abhisambuddhagāthā*. For a character to change sex from one life to another is not unheard of, as when Ānanda appears to be a female tree spirit in an earlier life (See *Kusanāli-jātaka*, J121; Introduction 10 n. 8; Appleton 2011; Shaw 2006a: 90–4). The Thais apparently preferred a female here: in the eighteenth-century manuscript MS. Pali a. 27(R), held in the Bodleian Library, for instance, the ascetic is shown as a woman (see Appleton, Shaw, and Unebe 2013: 34–5), reproduced here as Fig. 5.14. A female attribution would certainly fit thematically, as the Bodhisatta also communicates with his future wife through hand gesture. His deep affinity with both his wife, and the ascetic life as represented by Bherī, is then made clear by their 'speaking the same language'. Further sources involving the subject of changing sex from life to life can be seen in *Petavatthu* 25, 'Story of Ubbarī', especially vv. 11–12. For the story see Gehman 1974: 63–6 and 167–76. For commentary see Pva 160–8, especially pp. 165–6. I am grateful to Steven Collins for pointing these passages out to me.

153. As an ascetic her head would be shaven.

him to cut off your head, by lifting her hand and rubbing her head. Then Mahosadha indicated that he would cut you right through the middle, by rubbing his stomach. So be vigilant, great king! It is Mahosadha's plan to kill you.'

Now the king listened to what they said and thought, 'It just is not possible for my wise man to harm me. I will ask the female renunciate.' So the next day, when the female renunciate was having her meal, he approached her and asked, 'Venerable lady, have you ever seen Mahosadha?'

She said, 'Yes, Great King. I saw him yesterday when I had eaten my meal, as I was leaving.'

'What did you discuss?' he asked.

'It was not really a conversation. I had heard he was a wise man, and wanted to know if he was indeed wise. I asked him a question with his hands: "Wise man, is the king open handed or tight fisted? Is he agreeable or not?" And I opened my hand. But he closed his fist, meaning that the king had brought him here on his earlier promise, but now gave him nothing. Then I asked him why, given that he had become weary of this, he did not become an ascetic. And I rubbed my head. He replied that he had too many people to look after, and many stomachs to fill, so he could not become a renunciate. And he rubbed his stomach.'

'And this definitely was Mahosadha?'

'Oh yes, Great King. For there is no one such as he in wisdom across the whole face of the earth.' The king listened to her words and paid his respects, and sent her on her way.

When she had gone, the wise man entered to pay attendance upon the king, and he asked him, 'Wise man, have you ever seen the female ascetic, Bherī?'

'Oh yes, Great King. Yesterday I saw her as she was leaving, and she asked me questions with gestures of her hands. And I answered her in the same way, right there.' And he explained it all in the way that she had explained it just before. The king put his trust in him on that day, and gave the wise man the custodianship of the army and entrusted to him the running of all his business. He acquired the greatest renown, second only to that of the king.

Now he reflected, [469] 'In one stroke the king has given me the greatest lordship. But kings still do this, even if they wish to kill. Why don't I test the king to see if he has good heart or not? No one else will be able to find this out but the renunciate Bherī. She will find out by some stratagem.'[154] So he took large amounts of perfumes and garlands and went to the ascetic's dwelling place, saluted her, and paid her homage, saying, 'Venerable lady, the king has bestowed great glory on me; indeed he has overwhelmed me since the day that you explained my good qualities to him. But I do not know if he does this through his own natural volition or not. It would be good if you were to find out his disposition to me, by some means.'

She agreed to do this, and the next day as she was going to the palace she thought of the Question of the Water Spirit: and they say it just came into her mind. She thought, 'I must not put the question to the king in such a way as if I were a spy. I'll find out though if he has a good heart[155] towards the wise man or not.' So she went and had her meal and stayed sitting down. Then the king came and paid his respects to her, and sat down to one side, and this thought came to her: 'If the king does not have a good heart for the wise man, then when asked the question, he will speak of his lack of a good heart in the middle of the big assembly. It is not fitting: I'll ask him this question to one side.' So she said, 'Great King, I wish to ask you about something in confidence[156] (*raho*) with you.' The king dismissed the people present. 'Ask me now, venerable lady, and once I know, I can tell you.' So she recited the first verse of the Water Spirit Questions:

> 'If there were seven people carried away on the high seas with you,
> And a spirit seized the boat, searching for the sacrifice of a human being,
> In what order would you appease the water spirit?' (196)

[470] The king listened to her and told her how his inclination would go, reciting this verse:

> 'I would give my mother first, then my wife, then my brother;
> Then I'd give my friend, and fifthly, I'd give a brahmin.
> The sixth person I would give would be myself,
> And only then would I offer Mahosadha.' (197)

It was clear to the lady renunciate that the king was in a state of very good heart towards the Great Being. But the extent of the wise man's great excellency had not been made public. So then this thought came to her: 'I

154. Ja VI 469–78 and the questions of the water spirit make the episode linked to the *Sirimanda-jātaka* (J 500).

155. The contrast here is between literally having a good heart (*suhadayo*) or a 'bad', in this case a hostile, one (*duhadayo*).

156. The word translated here as 'in confidence' is a 'secret' (*raho*), used in The Questions of the Five Wise Men, concerning the keeping of a secret, earlier in the story.

will ask about the excellency of these people in the midst of a large number of people, and the king will then explain the virtues of the wise man, and their deficiency in these. In this way he will make the wise man's excellency public, like the moon shining in the sky. And she had called together all the people of the inner quarters of the palace and asked the same question of the king, from the beginning, and it was answered in just the same way. 'Great King, you say that you would give your mother first. But your mother has great virtues, and she is a mother that is not like others. She is very helpful to you.' And she then spoke two verses explaining this:

'She nourished you and gave you birth;
And through many long nights she showed compassion to you.
When Chambī behaved badly towards you,
She was wise and looked out for your good.
By putting another in your place, she rescued you from death. (198)
For what fault of your mother,
Who bore you in her womb and nurtured you, giving you life,
Would you hand her over to the water spirit?'[157] (199)

[471] [472] The king heard this, and said, 'Venerable lady, my mother certainly has many virtues. I know of her helpful nature, but my virtues are greater than hers.'[158] And he recited two verses about his mother's lack of virtue:

157. A long story in small type in F, which runs from the end of page 470 to halfway through page 472, explains how his mother had had an affair and killed her husband, marrying her lover. She saved him then from death by pretending he was the cook's son. This is an instance where Fausbøll's decision to put in small type stories that seem commentarial rather than central to the tale seems well justified. Although the stories do help to explain the verses, the response by the king to Bherī that comes after it clearly relates to the verse rather than the lengthy anecdotal explanation. Such stories seem to occupy a curious area between prose and commentary, suggesting the fluid relationship between written word and the spoken in a still largely oral tradition; perhaps the story is told within the prose as something to be recounted at the discretion of the storyteller. In the case of the nineteen problems, and the backstories concerning the verses, the text has been translated, as seeming more central to the story.

158. Rouse rightly finds this passage odd, and suggests an emendation that omits *mam'eva* and adds a negative, to make 'lack of virtues' *pan' ev'agunā*. So perhaps it should read that her bad qualities are more numerous than her good. Either way it is rather a stark statement, but given the shock that the verse suggests the mother should be forfeit first, no explanatory prose comment would really make amends! In a collection where parents are accorded the greatest respect and honour, this story, with its incident earlier on in which the Bodhisatta takes precedence over his father when he first enters the court, is out of the ordinary; the intent seems, however, not to denigrate parents, but to emphasise the worth of the Bodhisatta.

'She puts on ornaments, as if a young girl, which are not suitable for her.
She berates gatekeepers and bodyguards far too much. (200)
She sends, on her own volition, messages to rival kings,
And because of these faults I would give her to the water spirit.' (201)

[473] 'Great King, then give your mother for these faults. But your wife is most excellent.' And she spoke this verse about her:

'She is the most excellent in a crowd of women. She is always dear and kind in speech.
She is not haughty, is virtuous, and follows you like a shadow. (202)
She never becomes angry; she is wise, accomplished, and looks out for your good.
For what fault would you hand over her, your favourite wife, to the water spirit?' (203)

He replied, recounting her lack of good qualities:

'Because she is endowed with so much sexy playfulness, she leads me to no good!
And she does go on, asking for things she should not for her children. (204)
And I, in my passion for her, give her far too much wealth.
For this fault I would hand her, my favourite wife, over to the water spirit.' (205)

And then the female ascetic asked him, 'Alright, give her to the water spirit for this fault. But what about your younger brother, Prince Tikhiṇamantī? For what fault would you hand him over?

[474] He brought an increase of wealth for the country,
And when you were in far kingdoms brought you back,
Not succumbing to great wealth, (206)
A most excellent archer, the very best, a hero, Tikhiṇamantī.[159]
For what fault would you give him to the water spirit?' (207)

The king then described his fault.

'It is *because* he thinks: "I brought an increase of wealth for the country,
And when he was in far kingdoms brought him back,
Not succumbing to great wealth, (208)
A most excellent archer, the very best, a hero, Tikhiṇamantī!
It was because of me that the king is happy."
The young man exceeds himself. (209)
And he does not pay attendance to me as he used to in the past.
For these faults, I would give my brother to the water spirit.' (210)

159. A long story explains that the boy is born just after their father has died and their mother has a new husband. The boy later kills the usurper to the throne.

[475] So the female renunciate said, 'So be it: let the brother be at fault. But what about Prince Dhanusekha, who is of great service and who is deeply affectionate towards you?' And she described his great quality:

'In one night, you and Dhanusekha were both born,
Pañcālans, friends, and confidantes. (211)
His whole way of life is to follow you, and he shares your sorrow and happiness.
By day and by night he is eager to do service and diligent in his business.
For what fault would you hand your dear friend over to the water spirit?' (212)

And then the king described his fault:

'Venerable lady, yes, he laughs with me as a friend,
But today in his manner he has been laughing much too excessively! (213)
When I go in secret with my favourite wife, a venerable lady,
He comes in without arranging it and announcing himself before. (214)
He takes any chance he can, and acts without shame or respect.
For this fault I would hand my friend over to the water spirit.' (215)

The female renunciate then said, 'So there is a fault in him for you too. But your priest does really great service to you.' And she extolled his virtues:

'Skilful in reading all signs, he knows the cries of all animals,
And has mastered all omens, can read dreams and comings and goings.[160] (216)
[476] He can read the omens of the earth and the sky
And is skilled in understanding the movements of the stars.
For what fault would you hand the priest over to the water spirit?' (217)

The king described his faults too.

'In the assembly he stares at me with unblinking eyes,[161] and his eyebrows are cruel.
I'd give him to the water spirit.' (218)

Then the female renunciate asked, 'Great King, you say, starting with your mother, that you would give these five people to the water spirit, and you say, not taking into account your great glory, that you would give your own life for the sake of Mahosadha. What virtue do you see in him?' And she spoke these verses:

160. The commentary explains the 'comings and goings' as the movements of the stars, which would mean knowledge of the auspicious and inauspicious times for particular events.

161. The commentary says that this makes him look as if he is angry with the king.

'You live on the earth, the bearer of wealth, surrounded by the great ocean
And ringed by waters, and are encircled by your assembly. (219)
In the four continents and the islands, you have a magnificent kingdom,
Great power, and are a conqueror, the sole king of the earth. You live in great glory. (220)
Sixteen thousand women, with pearls and jewels as earrings, are yours,
Women from so many regions, as beautiful as divine nymphs. (221)
So in this way you are endowed with everything you could want and whatever you wish;
You have had a long and dearly loved life, in happiness, warrior. (222)
Then in what capacity, and for what reason, would you guard your wise man,
And give up what is so hard to give up, even your own life?' (223)

[477] He listened to what she had to say and spoke these verses in praise of the wise man:

'Since Mahosadha, venerable lady, came to me,
I have never known him to do even the slightest thing wrong. (224)
If I should die before him, Mahosadha would bring happiness
To my children and their children. (225)
He knows the future and the past, indeed everything,
And I would not hand over this man, who is without any kind of blame,
To the water spirit.' (226)

In this way this *jātaka* has moved along to its conclusion.[162] Then the female renunciate thought, 'Even so this is not enough to make known the wonderful qualities of the wise man. I will make them known in the midst of all the citizens of the city, as if spreading scented oil across the entire surface of the ocean!' And she led the king out of the palace and set him on his throne, and calling together the people of the city, she asked him the question of the water spirit, right from the beginning, and when he had answered it in the way that has just been described, she said:

'Hear this statement of the Pañcālan, King Cūḷani:
He would guard the wise man and even give up what is so hard to give up—his own life! (227)
[478] The life of his mother, his wife, his brother, his friend, and his brahmin,
And indeed himself: these six the Pañcālan would give up. (228)

162. In a style familiar in this *jātaka*, self-referential observation brings the story to its conclusion. This self-conscious formula is not found in others of the Great Ten.

Such is the magnificent power of wisdom, such the cleverness, and
such the good-heartedness,
For the welfare of things that can be seen in this world, and for
happiness in the future!' (229)

So, as if picking out the topmost of a heap of jewels, in a house of treasures, she picked out the topmost of her teaching, about the wonderful qualities of the Great Being.

The question of the water spirit is finished. And the entire description of the Great Tunnel is ended too.

This is the connection for this *jātaka*:[163]

Uppalavaṇṇā was Bherī, Suddhodana was the father;
Mahāmāyā was the mother, and Beautiful Bimbā was Amarā.[164] (230)
Ānanda was the parrot, and Sāriputta was Cūḷani,
The lord of the world was Mahosadha: so remember the *jātaka* in this
way. (231)
Devadatta was Kevaṭṭa, Cullanandikā was Talatā;
Sundarī was Pañcālacaṇḍī, Yasassikā was the queen. (232)
Ambaṭṭha was Kāvinda, Poṭṭhapada was Pukkusa,
Pilotika was Devinda, and Saccaka was Senaka. (233)
The auspicious Sāḷikā was Queen Udumbarā,
Kuṇḍalī was the mynah bird, and Lāḷudayī was Videha. (234)

163. This is the unusual but ancient *samodhāna* in verse, known as *abhisambuddha-gāthā* (see Geiger 1943: 31). In the *Mahānipāta*, only *Nārada-jātaka* also ends in this way (Chapter 8: 453; Ja VI 255), but the presence of such verses indicates the antiquity of the connections with earlier lives in the tales.

164. The rationale behind the attributions and the characters in the Buddha's lifestory is not clear. Some are family members and followers: Suddhodhana, for instance, is the Buddha's father; Bimbā is another name for Rāhulamātā, the Bodhisatta's wife in their final life together. Cullanandikā is unknown; she is not mentioned in known texts. Sundarī could be a number of people of that name; Yasāssikā is unknown. Ambaṭṭha could be the haughty brahmin of the same name who challenges the Buddha on questions of birth and is routed (*Ambaṭṭha Sutta*, DN 3). Poṭṭhapāda is known: he elicits a *sutta* from the Buddha, concerning the nature of 'self', which takes his name, *Poṭṭhapāda Sutta*, and he also becomes a follower of the Buddha (DN 9). Most name references may be found in DPPN.

The Ten Great Birth Stories of the Buddha

Carmel G

The Ten Great Birth Stories of the Buddha

The *Mahānipāta* of the *Jātakatthavaṇṇanā*

VOLUME TWO

Translated and introduced by

Naomi Appleton and Sarah Shaw

Chulalongkorn University Press

Silkworm Books

Cloth ISBN: 978-616-215-112-5
Paper ISBN: 978-616-215-113-2

First published in 2015 by
Silkworm Books
6 Sukkasem Road, T. Suthep
Chiang Mai 50200 Thailand
info@silkwormbooks.com
www.silkwormbooks.com

and

Chulalongkorn University Press
Phayathai Road, Pathumwan
Bangkok 10330 Thailand
ChulaPress@chula.ac.th
www.ChulaPress.com

Typeset in Gentium Book Basic 10.5 pt. by Silk Type

Printed and bound in China

5 4 3 2 1

Contents

Abbreviations

AN	*Aṅguttara Nikāya*
BHSD	*Buddhist Hybrid Sanskrit Dictionary*, ed. Edgerton
DN	*Dīgha Nikāya*
DP	*A Dictionary of Pāli*, ed. Cone
DPPN	*Dictionary of Pāli Proper Names*, ed. Malalasekera
F	Fausbøll's edition of the *Jātakatthavaṇṇanā*
J	*Jātakatthavaṇṇanā* stories by number, or volume and page as in the Cowell/Rouse translation.
Ja	*Jātakatthavaṇṇanā* references to F by volume and page number
MN	*Majjhima Nikāya*
PED	*Pāli-English Dictionary*, ed. Rhys-Davids and Stede
PGPV	*The Perfect Generosity of Prince Vessantara*, trans. Cone and Gombrich
PTS	Pāli Text Society
Pva	*Petavatthuattakathā*
SED	*Sanskrit English Dictionary*, ed. Monier-Williams
SN	*Saṃyutta Nikāya*
UJST	*Ummagga Jātaka: The Story of the Tunnel*, trans. (from Sinhalese) Karunaratne
Vsm	*Visuddhimagga*, referred to by section divisions as found in Ñāṇamoli's translation.
VRI	Vipassana Research Institute electronic edition of the Pāli scriptures

6

The Birth Story of Bhūridatta

(*Bhūridatta-jātaka*)

INTRODUCTION

The *Bhūridatta-jātaka* is immediately recognizable in Southeast Asian temple murals by the depiction of a colourful serpent entwined around an anthill, the image which has come to represent the attempts by the hero, the Bodhisatta, to keep the moral precepts even though he is a *nāga*, a mythical being that is half snake and lives beneath the waters. *Nāgas* form a central part of Southern Buddhist culture, with their snakelike forms often adorning shrines as well as appearing frequently in temple art. They share many characteristics with Western dragons: they guard hidden treasures, have great power, and their breath can prove fatal to human beings. Like the Chinese dragon, however, their connotations are almost entirely auspicious. Their realms occupy a kind of halfway house between the animal and the godlike; in Southern Buddhist mythology *nāgas* have miraculous powers, can remember their past lives, and can assume, as we see in this story, any form at will.[1] They are also possessors of prized wish-fulfilling jewels that they sometimes pass on to humans, a treasure their role as granters of wishes and aspirations suggests. Despite *nāgas*' great auspiciousness—the *nāga* Mucalinda for instance rises from

Introduced and translated by Sarah Shaw.

1. For some study of this see Jones 1979: 186–8 and, with a translation of the *Campeyya-jātaka*, Shaw 2006a: 158–78.

the depths of the river after the Buddha's final awakening to protect him for a week from rains and storms (Ja I 70)—rebirth in this realm is not considered as honourable as that of the sense-sphere gods and humans. Although sometimes aligned with the lowest sense-sphere heaven, that of the Four Kings, it is technically considered a lower rebirth, below that of humans. This is indicated in this story by the human king's reluctance to let his daughter marry a *nāga* herself. The Bodhisatta is frequently reborn as a *nāga* in *jātaka* stories, often on the basis of a wish that arises in him in a human rebirth, when he sees and aspires to their magnificent palaces, jewels, and hedonistic lifestyle. Once born there, he is always ashamed that he has taken a form in that realm, and does his utmost to regain a human rebirth.

His undertaking to regain a human rebirth is significant. It is because of the *nāgas*' capacity to remember past lives that the Bodhisatta recalls lives when he has not been a *nāga*: in the *Campeyya-jātaka* he is deeply ashamed to recollect the resolve that had brought him to his royal but lower rebirth. This aspect is not mentioned by Bhūridatta, but it is an essential and emphasized aspect of all *nāga* stories involving the Bodhisatta that he is dissatisfied with his rebirth, a feature that does not intrude in the tales where he is an animal, perhaps because as an animal he would not be able to remember his earlier lives. Because of the limitations imposed on spiritual practice by not having a stable human body for the extent of a rebirth, the scope for *nāgas* for bodily and verbal action leading to human and higher rebirth, and hence the cultivation of a full spiritual path, is limited. *Nāgas* can assume the bodies of humans or gods, but they are not able to participate in those realms except as outsiders. In this regard it is like the other lower rebirths of animal or ghost: only the practice of *sīla* and wisdom will help them find a higher rebirth. This is crucial to the plot in all the *jātaka nāga* stories. Because of this limitation, and the great and enticing pleasures of the *nāga* realm, the Bodhisatta cannot keep the precepts in that realm easily whilst living with other *nāgas*. Indeed when he tries, as in the story here, he is chased by ever eager and sexually enticing *nāga* girls anxious to dissuade him from this path. So the only recourse he has to try and keep the precepts is in the world of humans, above land, where, in snake form, he will be vulnerable to attack. This is where he keeps the *uposatha* days, which fall on the days of the full and new moons and the mid-point days in between. In modern practice *uposatha* days are festive temple events, when the laity, dressed in white, can take on extra precepts and can offer food and drinks to the monastic orders, enjoy food themselves, and spend the day in a mixture of activities involving chanting, listening to chanting, hearing *dhamma* talks—including *jātaka* stories such as this one—and perhaps participating in various types of meditation. That this was the case in ancient times is also demonstrated by the 'story from the present' in this story, where lay participants in an *uposatha* day celebration offer food, eat, offer garlands and flowers, and generally engage in *dhamma* activities such as listening to talks and paying respect to their teacher. All of these, then and now, come under the classification of *bhāvanā* in Southeast Asia, a term that is difficult to translate but which covers many such activities felt to contribute to the rounded practice of the eightfold path and the development of concentration and wisdom. Keeping the *uposatha* has a broader sense in the sections of *jātaka* stories that describe 'the present' when Buddhist practice is possible, as it does in modern practice, than it does within *jātaka* stories themselves, set 'in times past'. This is usually a time when there is no Buddhist teaching, and keeping the *uposatha* days are framed slightly differently, without the festive element, and usually appear to involve fasting, though occasionally gifts of food are made to ascetics (J 316).

In *jātaka*s where the Bodhisatta is a *nāga*, he escapes from his exciting but spiritually unsupportive environment in the *nāga* realm to the world above ground, where in this and the other tales he tends to wrap himself around an anthill and spend the day fasting and at rest, thus avoiding any transgression of the precepts. It is worthy of note, however, that he never practises any form of meditation as a *nāga* as participants in a modern *uposatha* day ceremony might. *Jātaka* stories tend to keep closely to the understanding of the possibilities of different realms, delineated in the third basket of the teaching, the philosophical *Abhidhamma*. According to this system, for *nāga*s, technically a lower rebirth, no form of *jhāna* is accessible, as it is not for any animal. *Jātaka*s are scrupulous in their depiction of the Bodhisatta in this regard, and as a *nāga* he never attains to any of the meditative states, requiring, like other beings, a human or higher rebirth to do so.

In this, as in other *nāga* stories, the Bodhisatta becomes vulnerable while keeping the *uposatha*, either to *garuḷa* birds, the traditional enemies of *nāga*s, who wait to swoop and eat *nāga* young, or more commonly in *jātaka*s, to snake charmers. Because the Bodhisatta has undertaken the vow of keeping the precepts, he cannot harm any snake charmer who comes to try his spells upon him, and must wait passively until a member of his family (J 506) or a passer-by (J 524) comes to rescue him. In these and other *nāga* rebirths, he has to endure a humiliating life kept in the snake charmer's basket, performing in public by dancing and making his hoods transform through his magical powers. Rescue comes in the end, however, and he is always described after this event addressing bystanders, usually royal, as a human whose handsome and noble appearance is compared sometimes, as in this story, to Lord Sakka, the king of the Tavatiṃsa heaven. This is a momentary appearance and reminder of his true, Bodhisatta self, capable of behaving and acting as a fully human being, before his necessary return to the realms below, where in all such stories he continues to observe the *uposatha* until his death releases him to a heavenly or a human rebirth. This story, which represents the perfection of his *sīla*, or moral virtue, shows him also delivering a *dhamma* talk in the human realm, and then in the *nāga* realm an eloquent and poetic denunciation of the brahmins and the practice of harming other beings through sacrifice.

So all stories involving the Bodhisatta as a *nāga* describe the hero perfecting and working upon *sīla*, in intention (*cetanā*) as well as deed. This is in part through his refusal to become lost in the sensory delights of this lower realm, where there is endless temptation to indulge in sexual activity and fine eating and drinking. It is primarily, however, through the need to practise non-harm, in a restraint that can be exercised even when he is captured, tortured, and humiliated, as in this tale. The Bodhisatta never breaks precepts in *jātaka*s where he is keeping the *uposatha* as a *nāga* and does not use the miraculous powers associated with his existence in this form to free himself or to cause harm to others. As is indicated in this story, *nāga*s can kill, either through their poisonous breath or their magical powers. The Bodhisatta never resorts to this option, thus demonstrating his perfection of the five precepts of non-harm, of which the other four are not stealing, not indulging in sexual misconduct that would harm others, not lying, and not becoming intoxicated.

The story itself is the only one of the Great Ten that involves a lower rebirth for the Bodhisatta, though others are remembered at the outset of the *Mahānipāta* by Temiya, where his horrified recollection of aeons in hell realms provide a stark reminder of the most unhappy depths of existence at the outset of the Great Ten and the Bodhisatta's search for the perfections. Both these recollections prompt action: for Temiya to renounce kingship, and for Bhūridatta to aim for a human birth. The only other story in the series that involves a non-human existence for the Bodhisatta is the *Nārada-jātaka* (Chapter 8), in which he has been reborn as Lord Brahmā and comes to intercede in the affairs of humans. He is however, in this lowly *nāga* rebirth, royal, and his actions suggest his capacity for leadership and the exercise of good governance. He also visits the Heaven of the Thirty-Three, where he demonstrates his capacity for argument and understanding and is praised by the king of the gods, Sakka.

The story itself is in some ways less unified than others of the Great Ten, in the main because of the late appearance of the Bodhisatta, who comes to play a prominent role but does not feature in the adventures of the first part of the story. The first part does, however, set the scene for the curious mixed nature of the Bodhisatta's double ancestry, as well as giving us a lively and engaging depiction of *nāgas*, their ethos and way of life, and how they interact with humans. The tale is divided into a number of sections,[2] as some of the other longer Great Ten stories are. There are eight in the F version and in the VRI, with only slight differences.[3] These sections offer natural breaks for those chanting the story on a festive occasion; some literary care is also evident in the way each section works as an episode, complete in itself, and within the sequence of sections as a kind of chapter, or scene, in which the action is propelled to the next stage of the narrative whole.

The Story

The story from the present describes the Buddha extolling the laity keeping the *uposatha* day, as wise men did in the past, the usual introduction for *nāga* rebirths.

2. The story sections according to F:
    1. *Nagarakhaṇḍa* (The section about the city) to 167
    2. *Uposathakhaṇḍa* (The section about the *uposatha*) to 170
    3. *Vanapavesana* (The section about entering the forest) to 177
    4. *Sīlakhaṇḍa* (The section about *sīla*) to 184
    5. *Kīḷanakhaṇḍa* (The section about the performance) to 186
    6. *Nagarapavesanakhaṇḍa* (The section about entering the city) to 197
    7. *Mahāsattassa pariyesanakhaṇḍa* (The section about the search for the Great Being) to 200
    8. Last section

3. The main differences are that VRI stresses the *garuḷa* element in section 3, where F stresses the entrance into the forest, and that there is a small *sīla* section in F, where the Bodhisatta's adoption of his *uposatha* vow is made into a small section on its own.

The first section, like the openings of the *Vessantara-jātaka* and the *Sāma-jātaka*, then gives the background to the Bodhisatta's rebirth—here the circumstances of his grandparents' meeting: A *nāga* lady entices an exiled prince who has become a reluctant ascetic and they have two children. When the prince, Brahmadatta, is invited back to his kingdom, the *nāga* maiden will not go, so he takes their two children. One day the children find a tortoise, who frightens them so much the king orders his execution. Through an amusing trick, the tortoise escapes and engineers a match between the king of the *nāgas* and Samuddajā, Brahamadatta's daughter. The princess is ingeniously deceived into marrying the king of the *nāgas*, without realizing that she has left the human realm. The outset of this story is different in tone from the rest of the narrative, but with a lighthearted tone that establishes a sense of the sexual directness of the *nāga* realm and some ways ingenuity and stratagem can be used to good effect.

Section 2 describes the new queen giving birth to four sons, the second of whom, Datta, is the Bodhisatta. She finds out the true nature of the realm only when her fourth son terrifies her by biting her. The Bodhisatta, meanwhile, grows up as a *nāga* prince, and his distinction is emphasized by a visit to the Heaven of the Thirty-Three (Tāvatiṃsa), where he earns the name Bhūridatta, the only being capable of answering Sakka's questions. The Bodhisatta is reminded of the shamefulness of his rebirth by his visit to the heavens, and resolves to keep the *uposatha*.

In Section 3, a hunter, Somadatta, and his son find the Bodhisatta, who takes them to the *nāga* realm and entertains them. He offers them the wish-fulfilling jewel when they go, but they do not take it, and upon their return home are abused by Somadatta's wife for this.

Section 4 opens with a *garuḷa*, the traditional enemy of the *nāgas*, who gives an ascetic a special spell, the *Ālambāyana*; he in turn gives it to an impoverished brahmin who waits on him, henceforth known as Ālamba or Ālambāyana. When Ālamba sees some *nāga* youths dancing around the wish-fulfilling gem belonging to the Bodhisatta, he takes it. He then meets Somadatta, who now wants the jewel: to the disgust of his son, who leaves to become an ascetic, Somadatta in return shows Ālamba the Bodhisatta as a snake keeping the *uposatha*.

VRI goes: 1. *Nagarakhaṇḍa* to 167; 2. *Uposathakhaṇḍa* to 170; 3. *Garuḷakhaṇḍa* to 178; 4. *Kīḷanakhaṇḍa* to 186; 5. *Nagarapavesanakhaṇḍa* to 197; 6. *Mahāsattassa pariyesanakhaṇḍa* to 200; 7. *Micchākathā* to 205; and a final unnamed section to the end.

Section 5 starts with Somadatta demanding the jewel from Ālamba; he does not catch it when it is thrown, however, so it disappears back into the *nāga* realm, and Somadatta loses everything. With the charm, Ālamba the snake charmer cruelly captures the Bodhisatta, who nonetheless keeps his resolve on non-harm.

In Section 6, the Bodhisatta's mother and wives realize a month later that he has been captured and send the other three sons to find him: Sudassana, dressed as an ascetic, goes to search the human realm, accompanied by his half-sister, disguised as a frog, in his hair. He reaches Vārāṇasī as the Bodhisatta is being made to dance, and he and his sister rout Ālamba by terrifying tricks; the Bodhisatta is released.

Section 7 describes the Bodhisatta, ill after his ordeal. He is given a doorman, Ariṭṭha, who is fearsome enough to prevent too many visitors. One brother, Subhaga, finds and brings back Somadatta, who was in the river trying to wash away his guilt over his betrayal.

In section 8, they are met in the *nāga* realm by Ariṭṭḥa, who defends brahminical practices, such as the sacrifice, saying that is why brahmins, and so Somadatta, should not be harmed. The Bodhisatta rises from his sickbed to make an impassioned critique of the deceits and trickeries of the brahmins, who use them for harmful sacrifices. Somadatta is sent away, while *nāgas* and humans meet joyfully, before going their separate ways.

Despite the large cast of varied characters and apparent diversity of the various plot strands, the use of trickery, deception, and illusion in relation to intention (*cetanā*), underlies and propels the plot and unifies this exploration of the practice of moral virtue. In this world of shape-shifting, illusions, and magic, intention that is not pure or is influenced by desire for personal gain, is, in the end, unsuccessful. Trickery to gain one's ends is not conveyed as wrong: the *nāga* girl wants a husband and the tortoise wants his freedom. Both these straightforward wishes are granted, in both cases by trickery based on a resourcefulness that is reminiscent of the lighthearted ingenuity of so many earlier *jātakas* in the collection and in the *Mahosadha-jātaka.* The magical deceptions the *nāgas* play on Samuddajā, a human princess who unknowingly marries a *nāga*, are based on a wish for her happy acquiescence: they also meet with success, as she does not see through them until she has had four sons. One of her sons also resorts to bluff and trickery by enlisting the king on his side and outfacing the brahmin. Even the *garuḷa* bird, who does not at first confess that he has uprooted the ascetic's tree, is reassured that he had no harmful volition in what he was doing, a crucial feature of the practice of *sīla* that makes this apparent excursion into another narrative important to the overall presentation of that perfection in the tale.

But where trickery is based on greed for money or personal gain in this magical world, it encounters its just deserts. So the brahmin Somadatta, who is understandably homesick in the *nāga* realm, needs to resort to stratagem to extricate himself; this intent finds more than ample reward when he is offered the wish-fulfilling gem, which he refuses. After being browbeaten by his wife—a brahminic wife of a type we see later in the *Vessantara-jātaka*—he decides he does want it, and barters for it with Ālamba, another brahmin. Here, motivated by excessive greed and acting ungratefully to a host by betraying a friendly *nāga*, he cannot catch the elusive wish-fulfilling gem that had once been his for the taking, and he loses his son as well as the gem. Magical jewels are too elusive to be caught in the air by the unskilful; such a precious jewel slips out of Kevaṭṭa's grasp, because of his base and self-serving motives, in the *Mahosadha-jātaka* too (Chapter 5 000).[4] Deception also goes badly for the snake charmer, who has used his skills improperly and then loses the battle with Sudassana.

In line with several other tales of the Great Ten, it is the great malevolent deceptions of brahmins, however, that lead to the climax of the tale, when the Bodhisatta passionately repudiates their practices, which are grounded, he says, on their lies and cruel exploitation of other beings.[5] We have already seen three brahmins, Ālamba, Somadatta, and his wife, behaving for base motives. Here, the Bodhisatta embarks on a generalised, impassioned attack on the caste and the tenets of its hegemony: their use of sacrifice, which harms and deceives other beings, and what he regards as their ridiculous pretences about the universe and future rebirths. The brahmins are deluded, and importantly, they use deception to break *sīla* and bring ruin and harm other beings too. The deceptions of the early part of the tale are only a preparation: their lies and subterfuges are presented as the most corrupt of all the layers of the make-believe, dishonesty, and intrigue that characterise the behaviour of so many beings in this tale, and when the Bodhisatta has finished his rebuttal, his prowess in argument as well as his practice of *sīla* is vindicated to his fellow *nāgas*.

4. Both the hunter in this lifetime, and Kevaṭṭa in the *Mahosadha-jātaka* (Chapter 5), are earlier births of Devadatta.

5. For discussion of this, see Alsdorf 1957.

These complex layers of apparently disparate plots, together with beings who interact with varied degrees of truthfulness and honour, make this the most mobile of all the Great Ten in terms of free movement between realms and conditions of existence. King Nemi acts only as a kind of tourist when he visits the other realms: while he interacts in the Heaven of the Thirty-Three, his role is primarily that of a viewer and commentator, and he does not have interchange with the beings he encounters on his tours of the hells and the heavens. In the *Nārada-jātaka*, the intervention of the Bodhisatta in the plot, as Lord Brahmā, a *deus ex machina*, introduces the perspective of the meditative heavens to the unfortunate circumstances in the human realm below. In this story, however, the Bodhisatta, while born as a *nāga*, is protected by his virtue and his wisdom, and visits and converses in all three realms. He shows himself in a good light in the Heaven of the Thirty-Three, and acquits himself with bravery, wisdom, and honour in the realm of the humans, giving *dhamma* teaching when released from bondage as well as doing so in the *nāga* sphere. Creatures in animal form feature also in this tale, moving the plot in ways that are less apparent in others of the Great Ten, apart from the interventions of the wild animals in the *Vessantara,* or, in the *Mahosadha*, the flirting parrot and mynah-bird. Here a clever tortoise sets the whole complicated story in motion; the *nāga* princess disguised as a frog gives the venom that terrifies the brahmin Ālamba into freeing the Bodhisatta. But it is the Bodhisatta who shows himself the master in all realms. Amongst the *nāga*s, he exhibits pre-eminent loyalty to his parents in his frequent visits to his mother and skill in debate and leadership. This tale is attributed to *sīla*, but here it is a moral code that shows him an equal in all his interactions, responding with wisdom even amongst the kings of humans and gods. In the search for the perfections, the vitality of the *nāga* existence provides a rich background of the world of magic, transformation, and the different kinds of intention that govern the use of these and other powers and skills. It is fitting that one of the Great Ten involves this richly fluid and colourfully powerful, if lower, existence.

Metre

The metre of this story has excited some comment, as it raises interesting issues about the dating of various levels of the text.[6] Many of the verses,

6. Thomas Oberlies (2002) has also made study of some related issues in the *Campeyya-jātaka*.

primarily those involving the praise and the denunciation of the brahmins and their practices, towards the end of the story, are in the eleven- or twelve-syllable *tuṭṭubha* (*triṣṭubh*) metre, often found in the *Ṛg Veda*. The use of such an ancient metrical form could be suggestive of older levels of the text (vv. 14, 15, 113–17, 123–84). The rest of the verses, primarily those that narrate the story up to the debate between Ariṭṭha and the Bodhisatta, and the concluding verses that describe the arrival of the Bodhisatta at the end, are in the classic sixteen-syllable *vatta* form so common in Pāli and indeed *jātaka* texts. It has been argued that the verses in the archaic metre represent an older level of the text than the other ones. This raises difficult issues: the verses in the ancient metre may have been composed for their rhetorical associations, with a deliberate usage of an older form and more archaic language. Just as Victorian British poets tended to like archaic language to evoke a specific response, it is possible that a comparable method was used by early Pāli composers. So in the *Bhūridatta-jātaka* we do not have to infer that an archaic form of language and metre automatically indicate an earlier composition date. The apparently older verses also do not make any kind of story as they stand; there must have always been a strong prose content associated with the tale if they were the earliest level of the story. Taken as a whole they certainly do not propel the action in the way the verses do in other long *jātaka*s, and lack any narrative content. They do include mention of Ariṭṭha, addressed in the vocative, so given the way this address is embedded in the metre, it seems likely that they are part of the original story and were formulated for it, though in this regard they perhaps need not be earlier than other verse sections. But this is all conjecture; the subject has been extensively explored by K. R. Norman (1991: 82–3), who argues that an earlier version can be restored from the metre.[7]

*Nāga*s in Southern Buddhism

As mythical underwater creatures who guard treasure and have special powers but who inhabit a realm considered less literally upright than the human, *nāga*s feature frequently in Pāli texts, Southern Buddhist folklore, and ritual practice. The monastic ordination ceremony still requires that the candidate acknowledges that he is not a *nāga* but is indeed a

7. For an extensive study of the repudiation of brahmins in passages in the older metres, see Alsdorf 1957.

full human being.[8] Epigraphic and archaeological evidence indicate *nāga* worship in early Indian shrines, suggesting some early accommodation of earlier snake cults into Buddhist practice.[9] In Burmese regions, *nāgas* feature prominently, particularly in a protective association. They are shown throughout the central temple of Mindon in this role (Stadtner 2011: 258). An early Mon chronicle, known only in a Burmese translation, describes the Buddha visiting Thaton, in Southern Myanmar, and then going to Singuttara Hill in Yangon, where he says he gives eight of his hairs as relics: 'The snake king Gavanna hid two of the hairs . . . and built a pagoda in the land of the *nāgas*.'[10] The *arahat* Upagutta, protector from floods, is shown with *nāgas* in attendance, and there are floating shrines to him on Burmese riversides. Throughout coastal regions of Myanmar, local stories abound of *nāga* princesses marrying humans to produce lines of human kings, a feature anticipated and very likely suggested by the *Bhūridatta-jātaka*. In Thailand, *nāga* protection is considered to promote a plentiful and well-regulated rainfall, needed for rice-growing areas, as well aiding and protecting against untimely or excessive floods. The 'merit of (firing) rockets' (*bun bang fai*) festival involves an extensive mythology of *nāgas* (see Tambiah 1970: 285–311); here they are regarded as symbols of fertility and the powers of nature, ensuring an abundance of rice and good health. Indeed in early Pāli texts their key role as protector is emphasized: they meet happily with their traditional enemies the *garuḷas*, as they do after the enlightenment (Ja I 70), in order to praise the Buddha in the *Mahāsamaya Sutta* (DN 20, PTS edn II 253–62), a *paritta* text that is considered particularly restorative and auspicious to this day in Southeast Asia.[11] The *nāgas* are under a king also called Dhataraṭṭha (Whose Empire is Firm), the name also given to one of the Four Great Kings that protect the four directions: he rules the East.[12] His entourage is supposedly made up of the descendants of the union of Samuddajā and King Dhataraṭṭha in

8. See Gombrich 1996: 72 ff.

9. See Hartel 1993: 426–7.

10. For discussion of this and quote see Stadtner 2011: 81.

11. It was chanted, for instance, in a 2007 ceremony organized by Achan Maha Laow in Phuket, Thailand, after work was undertaken to rebuild after the tsunami, to restore the equilibrium of the area and the spirits and people around.

12. It may not be the same character as in this story: see DPPN. Varied forms of this figure are frequent in Indian literature: Dhṛtarāṣṭra appears in the *Mahābharata*, the *Bhagavadgītā*, and the *Sanatsujatiya*.

this *jātaka*, a feature that sets the chronology of the *Bhūridatta* in the distant past of the Bodhisatta path,[13] and demonstrates the intertextuality and knittedness in the depiction of canonical mythical beings. In this protective capacity, this king of the Eastern direction, and *nāgas*, also pay homage to the Buddha in another great and still widely chanted *paritta* text, the *Āṭānāṭiyā Sutta* (DN 32, PTS edn III 194–206), used in extreme situations to dispel fear and bad spirits. Both the *Mahāsamaya Sutta* and the *Āṭānāṭiyā Sutta*, with specific variations in chanted style, are considered amongst the most auspicious and powerful of the monastic chanted repertoire in Southeast Asia today. They are usually chanted in all-night *Mahāparitta* festivals, where a selection of monks expressly trained in these texts chant within a specially constructed *maṇḍapa*, or temporary decorated canopy, to bring blessings and protection to the assembly and beings around. This prominence gives testimony to the role *nāgas* still play in Southern Buddhist ritual and practice.

The name Bhūridatta was the monastic choice of the great forest monk Achan Mun (1870–1949), whose austere practices, extended treks through often harsh terrain, sleeping out in the open, and *dhūtaṅga* practices, along with encounters with beings such as *nāgas*, are described in his biography.[14] Of Laotian descent, he grew up in the village of Ban Khambong, in Khong Chiam District, Ubon Ratchatani, in north-eastern Thailand. Here, *jātakas* were still the lifeblood of Buddhist teaching at the end of the nineteenth century, according to the disgusted reports of a rationalist reforming mission sent in 1898–1900, which complained that *jātakas* comprised most of the teaching given in such rural settlements (See Tiyavanich 1997: 30). Road and river connections were very poor, so royal wariness about *jātakas* as not truly Buddhist, and the downplaying of their role in Buddhism advised by the monastic administration in Bangkok, had little impact on this then-remote region. Achan Mun does not seem to have followed a

13. This is also suggested by the fact that the *garuḷa* bird has not yet found out how to catch *nāgas*, knowledge they gain in the *Paṇḍara-jātaka* (J 518). In this story an ascetic finds out from *nāgas* that the secret of their strength against *garuḷas* is that they swallow large stones, so that they are too heavy to carry. Caught by the tail, the stones would fall out and their capture would be easy. The birds find this out and capture the *nāga* king, who is told not to give his secrets away again, and is set free.

14. *Dhūtaṅga* (Thai *thudong*) practices are ascetic practices sanctioned by the Buddha for monks who wish to follow them. They include wearing rags, sleeping out in the open and staying in forests, often under trees.

Bodhisatta path, according to his biography, rather that of the teaching *arahat*. But he does seem to have maintained a special affinity with *nāgas*, always attempting to propitiate the beings he believed inhabited the lonely caves and rivers where he liked to stay on his travels and walks. One such *nāga*, of a bad-tempered disposition, apparently required considerable discussion on Buddhist subjects and a searching examination of his own angry nature before he was able to tolerate the presence of a human being in his cave. Despite winning this recalcitrant host over, Achan Mun thought in the end the *nāga* could receive little teaching in this lifetime, and decided to move on (Nyanasampanno 1976: 184–7).

Myths around the world have given special status to the serpent or the snake also as exemplifying not only some principle at the base of human existence, but freedom within existence too, as in the Western *ourobouros* serpent who eats his tail, or the Chinese dragon. In this connection a curious and enigmatic *sutta* in the *Majjhimanikāya*, the *Vammika Sutta* (MN 23) seems apt. Here, in an unusually symbolic approach for the *suttas* of that collection, the Buddha speaks of the body as a 'smoking anthill that smokes by night and flames by day' (MN I 142). He then gives images for the obstructions which need to be sliced away with a knife and thrown out: a bar, a toad, a fork, a sieve, a tortoise, a butcher's knife and block, a piece of meat. In this riddle, the bar is compared to ignorance, the toad to despair prompted by anger, the fork to doubt, the sieve to the five hindrances, the tortoise to the five aggregates fuelled by clinging, the butcher's knife and block to the five strands of sense desire (the five material senses and their objects), and the meat to lust.[15] At the end, however, the one digging finds the *nāga* serpent. 'This is a symbol for a *bhikkhu* who has destroyed the taints.' The Buddha enjoins, 'Leave the *nāga* serpent; do not harm the *nāga* serpent; honour the *nāga* serpent.'[16]

'Whatever jewel there is . . . '

1. THE SECTION ABOUT THE CITY

This story the Teacher told whilst he was staying at Sāvatthi, about lay

15. The commentary to this text says that the five sense desires are the knife, and the objects they perceive the block.

16. MN I 142–5; Ñāṇamoli and Bodhi 1995: 237–9.

followers who observe *uposatha* days. One such day, it is said, some lay followers rose early, gave *dāna*, and after the meal had been eaten they went with perfumes and garlands to the Jeta Grove; at the time for hearing the teaching they sat down to one side. The Teacher went to the *dhamma* hall, sat down in the adorned seat of the Buddha, and regarded the assembly of monks. [158] The Tathāgata liked to carry on *dhamma* talks with monks, and anyone else, concerning anyone about whom *dhamma* talk arises. On that day he knew that *dhamma* talk concerning wise men who lived in the past would come up and would be about lay followers, so as he was chatting with them he asked them: 'Lay followers, do you observe the *uposatha* days?'

'Yes, Bhante,' They replied.

'That is very good, lay followers, you have done well. But it is no great wonder that you, who have such a person as a Buddha to instruct you, keep the *uposatha* day. In days long ago wise men without a teacher abandoned great glory and observed such a day.' Saying this, at their request he told a story of long ago.

In times past in Vārāṇasī, Brahmadatta was king and made his son viceroy, but seeing his son's great glory he became suspicious that he might seize the kingdom. So he said to him, 'Please leave the kingdom and live wherever you please, and when I am gone take over the kingdom that belongs to our family.' The son agreed and, paying respects to his father, departed. In the course of time he came to the Yamunā River, built a hut from leaves between the river and the sea, and survived on roots and fruits from the forest. Now in the *nāga* world under the ocean, there was a young *nāga* woman who was single after her husband's death. She watched the happiness of others who did have husbands, and because of her defilements, left the *nāga* world and wandered by the shore of the ocean. Noticing the prince's footprints and following their trail, she came upon the hut of leaves. At that time the prince had gone to look for various kinds of fruit. She entered the hut and, seeing the mat made from twigs and the requisites left behind, thought to herself, 'This is the dwelling place of a lone recluse. I will test him out, and see if he has gone forth from faith or not. If he really has his heart in being a recluse and is intent upon renunciation, he will not like his bed being decorated by me. But if he does delight in sense pleasures and does not have his heart on being a recluse, he will lie down on my bed. Then I'll take him, make him my husband and we will live right here. So she went to the *nāga* kingdom, brought back heavenly flowers and perfumes, and prepared a bed of flowers and made an offering of flowers. She then sprinkled perfumed powders, decorated the leaf hut, and went back to the *nāga* kingdom. The prince came back in the evening and entered the leaf hut and, when he saw what she had done, thought, 'Who has decorated my bed?' [159] He ate the various fruits and thought, 'Ah! What lovely smelling flowers. And who has made my bed so charming?' Feeling delighted—for he had not become a recluse out of faith—he lay down and slept on the bed of flowers and fell asleep.

The next day he got up at sunrise and without sweeping his hut went to look for various fruits. At that moment the *nāga* maiden came back and saw the withered flowers, and knew immediately, 'He is intent on pleasure. He is not a true recluse, and so I can have him.' So she cleared out the old flowers, brought some other flowers and decorations, and prepared a new bed. Then she decorated the leaf hut, sprinkled flowers on the approach, and went back to the *nāga* kingdom. He lay down that night again on a bed of flowers and the next day thought, 'Now, who is decorating this leaf hut?' So he did not go in search of fruit but remained hidden not far from the hut. The woman, bringing strong perfumes and flowers, came along the path to the hermitage. The prince saw the great beauty of bearing of the young *nāga* woman and his heart was bound by love. Not letting himself be seen, he entered the hut as she was arranging the bed and asked her who she was.

'I am a *nāga* woman, my lord.' She replied.

'Have you got a husband or not?' he asked.

'I am a widow and have no husband; where do you live?' she answered.

'I am Prince Brahmadatta, the son of the king of Vārāṇasī; why have you abandoned the *nāga* kingdom and why do you wander around here?'

'Lord, I watched the happiness of the *nāga* women who had husbands and because of lust I became full of yearning, so I left there and wandered around searching for a husband.'

'I did not become a recluse out of conviction,' explained the prince. 'I came to live here because my father drove me away. So don't worry, I'll be your husband, and we two will live peacefully here together.'

Agreeing, she said, 'Yes'. So from that time the two lived peacefully together. She, using her own powers, made a valuable house and a valuable couch and prepared a bed. From that time he did not eat roots and fruit but only divine food. After some time, the *nāga* woman conceived and gave birth to a son, whom they named Sāgara (Ocean) Brahmadatta. [160] Then, when he was able to walk, the *nāga* woman gave birth to a daughter, and as she was born on the shore of the ocean they gave her the name Samuddajā (Ocean-born, or Marina).

Now a forester who lived in Vārāṇasī came to the spot and, when he made friendly greetings, recognised the prince and stayed there for a few days. 'Your majesty, I will tell the royal family that you are staying here,' he said, and then he went on his way back to the city. At that time the king died, and the ministers conducted the funeral for his body. On the seventh day they met together and deliberated: 'A kingdom cannot survive without a king. We do not know where the king is, or even if he is alive or dead. Let's send out a splendid carriage and bring him back.' At that moment the forester came to the city, heard the story and went into the presence of the ministers. 'I have just come from spending three or four days near the prince.' He related what had happened. The ministers heard this, paid homage to him and went there with him as a guide. They gave greetings and informed the prince of the king's death. 'Your majesty, take on your kingdom,' they said. He thought, 'I'll find out what the *nāga* lady feels about this,' and went up to her. 'My dear, my father has died, and my ministers have come to raise the royal parasol. Let's go, my dear, and we will both rule a kingdom in Vārāṇasī that extends for twelve *yojanas*. You will be foremost amongst sixteen thousand women.'

'My lord, I cannot go,' she said.

'Why is that?' he asked.

'My kind have a horrible poison and are quick to anger. We become angry at the slightest thing. The anger felt by a co-wife is dreadful: if I see or hear or look with anger at anything it is scattered like a handful of chaff. Because of this I cannot go.' So the prince asked again on the following day but then she said, 'Whichever way you look at it I will not go. But these children are not *nāga* children. They have been born with human natures. If you have any love for me, be kind to them, for they are of a watery nature and tender. They'll die if tired out by winds and heat. So have a boat dug out and fill it with water.[17] Take them so that they can play in the water and [161] when you have brought them into the city have a pool made for

17. All three MSS in the F edition, and VRI, have 'getting dug' (*khaṇāpetvā*) to create this mobile splash pool, which does seem odd. Perhaps it is dug out of some hard dead wood, and foisted on to a cart; or maybe earth is to be put in a cart and then dug into a pool.

them in its precincts; then they will not become tired.' Saying this, she bade farewell to the prince and walked around him, keeping him to her right as a gesture of respect; she then hugged her children and folded them to her breast and kissed their heads, and gave them to the prince, and, weeping and grieving, disappeared right there and returned to the *nāga* kingdom. The prince, stricken with sorrow and with tears streaming from his eyes, left the dwelling and after drying his moist eyes went up to the ministers, who anointed him there and then. 'Sire, let's go to our city.' He ordered them, 'Hollow out a boat and put it on a cart and fill it with water. Strew all sorts of flowers of various colours and perfumes onto the surface of the water. My children have a watery nature, and they will go happily while playing there.' The ministers did this. When the king came to Vārāṇasī he entered a city that was all adorned, and, surrounded by sixteen thousand dancing girls and his ministers, he sat on the great terrace and held a great drinking festival for seven days. He had a lake prepared for his children and they played there constantly.

Now one day as water was being poured into the lake a certain tortoise entered it, and, not seeing any way out it made its way to the surface of the lake. While the children were playing it emerged and popped its head out, looked at the children, and then sank back down into the water. The children had seen him and were terrified and went to their father and said, 'Daddy, a *yakkha* has scared us in the lake!' The king gave an order to his men to go and catch it, and they obeyed, putting out a net, and took the tortoise to show the king. When the children saw it they shrieked, 'Daddy, it's a demon!' The king, through his affection for his sons, was angry, and gave the order, 'Go and make a punishment for him.'

Some of them said, 'This is an enemy to the king. It should be pounded into powder with a pestle and mortar.'

Others said, 'It should be cooked three times for eating.' Some said it should be grilled on charcoal embers, and others that it should be stewed in a pot.

But one minister, who was afraid of water, suggested, 'It should be thrown into the Yamunā whirlpool: there it will perish completely; there is no punishment for him like that.'

The tortoise [162] heard his words and popping his head out said this: 'Sir, what great sin have I done that you ponder over a punishment like that! The other punishments I could endure, but this one is too terrible, please do not suggest it!'

The king heard this and commanded, 'This is the one to execute.' So they threw him into the Yamunā whirlpool.

He found a current feeding the abode of the *nāga*s and through it entered the kingdom and saw *nāga* youths, the children of the *nāga* King Dhataraṭṭha, playing there. When they saw him they said, 'Seize the slave!' He thought, 'I have escaped from the hands of the king of Vārāṇasī only to fall into the hands of such harsh *nāgas*. What trick shall I use to free myself?' Then he thought, 'Here is a trick,' and told a lie: 'Why are you, from the court of the *nāga* King Dhataraṭṭha, speaking in such a way? I am Cittacūḷa (Multicoloured Topknot) and I have come as a messenger from the court of the King of Vārāṇasī, who has sent me as he wishes to give his daughter to our king, Dhataraṭṭha. Show me to him.' They were very happy with this and took him to the king's court and informed him about this matter. The king asked him to be led in, but was angry when he saw him, saying, 'No one with such a miserable body can act as a messenger!' The tortoise heard this and said, 'But why should king's messengers be as tall as palm trees? Whether the body is small or large or without limits, the accomplishment of the job, in any given realm of existence,[18] is the only measure. Great King, many messengers belong to our king: humans do their business on dry land, birds in the sky, and I in water. I am Cittacūḷa by name, and I have reached the position of favourite amongst those around the king: do not mock me.' In this way he extolled his own virtues.

Then King Dhataraṭṭha asked, 'So, on what matter have you been sent by the king?'

'Great King, my king said this to me: "I have now made a friendship with all the kings of Jambudīpa, and I now wish to give my daughter Samuddajā in order to make friendship with the *nāga* king, Dhataraṭṭha." With these words he sent me. So, putting aside evil, you should send a company with me immediately, set a day, and then receive his daughter.'

Now the king was delighted at this and [163] paid him great honour, and sent four young *nāga* men with him. 'Go, hear what the king has to say, and set a day.' They agreed and taking the tortoise with them left the *nāga* kingdom. The tortoise saw a lotus pond between the Yamunā and Vārāṇasī, and wishing to escape by means of a skilful trick, said this: 'Sirs, *nāga* gentlemen, our king and queen and his son saw me coming out of

18. The Bd reading of *gatagataṭhāne*, suggesting 'whatever' realm, is clearer than the F *gataṭhāne*.

the water in his palace, and said, "Do get us some lotuses and some lotus stalks." So I'll get some for them. Just let me go here and if you don't see me, just go further on into the king's presence, and I'll see you there.' They agreed to this and set the tortoise free, and he hid there, so they did not see him. 'He will have gone on to the presence of the king,' they thought, and they made their way to the king in the form of young men.[19]

The king received them and asked, 'Where have you come from?'

'From the court of King Dhataraṭṭha.'

'Why?' he asked.

'O King, we are his messengers. Dhataraṭṭha has asked after your health, and he will give you whatever you desire. It was said that you would give your daughter Samuddajā as a wife.' Explaining this matter, they recited this first verse:

> 'Whatever jewel there is in the palace of King Dhataraṭṭha,
> All come to you: give us your daughter, sire.' (1)

Hearing this, the king spoke the second verse:

> 'At no time before has the marriage of one of us to *nāgas* been made.
> How could we make such an unsuitable marriage?' (2)

The youths heard him, and said, 'If you are so unwilling to contract a union with Dhataraṭṭha then why did you send a message with your servant, Cittacūḷa, the tortoise, that you would give your daughter Samuddajā to him?' [164] Since you have now treated our king with contempt, we know what we should do according to what you deserve. For we are *nāgas*.' So, threatening the king, they uttered two verses:

> 'What is your life, your throne, and your kingdom, lord of men?
> The one who has offended a *nāga* does not live long. (3)
> You, King, are just a human, without power,
> Who pour scorn on Varuṇa's own son, Yamunā, of great power.'[20] (4)

And then the king spoke two verses:

> 'I do not despise King Dhataraṭṭha, of wide fame:
> Dhataraṭṭha is the lord of many *nāgas*. (5)
> But a snake, even a powerful one, a warrior of the Videhans,
> Is not worthy to marry my daughter, the well-born Samuddajā!'[21] (6)

19. *Nāgas* are renowned for their ability to change shape at will.

20. For the suggestion that these lines could be from another poem (in Sanskrit), see J VI 85 n. 1.

21. The king seems to have forgotten his daughter's ancestry.

The young *nāga* men wished to kill him right there and then with a blast of their breath, but thought, 'Given we have been sent to fix a day for the wedding, it would not be right to kill him: let's go and tell the king all about this.' And they disappeared from the spot.

'Well, dear ones, have you brought the king's daughter?' Asked by the king, they became angry.

'Why, sire, did you order us to go here, there, and everywhere without good reason? If you want to kill us, then do it here. [165] He insults and speaks scornfully of you, and places his own daughter on high through pride of birth.' And they stirred up the king's anger, bringing up things said and unsaid. He ordered them to assemble his retinue together:

> 'Let the Kambalas and Assataras stir themselves; inform all the *nāgas*.[22]
> Let them enter Vārāṇasī, but let them not harm any one. (7)

Then the *nāga* said to him, 'And if any humans are not to be harmed, then what are we to do when we get there?'

Then, 'Well, you are going to do this; I however will do this.' And he said two verses giving explanation:

> 'In dwellings, and in pools, and in the cross roads of highways,
> In the tops of trees, let them hang stretched out in the archways of doors. (8)
> Meanwhile, I will encircle the great city with my white hood and coils,
> Bringing fear to the people of Kāsi.' (9)

And the *nāgas* did this. [166] Explaining the matter the Teacher said:

> When they heard his announcement, snakes of all kinds
> Entered Vārāṇasī and did not harm anyone. (10)
> In dwellings, and in pools, and in the cross roads of highways,
> In the tops of trees, they hung stretched out in the archways of doors.[23] (11)
> The women saw them hanging down everywhere and screamed;
> They saw the *nāgas* and their hoods, hissing again and again. (12)
> The people of Vārāṇasī became terrified and miserable;
> They stretched out their arms and cried, 'Give your daughter to their king!' (13)

Meanwhile the king, lying in his palace, heard the great wailing of the women and the citizens, and terrified of death from the threats of the

22. The commentary says the Kambalas and Assataras are *nāgas* who live at the bottom of Mount Sineru.

23. This verse is the same as verse 8, but is given an active rather than an imperative sense here.

four *nāga* youths, said three times, 'I will give my daughter Samuddajā to Dhataraṭṭha!' When they heard this all the *nāga* kings retired for the distance of a *gāvuta* and built a city there that was like the city of the gods. They remained there, and sent a special message, with a gift, saying, 'Let him send his daughter.' [167] The king received the gift and message brought to him, and sent them away, saying, 'You go, and I will send my daughter under the protection of ministers.' Then he sent for his daughter, and taking her to the upper storey of the palace, opened a window and said, 'Just look at that beautifully arranged city. They say that you are going to be the chief queen there. The city is not far, and you can come home when you feel homesick, but now you are to go there.' Then he called them to bathe her by pouring water over the head and adorning her with all kinds of jewelry, and sat her in a suitable carriage and sent her off under the protection of his ministers. The *nāga* kings came to welcome her and treated her with great honour. The ministers entered the city and entrusted her to him, and left taking great wealth with them.

They took the king's daughter into the palace and got her to lie down on an ornate divine bed, and *nāga* women all at once assumed the appearance of hunchbacks and such like and waited on her as if they were human attendants. As soon as she lay down on the divine bed she was touched by a divine touch and went straight to sleep. Dhataraṭṭha took her with the *nāga* assembly and disappeared in a moment and went down back into the *nāga* realm. When the princess woke up she saw the beautifully adorned divine bed, the palaces and suchlike made all from gold, and the lotus ponds, of the *nāga* realm, as if they were a divine city. She asked her deformed attendants, 'This city is so beautifully laid out; it is not like our city: to whom does it belong?'

'To your husband: people do not get this kind of glory with only a little merit! He has acquired very great merit indeed.'

Then Dhataraṭṭha had a drum beaten for five hundred *yojana*s around, with the proclamation, 'If anyone shows Samuddajā their snake-like form there will be a royal punishment for him!'[24] So on account of this, no one was able to assume the form of a snake in front of her. So she lived in great harmony and affection with him.

The section about the city is finished.

24. Reading *rājadaṇḍo* 'royal punishment' (Bd) rather than *rājāṇā* 'royal order' (F).

2. THE SECTION ABOUT THE *UPOSATHA*

In the course of time Dhataraṭṭha's queen gave birth to a son, and because of his pleasing appearance, they gave him the name Sudassana (Pleasing to the Eye). Then again she gave birth to a son, and they called him Datta (Gift), [168] and he was the Bodhisatta. And then she gave birth to another son, and they named him Subhaga (Good Fortune), and then she gave birth again, and this boy's name was Ariṭṭha (Unharmed).[25] And although she had given birth to the four children, she still did not realise it was a *nāga* realm. Then one day they said to Ariṭṭha, 'Your mother is a human, not a *nāga*.' Ariṭṭha said, 'I'll test her.' And one day while drinking from his mother's breast he assumed the body of a *nāga* and rubbed the back of her foot with his tail. She, seeing him in a serpentine body, was frightened and gave out a great screech, threw him to the ground, and clawed his eye with her nail, so that blood poured out from it. The king heard the racket and asked, 'Why did she scream?' Hearing what had happened with Ariṭṭha he came up, making threats, and saying, 'Seize this slave! Put him to death!' But the king's daughter, knowing his tempestuous nature, out of love for her son, said, 'Sire, I hit my son's eye—forgive me.' Because she had spoken in this way, the king did forgive and said, 'What is there to do?' So that day she knew that it was a *nāga* realm, and from that time Ariṭṭha was known as Ariṭṭha Kāṇāriṭṭha (Unharmed but One-Eyed).

The four sons reached the age of understanding. Then their father gave each one a kingdom of a hundred *yojanas*. Their renown was great, and they were each attended by sixteen thousand *nāga* girls. Now their father's kingdom was also a hundred *yojanas*, and three sons went each month to see their father and mother. But the Bodhisatta went each fortnight and discussed any question which had arisen in the *nāga* realm. And he used to go with him for an audience with King Virukkha,[26] and with him he also used to discuss any question that had arisen. Then one day King Virukkha, with an assembly of *nāgas*, went to Tidasapura, the City of the Thirty-Three Gods, and, sitting in attendance on Sakka, raised a question[27] in front of the *devas*. No one could answer it. But the Great Being, sitting in the most

25. See PED 77; the word *ariṭṭha* has mixed connotations: it can mean good or bad fortune, a spirituous liquor, the sign of the approach of death, as well as the soapberry tree, the *nimba* tree, and buttermilk (DP I 235).

26. Cowell and Rouse take this to be King Virupakkha (see their note: J VI 87 n. 1).

27. Reading *pañhaṃ* (Cks).

dignified cross-legged position, could answer it. The king of the gods paid respects to him with divine perfumes and flowers, and said, 'Datta, you are endowed with wisdom as broad as the earth. From now on you will be called Bhūridatta (Gift of the Great Wise Earth).'[28] And they gave him the name Bhūridatta.

[169] From that time he used to go for audience with Sakka, and when he saw the beautifully adorned palace of Vejayanta, graced with heavenly nymphs, and the charming good fortune of Sakka, he conceived a desire for the *deva* realm. 'What is there for me in this frog-eating state? I'll go to the *nāga* realm and live the *uposatha* way of life, and I'll make conditions for a rebirth in a heaven realm.' Thinking this, he went back to the *nāga* realm and informed his mother and father, 'Dearest ones, I am going to do the work of the *uposatha*.'[29]

'That is very good: do this, dear one, but keeping it, stay in an empty pavilion right here in the *nāga* realm, and do not go outside, for there is a great fear of *nāga*s outside.' He listened to them, saying, 'Very well,' and stayed keeping the *uposatha* right there in an empty pavilion, in the pleasure groves and parks. But then the *nāga* girls with various musical instruments surrounded him, and he thought, 'If I stay here my *uposatha* observance will never reach completion. I'll go in the ways of humans, and keep the *uposatha* there.' So, through fear of being hindered, he did not tell his mother and father but said to his wife, 'Dear one, I am going to go to the human world. There is a great banyan tree by the banks of the Yamunā. I will lie down and, folding my coils on the top of an anthill nearby, I'll make a resolve on the four-limbed *uposatha*[30] and observe the *uposatha*. When I have lain there every night, keeping the *uposatha*, each time the dawn comes up let ten *nāga* women[31] with musical instruments in their hands

28. *Bhūri* means 'earth' and so, adjectivally, 'wide, extensive abundant'. Another meaning is knowledge, understanding, and intelligence, with an acquired sense that it is as broad as the earth (PED 508, citing examples in the *Dhammasaṅgaṇī* and *Dhammapada-aṭṭhakathā*).

29. For *uposathakamma* see DP I 490. It refers either to the formal act of the *saṅgha* on the *uposatha* day, or lay observances on that day.

30. See Cowell's note, J VI 88 n. 1. It is possible that the four limbs of the *uposatha* could be related to the four limbs of the holy life (as found, for example, in MN 12, PTS edn I 77), where various degrees of asceticism are described.

31. Reading *itthiyo* with Bd.

come near me. Let them come with perfumes and flowers, paying respects, singing and dancing, to lead me right back here to the *nāga* realm.'

So, going there, he folded his coils around at the top of an anthill, and declared, 'Whoever wishes may take my skin, or sinews, or bone or blood!' And making a resolve on the four-limbed *uposatha* he assumed a body that had only a head and a tail, and used to lie there and keep the *uposatha*. And as dawn came the *nāga* girls used to come and do as they were instructed, and then they used to lead him back to the *nāga* realm. And while he kept the *uposatha* in this way, [170] a long time passed.

The section about the uposatha is finished.

3. THE SECTION ABOUT ENTERING THE FOREST

Now at that time a certain brahmin who lived in a village by the gate to Vārāṇasī went to the forest with his son, called Somadatta, and throwing out stakes, nets, and snares, killed wild animals. Carrying the meat away on a pole and selling it, he made his livelihood. One day he did not manage to get even a lizard or its young, and said, 'Somadatta, if we go empty-handed your mother will be furious. Let us go and catch at least something.' He approached the anthill where the Bodhisatta was, and seeing the tracks of a deer who went down to the Yamunā to drink, he said, 'Dear one, the path of the deer can be seen. You go back and wait. I am going to shoot with an arrow a deer who has come for a drink.' Taking his bow he stood looking out for the deer at the root of a tree. Then a deer came to drink water in the evening and he shot an arrow at it. The deer, spurred on with urgent desperation but not falling, made a getaway, streaming with blood. The father and son chased it to the place where it did fall, took its flesh and, leaving the forest, reached the banyan tree as the sun was setting. 'It is a bad time. We cannot go on. We'll stay here.' Saying this, they laid the flesh to one side and climbed the tree and lay in its branches. The brahmin woke at the time of the dawn and gave his ear attentively for the sound of deer. At that moment, the *nāga* girls came and prepared a seat of flowers for the Bodhisatta. He laid aside his snake's body and assuming a divine body, adorned with all kinds of ornament, sat on the seat of flowers with all the graceful poise of Sakka. The *nāga* girls paid respects to him with perfumes and garlands and the rest, and played their heavenly instruments and performed dances and songs. The brahmin heard the sound and said, 'Who is this? I'll find out.'

'Son!' he called; but he could not rouse his son. 'Let him sleep. He'll be tired. I'll go on myself.' Getting down from the tree he came nearby, but the *nāga* ladies saw him and, with their musical instruments, sank down to the ground and went right back to the *nāga* realm. The Bodhisatta [171] was left alone. The brahmin, standing near, questioned him and recited two verses:

'Having been brought flowers in the middle of the wood, Who is this,
red eyed and broad shouldered?[32]
And who are these ten ladies, who stand around honouring him,
In beautiful clothes, with golden bracelets? (14)
You whose arms are stretched out in the middle of the wood,
Shine like a flame in a vase of ghee.
Are you some being of great power,[33] or a *yakkha*,
Or a *nāga*, a prince of great glory?' (15)

Hearing this the Great Being thought, 'If I say I am one of the Sakkans, or the like, he will believe me, but today it is necessary for me to speak only the truth.' So he explained that he was the king of a *nāga* realm.

'I am a *nāga*, powerful and hard to overcome.
Angered, I could devastate a prosperous land with my power. (16)
Samuddajā is my mother, Dhataraṭṭha my father.
I am a younger brother of Sudassana. I'm known as Bhūridatta.' (17)

Saying this the Great Being thought, 'This brahmin is cruel and harsh; he may inform a snake charmer, and so make an obstruction to my keeping the *uposatha*. Why don't I take him to the *nāga* kingdom, treat him with great honour, and carry on keeping the *uposatha* without interruption?' Then [172] he said, 'Brahmin, I will accord you great honour. Come to my delightful *nāga* realm. Let us go!'

'My lord, I have a son; I'll go if he comes too.'

Then the Bodhisatta said, 'Go and bring him, brahmin.' And he described to him his own home:

'That deep, perpetually churning, terrible lake you look down upon:
This is my divine home, with many hundreds of attendants. (18)
Dark blue waters in the middle of the woods,

32. For some reason red eyes are considered a sign of a handsome appearance. See the end of the *Campeyya-jātaka* (Ja VI 466 and Shaw 2006a: 177). For phrase *lohitakkho vihat' antaraṃso* see PED 57.

33. For comment on *mahesakkha* see PED 527: 'possessing great power or authority' (*mahā* + *īsa* + *khyaṃ*). The commentary does not pick up on this word, but the Bodhisatta's first words in the prose section suggest that it was taken later to be a reference to the Sakkas. The Rouse/Cowell translation puts 'Sakka' in the verse.

Where there is the cry of peacocks and herons:
Enter the Yamunā and do not be afraid;
Enjoy the auspicious safety of those who keep the precepts!' (19)

The brahmin went and told his son about the matter and brought him. The Great Being took them both down to the shore of the Yamunā, and standing on the shore said:

'When you have got there, with a companion, with your son, brahmin,
You will be given great honour in my home, brahmin,
And you will live in happiness, with the pleasures of the senses.' (20)

When he had said this the Great Being through his power led the father and son into the *nāga* realm, and there was a divine state of affairs for them, and the Great Being gave them four hundred *nāga* girls each, and they enjoyed magnificent splendour. Now the Bodhisatta was diligent in keeping the *uposatha*, and going on his fortnightly visit to his mother and father he gave a talk on the *dhamma*, and then went to the brahmin to inquire about his well being and said, 'Whatever you want, tell me about; take delight and do not be stinting.' With these words he extended a friendly welcome also to Somadatta, and went to his own home. The brahmin stayed in the *nāga* realm a year, but through the laxness of his merit started to fret [173], and wished to go back to the world of humans. The *nāga* realm seemed like a hell realm to him, the decorated palace a prison, and the *nāga* girls seemed like *yakkhas*. He thought, 'I am not happy; I'll find out Somadatta's feelings.' He went to him and said, 'Are you not homesick, dear son?'

'Why should I be homesick? Let's not be unhappy. Are you fretting, dear one?'

'Yes, I am.'

'But why?' he asked.

'Through not seeing your mother and brothers. Come, Somadatta, let's go.'

He replied, 'I am not going.' But being entreated by his father again and again, he eventually agreed. The brahmin considered. 'I have won the agreement of my son, but if I let Bhūridatta know that I am discontented, he will give me more glory and I will not go. There is only one way to do it. I'll praise the splendour of this realm, and ask him, "Why do you abandon this splendour to go to the human world to keep the *uposatha*?" He'll answer, "for the sake of a heaven." And I'll let him know, saying, "You observe the *uposatha* for the sake of attaining a heaven realm. But what about us, who have made our livelihood from hunting? I am going to go to the human world to see my family and then I will take the going forth and live the *dhamma* of an ascetic." Then he'll give permission for my departure.' Thinking this, one day, when the Bodhisatta came to him and asked him whether he was unhappy, he assured him, 'There is nothing lacking here at all from you.' And without mentioning his departure, at first he just extolled his good fortune and said:

'Even is the land on every side filled with *tagara* flowers.
It looks lovely, covered with red insects, and of the richest green, (21)
With delightful woodland shrines, and calling geese,
And lakes with beautiful aspects, strewn with lotus blossoms. (22)
Wonderfully worked eight-faceted columns, decorated with all kinds of jewels:
The palace, filled with nubile girls, has a thousand columns and has been made to shimmer. (23)
[174] The pavilion that has arisen for you is filled with divine merits.
Untrammeled, auspicious delight, possessed with uninterrupted happiness. (24)
Consider this—you cannot yearn for the palace of Sakka;[34]
Your power is more abundant and brilliant even than his.' (25)

When he heard this the Great Being said, 'Do not say this, brahmin, for our splendour compared to that of Sakka is like a mustard seed next to Mount Meru: we are not worth as much even as his attendants. And he recited this verse:

'The shining power of Sakka cannot be reached, even by thought,
And his attendants, the Kings of the Four Directions.'[35] (26)

Speaking in this way, when he had heard the other saying 'This is for you the palace of King Sakka,' he said, 'I remembered that desiring the Vejayanta I keep the *uposatha*.' And he repeated this stanza, describing his great wish:

'Longing for this pavilion of those seeking for happiness, those who are undying,
I lie, always keeping the *uposatha* on the top of an anthill.' (27)

[175] Hearing this the brahmin thought, 'Now I have found my opportunity.' Filled with joy he repeated two stanzas, asking to leave:

'I also entered the forest with my son for deer,
But my relatives do not know if I am dead or alive. (28)

34. The commentary relates this to Sakka's palace, Vejayanta.
35. The commentary explains that their power is not worth even a sixteenth part of the Four Guardians.

Bhūridatta, I ask your permission to leave, glorious born from the daughter of the king of Kāsi.
With your permission, maybe we will get to see our relatives.' (29)

Then the Bodhisatta replied:

'It is my wish that you stay here with me,
For such sense pleasures are not easy to obtain in the world of men. (30)
And if you wish to dwell with me, honoured with sense pleasures, another time,
Then you have my permission to go and see your relatives in safety.' (31)

Saying these two verses he thought, 'So that he lives in happiness and does not tell anyone else, I'll give him the wish-fulfilling jewel.' And he gave it to him, saying:

'The one who possesses this divine jewel knows and finds his kin and his children.
Healthy and free from harm is he: go and take this with you, brahmin.' (32)

Then the brahmin said this verse:

'Bhūridatta I delight in this offer of yours.
But I will take the going forth as an old man, and shall not want the pleasures of the senses.' (33)

The Bodhisatta replied,

'And if you put an end to the brahma-faring life, and wish for sense pleasures,
Please don't hesitate to come and see me for more wealth.'[36] (34)

[176] The brahmin said:

'I delight in this offer of yours.
And if I need to, I will come back.' (35)

Then the Great Being, seeing that he did not desire to stay, asked some young *nāga* men to take him back to the world of men.

Explaining the matter the Teacher said:

Saying this Bhūridatta ordered four men,
'Get up and go there as quickly as possible to get the Brahmin there.' (36)
The four men heard the instruction and roused themselves,
Ordered by Bhūridatta to get the Brahmin there quickly. (37)

As they went on their way, the brahmin pointed out to his son, 'Dear

36. The commentary notes that living as a celibate is difficult, which is why the Bodhisatta reassures him about any return to the householders' life.

Somadatta, here we shot a deer, and here a pig.' And he saw the lake, 'Dear Somadatta, let us wash.'

'Very well,' he replied. And both wrapped their divine ornaments and clothes into a bundle and laid it on the banks of the lake, and bathed. At that moment the ornaments and clothes vanished and went back down to the *nāga* realm. And their earlier yellow ragged clothes came back and were wrapped around their bodies, and their bows, arrows and spears appeared again.

Somadatta lamented, 'You have ruined us, dear one!'

But his father consoled him, 'Do not think that. While there are deer in the forest we'll make a living killing them.'

Somadatta's mother heard them coming, and going to meet them, brought them food and drink. When the brahmin had eaten he went to sleep, and then she questioned her son: [177] 'Dear one, where did you go for such a long time?'

'We were taken to a magnificent *nāga* realm by the king of the *nāgas*, Bhūridatta. And there we were homesick, and now we have come home.'

'And did you bring any jewels?'

'We did not, Mother.'

'Why did he not give you any?' she asked.

'My father was given a wish-fulfilling jewel, but he did not take it.'

'Why?'

'Apparently he is going to take the going forth.'

She was furious, and said, 'After leaving me for such a long time with the responsibility of the children, he goes and lives in a *nāga* realm and now they say he is going to take the going forth!' And she struck him on the back with the spoon she used for cooking the rice and let rip at him, 'You wretched brahmin! They say you have said you are going to take the going forth; you did not bring back any jewel. Why did you not become an ascetic instead of coming here! Get out of my house, immediately!' And the brahmin replied, 'Don't fly off the handle, my dearest one; while there are deer in the forest I will take care of you, and the children too.' And the very next day he went into the forest with his son, just as before, and made his living.

The section about entering the forest is finished.

4. THE SECTION ABOUT *SĪLA*[37]

Now at that time, in a region in the Great Southern Ocean, in the Himalayas, there lived a certain *garuḷa* on a silk-cotton tree. With his wings he swept up water from the ocean and swooped down to the *nāga* realm, and seized a *nāga* king by the head. For this was a period when *garuḷas* did not know how to catch *nāgas*, but they learned how to do this in the *Paṇḍara-jātaka*.[38] When he did seize him by the head, he was not submerged by water when he picked him up, but he took him dangling and proceeded to the top of the Himalayas.[39] Now at that time a certain brahmin in the region of the Himalayas had taken the going forth as a seer, and built a leaf hut. At the end of his covered walkway there was a great banyan tree, and he used to spend the daytime at its roots. The *garuḷa* carried the *nāga* to the top of the banyan tree. The *nāga*, hanging down, wound his tail around a branch of the banyan in an attempt to get free. The *garuḷa* did not notice this, but flew up into the sky, and with his great strength pulled up the banyan tree by the roots.[40] The *garuḷa* took the *nāga* to a silk-cotton tree forest, split open its belly with his beak, ate the fat, and then threw his body into the middle of the ocean. [178] The tree roots had made a great crash as they had fallen, and the *garuḷa* wondered, 'What is that noise?' Looking down below he saw the uprooted tree, and wondered, 'Where did I get that from?' And then he remembered, 'There is a banyan tree by the ascetic's covered walkway. This tree was a great benefit for him. I wonder if an unskilful consequence is following on for me? I'll ask him and find out.' So he went near to him

37. In VRI this section is entitled the *garuḷakhaṇḍa*, and continues to Ja VI 178, so that the *kīḷanakhaṇḍa* is longer, but finishes also at Ja VI 186.

38. Intertextuality is frequent in *jātaka* commentarial prose. The *Paṇḍara-jātaka* (J 518) describes *garuḷas* finding out how to capture *nāgas*. A foolish *nāga* betrays the secret of his tribe's ability to withstand the birds: they load themselves with stones, and because they are taken by the head, the birds are weighed down when they try to pick them up, so they sink into the water and drown. But a certain *garuḷa* finds out this secret and captures a *nāga* by the tail, so that the stones come out and he can be captured. The reference to this earlier story demonstrates further that temporal sequence does not play a part in the original arrangement of the *Mahānipāta*.

39. In this and J 518 the weight of the water the *garuḷa* is carrying seems to be important, in this story in avoiding bringing him to his death, but it is not made clear how or why the water is there and what role it plays. The main point still seems to be that the *garuḷa* did manage to capture him, but even though he took him by the head rather than the tail, he managed to avoid being pulled down to the ground.

40. Reading *samūlo* 'with its roots' with Bd rather than *nimmūlo* 'without roots' (F), as the emphasis appears to be on how forceful his pull was.

disguised as a young man. At that moment the ascetic was smoothing out the ground. The *garuḷa* king paid homage to the ascetic and sat down to one side as if he did not know, and asked whose it was.

'It was the feeding ground for a certain *garuḷa*.' he replied. 'The *garuḷa* brought a *nāga* to the top of the banyan tree. The *nāga*, hanging down, wound his tail around a branch of the banyan in an attempt to get free. The *garuḷa* flew up, and with his great strength pulled up the banyan tree by the roots. This is the place where it was uprooted.'

'Then, sir, was there any unskilful behaviour in the *garuḷa*?'

'No: as he did not know this, there was no volition, and so it was not unskilful.' 'And what about the *nāga*, sir?'

'He did not take it to destroy it, so there was nothing unskilful in his behaviour either.'[41]

The *garuḷa* was pleased at what the ascetic had said. 'Sir, I am indeed that *garuḷa* king. I am very pleased with your answer to my question. Now, you live in the forest, and I know the Ālambāyana spell, a priceless spell. I am going to give this to you as a teacher's portion. Please take it.'

He replied, 'Enough of your spell! Be off with you.' But he requested him repeatedly and eventually made him agree and he gave him the spell, and explained the medicinal herbs and departed.

Now at that time in Vārāṇasī a certain impoverished brahmin took out a loan, and, being urged for payment by his creditors, thought, 'What is there for me living here? I'd better go to the forest and die.' So leaving his home, in the course of time he eventually arrived at the hermitage and pleased the ascetic by his success in his vows. The ascetic thought, 'This brahmin does a great service for me. I'll reveal to him the divine spell given to me by the *garuḷa* king.' So he said to him, 'Brahmin, I know the Ālambāyana spell. I'll give it to you, so please take it.' The brahmin replied, 'Oh no, sir, this spell is not for me.' [179] But he asked him repeatedly, and eventually, urging him again and again, he got him to agree and gave it to him, and showed him the all the necessary herbs and preparatory work for the spell.

41. This short episode importantly accords pre-eminence to the aspect of volition (*cetanā*) in keeping *sīla*, a feature crucial to this tale and other *jātaka* stories pertaining to this perfection: the *Kurudhamma-jātaka* (J 276) for instance involves a number of people who think they have not kept *sīla*, as each in some way has inadvertently caused harm. In each case the person is reassured that since the harm was not intended, no breach of *sīla* has taken place.

The brahmin thought to himself, 'I have now obtained a means of livelihood!' So he stayed a few days, and then pleaded illness, giving a false story: 'I have got bad wind.' Allowed by the ascetic to go, he asked him to forgive him, bade him farewell, and departed into the forest. Eventually he reached the shores of the Yamunā, and, chanting the spell, went on the main road.

At that moment a thousand *nāga* youths from Bhūridatta's entourage were carrying the jewel that granted all desires. They had come out of the *nāga* realm and had placed it on top of a heap of sand, and played water games in the water all night by the light of its radiance. When dawn came they put on all their ornaments and encircled the jewel, and then sat down, bringing its splendour amongst them. Now the brahmin, chanting the spell, reached that place, and, hearing it, the *nāga* youths thought that it must be a *garuḷa*. So they were terrified, and plunged into the ground and went back to the *nāga* realm, without taking the jewel. The brahmin saw the jewel, and was overjoyed. 'My spell has been very successful!' And he took the jewel and left.

Now at the same time the hunting brahmin had entered the forest to kill deer with his son, Somadatta. He saw the jewel in this man's hands and said, 'Is this not the jewel that Bhūridatta gave us?'

'Yes,' said his son, 'it is.'

'Well, I will tell him its bad properties, and so deceive him and get the jewel.'

'Dear father, you did not keep the jewel before when offered it by Bhūridatta. Now this brahmin will deceive you! Just keep silent.'

The brahmin said, 'Let it be, dear son. You will see who turns out to be the cheat: me or him.' So he went up to the one who knew the Ālambāyana spell[42] and addressed him:

'Who is holding out this auspicious jewel, of the highest water and
pleasing to the eye?
Who has come with this stone, endowed with certain characteristics,
this jewel?' (38)

[180] And then the one who knew the Ālambāyana said to him:

42. The impoverished brahmin now seems to have acquired the name of the spell whose properties he has been taught, and is termed in the text Ālambāyana, so to make it clear he is called here 'the one who knew the Ālambāyana spell', and after that 'Ālambāyana'.

'I came across this jewel today: a thousand red-eyed youths were gathered all around
And I came up and approached them, and they went away and left the jewel.' (39)

The hunter's son, wishing to deceive him about the jewel and explain its worthlessness, uttered these three verses in the hope of seizing it for himself:

'This stone is well-known, always revered, and honoured;
If it is worn well and placed down well it achieves every purpose. (40)
Treated carelessly, in the wearing of it or in the putting down of it,
Or improperly treated, it leads to destruction. (41)
But it is not possible for someone who is unskilled to bear this divine jewel.
Go, and for a hundred coins give me this jewel.' (42)

Then Ālambāyana said this verse:

'This jewel of mine is not for sale, for cattle or jewels.
The stone is endowed with all sorts of properties, but I would not sell my jewel.' (43)

[181] The brahmin said:

'If the jewel is not for sale, for cattle or jewels.
For whom is it for sale? Tell me that when I ask you.' (44)

Ālambāyana said:

'Whoever points me to the magnificent *nāga* whose power is hard to overcome,
Then I'll give him this stone that shines with its light all around.' (45)

The brahmin said:

'Who is the *garuḷa*, the best of birds, in the guise of a brahmin?
Wishing to find the *nāga*, he seeks his own food for himself.' (46)

Ālambāyana said:

'I am not a bird: I have never seen the *garuḷa;*
They know me as a brahmin, in learned texts, and a doctor specializing in curing snake poison.'[43] (47)

The brahmin said:

'What is your power? What learned speciality do you have?
On what do you rely, that you are not daunted by the snake?' (48)

He said this, explaining his power:

43. Reading *vejjo*, which signifies a physician or a doctor, with F.

'While the legendary seer Kosiya was keeping the austerities for a long time in the woods,
A *garuḷa* revealed to him knowledge about poisons. (49)
I waited respectfully, tirelessly, night and day on this one,
Who lived at the top of the mountain. (50)
Then he, for keeping the brahma-faring devotion, rewarded me:
My exalted teacher willingly revealed the divine spell to me. (51)
[182] Trusting in this spell, I do not fear snakes,
I am Ālambāyana the sage, with knowledge about the destruction of poisons!'[44] (52)

Hearing this, the hunter brahmin thought, 'This Ālambāyana is going to give this jewel to the one who shows him the *nāga*. And I'll show him Bhūridatta and take the jewel.' Then discussing it with his son, he said this verse:

'Let's get this jewel, my dear Somadatta: get smart!
Let's not be like the one who hit the auspicious bowl with a stick to please himself.'[45] (53)

Somadatta said:

'Brahmin, but this is the one who honoured you when you came to his dwelling:
How can you wish to give an injury to someone who has behaved so kindly? (54)
If you wish for wealth, then Bhūridatta will give you it.
Just go there and ask, and he will give you great wealth.' (55)

The brahmin said:

'It's best to eat the food that lies in the hand and in the bowl:
Do not Somadatta, give up this thing that is in sight.' (56)

[183] Somadatta said:

'He cooks in a Niraya hell and the earth splits up,
Or will be parched with thirst, who is a bad friend, sacrificing his goodwill. (57)
And if you wish for wealth, Bhūridatta will give it to you.
Think about it. For soon you will be experiencing back the hostility done by you.' (58)

The brahmin said:

'Through a grand sacrifice brahmins can sin and still be clean.

44. As so often in *jātaka* prose, the commentary here seems to be giving instructions to a narrator of the story: 'the matter is to be told in full by expanding this.'
45. Cowell and Rouse (J VI 96 n. 1) note that this story is in the *Hitopadeṣa* (IV, story 8).

Let's make a grand sacrifice, and we'll be free from evil.'[46] (59)

Somadatta said:

'Now I just cannot stay with you any longer.
I will not go one step on the way of your dirty work.' (60)

With these words, the wise youth could not accept his father's words, and exclaimed in a loud voice that let all the *devas* around know, 'I'll not come with you in your evildoing!' As his father watched he fled and entered the Himalayas, and took the going forth. He attained the higher knowledges and lived in undiminished meditative attainment, and then was reborn in the Brahmā realm.

The Teacher, explaining the matter, said:

Saying this the learned Somadatta addressed his father,
Startled the local spirits, and went on his way. (61)

The hunter brahmin thought, 'Where will Somadatta go, except to his own home?' When he saw that Ālambāyana was concerned [184], he said, 'Do not worry, Ālambāyana, I'll show you Bhūridatta.' Taking him he went to the place where the *nāga* king kept the *uposatha*, and he saw the *nāga* king lying there bending his coils around the top of the anthill. Standing nearby he stretched out his hand and said these two verses:

'Seize this great *nāga*, and take this jewel,
Which shines auspiciously with a bright red light, the colour
of insects. (62)
His body is seen like a heap of cotton from a cotton tree;[47]
He lies on the anthill, now, brahmin, you seize him.' (63)

The Great Being, opening his eyes, saw the hunter and thought, 'This could be an obstruction to me keeping the *uposatha*. I led him into the *nāga* realm and set him up in great magnificence. He did not wish to take the jewel that I wanted to give him. But now he has come here with a snake charmer. If I get angry with him for his lack of friendship then there would be a breach of the precepts for me. I made a resolve at first on keeping the *uposatha*, with all its four limbs. This must remain as it is. So even if Ālambāyana cuts me, or cooks me, or puts me on a spit, I must not get in any way angry with him. Then he thought, 'But even if I look at him the *uposatha* would be broken for me.' So he shut his eyes and put his perfection

46. An anti-brahminical element is never far from early Buddhist depictions of this caste following their usual practices.

47. *Kappāsapicurāsi* 'heap of cotton from a cotton tree'.

of resolve (*adhiṭṭhāna*) before everything else.[48] Placing his head in his coils, he lay there completely motionless.

The section about *sīla* is finished.

5. THE SECTION ABOUT THE PERFORMANCE

Now the hunter brahmin spoke. 'Sir Ālambayana, take this *nāga*, and give me the jewel.' Ālambāyana saw the *nāga* and was delighted. Not grasping on to the jewel at all, he tossed it into his hand, saying, 'Here, catch, brahmin!' But as soon as it dropped out of his hand it went on the ground, and then entered into the earth and went right back to the *nāga* realm. And so the brahmin was deprived of three things:[49] the jewel, Bhūridatta's friendship, and his son. 'I have lost everything through not listening to my son's advice!' he wailed, and then went home.

Now Ālambāyana [185] anointed his body with divine herbs, and eating a little too, keeping it in his body, he muttered the divine spell and approached the Bodhisatta. Then he seized him by the tail, dragged his head and forcing his mouth open, spat the herb that he had been keeping in his own mouth into it. The pure-natured *nāga* king did not become angry, through fear of breaking the precepts, and although he opened his eyes did not open them completely.[50] Then Ālambāyana performed the herb spell and, seizing his tail, keeping his head down, forced him to leave the place where he had been. He then dragged him along, made him vomit and laid him out stretched full length on the ground. He pummelled him with his hands like a bolster, and his bones were as if they had been ground to pieces. Then seizing his tail again he hit him as if he were beating cloth. But the Great Being, despite such suffering, still betrayed no anger.

The Teacher explained the matter in this way:

48. This is an interesting comment, perhaps dating from a different period from the *Jātaka-nidāna*, which associates the story with *sīla*, as indeed has the tradition for as long as we have records. The association with resolve has not been made by Southeast Asian Buddhists (see Introduction 5, Table 2). The words *purecārika katvā* mean 'putting before everything else' (see PED 470).

49. This is a classic *jātaka* method of summarizing an important event: see for instance Sāma's revival, where the miraculous things that happened as he is revived are also made into a short numerical list (see Chapter 3: 141).

50. As Cowell notes, this must be through fear that his glance would harm the man. The *nāga* lady who is mentioned at the beginning of the story had comparable compunctions about the potentially harmful effect of her power.

Murmuring, with divine herbs and spells,
Still he could not overpower him, after chanting his spell.[51] (64)

Then, having rendered the Great Being helpless, he prepared a basket of creepers and tossed him into it. But the vast body would not fit into it, so he kicked him with his heels and pushed him in. Then he took the basket to a certain town, and putting it down in the middle of the town, gave out a great cry. 'Let anyone come who wants to see the dance of a *nāga*!' All of the inhabitants of the town gathered together, and at that moment, Ālambāna[52] gave the order, 'Get out, big *nāga*!' The Great Being thought to himself, 'It is best if I satisfy the public today. Then Ālambāna will get plenty of money and be pleased and set me free. So whatever he wants me to do, I'll do it.' And then he left the basket. 'Become big!' said Ālambāna, and he became big. 'Become small!' And he told him to become flat, one hooded, two hooded, three hooded, four hooded, five, six, seven, eight, nine, ten, twenty, thirty, forty, and fifty hooded, hundred hooded, to become high or low, visible or invisible, blue, yellow, red, white, or crimson, or to emit flames, or water and smoke. He transformed his body into these various forms [186] just as he was ordered, and demonstrated his dance. Seeing him, no one could keep back their tears, and people gave gold and silver, clothes and ornaments and the like. In that village alone he made a hundred thousand coins.

When he had captured the Great Being, Ālambāna had thought, 'I'll set him free when he has made me a thousand pieces.' But he had made such a windfall that he thought again. 'I can make this much wealth in this village. How much more I could make in a city?' So through greed for money he did not set him free, and, after settling his household there, he made a basket covered in jewels, threw the Great Being into it and got into a splendid carriage, with a large retinue, and left for all different kinds of towns and villages, making him perform, until he reached Vārāṇasī. He gave the *nāga* king honey and puffed rice and killed frogs for him, but he did not take the

51. It seems that here the infinitive *saṭṭhuṃ* must mean 'to overpower', as has been suggested, rather than 'to loose' as Rhys Davids prefers (see PED 671 for discussion of this passage and the use of *saṭṭhuṃ*). This still poses problems. An alternative would be to say 'Still he could not overpower him, as he [the Bodhisatta] had made a protection for himself', though this would mean a new subject for the subsidiary clause, and there is no indication that this is the case. The commentary equates the word with *gaṇhitum* 'to take', which perhaps supports 'to overpower' as a translation for *saṭṭhuṃ*.

52. For unclear reasons the text from this point onward makes his name Ālambāna.

food, for fear of not being released from his captivity. Even so, Ālambāna made him perform at the four villages at the gates of the city, where he stayed a month. Then, on the full moon day he thought, 'Today I'll have it announced to the king that I will get him to perform for him.' And the king had a kettle drum beaten and called together the citizens, and prepared couch upon couch in the royal courtyard.

The section about the performance is finished.

6. THE SECTION ABOUT ENTERING THE CITY

Now on the very day that the Bodhisatta was seized by Ālambāna, his mother had a dream that a black man with red eyes had cut off her arm with a sword and was carrying it away, streaming with blood. She was terrified and got up and rubbed her arm and realised it was a dream. But she thought, 'I have had the most terrible nightmare. There must be some danger lying in wait for my four sons, or for King Dhataraṭṭha, or for myself.' She worried in particular about the Great Being: 'The rest are all living in the *nāga* realm. But he has gone to the human realm intent on moral restraint. I wonder if some snake charmer or *garuḷa* might have seized him?' And then after another fortnight [187] she became increasingly worried. 'My son cannot let a fortnight pass without visiting me. Something terrible must have happened to him.' And she was very unhappy. After a month had passed there was no time when tears were not flowing from her eyes in her terrible grief. 'He'll come now, he'll come now!' And she sat watching by the only way he would come. Then, after a month away, her eldest son Sudassana came to see his mother with a great retinue. He left his followers outside and went up into the palace, paid respects to his mother and stood to one side. She was grieving and said nothing to him. He thought, 'My mother always used to give me a big welcome in the past, but today she is in great distress. What is the reason?' And asking her he said this:

> 'You see me rich in all pleasures of the senses and power,
> But your faculties are not delighted, and your face has gone dark. (65)
> Just as a lotus which has been crushed by the hand,
> Seeing me your face has become so dark.' (66)

Even though he had spoken in this way, she still did not speak. Sudassana thought, 'Perhaps she has been abused or treated with contempt by someone?' And then asking her he spoke another verse:

> 'Has someone abused you? Is there not some painful feeling in you?
> Even when you see me arrive, your face has gone dark!' (67)

She, replying to him, explained:

'Dear one, I had a dream a month ago. [188] A man cut off my right arm,
Smeared with blood, and left, with me weeping. (68)
Know this dream I saw, Sudassana, and since that time,
Neither by day nor by night has there been any peace for me.' (69)

When she had spoken, she added, 'Dear one, my beloved younger son has not been seen. Something terrible must have happened to him.' And she lamented:

'He whom the young girls, who take on beautiful forms, covered in golden netting,
Used to wait on before—Bhūridatta—has not been seen! (70)
He whom young soldiers, like full-blown *kaṇikāra* flowers, who bear the most excellent swords,
Used to wait on before—Bhūridatta—has not been seen! (71)
But now I'll go to Bhūridatta's dwelling place,
Let us go and see your brother, who fulfils his precepts, firm in the *dhamma*.' (72)

And when she had said this, she set out with his entourage as well as her own. And Bhūridatta's wives, not seeing him on top of the anthill, had not been worried, thinking, 'He'll be in his mother's house.' But when they heard people say that she was coming, grief-stricken because she had not seen her son, they went to meet her and lamented, 'Lady, we have not seen your son for a month today!' And they fell at her feet, also deeply distressed.

The Teacher, explaining the matter, said:

The women saw Bhūridatta's mother coming near,
And stretching out their arms they went forward. (73)
'Lady, we do not know where your son has been in this month that has passed,
And whether the renowned Bhūridatta is alive or dead.' (74)

[189] Bhūridatta's mother joined in the grieving with her daughters-in-law in the middle of the road, and went up with them to the palace and looked at her son's bed, and poured out her grief:

'Like a bird whose chicks have been killed, who sees an empty nest,
Not seeing Bhūridatta for a long time, I burn with grief. (75)
Like a bird whose chicks have been killed, who sees an empty nest,
I run out, hither and thither, not seeing my dearest son. (76)
Like a female osprey whose young have been killed, who sees an empty nest,
Not seeing Bhūridatta for a long time, I burn with grief. (77)

Like a female *cakra* bird[53] in a pond without water,
Not seeing Bhūridatta for a long time, I burn with grief. (78)
Just as a smith's firebrand burns, wherever it is outside,
In this way I burn with grief, not seeing Bhūridatta.' (79)

As Bhūridatta's mother lamented, Bhūridatta's house was filled with a single noise, like the depths of the ocean, and no one could be unmoved, and the entire house was like a *sāl* forest struck by the storm of the end of the world.[54]

Explaining the matter the Teacher said:

Like *sāl* trees hurled and crushed by the wind,
Children and wives lie prostrate in the home of Bhūridatta. (80)

The brothers Ariṭṭha and Subhaga, who had come to pay attendance to their mother and father, heard the noise and entered Bhūridatta's home, and tried to comfort their mother.

Explaining the matter the Teacher said;

Hearing these deep laments in Bhūridatta's home,
Ariṭṭha and Subhaga hurried inside. (81)
'Do not grieve, dear mother, this is how it is with all living beings: they die and come into being; these are the changes of the world.'[55] (82)

[190] Samuddajā said:

'I know this, dear ones. All living beings are of such a nature,
But not seeing Bhūridatta I am overcome with grief. (83)
Today and this very night for me—know this, Sudassana—
I think I will take my life.' (84)

The sons said:

'Do not grieve—we'll bring our brother!
We'll go, wandering from district to district, searching for him. (85)
In mountains, difficult terrains,[56] in towns, and villages.
Within ten nights, you'll see our brother return.' (86)

Then Sudassana thought, 'If we three go just to one area it will be bad; it is better for the three to go to different places. So one can go to the *deva* world, one to the Himalayas, and one to the world of humans. But if Kāṇāriṭṭha goes to the world of men he will set that village or town on

53. See DP II 92, where Cone suggests the ruddy sheldrake could be meant.
54. PED 556. This is the storm that brings about the end of a single world system.
55. The commentary suggests that *assa* refers to *lokassa* 'of the world' in this verse.
56. For this translation of *giridugga* see DP II 51.

fire where he should chance to see Bhūridatta, for he has a harsh nature. It would not be good to send him.' So, thinking this, he said, 'Dear Ariṭṭha, you go to the world of *devas*, and if the Bodhisatta has been taken to the *deva* world by the gods so they can hear the *dhamma* from him, then bring him back from there.' And Ariṭṭha went to the *deva* world. But he said to Subhaga, 'You, dear one, go to the Himalayas and search for Bhūridatta in the five great rivers, and if you find him bring him back.' And he left for the Himalayas. But as he was resolving to go himself to the world of men he thought, 'If I go in the guise of a young man, men will withdraw from me. It is better to go in the guise of an ascetic, for those who go forth are dear to humans.' And he assumed the form of an ascetic, bade farewell to his mother, and left.

But the Bodhisatta also had a sister from a different mother, called Accimukhī (One whose Face is like a Ray of Light). And she held the Bodhisatta in her deepest affection. She saw Sudassana going and said [191], 'Brother, I am profoundly distressed. I'll go with you.'

He replied, 'Dear sister, you cannot come. I am going in the guise of an ascetic.'

So she said, 'And I'll be a little frog, and I'll go by lying in your matted hair!'

'Oh, alright, come then,' he agreed, and she turned into a young frog and lay down in his matted hair. Sudassana thought, 'I'll go looking for him from where he started.'[57] So he asked the Bodhisatta's wife where the place was that he kept the *uposatha* and went there first. He saw the blood on the spot where the Bodhisatta had been taken by Ālambāna and the place where he had made the basket from creepers, and realised that Bhūridatta had been taken by a snake charmer. Filled with grief, and with tears pouring from his eyes, he followed the route that Ālambāna had taken. At the first village where he had performed his dance, he asked people, 'Has such-and-such a snake been made to perform dances here by a snake charmer?'

'Yes, he was made to perform here about a month ago, by Ālambāna.'

'What did he earn?'

'He earned about a hundred thousand coins just here.'

'Now where has he gone?'

57. The word is *mūlato*, literally 'from the root'.

'To such-and-such a town,' they replied. So from there he asked along the way and eventually arrived at the royal gate.

At that moment, Ālambāna had arrived there, freshly bathed and anointed, having decked himself up in fine cloth. He had the jewelled basket brought along right by the king's gate. A crowd of people gathered, a seat laid out for the king, and standing inside the palace, he announced, 'I am coming! Let the command be given for the king of the *nāgas* to perform!' He gave the order. Ālambāna had the multicoloured jewelled basket set down on a coloured rug and opened it. 'Come, *nāga* king!' he said. He gave the sign, and at the same time as Sudassana was standing in the assembly, the Great Being put his head out and looked over the assembly. Now *nāgas* look over assemblies for two reasons: either on the lookout for the danger of *supaṇṇas*,[58] or to see relatives. Seeing *supaṇṇas* they are frightened and do not dance; seeing relatives, they feel shame. But the Great Being, looking out, saw his brother in the crowd. Keeping down the tears that filled his eyes, he crept out of the basket and went in front of his brother. People saw him and, frightened, stepped out of the way, so Sudassana stood alone. He went up to him and placing his head on the back of his foot, he wept, and Sudassana also wept, and the Great Being, still weeping, returned and slithered back into his basket. Ālambāna thought, 'This ascetic will have been bitten by this *nāga*, I will reassure him.' Approaching him, he said:

> [192] 'The snake slipped from my hand and has fallen on your feet badly.
> Has it bitten you, sir? Do not be frightened; it does not have a harmful
> nature.' (87)

Sudassana, wishing to speak with him, said:

> 'This *nāga* does not have enough power to bring bodily suffering to me.
> You'll not find a snake charmer better than me.' (88)

Ālambāna, not knowing who he was, was furious:

> 'Who is this who comes to the assembly in the guise of an ascetic?
> Let them challenge a good fight! Let the assembly hear me.' (89)

Then Sudassana addressed him:

> 'Your support will be the snake; mine a young frog.
> Let there be a display of power, with five thousand coins as
> guarantee.'[59] (90)

58. *Supaṇṇas* are the same as *garuḷas*, or *garuda* birds.
59. The commentary says this refers to a gambler's stake.

Ālambāna replied:

'I am rich, with plenty of money; you are just an impoverished youth.
Who is your sponsor for this? What would be your guarantee?[60] (91)
Such a one as me will be the sponsor of my guarantee!
It would be a great thing to marvel at[61] for us, with five thousand coins there.' (92)

[193] Sudassana heard this from him, and said, 'Then let there be something to marvel at, with five thousand coins!' Unafraid, he went up into the king's palace and, standing in the presence of his father-in-law spoke the following verse:

'Listen to what I have to say, Great King, and may there be good fortune for you.
Will you be the sponsor in my name for me, with five thousand coins?' (93)

The king thought, 'This ascetic asks me for a great deal of money! What is this?' and spoke this verse:

'Is this some debt of your father's, or is it one you have incurred yourself?
Why do you ask me for so much in this way, brahmin?' (94)

When he had spoken in this way, Sudassana said two verses:

'Ālambāna wishes to overcome me with a snake;
But I will sting the brahmin with a young frog! (95)
You, Great King, the strengthener of your kingdom,
Attended by a crowd of warriors: come out today to see this.' (96)

The king decided to go, and left with the ascetic. When Ālambāna saw this he thought, 'This ascetic has come and brought the king: the king must be a member of his family.' Frightened, he started to follow him, saying this verse:

'Young man, I do not want to humiliate you by speaking of your skill,
You dishonour the snake, with your skill, and do not pay him respects.' (97)

[194] At that Sudassana spoke two verses:

'I do not want to humiliate you either by speaking of your skill:

60. This is unclear. The Pali reads, *ko nu te pāṭibhog'atthi, upajūtañ ca kiṃ siyā*, and, in the next verse: *Upajūtañ ca me assa pāṭibhogo ca tādiso*. PED 450 says the word *pāṭibhogo* is uncertain, and perhaps a gerund formation; *prati-bhogya* is something 'counter-enjoyable' or 'one who has to be made use of in the place of someone else'. The idea of substitution seems to be there. Cowell translates it as 'stake'. Geiger 1943: 73 translates it as 'surety'.

61. *Abbhutaṃ* usually means 'miracle', or a spectacular display of psychic power.

But you are practising a big deceit on people with a *nāga* who is
harmless. (98)
If people knew about this, as I know it, Ālamba, you would not get
A fistful of barley meal, so where does the wealth come from?' (99)

Ālambāna was enraged at this and said:

'You dirty, rough clothed ascetic, you come to this assembly
And cast aspersions on the snake in this way saying, "It's harmless!" (100)
Just come and find out for yourself the full power of the snake,
And think about it: it will quickly make you into a heap of dust.' (101)

Sudassana spoke a verse making fun of him:

'The poison of a whip snake, a rat snake, or a water snake
Might do, but that of the red-headed *nāga* will not do this.' (102)

And then Ālambāna addressed him with two verses:

'I have heard from ascetics who are *arahats*,[62] who have discernment,
Those benefactors who give gifts here go to heaven.
While you are alive, be generous with gifts, and whatever you have to
give. (103)
This *nāga* with great powers and ascetic energy, hard to overcome:
He will bite you and turn you into dust!' (104)

[Sudassana:]

'I also have heard this from ascetics who are skilled in what is right.
Those benefactors who give gifts here go to heaven
While you are alive, be generous with gifts and whatever you have to
give. (105)
[195] This Accimukhī by name, full of the power of the snake,
Will bite you, and she will turn you into dust. (106)
For she is my half-sister, from the same mother,
Let her be seen! Accimukhī, full of the power of the snake!' (107)

When he had said this, he said, 'Dear Accimukhī, please leave my tangled ascetic's hair and come and stand on my hand.' And, in the midst of the people, he extended his hand and called her. And when she heard his call, lying in his hair, she croaked three times with a frog croak, and then left and sat on his shoulder. And, springing up, she emitted three drops of venom onto the palm of his hand, before going back into his ascetic's tangled hair. Sudassana standing there seized the venom. 'This will destroy

62. These are perhaps ascetics or *paccekabuddhas*, though *arahats* are unlikely when there is no Buddha, which was usually the case at the time of the *jātakas*. *Paccekabuddhas* are never explicitly mentioned in *jātaka* verses.

the kingdom; this will destroy the kingdom!' And he said this three times, and the sound of his voice was thrown throughout the whole of Vārāṇasī, to the extent of twelve *yojanas*. And the king asked, 'But what will destroy the kingdom?'

'Great King, I do not see anywhere where I could sprinkle this venom.'

'What about the ground, the earth: sprinkle it there.'

He said, 'I cannot, Great King.' And, refusing, he spoke this verse:

> 'If I sprinkle this on the ground—and think about this, Brahmadatta –
> The active agent[63] would shrivel grass and creepers, without
> a doubt.' (108)

'Then why don't you throw it up into the sky?'

'I cannot do that.' And he gave this verse in explanation:

> 'If I throw it upwards—and think about this, Brahmadatta—
> The rain god will not let either rain or snow fall for seven years.' (109)

'Then sprinkle it in the water.'

'I cannot do it there,' he replied, and spoke this verse in explanation:

> [196] 'If I were to sprinkle it in the water—and think about this,
> Brahmadatta—
> Whatever water-born beings there are, and fish and tortoises,
> Would die.' (110)

Then the king said to him, 'Dear sir, I just don't know anything about this. You tell us some way our kingdom will not perish.'

'Well, Great King, have three holes in the ground dug alongside one another right here.'

The king had them dug. Sudassana then had the middle hole filled with various herbal medicines, the second with cow-dung, and the third with divine herbs. In the middle hole he let fall the drops of venom. Fire burst out, filling the hole with smoke. This fire took hold in the hole filled with cow-dung, and then flared up after taking hold of the hole filled with divine herbs. It consumed them all, and then went out. Ālambāna stood by the farthest hole, and the heat of the venom struck him, so that the skin on his body was removed and he became white as a leper. He was gripped with fear. 'I'll set the *nāga* king free!' he blurted out three times. When he heard this the Bodhisatta left the jewelled basket and, assuming his own

63. DP I 593 relates the word *osajjho* to *osadhī*, a medicinal herb: presumably it means then the active agent in the venom. The commentary also relates the word to *osadhī*.

form, stood there with the bearing of Sakka, the king of the *devas*, adorned with every kind of ornament. Sudassana and Accimukhī also stood there.

Then Sudassana addressed the king: 'Do you recognize us, Great King, as anyone's children?'

'I do not,' he said.

'You do not recognize us, but you do know the king of the Kāsi's daughter, Samuddajā, who was given to Dhataraṭṭha.'

'I certainly do, as she is my younger sister.'

'And we are her sons, and you are our uncle!'

When the king heard this he embraced them, kissing their heads, and wept. And he had them led into the palace with great honour and he arranged the warmest of welcomes for Bhūridatta. Then he asked, 'Dear one, tell me how Ālambāna caught you, when you possessed such great power?' The Bodhisatta related to him the whole story and then said, 'Great King, a king should rule his kingdom in this way.' And he gave a *dhamma* teaching to his uncle. And then Sudassana said, 'Uncle, my mother is grieving through not seeing Bhūridatta. We cannot spend a long time away from her.'

'Very well then, dear one, you go then, but I also wish to see my sister. So how shall I see her?'

'Uncle, where is our grandfather, the king of Kāsi?'

[197] 'Dear one, he could not bear it without his sister, so he gave up the kingdom and took the going forth, and lives in such-and-such a forest thicket.'

'Uncle, my mother wishes to see you and our grandfather. You, go to my grandfather. We'll collect my mother, and let's go to his hermitage on such-and-such a day, and then you will see him too.' So they set a day and left the uncle's royal palace. The king, after parting from his daughter's sons, retired in tears. They disappeared into the earth and went into the realm of *nāgas*.

The section about entering the city is finished.

7. THE SECTION ABOUT THE SEARCH FOR THE GREAT BEING[64]

When the Great Being came into the city, the entire population were at one in their outpouring of grief. He was tired out after a month in the

64. This section heading is surely a misnomer.

basket, and lay down in a sick bed. But there was no limit to the amount of *nāgas* who came to visit him, and he became exhausted through having conversations with them. Kāṇāriṭṭha had gone to the world of the gods and had not found the Bodhisatta there, so had been the first back. Thinking, 'He is a rough and fierce fellow: he will be able to keep the *nāgas* en masse at bay,' they made him the doorkeeper for the Great Being. Then Subhaga, after searching the entire Himalayan region and the great ocean and other rivers, came in the course of his searches to the Yamunā. Meanwhile, the hunter brahmin, when he saw Ālambāna with his skin disease, had thought to himself, 'He has got this skin disease from tormenting Bhūridatta. I also, through greed for the jewel, showed him the one who had done all kinds of generous things for me. Some evil will come my way, if I don't go to the river Yamunā and make a purificatory rite at the bathing place for purifications.' So he went there, 'I'll wash away my bad actions and betrayal of Bhūridatta!' And he went to wash away the effects of his actions.

At that moment Subhaga reached that place too, and heard what the brahmin was saying. 'This evildoer betrayed my brother, who had given him so much in the way of glory, for the sake of the jewel spell. I will not spare his life.' So he twisted his tail around the brahmin's feet and dragged him into the water and held him down. When he had made him quite breathless, he left him limp, and then, when he raised his head, [198] he pushed him down again, and did this several times, until the exhausted brahmin lifted his head and spoke this verse:

'I was just standing splashing myself with the water, at the Pāyaga ford;[65]
Who is the being who is eating me up, immersing me in the river Yamunā?' (111)

And then Subhaga addressed him with this verse:

'That lord of the world, of great repute,
Who could destroy Vārāṇasī on all sides:
I am the son of that lord of the serpents.
They call me Subhaga, brahmin.' (112)

65. A bank for bathing in the Ganges, between Verañjā and Vārāṇasī, one of the river *ghats* where purification by washing took place (DPPN). The word *sajantaṃ* is glossed by the commentary as meaning 'sprinkling with such water' (*evarūpaṃ udakaṃ abhisiñcantaṃ*). See also verse 135.

And then the brahmin thought, 'This brother of Bhūridatta's will not spare my life, so why don't I soften his heart by speaking some fulsome praise of his mother and father? When I have done that I'll beg for my life.' And he spoke this verse:

'And if the son of the lord of the serpents, of the vessel of the Kāsis,[66]
Chief amongst the deathless, of a noble line, is your father,
And the incomparable woman amongst humans, your mother:
Then such a man, of magnificent glory, would not be able
To push the slave of a brahmin down into the water!'[67] (113)

[199] And then Subhaga said, 'You evil brahmin! You think that by deceiving me I will set you free, but I'll not let you live!' So he made clear to him the *kamma* of what he had done:

'With a tree trunk as your support, you struck an antelope that had
 come into sight.
It was hit and in desperation, hastening, ran quickly, far away. (114)
You saw where it fell in the great forest, took it on your carrying pole,
And in the evening went to a banyan tree, (115)
Resounding with calling birds,[68] strewn with yellow brown new twigs,[69]
Full of the sounds of cuckoos, grassy green, constantly delightful. (116)
And there before you appeared my water-born brother,
Who is of great power, glory, and magnificence, with a retinue of
 maidens. (117)
You committed violence towards him, when he was surrounded by this
 retinue
And delighted with all kinds of sense pleasures, although he had done
 you no harm. (118)
Put out your throat quickly; I'll not spare your life,
Remembering your violence to my brother, I'll cut off your head!' (119)

And then the brahmin said, 'He will not spare me my life, so what is there for me to do to exert myself?' And he said this verse:

'A brahmin is learned in the texts, open handed to requests, and
 honours the sacred fire:[70]

66. The word is *kaṃsa*, usually a vessel, glossed by the commentary as a name for the king of the Kāsis.

67. The commentary suggests *ohātuṃ*, to push down, refers to his submerging.

68. *Suvasālika* appears in the *Vessantara-jātaka* (Ja VI 539 v. 421), and seems to be some kind of calling bird.

69. The commentary describes *santhatāyutan* as *pārohaparikiṇṇaṃ* 'strewn with new twigs'.

70. *Ajjhayako yācayogo āhutaggi ca brāhmaṇo.*

For these three reasons the brahmin is not to be killed!' (120)

[200] When he heard this Subhaga became doubtful: 'I'll take him to the *nāga* realm and find out what to do by asking my brothers.' Thinking this, he said two verses:

'Deep within the River Yamunā is Dhataraṭṭha's city,
The mountain that is entirely gold shines, reaching out across the Yamunā: (121)
That is where my brothers are, tiger-like men, all from the same stock—remember!
They will say what is to become of you, brahmin!' (122)

When he said this he grabbed him by the throat, shouted abuse at him and shook him, and led up to the gate of the Great Being's palace.

The section about the search for the Great Being is finished.

8. FINAL SECTION

As Kāṇāriṭṭha, who had become the doorkeeper, was sitting there, he saw Subhaga coming along the way, leading the brahmin and mistreating him. He said, 'Subhaga, do not harm him, for brahmins are the sons of Great Brahmā, and if Great Brahmā finds out that someone is harming his son, he will be angry and destroy the whole of our *nāga* realm. For brahmins have great power as elders in the world. You do not know their power, but I do.' For they say that in the life preceding that one Kāṇāriṭṭha had been a brahmin who conducted sacrifices, and that was why he said this. As he was practised in sacrifice from his experience in an earlier life, he addressed Subhaga and the assembly of *nāgas*. 'I will explain to you the particular features of brahmins who conduct sacrifices.' Embarking upon a praise of sacrifice, he said this:

'The sacrifices, the *Vedas*, and things of high regard in the world
Are not transient, though they are associated with the transient.
The one who censures the householder brahmin lives in great reproach,
And loses happiness, self-possession, and *dhamma*.'[71] (123)

[201] And then Kāṇāriṭṭhā asked. 'Subhaga, do you know who organised the world?'

'I do not know', was the reply.

71. See DP I 371 for *anittara*. My translation is very different from Cowell here. The word *aggarayhaṃ* is unclear. Perhaps it is a corruption of 'householder' (*agāri*).

'It was Brahmā, grandfather of the brahmins.' To explain this further, he said this verse:

'Those who are most noble he made for study of the *Vedas*, while some are lords of the earth;
Vessas are for ploughing, and the *suddas* for service:
Each has gone to its separate domain.
This was what the Lord arranged.' (124)

He continued: 'Great are the qualities of the brahmin, who, through these, makes his mind clear, he is generous with gifts. For him there is no further rebirth, or he goes to a *deva* realm.' Then he said:

'Dhātā, Vidhātā, Varuṇa, and Kuvera,
Soma, Yama, the Moon, and the Sun:
These all offered extensive sacrifices,
And all the pleasures of the senses, to those who studied the *Vedas*. (125)
With five hundred bows drawn out for action,
And a thousand arms, incomparable,
The one who is powerful, Ajjuna, with a terrifying army,
Lit the sacrificial fire.'[72] (126)

[202] And he gave this verse, extolling the virtues of the brahmins further:

'The one who regally entertained brahmins for a night long,
Giving them as much of food and drink as was in his power,
With a confident mind, joyful,
Was reborn as a *deva*, with great wealth.[73] (127)

It is in this way that the brahmins are worthy of offerings!' And then he brought up another example to illustrate the point:

'A magnificent divine feast of supreme excellence,[74]
The one who himself fed the sacred fire,
Mujalinda, conducted the sacrificial ceremony in the best way
And then went to a divine rebirth!'[75] (128)

72. Ajjuna was king of Kekakā, and an archer, who used to offer sacrifices to the gods. He is mentioned in the *Saṃkicca-jātaka* (J 530; Ja V 267). This must surely be a reference to Arjuna, the hero of the *Mahābhārata*, who is said to be the finest archer in the world.

73. The commentary describes this as an ancient king of Vārāṇasī, who became a king of the gods.

74. For *mahāsanaṃ* I am taking the commentary's suggestion of *mahābhakkhum*, a great feast. The reading is *yo sappināsakkhi bhojetum aggiṃ*, with Cone. For comment on this line, see DP II 209.

75. The commentary says that Mujalinda made his offering to the god of fire, Aggi.

Explaining the matter he said this verse:

'The one of great glory, who lived for a thousand years,
The noble one, handsome to behold, took the going forth,
Abandoning his army of boundless chariots
[203] O yes—King Dujīpa went to heaven too.' (129)

And then he provided even more examples:

'Sāgara, the one who conquered the earth that is bounded by the ocean,
Raised a lofty sacrificial post, shining and made of gold,
And kindled the fire.
And then he became a greatly fortunate *deva*. (130)
Aṅga poured flowing offerings of milk and curds,[76] while tending the fire,
And by this power, Gangā became full,
And he attained the state of Sakka, the thousand-eyed lord.' (131)

Then, having introduced this history, he said:

'Of great potency, and repute, the most excellent,
A general in the third *deva* world[77] of Vāsava,
[204] He removed his stain by means of the *soma* sacrifice,
And is worthy to be called a god.' (132)

Explaining the matter he said:

'The one who did this, in this and the other world,
In Bhāgira, the Himavanta, and Gijjha,[78]
He is of great potency, and repute, the most excellent,
Because he kindled the sacred fire. (133)
Mālāgirī, the Himavanta, and Gijjha,
Sudassana, Nisabha, and Kākaneru,
These other great mountains were built, in layers,
By those conducting sacrifices.' (134)

And then he went on further: 'Brother, do you know how the ocean came to be salty and unfit to drink?'

'I do not know, Ariṭṭha.'

76. The commentary says that this was milk as well; taking *sanna* as the past participle of *sandati* 'to flow'.

77. See DP II 312. The third world of the *deva*s is not specified, but presumably it is the one above the Tāvatiṃsa realm, of the Yāmā gods—this is the realm below the realm where the Buddha is reborn before his final life and where in his final life his mother is reborn after her death, the Tusita heaven. The mention of Vāsava, an epithet for Sakka, however, suggests the Tāvatiṃsa heaven.

78. Bhāgira is a name for the Ganges; Gijjha is one of five hills encircling Rājagaha, particularly associated with sages.

'You know only how to harm brahmins, so listen.' And saying this he pronounced this verse:

'There was a scholar of the *Vedas*, possessed with mantras and virtues,
Who was liberal to ascetics, it is said;
[205] He was splashing himself on the banks of the ocean,[79]
And the ocean swallowed him, and because of this it became
undrinkable.' (135)

'These are the ways of brahmins', he said, and then added:

'There were men in the world,
Brahmins who were worthy recipients of offerings from Vāsava;
In the eastern, the western and the southern direction,
Stirred up, they brought into being the *Vedas*.' (136)

In this way Ariṭṭha praised brahmins, their sacrifices, and their *Vedas* in fourteen verses. Plenty of *nāgas* heard this and then went to the Bodhisatta's sickbed and told him, 'He is describing a miracle.' They were becoming receptive to a false doctrine.[80]

Now the Great Being, lying in his sick bed, heard all this, as the *nāgas* told him about what they had heard. The Bodhisatta reflected on this. 'Ariṭṭha is praising a wrong path. I will cut through his argument and present right view to the assembly.' So he got up, washed, adorned himself in every way, and sat on the *dhamma* seat, and called the entire *nāga* assembly together. He then told Ariṭṭha off: 'Ariṭṭha, you say what is not the case, and extol the virtues of the *Vedas*, and sacrifice and the brahmins, when the making of sacrifice by means of the *Vedas* is not thought to be at all desirable or to be revered, and does not lead to heaven: so you have said something that is not the case.' And he embarked upon a critique of the practice of sacrifice:

[206] 'It is a losing throw of the dice for the strong, done by fools:
They go into the *Veda*, Ariṭṭha, a glittering mirage of *dhamma,*
Based on lack of reflection.
Its qualities are imaginary and do not lead to wisdom. (137)
The *Vedas* do not give a refuge to a man who is a betrayer of friends
Or the destroyer of other beings.[81]
Fire that is worshipped does not save the one who bears evil in his heart
Or who does an ignoble thing. (138)

79. See v. 111. Verse 173 is the same as v. 135.

80. In VRI a section divider is made at this point, but not in the F version. VRI reads: 'The teaching based on wrong view is finished' (*micchākathā niṭṭhitā*).

81. See PED 508.

If men of wealth and good fortune burnt all the wood
In the world mixed with grass, the fire would not be satiated:
What person without common sense would find a good meal there? (139)
Just as milk is always anxious to change, and becomes curds and fresh butter,
In this way a flame is also anxious to change,
And fire, bent on attachment, takes light [all around]. (140)
Fire that just bursts out in dry wood and new twigs is not seen:
Without someone rubbing the kindling wood, fire does not come into being. (141)
If fire could live within dry or new wood, all the forests in the world
Would be parched up, and dry wood would burst into flames. (142)
If a man makes merit with wood and grass, feeding[82] a plume of smoke,
However splendid, then charcoal burners, salt makers and cooks,
And those that burn bodies, make merit too! (143)
[207] They just do not make merit in this.
The fire, with all the *Vedas*, is soon satiated;
And no one makes merit just by feeding
A plume of smoke, however splendid. (144)
How can fire be a being, honoured in the world,
If it eats many foul-smelling and ugly things
Which human beings avoid, and which even someone without common sense
Would be little able to stomach? (145)
They say that the plume of smoke is amongst the ranks of *devas*;
Barbarians say that water is a god.
But both of these are way off the mark in their speaking!
Fire is not a god! (146)
How does anyone go to a good rebirth,
If he has been performing evil deeds,
By worshipping fire, which has no faculties,
No body that perceives, and does any old job for humankind?[83] (147)
And they who perform all kinds of livelihood
Say that Brahmā, the all-powerful, worships fire;
But how can the uncreated worship what has been created?[84] (148)
In former times, they followed, for the sake of honour,

82. For *bhojaṃ* 'feeding', the present participle; see PED 206, which cites this passage.

83. These verses critique the Vedic worship of Agni, the fire god. As the verses point out, fire burns all sorts of impure things, is usually caused by humans, and is ever-changing. It therefore makes no sense to worship fire.

84. In other words why would Brahmā, who is believed by brahmins to be 'self-born', worship a being that has been created by him?

Something that is quite ridiculous, does not stand up to scrutiny, and is not true;
They stubbornly stuck to invisible gains and honours
In their teaching amongst people: (149)
"Those who are most noble he made for study of the *Vedas*, while some are lords of the earth;
Vessas are for ploughing, and the *suddas* for service:
Each has gone to its separate domain.
This was what the Lord arranged."[85] (150)
[208] This is a statement of truth, the creed amongst the brahmins:
That no one but a warrior by birth rules the kingdom,
No one but a brahmin is trained in the mantras,
No one other than a *vessa* ploughs the field;
The *suddas*, not free, serve the others. (151)
With this statement of what is not the case,
These gluttons speak falsely, and
Those with little wisdom have faith in this,
Even though wise men see right through it. (152)
Warriors and merchants do not bring oblations:[86]
Adopting this view, brahmins live as teachers,
But why does Brahmā not make the world,
So shaken and divided in this way, straight? (153)
And if this Brahmā, lord of all worlds,
Is such a magnificent lord of beings,
Why does he arrange bad luck for the whole world?
Why does he not make the whole world happy? (154)
And if this Brahmā, lord of all worlds,
Is such a magnificent lord of beings,
What was the point in making the world filled with lack of a teaching,
And with delusions, lies, and madness? (155)
And if this Brahmā, lord of all worlds,
Is such a magnificent lord of beings,
Then the lord of beings is unjust himself, Ariṭṭha,
A being who arranges unfairness and a lack of teaching amongst the just![87] (156)
How does he become pure,
If he is killing worms, winged insects, snakes and frogs, and flies?

85. This verse is the same as verse 124.

86. The word used is *bali*, used for offering of food in a sacrifice (PED 483).

87. These verses offer a Buddhist perspective on the 'problem of evil' that has beset Western philosophy of religion for centuries: if there is an all-powerful, all-good god (as brahmins arguably believe Brahmā to be), then why is the world so apparently unfair and full of suffering?

These are not noble teachings. They are untrue,
Such as those of the Kambojan rabble!'[88] (157)

[209] [210] And[89] then the Great Being explained the nature of this untruthfulness:

'And if he who kills someone is considered pure,
And the one who is killed is sent to a heavenly place,
[211] Then let the hoity-toity brahmin[90] kill another hoity-toity brahmin,[91]
And those who have put their trust in them. (158)
And what wild animals or cattle beg for death?
Although they are quivering in fear for their lives in this world,
Still they take these cattle and living beings to the sacrifices. (159)
The brahmins lead them forwards, describing the sacrificial post,
The victims, and the blows with colourful euphemisms:
"This sacrificial post will be a granter of wishes in the hereafter,
And forever, in the future." (160)
But if the sacrificial posts really were filled with jewels and mother-of-pearl,
Grain and wealth, silver and gold, amongst the dry new twigs,
And if they granted all the pleasures of the senses in the third heaven,
The community of those with threefold knowledge (*tevijja*) would sacrifice humans,
And would not sacrifice anyone except brahmins! (161)
Where do the jewels and mother-of-pearl,
Grain and wealth, silver and gold come from, amongst the dry, new twigs?
And where do all the pleasures of the senses in the third heaven come from? (162)
Crafty, cruel, and childish in understanding,
They lead them forward with colourful euphemisms:
"Bringing the fire, give me joy: (163)
Then you will be happy from that with all the pleasures of the senses!"
So they lead them forward, entering the refuge of the sacred fire,

88. The Kambojans, inhabitants of one of the early Janapadas, or sixteen territories, offer a paradigm of bad behaviour, being of a north-western tribe who supposedly lost Aryan customs and degenerated. The region is mentioned in Aśoka's Rock Edict XIII and is thought to be on the banks of the Kabul River (see DPPN).

89. Page 209 and most of page 210 are taken up by extensive commentarial explanation of the terminology of this difficult and complex passage.

90. *Bhovādin* refers to a brahmin, as he addresses others as *bho,* but implies that he is superior (PED 509); See *Suttanipāta:* 620 and Norman 1995: II 263.

91. VRI and all MSS consulted for the F version give *bhovādina.*

With colourful euphemisms, and, getting them to offer up their hair and beard and nails,
They make all their happiness and wealth go away, justified by the *Vedas*. (164)
Like crows setting on an owl in secret, many come together for one person.
[212] Deceitful, they trick him and eat his food,
And then strip him bare and abandon him to the way of sacrifice. (165)
When this individual has been deceived by the brahmins in this way,
Many of them come together and plunder his understanding
With the bonds of their doctrine:
They make off with his wealth by means of wrong view. (166)
They issue instructions like royal taxmen,[92]
And carry his wealth and take it away;
They are the same as thieves, but although they merit execution,
No one in the world harms them, Ariṭṭha![93] (167)
They cut a stick from a Judas tree and call it "the right arm of Indra",[94]
But if this really is true and Indra did cut his arm off,
How did he conquer the *asuras*? (168)
This is just empty talking, as Indra,[95] the supreme of the *devas*,
Has his limbs intact and is invincible;
These brahmin mantras are quite empty,
And are falsehoods in this visible world. (169)
"Mālāgirī, the Himavanta, and Gijjha,
Sudassana, Nisabha, and Kākaneru,
These other great mountains were built in layers
By those conducting sacrifices," they say.[96] (170)
Whatever bricks they say were built in layers
As arrangements by those conducting sacrifices,
These did not make mountains!
Immoveable stones are put in place through other causes. (171)

92. The Cowell/Rouse translation suggests 'grasping strangers' for *akāsiyā*; Cone however suggests 'royal taxmen' here (DP I 2).

93. Several standard Buddhist arguments against Vedic sacrifice are offered here: (1) If sacrificial victims really go to heaven then why do brahmins not sacrifice other brahmins? (This argument is also found in the *Candakumāra-jātaka*.) (2) The symbolism of the sacrifice is all plain lies. (3) Sacrifices are largely orchestrated by brahmins in order to make money.

94. *Pālasa*, or the Judas tree, used to be known as *Butea frondosa* but is now known as *Cercis siliquastrum*. It has a very hard wood. Search 'cercis siliquastrum' at nhm.ac.uk.

95. Indra is called by his epithet Maghavā here and in the third line of the preceding verse.

96. This verse repeats the assertion made by Ariṭṭha in v. 134 (Ja VI 204).

Bricks are not stones, even after a long period of time;
There is no red iron to be seen there.
[213] Yet these people extol the sacrifice, and say that the mountains
Were built in layers by those conducting the sacrifices. (172)
"There was a scholar of the *Vedas*, possessed with mantras and virtues,
Who was liberal to ascetics," it is said.
"He was splashing himself on the banks of the ocean,[97]
And the ocean swallowed him, and because of this it became undrinkable." (173)
But the rivers have swallowed up a thousand of them, with all their *Vedas*,
Endowed with mantras, and their waters are not corrupted by this,
So why should the ocean become undrinkable because of this? (174)
Whatever wells there are in this world here that have saltwater
Are dug out by spades, and not through the swallowing up of brahmins.
The water is undrinkable because of these methods,
Not because someone without common sense has said so. (175)
Formerly who were the women and to whom did they belong?
Mind-made, the mind did not know humans in times past.
There was no law that made someone an inferior in this way—
There was just a difference in what people did. (176)
The low-caste boy, with skilful mind, might say mantras
And live according to the *Vedas*,
It would not be the case that his head is smashed into seven pieces
And that these mantras lead to destruction! (177)
Speech and actions taken by foolish people,
Following the way of poetry,[98] are hard to relinquish.
The mind settled on a wrong way, with foolishness:
Only those with little wisdom have faith in this. (178)
Human nature does not even match the lion, the tiger, and the leopard in power:
The power of men is what is to be expected in a cow.
By nature they are of the same intelligence, although they look different. (179)
[214] And if a king were to conquer the earth
And live together with a loyal assembly,
Then he should conquer too the enemy gathering in himself,
And his people would live in constant happiness. (180)

97. See vv. 111 and 135.

98. For *kavyāpathānupannā* here, see DP I 637 under *kabba*. The meaning is unclear: it could mean that they pay too much attention to what later became *kavyā*, the classical Sanskrit poetic form, or perhaps that they are as described in such poetry.

The spells of warriors and the three *Vedas* are the same in meaning:
Not investigating their meaning,
He sleepwalks onto a path that is flooded or completely obscured. (181)
The spells of warriors and the three *Vedas* are the same in meaning;
Gain, loss, lack of reputation, and reputation:
All of these four things apply to all beings. (182)
Just as wealthy people on earth pursue many kinds of jobs
For the sake of wealth and grain,
So the community of those with threefold knowledge on earth
Today pursue many kinds of jobs too.[99] (183)
And wealthy people are the same in this, always moving forwards,
Attached by the pleasures of the senses.
They pursue many kinds of jobs on earth: and this, with little wisdom,
Is what those without any common sense are doing too.' (184)

[217] In this way the Great Being refuted their argument, and set down his own argument, and when the *nāga* assembly heard his *dhamma* talk, they were delighted. The Great Being had the hunter brahmin led out of the *nāga* realm and did not make any scornful attack on him. Sāgara Brahmadatta did not miss the appointed day and, surrounded with his four-limbed army, went to his father's palace. The Great Being said, 'I will go and see my uncle and my father-in-law,' and had a drum beaten with great pomp and magnificence and went on ahead to the hermitage. The rest of his brothers and his mother and father followed behind. And at that moment Sāgara Brahmadatta, not recognising the Great Being as he arrived with his great retinue, spoke asking his father:

'Whose are the tabors, the little drums, the conches, and the kettle drums?
Proceeding out in front, they bring joy to the lord of charioteers! (185)
Who is the young man, armed with a quiver of arrows, and with a golden crown
Like a flash of lightning, who approaches, shining in majesty? (186)
Whose handsome face glows, like a firebrand of acacia in the mouth of a crucible,
Rejoicing: who approaches, shining in majesty? (187)
[218] Whose is the golden parasol, with delightfully worked ribs,

99. For discussion of the 'three knowledges' (*tevijja*) see Gombrich 1996: 29, 129–30. In Buddhism the three are knowledge of one's former lives, knowledge of the rebirths of others, and the knowledge that has found the four noble truths and eliminated the corruptions. In a brahminic context, the three are knowing by heart the *Ṛg Veda*, the *Sāma Veda*, and the *Yajur Veda*.

That makes a rampart of protection against the beams of the sun:
Who approaches, shining in majesty? (188)
Whose is the arm, stretching out, with a yak's tail fan held on high,
That makes a peacock feather shade above the head? (189)
Whose are the peacock feathers, held in the hand, of many colours, and soft,
And the shining gold, jewelled sticks that move on either sides of his face?[100] (190)
Full of gladness, he is like a firebrand of acacia in the mouth of a crucible.
Whose are these lovely earrings, which shine on both sides of his face? (191)
Whose soft curls, touched and moistened by the wind,
Make the edge of the forehead shine like lightning in the sky? (192)
Whose are the eyes, long and stretched out, and broad too?
Who shines with large eyes, whose is this face with the wisp of hair between the eyebrows?[101] (193)
Whose are the teeth, clean, like the best clean mother-of-pearl?
While he is speaking, his teeth shine like white flowers! (194)
Whose are the hands and feet, well cared for and coloured with essence of lac?
Who is this man, endowed with red lips, who shines like the sun god? (195)
Like a large *sāl* blossoming on a snowy peak in the Himalayan snows,
Who shines like Indra, triumphant, in a white cloak? (196)
Who, like a lord plunging into the assembly, draws out his sword,
A jewelled stick of many colours, in a golden sheath? (197)
Who is it that takes off his many-coloured shoes, which are inlaid with gold and jewels,[102]
Finely embroidered and well made, and pays homage to the great sage?' (198)

100. I share Cowell's puzzlement about this, though the idea that they are whiskers sounds a bit odd (See J VI 113 n. 1). Could they be some sort of decorative hangings?

101. See DP I 406 for *uṇṇa* (*ūṛṇā*). The tuft of hair between the eyebrows is associated with great auspiciousness, when, soft like white cotton, it is the thirty-first of the thirty-two *lakkhaṇas*, or marks, of the *mahāpurisa*, the Great Man. These are the physical manifestations of the auspicious karma created throughout the lives of the Bodhisatta in his preparation for Buddhahood. Interestingly, for a story in which deceit and crookedness are so central, it is said to be the good karmic result of great truthfulness (DN 30, PTS edn III 170–1; Walshe 1995: 445–6). At various times in the *Mahānipāta*, the Bodhisatta's appearance is described in terms that evoke these marks, as if his auspiciousness is being impressed upon his physical body too.

102. The commentary glosses *suvaṇṇacitakā*, which has the sense of 'heaps' of gold, as *suvaṇṇakhacitā* 'inlaid with'.

In this way, when he was asked by his son, Sāgara Brahmadatta, the powerful ascetic who had grasped the psychic powers, said, 'O my son, these are the sons of Dhataraṭṭha, your sister's *nāga* sons!' And he gave this verse of description:

> 'These are Dhataratṭṭha's *nāgas*, of great power and glory;
> They were born from Samuddajā and are *nāgas* of great power!' (199)

As they were talking in this way the *nāgas* came up to them and paid their respects, and sat to one side. Weeping, Samuddajā paid her respects to her father and then went with the *nāga* assembly back to the *nāga* realm. Sāgara Brahmadatta stayed there for a day and then went to Vārāṇasī. And Samuddajā eventually died in the *nāga* realm. The Bodhisatta guarded his *sīla* for the rest of his life and kept the *uposatha*, and at the end of his life he, and the rest of the *nāga* assembly, made the heaven realms full.

The Teacher, when he had given this *dhamma* talk, said, 'In this way lay disciples and wise men in ancient times kept the *uposatha*, even when there was no Buddha, and abandoned the glory of the *nāga* realm. And he made the connections with the births: 'At that time the royal family were the mother and the father, Devadatta the hunter brahmin, Ānanda was Somadatta, Uppalavaṇṇā was Accimukhī, Sāriputta was Sudassana, Moggallāna was Subhaga, Sunakkhatta was Kāṇāriṭṭha,[103] and I was Bhūridatta.'

103. Sunakkhatta is a significant later rebirth here for Ariṭṭha. Sunakkhatta was a Licchavi prince who converted to the Buddha's order of monks, but became dissatisfied with his teachings because he felt there ought to be more stress on psychic powers, and some indication of the beginning of things. He then drifted without result from one teacher to another (See *Pāṭika Sutta* in DN 24; and DPPN).

7

CANDA

The Birth Story of Prince Canda, or of Khaṇḍahāla

(*Candakumāra-jātaka* or *Khaṇḍahāla-jātaka*)

INTRODUCTION

The seventh *jātaka* of the *Mahānipāta* is known by two names, *Candakumāra* (Prince Canda) and *Khaṇḍahāla*, which refer to the characters of the Bodhisatta and his arch-enemy Devadatta, respectively. Though ostensibly a tale of the Bodhisatta's mastery of the perfection of *khanti*, or forbearance, the main character of the action is really Khaṇḍahāla, an evil brahmin who wishes to have Canda killed and so convinces King Ekarāja (Canda's father) that sacrificing his family members will lead him to heaven. Prince Canda's main role is to question the king's faith in Khaṇḍahāla's advice, and to beg for his life (and, secondarily, for the lives of the other people lined up ready for slaughter). The story is thus strongly focused upon the character of Devadatta, whose hatred of the Buddha has led to him striving to kill many people, both in the 'present' time of the Buddha and in the past time of Prince Canda.

Devadatta in *Jātaka* stories

Devadatta is a frequent character in *jātaka* stories, where he performs the role of villain with admirable consistency. He is selfish, power hungry, dishonest, disloyal, and mean. Many *jātaka* stories show him acting in

Introduced and translated by Naomi Appleton.

one of two ways: trying to kill the Bodhisatta; or unsuccessfully leading a rival group to that of the Bodhisatta. Examples of the former include a particularly popular set of tales where Devadatta is a crocodile trying to capture the Bodhisatta, who is in the form of a wily monkey (J 57, 208, 342). In many stories it is jealousy of the Bodhisatta that leads to Devadatta's murderous intentions, even when the Bodhisatta is born as Devadatta's own son (as in J 58). While on most of these occasions the Bodhisatta outwits Devadatta and escapes, sometimes Devadatta succeeds in killing the Bodhisatta. The most famous of such stories is the *Khantivāda-jātaka* (J 313) in which Devadatta is an angry king who mutilates and kills an ascetic (the Bodhisatta) whose doctrine is forbearance; the king of course meets a suitable punishment in the hell realms after the earth splits and a flame reaches up to drag him down there. Demonstrating Devadatta's recurring ambition to lead, the very first *jātaka* of the *Jātakatthavaṇṇanā* sees him born as a foolish caravan leader whose merchants are all eaten by demons, while the Bodhisatta's caravan successfully crosses the wilderness. In a later story when born as a stag who is the son of the Bodhisatta, Devadatta endangers the lives of his herd while his brother (Sāriputta) keeps his herd safe (J 11). Many other stories show Devadatta's strong ambition, and the inappropriate ways in which he tries to fulfil it.[1]

These two patterns of behaviour of course reflect the character and actions of Devadatta during the time of the Buddha. In the Pāli *Nikāyas* as well as in many stories of the present in the *Jātakatthavaṇṇanā*, Devadatta is described as attempting several times to kill the Buddha and trying to take over leadership of the *saṅgha*. He is also credited with encouraging Ajātasattu to murder his father King Bimbisāra, as is mentioned in the introduction to the *Candakumāra-jātaka*. Many *jātaka*s show that people would be very foolish to follow Devadatta's example, instructions, or leadership: the Buddha's life-saving advice to the archers during this *jātaka*'s story of the present—'Friends, don't follow the path described by Devadatta, but go by this path!'—has a wide implication.

The *Candakumāra-jātaka* draws on both patterns, by showing Devadatta's ambition and desire for influence, as well as his perennial hatred of the Buddha and desire to kill him. More specifically, in this *jātaka* we discover that Devadatta's hatred of the Buddha alone leads him to attempt the

1. More references to stories containing Devadatta, as well as a general discussion of his character, can be found in Jones 1979: 31.

destruction of many other people. As is so often the case in *jātaka* stories, the story of the past is a demonstration that such behaviour is not limited to the present, but has deeper and more long-lasting roots. The question naturally arises as to whether or not Devadatta is capable of change. More than any other character in the *jātakas*, Devadatta seems fixed in his karmic patterns, consistently causing trouble wherever he goes. Even the Bodhisatta has a variable past, with some stories showing him gambling, committing adultery, or even killing, creating a dramatic contrast to his more usual exemplary behaviour. No such variety is present in Devadatta's actions.

Devadatta's consistent villainy also prompts another question: why does he so often have a human or animal birth, when he should be suffering aeons in the hell realms for his villainy? Not only is he frequently human, he sometimes has senior births to the Bodhisatta. This was clearly a worry to some early Buddhist communities, since it is discussed in the *Milindapañha* ('The Questions of King Milinda'), a text composed in north India but preserved in Pāli and given very high status within Theravāda countries. The text takes the form of a series of questions posed by the Bactrian king Milinda to a monk named Nāgasena, and the latter's responses. One of the questions concerns whether or not good and bad actions result in the same fruit.[2] The king points out that in many previous births (he gives sixteen examples) Devadatta, though behaving badly, occupies a higher status than the Bodhisatta, and in some other cases (he cites six) the two are on a par. Thus, he argues, good and evil actions lead to equal results. As Nāgasena points out, however, Devadatta did a variety of bad and good things, and his karmic fruit was a lot more complicated and long lived than this small number of births. His intervening time in hell is left unnarrated, but can surely be vividly imagined.

Evil Brahmins

While Devadatta is singled out for criticism in this story, the general role of brahmins is also commented upon. Khaṇḍahāla is described as being a brahmin in name only, which echoes such texts as the final chapter of the *Dhammapada*, where the Buddha describes the *true* brahmin in Buddhist terms; a true brahmin of course need not be a brahmin by birth. Khaṇḍahāla is shown to be following a long tradition of bad brahmins,

2. This passage is found in *Meṇḍakapañha* IV 7 (Trenckner 1997: 200–1).

whom Prince Canda describes as greedy, ungrateful, and deceitful. We are told that brahmins of old put fences around the sacrificial area in case righteous men should interfere (with the implicitly unrighteous action).

There appear to be three main points being made here. Firstly, brahmins are not worthy recipients of gifts; in this sense they contrast with the monks of the present time and various holy men in many stories of the past. Secondly, brahmins are not to be trusted. The king believes Khaṇḍahāla to be pious, to have mastered religious truth and law (*dhamma* and *vinaya*), and thus to know the way to heaven. All this faith is ill-founded, and is in danger of leading the king straight to hell. Thirdly, brahmanical sacrifice is shown to be terrible, not only for the victims but also for those who 'sacrifice, bring about a sacrifice, or rejoice in it', all of whom are said to go to hell. Hell is the destination for these people even when the victims are animals, not only in the more extreme case of human sacrifice.

Giving and Sacrificing

The evil brahmin Khaṇḍahāla advises the king to do something so horrendous that every person both within and outside the story is aware that it is wrong. The suspense builds as person after person tries and fails to convince the king of the immorality of this sacrifice. Yet despite being so clearly in the wrong, the king is not far from the truth, for Buddhist doctrine would hold that renouncing your family is essential to achieving the ultimate religious goals. Whether giving away your sons (who are difficult to obtain and much loved) to the *saṅgha*, or renouncing your family ties and becoming a monk yourself, the Buddhist path is difficult. Faint-hearted people cannot do such difficult acts, especially since many friends and relatives are likely to disapprove.

The difficulties of detaching from your family are dramatically exemplified in the *Vessantara-jātaka*, the final *jātaka* of the *Mahānipāta* (Chapter 10). In this, the most famous of all *jātaka*s, the Bodhisatta gives away his children and wife in the perfection of his generosity. The parallels between this story and the *Candakumāra-jātaka* are striking. Both stories hinge upon the difficulties of detaching from your family, and the likelihood that others close to you will try to dissuade you from doing so. In the *Candakumāra-jātaka* King Ekarāja's wives and daughters-in-law try to dissuade him from his sacrifice. Vessantara's wife, on the other hand, is unable to argue with him as she is kept away by beasts of the forest while Vessantara completes the very difficult act of giving away their children; the implication is that she would have prevented him if she could. The extreme difficulty of detaching from one's family is portrayed as good evidence of its benefits and of the great strength of a person who can manage it. Yet both stories also conjure up strong moral feelings in the audience. Khaṇḍahāla is plainly wrong in his advice to the king, but the king is blind to reason and feeling, leaving the audience horrified by the potential outcome. Even Vessantara, who is the Bodhisatta in his antepenultimate birth, has had his actions questioned by Buddhist communities at least from the time of the *Milindapañha*, and many contemporary Buddhists struggle to make sense of the example being set in this tale. As Vessantara's young children beg him not to give them away as slaves to an evil brahmin, the audience would be forgiven for wishing him to relent.

Though giving away and sacrificing might seem worlds apart, the link between the *Candakumāra*- and *Vessantara-jātaka*s allows the former story to function as a warning about how *not* to go about detaching from your family. As Prince Canda entreats his father, 'send your family away to foreign lands' (as Vessantara's father does to Vessantara), 'or give them as slaves to an evil brahmin' (as Vessantara does with his children), 'but do not slaughter them.'

The Perfections

Whilst Vessantara is said to demonstrate the perfection of *dāna* 'giving' or 'generosity', according to Southeast Asian tradition Prince Canda is perfecting his *khanti*, 'patience' or 'forbearance'. This perfection is perhaps only clear at the end of the story, when Canda insists on supporting his exiled father, despite the latter's earlier attempts to kill him. The text describes him embracing his father in order to prevent the angry citizens from killing their king. It is notable also that Prince Canda has nothing to do with the killing of Khaṇḍahāla, who is stoned to death by the same crowd of angry citizens.

As discussed in the general introduction, the associations between stories and particular perfections can be very fluid. In the case of the *Candakumāra-jātaka*, we have a difference between the Southeast Asian tradition that the story illustrates forbearance, and an alternative tradition that associates it with the perfection of giving. Both the *Jātaka-nidāna* and the *Cariyāpiṭaka* mention the story as an illustration of *dāna*. In the *Cariyāpiṭaka* version of the story, which amounts to only six verses, Prince Canda frees everyone from the sacrifice and then proceeds to give great gifts to worthy recipients.

The emphasis in the *Cariyāpiṭaka* is clearly upon King Canda's generous acts *after* the set of events narrated in this lengthy *jātaka*.

The Bodhisatta as Prince Canda

Whether he is perfecting his forbearance or generosity, or both or neither, this *jātaka* demonstrates the Bodhisatta's impressive ability to inspire love and admiration. For much of the story he is in the background, whilst members of his family entreat the king to release him, and the citizens at large lament his imminent demise. He is described as beautiful, adorned in all the accoutrements of royalty, with noble steeds appropriate to his station and bearing. He praises himself at length, pointing out his own courage and nobility, and begging the king to send him to battle rather than slaughter him in the sacrificial arena.

It is notable that the entreaties of Prince Canda's family are inspired primarily by their love of Canda (and also his brother Suriya) and the wrongness of killing sons. While the wives and daughters of King Ekarāja are also lined up for the slaughter, they receive little attention. Even Prince Canda pleads only for his own life, although the prose mentions several times that he feels responsible for ensuring the safe release of all the innocent victims of the sacrifice. Devotion to Prince Canda inspires Candā to offer her own sons as a replacement sacrifice, and to demand that she be killed before the prince. Although Candā is described as the 'chief queen', implying that she is one of Ekarāja's wives, her role within the story and her identification as a past birth of the Buddha's wife suggest that she is in fact Canda's wife. Her devotion to her husband is truly impressive.

The people's devotion towards Prince Canda thus forms a strong focus for this story. The large sacrifice planned by King Ekarāja is clearly horrific and will lead to many innocent deaths, yet it is one innocent victim that is the motivation for everyone's lamentations. In this way the Bodhisatta is not an active hero so much as an object of devotion for the characters within the story as well as the audience in the story of the present who are listening to the Buddha's narration (or other audiences listening to subsequent retellings). This biography is not simply a story of events, but is a vehicle for expressing love and admiration for the Bodhisatta and Buddha.

Further evidence of the Bodhisatta's rather passive role in this *jātaka* is found in the climactic moment, for he has nothing to do with the last-minute disruption of the sacrifice. In addition to the devotional tone already discussed, another possible message here is that the Bodhisatta is ultimately inferior to the Buddha. In the story of the present the Buddha prevents his own murder and helps his would-be murderers achieve awakening. Prince Canda tries to prevent his murder, but is ultimately rescued by the truthfulness of Candā and the impressive power of the god Sakka. The Bodhisatta's inferiority to the Buddha is a theme that pervades the early birth stories embedded in the *suttas*, and continues in some stories within the *Jātakatthavaṇṇanā*.[3] Another explanation for the Bodhisatta's passivity is of course that a large focus of the story is the character of Devadatta, whose actions—along with those of the king (who remains unidentified with any person from the time of the Buddha)—move the story along.

This Translation of the *Candakumāra-jātaka*

This story is rather slow moving, filled as it is with long repeated passages that are characteristic of many of the longer *jātakas*. Several groups of verses are repeated verbatim by different characters, or by the same characters at different times. Other parts of the text contain verses modelled on a repeated pattern, with as little as one word changed between consecutive verses. Cowell and Rouse chose to omit much of this repetition in their translation, and to compress many of the verses into shorter passages. Whilst this arguably makes their translation more pleasant for the average reader, much is also lost by this approach. The repetitious dialogue conjures up images of an oral or performative tradition for the story, as such repetition does with many of the *jātakas*. The repeated entreaties and increasingly despairing laments of different characters also heighten the suspense of the story, as the audience wait impatiently to see if this gruesome sacrifice really will go ahead. The very sudden and dramatic ending is effective only because of the long lamentations that precede it.

As well as many repeated passages, the *Candakumāra-jātaka* contains long lists of names of the sacrificial victims both human and animal, and of their relations. Once again differing in my approach from Cowell and Rouse, all these names have been preserved in this translation. The inclusion of the names for characters that play little or no part in the action of the story may seem odd; however, the specific historical setting of this story is underpinned by such lists of names, which are carefully preserved in the canonical verses. We are led to believe that these events really did

3. For a discussion see Appleton 2010a: 47–51.

take place, and are thus transported into a whole new world of intrigue surrounding the court of King Ekarāja.

'THERE WAS A WICKED KING . . . '

[129] While he was staying on Vulture Peak, the Teacher related this about Devadatta. The story of Devadatta comes from the 'Schism in the *saṅgha*' section [of the *Vinaya*] and the story can be fully understood from narrations therein of the conduct of the Tathāgata from the time of Devadatta's going forth until the death of King Bimbisāra.[4] After Ajātasattu had killed Bimbisāra, Devadatta approached him and said, 'Great King! You have attained your desire, but I have not yet attained mine.'

'What is your desire, Bhante?'

'To kill the Ten-Powered One, and become Buddha.'

'What are we to do?'

'Be so good as to call together some archers.'

'Very good, Bhante' said the king, and he assembled five hundred archers who were skilled marksmen, picked out thirty-one men, and sent them to Devadatta saying, [130] 'Do as the Elder tells you.' Devadatta addressed the foremost of them: 'Friend, the recluse Gotama lives on Vulture Peak, and he walks up and down at a certain time of day. Go there, and shoot him with a poison arrow, and having brought about his death return by such-and-such a road.' Having said this and sent him off, he sent two archers down that road, saying, 'You will meet a man coming up your road. Deprive him of his life and come back by such-and-such a road.' Then he sent four men on that road, saying, 'You will meet two men coming up your road. Kill them and return by such-and-such a road.' Then he sent eight men along that road, saying, 'You will meet four men coming up your road. End their lives and return along such-and-such a road.' Then he sent sixteen men along that road, saying, 'You will meet eight men coming up your road. Kill

4. The 'Schism in the *saṅgha*' (*saṅghabhedaka*) section is the seventh chapter of the *Culla Vagga* of the *Vinaya*. In it we find the full story of Devadatta from his going forth to his attempt to split the *saṅgha*. Devadatta's increasing influence over Ajātasattu, which allows him to persuade Ajātasattu to kill his father, King Bimbisāra, is narrated here. His attempt to have archers kill the Buddha is also found in this text, in very similar wording, but without the story of the past that follows. See Horner 1952, chapter 7, especially pp. 268–71.

them and return along such-and-such a road.' Why did he do this? In order to cover up what he had done.

So the foremost archer hung his sword on his left side, bound his quiver to his back, seized his great bow of ram's horn and went towards the Tathāgata, thinking, 'I will shoot him'. But though he strung his bow, fastened his arrow and drew it, he was not able to shoot it. His entire body became rigid as if it was being crushed, and he stood there, filled with the fear of death. Seeing him, the Teacher spoke in a soothing voice and said, 'Don't be afraid—come here.' At that moment he threw down his weapons, and bent his head at the feet of the Blessed One. 'Bhante, I have committed a fault, as if a fool, confused, and unskillful, not knowing myself of your qualities! Because of the words of foolish Devadatta I came here to kill you. Forgive me, Bhante!' Having asked pardon, he sat to one side. Then the Teacher explained the Truths and established him in the fruit of stream entry. After that he dismissed him, saying, 'Friend, don't follow the path described by Devadatta, but go by another path.' Then he descended from the walkway and sat at the foot of a certain tree.

So while the archer was not returning, the next two were coming to meet him, saying, 'What's delaying him?' They saw the Ten-Powered One, approached him, greeted him respectfully, and sat to one side. The Teacher explained the Truths to them too and established them in the fruit of stream entry. He dismissed them, saying, 'Friends, do not follow the path described by Devadatta, but go by this path.' In the same way, when the others came and sat he established them in the fruit of stream entry and dismissed them down another path. Then the foremost archer who had been the first to come [131] approached Devadatta and said, 'Bhante Devadatta, I was not able to kill the Fully Awakened Buddha—the Blessed One has great powers and majesty.' They all agreed, 'Our lives were preserved because of the Fully Awakened Buddha.' They renounced the worldly life in the presence of the Teacher, and achieved arahatship.

This incident became well known amongst the community of monks. The monks raised the story in the *dhamma* hall: 'Friend, Devadatta at this time tried hard to kill many people because of his hatred of the Tathāgata, but because of the Teacher their lives were all preserved.' The Teacher came and asked, 'Monks, what matter are you talking of as you sit here together?'

'Of this particular incident,' they said.

'Monks, not only now but also in former times has Devadatta tried hard to kill many people because of his hatred of me alone.' He told a story of the past.

In times past, this Vārāṇasī was called Pupphavatī. There the son of King Vasavatti, called Ekarāja, reigned, and his son, called Prince Canda, was viceroy. A brahmin called Khaṇḍahāla was the chaplain, and he advised the king on worldly and religious matters. Thinking him to be wise, the king invited him to sit in the courthouse. But Khaṇḍahāla was inclined to get rich through bribes: having taken bribes he deprived rightful owners of their possessions and made wrongful owners the proprieters. One day, a man who had lost his case left the courthouse complaining. He saw Prince Canda coming to attend the king, and fell at his feet. 'Good man, what's the matter?' Canda asked. 'Lord, Khaṇḍahāla lives by plundering the courthouse. He took my bribe yet still I lost my case!' Prince Canda comforted him, saying, 'Don't fear.' He led him into the courthouse and restored ownership to him. The people loudly declared their approval. Hearing this, the king asked, 'What is this noise?'

'Prince Canda has correctly decided a case that Khaṇḍahāla had wrongly decided, and the noise is in approval of this.' When the prince had approached and bowed, the king said, 'Son, they say you have decided a case.'

'Yes, Your Majesty.'

'Then, son, from now on you alone are established in the courthouse.' Saying this he gave him jurisdiction.

Khaṇḍahāla's earnings were cut off, and so from then onwards he began to bear malice towards the prince, and kept watch for an opportunity. Now the king was foolish in his piety. One day at dawn, while dreaming, [132] he saw the Heaven of the Thirty-Three (Tāvatiṃsa), complete with palaces such as Vejayanta, a thousand leagues high and beautifully decorated, with an ornamented gatehouse and a rampart made of the seven treasures. There was a great road of sixty leagues made of gold, and many delightful lotus pools such as Nandā and groves such as Nandana, and the place was filled with gods.[5] He wanted to go there and thought, 'Tomorrow when the

5. These are the standard names of some of the favourite locations in the Tāvatiṃsa heaven. Nandā and Nandana both mean 'delightful'.

teacher Khaṇḍahāla comes I will question him about the path that goes to the realm of the gods, and I will go there along the path described.'

Khaṇḍahāla entered the king's residence very early and enquired about the health and happiness of the king. The king granted him a seat and asked his question. Explaining this matter the Teacher said:

There was a wicked king, Ekarāja of Pupphavatī.
He questioned his erring chaplain Khaṇḍahāla, a brahmin in name only: (1)
'Tell me the path to heaven,
You brahmin skilled in religious truth and discipline,[6]
By which the men who have made merit proceed to the good realm.' (2)

Now he would have been right to pose this question to an all-knowing *buddha*, or disciples of his, or in the absence of these then a *bodhisatta*, but the king asked Khaṇḍahāla, just as a man who has lost his way for a week might ask the way from another who has been lost for a fortnight. Khaṇḍahāla thought, 'It is time to see the back of my enemy, for having killed Prince Canda I will have fulfilled my desire.' So he addressed the king and spoke the third verse:

'Having given the ultimate gift,
Having slaughtered that which is inviolable,
In this way the men make merit and proceed to heaven, Your Majesty.' (3)

Then the king asked him to explain:

'But what is the ultimate gift? And what in this world is inviolable?
Declare this now! I will make the sacrifice, I will give the gifts.' (4)

[133] Khaṇḍahāla explained:

'Your Majesty, you must make a fourfold sacrifice:
You must sacrifice with four each of your children and queens,
Four of your citizens, four pure-bred horses, and four bulls.' (5)

And so, asked by the king to explain the road to the realm of the gods he explained the road to hell.

Thinking, 'If I seize Prince Canda alone they will think it is because of ill-feeling,' Devadatta included him amongst other people. But when this was

6. *Dhamma* and *vinaya*, which refer, amongst other things, to the teachings of the Buddha and the discipline he laid down for his monks. Here they have a broader meaning, referring to two branches of knowledge that religious advisers might be expected to have mastered.

related to those in the ladies' apartments, they all trembled with fear, and all at once cried out a great wail. Illustrating this matter the Teacher said:

> The royal ladies heard, 'The chief queens and princes are to be killed!'
> There was a single loud shout—the sound of fear. (6)

All the royal family were like a grove of *sāl* trees destroyed by the storm at the end of the world, and the brahmin asked the king, 'Great King, are you able to make this sacrifice or not?'

'Why do you ask this, teacher? Having made the sacrifice I will go to the realm of the gods.'

'Great King, the cowardly and those of weak intention are not strong enough to make the sacrifice. You should assemble everyone here, and I will perform the act in the sacrificial enclosure.' Taking a sufficient army for himself, Khaṇḍahāla left the city, had the sacrificial arena made level, and enclosed it with a fence. Why? It was a practice established by brahmins of old [134] that a fenced enclosure was prepared in the sacrificial arena, lest a righteous recluse or brahmin come and obstruct the sacrifice.

Meanwhile the king had the people sent for, saying, 'Friend, I will have my own sons and daughters and wives killed, and having offered them as a sacrifice I will go to the realm of the gods. Go and explain this to them and bring them here.' And he said for the purpose of bringing his sons:

> 'Go tell the princes—Canda, Suriya, and Bhaddasena,
> And Sūra Vāmagotta—you are all to be sacrificed!'[7] (7)

First they approached Prince Canda and said, 'Prince, your death has been ordered. Your father wishes to go to the realm of the gods, and sent us to seize you.'

'Who told him to have me seized?'

'Khaṇḍahāla, your highness.'

'Is it only me that is to be seized, or others as well?'

'Others are to be seized as well, for he wishes to make the fourfold sacrifice.'

Canda thought, 'He has no hatred of the others. He is angry towards me

7. F has *Canda-Suriyaṃ Bhaddasenañ ca / Sūrañ ca Vāmagottañ ca*. Cowell has a note on this, commenting on the apparent presence of five princes rather than four, and suggesting that Candasuriya could be one name. However, since Canda and Suriya seem clearly to be two separate princes in later verses, and have separate identifications with characters in the present, this is not really a tenable position. On the other hand, the identification of the births says that Sūra Vāmagotta (as one name) is Kassapa. I have therefore chosen to translate this verse accordingly.

alone because I have stopped him living by plundering in the courthouse, yet he will have many killed. When I am able to see my father, it is my duty to ensure all those people are released.' Then he said, 'Do as my father says.' They led him off, and put him to one side in the palace. Then they brought the other three and put them with him, and announced to the king, 'Your Majesty, your sons have been fetched.' Hearing their words, he said 'Friends, now bring my daughters and put them with their brothers!' and spoke the next verse:

> 'Tell the princesses—Upasenā, Kokilā, Muditā,
> And Princess Nandā—you are all to be sacrificed!' (8)

'We will do so!' They went to them and led them crying and lamenting and put them with their brothers. Then in order to have his own wives seized, the king spoke the next verse:

> 'Tell my chief queen Vijayā, and Ekapatī,[8] Kesinī, and Sunandā,
> Endowed with auspicious marks, you are all to be sacrificed!' (9)

[135] They led them lamenting and put them also with the princes. Then the king, having four merchants fetched, spoke the next verse:

> 'Tell the gentlemen—Puṇṇamukha, Bhaddiya, and Siṅgāla
> And also Vaḍḍha—you are all to be sacrificed.' (10)

The king's men went and led them off too.

When the king's wife and children were seized, nobody in the whole city spoke, but the families of the merchants were a large group, so when they were seized, the whole city was agitated, saying, 'Let's not watch the king's merchants being killed as a sacrifice!' And so the merchants came to the king's court surrounded by a group of their relatives. The merchants, surrounded by a multitude of family, begged the king for their lives. Explaining the matter the Teacher said:

> Those gentlemen, surrounded by their families, assembled there and spoke:
> 'Your Majesty, make us all ascetics, or else announce us to be slaves!'[9] (11)

But despite begging in this way, they were not able to obtain their lives.

8. In the VRI edition she is called Erāvatī. F and Cowell do not treat this as a name, but given the repeated fourfold lists of names, I feel inclined to disagree.

9. The commentary explains that *sabbasikhino* is a reference to shaving the heads except for the tuft (usually indicative of asceticism) but then proceeds to explain it as indicating slavery (*ceṭaka*), rather than asceticism. The presence of *atha vā* seems rather to imply that these are two alternatives, not the same one.

The king's men, making the others retreat, seized the four merchants and put them with the princes.

Then the king, in order to have the elephants and so on brought, ordered them to be fetched, saying:

'Now quickly fetch my elephant Abhayaṅkara, and Rājagiri,[10]
Accuggata, and Varuṇadanta![11] They will be used for the sacrifice. (12)
And quickly fetch the horse Assatara, and Suraṃmukha,
Puṇṇaka, and Vindaka! They will be used for the sacrifice. (13)
[136] And fetch me the bulls Yūthapati, Anoja, Nisabha, and Gavampati!
Heap them all up. I will sacrifice. I will give the gifts.[12] (14)
Prepare everything for the sacrifice, when the sun is rising.
And tell the princes to enjoy themselves this night. (15)
Prepare everything for the sacrifice, when the sun is rising.
Speak now to the princes, for tonight is their final night.' (16)

The king's mother and father were still alive, so his advisers went and spoke to his mother: 'My lady, your son is having his sons and wives killed, wanting to make a sacrifice.'

'Friends, what are you saying?' Clutching at her heart with her hand and crying, she came and asked, 'Son, is it really true that such a sacrifice is to take place?' Explaining the matter the Teacher said:

The mother spoke to each one, and crying she came from the palace:
'Son, they say there will be a sacrifice with your four sons.' (17)

The king said:

'When Canda dies all my sons will be sacrificed.
Having sacrificed my sons, I will go to the good realm of heaven.' (18)

Then his mother said:

'Son, don't believe that the good realm is attained by sacrificing sons.
This is the path of the hells; this is not the path of the heavens. (19)
[137] Koṇḍañña,[13] give gifts, and do not harm living things.
This is the path to the good realm—not the path of sacrificing sons.' (20)

10. The VRI edition and some of F's manuscripts have Nāḷāgiri, the name of the elephant which Devadatta let loose on the Buddha in yet another attempt to kill him.

11. This is according to the VRI reading. F has *Accutavaruṇadanta* but then there are only three elephants.

12. Again using the VRI reading. F has only two bulls (omitting the middle two) and has the king ordering 'Let them serve!' (*samupakarontu*) rather than 'Heap them up!' (*samūha karontu*). The latter fits better with the context as well as with the commentary's explanation that the different kinds of animals should be made into a heap (*rāsiṃ*).

13. This is the name of the king's *gotta* 'clan, lineage'.

The king said:

'According to the words of my teachers,
Canda and Suriya should be killed.
Having sacrificed my sons, difficult to give up,
I will go to the good realm of heaven.' (21)

Unable to convince him with her words, his mother left. Then his father heard about the matter and came to question him. Explaining this matter the Teacher said:

In turn, the father Vasavatti also spoke to his own self-begotten son:
'Son, they say there will be a sacrifice with your four sons.' (22)

The king said:

'When Canda dies all my sons will be sacrificed.
Having sacrificed my sons, I will go to the good realm of heaven.' (23)

Then his father said to him:

'Son, don't believe that the good realm is attained by sacrificing sons.
This is the path of the hells; this is not the path of the heavens. (24)
Koṇḍañña, give gifts, and do not harm living things.
This is the path to the good realm—not the path of sacrificing sons.' (25)

The king said:

'According to the words of my teachers,
Canda and Suriya should be killed.
Having sacrificed my sons, difficult to give up,
I will go to the good realm of heaven.' (26)

[138] Then his father said to him:

'Koṇḍañña, give gifts, and do not harm any living beings.
Surrounded by your sons, protect this country and its people.' (27)

But he was not able to convince him.

Then Prince Canda thought, 'All these many people are suffering on account of me alone. Having begged my father I will have all these people freed from the suffering of death.' Talking with his father he said:

'Slay us not, Your Majesty, but make us Khaṇḍahāla's slaves.
Bound in chains we will guard the elephants and horses. (28)
Slay us not, Your Majesty, but make us Khaṇḍahāla's slaves.
Bound in chains we will clear up the elephants' dung. (29)
Slay us not, Your Majesty, but make us Khaṇḍahāla's slaves.
Bound in chains we will clear up the horses' dung. (30)
Slay us not, Your Majesty, but make us slaves.
Or if you so wish we will go forth from the kingdom,
And wander as mendicants.' (31)

Hearing his various lamentations the king felt as if his heart had burst, and with eyes full of tears he said, 'Nobody will kill my sons! What need have I of the realm of the gods!' And he said to free them all:

'This pleading for their lives makes me suffer.
Now free the princes! Enough of me sacrificing my sons!' (32)

Hearing the speech of the king, they freed all of the creatures beginning with the princes and ending with the birds.

Meanwhile Khaṇḍahāla [139] was preparing everything in the sacrificial enclosure, when one man said, 'Hey evil Khaṇḍahāla! The king's sons have been released. You kill your own sons and sacrifice with the blood from their throats!' Exclaiming, 'What has the king done?' Khaṇḍahāla went hastily to the king and said:

'Didn't I tell you before that this is hard to do, this is hard to master?
Why do you create a disturbance when the sacrifice is already prepared? (33)
All proceed to the good realm, performing such a great sacrifice:
Those that sacrifice, or bring about a sacrifice, or rejoice in it.' (34)

The foolish king was convinced by the words of the enraged man, and becoming religious once more he had his sons seized once again. Then Prince Canda, instructing his father, said:

'Why did you have the brahmin recite a birth blessing for us?
For no reason Your Majesty slaughters us for the sake of the sacrifice. (35)
Formerly, when we were small, you did not harm nor slaughter us.
From babies to youths we have grown. Innocent, Father, we are harmed. (36)
Great King, see us armed and mounted on elephants and horses,
Fighting in the battle, for valiant men like me are not meant for sacrifice. (37)
During trouble on the borders or in the forests, men like me are urged onwards.
Without a reason, Father, we are being killed groundlessly. (38)
Even the birds are kind, who live in houses made of grass.
Their sons are dear to them—yet you, Your Majesty, slay us. (39)
[140] Don't trust him! Khaṇḍahāla must not have me killed,
For having killed me he would kill you next, Your Majesty. (40)
Great King, they are given the best villages and best towns for their enjoyment,
And receiving the choicest alms they feed on every family. (41)
But, Great King, they wish to deceive such people;
Your Majesty, as a rule these brahmins are ungrateful. (42)

Slay us not, Your Majesty, but make us Khaṇḍahāla's slaves.
Bound in chains we will guard the elephants and horses. (43)
Slay us not, Your Majesty, but make us Khaṇḍahāla's slaves.
Bound in chains we will clear up the elephants' dung. (44)
Slay us not, Your Majesty, but make us Khaṇḍahāla's slaves.
Bound in chains we will clear up the horses' dung. (45)
Slay us not, Your Majesty, but make us slaves.
Or if you so wish we will go forth from the kingdom,
And wander as mendicants.' (46)

[141] Having heard the entreaties of the prince, the king had them freed again, saying:

'This pleading for their lives makes me suffer.
Now free the princes! Enough of me sacrificing my sons!' (47)

But Khaṇḍahāla came and once more said:

'Didn't I tell you before that this is hard to do, this is hard to master?
Why do you create a disturbance when the sacrifice is already
prepared? (48)
All proceed to the good realm, performing such a great sacrifice:
Those that sacrifice, or bring about a sacrifice, or rejoice in it.' (49)

Having heard this he had them seized again. Trying to persuade him the prince said:

'King, if sacrificing sons leads one after death to the realm of the gods,
Let the brahmin sacrifice his sons, and afterwards you sacrifice yours! (50)
King, if sacrificing sons leads one after death to the realm of the gods,
Let Khaṇḍahāla sacrifice with his own sons. (51)
Knowing this, why does Khaṇḍahāla not slaughter his sons?
And all his relations, and why not slaughter himself? (52)
All proceed to hell, performing such a great sacrifice:
Those that sacrifice, or bring about a sacrifice, or rejoice in it.' (53)

But despite speaking all of this the prince was unable to convince the king. Turning his attention to the assembled people who surrounded the king, Canda said:

[142] 'Now these gentlemen and ladies of the city, loving their sons,
How can they not cry out to the king,
"Don't slaughter your own son"? (54)
Now these gentlemen and ladies of the city, loving their sons,
How can they not cry out to the king,
"Don't slaughter your self-begotten son"? (55)
Desiring the welfare of this king, and the welfare of all of the country,
There is nobody repulsed by this, nor a citizen protesting with me!' (56)

But even after he said that, nobody spoke. Then the prince, sending off his own wives in order to entreat the king, said:

'Go, ladies, speak to my father and Khaṇḍahāla,
"Slay not the princes, innocent and with the appearance of lions." (57)
Go, ladies, speak to my father and Khaṇḍahāla,
"Slay not the princes, who are respected by the whole world."' (58)

They went and begged, but the king did not even look at them. Then the prince became helpless and lamented:

'Had I been born in a family of chariot makers,
Or of outcastes, or had I been born amongst farmers,
I would not today be slain for the king's sacrifice!'[14] (59)

But after saying this he sent off his wives saying:

'All you women go, throw yourselves at the feet of noble Khaṇḍahāla,
And say, "I have not sinned." (60)
[143] All you women go, throw yourselves at the feet of noble Khaṇḍahāla,
And say "Bhante, have we done you harm?"' (61)

Then Prince Canda's younger sister, Princess Selā, was unable to bear the grief, and she fell at her father's feet lamenting. Explaining this matter the Teacher said:

Wretched Selā lamented, seeing her brothers sentenced by him:
'They say my father, desiring heaven, performs this sacrifice.' (62)

But the king was unmoved by her words. Then Prince Canda's son, Vasula, saw his suffering father and fell at the king's feet lamenting, 'I beg my grandfather, please grant my father's life.' Explaining this matter the Teacher said:

With wandering uneven steps Vasula came face to face with the king:
'Don't kill our father,
For we are children who haven't even reached the prime of youth.' (63)

The king heard his lament and felt as if his heart was broken. He embraced the prince with his eyes full of tears, and saying, 'Friend, receive this comfort, for I will set your father free!' he spoke the verse:

'Vasula, here is your father! Your words make me suffer.
Now free the princes—enough of me sacrificing my sons!' (64)

14. Chariot makers are considered a very low caste, and *pukkusa*—the term I have translated here as 'outcaste'—is a mixed non-Aryan caste often responsible for dealing with waste.

But Khaṇḍahāla came and once more said:

'Didn't I tell you before that this is hard to do, this is hard to master?
Why do you create a disturbance when the sacrifice is already prepared? (65)
[144] All proceed to the good realm, performing such a great sacrifice:
Those that sacrifice, or bring about a sacrifice, or rejoice in it.' (66)

And the blind king once again had his sons seized because of Khaṇḍahāla's words. Then Khaṇḍahāla thought, 'This king is weak-minded, now capturing them, now releasing them—indeed he would release his sons because of the words of children. I will lead him right now to the sacrificial arena.' In order to proceed there he spoke the verse:

'The sacrifice of all the jewels is prepared for you, Ekarāja.
Your Majesty, go forth from the palace! You will be delighted in heaven!' (67)

When they took the Bodhisatta away to the sacrificial arena, his womenfolk also went forth together. Explaining this matter the Teacher said:

These seven hundred young wives of Prince Canda
Let down their hair and, weeping, followed on the path. (68)
And others too, grieving, going forth like gods in Nandana Grove,[15]
Let down their hair and, weeping, followed on the path. (69)

And as they went they lamented:

'Wearing pure Kāsi cloth and earrings,
Anointed with aloe and sandalwood paste,
Canda and Suriya are led away to be used in Ekarāja's sacrifice. (70)
Wearing pure Kāsi cloth and earrings,
Anointed with aloe and sandalwood paste,
Canda and Suriya are led away, making their mother's heart grieve. (71)
Wearing pure Kāsi cloth and earrings,
Anointed with aloe and sandalwood paste,
Canda and Suriya are led away, making the people's hearts grieve. (72)
Carefully bathed, wearing earrings,
Anointed with aloe and sandalwood paste,
Canda and Suriya are led away to be used in Ekarāja's sacrifice. (73)
[145] They used to travel on noble elephants, but now proceed on foot!
Today Canda and Suriya are both walking. (74)
They used to travel on noble horses, but now proceed on foot!

15. The foremost of the parks in the Heaven of the Thirty-Three, where the gods go—led by Indra—for their amusement.

Today Canda and Suriya are both walking. (75)
They used to travel in noble chariots, but now proceed on foot!
Today Canda and Suriya are both walking. (76)
They used to lead on swift horses in shining harnesses,
Today Canda and Suriya are both going on foot.' (77)

While they were lamenting in this way, the Bodhisatta was taken out of the city. Having become agitated, the whole city began to leave too. The people went forth and proceeded to the gates. The brahmin saw the very large crowd of people and had the city gates closed, saying, 'Who knows what will happen?' The people, unable to leave, assembled in a park near the city gates and let forth a great cry. A group of birds was disturbed by this cry and took to the sky. The people addressed each of the birds and lamenting said:

'Bird, if you want meat, fly east from Pupphavatī!
There mad Ekarāja is sacrificing his four sons. (78)
Bird, if you want meat, fly east from Pupphavatī!
There mad Ekarāja is sacrificing his four girls. (79)
Bird, if you want meat, fly east from Pupphavatī!
There mad Ekarāja is sacrificing his four wives. (80)
Bird, if you want meat, fly east from Pupphavatī!
There mad Ekarāja is sacrificing four gentlemen. (81)
[146] Bird, if you want meat, fly east from Pupphavatī!
There mad Ekarāja is sacrificing four elephants. (82)
Bird, if you want meat, fly east from Pupphavatī!
There mad Ekarāja is sacrificing four horses. (83)
Bird, if you want meat, fly east from Pupphavatī!
There mad Ekarāja is sacrificing four bulls. (84)
Bird, if you want meat, fly east from Pupphavatī!
There mad Ekarāja is sacrificing all the groups of four.' (85)

The citizens, having lamented there in that way, went to the Bodhisatta's residence and respectfully circumambulated the palace. They saw the inner chambers, the belvedere, and pleasure groves and so on, and grieved with verses:

'This is his palace, this is his delightful inner apartment.
Now those four noble sons are led to the slaughter. (86)
This is his golden belvedere, strewn all over with garlands and flowers.
Now those four noble sons are led to the slaughter. (87)
This is his pleasure park, delightful, full of flowers that are always in season.
Now those four noble sons are led to the slaughter. (88)

This is his Asoka grove, delightful, full of flowers that are always in season.
Now those four noble sons are led to the slaughter. (89)
This is his Kaṇikāra grove, delightful, full of flowers that are always in season.
Now those four noble sons are led to the slaughter. (90)
This is his Pāṭalī grove, delightful, full of flowers that are always in season.
Now those four noble sons are led to the slaughter. (91)
This is his mango grove, delightful, full of flowers that are always in season.
Now those four noble sons are led to the slaughter. (92)
[147] This is his lotus pool, covered with lotuses of many colours
And a boat made of gold, delightful and decorated with a flower garland.
Now those four noble sons are led to the slaughter.' (93)

And having lamented in these various places, they approached the elephant stables and so on and said:

'This is his jewel of an elephant, the mighty tusker elephant Erāvaṇa.
Now those four noble sons are led to the slaughter. (94)
This is his jewel of a horse, the horse Ekakhura.[16]
Now those four noble sons are led to the slaughter. (95)
This is his horse chariot Sāḷikanigghosa,[17]
Shining and ornamented with jewels,
In which the noble sons shone like gods in Nandana.
Now those four noble sons are led to the slaughter. (96)
How indeed can the mad king sacrifice his four sons,
Who are beautiful, serene, and golden coloured,[18]
And whose limbs are smeared with sandalwood paste?[19] (97)
How indeed can the mad king sacrifice his four daughters,

16. The commentary explains *ekakhuro* as 'having unbroken hooves' and accordingly F does not record this as a name. However, given the pattern of the verses I am inclined to disagree.

17. Again the commentary does not explain this explicitly as a name, but rather explains that *sāḷikanigghoso* means that when it is time to go, people flock around it like birds (*sāḷika viya*) to shout out (*nigghosa*) praise of it. But as in the previous case I am inclined to translate it as the name of the prince's chariot.

18. The commentary explains that *sāmasamasundarehi* means they are shining golden, calm about rebirth in one or another realm, and beautiful with non-hatred.

19. This phrase *candanamarakatagattehi* is somewhat problematic. In place of the unclear component *marakata* VRI has *muduka* ('soft'), giving an overall meaning of 'with limbs soft [as? with?] sandalwood'. The commentary says the limbs are smeared with red sandalwood paste.

Who are beautiful, serene, and golden coloured,
And whose limbs are smeared with sandalwood paste? (98)
How indeed can the mad king sacrifice his four wives,
Who are beautiful, serene, and golden coloured,
And whose limbs are smeared with sandalwood paste? (99)
How indeed can the mad king sacrifice his four gentlemen,
Who are beautiful, serene, and golden coloured,
And whose limbs are smeared with sandalwood paste? (100)
Some towns and villages become vast forests—empty and haunted.
Pupphavatī will become like this when Canda and Suriya
are sacrificed.' (101)

[148] And in this way those many people, unable to go outside, wandered within the city, lamenting.

Meanwhile the Bodhisatta was led to the sacrificial arena. His mother, the queen named Gotamī, fell at the feet of the king, saying, 'Give me my sons' lives, Your Majesty!' Crying, she said:

'Because of you killing these beings,[20]
I will become mad, and scattered with dust!
If they kill noble Canda, these creatures destroy me, Your Majesty. (102)
Because of you killing these beings,
I will become mad, and scattered with dust!
If they kill noble Suriya, these creatures destroy me, Your Majesty.' (103)

Despite lamenting in this way, she didn't receive a response from the king, so she went and embraced the prince's four wives, and saying, 'My son being angry with you will be gone. Why don't you make him turn back?' she lamented:

'Shouldn't these women, Ghaṭṭiyā, Oparikkhī, Pokkharakā, and Gāyikā,
Give pleasure, speaking amiably to one another
And dancing for Canda and Suriya? Their equal cannot be found.' (104)

Having lamented with her daughters-in-law, she could not see anything else to be done, and began abusing Khaṇḍahāla. She spoke eight verses:

'This heart of mine grieves! Khaṇḍahāla, may your mother experience
The pain my heart feels when Canda is led to the slaughter. (105)

20. The term *bhūnahatā* is very tricky. PED defines *bhūnaha* and variants as 'a destroyer of beings' but notes the problems of interpretation and origins. The commentary glosses with *hatavaḍḍhi*, which might mean a person who profits from killing. The implication, therefore, is that the term refers to the king, rather than to Gotamī, but it is not possible to be completely certain about this.

[149] This heart of mine grieves! Khaṇḍahāla, may your mother experience
The pain my heart feels when Suriya is led to the slaughter. (106)
This heart of mine grieves! Khaṇḍahāla, may your wife experience
The pain my heart feels when Canda is led to the slaughter. (107)
This heart of mine grieves! Khaṇḍahāla, may your wife experience
The pain my heart feels when Suriya is led to the slaughter. (108)
Khaṇḍahāla, may your mother see neither her sons nor her husband again!
For you would kill the princes, innocent and with the appearance of lions. (109)
Khaṇḍahāla, may your mother see neither her sons nor her husband again!
For you would kill the princes, who are loved by the whole world. (110)
Khaṇḍahāla, may your wife see neither her sons nor her husband again!
For you would kill the princes, innocent and with the appearance of lions. (111)
Khaṇḍahāla, may your wife see neither her sons nor her husband again!
For you would kill the princes, who are loved by the whole world.' (112)

Then the Bodhisatta, in the sacrificial arena, begged his father saying:

'Slay us not, Your Majesty, but make us Khaṇḍahāla's slaves.
Bound in chains we will guard the elephants and horses. (113)
Slay us not, Your Majesty, but make us Khaṇḍahāla's slaves.
Bound in chains we will clear up the elephants' dung. (114)
Slay us not, Your Majesty, but make us Khaṇḍahāla's slaves.
Bound in chains we will clear up the horses' dung. (115)
Slay us not, Your Majesty, but make us Khaṇḍahāla's slaves.
Or if you so wish we will leave the kingdom! (116)
[150] Your Majesty, even the poor, desirous of sons, entreat the gods.
Losing even their faith some do not obtain sons. (117)
People make an aspiration: 'May sons and grandsons be born!'
Yet Your Majesty slaughters us for the sacrifice with no reason. (118)
With begging one obtains a son—don't slaughter us, Father.
Don't perform this sacrifice with sons that are difficult to obtain. (119)
With begging one obtains a son—don't slaughter us, Father.
Don't sacrifice with sons that are painful to obtain,
Don't take us from our mother!' (120)

But despite speaking in this way, he received no response from his father, and so he went and bowed at the feet of his mother. Lamenting he said:

'Having nourished him through great hardships,
You are deprived of your son Canda.

I bow at your feet, Mother. May Father obtain the next world. (121)
Oh embrace me! Allow me to bow at your feet, Mother.
Now I go away, for Ekarāja's sacrifice. (122)
Oh embrace me! Allow me to bow at your feet, Mother.
Now I go away, making my mother's heart grieve. (123)
Oh embrace me! Allow me to bow at your feet, Mother.
Now I go away, making the people's hearts grieve.' (124)

[151] His mother, lamenting, spoke four verses:

'And now, son of Gotamī, bind lotus leaves into a headdress
Mixed with *campaka* and plantain, as used to happen. (125)
And now apply the final sandalwood paste,
Anointed by which you shine in the royal assembly. (126)
And now put on the last soft Kāsi clothes,
Clothed in which you shine in the royal assembly. (127)
Take the hand ornaments, adorned with pearls, jewels, and gold,
Wearing which you shine in the royal assembly.' (128)

Then his chief queen, called Candā,[21] threw herself at the feet of the king and crying said:

'Oh is this the protector of the kingdom,
Lord of the earth, inheritor of the country,
The great lord of the world, who has such affection for his sons?' (129)

Hearing this the king spoke the verse:

'My sons are dear to me indeed, as are my wives and myself.
But, wishing for heaven, I will slaughter them.' (130)

[152] Candā said:

'Slay me first, don't break my suffering heart.
Beautiful and adorned, your son is tender, Your Majesty! (131)
And so, sire, kill me—I will go to the next world with Canda.
You will make abundant merit,
And the two of us will wander in the next world.' (132)

The king said:

'No Candā—please don't wish for death!
You have many brothers-in-law, large-eyed one,
Who will comfort you when Gotamī's son is sacrificed.' (133)

21. I am deliberately reproducing the text's ambiguity about whether Candā is wife of Canda (as seems likely from her role in the story and her identification as a past birth of the Buddha's wife) or of Ekarāja (as is arguably implied by calling her the chief queen (*aggamahesī*)).

The Teacher further said this half verse:

Saying this Candā beat herself with the palms of her hands. (134a)

Then she lamented further:

'Enough with this life; I will drink poison, I will die! (134b)
For indeed there are no friends or courtiers of this king to be found,
Good hearted, who would tell the king, "Slay not your own sons!" (135)
For indeed there are no friends and relatives of this king to be found,
Good hearted, who would tell the king, "Slay not your own sons!" (136)
[153] King, these are my sons, armoured and in royal ornaments,
With these make your sacrifice, but free Gotamī's sons! (137)
Great King, chop me into a hundred pieces, and sacrifice me in seven portions,
But don't kill your eldest son, innocent and with the appearance of a lion. (138)
Great King, chop me into a hundred pieces, and sacrifice me in seven portions,
But don't kill your eldest son, loved by the whole world.' (139)

Though lamenting with these verses in the king's presence, she did not receive any consolation, and so she approached the Bodhisatta and stood there weeping. Then he said to her, 'Candā, on various notable occasions during my lifetime I brought and gave you many varieties of pearls and jewels and so on. But today there is this final gift: I am giving you this ornament from my body—take it!' Explaining this matter the Teacher said:

'Many and various jewels were given to you, at notable times:
Pearls, jewels, and lapis lazuli. This is your final gift.' (140)

Hearing this Queen Candā cried and uttered nine further verses:

'Previously, blossoming garlands fell across their backs,
But today a poison-sharpened[22] sword will fall across their backs. (141)
Previously, shining garlands fell across their backs,
But today a poison-sharpened sword will fall across their backs. (142)
Surely the sword will fall on the princes' backs very soon!
But my heart will not burst, as long as it is steadfastly bound. (143)
[154] Wearing pure Kāsi cloth and earrings,
Anointed with aloe and sandalwood paste,
Lead Canda and Suriya away to be used in Ekarāja's sacrifice. (144)
Wearing pure Kāsi cloth and earrings,
Anointed with aloe and sandalwood paste,

22. The term *pītanisito* could also mean 'golden and sharpened'—see PED entries 1 and 2 for *pīta*. The VRI edition has *sunisito* 'well-sharpened'.

Lead Canda and Suriya away, making their mother's heart grieve. (145)
Wearing pure Kāsi cloth and earrings,
Anointed with aloe and sandalwood paste,
Lead Canda and Suriya away, making the people's hearts grieve. (146)
Carefully bathed, wearing earrings,
Anointed with aloe and sandalwood paste,
Lead Canda and Suriya away to be used in Ekarāja's sacrifice. (147)
Carefully bathed, wearing earrings,
Annointed with aloe and sandalwood paste,
Lead Canda and Suriya away, making their mother's heart grieve. (148)
Carefully bathed, wearing earrings,
Anointed with aloe and sandalwood paste,
Lead Canda and Suriya away, making the people's hearts grieve.' (149)

While she was lamenting in this way, all the preparations in the sacrificial ground were finished. The king's son was led forward, had his neck bent, and was made to sit. Khaṇḍahāla held a golden vessel close, took his sword, and stood there saying, 'I will cut his neck'. Seeing this, Queen Candā thought, 'There is no other refuge for me! I will ensure my lord's safety with the power of my own truth.' She made a respectful salute, and wandering amongst the assembly she performed an Act of Truth. Explaining this matter the Teacher said:

While everyone drew near, and Canda was sat down ready for the sacrifice,
The king of Pañcāla's daughter, holding up clasped hands,
Wandered all through the assembly: (150)
'By the truth "foolish Khaṇḍahāla is doing an evil act"—
By this spoken truth, may I have my lord. (151)
You non-humans who are here, and *yakkha*s and other beings,[23]
Perform what I desire: let me have my lord. (152)
[155] Those *devatā*s that have come here, and spirits and beings,[24]
Be a refuge for the helpless! Protect me, I entreat you.' (153)

Sakka, king of the gods, heard the sound of her lament, understood what was going on, and went there with a flaming iron hammer. He terrified the king and dispersed everyone. Explaining the matter the Teacher said:

23. *Yakkhabhūtabhavyāni*. A *yakkha* is a demon or spirit deity. *Bhūta* and *bhavya* refer rather vaguely to 'beings' but can more specifically be categories of spirits and creatures that are neither human nor animal nor fully divine. The commentary has specific definitions, but these seem unhelpful for the translation of the verse.

24. Again the term here is *bhūtabhavyāni*. A *devatā* is also a form of spirit or demigod, often a god that inhabits an earthly place, for example a tree or pond.

Hearing that, a god wielded his iron hammer.
Filling him with fear, he said this to the king: (154)
'Recognise me, sinful king, lest I strike you on the head.
Don't kill your eldest son, innocent with the appearance of a lion. (155)
Sinful king, who do you see? Your sons and wives are being killed!
And the householder merchants, innocent and desirous of heaven!' (156)
Hearing that and seeing this marvel, Khaṇḍahāla and the king
Freed all those who were bound, and did not hurt them. (157)
When they were all released, those who were assembled there
All took clods of earth and one by one they punished him,
And brought about the destruction of Khaṇḍahāla. (158)

[156] And having killed him the people began to kill the king. But the Bodhisatta embraced his father and would not let them kill him. The citizens said, 'Grant this evil king his life, but we will not see his royal canopy abiding in the city. We will make him an outcaste and have him dwell outside the city.' Having removed his royal apparel they dressed him in yellow robes, wrapped his head with turmeric rags, made him an outcaste and sent him to a settlement of outcastes. And those who made sacrifices even with slaughtered cattle, and those who brought about a sacrifice or rejoiced in it, all met their end in hell. Explaining this matter the Teacher said:

All those who make demerit fall into hell,
But those who don't are able to go from here to heaven. (159)

And the citizens, having removed the two black-eared (ill-omened) ones, arranged for a consecration and crowned Prince Canda. Explaining this matter the Teacher said:

When all were freed, there was a great gathering:
An assembly of royals gathered there and consecrated Canda. (160)
When all were freed, there was a great gathering:
The royal daughters assembled there and consecrated Canda. (161)
When all were freed, there was a great gathering:
A divine assembly gathered there and consecrated Canda. (162)
When all were freed, there was a great gathering:
The daughters of the gods assembled there and consecrated Canda. (163)
When all were freed, there was a great gathering:
The royal assembly gathered and waved their garments in applause. (164)
When all were freed, there was a great gathering:
The royal daughters assembled and waved their garments in applause. (165)
When all were freed, there was a great gathering:
A divine assembly gathered and waved their garments in applause. (166)
When all were freed, there was a great gathering:

The daughters of the gods assembled and waved their garments in applause. (167)
When all were freed, there was a great rejoicing amongst the family.
Joy was ushered into the city when their release was announced. (168)

[157] The Bodhisatta provided for his father's needs, but he was not allowed inside the city. When his allowance ran out he would approach the Bodhisatta while he was sporting in the parks and so on. Thinking, 'I am the lord,' he did not bow to him, but he made a respectful salutation and said, 'Live long, sire.' The Bodhisatta would ask him what he needed, and give him funds. The Bodhisatta ruled the kingdom righteously, and when his life was concluded he went to fill the realm of the gods.

Having spoken this *dhamma* teaching the Teacher said, 'It is not only now, monks, but also in the past that Devadatta on account of me alone tried to kill many.' He made the connections of the birth story: 'At that time Devadatta was Khaṇḍahāla, Mahāmāyā was Queen Gotamī, the mother of Rāhula was Queen Candā, Rāhula was Vasula, Uppalavaṇṇā was Selā, Kassapa was Sūra Vāmagotta, Moggallāna was Bhaddasena,[25] Sāriputta was Prince Suriya, and I myself—Fully Awakened Buddha—was King Canda.'

25. F has *Candasena*, but earlier in the text he is called Bhaddasena. The VRI edition and one of F's manuscripts have *Bhaddasena*.

8

The (Great) Birth Story of Nārada (Kassapa)

(*Nārada-jātaka* or *Mahānāradakassapa-jātaka*)

INTRODUCTION

The eighth story of the *Mahānipāta* is said to address the perfection of equanimity (*upekkhā*), though quite how this is displayed is unclear. The story tells of a king led astray by the fatalist teachings of a wandering ascetic, the attempts of his daughter to bring him to a correct understanding of karma, and the final intervention of a divine sage (the Bodhisatta) called Nārada Brahmā. The main focus would appear to be the workings of karma, and it is here, perhaps, that the teachings on equanimity are implicit: understanding that all beings are the heirs to their karma is said to cause equanimity to arise.[1]

Seeing all beings as heirs to their karma can be made easier by being able to see one's own past lives, as several characters in this story do. However, this *jātaka* also demonstrates that past-life memory can be dangerous if incorrectly mediated, or if only a limited view of the past is gained. According to the Theravāda understanding, the ability to recall

Introduced and translated by Naomi Appleton.

Translator's note: I am grateful to L. S. Cousins, who read this story with myself and Sarah Shaw during the summer of 2010. Many of the more difficult passages were made intelligible thanks to his expert eye. For a more detailed discussion of this story in relation to karma, rebirth, and the early Indian religious scene, see chapter 1 of Appleton 2014.

1. For example in Buddhaghosa's Vsm IX 96.

one's past lives is attained through advanced meditation, specifically the fourth *jhāna.* As such it is open to all meditators, and not limited to the Buddha or even Buddhists. Buddhaghosa records that sectarians too can have limited vision of their past lives, but that this is far inferior to the vision of the Buddha or his chief followers.[2] This distinction is amply demonstrated by the various characters in the *Nārada-jātaka* and the use they make of their limited recollections. And in this story of human lives in a time without Buddhism, the Bodhisatta, Nārada Brahmā, might be seen as in some way representing the Buddhist meditative perspective when he demonstrates a balanced equanimity, combined with compassion, in his intervention in the royal dispute.

The Ascetic Guṇa

The naked ascetic who leads the king into a hedonistic immorality is said to be an Ājīvika. This term denotes a religious group contemporary with early Buddhism (and indeed Jainism) who are described as fatalists. Although Ājīvikism survived in India until at least the fourteenth century, none of their texts or teachings survive, and so what we know of the tradition is reconstructed from descriptions in Buddhist and Jain texts, which hardly preserve impartial accounts. One key source for Ājīvika teachings is the *Sāmaññaphala Sutta*, the second discourse of the *Dīgha Nikāya*. In this text Ajātasattu, the patricidal king of Magadha, explains to the Buddha what teachings he has received from six wandering ascetics of the time. Amongst these six 'heretics' we find the leader of the Jains, a materialist, and three teachers that can be associated with the Ājīvika school.[3] The *Sāmaññaphala Sutta* would appear to be the source for much of the material found in Guṇa's teachings. Ideas placed in the mouths of diverse teachers are here combined and attributed to a single, dangerously influential ascetic.

Although the story labels Guṇa as an Ājīvika, his doctrines include materialism (the lack of another world, the denial of rebirth) as well as ideas associated with the Ājīvika tradition, such as the inability to alter one's destiny, the seven eternal substances, and the gradual purification of beings. Materialism and Ājīvikism are inconsistent with one another, suggesting that Guṇa is really a catch-all heretic, a narrative device.

2. See discussion in Vsm XIII 13 ff.
3. For a very useful discussion see Basham 1951, especially chapter 2.

However, one feature of his teachings is consistent: he denies the efficacy of karma, and therefore teaches that it makes no difference how you behave.[4] It is this teaching that is so dangerous not only to Buddhism but also to ordinary moral human society.

Karma and Rebirth

As the character of the ascetic highlights, a key focus for this story is the way in which karma operates. The ascetic's teaching is considered particularly dangerous because it denies the efficacy of karma; in other words, it suggests that moral behaviour brings no rewards. It therefore encourages the king to indulge his every desire, which not only brings the kingdom into disarray but also stores up a large amount of bad karma for the king himself.

The only person in the palace who understands the proper workings of karma is the king's daughter, Rucā. Her advanced understanding is at least in part due to her ability to see her past and future lives. In contrast to two other associates of the king, Alāta and Bījaka, who can see only a single past life and thus misinterpret what they see, Rucā has enough vision to see the delayed fruiting of different karmic deeds over multiple lives. Her superior vision is complemented by the explanations of the commentator about the longer karmic histories of Alāta and Bījaka. That these commentarial explanations are embedded in word commentary (and thus left untranslated by Cowell and Rouse) suggests they may not be intended as part of the narrative itself. However, they do demonstrate the concern the commentator had to ensure the audience understands that karma works itself out over multiple lifetimes, and thus that Alāta and Bījaka's simplistic understandings are incorrect. I have therefore included these passages in my translation but placed them inside parentheses. (The same applies to several other passages of narrative that are embedded within word commentary in this story.)

4. It is highly unlikely that a religious tradition teaching that one's actions are irrelevant would survive, with a community of renouncers, for so many centuries, so this must be a caricature of the Ājīvika teachings. Bronkhorst (2011: 15) has suggested that the real teaching of the Ājīvikas may have been that one's existing karmic load cannot be removed through any means but that one can still prevent further influx of karma from occurring through careful ascetic practice.

Rucā's karmic history, related by her to the king, provides evidence for the efficacy of karma and the importance of behaving in a moral way. In Rucā's past lives we see the consequences of going after other men's wives: rebirth in hell, followed by birth as a series of castrated animals, then as a neuter, then as a female human or god. The human and divine births are good in some ways, and this is due to past good deeds, but her female state limits her abilities. As discussed in the Introduction, Rucā is just one of several strong female characters in the *Mahānipāta*, and the story's ambivalence towards her female state is very revealing about attitudes towards women in early Buddhism. It is no coincidence that her karmic history is dominated by sexual impropriety, for this is the very same fault that now afflicts her father, and thus Rucā is well aware of the suffering that awaits him in future lives. The poetic justice of the karmic fruits is common in narrative materials, and is—one assumes—particularly potent for the audience.

As well as commenting on the importance of being a believer in karma, understanding its workings over multiple lives, and the poetic nature of its consequences, the *Nārada-jātaka* also has something to tell us about the different realms of rebirth. Rucā narrates past lives in hell and as an animal—both realms of severe suffering, even without the specific results of her adulterous actions. In addition, a god comes to pay a visit and describes the hells in great and gory detail. This story thus draws on references to the main realms of rebirth in order to instruct human beings in how to avoid negative states of existence. The audience is left in no doubt of the existence of these realms, and thus is cured of any potential materialist tendencies. Crucially, the audience is also taught that actions affect one's future experiences, and should therefore be considered very carefully.

The Characters

The *Nārada-jātaka* is said to have been told by the Buddha about his conversion of Uruvela Kassapa, a leading rival ascetic of the time. It is therefore no surprise that in the identification of the births, the king who was converted by Nārada Brahmā (the Bodhisatta) is identified as Uruvela Kassapa. The ascetic is said to be Sunakkhatta the Licchavi, who was at one time a follower of the Buddha but later transferred his allegiance to another teacher. He criticised the Buddha, saying he could not possibly be awakened because he did not display any supernormal powers. Sunakkhatta's fickle commitment to a number of rival teachers and doctrines may be reflected in Guṇa's various inconsistent views.[5] Devadatta, the Buddha's infamous cousin who caused a schism in the Buddhist community, is identified as Alāta, the courtier who bolsters his fatalist teaching by recalling a single past life. Alāta's limited memory may be intended as a mockery of Devadatta's incomplete mastery of the teaching. Curiously, the courtier responsible for leading the king to the ascetic is identified with the senior monk Sāriputta.

The most interesting revelation in the identification of the births is the statement that 'Ānanda was Rucā who reconciled the king'. This simple line tells us two important things: Firstly, the princess, whose superior understanding of karma is praised by Nārada Brahmā himself, is a past life of Ānanda, the Buddha's male personal attendant, noted for his loyalty but not, perhaps, his intellect. Is this identification intended as a mockery of Ānanda, whose sympathy towards women led to him convincing the Buddha to create an order of nuns, and whose emotional attachment to the Buddha prevented him from attaining arhatship until after the Buddha's death?[6] Secondly, the line suggests that Rucā succeeded in her attempts to convince her father, whereas in fact she fails and has to call upon the gods to help her. The term used—*pasādayi*, from *pasādeti*—means to reconcile or make glad, but cognate terms are often used in stories of conversion or the engendering of faith. The identification of the births thus accords Rucā a more important place in the narrative than she actually has.

Like many of the other stories of the *Mahānipāta*, the *Nārada-jātaka* has only a few key characters: the king, his three courtiers, the false ascetic, the princess, and the divine sage Nārada, who is identified as the Bodhisatta. While much of the dramatic tension revolves around the king and his discussions with his courtiers, the ascetic, and then his daughter, one cannot forget the role of the Bodhisatta in his spectacular entrance, witty instruction, and spine-tingling account of the hells. In addition, we must bear in mind the wider significance of the character Nārada, who appears in Hindu and Jain narratives too, often visiting the world of men to offer advice on correct living.[7] By declaring that a divine sage familiar from the

5. Sunakkhatta's fickle-minded adherence to rival religious traditions is also referred to in his identification as Ariṭṭha in the *Bhūridatta-jātaka* (Chapter 6).

6. I discuss this possibility, as part of a wider exploration of sex-change in Buddhist literature, in Appleton 2011.

7. For a discussion of Nārada's role in Hindu and Jain narrative, in which he is often closely involved in discussions of non-Vedic ideas, see Geen (forthcoming).

wider Indian story-pot was actually the Buddha in a past life, the *Nārada-jātaka* once again reinforces its message about the central importance of karma (and the concomitant impermanence of divine birth) as well as gaining some serious heroic weight for the Bodhisatta.

Although the number of key characters in this story is few, in another version found in Āryaśūra's *Jātakamālā* (number 29) it is simplified even further. In that version, a god from a high heaven (the Bodhisatta) comes to visit the king because the king has a wrong view. There is no ascetic to demonstrate the views of rival schools, and there is no princess to teach the truth or call on the gods. The setting is a simple dialogue between king and god—not explicitly Nārada, though he is a divine sage. The content of the dialogue is similar to that in our *jātaka*, with the king denying the existence of the other worlds and the god describing the hells. However, while the teaching is present, the dramatic tension is lost: we only see the great compassion of the Bodhisatta who, even when born in the highest heavens, wishes to help all beings. In contrast, in the *Nārada-jātaka* we witness a good king led astray due to his association with bad advisers, a heretic that represents all the dangerous and opposing views, a princess who explains the gradual fruiting of karma and the great danger of philandering, and then—at the climax—the intervention of a divine sage.

'There was a king of Videha . . .'

[219] This story about the conversion of Uruvela Kassapa was told by the Teacher while he was dwelling in the Laṭṭhivana Park.[8] The Teacher, who had set in motion the glorious wheel of the *dhamma*, [220] converted the ascetics beginning with Uruvela Kassapa, and then came to the Laṭṭhivana Park accompanied by the thousand former ascetics to discharge[9] a promise to the king of Magadha.[10] The king of Magadha came with an assembly of twelve myriads, and after he had honoured the Ten-Powered One, a thought occurred to the brahmins and householders within his assembly: 'Is Uruvela

8. A park southwest of Rājagaha. See DPPN.

9. Following F's Burmese manuscript's reading of *mocetuṃ*. F has *muñcetuṃ*, while VRI *locetuṃ* is difficult to make sense of.

10. The Buddha, as a Bodhisatta, had promised the king of Magadha (Bimbisāra) that he would return after his awakening.

Kassapa practising the religious life under the great renouncer,[11] or is the great renouncer under Uruvela Kassapa?' The Blessed One thought, 'I will make it known that Kassapa has gone forth in my presence,' and spoke this verse:

> Resident of Uruvelā! The ascetic and teacher[12]
> Renounced the fire after having seen what?
> I ask you this, Kassapa:
> How is it that your fire sacrifice is abandoned?'

Understanding the Blessed One's intention, the Elder said:

> 'They say that forms, sounds and flavours,
> And women for sensual pleasure come from sacrifices.
> Knowing these to be dirt, as worldly attachments,
> I thus find pleasure neither in sacrifice nor oblation.'

Having spoken this verse, wanting to make it clear that he was the disciple, he touched his head to the Tathāgata's feet and saying, 'Bhante, the Blessed One is my teacher, I am his disciple,' he rose seven times into the air, to the height of one palm tree, two trees, three, all the way up to seven palm trees high. Having descended he bowed to the Tathāgata and sat to one side. Seeing that miracle the people began to talk of the Teacher's qualities, saying, 'Oh the Buddha is mighty! Even Uruvela Kassapa, who had entrenched views and thought himself an *arahat*, has been converted by the Tathāgata, who has broken his net of views.' Hearing this the Teacher said, 'It is not marvelous that I should convert him now, when I have attained omniscience. Formerly, when I was still subject to passion, I became a Brahmā called Nārada and broke his net of views, making him humble.' Entreated by the assembly he told a story of the past.

In times past, a righteous and just king called Aṅgati ruled in Mithilā in the kingdom of Videha. A daughter called Rucā[13] was conceived in the

11. *Samaṇa* is cognate with Sanskrit *śramaṇa*, and means a striver or one who exerts himself. It is used to refer to the various religious wanderers, ascetics, and recluses of the time, including the Buddha.

12. Reading *kisakovadāno* as a compound of *kisaka* 'emaciated person' (possibly a specific type of ascetic) and *ovadāna* 'instructor'. An alternative, following F's printing of *kisako vadāno*, would be 'the so-called ascetic' or 'the one called an ascetic'.

13. F has Rujā but here I follow the VRI Rucā. The name is probably intended as a variation of *ruci* 'light, splendour, pleasure'.

womb of his chief wife, and she was beautiful, charming, and of great merit, having made aspirations[14] for a hundred thousand aeons. All the rest of his sixteen thousand wives were barren, so this daughter became dear and pleasing to him. Every day he sent twenty-five flower baskets filled with various flowers to her, along with exquisite clothes, saying, 'Let her adorn herself with these.' [221] There was no limit to her hard and soft food, and twice a month he sent a thousand pieces saying, 'Let her give alms.'[15] Now he had three courtiers called Vijaya, Sunāma, and Alāta. During the Komudi festival of the fourth month,[16] when the city and inner palace were adorned like the city of gods, he was bathed, perfumed, and adorned with all his ornaments and stood on the terrace by an open window surrounded by his courtiers. He saw the moon's disc rising into the expanse of pure sky and asked his courtiers, 'Friends, this is indeed a delightful moonlit night. With what pleasures should we amuse ourselves today?' Explaining the matter the Teacher said:

> There was a king of Videha, a warrior named Aṅgati,
> Wealthy, with abundant carriages and an innumerable army. (1)
> When the first watch of the fifteenth night arrived,
> During the full moon of the fourth month, he gathered together his courtiers: (2)
> Wise and learned ones, skilful, who smile before speaking,[17]
> Vijaya, Sunāma, and the general Alātaka. (3)
> Then the Videhan asked each of them to explain their own liking:
> 'Today is the Komudi of the fourth month, moonlit, with darkness dispelled.
> On this occasion, for this night, with what pleasures should we occupy ourselves?' (4)

Questioned by him, each one spoke of his own inclination. Explaining the matter the Teacher said:

14. Presumably she was aspiring to be born as a princess, or at least as a human with certain beauty and wealth.

15. Alternatively: 'He sent her a thousand pieces saying, "There is no limit to the hard and soft food. Let her give alms every fortnight."'

16. A full moon festival that marks the end of the four months of the rainy season. This is traditionally one of the most important festivals in Buddhist countries, and may have its origins in pre-Buddhist times. It is called Komudi after the white water lilies that bloom at that time.

17. *Mihitapubbe* 'smile before' is glossed in the commentary as *pathamaṃ sitaṃ katvā pacchā kathanasīle* 'those whose nature is to smile first and then talk'.

Then the general Alāta said this to the king:
'Let us array the army, the army that is entirely willing and able. (5)
[222] Let us go out to battle, Your Majesty, who has an innumerable army.[18]
Let us bring under your control those who have not come under your control.
This is my own view: let us conquer the unconquered!' (6)
Hearing Alāta's words, Sunāma said this:
'Great King, all your enemies are gathered here. (7)
They have laid down their weapons themselves, and are submissive.
Today is the best festival, so I do not delight in war. (8)
Let them quickly bring food and water and nourishment.
Delight in sense pleasures, Your Majesty, in music, song, and dance.' (9)
Hearing Sunāma's words, Vijaya said this:
'Great King, all the sense pleasures are permanently close at hand. (10)
Your Majesty, they are not hard to get, to enjoy yourself with sense pleasure.
Sense pleasures are always obtainable, so this is not my idea. (11)
Let us attend on a learned brahmin or renouncer,
A seer,[19] learned in practical and religious matters,[20] who can remove our doubt today.' (12)
Hearing Vijaya's words, King Aṅgati said:
'What Vijaya said, this pleases me. (13)
Let us attend on a learned brahmin or renouncer,
A seer, learned in practical and religious matters, who can remove our doubt today. (14)
Make it all happen![21] What wise man should we attend to?
Which seer, learned in practical and religious matters, can remove our doubt today?' (15)
Hearing the Videhan's words, Alāta said this:

18. *Anantabalaporisā* is likely a vocative here, as an epithet of the king.

19. The term for seer is found in the form *ise* which would normally be vocative. However, in this verse, as in vv. 14 and 15, it must instead be read as nominative singular (usual form isi). The vocative term is used frequently at the end of verses addressed to seers in epic verse, so perhaps its frequent appearance thus has influenced the use of the term here. I am grateful to L. S. Cousins for a discussion of this matter.

20. *Atthadhammavidū* 'learned in *attha* and *dhamma*', with *attha* holding a range of meanings relating to profit and purpose, but also meaning and aim, and *dhamma* referring to anything from duty and righteousness to religious teaching and truth.

21. To make this verse metrical one must remove either *santā* (the present participle of the verb 'to be', thus meaning 'existing' or 'happening') or *matiṃ* (here in the sense of 'wish' or 'desire'); the latter may have crept in from the commentary. The resulting meaning is much the same whichever word is elided.

'There is in the deer park a naked ascetic, endowed with wisdom, (16)
Wise and eloquent, with a great following, this Guṇa from the Kassapa clan.
Your Majesty, let us honour him—he will remove our doubt!' (17)
Hearing Alāta's words, the king summoned his charioteer:
'Let us go to the deer park! Bring a suitable carriage here!' (18)
[223] They yoked his carriage of ivory with silver trimmings,
With clean, bright accessories, pale as a moonlit face. (19)
Yoked to that were four Sindh horses, lotus-white,
Swift as the wind, well trained, and garlanded with gold. (20)
White was the parasol, white the chariot, white the horses, and white the fan:
The Videhan, going out with his courtiers, shone like the moon. (21)
Many strong men bearing swords and spears,
And valiant[22] men on horseback followed him, the highest ruler. (22)
Having driven there in merely a moment, the warrior descended from his carriage;
The Videhan, along with his courtiers, approached Guṇa on foot. (23)
Those brahmins and lords[23] who were already assembled there,
The king did not have them moved, though the place was unprepared when he came. (24)

[224] Surrounded by a multifarious assembly, having sat at one side he made a polite greeting. Explaining the matter the Teacher said:

When a soft multicoloured blanket with soft cushion was spread out
The king approached on one side. (25)
The king greeted him with a courteous speech:
'I hope you have sufficient, Bhante, and that your winds are undisturbed. (26)
I hope your livelihood is not distressing, and that you acquire sufficient alms.
I hope you are little ill, and that your vision does not deteriorate.' (27)
Then Guṇa in turn greeted the Videhan, who delighted in discipline:
'Great King, all this is sufficient, and the last two as well.[24] (28)
I hope you are also well, Videhan, that your neighbours are not overpowering.

22. Following VRI *vīrā*. F has *dhīrā* 'wise'.

23. *Ibbhā* refers to dependents, usually of the king, suggesting perhaps courtiers or wealthy landowners. 'Lords' may be a stretch, but communicates the sense in which it is used paired with brahmins to mean 'the great and the good'.

24. The commentary confirms that *ubhayaṃ* 'both' refers to the last two questions put to him.

I hope your yoked animals are free of disease, that your steed carries
you well,[25]
That you have no illnesses, and no afflictions of the body.' (29)
After this greeting the king, lover of *dhamma* and bull of warriors,
Immediately asked about worldly and spiritual matters, and propriety: (30)
'Kassapa, how should a mortal behave properly towards his parents?
How should he behave towards teachers? How towards his wives and
children? (31)
How should he behave towards the elderly? How towards renouncers
and brahmins?
How should he behave towards his forces, and the populace? (32)
How should he live righteously and go after death[26] to heaven?
How do some, established in unrighteousness, fall into hell below?' (33)

[225] This powerful question was suitable to be asked of a *buddha*, first of all, or failing that a *paccekabuddha*, disciple of a *buddha*, or a *bodhisatta*, but the king asked it of an ignorant, naked and bent[27] Ājīvika ascetic, a blind fool who had lost his splendour. He, thus asked, did not give a suitable answer to that question, but like hitting an ox that is progressing or throwing rubbish in a food bowl, said, 'Hear, Great King!' and took the opportunity of giving his own false views. Explaining the matter the Teacher said:

Having heard the words of the Videhan, Kassapa said this:
'Great King, listen to my true and correct path. (34)
There is no fruit, good or bad, in righteous conduct.
Your Majesty, there is no other world—for who has come back from
there? (35)
There are no ancestors. How are there mothers? How fathers?
There is no one to be called "teacher", for who will tame
the untamed? (36)
Beings are all equal—there is no respect for the elders.
There is no strength and vigour—so whence comes exertion and effort?[28]

25. Taking *yogga* as an animal that is yoked to a vehicle and *vāhana* as an animal that is ridden. The commentary glosses the former as horse and the latter as elephant.

26. VRI has *maccā* 'mortals' in place of F *pecca* 'after death'.

27. *Naggabhoggam* 'naked and bent' may be a technical term, possibly the name of a type of ascetic. See the PED corrigenda, which makes reference to an inscription citing *nagnabhagna* as a class of ascetic.

28. These verses do not in fact represent the Ājīvika position, but rather that of the materialists.

For beings are fixed in their destiny,[29] as if tied to a boat.[30] (37)
A man receives what he should receive—how then can there be fruit of giving?
There is no fruit of giving, Your Majesty. There is no vigour or capacity for action. (38)
Giving is ordered by fools, and accepted by the wise.
Without choice, fools, imagining themselves learned, give to the wise.' (39)

[226] Having thus described the non-fruiting of giving, in order to explain the non-fruiting of evil he said:

'There are these seven eternal substances that are indestructible and undisturbed:
Fire, earth, water, and wind, happiness and suffering,
And soul[31]—a destroyer of these seven bodies cannot be found. (40)
There is no killer and no destroyer; and nobody is harmed.
Weapons proceed between these substances. (41)
He who takes others' heads with a sharp sword,
He does not cut these substances, so where is the evil fruit in that? (42)
All during eighty-four great aeons become purified as one transmigrates.[32]
Before that time has passed not even the well restrained are purified. (43)
Even those who have done great good are not purified before then,
And even those who have done great evil would not go beyond that moment. (44)
In the course of time during eighty-four aeons we become pure;
We cannot escape our destiny, as the ocean cannot escape the shore.' (45)

[227] In this way the annihilationist[33] comprehensively and with determination taught his own view.

Hearing the words of Kassapa, Alāta said this:
'What the venerable sir says, this pleases me. (46)

29. The term *niyata* simply means 'fixed', but this is a clear reference to *niyati*, the doctrine of destiny or fate.

30. *Goṭaviso* is not clear but must refer to some part of a boat or something that is tied to the back of it. The commentary glosses it as *nāvāya pacchimabandho* 'bound to the back of a boat'.

31. The term here is *jīva*, which is the preferred term for soul amongst the Ājīvikas and Jains, both of whom consider it to be permanent.

32. Other sources on Ājīvika doctrine say that this process of purification takes eighty-four *thousand* great aeons (*mahākalpas*).

33. *Ucchedavādo*. According to the views just stated, Guṇa is not actually an annihilationist. However, some annihilationist doctrines were stated by him at the beginning of his discourse.

I too remember a former birth, journeyed through by me.
I was formerly a cruel butcher called Piṅgala.[34] (47)
In prosperous Vārāṇasī I did much evil.
I killed a great many beings—buffaloes, pigs and goats. (48)
Disappearing from there I am born now in a wealthy general's family.
There is indeed no evil fruit, for I am not gone to hell.' (49)

(It is said that having honoured the reliquary of Ten-Powered Buddha Kassapa with a garland of *anoja* flowers, at the time of death he was impelled by a different *kamma*. Transmigrating in *saṃsāra*, by the result of a certain evil deed he took birth in a butcher's family, where he did great evil. At the time of his death, the meritorious *kamma*, which had remained for a long time, like fire covered by dust, made an appearance. Having been reborn here in accordance with that he attained this splendour. Remembering that birth, but unable to remember beyond the immediate past, he thought, 'I am reborn here having made butcher *kamma*,' and having established that view he said, 'What the venerable sir says . . .' and so on.)[35]

In this place there was a poor servant called Bījaka.
Observing the *uposatha*, he had approached Guṇa. (50)
Having heard Kassapa's words and the speech of Alāta,
He suddenly sighed and cried hotly, bursting into tears. (51)
The Videhan questioned him, 'Friend, why do you cry?
What have you heard or seen? Why do you make your feelings known to me?' (52)
[228] Hearing the Videhan's words, Bījaka said this:
'Hear me, Great King, I feel no suffering. (53)
I too remember a former birth, and my happiness.
Formerly I was Bhāva the treasurer in Sāketa, delighting in excellence, (54)
Honoured by brahmins and lords, delighting in distribution, pure.
I do not remember doing any evil myself. (55)
Disappearing from there, Videhan, now I am born of a bad woman,
Born in a very bad destiny in the womb of a water-pot slave. (56)
Being in a bad realm thus, I resolved upon good conduct:
Whoever asks of me, I give him half of my food. (57)

34. His name means 'Red Eyes', likening him perhaps to a *yakkha* (demon).

35. This passage is sandwiched between two parts of the word commentary, and so F placed it in small type, and Cowell and Rouse did not include it in their translation. However, it adds interesting background to the narrative and so is worthy of inclusion. Clearly the commentator was not willing for the audience to think that Alāta might be right in his understanding of karma.

I always observe the fourteenth- and fifteenth-day holy days,
And I do not harm any beings, and I avoid theft. (58)
But all this, well performed, has indeed no fruit.
I believe this virtue is pointless, as Alāta said. (59)
Indeed I have gained the losing dice, like an untaught gambler.
Alāta has gained the winning dice, like a professional dicer.[36] (60)
I do not see the door by which I can go to the good realms.
This is why I cry out, O King, having heard Kassapa's speech.' (61)

(It is said that in the past time of Kassapa Buddha, he was searching for an ox that had perished in the forest when he was asked the way by a certain monk who had got lost. He was silent, and when asked again he became angry and said, 'So-called slave-mendicants are noisy! You must be a slave—you are so garrulous!' Not giving fruit then, that action remained like a fire covered with ashes. At the time of death another *kamma* attended. He transmigrated in *saṃsāra* according to his *kamma* and by the fruit of one skilful action he became the aforementioned treasurer in Sāketa and was generous and so on and made merit. Then his *kamma*, which had remained like treasure buried in the earth, gained an appearance and saw fruit. The bad *kamma* made by being rude to that monk gave its results in his present birth. Thinking, 'I was born in the womb of a water-pot slave by the fruit of preceding good action,' he spoke thus.)[37]

[229] Hearing Bījaka's words, King Aṅgati said:
'There is no door to the good realms. Await your destiny Bījaka! (62)
Happiness or suffering will surely be gained according to destiny.
All are purified through faring on. Do not hurry when the time is not yet come. (63)
I was also previously morally good, serving brahmins and lords,
Administering justice, having no pleasure meanwhile.' (64)

And then he said, 'Bhante Kassapa, we have wasted so much time! But now we will take you as our teacher, and from now on we will partake of love and pleasure and so on. Henceforth even listening to the *dhamma* in your presence will be no obstacle.' Asking leave with the words, 'Please stay—we will go,' he said:

'Bhante, we may see you again, if there is a conjunction of the fates.'

36. The four possible rolls of the dice are named after the four *yugas* (world ages) of Hindu mythology, thus the winning roll (in which the number is exactly divisible by four) is called *kaṭa* (Sanskrit *kṛita*) and the losing roll (in which there is a remainder of one) is called *kali*.

37. Again, F includes this passage in the word commentary.

Having said this the Videhan left and went home. (65)

[230] When the king first approached Guṇa he honoured and questioned him, but when he left he paid him no honour—he was simply gone. Guṇa, because of his own lack of excellence,[38] did not receive even honour, so how would he receive any alms and so on or hospitality?

After that night had passed, the next day the king assembled his courtiers, saying, 'Prepare the different kinds of sense pleasures for me! From now on I will partake only in the happiness of sense pleasures—other duties are not to be spoken of to me. Let this and that person perform the duty of jurisdiction.' And he became immersed in the enjoyment of the sense pleasures. Explaining the matter the Teacher said:

When night turned to dawn, Aṅgati assembled his courtiers
In the audience hall and said this: (66)
'In the Candaka Palace let them prepare continual pleasures for me!
Let them not approach me about matters public or private! (67)
Vijaya and Sunāma and General Alāta,
Let these three, skilled in jurisprudence, sit with regard to these matters.'[39] (68)
Having said this the Videhan thought much of pleasures
And did not busy himself with any matters related to the brahmins and lords. (69)
Then on the fourteenth night the Videhan's own dear daughter,
Called Princess Rucā, said to her nurse: (70)
'Quickly adorn me, and let them adorn my companions.
Tomorrow is the holy fifteenth day; I will go into the lord's presence.' (71)
They fetched a flower garland for her, and costly sandalwood,
Jewels, gems, and mother-of-pearl, and cloths of various colours. (72)
The many women surrounded her as she sat on a golden seat,
And they made the beautiful Rucā resplendent. (73)

[231] (It is said that on each fourteenth day, surrounded by five hundred royal women and with a company of nurses, with great beauty and charm she descended from her own seven-storeyed Rativaḍḍhana Palace and went to the Candaka Palace to see her father. Her father, having seen her, became pleased and paid her great honour, and as she was leaving he gave

38. This is a pun on the ascetic's name—*guṇa* means quality or excellence. Further humour arises from the fact that it is the ascetic's own teaching that has led the king to pay him no attention!

39. The commentary glosses *atthe* as *atthakāraṇe vinicchayaṭṭhāne*, in other words a courtroom. Although this seems a stretch, the meaning is clear—the king wishes his courtiers to take over his duties.

her a thousand pieces and took leave of her saying 'My dear, give gifts!' She, having returned to her own dwelling, the next day became an observer of the *uposatha* and gave great gifts to the poor, travellers, wayfarers, and beggars. Then the king gave a province to her and she had all duties done with the income. But then there was an uproar across the whole city: 'The king because of the Ājīvika Guṇa has adopted a wrong view!' Having heard that, Rucā's women announced to the king's daughter, 'My lady, apparently your father, having heard the speech of the Ājīvika and adopted a wrong view, has had the alms halls at the four gates knocked down, and he has had women and girls belonging to other people taken by force and brought to him! He doesn't administer the kingdom but has become entirely intoxicated with sensual pleasures.' Hearing this she was displeased and thought: 'How can my father, having approached the shameless, naked and bent Ājīvika who is lacking in pure *dhamma*, question him?[40] Surely a righteous recluse or brahmin who holds the doctrine of *kamma* should be approached and questioned. But aside from me there is certainly no one else who is able to lead my father away from wrong views and establish him in correct views. I remember fourteen births—seven past and seven future—so having related the bad deeds I did formerly, demonstrating the fruit of evil action I will awaken my father. But if I go today he will say to me, "My dear, you previously came at the fortnight, so why have you come early today?" and if that happens I will say, "I have come having heard that you have adopted a wrong view" and then he will not take my words seriously. Therefore I will not go today, but on the fourteenth day from now—the dark fourteenth day—as if unaware of anything I will go in the former manner and when the time has come I will ask for the thousand pieces for the purpose of almsgiving. Then my father will explain the views he has adopted, and I by my own strength will cause him to cast the wrong views away.' Therefore on the fourteenth day she wanted to go into the presence of her father and spoke thus.)

And in the midst of her companions, adorned with all adornments,
Rucā entered the Candaka Palace, like lightning entering
a storm cloud. (74)

40. Following the VRI reading *kathañhi nāma me tāto* 'how indeed can my father' in preference over F *me pitā tādisan nāma*, which is harder to make sense of since it is lacking any interrogative.

Having approached the Videhan and honoured him that delighted in discipline,
She sat to one side on a chair adorned with gold. (75)
[232] And the Videhan, seeing Rucā in the midst of her companions
Like an assembly of celestial nymphs, said this: (76)
'I hope you enjoy yourself beside the lotus pool in the palace.
I trust they always bring you many kinds of food. (77)
I hope the young women gather many kinds of flowers,
And that you each make bowers, intent on pleasure and amusement for a time. (78)
What are you lacking? Let them bring it to you immediately!
Set your mind on it, painted-face one, even if it is equal to the moon.' (79)
Hearing the Videhan's words, Rucā said to her father:
'Great King, all this is obtained in the presence of the lord. (80)
Tomorrow is the holy fifteenth day. Let them bring the thousand pieces to me
And as they are given to me, I will give gifts to all that request them.' (81)
Hearing Rucā's words, King Aṅgati said,
'Much wealth has been pointlessly and fruitlessly destroyed by you. (82)
Constantly observing the *uposatha* you do not enjoy the food and drink.
That you do not eat it is destined—there is no merit from not eating. (83)
[233] For having heard Kassapa's words, Bījaka then
Sighed, and weeping hotly for a moment, he shed tears.[41] (84)
Rucā, as long as you live don't take away our food.
Fortunate one, there is no other world, so why suffer pointlessly?' (85)
Hearing the words of the Videhan, the beautiful Rucā,
Knowing the *dhamma* from start to finish,[42] said this to her father: (86)
'I previously heard the teaching, and now I see it with my own eyes:
He who follows a fool becomes the same—a fool! (87)
For a fool, relying upon a fool, approaches further delusion.
It is fitting to be deluded by Alāta and Bījaka! (88)
[234] You, Your Majesty, are wise, sagacious, insightful in business.
How was such an ignoble view obtained on account of fools? (89)
For if one is purified by the path through *saṃsāra*,
Guṇa's asceticism would be pointless.
Like an insect falling into a blazing fire,

41. It is not quite clear why Bījaka's actions are mentioned here, but since the verse is present in both F and VRI, and commented on in the word commentary, its removal would be difficult to justify.

42. *Jānaṃ pubbāparaṃ dhammaṃ*. While *pubba* + *āpara* can mean simply 'what precedes and what follows', it seems likely that the more specific meaning of 'what comes first and what comes last' is meant here, qualifying the *dhamma* as referring to scriptures.

The deluded one has adopted the naked state. (90)
Devoted first to purification by *saṃsāra*, ignorantly many harm their *kamma*.
Having wrongly grasped at demerit[43] in former lives,
Like a fish caught on a hook, it is difficult to escape from that destruction.[44] (91)
I will make a simile for you, for your benefit Great King!
Some wise men understand matters through a simile. (92)
Just as a boat belonging to merchants, heavy from an excessive burden,
Having taken on too great a load, sinks down into the ocean, (93)
In just the same way a man who has accumulated evil little by little,
Having taken on too great a load, sinks down into hell. (94)
Lord of the earth, Alāta's load is not yet complete:
He accumulates this evil, on account of which he will go to a bad realm. (95)
Lord of the earth, Alāta formerly did a good deed,
And this happiness he has obtained is the result of that, Your Majesty. (96)
Delighting in inexcellence he wears down his merit,
Leaving the straight road he follows the wrong path. (97)
[235] Just as the scales are held up when a load is placed in the pan,
And when the load is removed, the near end of the scales rises up,[45] (98)
In the same way rises a man who has accumulated good little by little,
Delighting in good results, like the slave Bījaka who is intent upon heaven.[46] (99)
The suffering that today Bījaka the slave sees in himself,
That was formerly an evil deed he indulged in. (100)
That evil of his is worn away for he delights in discipline,
But don't let him enter the wrong path having encountered Kassapa!'[47] (101)

Next, demonstrating the fault of associating with evil and the benefit of associating with spiritual friends, she said:

'O King, whoever one associates with, whether good or bad,
Moral or immoral, one goes into his power. (102)
Whatever friend he makes, whoever he pays honour to,
Keeping company in such a way, he becomes like him. (103)
[236] An associate defiles his associate, an intimate the other party,

43. The term used here is *kalī*, which can refer literally to an unlucky dice, as in the earlier metaphor.

44. This verse is obscure and the translation is tentative.

45. This is a tricky image, and I am grateful to L.S. Cousins for unfolding it in this way.

46. Reading *saggādhimano* for *saggātimāno* 'heaven-conceit'. The commentary gives *saggādhimāno* as an alternative gloss.

47. The commentary reads this as a second person imperative, not third person, making the prohibition directed at the king rather than Bījaka.

Just as a poison arrow defiles the undefiled quiver.
A wise person, fearing defilement, would not be friends with the evil. (104)
If a man ties up some stinking fish with a blade of *kusa* grass,
As the grass smells bad, thus become those who honour fools. (105)
If a man ties up incense with a leaf,
As the leaves smell fragrant, thus become those who honour
the wise. (106)
Therefore, knowing the ripeness of his own deeds to be like a basket of
fruit,[48]
A wise person would not keep company with the bad, but would
associate with the good,
For the bad lead us to hell, while the good help us to attain the good
realm.' (107)

Thus the King's daughter, having spoken the *dhamma* for her father with six verses, now illuminating the suffering experienced by herself in the past, said:

'I remember my own faring on through seven births,
And seven yet to come, where I will go when I pass on from here. (108)
In that seventh previous birth of mine, king of men,
I was the son of a goldsmith in the city of Rājagaha in Magadha. (109)
Having acquired an evil friend, I did great evil:
Harrassing the wives of others, we lived as if we were immortals. (110)
That *kamma* laid down remained like fire covered with ash,
And by other actions I was born in the Vaṃsa country. (111)
[237] In a rich, wealthy, and prosperous treasurer's family in Kosambī,
I was the only son, Great King, honoured and revered constantly. (112)
There I associated with a friend who delighted in good works;
Wise and learned, he established me in good. (113)
I observed the fast on many fourteenth and fifteenth nights;
That *kamma* laid down remained like treasure hidden near water. (114)
Then this fruit of the evil actions done in Magadha
Caught up with me, as if I had enjoyed a ruinous poison. (115)
Falling from there, Videhan, I for a long time in the Roruva hell
Boiled on account of my own actions. That memory gives me no
pleasure. (116)
Having endured great suffering there for many years,
O King, I became a castrated billy goat in Bhennākaṭa.' (117)

[238] Explaining the matter she spoke a verse:

48. This is a tricky passage, but is suggestive of the metaphor of deeds ripening and bearing fruit. Alternatively, the VRI reading gives leaf basket, which instead implies that we are still in the metaphor of fragrances wrapped in leaves.

'Noble sons[49] were carried by me, in carts and on my back.
This was the result of my action of going after the wives of others.' (118)

Falling away from there she attained rebirth in the womb of a monkey in the forest. On the day of his birth they showed him to the leader of the herd, who said, 'Bring me my son!' He grasped him strongly, and roaring ripped out his testicles with his teeth. Explaining the matter she said:

'Passing on from there I became a monkey in the vast forest, Videhan,
Castrated[50] by the bold leader of the troop.
This was the consequence of my action of going after the wives of others.' (119)

Then explaining her next births she said:

'Videhan, falling away from there I became an ox amongst the Dasaṇṇas,
A swift castrated bullock, I carried the cart for a long time.
This was the consequence of my going after the wives of others. (120)
Passing away from there, Videhan, I was born in a family amongst the Vajjis,
But I was neither male nor female, in the human existence that is so hard to obtain.[51]
This was the consequence of my going after the wives of others. (121)
Falling away from there, Videhan, I was born in the Nandana grove,
In the Heaven of the Thirty-Three, as a celestial nymph able to take any form at will. (122)
In various clothes and ornaments and wearing jewelled earrings,
Skilled at singing and dancing I attended Sakka. (123)
Established there, Videhan, I remembered these births,
As well as seven future births, where I will go having fallen from here. (124)
The good done by me in Kosambī has come around;
Passing away from here I will transmigrate amongst gods and humans. (125)
Great king, for seven births I will be constantly honoured and served,
But in these six destinies I will not be freed from female form. (126)

49. This appears to be the only occurrence of the Pāli term *sātaputta*. L. S. Cousins suggests an abstraction from *sataputta* (Sanskrit *śataputra*), referring to a person of a hundred sons, found in this meaning in some Sanskrit texts. The commentary glosses *amaccaputtā* 'sons of courtiers'.

50. Where F has *nilicchitaphalo* VRI has *niluñcitaphalo* - these may simply be alternative forms of the same term. PED suggests a link to *nirlañcayati* 'to deprive of the marks' (of sex), but one would expect a double *l* in such a case; plus it is not clear how this interpretation would work in compound with *phalo*.

51. In other words, although human birth is good, being neither male nor female deprived her of spiritual capabilities such as the ability to enter *jhāna* meditation states or be ordained into a Buddhist community.

[239] My seventh existence, Your Majesty, will be as a god of great power;
I will be a male god, in a supreme divine category. (127)
Even today they bind garlands from celestial flowers[52] in the Nandana Grove,
A god called Java is the one who receives my garland.[53] (128)
For a divine moment is sixteen years here,
And a day and night for the gods is a hundred autumns amongst men. (129)
Thus actions follow you, even through incalculable births;
Actions do not disappear whether good or bad.' (130)

(It is said that she, established in that *deva* world, reflected, 'Coming to the *deva* world like this, from where indeed did I come?' and saw that she had attained that rebirth realm having fallen from the state of being a neuter in a wealthy family in the Kingdom of Vajji. Then she reflected, 'By what action was I reborn in such a pleasant state?' She saw the skilful actions of giving and so on done having been born in a treasurer's family in Kosambī. Knowing, 'I was reborn here as a fruit of this action,' she wondered, 'How has it come about that I was reborn in the immediate past birth as a neuter?' and knew of the state of much suffering in a bovine birth in Dasaṇṇa. Then recollecting her next birth she saw the birth as castrated monkey, and then remembered the next as a castrated ox in Bheṇṇakaṭa, and then remembered the Roruva realm of rebirth. Whilst she was remembering the suffering experienced by her in hell and animal births, fear arose. Thus she thought, 'On account of what action was this suffering experienced by me?' Having considered the six births and seen the wholesome action done during her birth in Kosambī city, she considered her seventh, saw the action of going after the wives of others done because of associating with an evil friend in the Kingdom of Magadha. She realised, 'This experience of great suffering was my fruit from that.'

52. The term *santāna* is rare in Pāli texts. SED explains that it is one of the five trees in Indra's garden.

53. This verse is rather ambiguous. Since the previous verse mentioned Rucā's future birth as a *devaputta*, it seems logical to assume that this is the *devaputta* Java mentioned here, who will soon be receiving garlands. However, the commentary takes this as referring to Rucā's previous birth as the wife of Java, which hasn't been mentioned in the verses. The commentator understands that Rucā remembered seven past and seven future births whilst as a nymph in Nandana—in other words the 'future' births are actually almost all in the past by the time Rucā relates them. This seems awkward given Rucā's frequent insistence that she can remember seven past and seven future births.

Then considering, 'Having fallen from here where will I be born in the future?' she realised, 'Having been established here for a lifetime, next I will be reborn and become an attendant of Sakka himself.' Considering again and again in this way, 'In my third form I will be reborn as an attendant of Sakka, and likewise in the fourth, but taking birth in the fifth I will become the chief queen of the god Javana in the *deva* realm.' Knowing that, she considered further and realised, 'In my sixth existence, having fallen from the Tāvatiṃsa realm, I will be reborn in the womb of the chief wife of King Aṅgati, and I will be called "Rucā".' Reflecting, 'Further than there, where will I be reborn?' she knew, 'Having fallen from there in my seventh birth I will become a god of great power in the Heaven of the Thirty-Three—I will be freed from the female form.')

[240] Then she taught the *dhamma* further, saying:

'He who wishes to be a man, again and again in birth after birth,
Should avoid the wives of others, as one who has washed his feet avoids the dirt. (131)
She who wishes to be a man, again and again in birth after birth,
Should honour her husband, like the attendants honour Indra. (132)
And whoever wishes for heavenly enjoyment, divine lifespan, glory, and happiness,
Having shunned evils, should practice the threefold *dhamma*, (133)
Be watchful and careful with body, speech, and mind,
For the sake of the self, whether women or men. (134)
Whichever men among living beings are glorious and have all complete enjoyments,
Without a doubt they formerly did good.
For all beings one's *kamma* is one's own. (135)
Look here, Your Majesty! Consider your own situation.
Lord of men, for what reason do you have these women who resemble celestial nymphs, adorned and covered with a blaze of gold?'[54] (136)

[241] In this way she advised her father. Explaining the matter the Teacher said:

With these words the maiden Rucā pleased her father Aṅgati;
The virtuous one spoke of the path and of the *dhamma* to the bewildered one. (137)

Having explained the *dhamma* to her father in this way from the morning

54. In other words, as the commentary explains, the king should consider whether he acquired his many women whilst sleeping, or as a result of having been a thief, or as a result of good actions.

throughout the night, she said, 'Your Majesty, don't accept the words of the naked one with wrong views, but take on board the words of a skilful friend like me, who says that there is this world, there is the other world, there is fruit of actions well and badly done. Don't rush along the wrong road.' But even though this was the case, she was not able to free her father from wrong views. He was merely pleased having heard her sweet speech, for parents are fond of the words of their dear children, but he did not give up that view. But in the city there was one hullabaloo: 'They say that Rucā the king's daughter, having taught the *dhamma* to her father, has made him give up wrong views!' The populace were pleased: 'The wise princess having today released her father from wrong views will ensure the safety of the city's inhabitants!' Though she was unable to awaken her father, she did not give up her efforts, but thought, 'By some means or another I will ensure my father's well-being!' She raised her hands in salutation above her head and having bowed to the ten directions, she worshipped, saying, 'In this world there are bearers of the world, namely righteous renouncers and brahmins, the guardian deities of the world, and the Great Brahmās. Let them come and, with their own strength, cause my father to give up his wrong view! [242] And regardless of his absence of quality, let them come on account of my virtue, my strength, and my truthfulness. Having caused my father to give up this wrong view, let them ensure the welfare of the whole world!'

At that time the Bodhisatta was a Great Brahmā called Nārada. Now *bodhisattas* survey the world time and time again because of the greatness of their compassion and their cultivation of loving-kindness, in order to see beings that are good and bad in their conduct.[55] That day he was surveying the world and saw the homage being made towards the gods that are supporters of the world for the purpose of freeing the princess' father from wrong views. He thought, 'Besides me, there is nobody else who is able to cause this wrong view to be rejected. It is fitting that today I should go to assist the princess, and ensure the welfare of the king and his retinue.

55. Or 'through their greatness and on account of their compassion and cultivation of loving-kindness', or 'through the greatness of their compassion on account of their cultivation of loving-kindness'. The verb 'surveys' is *oloketi*, which is cognate with Sanskrit *avalokayati*, from which the name of the compassionate Mahāyāna *bodhisattva* Avalokiteśvara is formed. Avalokiteśvara is said to be called thus because he surveys the world for people in need of his help, very much as Nārada is doing here.

But in what disguise should I go? Renouncers are dear to men, as is the welcome speech of the teacher. Therefore I will go dressed as a renouncer.' Having decided he made himself a human body of lovely golden colour and arranged his circle of delightful braided hair and placed a golden hairpin in it. He dressed himself in a red undergarment and red overgarment of bark, and placed over one shoulder an antelope hide worked in silver and adorned with golden stars. Taking his begging bowl made of gold, with a string of pearls tied onto it, he placed on his shoulder a golden carrying pole that was curved in three places, and he took a coral water pot also with a string of pearls. With this guise of a sage he came through the sky shining forth like the moon coursing through the heavens. He entered the terrace of the adorned Candaka Palace and stood in the sky in front of the king. Explaining the matter the Teacher said:

Then Nārada, coming from the Brahmā realm to the realm of humans,
Looked around at Jambudīpa, and saw King Aṅgati. (138)
He stood himself in the palace in front of the Videhan.
Seeing him arrived there, Rucā worshipped that sage. (139)

[243] Seeing him, the king, moved by the power of the Brahmā, was unable to remain seated, and getting up he stood on the ground. He asked his name and clan and from whence he had come. Explaining the matter the Teacher said:

Then the king, with mind full of awe, rose from his seat,
And questioning Nārada said these words: (140)
'From where have you come, you with divine appearance,
Radiant like the moon at night?
Questioned by me, declare your name and clan.
How do they know you in the world of men?' (141)

And he, thinking, 'This king imagines there is no other world, so I will show him a little of the other world,' spoke the verse:

'I have come now from a heavenly realm,
Radiant like the moon at night.
Questioned by you, I declare my name and clan:
They know me as Nārada Kassapa.' (142)

Then the king, thinking, 'I will ask later about this other world, but now I will ask him about how he acquired his superpowers,' spoke the verse:

'Marvellous indeed is such an appearance,
And you go about and stand in the air!
I ask you, Nārada, about this matter:

What is the reason for this power of yours?'[56] (143)

[244] Nārada said:

'Truth, *dhamma*, self-control, and generosity[57]—
By these qualities of mine, formerly done,
By these *dhammas*[58] well practised,
I am gone where I wish, as quick as a thought.' (144)

But even when he spoke in this way the king remained strongly attached to his wrong view and did not have faith in the other world. Saying, 'Is there indeed fruit of meritorious deeds?' he spoke the verse:

'You explain this marvelous power through merit,
Whether it is indeed as you say,
I ask you, Nārada, about this matter.
Asked by me, explain well.' (145)

Nārada said:

'King, ask me, for this is for your benefit,
That which—lord of the earth—makes you doubt. I will lead you to a state without doubt,
With methods, knowledge, and causal discourse.'[59] (146)

[245] The king said:

'I ask you, Nārada, about this matter.
Questioned by me, Nārada, don't speak falsely.
Are there gods and ancestors,
Or indeed another world, as people say?' (147)

Nārada said:

'There are indeed gods and ancestors too
And there is another world as people say.
Men, infatuated and greedy for sense pleasures,
Yoked to delusion do not know the other world.' (148)

Hearing this the king, mocking him, spoke the verse:

'If they exist, as you say Nārada,

56. The commentary explains that the king, not believing in the *deva* realm, thinks he is a magician.

57. The commentary glosses *dhamma* as both the threefold good conduct and the preparatory *kasiṇa* practice. *Cāga* is glossed as giving things to be given and giving up defilements.

58. The commentary explains that this means *guṇas* 'qualities'.

59. *Nayehi ñāyehi ca hetubhī ca*. The precise difference in meaning of these three terms is not clear. The commentary glosses them as *kāraṇavacanehi* (causal discourse), *ñāṇehi* (knowledge) and *paccayehi* (conditions) respectively.

If you have faith in the abode of the dead in the next world,
Give me now five hundred pieces,
And I will give you a thousand in the next world!' (149)

Then the Great Being reproached him in the midst of his assembly, saying:

'Sir, I would indeed give you five hundred pieces,
If I knew you were virtuous and liberal.
But who would collect the debt of a thousand
When sir is a rogue living in hell? (150)
He who is unvirtuous, of evil conduct,
Idle and cruel of action,
Wise men do not lend to him,
For there is no repayment from such people. (151)
[246] Having found a man who is skilful,
Energetic, virtuous, and liberal,
People invite him with possessions.
After he has done his work, they receive it back again.' (152)

Thus rebuked by him, the king was at a loss for an answer. The populace became joyful and pleased, and there was a single uproar in the entire city: 'Today a god-sage of great power will make the king give up his wrong view!' By the greatness of the Great Being in Mithilā for the extent of seven miles there was nobody indeed who did not hear his *dhamma* teaching. Then the Great Being thought, 'This king has taken on false views with excessive steadfastness. I will frighten him with the fear of the hells, and having caused him thus to reject wrong views I will comfort him with the realm of the gods.' He said, 'Great King, if you do not give up this view you will go to a hell of extreme suffering,' and he furnished a discourse on the hells:

'O King, gone from here to there you will see:
Being dragged around by groups of ravens,
Living in hell and being eaten up
By crows, vultures, and hawks,
With body destroyed and blood streaming—
Who would press you for a thousand in the next world?' (153)

[247] Having described the raven hell, saying, 'If you are not reborn here you will be reborn in an in-between-worlds hell,' he spoke a verse to explain that hell:

'There is blinding darkness, no sun or moon.
The hell is always tumultuous[60] and of terrible form.

60. *Tumulo* usually means noisy or uproarious, though in the commentary it is

Neither night nor day is perceived.
Who wanders in such a place for the sake of wealth?' (154)

And having described to him in detail the hell between the worlds, he explained, 'Great King, not giving up wrong view, you will not only experience this, but also another suffering!' and spoke a verse:

'The two dogs, Spotted and Black,[61]
Large-bodied and great in strength,
Devour with their teeth of iron!
Driven away from here, that other world is attained.[62] (155)
Dwelling in hell, being eaten
By fierce beasts and wild animals,
The body cut, blood flowing—
Who would press you for a thousand in the next world? (156)
[248] With arrows and with well-sharpened swords,
The enemies strike and shoot,
In the frightful Kāḷūpakāla hell,[63]
The man who was formerly the doer of bad deeds. (157)
Running through hell, being struck,
Belly split open, in the stomach and the ribs,
The body cut, blood flowing—
Who would press you for a thousand in the next world? (158)
Swords, arrows, pikes, and spears:
Your Majesty, these various weapons rain down there.
They fall, glowing like cinders;
A stone thunderbolt rains onto the evildoer. (159)
And the hot wind in hell is hard to endure.
Not even the briefest happiness is obtained there.
Running about here and there without shelter, miserable—
Who would press you for a thousand in the next world? (160)
Running through there yoked to chariots,
Travelling the flaming earth,
[249] Urged on by goad sticks—
Who would press you for a thousand in the next world? (161)

---

glossed with *bahalandhakāro* 'thick darkness'.

61. The two dogs of Yama, guardian of hell.

62. Here we find, 'This is also the method with regard to the hells to come. Thus having explained all those states, along with the assaults of the hell guards, by the means of the words above, the unexplained words in each of the verses should be explained.' This is really word commentary, an instruction to apply the same explanations to the descriptions of subsequent hells as have been given thus far.

63. The commentary explains that this is the name both of the hell and of the beings that attack its inhabitants.

Climbing a mountain of razors,
Horrific, frightful, and flaming,
The body cut, blood flowing—
Who would press you for a thousand in the next world? (162)
Climbing a mass of cinders
That resembles a mountain, flaming and frightful,
The body burnt, miserable and lamenting—
Who would press you for a thousand in the next world? (163)
There are trees, high as the top of a storm cloud, dense with thorns,
Sharp and made of iron, that bring forth the blood of men. (164)
Climbing them are women and men who went after others' wives,
Urged by those with swords in hand, doers of the orders of Yama. (165)
Climbing that hellish *simbali* tree, smeared with blood,
The body damaged, without skin, miserable and deeply suffering; (166)
Breathing a hot sigh, is one who is guilty of former actions.
Body and skin cut up at the top of the tree—who would ask you for the debt? (167)
[250] Trees, high as the top of a storm cloud, are lined with sword leaves,
Sharp and made of iron, that bring forth the blood of men. (168)
Having reached that sword-leafed tree,
Tortured with sharp spears,
The body cut, blood flowing—
Who would press you for a thousand in the next world? (169)
As soon as he has departed from there, from that sword-leafed hell of suffering,
He falls into Vetaraṇī. Who would seek wealth there? (170)
The river Vetaraṇī, which is difficult to traverse, hot, harsh, and of caustic water,
Covered in iron lotus plants with sharp leaves, flows on. (171)
Who would ask you for a debt, when you are in Vetaraṇī without support,
Drowning, smeared with blood, with body thoroughly cut up?'[64] (172)

Then after hearing the discourse on hell from the Great Being, the king was agitated of heart and by way of seeking refuge in that same Great Being, said:

'I tremble like a tree being cut down.

64. This section describing the hells seems to be a unit in its own right and has more metrical variation than is common in the *jātakas*, suggesting that it may have had an independent existence. It is not clear whether it is an enumeration of a specific list of hells or just a selection for narrative effect. Compare the long description of hell torments in the *Nemi-jātaka* (Chapter 4).

With bewildered mind I know not the directions.
I feel remorseful and afraid—great indeed is my fear
Having heard the verses you have spoken, O sage. (173)
Like the middle of the sea when on fire,
Like an island in the great ocean,
Like light in the blinding darkness,
You are our refuge, O sage. (174)
[251] Sage, teach me of worldly and spiritual good,
Which I have certainly transgressed for a long time.
Explain to me, Nārada, the path of purity,
So that I may not fall into hell.' (175)

Then the Great Being, in order to explain the path of purity, teaching by means of the example of former kings whose conduct was correct, said:

'Just like Dhataraṭṭha, Vessāmitta, Aṭṭhaka, Yāmataggi,
And Usinnara and King Sivi,[65] who attended upon brahmins and
 renouncers, (176)
These kings and others who have gone to the heaven realm,
Avoid unrighteousness and practise the *dhamma*, O lord. (177)
And have people with food in their hands proclaim in your palace and
 your city,
"Who is hungry? Who is thirsty? Who needs a garland or perfume?
Who, being naked, would put on clothes of various hues? (178)
Who would take up a sunshade for the road, and beautiful soft
 slippers?"
In the evening and morning have it proclaimed thus in your city. (179)
And don't indeed yoke old men or horses or cows in the city.
Provide honour for the one who has done his duty when strong.' (180)

[252] Thus the Great Being, having spoken discourses on giving and morality to the king, because the king is pleased when his person is compared with a carriage, taught the *dhamma* with the simile of the carriage that is the bringer of all happiness:

65. These are legendary figures of the past. Dhataraṭṭha is one of the four Great Kings or Guardians of the World (*lokapālas*) and guards the Eastern direction, but his name is also cognate with Dhṛtarāṣṭra, the patriarch of the *Mahābhārata* war. Vessāmitta, Aṭṭhaka, and Yāmataggi are three of the ten great seers of the past, who are said to have incorporated the teachings of Kassapa Buddha into their brahmanical tradition. Usinnara, or Usīnara, is also mentioned as an exemplary king in the *Nemi-jātaka*, and is said in the *Mahākaṇha-jātaka* (J 469) to have been king of Varanasi in the time of Kassapa Buddha. The *Mahābhārata* identifies Usīnara as the father of King Sivi, who himself is the hero of a story cycle involving bodily self-sacrifice that is familiar to Buddhist, Jain, and Hindu sources. In Buddhist sources Sivi is usually identified with the Bodhisatta.

'Your body is known as a carriage, the mind its agile coachman,
Its turning axle is a lack of cruelty and its covering is generosity. (181)
The rim of the wheel is restraint of the feet, the trimming restraint of the hands,
The nave is restraint of the belly, and its soft noise is restraint of speech. (182)
The completeness of its parts is true speech, and it is well held together by lack of slander,
Its faultless parts are kind speech and it is bound with measured speech. (183)
Its ornaments are faith and non-greed, and the frame is humble reverent greetings,
The unbent pole is lack of hardness, and the strap is moral restraint. (184)
Its not shaking is the lack of anger, the pale sunshade is virtue,
The brakes are great learning, and the cushion a steady mind. (185)
Its heart is a mind that knows the appropriate time, the triple rod is self-confidence,
The tie of the yoke is humble conduct and the light yoke non-pride. (186)
The flooring is sincerity of mind, the lack of dust is the increase of wisdom,
The goad is the mindfulness of the wise, resolve and spiritual work are the reins. (187)
The tame mind follows the path with evenly tamed horses.
Greed and desire are the wrong path; restraint is the straight path. (188)
[253] Whilst the vehicle is running forth at forms, sounds, tastes, and smells,
Wisdom is the spur, O King, and he himself is the charioteer. (189)
If he goes in such a vehicle, peaceful living is firmly established;
The bringer of all happiness will not lead to birth in hell, O King.' (190)

[254] Thus[66] having taught the *dhamma* to him, having caused him to retract his wrong view and established him in moral conduct, he exhorted him thus: 'From now on forsake evil friends and associate with good friends, and always be diligent!' After praising the virtues of the king's daughter [255] and advising the assembly of the king and the harem, even as they watched he was gone to the Brahmā realm by his great power.

66. I have omitted a sentence before this one, as I believe it belongs in the word commentary.

The Teacher, having given this *dhamma* teaching said, 'Monks, not only now but also in the past did I destroy the net of views and tame Uruvela Kassapa.' Connecting the birth, in conclusion he spoke these verses:

'Devadatta was Alāta, Bhaddaji was Sunāma,
Sāriputta was Vijaya, Mogallāna was Bījaka, (191)
Sunakkhatta the Licchavi was Guṇa the naked ascetic,
Ānanda was Rucā who reconciled the king, (192)
Uruvela Kassapa was the king who had evil views,
And the Bodhisatta was Mahābrahmā; in this way understand the birth.'[67] (193)

67. It is very rare for a *samodhāna* (identification of the births) to be in verse. It may be a sign of its antiquity.

6.1

6.2

6. The Birth Story of Bhūridatta

Fig. 6.1 Although there is a long narrative before the birth of Bhūridatta, the Ananda series starts, as with most of the others in the Great Ten, with his birth, and focuses on incidents when the Bodhisatta is present. All characters here appear as humans, in line with the deception the *nāga*s carry out on his human mother. **Fig. 6.2** In the Heaven of the Thirty-Three, Bhūridatta is the only one capable of answering King Sakka's question.

Bhūridatta-jātaka, terracotta tile, Ananda Temple, Pagan, Myanmar, late 11th or early 12th century. Photographs copyright Lilian Handlin, 2004.

6.3

6.4

Fig. 6.3 The Bodhisatta asks his father for permission to observe *sīla* above the ground; when they are under the water he and other *nāga*s are shown with snake-like hoods. **Fig. 6.4** The Bodhisatta here is observing the *uposatha*; the *nāga* dancers appear at their most animated and enticing.

Bhūridatta-jātaka, terracotta tile, Ananda Temple, Pagan, Myanmar, late 11th or early 12th century. Photographs copyright Lilian Handlin, 2004.

6.5

6.6

Fig. 6.5 Bhūridatta gives the jewel to the brahmin and his son.
Fig. 6.6 Ālamba finds the Bodhisatta as he keeps the *uposatha*.

Bhūridatta-jātaka, terracotta tile, Ananda Temple, Pagan, Myanmar, late 11th or early 12th century. Photographs copyright Lilian Handlin, 2004.

6.7

6.8

Fig. 6.7 The Bodhisatta returns to his *nāga* realm. **Fig. 6.8** Resting after his ordeal, the Bodhisatta lies on his side in the *nāga* realm.

Bhūridatta-jātaka, terracotta tile, Ananda Temple, Pagan, Myanmar, late 11th or early 12th century. Photographs copyright Lilian Handlin, 2004.

6.9

6.10

Fig. 6.9 Bhūridatta teaching in the *nāga* realm. *Bhūridatta-jātaka*, glazed terracotta tile, Shwedagon Pagoda, Yangon, Myanmar, c. 1900. Photograph copyright Lucy Shaw. **Fig. 6.10** *Nāga*s are central to the mythology, storytelling, and ritual of coastal and rice-growing regions of Southeast Asia. They are often shown flanking Shin Upagutta, or Upagupta, an *arahat* believed to protect against floods and promote good rainfall, as at this devotional shrine found on the riverside in Yangon (see Tambiah 1970 176–8).Photograph copyright Sarah Shaw.

Fig. 6.11 Here the *nāga* form is used to dramatic effect for decoration as well as narration. The picture, a composite of events, gives a central focus in the straight structure of the palace in the middle, but also a pair of underlying green snake-like swirls that complement the strong green lines of the palace, where the king is being scared by the *nāgas*. Bhūridatta is being shown off by the snake charmer on the left, while on the right this grappling with the snake is echoed in the graceful movement of the court dancer serpentine curves around straight lines unify the whole mural. *Bhūridatta-jātaka*, painted mural, Minyegyi complex, Amyint Village, Myanmar, late 18th or very early 19th century. Photograph copyright Alexandra Green.

Fig. 6.12 In this picture the dancing girls are all firmly above the ground. This synoptic presentation makes a dramatic tableau of the nymphs, Ālamba finding the Bodhisatta, and then, in the lower right of the picture, Ālamba capturing and mastering the *nāga* prince. *Bhūridatta-jātaka,* painted mural, Wat No Phutthangkun / Wat Makham No, Suphanburi Province, Thailand. Photograph copyright Naomi Appleton.

Next page
Fig. 6.13 From the right of the page, this picture shows the enticing dance of a *nāga* girl, accompanied by male and female *nāga* musicians, who all appear here in human form. **Fig. 6.14** Bhūridatta is coiled around his mound while the hunter points him out to Ālamba, the snake-charmer, and his son turns his head away in shame.

Bhūridatta-jātaka, painted *khoi* manuscript, MS. Pali a. 27 (R), fol. 13, mid-18th century, Central Thailand. Copyright Bodleian Library, University of Oxford, 2013. Taken from Appleton, Shaw, and Unebe, *Illuminating the Life of the Buddha* (Oxford Bodleian Library Publishing, 2013).

6.11

6.12

6.13

6.14

6.15

Fig. 6.15 Bhūridatta coils himself around the mound, while beautiful *nāga* girls, in human form, dance and swim near the waves below. The waves and the material of the dress of the nymph on the left seem to fall in the same patterns together, showing their watery nature. *Bhūridatta-jātaka*, painted mural, Wat Nak Prok, Bangkok, Thailand. Photograph copyright Ven. Piyobhaso Bhatsokorn.

Fig. 6.16 Another twentieth-century depiction of this scene shows a far darker and more dramatically intense sense of the two figures, with storm clouds apparently brewing above an ominous sign of what is to come. *Bhūridatta-jātaka*, painted mural, Wat Rang Si Sut Thawat, Chiang Mai Province, Thailand. Photograph copyright Sébastien Tayac.

Fig. 6.17 This scene with the brahmin about to seize the Bodhisatta is emblematic now in twentieth-century depictions. *Bhūridatta-jātaka*, painted mural, Wat Upakhut, Chiang Mai Province, Thailand, 1933. Photograph copyright Sébastien Tayac.

7.1

7.2

7. The Birth Story of Prince Canda

Fig. 7.1 Prince Canda passes judgement on cases. **Fig. 7.2** Prince Canda entreats his father to cancel the sacrifice.

Candakumāra-jātaka, terracotta tile, Ananda Temple, Pagan, Myanmar, late 11th or early 12th century. Photographs copyright Lilian Handlin, 2004.

7.3

7.4

Fig. 7.3 Prince Canda awaits slaughter by Khaṇḍahāla in the sacrificial pit.
Fig. 7.4 The people attack Khaṇḍahāla.

Candakumāra-jātaka, terracotta tile, Ananda Temple, Pagan, Myanmar, late 11th or early 12th century. Photographs copyright Lilian Handlin, 2004.

7.5

7.6

Fig. 7.5 Khaṇḍahāla, sword in hand, prepares to kill Prince Canda. Behind, Candā calls on the gods, and Sakka appears in the sky. *Candakumāra-jātaka*, glazed terracotta tile, Shwedagon Pagoda, Yangon, Myanmar, c. 1900. Photograph copyright Lucy Shaw. **Fig. 7.6** In this pivotal moment in the story, Khaṇḍahāla stands ready to kill Prince Canda in front of the sacrificial fire, while the king looks on. The other human sacrificial victims await their turn. Behind the prince, Candā entreats the gods for assistance, and Sakka descends carrying a flaming trident, rather than the hammer mentioned in the story. *Candakumāra-jātaka*, painted mural, Wat Thung Yu, Chiang Mai Province, Thailand, 1967. Photograph copyright Sébastien Tayac.

7.7

7.8

7.9

Fig. 7.9 This delightful mural shows the various animals that have been assembled ready for the sacrifice. The writing, translated by Alexandra Green, reads 'The bodhisattva Candakumara prince together with 100 elephants, 100 horses, 100 cows, 100 buffalo, 100 goats, chickens and ducks 100 each, [illegible] . . . preparing to make a sacrifice.' *Candakumāra-jātaka*, painted mural, Zedidawdaik complex, Anein Village, Myanmar, 18th century. Photograph and translation copyright Alexandra Green.

Previous page
Fig. 7.7 The king sits on his throne, listening to the advice of his brahmin Khaṇḍahāla. **Fig. 7.8** This is the classic scene of the sacrifice being disrupted by Sakka. The animals lined up for slaughter are particularly charming in this image.

Candakumāra-jātaka, painted *khoi* manuscript, MS. Pali a. 27 (R), fol. 14, mid-18th century, Central Thailand. Copyright Bodleian Library, University of Oxford, 2013. Taken from Appleton, Shaw, and Unebe, *Illuminating the Life of the Buddha* (Oxford Bodleian Library Publishing, 2013).

7.10

Fig. 7.10 The story is shown here in several interconnected scenes across a whole wall. The disruption of the sacrifice by Sakka takes centre stage, with the people and animals dispersing below. *Candakumāra-jātaka*, painted mural, Wat Nak Prok, Bangkok, Thailand. Photograph copyright Ven. Bhatsakorn Piyobhaso.

7.11

Fig. 7.11 In this mid-nineteenth-century mural, Sakka descends to disrupt the sacrifice, prompting the citizens to attack Khaṇḍahāla. *Candakumāra-jātaka*, painted mural, Wat No Phutthangkun / Wat Makham No, Suphanburi Province, Thailand, 1848. Photograph copyright Naomi Appleton.

8.1

8.2

8. The Birth Story of Nārada

These are the only two scenes from the *Nārada-jātaka* shown at Pagan, suggesting the story did not have the popularity or currency of the other tales of the Great Ten during this period of Myanmar's history.
Fig. 8.1 The hermit Nārada converses with the king. **Fig. 8.2** Nārada returns to the Brahmā world.

Nārada-jātaka, terracotta tile, Ananda Temple, Pagan, Myanmar, late 11th or early 12th century. Photographs copyright Lilian Handlin, 2004.

8.3

8.4

Fig. 8.3 Here the king is shown receiving a teaching from the false ascetic.
Fig. 8.4 Nārada Brahmā, looking very much like a Buddhist monk, stands in the sky to teach the king, while Princess Rucā pays him honour.

Nārada-jātaka, glazed terracotta tile, Shwedagon Pagoda, Yangon, Myanmar, c. 1900. Photographs copyright Lucy Shaw.

Fig. 8.5 The middle row of this mural shows the scene in the palace as the king gains a wrong view, Rucā tries to cure him, and Nārada arrives to instruct the king. Though Nārada is recognisable from his ascetic's carrying pole, his appearance otherwise looks more like a Buddhist monk than a divine sage. The caption reads 'A representation of King Angati consulting with heretics. A representation of Rujā practising the *sīlas*.' *Nārada-jātaka*, painted mural, Payani temple, Pakhangyi, Myanmar, 18th century. Photograph and translation copyright Alexandra Green.

Facing page

Fig. 8.6 Nārada Brahmā, carrying his ascetic's pole, descends at the request of Princess Rucā to teach the king. *Nārada-jātaka*, painted mural, Wat Kongkaram, Ratchaburi Province, Thailand. Photograph copyright Naomi Appleton.

Fig. 8.7 King Aṅgati sits on his throne in the centre of this mural, as Nārada Brahmā, shown here with the four faces that distinguish the god Brahmā, descends from the sky. *Nārada-jātaka*, painted mural, Wat Nak Prok, Bangkok, Thailand. Photograph copyright Ven. Bhatsakorn Piyobhaso.

8.6

8.7

8.8

Fig. 8.8 Nārada Brahmā descends from the sky amidst coloured flames. He has the four faces characteristic of Brahmā but not the carrying pole that usually indicates his ascetic disguise. **Fig. 8.9** Rucā entreats the gods for help, as the king sits unmoved upon his throne.

Nārada-jātaka, painted *khoi* manuscript, MS. Pali a. 27 (R), fol. 15, mid-18th century, Central Thailand. Copyright Bodleian Library, University of Oxford, 2013. Taken from Appleton, Shaw, and Unebe, *Illuminating the Life of the Buddha* (Oxford Bodleian Library Publishing, 2013).

8.9

Fig. 8.10 Entreated by Princess Rucā, the ascetic Nārada arrives through the palace window to the surprise of the king. *Nārada-jātaka*, painted mural, Wat Santon Mueang Nua, Chiang Mai Province, Thailand, 1977. Photograph copyright Sébastien Tayac.

Fig. 8.11 The king and the princess are seated on the palace terrace as the ascetic Nārada descends from the sky. *Nārada-jātaka*, painted mural, Wat Chai Sathan, Chiang Mai Province, Thailand, 1980. Photograph copyright Sébastien Tayac.

9.1

9.2

9. The Birth Story of Vidhura

Fig. 9.1 Vidhura answers the question of the four kings.
Fig. 9.2 Puṇṇaka carries Vidhura away.

Vidhura-jātaka, terracotta tile, Ananda Temple, Pagan, Myanmar, late 11th or early 12th century. Photographs copyright Lilian Handlin, 2004.

9.3

9.4

Fig. 9.3 Puṇṇaka swings Vidhura upside down. **Fig. 9.4** Vidhura teaches the *nāga* king and queen.

Vidhura-jātaka, terracotta tile, Ananda Temple, Pagan, Myanmar, late 11th or early 12th century. Photographs copyright Lilian Handlin, 2004.

9.5

9.6

Fig. 9.5 Puṇṇaka plays the king at dice. **Fig. 9.6** Vidhura is carried by Puṇṇaka on his horse. Though most depictions show Vidhura clinging to the horse's tail as in the text, here Puṇṇaka holds Vidhura by the ankles and drags him behind.

Vidhura-jātaka, glazed terracotta tile, Shwedagon Pagoda, Yangon, Myanmar, c. 1900. Photographs copyright Lucy Shaw.

9.7

9.8

Fig. 9.9 In the bottom row of this mural we see Vidhura adjudicating on the comparative merit of the four kings. The writing reads 'Minister Vidhura solving the problem of the four kings Korabba king, Sakka king, Galon king, and Naga king.' *Vidhura-jātaka*, painted mural, Monywe complex, Salingyi, Myanmar, 18th century. Photograph and translation copyright Alexandra Green.

Previous page
Fig. 9.7 The iconic image of Vidhura being carried away by Puṇṇaka. Here he clings calmly to the horse's tail and seems to float along behind the demon.
Fig. 9.8 Vidhura teaching Puṇṇaka and a woman, who is presumably either Puṇṇaka's bride Irandatī or the *nāga* queen Vimalā.

Vidhura-jātaka, painted *khoi* manuscript, MS. Pali a. 27 (R), fol. 16, mid-18th century, Central Thailand. Copyright Bodleian Library, University of Oxford, 2013. Taken from Appleton, Shaw, and Unebe, *Illuminating the Life of the Buddha* (Oxford Bodleian Library Publishing, 2013).

9.10

9.11

Figs 9.10, 9.11 These two images form part of a wall that depicts the full story of Vidhura. In the first, the demon Puṇṇaka plays the king at dice. Puṇṇaka's magical horse is behind him. The second shows Vidhura being tied to the horse by Puṇṇaka while his friends and family lament. Just above this scene we see the *nāga* realm, in which Vidhura is giving a teaching.

Vidhura-jātaka, painted mural, Wat Buak Khrok Luang, Chiang Mai Province, Thailand. Photographs copyright Sarah Shaw.

9.12

9.13

Fig. 9.12 Vidhura holds on to the tail of Puṇṇaka's horse as they travel through the air. *Vidhura-jātaka*, painted mural, Wat Kongkaram, Ratchaburi Province, Thailand. Photograph copyright Naomi Appleton. **Fig. 9.13** In this early 21st-century depiction, Vidhura lies peacefully as the *yakkha* Puṇṇaka—here pictured with bright green skin—tries to frighten him to death. In the background we see Puṇṇaka listening to a teaching from the wise Vidhura. *Vidhura-jātaka*, painted mural, Wat Amphawan, Chiang Mai Province, Thailand, 2008. Photograph copyright Sébastien Tayac.

10.1

10.2

10. The Birth Story of Vessantara

Fig. 10.1 The Birth of Vessantara. The Bodhisatta asks for gold so that he can make gifts. **Fig. 10.2** The royal steward delivers his message to Vessantara; he can be seen wearing the jewelled earrings described in the story.

Vessantara-jātaka, terracotta tile, Ananda Temple, Pagan, Myanmar, late 11th or early 12th century. Photographs copyright Lilian Handlin, 2004.

10.3

10.4

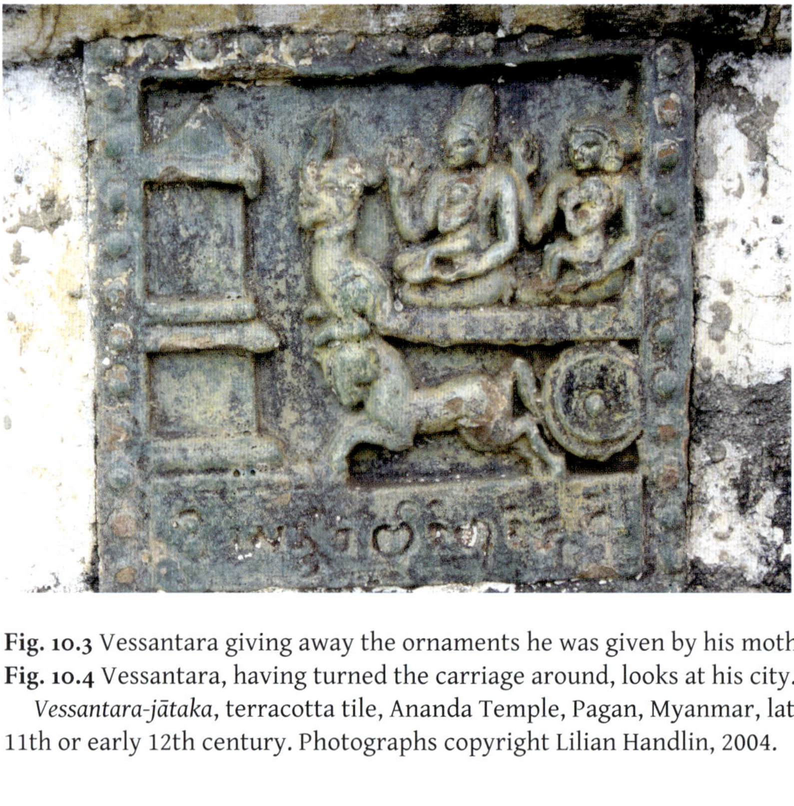

Fig. 10.3 Vessantara giving away the ornaments he was given by his mother.
Fig. 10.4 Vessantara, having turned the carriage around, looks at his city.
Vessantara-jātaka, terracotta tile, Ananda Temple, Pagan, Myanmar, late 11th or early 12th century. Photographs copyright Lilian Handlin, 2004.

10.5

10.6

Fig. 10.5 The red deer drawing the carriage. **Fig. 10.6** King Sakka comes as a brahmin to ask for Maddī.

Vessantara-jātaka, terracotta tile, Ananda Temple, Pagan, Myanmar, late 11th or early 12th century. Photographs copyright Lilian Handlin, 2004.

10.7

10.8

Fig. 10.7 Maddī mounts her elephant. **Fig. 10.8** The giving of the ornaments. *Vessantara-jātaka*, terracotta tile, Ananda Temple, Pagan, Myanmar, late 11th or early 12th century. Photographs copyright Lilian Handlin, 2004.

10.9

10.10

Fig. 10.9 Vessantara giving away the elephant. **Fig. 10.10** The children being redeemed by their grandfather. The other two tiles in this Vessantara series show Maddī in the forest with the wild animals and the brahmin asleep in the tree while the children are being tended by the *devas*.

Vessantara-jātaka, glazed terracotta tile, Shwedagon Pagoda, Yangon, Myanmar, c. 1900. Photographs copyright Lucy Shaw.

10.11

Fig. 10.11 In both registers Vessantara offers gifts. The words that can be read say ' . . . Young daughter and son gold and silver male and female servants longyi gold and silver boxes precious elephants and horses . . . elephants horses buffalo cows goats pigs chickens geese being given away.' *Vessantara-jātaka*, painted mural, cave 284, Powindaung, Myanmar, 18th century. Photograph and translation copyright Alexandra Green.

10.12

Fig. 10.12 A sense of tranquil rest, under the light of a new moon, is being suggested by this depiction of the *deva*s tending to the children, while the brahmin sleeps. *Vessantara-jātaka*, painted mural, Wat Ping Noi, Chiang Mai Province, Thailand. Photograph copyright Sébastien Tayac.

10.13

10.14

Fig. 10.13 Vessantara makes the gift of the carriage. Forest and soft foliage separate incidents in this downwards pendulum depiction. **Fig. 10.14** Women gathering water in the brahmin village, teasing the brahmin's wife.

Vessantara-jātaka, painted mural, Wat Saket, Bangkok, Thailand. Photographs copyright Sarah Shaw.

10.15 

In the gracefully balanced pair of pictures on these two pages, a sense of the ceremony of these gift-giving occasions is communicated by the mirroring placement of key figures in these scenes, which in the manuscript flank the text of an *Abhidhamma* chant. **Fig. 10.15** Vessantara pours water to signify his gift of the children to the brahmin, who sits on the extreme left. In the top left corner, Maddī makes her entreaties to the beasts in the forest. Copyright Bodleian Library, University of Oxford, 2013. Taken from Appleton, Shaw, and Unebe, *Illuminating the Life of the Buddha* (Oxford Bodleian Library Publishing, 2013).

10.16

Fig. 10.16 Vessantara makes the gift of his wife, who is sitting paying respect as her children did before, behind the Bodhisatta. Sakka, still showing his green body though disguised as a brahmin, sits before him. In the top right corner, he is seen in his heaven before making his request. *Vessantara-jātaka*, painted *khoi* manuscript, MS. Pali a. 27 (R), fol. 17, mid-18th century, Central Thailand. Copyright Bodleian Library, University of Oxford, 2013. Taken from Appleton, Shaw, and Unebe, *Illuminating the Life of the Buddha* (Oxford Bodleian Library Publishing, 2013).

10.17

10.18

Fig. 10.17 Vessantara pours water on the ground, a symbolic act signifying the irrevocability of a gift, when giving the carriage to the brahmins after he has left the palace. **Fig. 10.18** Vessantara and Maddī carry the children as they go on foot after Vessantara has given the carriage.

Vessantara-jātaka, painted mural, Wat No Phutthangkun / Wat Makham No, Suphanburi Province, Thailand. Photographs copyright Naomi Appleton.

Fig. 10.19 Vessantara giving away the children. *Vessantara-jātaka*, painted mural, Wat Nak Prok, Bangkok, Thailand. Photograph copyright Ven. Bhatsakorn Piyobhaso.

Fig. 10.20 Detail showing the brahmin visiting the seer Accuta. *Vessantara-jātaka*, painted mural, Wat Saket, Bangkok, Thailand. Photograph copyright Sarah Shaw.

10.21

10.22

Fig. 10.21 Vessantara, Maddī, and the children on their journey.
Fig. 10.22 Detail of the brahmin in his hammock.

Vessantara-jātaka, painted mural, Wat Saket, Bangkok, Thailand. Photographs copyright Sarah Shaw.

10.23

10.24

Fig. 10.23 This mural shows several scenes the brahmin and the hunter, the horses being given away, and the brahmin in his hammock above. *Vessantara-jātaka*, painted mural, Wat Buak Khrok Luang, Chiang Mai Province, Thailand, 19th century. Photograph copyright Sarah Shaw.
Fig. 10.24 Vessantara giving away his horses. *Vessantara-jātaka*, painted mural, Wat Buak Khrok Luang, Chiang Mai Province, Thailand, 19th century. Photograph copyright Sébastien Tayac.

10.25

10.26

Fig. 10.25 This favourite scene from the story shows the craven brahmin hiding from the hunter and his dogs. **Fig. 10.26** Maddī paying homage to the wild beasts of the forest.

Vessantara-jātaka, painted mural, Wat Buak Khrok Luang, Chiang Mai Province, Thailand, 19th century. Photographs copyright Sébastien Tayac.

10.27

10.28

Fig. 10.27 In this depiction of Accuta's guidance to the brahmin the artist has chosen to emphasize the grandeur and loneliness of the hills and forest beyond. *Vessantara-jātaka*, painted mural, Wat Si Soda, Chiang Mai Province, Thailand. Photograph copyright Sébastien Tayac. **Fig. 10.28** This scene of the brahmin's wife being teased by the other women shows the earthy humour characteristic of much Thai temple art, from the nineteenth century to the present. *Vessantara-jātaka*, painted mural, Wat Si Ping Mueang, Chiang Mai Province, Thailand, 2010. Photograph copyright Sébastien Tayac.

10.29

10.30

10.31

In some parts of northeastern Thailand, the twelfth section of the *Vessantara*, describing Vessantara's reunion and agreeing to return, is chanted the day before the full recitation. The recitation takes place outside the village in a location reached by a long procession the bower has been specially constructed so that the monk who chants the section, using a palm-leaf manuscript popularly referred to as a *samut khoi*, can sit and face the assembled listeners. He takes on the persona of Vessantara, and is invited by a village elder, acting as the king, to return to his own city.
Fig. 10.29 Spectators wait for the chanting of the twelfth section to begin.
Fig. 10.30 A village elder makes the request for Vessantara, represented by the monk who has just recited the twelfth section, to come home.
Fig. 10.31 Celebrations and dance accompany the homecoming after the recitation is finished. Si Sa Ket Province, Thailand, May 2011. Photographs copyright Ian Rose.

10.32

10.33

Fig. 10.32 Maddī laments in the foreground; the officiating monk recites the story. *Vessantara* performance, Bangkok, Thailand, 2009. Photograph copyright Arthid Sheravanichkul. **Fig. 10.33** Procession of a *Vessantara* scroll during a Bun Phra Wet festival in northeastern Thailand. Copyright Sandra Cate, 2011. Taken from Leedom Lefferts and Sandra Cate, *Buddhist Storytelling in Thailand and Laos*. Singapore Asian Civilisations Museum, 2012.

Fig. 10.34 Moving downwards from the top, the central part of the image depicts the brahmin being shown the way by the Cetan, hiding from the dogs and the hunter, meeting with Accuta, and making his request for and then taking the children, who are also shown hiding in the lotus pond. Several other scenes are painted to the sides. *Vessantara-jātaka*, painted mural, Wat Si Koet, Chiang Mai Province, Thailand. Photograph copyright Sébastien Tayac.

9

The Birth Story of (Wise) Vidhura

(*Vidhurapaṇḍita-jātaka* or *Vidhura-jātaka*)

INTRODUCTION

The Birth Story of Vidhura tells of a wise and truthful adviser who survives a number of challenging situations with bravery and wit. He is, unsurprisingly, identified as the Bodhisatta, and the perfection he is said to be cultivating is that of truthfulness. However, alongside a celebration of the Bodhisatta's wisdom and honesty this story introduces us to a myriad of entertaining characters from various worlds. The story begins in the realm of King Dhanañjaya, who can in some sense be identified as Arjuna, one of the Pāṇḍava brothers and a hero of the Indian epic *Mahābhārata*. The drama, however, unfolds in the realms of the *nāgas* (serpent deities) and of the *yakkhas* (demons or spirit-deities). Such creatures might exhibit fantastic abilities, such as flying through the air, changing their form at will or summoning winds, but they also experience very human desires and family dramas: wives make unreasonable demands of husbands, daughters are pressured by fathers into attracting suitors, and uncles ignore their overenthusiastic nephews. By bringing together all three categories of being—human, *nāga*, and *yakkha*—the story has a lot of delightful narrative tricks at its disposal. Supplement this with a magical jewel that contains all of the universe and a horse that can walk on water and you have an adventure of the most entrancing kind.

Introduced and translated by Naomi Appleton.

It is often said that religious narratives are a way of issuing a moral pill in story jam. If that is the case then in the *Vidhura-jātaka* we have both lots of jam and lots of pills. In amongst the tales of demons and magical horses we find several self-contained passages of teaching. The story opens with what appears to have been considered a separate *jātaka*—that of the four observers of the *uposatha*. A story entitled the *Catuposathika-jātaka* is included as number 441 in the *Jātakatthavaṇṇanā*, but it contains no story, only a reference to the *Puṇṇaka-jātaka*, which is presumably another name for the *Vidhura-jātaka*. The first eleven verses found in the *Vidhura-jātaka* are really considered to be part of that *Catuposathika-jātaka*. The story concerns a debate between four observers of the holy day who cannot decide which one of them is most holy, and so they turn to Vidhura to judge. This self-contained moralizing preface is followed later on in the narrative by four sets of teaching: Firstly Vidhura advises his king about the appropriate conduct for a householder, secondly he advises his children about how to live happily in the royal household in service to the king, thirdly he teaches Puṇṇaka about the four *dhammas* of a virtuous man, and fourthly he shows the *nāgas* how to ensure they attain a future rebirth in heavenly glory. However, these teachings are interspersed with plenty of pure jam, from long descriptions of the *nāga* realm or the qualities of the supreme jewel offered as gambling stake, to the tense unfolding of events as Vidhura's life comes under threat.

The Perfections

Another aspect of religious teaching that is found in the *Vidhura-jātaka*, as in all the *jātakas* of the *Mahānipāta*, concerns the ten perfections. The *Vidhura-jātaka* is associated in the Thai tradition with truthfulness (*sacca*). This is presumably a reference to the moment in the narrative when Vidhura is asked by Puṇṇaka whether or not he is owned by the king. If he is, then he has been won by the demon and must leave his home and family and go wherever his new master desires. If he is not, then he may stay. Despite the obvious temptations, Vidhura reasons that there is no refuge in this world better than the truth, and so admits to being owned by the king. His honesty is immediately rewarded, as Puṇṇaka then allows him to stay long enough to provide some guidance to his family. However, although his truth-telling is clearly relevant to the story, the *Vidhura-jātaka* does not contain any of the more obvious examples of the power of truth, such as the curing of Sāma by truth declarations in the *Suvaṇṇasāma-jātaka*

(Chapter 3) or the intervention of the gods due to Candā's Act of Truth in the *Candakumāra-jātaka* (Chapter 7).

The story itself mentions two other perfections: wisdom (*paññā*) and determination or resolve (*adiṭṭhāna*). The former is the perfection associated with this story in the *Jātaka-nidāna*, and is the subject being discussed by the monks just prior to the Buddha's telling of the story in the *Jātakatthavaṇṇanā*. The latter is mentioned at the moment when Vidhura takes hold of the tail of Puṇṇaka's horse, when he 'put the perfection of resolve before everything else' (*adiṭṭhānapāramiṃ purecārikaṃ katvā*). Clearly Vidhura's great wisdom and skill as a *dhamma* teacher as well as his courage and determination are key to the narrative. Without the former he would not have been desired by the *nāgas* and without the latter he would not have survived his ensuing ordeal. It would appear that this story is therefore exploring several of the Bodhisatta's qualities at once: his skill in teaching, courage, wit, wisdom, honesty, determination, and sense of duty to his family and king. In this story he is a truly admirable character, and a well-rounded one. But to understand the full implications of Vidhura's heroism we must briefly comment on his wider South Asian presence.

Vidhura in the Mahābhārata

The wise Vidhura of the *Vidhura-jātaka* is also known to wider South Asian tradition as the uncle of the two sets of warring cousins in the Indian epic *Mahābhārata*, which was composed over a similar period to the *Jātakatthavaṇṇanā*. Vidhura is half-brother of the blind king Dhṛtarāṣṭra and his predecessor Pāṇḍu. The main story of the epic is of the struggle of the sons of Pāṇḍu, the five Pāṇḍava brothers, to maintain their claim to half of the kingdom against the wishes of their cousins, the sons of Dhṛtarāṣṭra. Being born of a slave woman, Vidhura has no entitlement to the throne himself, and so simply acts as adviser. He is said to be the god Dharma reborn as a human, and so offers the best possible advice, saving the Pāṇḍavas from their murderous cousins and repeatedly trying to reconcile the two sets of brothers. He offers several speeches on correct kingship and appropriate behaviour towards teachers and relatives, some of which are similar in sentiment to those preserved in this *jātaka* story.

That the *Vidhura-jātaka* refers to the same Vidhura (spelled Vidura in the *Mahābhārata*) is clear from his wisdom and role as steward (*kattar*), his status as slave, and his service to a gambling Kuru king named Dhanañjaya at his capital Indapatta (Indraprastha in Sanskrit). Even Vidhura's association with truth is found in the *Mahābhārata*, where he is called 'bearer of the truth', 'seer of the truth', and 'truth-speaking Vidura'.[1] However, despite the use of common names and terms, the *jātaka* does not reproduce the circumstances of the epic. So, for example, Dhanañjaya is a name often given to Arjuna, the middle of the five Pāṇḍava brothers, whereas in the *Mahābhārata* it is the eldest brother, Yudhiṣṭhira, whose passion for gambling lands him in trouble. In addition, although a dicing match plays a pivotal role in both stories, the stakes, players, and consequences are rather different.[2] Thus the *jātaka* blends several characters and motifs together and adds to them the entirely new story of Puṇṇaka's attempt to abduct Vidhura at the request of a *nāga*. The character of Vidhura is thereby incorporated into Buddhist legend through his identification not as the god Dharma, but as the Bodhisatta, who is himself the paragon of truth and morality. Once again the *Mahānipāta* draws on a wide set of narrative characters and motifs in order to praise the Bodhisatta and demonstrate the superiority of Buddhism.

'You are pale, thin, and weak . . .'

[255] The Teacher related this, concerning his perfection of wisdom, while dwelling in the Jeta Grove. One day the monks raised this subject in the *dhamma* hall: 'Friend, the Teacher's wisdom is great, broad, bright, swift, sharp, and penetrating. He defeats the words of others through the power of his own wisdom. He breaks open the subtle questions prepared by warriors and wise men and so on, making them meek, and having established them in the refuges and precepts, he brings them onto the path

1. For example *satyadhṛtiḥ, satyadarśanaḥ*, and *satyavādinaḥ* are all used to refer to Vidura in the *Śalya Parvan*; see Meiland 2005: 334–5, 276–7, and 50–1.

2. For a more detailed comparison of the *Vidhura-jātaka* with the *Mahābhārata* see Moačanin, 2009. While I find some of Moačanin's observations interesting, her comparison is too rigid and her argument for a common source for both stories is somewhat unconvincing. She sees the gambling episode as a parallel to Yudhiṣṭhira's gambling away his kingdom in the *Mahābhārata*, even though the stake, process, and consequences in the *jātaka* are very different. I find it more fruitful to talk of the two stories drawing on similar characters and motifs, rather than understanding them as different versions of the same story. That said, the question of the gambling king's ownership of the stake (Vidhura in our story, the Pāṇḍavas' wife Draupadī in the *Mahābhārata*) is central to both versions, suggesting a fairly close link.

that leads to the deathless.' The Teacher came and asked them, 'Monks, what are you talking of as you sit here together?' Hearing their response he said, 'It is not a marvel, monks, that the Tathāgata, having attained the perfection of supreme Buddhahood, can defeat the words of others and instruct warriors and so on. For in an earlier existence, when still seeking the knowledge of awakening, the Tathāgata was endowed with wisdom and crushed the words of others. At the time when I was the young man Vidhura, on top of Black Mountain sixty *yojana*s tall I tamed a *yakkha* general called Puṇṇaka, made him meek, and induced him to grant me my life.' Entreated by them he spoke of the past.

In times past, in the city of Indapatta in the Kuru country, the Kuru descendent Dhanañjaya ruled the kingdom. There was a minister named Wise Vidhura, who was his adviser on worldly and religious matters.[3] He spoke sweetly and was a great preacher, and the kings in all Jambudīpa were like elephants [256] seduced by the sound of an elephant-enticing lute. Since they each desired a sweet *dhamma* teaching themselves, he would not let them go each to their own kingdoms. He lived in the city with great fame, teaching the *dhamma* to the populace with the mastery of a Buddha.

And at that time in Vārāṇasī four householder friends, who were brahmins possessing great halls,[4] saw the danger in sense pleasures and entered the Himalayas to take up the holy life of a sage. They cultivated the higher knowledges and attainments, and after living there for a long time, eating the fruits and roots of the forest, they set out wandering in search of salt and vinegar. They reached the city of Kālacampā in the Aṅga country and entered the city in search of alms. There four householder friends who were pleased with their deportment paid them honour. They took their alms bowls and each of them served one with food and drinking water in his house. Obtaining their agreement, they had them live in the royal park.

The four ascetics ate at the houses of the four householders, then for their daytime abodes one went to the Heaven of the Thirty-Three (Tāvatiṃsa), one to the *nāga* realm, the third to the realm of the *supaṇṇa*s, and the fourth

3. The terms here are *attha* (aim, wealth, good) and *dhamma* (truth, religion, duty).
4. In other words they were very wealthy. VRI adds that they renounced 'when they were elderly'.

to the Migācira Park in the kingdom of the Kurus. Of them the one who went to the godly realm and made his daytime abode there, he saw the glory of Sakka and described it to his own attendant. The one who went to the *nāga* realm for his daytime abode saw the fortune of the *nāga* king and described it to his attendant. The one who went to the *supaṇṇa* realm for his daytime abode saw the splendour of the *supaṇṇa* king and described that to his own attendant. The one who made his daytime abode in the park of the Kuru saw the majesty and prosperity of Dhanañjaya's kingdom and described it to his attendant. And so those four men desired each of those places,[5] and having made merit through gift-giving and so on, when their lives were concluded one became reborn as Sakka, one was reborn, with his wife and child, in the *nāga* realm,[6] one became the king of the *supaṇṇas* in Lake Simbali palace, and one took rebirth in the womb of the chief wife of King Dhanañjaya. The ascetics arose in a Brahmā realm.

The Kuru prince, after he had grown up, was established on the throne by his father, and ruled the kingdom righteously, but he became rich through gambling. Abiding by the advice of Wise Vidhura he gave gifts, guarded morality, and observed the *uposatha*. One day when he was observing the *uposatha* he went to the park, thinking, 'I will devote myself to solitude!' [257] He sat down in a pleasant spot and observed the conduct of a renouncer. Sakka too, observing the *uposatha* and thinking, 'There is an obstacle in the godly world,' came to the same park in the world of men, sat down in a pleasant place, and observed the conduct of a renouncer. The *nāga* king Varuṇa also, observing the *uposatha*, thinking, 'There is an obstacle in the world of the *nāgas*,' came to the same place, sat down in a pleasant spot, and observed the conduct of a renouncer. And so too the king of the *supaṇṇas*, observing the *uposatha*, thinking, 'There is an obstacle in the *supaṇṇa* world,' came to the same place, sat down in a pleasant spot, and observed the conduct of a renouncer. In the evening the four of them came out from their own places, and came together on the banks of an auspicious lotus pond. Seeing one another, because of their former affection they all greeted each other warmly, and friendliness towards one another arose, and they gave each other a genial welcome and sat down. Sakka sat on an

5. Using VRI reading *tam tadeva ṭhānaṃ* rather than F *taṃ devaṭṭhānaṃ* since not all four states are *deva* realms.

6. VRI specifies that he becomes king of the *nāgas*. As we later find out, he is King Varuṇa and his wife and daughter play a key role in the narrative.

auspicious stone slab, and one after another each of them found a suitable place and sat down.

Then Sakka said to them, 'The four of us are kings. But which of us has the greatest virtue?' Then Varuṇa, king of the *nāgas*, said, 'My virtue is greater than the virtue of you three.'

'For what reason?'

'This king of *supaṇṇas* is the enemy of us all, whether born or not yet born, and yet seeing our enemy, the death-maker, like that, I do not get angry. For this reason my virtue is great.' He spoke the first verse of the *Jātaka of the Four Uposathas*, from the chapter of the tens:[7]

'He who does not lose his temper when provoked,
The good person who never gets angry,
And who even when angry does not show anger,
That man is surely called a renouncer in the world.'

[258] Hearing that,[8] this king of the *supaṇṇas* said, 'This *nāga* is my favourite food, and yet seeing my favourite food right here, I endure the hunger and do not harm him for the sake of food, therefore my virtue is surely greatest!' He spoke this verse:

'The hungry one who overcomes his hunger,
The restrained ascetic, moderate in food and drink,
Who does no evil for the sake of food,
That man is surely called a renouncer in the world.'

Then Sakka, king of the gods, said, 'I abandoned manifold causes of happiness, the bliss of the heaven realm, and came to the world of men for the sake of protecting my virtue. Therefore my virtue is greatest.' He spoke this verse:

'Having abandoned all pleasure and enjoyment,
He speaks no falsehoods in the world,
Abstaining from adornments and sexual intercourse,
That man is surely called a renouncer in the world.'

7. Here and below in F the declaration that he spoke the verse is made after the verse, which reads very awkwardly and is in contrast to the norm in the *Jātakatthavaṇṇanā*. I have therefore followed VRI in placing it as normal. The difference is perhaps due to the fact that these verses are considered to belong to another *jātaka* (the *Catuposathika-jātaka*; see discussion above) and do not actually form part of the *Vidhura-jātaka* verses.

8. Before this sentence, F includes a line reiterating the message of the verse, which VRI (rightly in my view) considers part of the verse commentary. I have therefore omitted it.

Hearing that,[9] King Dhanañjaya said, 'Today I gave up a great property—my harem complete with sixteen thousand dancing girls—and practised the conduct of a renouncer in the park. Thus my virtue is the greatest.' He spoke a verse:

[259] 'He who, in right knowledge, gives up
All possessions and objects of greed,
Tamed, steadfast, without ego, without desire,
They surely call that man a renouncer in the world.'

In this way they all praised their own virtue as the greatest. Sakka and the others asked Dhanañjaya, 'Great King, is there some wise person in your presence who could remove our uncertainty?'

'Yes, Great Kings, I have a steadfast adviser on worldly and religious matters named Wise Vidhura. He will remove our uncertainty. Let us go to him!'

'Very good!' they agreed. Then all of them left the park and went to the *dhamma* hall. They had the Bodhisatta adorned and seated in the middle of a couch, expressed cordial greetings, and then seated to one side said, 'Wise one, we have a doubt. Remove it for us!' They spoke this verse:

'We ask the steward of unsurpassed wisdom!
A dispute has been born in our verses.
Remove the uncertainty and doubts today.
We would all overcome that uncertainty today.'

[260] Hearing their speech the wise one said, 'Great Kings, how will I understand what has been well and ill spoken amongst the verses of disagreement that have arisen concerning your virtue?' He spoke this verse:

'Those wise men who are intent on the good,
They speak about that thoroughly at the appropriate time.
But how, when the verses have not been spoken,
Would the skilful understand the meaning, king of men?
How indeed does the king of *nāga*s speak?
And how the descendent of Vinatā, Garuḷa?[10]
And what does the king of the *gandhabbas*[11] say?

9. Again I omit a line repeating the message of the previous verse, following VRI in designating it as verse commentary.

10. A reference to the king of *supaṇṇa*s, also called *garuḍa*s or *garuḷa*s and said to be descended from the first divine bird Garuḍa, son of Vinatā.

11. The commentary explains that this means Sakka.

How the excellent king of the Kurus?'

Then they spoke this verse:

'The king of *nāgas* speaks of forbearance,
Garuḷa, descendent of Vinatā, of fasting,
The king of *gandhabbas* of abandoning pleasures,
And the excellent king of the Kurus of abandoning possessions.'

Then having heard their speech the Great Being spoke this verse:

'All these are well spoken,
Nothing here is poorly spoken.
And he in whom these are established
[261] like spokes well connected to the nave of the wheel,
Possessed of these four qualities,
That man they call a renouncer in the world.'

In this way the Great Being spoke of the similarities of the four virtues. Hearing that the four beings were joyful and praising him spoke this verse:

'You are indeed excellent and unsurpassed!
You are wise, knowledgeable in the *dhamma*, skilled in the *dhamma*!
Having mastered the question with wisdom,
The wise one has destroyed our doubts!
He has cut out the doubt and uncertainty,
Like an ivory worker cuts the tooth of an elephant with a saw!'

Thus the four beings became pleased of mind because of that explanation of their question. Sakka honoured him with divine *dukūla* cloth, Garuḷa with a garland of gold, Varuṇa the *nāga* king with a jewel, and King Dhanañjaya with a thousand cows and so on, saying:

'Pleased by the explanation of the question,
I give you eleven excellent villages,
A thousand cows, buffaloes and elephants,
And thoroughbred horses, and these ten chariots.'

[262] Sakka and the others, having honoured the Great Being, went back to their own abodes.

The wife of the *nāga* king was called Queen Vimalā. Not seeing the jewelled ornament around her husband's neck, she asked, 'Lord, where is your jewel?'

'My dear, having heard a *dhamma* talk by Vidhura the Wise, son of the brahmin Canda, my heart was delighted and I honoured him with that jewel. I was not alone: Sakka too honoured him with divine cloth, the king of the *supaṇṇas* with a garland of gold, and King Dhanañjaya with a thousand cows and so on.'

'Is he a *dhamma* teacher, lord?'

'My dear, what are you saying? He proceeds across the earth of Jambudīpa as if a Buddha has arisen. The one hundred kings of all Jambudīpa have been bound by his sweet speech, and do not return to their own kingdoms. They are like rutting elephants that have been seduced by the sound of the elephant-pleasing lute. He is that sort of teacher of sweet *dhamma*!'

Hearing of Wise Vidhura's great qualities, she became desirous of hearing his *dhamma* teaching, and thought, 'If I were to say, "Lord, I wish to hear his *dhamma* teaching—bring him here!" he would not fetch him. What if I were to make a pretence at illness, saying to him that a craving has arisen in my heart?'[12] She did this, and giving the sign to her attendants she lay down. The *nāga* king, not seeing her at the time of attendance, asked her maidservants, 'Where is Vimalā?' When they replied, 'She is unwell, Your Majesty!' he went into her presence, sat on the side of her bed and stroking her body spoke the first verse:

'You are pale, thin, and weak! You did not use to look like this.
Vimalā, asked, explain: how does your body feel?' (1)

Then she, explaining, spoke the second verse:

[263] 'There is a characteristic of mothers amongst men
Called craving, lord of beings.
Chief of *nāgas*, I long for the heart
Of Vidhura, obtained lawfully.' (2)

Hearing that the king of *nāgas* spoke the third verse:

'Crave the moon!
Or else the sun or even the wind!
When the sight of Vidhura is hard to obtain,
Who will lead Vidhura here?' (3)

Hearing his words, she declared, 'Not getting this, I will now die!' She showed him her back, covered her face with a corner of her cloak, and lay down. The *nāga* king went to his own quarters and, seated on the side of his bed, he considered, 'Vimalā calls for the flesh of Vidhura the Wise's heart!' He thought, 'Not getting the heart of the wise one, Vimalā will die! How on earth am I going to get his heart-flesh?' Then his daugher, the *nāga* princess named Irandatī,[13] came in attendance with great pomp and

12. A *dohaḷa* is a craving often associated with pregnancy. It is understood that if the craving is not satisfied then the woman will die.

13. VRI consistently spells her name 'Irandhatī'.

splendour, adorned with all her jewels. Having honoured her father she stood to one side. Seeing his disturbance of mind she asked, 'Father, you are extremely melancholy. What is the reason for this?' and spoke a verse:

'Oh why, Father, are you so consumed with grief,
Your face like a lotus held in your hands?
[264] Lord, why are you so downcast?
Do not grieve, torturer of enemies!' (4)

Hearing his daughter's words the king of the *nāga*s explained the matter thus:

'Irandatī, your mother
Desires the heart of Vidhura!
When the sight of Vidhura is hard to obtain,
Who will lead Vidhura here?' (5)

Then he sent her away, saying, 'My dear, there is nobody in my presence able to lead Vidhura here. You must give your mother life—seek a husband that is capable of fetching Vidhura!' He spoke this half verse:

'Go seek a husband
Who will lead Vidhura here!' (6a)

Out of love for depravity he spoke this improper speech.

And she, having heard her father's speech,
That night departed and full of desire she went.' (6b)

[265] And wandering in the Himalayas she gathered those flowers that had various fragrances and flavours, and adorned the whole mountain as if a precious jewel. Having covered the upper surface with flowers, she danced in a delightful way and singing a sweet song she spoke the seventh verse:

'Which *gandhabba*, *rakkhasa*, or *nāga*,
Which *kimpurisa* or human,
Which wise bestower of all desires
Will become my husband for a long time?' (7)

At that time the great king Vessavaṇa had a nephew called Puṇṇaka, who was a *yakkha* general. Having mounted his magical Sindh horse that was three-quarters of a *yojana* in length he was going to a *yakkha* gathering on Manosilā Rock at the top of Black Mountain when he heard the sound of her song. The sound of the song of the woman whom he had enjoyed in his immediately preceding life cut his skin and so on and struck at his bones. He stood there. Becoming enamoured he turned back and, seated on the back of his horse, consoled her: 'Noble one, through my wisdom, justice, and *dhamma* I am able to fetch the heart of Vidhura! Do not worry!' He spoke the eighth verse:

'I will be your comfort and your lord,
I will be your husband, you of faultless eyes!
For my wisdom is such
That you will be my wife and be comforted.' (8)
Then Irandatī said to him,
With her heart following its former conduct:[14]
[266] 'Come, let us go to see my father,
And he will declare on this matter.' (9)
Adorned and well dressed, garlanded and covered in sandal perfumes,
She seized the *yakkha* by the hand and went into the presence of her father. (10)

And Puṇṇaka the *yakkha* was announced[15] and went to the presence of the *nāga* king. Asking for Irandatī as his wife he said:

'Excellent *nāga*, hear my speech!
Take the appropriate bride price:
I wish for Irandatī.
Bestow her on me! (11)
A hundred elephants, a hundred horses, a hundred chariots pulled by mules,
A hundred covered wagons completely filled with various jewels.
Nāga, take this, and give me your daughter Irandatī!' (12)

Then the king of *nāgas* said:

'First I will consult friends and relations and the good-hearted people.
A deed done without consultation is later regretted.' (13)
[267] Then the *nāga* Varuṇa entered his dwelling,
Consulted his wife, and spoke these words: (14)
'This *yakkha* Puṇṇaka begs me for Irandatī,
With abundant wealth and possessions. Let us give our beloved to him!' (15)

Vimalā said:

'Not with wealth nor with possessions is our Irandatī to be gained!
But if the wise one's heart
Were lawfully obtained and brought here,
With this possession the princess will be gained.
We wish for no other wealth besides this.' (16)

14. In other words because of the affection remaining from being married to him in a previous lifetime.

15. For *paṭihāretvā* compare BHSD *pratihārayati* 'to announce'.

Then the *nāga* Varuṇa left her residence
And addressing Puṇṇaka he spoke these words: (17)
'Not with wealth nor with possessions is our Irandatī to be gained!
But if you lawfully gain
The wise one's heart and bring it here,
By this property the princess will be gained.
We wish for no other wealth besides this.' (18)

Puṇṇaka said:

'He whom some in the world call "wise"
Is nonetheless called "fool" by others.
Tell me their arguments in this case.
Which wise one do you speak of, *nāga*?' (19)

[268] The *nāga* king said:

'Surely you have heard the name of Vidhura,
Steward of the Kuru King Dhanañjaya?
Fetch that wise man, and justly acquired,
Irandatī will be your servant.' (20)
Having heard this speech of Varuṇa,
The *yakkha* got up, extremely delighted,
And right there he proclaimed to his man,
'Fetch my harnessed thoroughbred here! (21)
With ears made of unwrought gold, hooves of red crystal,
And breastplate of wrought Jambū River gold.' (22)

That man fetched the Sindh horse at once, and Puṇṇaka mounted it and went through the air to the presence of Vessavaṇa. Having described the *nāga* realm he announced his news. By way of explaining that matter this is said:

Puṇṇaka mounted his horse, the divine mount, the vehicle,
And adorned and with trimmed hair and beard,
He set out through the air and sky. (23)
That Puṇṇaka was hungry with the passion of sense pleasures,[16]
Wishing to win Irandatī the *nāga* maiden.
[269] Having gone to the glorious lord of spirits,[17]
He said this to Vessavaṇa Kuvera: (24)
'In the palace named Bhagavatī
The residences are said to be made from gold;

16. VRI reading *kāmarāgena* seems better than F *kāmavegena* 'with the impulse of sense plesures' here.

17. *Bhūtapati* means lord of *bhūtas*, the latter usually referring to spirit deities. According to wider mythology, Vessavaṇa/Kuvera is the overlord of the *yakkhas*.

In the city, created out of gold,
It is made ready for the circle of snakes. (25)
The watchtowers are like camels' necks,
With rubies and emerald crystals;
The palaces here are made of quartz,[18]
Covered with golden jewels. (26)
Mango, *tilaka*, and rose-apple trees,
Sattapaṇṇa, mucalinda, and *ketaka*,
Piyaka, uddālaka, sahakāra,[19]
Uparibhaddaka, and *sindhuvārita* trees; (27)
Campaka-like trees,[20] *nāgamālika*,[21]
Bhaginimāla, and jujube are here;
These trees, overladen with fruit,
Adorn the palace of the snakes. (28)
Here the date palms are made of quartz,
Constantly flowering gold.
Where many live, spontaneously arisen,
Is Varuṇa the king of the *nāgas*, of great supernormal power. (29)
He has a young wife
Vimalā, with a golden body,[22]
Lofty like a young sprouting creeper,[23]
Beautiful to behold, with breasts like fruits of the *nimba* tree, (30)
Lovely skin, coloured with lac dye,
Like a *kaṇikāra* tree blossoming in a sheltered place,
Like a celestial nymph that lives in the *deva* world,
Like lightning escaping from a dense cloud. (31)
[270] She, overcome by a craving,
Desires the heart of Vidhura.
Lord, if I give that to them,
They will give me Irandatī.' (32)

Now without Vessavaṇa's permission he was unable to go, so he spoke

18. *Silā*, translated here as 'quartz', can refer to stone or a range of precious stones. The commentary says that here it refers to jewels (*maṇi*).

19. The verse has *sahā* but the commentary glosses *sahakārā*, which according to PED is a type of fragrant mango.

20. *Campeyyakā*, i.e. relating to the *campaka* tree.

21. Presumably this is another type of tree, though it is not recorded in PED. Alternatively it could mean *nāga* garlands.

22. The term *velli* is only found in the *Jātakatthavaṇṇanā*, and its meaning is unclear, but it seems always to be connected with 'golden', as here: *kañcanavelliviggaha*.

23. *Kāla* is difficult to interpret in this context, but the commentary indicates that it is the *kālavalli* creeper that is meant.

these several verses to explain. But Vessavaṇa did not hear his speech, for he was deciding the case of the celestial palaces of two gods. Realising that his words had not been heard, Puṇṇaka [271] stood before the victorious god. Having judged the case and put aside the defeated, Vessavaṇa said to the other, 'You go, and live in your celestial palace.' At the very moment that he said 'You go!' Puṇṇaka called upon several gods as witnesses: 'You see that I have been sent forth by my uncle!' He sent for his Sindh horse in the manner described above and having mounted it he set off. Explaining the matter the Teacher said:

Having addressed Vessavaṇa Kuvera,
Glorious lord of the spirits, Puṇṇaka
Right there proclaimed to his man:
'Fetch my harnessed thoroughbred here! (33)
With ears made of unwrought gold, hooves of red crystal
And breastplate of wrought Jambū River gold.' (34)
Puṇṇaka mounted his horse, the divine mount, the vehicle,
And adorned and with trimmed hair and beard
He set out through the air and sky. (35)

Going through the sky he thought, 'Vidhura the Wise has a great entourage. I will not be able to seize him. But King Dhanañjaya the Kuru enjoys gambling. Having beaten him at dice I will take Vidhura. But in his house there are many jewels, so he will not play dice for a stake of little value. I will have to fetch a jewel of great value; the king will not take another jewel. In the neighbourhood of Rājagaha, inside Mount Vepulla, there is a gem of great majesty that belonged to a Universal Monarch. I will take it, the king will desire it, and I will beat the king.' So he did that. In order to describe that matter the Teacher said:

He went to beautiful Rājagaha,
The invincible city of King Aṅga,
Of abundant food, plentiful food and drink,
Like Masakkasāra of Vāsava.[24] (36)
[272] Where a multitude of peacocks and herons sound,
Birds cry out, birds assemble together,
Various birds sing in beautiful clearings,
Decked out with flowers like the Snowy Mountain. (37)
That Puṇṇaka ascended Vepulla,
The mountain adorned with *kiṃpurusas*,

24. Masakkasāra is the abode of the Tāvatiṃsa gods, headed by Sakka, also known as Vāsava.

And seeking the excellent jewel,
He saw it in the middle of the mountain's summit. (38)
Seeing the resplendent, noble jewel, bringer of wealth,
The superior gem,[25] resplendent, famous, and glorious,
Shining like lightning in the sky; (39)
He took that valuable gem,
Splendid, called Manohara (Charming);
And the one of excellent appearance mounted the thoroughbred,
And set off through the air and sky. (40)
Having come to the city of Indapatta
He descended and approached the assembly hall of the Kurus.
[273] The unwavering *yakkha* addressed
The one hundred assembled in the meeting: (41)
'Who here would win this excellent jewel of kings?
Who will we conquer with the best of wealth?
What unsurpassed excellent jewel will I win,
Or who would conquer our best possession?' (42)

In these four quarter-verses he offended the Kuru. Then the king thought, 'Until now I have never before seen someone speaking thus like a hero—who is this?' Questioning him he spoke the verse:

'What country were you born in?
This speech of yours is not that of a Kuru.
You overpower us all with your appearance.
Tell me your name and clan.' (43)

Hearing that the other thought, 'This king asks me my name, but Puṇṇaka is a servant. If I say, "I am Puṇṇaka," then he will disregard me, saying, "This is a slave. Why does he speak to me so boldly?" So I will tell him my name from my immediate past existence.' He spoke the verse:

'King, I am the young man Kaccāyana:[26]
They call me Anūnanāma.[27]
[274] My family and clan are of the Aṅgas.
Your Majesty, I have arrived here with dice.' (44)

Then the king, asking him, 'Young man, if you are conquered at dice what will you give, what do you have?' spoke the verse:

'What jewel does the young man have,

25. F places this phrase in square brackets to indicate his uncertainty, but the phrase is found in the VRI edition.

26. This is an alternative spelling for Kaccāna.

27. His name might be translated as 'not deficient in name'.

Which the victorious gambler would take?
The king has many jewels.
You, vagrant, what will you declare?' (45)

Then Puṇṇaka said:

'I have this gem named Manohara,
Bringer of wealth, the excellent jewel,
And this thoroughbred, harasser of enemies.
Having conquered me the gambler would take this.' (46)

Hearing this the king spoke a verse:

'Young man, what will one gem do?
And what will one thoroughbred do?
The king has a great many jewels,
And is not lacking thoroughbreds, swift as the wind.' (47)

[275] Having heard the words of the king, he said, 'Great King, why do you speak in this way? A single horse can be the stake for a thousand horses, and a single jewel for a thousand jewels, for not all horses are of the same kind. You should see the speed of this one!' He mounted the horse and rode it around the top of the ramparts. It was as if the seven-*yojana* city was encircled by horses neck to neck. Then in due course the horse could not be seen and neither could the *yakkha*, and the red cloth bound to his belly became like a single fence. Having got down from the horse he said, 'Great King, you have seen the speed of this horse.'

'Yes, I have seen it,' he replied.

'Now watch, Great King,' he said, and he rode the horse on top of the water in a park inside the city. He sprung forward without even the tips of the hooves becoming wet, and then wandered over the leaves of the lotus pools. He clapped and stretched out his hand, and the horse came and stood on the palm of his hand. 'Lord of Men, is this not a jewel of a horse?'

'Indeed so, young man.'

'Great King, leave aside this jewel of a horse. Now see the glory of the gem.' Explaining its excellence he said:

'See this, my jewel, best of the two-footed.
Here are the bodies of women and bodies of men, (48)
And here are the forms of animals and figures of birds,
And *nāga* kings and *supaṇṇas*—see the magical creation in the jewel. (49)
Elephant troops and an army of chariots, horses, infantry, and
banners—
See created in the jewel this fourfold army: (50)
Elephant drivers, soldiers, charioteers, and foot soldiers,

Massed and strong—see the magical creation in the jewel. (51)
[276] A city with a mound, with great ramparts and gateways,
And districts at crossroads—see the magical creation in the jewel. (52)
Pillars and moats, crossbars and bolts,
Watchtowers and gates—see the magical creation in the jewel. (53)
See great flocks of various birds on the tops of the gateways:[28]
Geese, herons, peacocks, *cakkavāka* birds, and ospreys; (54)
Cuckoos of many colours, crested birds, pheasants;
See the magical creation in the jewel, crowded with flocks of various birds. (55)
See a city with ramparts, extraordinary and thrilling,
With flags elevated, charming and strewn with golden sand. (56)
See the hermitages partitioned off in equal measure,
Abodes and houses grouped on junctions and busy roads.[29] (57)
Taverns and drunkards, butchers and rice kitchens,
Prostitutes and courtesans—see the magical creation in the jewel. (58)
Gardeners and dyers, perfumers[30] and cloth-makers,
Goldsmiths and jewelers—see the magical creation in the jewel. (59)
Cooks and chefs, dancers, acrobats, and singers,
Musicians and drummers[31]—see the magical creation in the jewel. (60)
[277] See the kettle drums, tabours, conches, *paṇava* drums, and *deṇḍima* drums,
And all the music—see the magical creation in the jewel. (61)
Cymbals and lutes, singing, dancing, and good music;
See the magical creation in the jewel, resounding with the striking of instruments. (62)
Acrobats, wrestlers, magicians, and clowns are here,
Bards and athletes—see the magical creation in the jewel. (63)
Fairs take place here, crowded with men and women,
Platform on platform as stages—see the magical creation in the jewel. (64)
See the wrestlers at the fair, striking with both their arms,
Destroyed and humiliated—see the magical creation in the jewel. (65)

28. Following the commentary's gloss of *toraṇamaggesu* with *toraṇaggesu* 'on the tops of the gateways', which makes it clear that the *m* is simply bridging *torana* and *agga* and not indicating a reading of *torana-maggesu* 'on the roads and the gateways'.

29. This line is not clear. Commentary glosses *sandhibbūhe* with *gharasandhiyo ca anibbiddharacchā ca*, which might be rendered as 'houses on junctions and not-broken-up (i.e. not busy) carriage roads'. *Patatthiyo*, which F suggests is meant to be *pathaddhiyo* (as it is in VRI), is glossed as *nibbiddhavīthiyo* 'broken up (i.e. busy) roads'.

30. Following VRI *gandhike*. F has *ganthike* which might be rendered as student, but the VRI reading is a much better fit with the context.

31. Strictly speaking, players of the *pāṇissara* instrument and players of the *kumbhathuna* drum.

See at the foot of the mountains there are many packs of various animals:
Lions, tigers, and boars; bears, wolves, and hyenas; (66)
Rhinos, oxen, buffaloes, and red deer,
Antelopes and hogs, herds of *niṃka* deer and pigs; (67)
Kadalī deer of many colours, cats and long-eared hares,
Crowded with herds of various animals—see the magical creation in the jewel. (68)
[278] Rivers with beautiful banks strewn with golden sand,
The clear water flowing, enjoyed by shoals of fish; (69)
Crocodiles and *makaras* are here, and alligators and turtles,
Pāṭhina and *pāvusa* fish, born of the water, *muñja* and *rohita*; (70)
Dense with groups of various trees furnished with flocks of various birds,
A forest made of beryl—see the magical creation in the jewel. (71)
See here the lotus pools, pleasantly arranged in the four directions,
Crowded with flocks of various birds, enjoyed by flat-fin fish. (72)
Furnished with water everywhere, the earth bounded by the ocean,
Provided with the king of forests—see the magical creation in the jewel. (73)
See Videha in front and Goyāniya behind,
And Kuru-land and Jambudīpa[32]—see the magical creation in the jewel. (74)
See the moon and the sun illuminating the four directions,
Travelling around Sineru—see the magical creation in the jewel. (75)
Sineru, the Himalayas, and the ocean of great power,
And the four great kings—see the magical creation in the jewel. (76)
Gardens and dense forests, plateaus[33] and mountains,
Crowded with charming *kimpurisas*—see the magical creation in the jewel. (77)
The celestial groves Phārusaka, Cittalata, Missaka, and Nandana,
And the Vejayanta Palace—see the magical creation in the jewel. (78)
Sudhamma and Tāvatiṃsa, and the Päricchataka tree in flower,
And Erāvaṇa the king of elephants[34]—see the magical creation in the jewel. (79)
See here the daughters of gods, lofty as the clouds and lightning,
Wandering through Nandana—see the magical creation in the jewel. (80)
[279] See here the daughters of gods and the desirous sons of gods,

32. As the commentary explains, this is a reference to the four continents: Pubbavidehadīpa in the East, Aparagoyānadīpa in the West, Utturakuru in the North and Jambudīpa (India) in the South.

33. *Pāṭiya* is obscure, but commentary glosses *piṭṭhipāsāṇe* 'plateaus' or 'ridges'.

34. All that has been mentioned in the last two verses belongs to Sakka/Inda (Sanskrit 'Indra'), king of the Heaven of the Thirty-Three.

Sons of gods wandering around—see the magical creation in the jewel. (81)
Over a thousand palaces, strewn with fruits and beryl,
Blazing forth with splendour—see the magical creation in the jewel. (82)
Those delighting in Tāvatiṃsa, Yāma, Tusita,
Nimmita, and Paranimmita[35]—see the magical creation in the jewel. (83)
See here the lotus pools, with water clear and pure,
Covered with *mandālaka*, *paduma*, and *uppala* lotuses. (84)
Here are ten white rows and ten delightful blue ones,
Twenty-one brown and fourteen turmeric. (85)
There are twenty golden and twenty made of silver,
And thirty appear shining with the colour of cochineal beetles. (86)
Here are ten and six black, and twenty-five crimson,
Various blue lotuses, mixed with *bandhuka* flowers. (87)
Thus, Great King, best of two-footed beings, see the stake,
Endowed with all parts, brilliant and resplendent.' (88)

[280] Having spoken in this way Puṇṇaka said, 'Great King, if I am conquered at dice I will give you this jewel. Now what will you give me?'

The king replied, 'Setting aside my body and my white parasol of state, let all my possessions be the stake.'[36]

'Then do not delay, Your Majesty, for I have come a long way. Have the dicing area prepared.'

The king instructed his courtiers and very quickly they prepared the dicing hall. They appointed a carpet of the finest cloth for the king and seats for the other kings,[37] and prepared[38] a suitable seat for Puṇṇaka. They announced to the king that it was time. Then Puṇṇaka spoke these verses to the king:

'King, having come here approach the mark;
You have no jewel of such a kind as this.
We will lose righteously, without violence,
And the loser will quickly discharge the debt.' (89)

Then the king said, 'Young man, since I am called "king" you should not fear. We shall have victory and defeat righteously and without violence.'

35. These are the five lowest heavens. Nimmita must be a reference to the heaven better known as Nimmānarati.

36. According to VRI he also excludes the queen from his stake, perhaps a deliberate reference to the famous episode in which Yudhiṣṭhira stakes his wife Draupadī, and loses her.

37. Following VRI *rājūnaṃ* rather than F *rājānaṃ*.

38. Following VRI *paññāpetvā* rather than F *ñatvā*.

Hearing this Puṇṇaka said, 'Know you that we will experience victory and defeat righteously!' Calling the kings to witness he spoke a verse:

'Illustrious Pañcāla, Surasena,
And those of Maccha, Madda, and Kekaka,
Let them see our battle with honesty.
He will not do nothing in our assembly hall.'[39] (90)

[281] Then the king, surrounded by a hundred kings, took Puṇṇaka and entered the gaming hall, and everyone sat down on the appropriate seats. Golden dice were placed there on a silver board. Quickly Puṇṇaka said, 'Great King, amongst the dice are lucky ones called *mālika*, *sāvaṭa*, and *bahula*, and there are twenty-four lucky throws and so on. You should take the lucky dice from among them as it pleases you.' The king replied, 'Very well,' and took the *bahula*; Puṇṇaka took the *sāvaṭa*. Then the king said to him, 'Now friend, young man, throw the dice.'

'Great King, it is not my place to go first. You should throw.'

'Very good,' the king accepted. Now a guardian deity who had been his mother three births ago controlled the king's play of dice with her power. She was stood nearby, and remembering the god the king sang a gambling song,[40] turned the dice over in his hand, and threw them into the air. Because of Puṇṇaka's power the dice were falling causing the king to lose. The king, very skilled in the art of dice-playing, [282] realized that the dice were falling to his own detriment, and scrutinizing them in the sky he grabbed them and threw them into the air again. Seeing that they were falling to his loss for a second time he seized them again. Then Puṇṇaka thought, 'This king, playing at dice with a *yakkha* like me, scrutinizes the falling dice and grabs them. Why is that?' He saw the power of the guardian deity, and opening his eyes he looked at her as if angry. She ran away in fear and stood shaking at the top of a Cakkavāḷa mountain.[41] For a third time

39. As the commentary explains, Puṇṇaka is insisting that the assembled people should not be able to say 'we didn't see that' when a dispute arises, but must oversee the game diligently.

40. VRI includes the gambling song in six verses. The first of these verses is also found in J 62: 'All rivers wind, all forests are made of wood; all women, given opportunity, do no good.' It is said to bring luck because it is a statement of the truth. The remaining verses are addressed to the goddess and entreat her—addressed as mother—to protect the king and ensure his victory. F also includes a selection of similar verses as found in his Burmese MS in the footnotes.

41. The Cakkavāḷa mountain range is said to encircle the very edge of the world.

the king threw the dice, and saw they were falling to his loss, but though he stretched out his hand, through Puṇṇaka's power he was unable to seize them. They fell to the detriment of the king. Then Puṇṇaka threw the dice and they fell to make him win. And knowing he was defeated he clapped his hands and with a great noise roared out three times, 'I have conquered him! I have conquered him!' The sound permeated the whole of Jambudīpa. Explaining the matter the Teacher said:

They entered, maddened by the intoxication of dice,
King of the Kurus and Puṇṇaka the *yakkha.*
The king scrutinised and seized his unlucky throw,
And Puṇṇaka the *yakkha* had a lucky throw. (91)
There they both assembled at dice,
In the presence of kings and in the midst of friends.
The *yakkha* conquered the best of strong men,
And there were uproarious shouts. (92)

The defeated king was displeased, and comforting him Puṇṇaka spoke a verse:

[283] 'Great King, victory and defeat
Are thrust forward for somebody.
King of men, you have lost with an excellent possession.
Defeated, you should pay up quickly.' (93)

Saying 'Take it!' he spoke a verse:

'Elephants and cows and jewelled earrings,
And that which is my jewel on the earth,
Take, Kaccāna, the best of my wealth.
Take as you wish and then go.' (94)

Puṇṇaka said:

'Elephants and cows and jewelled earrings,
And that which is your jewel on the earth,
Of these give to me your best steward,
Named Vidhura, for I was victorious.' (95)

The king said:

'He is my self, my refuge, and my direction,
My lamp, my shelter, and support.
He is not comparable with my possessions.
This steward is like my breath.' (96)

Puṇṇaka said:

'We may quarrel for a long time over him,
So let us ask his wish, having gone to him.

[284] Let him make this matter clear for us,
And let what he says be advice for us both.' (97)

The king said:

'Certainly you speak the truth and not arbitrarily, young man.
Having gone to him we will ask, then both of us are happy.' (98)

Having said this the king took the one hundred kings and Puṇṇaka, and with pleased mind he went quickly to the *dhamma* hall. The wise one got down from his seat, honoured the king, and stood to one side. Then Puṇṇaka addressed the Great Being: 'Wise One, you are praised throughout the whole world as one who is established in the *dhamma* and who would not speak falsely even for the sake of your life. But today I will know how firm you are in the *dhamma*.' He spoke the verse:

'The gods provided Truth amongst the Kurus,
A courtier named Vidhura, firm in the *dhamma*.
Who are you in the world, called "Vidhura":
Are you slave of the king or his kinsman?' (99)

Then the Great Being thought, 'He asks me this, and I could announce "I am the king's relation" or "I am the king's superior" or "I am nothing to the king". But in this world there is certainly no protection equal to the truth. [285] So I should speak the truth.' Explaining, 'Young man, I am not the king's relation nor his superior, but one of four slaves,' he spoke two verses:

'For there are slaves by birth,
And there are slaves that are bought with money,
And slaves that approach by themselves,
And slaves that are driven by fear. (100)
These are the four slaves of men,
And surely I was born one from the womb.
Being of the king and not being of the king,[42]
I am a slave of his majesty even when gone away.
It is lawful for him to give me to you.' (101)

Hearing that Puṇṇaka was pleased and delighted, and clapped his hands:

'This is my second victory today,
For the steward, asked a question, revealed it here;
The excellent king is surely not a righteous type;
You do not grant me what has been well spoken.' (102)

Hearing this the king was angry at the Great Being: 'Not looking to one

42. The commentary glosses 'let it be for the benefit of the king or for his detriment—I am not able to speak falsely'.

such as me to grant him fame, he looks now to this young man he has seen.' Saying, 'If he is a slave, take him and go!' he spoke a verse:

> [286] 'If he answered our question here in this way:
> "I am a slave, and I am not a relation",
> Take the best of my wealth, Kaccāna!
> Take as you wish and then go.' (103)

But having said this the king thought, 'Having taken the wise one this young man will go wherever he likes, and from the time that he leaves it will be very difficult to get a sweet *dhamma* talk. Having had him remain in his place let me ask about the question of household life.' Then he said to him, 'Wise one, when you are gone, it will be very hard for me to hear talks on the sweet *dhamma*. Having seated yourself on the adorned *dhamma* throne and established in your place, answer my question about the householder life.'

'Very well,' he assented, and having seated himself on the adorned *dhamma* throne he discharged the question asked by the king. And this was the question:

> 'Vidhura, for one dwelling in his own home as a householder,
> How is peace attained, and how a good disposition? (104)
> How does he gain freedom from suffering, a young man who speaks the truth,
> And going from this world to the world beyond after death, how does he not grieve?' (105)
> There the clever, courageous, intelligent one, who knew what is beneficial,
> With an understanding of all *dhammas*, Vidhura, said this: (106)
> 'He has no joint wife, and does not indulge in sweet things alone,[43]
> He does not indulge in pointless argumentation, understanding that this is not profitable. (107)
> Moral and a keeper of observances, diligent and attentive,
> Humble and not stubborn, loving, congenial, and mild, (108)
> [287] Kind to one's friends, generous and circumspect,
> One should satisfy brahmins and renouncers with food and drink. (109)
> Loving the *dhamma* and preserving the scriptures one should be enquiring;
> One should respectfully honour the virtuous and learned. (110)
> When living at home, as a householder in one's own home,

43. *Ekato* usually means 'together' but both the commentary and VRI edition gloss with *ekako* 'alone'. It is possible that the commentator misunderstood the meaning and the commentarial gloss was incorporated into VRI.

One should behave peacefully in this way: that will be for his advantage. (111)
In this way he becomes free from suffering, a young man who speaks the truth,
And going from this world to the world beyond after death, he does not grieve.' (112)

After the Great Being had explained the king's question about householders in this way, he got down from his couch and honoured the king. The king in turn paid him great honour and, surrounded by the one hundred kings, went to his own abode. [288] And the Great Being turned and Puṇṇaka said to him:

'Come, I will go now. You have been given to me by your master.
You should follow this for this is the eternal *dhamma*.' (113)

The wise Vidhura said:

'I know, young man, that I am yours.
I have been given to you by my master.
But for three days I should live at home,
And in that time I should instruct my sons.' (114)

Hearing that Puṇṇaka thought, 'The wise one spoke the truth and this was very helpful for me. Were he to say, "Be seated for seven days or half a month," I should consent.'

'Let it be so. For three days you may stay.
Today you should fulfil your duty towards your household.
Today you should instruct your wife and children.
But after three days you should be contented.' (115)

Having said this Puṇṇaka went with the Great Being and entered his house. [289] Explaining the matter the Teacher said:

Having assented, the lover of abundance,
The *yakkha*, set out with Vidhura;
Accompanied by elephants and thoroughbred horses,
The best of nobles entered the inner quarters. (116)

Now the Great Being had three palaces, for each of the three seasons, one named Heron, one named Peacock and one named Piyaketa.[44] This verse was spoken with reference to that:

He reached there, beautiful in appearance:

44. It is not clear what the meaning of this name is, and in the verse that follows the name is broken into two: Piya and Keta, the first meaning Dear but the second remaining obscure, perhaps related to the *ketaka* tree/flower.

Heron, Peacock, and Piya and Keta.
Of plentiful food, with much food and drink,
Like Masakkasāra of Vāsava. (117)

Having arrived he had the terrace prepared and an inner room with a couch in the adorned seven-storey palace. Having declared that to be the royal bed, he had him served with all kinds of food and drink and presented him with five hundred women resembling daughters of the gods, saying, 'May these be your foot servants, and may you stay here with all your wishes fulfilled.' He went to his own residence and when he had gone those women took up various instruments and attended on Puṇṇaka with dancing and so on. Explaining the matter the Teacher said:

There they danced and sang and addressed him according to his wishes,
Adorned women, like nymphs of the gods. (118)
Having provided the *yakkha* with women
And food and drink, Dhammapāla [Vidhura][45]
[290] reflected on what was good,
And then entered the presence of his wife. (119)
He said to his wife, anointed with fragrant sandalwood extract,
Resembling an ornament made of gold from the Jambū river,
'Come, noble one, and listen.
Summon our children, copper-eyed one.' (120)
Hearing the words of her husband, Anujjā
Said to her daughter-in-law, with copper-coloured nails and eyes,
'Cetā, summon the bearers of armour,
My sons, dark as the flowers of the blue water lily.' (121)

'Very good,' she said, and she made her way through the palace saying, 'Your father summons you, wishing to give you instruction. Surely this will be the last time you see him.' She assembled everyone—the sons and daughters and even their friends. But young Dhammapāla, hearing these words, came into his father's presence weeping and surrounded by his younger brothers. Seeing this his father was unable to compose his own countenance, and embraced him with eyes full of tears. He kissed his head and clasped his eldest son to his heart for a moment, then lowered him from his heart, left the royal inner chamber, and sat in the middle of a couch on

45. 'Protector of the *dhamma*'. This could be an epithet but it seems to be being used as an alternative name. The commentary tells us that Vidhura's son is called Dhammapāla, and it is likely that this is an (ill-executed) attempt to explain the presence of an extra name. In the verse, however, Dhammapāla refers to Vidhura himself.

the terrace. He gave a teaching to his hundred sons. [291] Explaining the matter the Teacher said:

When they came, Dhammapāla
Kissed his sons on the head, and without wavering
Summoned them and spoke this speech:
'I have now been given by the king to this young man. (122)
Today I am obedient to him, happy in myself,
And taking me he may go where he wishes.
But I have come to instruct you.
How could I go without this safeguard? (123)
If your king, resident of Kurukheṭṭha,[46]
Janasandha,[47] lover of plenty, should ask,
"What did you understand before, in the past?
Did your father instruct you previously? (124)
You should all sit together with me,
For which man here is not owned by the king?"
You should salute him and say,
"Do not speak thus, Your Majesty, for this is not right.
How could it be, Your Majesty, that one of lowly birth
Would sit together with this tiger king?"' (125)

[292] But having heard his speech, his sons and daughters, friends and relations, and slaves and servants were all unable to compose themselves and cried out with a great wail. The Great Being consoled them.

Then having approached his kinsmen and seen that they had become silent, he said, 'My dears, do not think this way. All conditioned things are impermanent. Even fame ends with misfortune, but I will speak about a reason for the acquisition of fame, namely royal residence. Listen with calm mind.' With the mastery of a Buddha he gave them what is called 'royal residence'. Explaining the matter the Teacher said:

Vidhura, his mind sincere in purpose, said this
To his allies and enemies,[48] kinsmen and friends: (126)

46. This is the Pāli form of Kurukṣetra 'the field of the Kurus', a term found commonly in the *Mahābhārata* and still used today to refer to the area associated with the great epic battle between the warring Kuru cousins. VRI has Kururaṭṭha 'the kingdom of the Kurus' which is perhaps a more normal Pāli construction.

47. Presumably this is meant as another name for King Dhanañjaya. The name is used for other characters in the *jātakas* and elsewhere. It is reminiscent of Jarāsandha, the name of one of the kings in the *Mahābhārata* who opposes the rule of the Pāṇḍavas and the Yadavas, but there does not appear to be a link.

48. VRI has *putte amacce ca* 'children and courtiers'.

'Sirs, sit here in this royal residence and listen to me,
How a man who has attained the royal court incurs fame. (127)
For having entered the court he does not achieve fame while unknown,
Nor if he is a coward, nor an idiot, nor a careless person. (128)
But when he acquires virtue and wisdom and purity,
Then he [the king] trusts him and does not guard his secret. (129)
He may live in the royal residence who, when requested, does not waver,
Just as the balance holds firm, the level stick bearing well. (130)
He may live in the royal residence who bears everything,
Just as the balance holds up, the level stick bearing well. (131)
[293] A wise man in service to the king may live in the royal residence,
If, when requested, by day or night, he does not waver. (132)
A wise man in service to the king may live in the royal residence,
If he bears everything, by day or night. (133)
And he who, even if told to, would not travel on the road that is well made
And properly prepared for the king, he may live in the royal residence. (134)
He who would not ever enjoy the same pleasures as the king;
And who goes everywhere behind him, he may live in the royal residence. (135)
He should have no clothes, garlands, or unguents equal to the king,
Nor should he indulge in deportment or intonation similar to the king,
But should make a different appearance. Such a one may live in the royal residence. (136)
In sport the king is surrounded by his courtiers and wives,
But a wise courtier does not pursue intimacy amongst the wives of the king. (137)
He who is modest, steady, prudent, having the senses under control,
Endowed with mental resolve, he may live in the royal residence. (138)
[294] He should not sport with the king's wives, nor talk privately with them,
Nor should he take wealth from the treasury. Such a one may live in the royal residence. (139)
He should not think much of sleep, nor drink liquor for intoxication,
Nor should he harm the king's deer in the forest. Such a one may live in the royal residence. (140)
He should not think, "I am honourable," and mount the king's seat, couch, or settee,
Nor his elephant[49] or chariot. Such a one may live in the royal residence. (141)

49. VRI has *nāvaṃ* 'boat' instead of *nāgaṃ* 'elephant', but the latter seems more

Attentive, he should be neither too far from nor too close to the king,
And he should stand in his presence, being seen together with his protector. (142)
Now the king is not a friend[50] and the king is not an associate;
Kings anger quickly, like the eye touched by a husk of grain. (143)
A wise and intelligent man, imagining he is honoured,
Should not reply harshly to a suspicious king. (144)
If he gains an opportunity he should take it, but he should not trust in kings;
He should remain self-controlled like fire. Such a one may live in the royal residence. (145)
If the warrior favours his own son or his brother,
With villages and towns or kingdoms and countries,
He should not speak good or ill but remain indifferent and silent. (146)
[295] If, because of their exploits, the king increases the wages
Of elephant riders, cavalry, chariot soldiers, and foot soldiers,
He should not interfere. Such a one may live in the royal residence. (147)
A wise person should be empty-stomached like a bow, and bend like bamboo;
He should not go against the grain. Such a one may live in the royal residence. (148)
Tongueless like a fish, with an empty stomach like a bow,
Eating little, prudent and courageous, he may live in the royal residence. (149)
One should not go to women too often, considering the loss of one's reputation;
A fool suffers a cough, asthma, and powerful sorrow. (150)
One should not talk too much, nor be silent all the time;
When it is time, one should speak words that are precise and measured. (151)
Not angry or provoking anger, truthful, mild, and not slanderous;
Not speaking frivolous words, he may live in the royal residence.[51] (152)
[296] Educated, master of a craft, restrained, accomplished, steadfast yet mild,
Diligent, pure, and dexterous, he may live in the royal residence. (153)
Humble, deferential, and respectful to his elders,
Devoted, and cohabiting in happiness, he may live in the royal residence. (154)

---

natural as a royal elephant is a mark of state.

50. Following VRI *sakhā* 'friend' rather than F *saṃkhā* 'shell'.

51. VRI adds another verse here: 'Supporting his mother and father and respecting the elders in the family, / Speaking mild and congenial words, he should live in the royal residence.'

He should keep his distance from people who have been sent away;
He should look out for his supporter and not for another king. (155)
He should respectfully honour renouncers and brahmins
Who are virtuous and learned. Such a one may live in the royal residence. (156)
He should respectfully attend on renouncers and brahmins
Who are virtuous and learned. Such a one may live in the royal residence. (157)
He should entertain with food and drink the renouncers and brahmins
Who are virtuous and learned. Such a one may live in the royal residence. (158)
Desiring his own prosperity he should approach and serve the wise ones,
Renouncers and brahmins who are virtuous and learned. (159)
He should not deprive renouncers and brahmins of a gifit that has been given to them,
Nor refuse anything of beggars when it is the time to give. (160)
Virtuous and intelligent, understanding the rites and provisions,
Knowing the proper times and occasions, he may live in the royal residence. (161)
[297] Energetic, diligent, and attentive regarding his duties,
Well appointed in his work, he may live in the royal residence. (162)
And going often to the threshing floor, the hall, the cattle, or the field,
He should have them set aside a measure of grain and cook a measure in the house. (163)
He should have his son or brother who is not firm in virtues
Give rags and alms to those seated,
For limbless fools are like the dead.[52] (164)
Slaves, servants, and menials that are well established in virtues,
Skilful, and industrious, he should place in powerful positions. (165)
Virtuous and unwavering and devoted to the king,
A friend openly and in secret,[53] he may live in the royal residence. (166)
Knowing the will of the king and firm in the king's thoughts,
Not doing to the contrary, he should live in the royal residence. (167)
[298] Rubbing him with perfumes, bathing him, and washing his feet with bowed head,

52. This verse is obscure. The commentary explains that although a brother is generally said to be like a limb of a man, and 'these of poor virtue are therefore are not like limbs, but like dead mothers abandoned in the cemetery. Therefore these types should not be established in a place of power, for they destroy the king's property. And when the king's property is destroyed and he is poor, cohabitation with the king will not succeed.'

53. Following VRI *āvī raho* 'openly and secretly' for F *avīraho*, the meaning of which is unclear.

And though afflicted, not getting annoyed, he may live in the royal
residence. (168)
He would circumambulate a crow and pay honour to a water pot,
How much more so to him that is generous in all sense pleasures and
unsurpassed in wisdom?[54] (169)
He who gives beds, clothes, vehicles, dwellings, and houses,
Raining down possessions on beings like Pajjunna;[55] (170)
That gentleman living in the royal residence, a man of that kind,
Wins the favour of the king and obtains honour from his protectors.' (171)

In this way did Vidhura of incomparable resolve speak about the royal residence with the charm of a Buddha.

Whilst instructing his children, wives, friends, and so on in this way, three days passed. Knowing that the days were complete, early in the morning he ate a selection of food of excellent flavours, and thinking, 'Having taken leave of the king I will go with this young man,' he went, surrounded by his relations, to the king's residence. Having honoured the king he stood to one side and spoke about what is appropriate to be done. Explaining the matter the Teacher said:

The skilful one instructed his relations assembled there
And surrounded by friends approached the king. (172)
[299] Vidhura bowed and placed his head at his feet, then
circumambulated him,
Then spoke, saluting the king. (173)
'This young man leads me, desiring to do what he will.
I will explain what this means for my relations. Listen, tamer of
enemies: (174)
Look after my sons and the other treasures in my house.
After my departure, when I am gone, do not allow my relations to
waste away. (175)
Just as he stumbles on the ground and then stands up again on that
same ground,
I see my passing away as the same as this stumbling.' (176)

Having heard this the king explained, 'Wise one, your going does not please me. Don't go! We should summon the young man, kill him, and conceal the matter—that would please me.' He spoke the verse:

54. This verse is obscure but the commentary explains that a person who wishes for benefit will pay honour to a water pot full of water or even to a bird, when these are unable to give anything to him. So why would he not pay honour to a wise and generous king, who is deserving of honour?

55. The rain god.

'It strikes me that it is not possible for you to go.
Having killed and destroyed this Kaccāna here,
You will remain here, and I will be pleased.
Do not go, you that are the best in broad wisdom.' (177)

Hearing that the Great Being said, 'Your Majesty, your wish is of an inappropriate kind,' and said:

'Do not direct your mind towards what is unrighteous.
May you be proper in worldly and religious matters.
Shame that there should be unskilful and ignoble actions,
After doing which you would proceed to hell. (178)
[300] This is not right and nor is it a duty
For a noble master of a slave, king of men,
To kill and murder and destroy.
I proceed without anger.' (179)

Having said this the Great Being honoured the king and instructed the royal women and the king's household. When they were unable to keep their own composure and cried out with a great wail he left the royal residence. The inhabitants of the whole city cried out, 'They say the wise one is going with the young man! We will see him!' They saw him in that very royal court, but he instructed them, 'Do not worry yourselves. All conditioned things are impermanent. Be diligent with regard to such things as gift giving.' He turned away from them and set out facing his home. At that moment the young Dhammapāla surrounded by a resplendent company had set out thinking, 'I will meet with my father,' and in the doorway to his residence he faced his father. Seeing him the Great Being was unable to control his grief, and having embraced him, clasping him to his chest, he entered his abode. Explaining the matter the Teacher said:

Embracing his eldest son, he gave himself up to the sorrow in his heart,
And with his eyes full of tears he entered the great house. (180)

But in the houses his thousand sons and thousand daughters, thousand wives and seven hundred courtesans, and with them the remaining slaves, servants, friends, and relations—the entire household—immediately fell down as if a grove of *sāl* trees killed by the storm at the end of the aeon. Explaining the matter the Teacher said:

Like *sāl* trees overwhelmed and crushed by the wind,
The children and wives lay prostrate in Vidhura's dwelling. (181)
[301] A thousand women and the wives' seven hundred slave women
Lamented with outstretched arms in Vidhura's dwelling. (182)
Women of the harem, princes, merchants, and brahmins

Lamented with outstretched arms in Vidhura's dwelling. (183)
Elephant riders, cavalry, charioteers, and infantry
Lamented with outstretched arms in Vidhura's dwelling. (184)
The country folk gathered together and the assembled city folk
Lamented with outstretched arms in Vidhura's dwelling. (185)
A thousand women and the wives' seven hundred slave women
Lamented with outstretched arms, 'Why do you abandon us?' (186)
Women of the harem, princes, merchants, and brahmins
Lamented with outstretched arms, 'Why do you abandon us?' (187)
Elephant riders, cavalry, charioteers, and infantry
Lamented with outstretched arms, 'Why do you abandon us?' (188)
The country folk gathered together and the assembled city folk
Lamented with outstretched arms, 'Why do you abandon us?' (189)

The Great Being comforted all the many people, fulfilled his remaining duties, advised his household, and explained all that is appropriate to explain. Then he approached Puṇṇaka and announced that his duties were complete. Explaining the matter the Teacher said:

Having performed his duties in his houses and instructed his people—
Friends and courtiers, companions, children, wives, and relatives; (190)
Having settled his affairs and explained the wealth of the house—
The treasure and the loans—he said this to Puṇṇaka: (191)
'You have stayed in my home for three days:
I have performed my duties in my houses,
I have instructed my wives and children,
So now do what you will, Kaccāna.' (192)

[302] Puṇṇaka said:

'If, steward, they have been instructed—
children and wives and dependents—
Then come along now quickly,
For there is certainly a long journey ahead. (193)
Fearless, take hold of the tail of my thoroughbred:
This is your last look at the world of the living.' (194)

Then the Great Being said:

'What would I be afraid of, when I have not done any wrong
In body, speech, or mind that would lead me to a bad realm?' (195)

The Great Being roared forth a lion's roar and was fearless as a bold lion. Thinking, 'I would not like to let my cloak fall,' he put the perfection of resolve before everything else, and dressed himself firmly. He took the horse's tail, seized the tail firmly with both hands, and wrapped his two feet around the horse's thighs. He said, 'Young man, I have taken hold of the tail. Go where you please.' At that moment Puṇṇaka gave the sign to his mind-made horse and sprung forward into the sky taking the wise one with him. Explaining the matter the Teacher said:

The king of horses, carrying Vidhura
Set out through the air and sky,
And not attached to branches or rocks,
They quickly approached Black Mountain. (196)

[303] After the Great Being had gone, taken away like this by Puṇṇaka, the Wise One's children and so on went to where Puṇṇaka had been staying, and not seeing the Great Being they fell as if cut down at the feet. Rocking back and forth they lamented loudly. Explaining the matter the Teacher said:

A thousand women and the wives' seven hundred slave women
Lamented with outstretched arms, 'A *yakkha* with the appearance of a brahmin[56] has taken Vidhura and gone!' (197)
Women of the harem, princes, merchants, and brahmins
Lamented with outstretched arms, 'A *yakkha* with the appearance of a brahmin has taken Vidhura and gone!' (198)
Elephant riders, cavalry, charioteers, and infantry
Lamented with outstretched arms, 'A *yakkha* with the appearance of a brahmin has taken Vidhura and gone!' (199)
The countryfolk gathered together and the assembled city folk
Lamented with outstretched arms, 'A *yakkha* with the appearance of a brahmin has taken Vidhura and gone!' (200)
A thousand women and the wives' seven hundred slave-women
Lamented with outstretched arms, 'Where has the Wise One gone?' (201)
Women of the harem, princes, merchants, and brahmins
Lamented with outstretched arms, 'Where has the Wise One gone?' (202)
Elephant riders, cavalry, charioteers, and infantry
Lamented with outstretched arms, 'Where has the Wise One gone?' (203)
The country folk gathered together and the assembled city folk
Lamented with outstretched arms, 'Where has the Wise One gone?' (204)

After he took[57] the Great Being, having seen and heard him going through the sky they lamented in this way. All of them lamenting with the inhabitants from the whole city went to the royal gate. The king heard the sound of their great wailing and opened his window. 'Why do you lament?'

56. In each of these verses F places *yakkho brahmaṇavaṇṇena* in brackets as it makes the verses unmetrical and looks like it could be an insertion. However, all of his manuscripts and VRI contain this phrase.

57. Correcting *ahetvā to gahetvā*—this looks like a typographical error in F, but it seems an odd construction and the whole phrase is omitted in VRI.

he asked, and they replied, 'Your Majesty, it is said that the young man is not a brahmin but a *yakkha* with the body of a brahmin. Having come here he has taken the Wise One and gone. [304] We have no life without him! If in seven days from now he has not returned, we will collect wood on one hundred or one thousand carts and all enter the fire!' Explaining the matter the Teacher said:

'If the Wise One does not return in seven nights,
We will all enter the fire, for there is no meaning to our lives!' (205)

Hearing their words the king said, 'The Wise One of sweet speech, having seduced the young man with righteous talk, will make him fall at his feet and will shortly return, gladdening your tearful faces. Do not grieve.' He spoke the verse:

'The Wise One is learned, intelligent, and skilful.
He will free himself quickly; do not fear—he will come.' (206)

Now Puṇṇaka placed the Great Being on the summit of Black Mountain and thought, 'While he lives I will have no happiness. Having killed him and taken his heart-flesh I will go to the *nāga* realm and give it to Vimalā. Then I will take Irandatī and go to the heavenly world.' Explaining the matter the Teacher said:

Having gone there he reflected
And had mixed intentions;
'But there is nothing while he lives,
So having killed him I will take his heart!' (207)

[305] But then he thought, 'I will not kill him with my own hands, for surely I can put an end to his life through displaying my frightful form.' He produced a body of a terrifying demon and coming and going he threw him down in between his fangs[58] as if he wanted to devour him. But he did not so much as raise a hair on the Great Being. Then he came in the form of a lion and in the form of a great rutting elephant and appeared as though he wanted to pierce him with tusks and teeth. Then he created the appearance of a great serpent as big as a boat[59] for the fearless one, and approached, hissing. He enveloped his whole body and spread his hood on his head, but he had no sign of fear. Then he thought, 'Having placed him

58. Following VRI *dāṭhānaṃ antare*. F makes no reference to the fangs and simply says 'in between', but the idea is implicit.

59. More literally, *ekadoṇikanāvappamāṇaṃ* should probably be rendered 'the size of a boat one *doṇa* [pail, vat, trough] in capacity'.

on the summit of the mountain I will knock him down and break him into pieces!' and he raised up a great wind, but it did not even shake the tips of his hair. Then he placed him there on the top of the mountain and shook the mountain to and fro like an elephant shaking a date-palm tree, but even then he was unable even to shake the tips of his hair from the place where they were standing. Then he thought, 'I will kill him by bursting his heart with a fearful noise!' and entering the interior of the mountain he roared out a great noise, making the clouds and the earth into a single sound. But even then he was not at all intimidated, for the Great Being knew, 'He comes in the disguise of a *yakkha*, lion, elephant, or king of snakes, and makes wind and rain and the trembling of the mountain. He enters the mountain and lets forth a cry. This is the young man and not another.' Then the *yakkha* thought, 'I am not able to kill him through external means, so I will kill him with my own hands.' He placed the Great Being on the top of the mountain, went to the foot of the mountain, and as if threading a pale thread through a large jewel emerged from the mountain yelling, took firm hold of the Great Being, spun him around, and discharged him headlong into the unsupported sky. It was said:

[306] Having gone there, into the interior of the mountain,
He entered the inside with wicked thoughts.
Unsupported by any spot in the world,
The Kaccāna carried him headfirst. (208)
Hanging down, on a cleft and precipice,
Terrible and difficult, hair-raising,
The best of the Kuru's stewards was not frightened,
And said this to the *yakkha* Puṇṇaka: (209)
'You have the appearance of a noble but not a noble body,
You are unrestrained though you appear to have restraint,
You do terrible and cruel actions,
And there is nothing skilful in your character. (210)
If you wish to hurl me from this cliff,
How will you benefit from my death?
Today you have the appearance of a non-human,
Explain to me what you are, deity.'[60] (211)

[307] Puṇṇaka said:

'Surely you have heard of a *yakkha* named Puṇṇaka,

60. Vidhura addresses him as *devatā*, which usually refers to the lower gods or spirit deities that dwell on the earth.

He that is a minister to King Kuvera.
There is a *nāga* named Varuṇa, bearer of the earth,
Lofty and pure, possessing various powers. (212)
I desire the daughter born of him,
A *nāga* maiden named Irandatī;
Because of her that is dear and well grown[61]
I strive to kill you, wise one.' (213)

Hearing this the Great Being thought, 'This world is destroyed because of what is difficult to understand.[62] What is the young *nāga* girl's purpose in desiring my death? I will find out the truth.' He spoke the verse:

'Don't be foolish, *yakkha*!
Much in the world is destroyed through misunderstanding.[63]
What need have you, for the dear and well-grown one,
To kill me? Come now, I would hear everything.' (214)

Explaining it to him Puṇṇaka said:

'I am entering the family, desiring the daughter
Of a great serpent of great power.
My father-in-law spoke, asking for this,
Therefore I am led by my desire for another: (215)
"We would give you the one with slender waist and beautiful eyes
With a pleasing smile and limbs smeared with sandalwood paste,
If you would obtain the heart of the wise one,
And bring it here lawfully.
[308] With this possession the princess is gained:
We do not ask for any other wealth besides." (216)
Thus I am no fool—hear this, steward—
And there is nothing that I have misunderstood!
Because of your heart, lawfully acquired,
The *nāgas* will give me the *nāga* maiden Irandatī. (217)
Therefore I am engaged in killing you,
And this is my benefit from your death.
Now having thrown you into hell[64]

61. *Sumajjhā* is a little obscure, literally meaning 'well-middling'. Since *majjha* (Sanskrit *madhya*) can mean 'mature' as opposed to young and old, 'well-grown' seems the best translation.

62. The term *duggahitena*, used several times in this conversation, could refer to something that is difficult to obtain (for example Vidhura's heart) or something that is misunderstood (for example Vimalā's true desire). The latter interpretation seems most likely.

63. Reading the locative *loke* 'in the world' for the nominative *loko*, as in VRI.

64. *Narake* could also mean 'into a pit'.

And killed you I will take your heart!' (218)

Hearing his speech the Great Being thought, 'Vimalā has no need of my heart. But after having heard my *dhamma* talk, honoured me with a jewel, and gone there Varuṇa will have explained to her my abilities as a *dhamma* teacher. Then Vimalā will have had a craving to hear a *dhamma* talk from me. Varuṇa, having misunderstood, will have commanded Puṇṇaka, and because of his misunderstanding, in order to kill me he will bring himself suffering of this kind. My wisdom is strength in finding a means right on the spot, but what can be done while he is killing me? Well then, I should say, "Young man, I know the *dhamma* of the virtuous man. While I am not dead why not sit down on the summit of the mountain and listen to the *dhamma* of the virtuous man, and after that do as you wish." Explaining the *dhamma* of the virtuous man I would make him grant me my life.' Even as he hung there head first he spoke the verse:

'If you have this need of my heart, Kaccāna,
Then quickly raise me up.
[309] Whatever are these *dhammas* of the virtuous man
I will make them all manifest to you today.' (219)

Having heard that Puṇṇaka thought, 'This will be the *dhamma* not previously spoken by the wise to gods and men. Having quickly raised him up I will listen to the *dhamma* of the virtuous men.' He raised up the Great Being and sat down on the top of the mountain. Explaining the matter the Teacher said:

That Puṇṇaka swiftly set down
The best of the Kurus' stewards on top of the mountain,
Checked he was comfortable and seated,
And questioned the steward of supreme wisdom: (220)
'I have rescued you from the cliff,
And today I have need of your heart,
But those *dhammas* of the virtuous man,
Make them all manifest to me today.' (221)

The Great Being said:

'I have been rescued from the cliff by you
And indeed you have need of my heart.
These *dhammas* of the virtuous man,
I will make them all manifest to you today.' (222)

Then the Great Being said, 'My body is dirty. First I must bathe.'

'Very good,' said the *yakkha*, and he fetched water for bathing. While he was bathing he provided divine cloth, divine scented garlands, and so on for the Great Being, and when he was dressed and adorned he gave him some divine food. Once he had enjoyed the food the Great Being had the top of Black Mountain decorated, assigned himself a seat, and sat down on that adorned seat. Teaching the *dhamma* of the virtuous man with the grace of a Buddha he spoke the verse:

'You should follow custom, young man,
And avoid a wet hand,[65]
[310] and do not ever betray your friends,
And do not enter the dwelling of unchaste women.' (223)

The *yakkha*, unable to understand the four *dhammas* of a virtuous man from this concise speech, asked for it to be expanded:

'How does one follow custom,
And how should he burn a wet hand?
Who is an unchaste woman, and who would betray his friends?
Thus asked, explain the meaning to me.' (224)

And the Great Being said to him:

'Even someone unfamiliar, not met with before,
A person should invite them to be seated
And look after his welfare:
This the wise call "following custom". (225)
One should not conceive of any evil towards
Him in whose home one dwells for one night,
And there obtains food and drink;
One who injures his friends burns a harmless hand.[66] (226)
If one sits or lies down in the shade of a certain tree,
One should not break off its branch, for to harm one's friends is evil. (227)
A man should give with possessions
This full earth to an honourable woman;
If he obtains an opportunity he should ignore it,
And should not go to the dwelling of those women who are unchaste. (228)
This indeed is following custom,
And this is burning the wet hand,
These are unchaste women and this is a betrayer of friends.

65. This is obscure. The commentary glosses *dahi* and *jhāpayi* 'burn' for the verb, but this meaning is not attested for *parivajjeti* so the interpretation is presumably inspired by the later verses. See also the following note.

66. The commentary explains: 'Burning the hand that feeds himself he is called an injurer of friends (*mittadūbhī*), and thus it is called burning a wet/clean hand'. Presumably the supporter's hand is wet from the giving of gifts, symbolised by the pouring of water.

This is in accordance with the *dhamma*. Renounce non-*dhamma*!' (229)

[311] In this way the Great Being spoke to the *yakkha* about the four *dhammas* of virtuous men with the charm of a Buddha. Hearing this Puṇṇaka considered, 'In relation to these four positions the Wise One begs for his own life, for he gave me hospitality even though I was not previously known to him. I stayed in his house, experiencing his great fame, for three days. Doing this evil on account of a woman, I am a harmer of friends in every way! If I offend against the Wise One then certainly I will not proceed according to the *dhamma* of a virtuous man. What is the *nāga* maiden to me? Gladdening the faces and eyes of the inhabitants of Indapatta I will speedily lead him there and bring him to the *dhamma* hall.' Thinking this he said:

'I stayed in your house for three days,
And I was served with food and drink.
You are my friend. I set you free:
You of unsurpassed wisdom, go home as you wish. (230)
[312] May the purpose of the *nāga* family disappear.
Enough of that *nāga* princess for me!
Wise One, today you are freed from slaughter
By your own good speech.' (231)

Then the Great Being said, 'Young man, do not send me back to my own home yet—take me to the *nāga* realm!' and spoke the verse:

'Well then, *yakkha*, lead me
To your father-in-law. Do as I wish:
I would see the palace of the lord of *nāgas*
That has not been seen before.' (232)

Puṇṇaka said:

'A wise person does not deserve to see
That which is not beneficial for that man.
So for what reason do you, of unsurpassed wisdom,
Wish to go to the house of the enemy?' (233)

The Great Being said:

'Truly I understand this,
That a wise one does not deserve to see that.
But I have not done any evil,
So I do not hesitate about approaching death.' (234)

[313] 'And anyway, god-king, a cruel type such as yourself, after desiring a *dhamma* talk from me, became soft. Now you said, "What is the *nāga* maiden to me? Go to your own home!" but I will soften the *nāga* king. This

is my task. So take me there!' Hearing that, Puṇṇaka assented to his words, saying, 'Very well,' and said:

'Well then, that place of incomparable glory
You shall see with me. Come, steward,
To where the *nāga* lives amongst song and dance
Like King Vessavaṇa in Naḷinī. (235)
The *nāga* girl wanders there with her company,
Constantly playing both day and night,
With abundant garlands and many bowers of flowers,
Shining like lightning in the sky. (236)
Provided with food and with drink,
With songs, dances, and music,
Complete with adorned girls,
She shines forth with the adornment of clothes.' (237)
So Puṇṇaka sat the Kuru, best of stewards,
On the seat behind him,
And taking the steward of unsurpassed wisdom
He brought him to the realm of the *nāga* king. (238)
Having arrived at that place of incomparable glory,
The steward stayed behind Puṇṇaka,
And the *nāga* king beheld the meeting
And addressed his son-in-law as before. (239)

[314] The *nāga* king said:

'You went to the realm of mortals
Seeking the heart of the Wise One.
Surely you have arrived here successfully,
Bringing the steward of unsurpassed wisdom?' (240)

Puṇṇaka said:

'He has come here as you wished,
Dhammapāla, obtained lawfully by me.
See him face-to-face, shining forth!
May the meeting of good men be happy! (241)

Seeing the Great Being the *nāga* king spoke a verse:

'Having seen what has not been seen before, the mortal is oppressed with the fear of death;
Frightened he pays no honour. It seems he is not possessed of wisdom!' (242)

The Great Being, questioned in this way by the *nāga* king, rather than saying, 'You are not for me to honour,' with his own insight and skill at strategy he said, 'I do not honour him with the nature of one condemned to death,' and spoke two verses:

[315] 'I am not scared, *nāga*, nor oppressed with the fear of death.
An object of execution does not pay honour, and nor is honour paid to the condemned. (243)
How should he honour us or make us pay honour,
A man whom he wishes to kill?
That action does not happen.' (244)

Having heard that the *nāga* king, praising the Great Being, spoke two verses:

'You speak the truth, Wise One, explaining it in this way:
"An object of execution does not pay honour, and nor is honour paid to the condemned. (245)
How should he honour us or make us pay honour,
A man whom he wishes to kill?
That action does not happen."' (246)

Then the Great Being, showing goodwill to the *nāga* king, said:

'This is temporary, not eternal,
Your power, splendour, and rebirth with power and energy.
I ask you the meaning of this, *nāga* king:
How did you obtain this celestial palace? (247)
Was it attained without cause, born from change,
Made by yourself, or given by the gods?
Explain this matter to me, *nāga* king,
Of how you obtained this celestial palace.' (248)

[316] The *nāga* king said:

'It was not attained without cause, born from change,
Nor made by myself nor given by the gods.
Through my own actions, free from evil,
Due to my merit I obtained this celestial palace.' (249)

The Great Being said:

'Was it your rites or your chaste living?
Of what, well done, is this the fruit,
your power, splendour, and rebirth with power and energy,
And your celestial palace, *nāga*?' (250)

The *nāga* king said:

'I and my wife in the world of men
Were both faithful and masters of generosity.
At that time my house was a wellspring,
And the renouncers and brahmins were satisfied. (251)
Garlands and perfumes and ointments,
Lamps, beds, and dwellings,

Clothing, couches, food, and water:
We gave gifts respectfully there. (252)
It was my rites and my chaste living,
Of that, well done, this is the fruit,
My power, splendour, and rebirth with power and energy
And this great celestial palace, Wise One.' (253)

[317] The Great Being said:

'Thus was your celestial palace obtained by you;
You know that your rebirth is the fruit of meritorious deeds.
Therefore live correctly with diligence,
And thus live in a celestial palace again.' (254)

The *nāga* king said:

'There are no renouncers and brahmins here
To whom we could give food and drink, steward.
Explain this matter asked by me,
So that we may live again in a celestial palace.' (255)

The Great Being said:

'There are these snakes, arisen here,
And sons and wives and dependents.
You should be constantly uncorrupted
In your actions and speech towards them. (256)
Nāga, preserving your innocence in this way,
In your actions and your speech,
You will stay here in this celestial palace all your life,
And go from here up to the *deva* realm.' (257)

[318] The *nāga* king, having heard the *dhamma* talk of the Great Being, thought, 'It is not possible to place obstacles outside the Wise One. Having shown him to Vimalā and made her listen to his good speech her craving will be suppressed, and then we can please King Dhanañjaya by sending the Wise One back to him.' He spoke a verse:

'Surely the best of kings grieves
Without you, his minister.
The suffering one will meet with you,
And that miserable man will know happiness again.' (258)

Hearing that the Great Being praised the *nāga* and spoke this other verse:

'Surely, *nāga*, you speak the *dhamma* that is peaceful,[67]
Unsurpassed, of purposeful sayings, and well performed.

67. Following the commentary's understanding of *sata as santa*.

For when in distress of this kind
The excellence of people like me is well known.' (259)

Hearing this the *nāga* king was exceedingly pleased and spoke the verse:

'Explain to us, were you obtained for free,
Or won at gambling with the dice?[68]
He said you were obtained lawfully.
How did you come into this one's hands?' (260)

The Great Being said:

'He who is king there, my lord,
This one beat him at gambling with the dice,
[319] And beaten the king gave me to him.
Thus I was obtained lawfully, without violence.' (261)
The great snake, delighted and joyful,
Having heard the good words of the wise one,
Seized the supremely wise one by the hand
And entered the presence of his wife. (262)
'Vimalā, the one because of whom you are pale and take no delight in your food,
Unmatched in his appearance, he is a dispeller of darkness; (263)
The one whose heart was sought, this light-bringer has come.
Listen to his speech and see his appearance hard to obtain.' (264)
Seeing the one of broad wisdom Vimalā
Held up her ten fingers in salutation.
With her being bristling, delighted in body,
She said this to the excellent steward of the Kurus: (265)
'Having seen what has not been seen before, the mortal is oppressed with the fear of death;
Frightened he pays no honour. It seems he is not possessed of wisdom!' (266)
'I am not scared, *nāgī*, nor oppressed with the fear of death.
An object of execution does not pay honour, and nor is honour paid to the condemned. (267)
How should he honour us or make us pay honour,
A man whom he wishes to kill?
That action does not happen.' (268)
'You speak the truth, Wise One, explaining it in this way:
"An object of execution does not pay honour, and nor is honour paid to the condemned. (269)
[320] How should he honour us or make us pay honour,
A man whom he wishes to kill?

68. Following VRI *akkhāhi* 'explain' in the first line. F has *akkhehi* 'with the dice' as in the second line, but his MSS are not in agreement.

That action does not happen.'" (270)
'This is temporary, not eternal,
Your power, splendour and rebirth with power and energy.
I ask you the meaning of this, *nāga* maiden:
How did you obtain this celestial palace?[69] (271)
Was it attained without cause, born from change,
Made by yourself, or given by the gods?
Explain this matter to me, *nāga* maiden,
Of how you obtained this celestial palace.' (272)
'It was not attained without cause, nor due to change,
Nor made by myself nor given by the gods.
Through my own actions, free from evil,
Due to my merit I obtained this celestial palace.' (273)
'Was it your rites or your chaste living?
Of what, well done, is this the fruit,
your power, splendour, and rebirth with power and energy,
And your celestial palace, *nāgī*?' (274)
'I and my husband
Were both faithful and masters of generosity.
At that time my house was a wellspring,
And the renouncers and brahmins were satisfied. (275)
Garlands and perfumes and ointments,
Lamps, beds, and dwellings,
Clothing, couches, food, and water:
We gave gifts respectfully there. (276)
It was my rites and my chaste living,
Of that well done, this is the fruit,
My power, splendour, and rebirth with power and energy
And this great celestial palace, Wise One.' (277)
[321] 'Thus was your celestial palace obtained by you;
You know that your rebirth is the fruit of meritorious deeds.
Therefore live correctly with diligence,
And thus live in a celestial palace again.' (278)
'There are no renouncers and brahmins here
To whom we could give food and drink, steward.
Explain this matter asked by me,
So that we may live again in a celestial palace.' (279)
'There are these snakes, arisen here,

69. F records *-pe-* here, which stands for *peyyāla* 'repetition, formula' and is the standard Pāli method of indicating that some formulaic passage should be added from an earlier instance. However, no verses are missing from the earlier occurrence of this passage.

And sons and wives and dependents.
You should be constantly uncorrupted
In your actions and speech towards them. (280)
Nāgī, preserving your innocence in this way,
In your actions and your speech,
You will stay here in this celestial palace all your life,
And go from here up to the *deva* realm.' (281)
'Surely the best of kings grieves
Without you, his minister.
The suffering one will meet with you,
And that miserable man will know happiness again.' (282)
'Surely, *nāgī*, you speak the *dhamma* that is peaceful,
Unsurpassed, of purposeful sayings, and well performed;
For when in distress of this kind
The excellence of people like me is well known.' (283)
'Explain to us, were you obtained for free,
Or won at gambling with the dice?
He said you were obtained lawfully.
How did you come into this one's hands?' (284)
'He who is king there, and my lord,
This one beat him at gambling with the dice,
[322] And beaten the king gave me to him,
Thus I was obtained lawfully, without violence.' (285)
Just as Varuṇa the *nāga* questioned the wise one,
So too the *nāga* maiden asked questions of the wise one. (286)
And just as the wise one, questioned, satisfied the *nāga* Varuṇa,
So too the wise one, questioned, satisfied the *nāga* maiden.[70] (287)
Both of them experienced delight
And the wise one, fearless, brave, and calm,
Said this to Varuṇa the *nāga* king,
To the great snake and the *nāga* maiden: (288)
'Do not worry, *nāga*, for I am the one
With this body that is your purpose.
Do what you need with the meat of my heart,
And I will myself do whatever you desire.' (289)

The *nāga* king said:

'The heart of the wise is their wisdom!
We are very pleased with your wisdom.
Today Anūnanāma [Puṇṇaka][71] will have our daughter,

70. F includes a short line of prose—'In this way they were satisfied.'—but this interrupts the flow of the verses and is not found in VRI.

71. See v. 44, in which Puṇṇaka introduces himself as called Anūnanāma in his past

And today he will return you to the Kurus.' (290)

[323] Having said this Varuṇa gave Irandatī to Puṇṇaka, and having taken her he was pleased and talked with the Great Being. Explaining the matter the Teacher said:

Puṇṇaka was pleased and delighted
At obtaining the *nāga* maiden Irandatī.
Rejoicing in body, with happy being,
He said this to the excellent steward of the Kurus: (291)
'You made me gain a wife.
Now I will do my duty by you, Vidhura.
I give you this jewel,
And this very day I will return you to the Kurus.' (292)

Then the Great Being praised him with another verse:

'May this love you have never grow old,
With your dear wife, Kaccāna.
Pleased, delighted, and joyful,
You give me this jewel and lead me to Indapatta.' (293)
Puṇṇaka sat the excellent steward of the Kurus
On the seat behind him,
And taking the steward of incomparable wisdom,
Brought him to the city of Indapatta. (294)
Just as the mind of a man goes,
He was that fast:
Puṇṇaka brought the excellent steward
Of the Kurus to the city of Indapatta. (295)

[324] Then he said:

'The city of Indapatta is visible,
And delightful well-apportioned mango forests.
I have obtained a wife
And you have obtained your own home.' (296)

Now on that day in the morning the king had a dream, and the form of this dream was this: At the door of the king's dwelling stood a great tree covered in horse and elephant ornaments, whose fruits were the five produce of the cow,[72] whose branches were morality and whose trunk was wisdom. The people were paying great honour to it and venerating it with

life. The name could be translated as 'not-lacking in name' or 'named not-lacking', which could be a reference to Puṇṇaka 'complete, full'. The commentary's explanation that Anūnanāma was Puṇṇaka's name in a past life seems unnecessary.

72. Namely milk, cream, buttermilk, butter, and ghee.

outstretched arms. Then a black man clothed in a red robe and with ear ornaments of red flowers arrived, weapon in hand, and cut at the root of that tree, even as the populace lamented. Dragging it out he took it and left. But then he brought it back, placed it in its original position, and departed. The king embraced this dream: 'Who else could the great tree be but Vidhura the wise? And this person who left taking him, after cutting the root even as the people lamented, is nobody else but the young man who has gone after seizing the wise one. But just as the one who left returned the tree and placed it back in its original place, so too the young man will lead the wise one back and place him at the door of the *dhamma* hall before departing. Surely today we will see the wise one!' Having come to this conclusion he was happy in mind and had the whole city adorned and the *dhamma* hall decorated. He had the *dhamma* seat appointed under an awning decorated with jewels. Surrounded by a hundred kings, his collection of courtiers, citizens, and country folk, he comforted the people: 'Today you will see the wise one, do not worry!' Looking for the arrival of the wise one he sat in the *dhamma* hall, and Puṇṇaka brought the wise one down and placed him in the middle of the assembly, at the door to the *dhamma* hall. Then taking Irandatī he went to his own heavenly city. [325] Explaining the matter the Teacher said:

> Puṇṇaka brought down the excellent steward of the Kurus
> To the middle of the *dhamma* hall,
> And mounting his thoroughbred he of peerless appearance
> Set out into the sky and air. (297)
> Seeing that, the king was exceedingly pleased.
> Having stood up he embraced him in his arms
> And had the steadfast one seated in front
> On a seat in the middle of the *dhamma* hall. (298)

Then, having exchanged friendly greetings with him and given him a warm welcome, he spoke a verse:

> 'You are our guide, as if fastened to our chariot.
> The Kurus rejoice at seeing you.
> Questioned, explain this matter to me:
> How were you released from the young man?' (299)

The Great Being said:

> 'He whom they call "young man", king of men,
> Is not a human, best of heroes.
> Perhaps you have heard of a *yakkha* named Puṇṇaka:
> He is a minister to King Kuvera. (300)

There is a *nāga*, bearer of the earth, named Varuṇa,
Gigantic and of pure appearance and strength;
He [Puṇṇaka] desired the daughter born from him,
A *nāga* girl named Irandatī. (301)
[326] Because of her that is dear and well grown
He tried to bring about my death.
But he is now possessed of his wife,
And I, given leave, obtained this jewel.' (302)

'Great King, that king of *nāgas* was pleased with my answers to the questions about the four *uposatha*-observers and honoured me with a jewel. Having gone to the *nāga* world his queen named Vimalā asked him, "Where is your jewel?" and he explained about my status as a *dhamma* teacher. She became desirous of hearing a *dhamma* talk, and displayed a craving for the meat of my heart. Because of misunderstanding that, the *nāga* king said to his daughter Irandatī, "Your mother has a craving for Vidhura's heart-meat. Seek a husband who is able to bring the meat of his heart." Seeking that she saw the *yakkha* called Puṇṇaka, nephew of Vessavaṇa. Knowing him to be enamoured with her she led him into her father's presence, and he said, "The one able to bring me the heart-meat of Vidhura the Wise will get Irandatī." Having fetched from Vepulla Mountain a jewel that was used by a Universal Monarch, he played with you at dice and won me. He stayed in my home for three days and then, with me hanging onto his horse's tail, he struck me on the trees and mountains of the Himalayas. Unable to kill me, he sprung forward seven massive winds, foremost of the *veramba* winds.[73] He placed me on the summit of Black Mountain, sixty *yojanas* high and made this and that appearance of lions and so on. While he was still unable to kill me I asked him why he wanted to kill me and he explained the whole matter. Then I spoke to him about the *dhamma* of virtuous men, and hearing that, his mind was pacified and he wanted to lead me back here, but I took him and went to the *nāga* realm. I spoke the *dhamma* to the *nāga* king and Vimalā, and the whole *nāga* assembly was pacified. After I had dwelled there for six days, the *nāga* king [327] gave Irandatī to Puṇṇaka, and having obtained her he was pleased and honoured me with a jewel. At the *nāga* king's command he placed me on his mind-made Sindh horse. He seated himself in the middle of the seat and seated Irandatī on the

73. PED suggests these are high altitude winds. BHSD *vairambha* notes 'name or epithet of certain very violent winds'.

seat behind. Having led me here he brought me down in the middle of the assembly and then taking Irandatī was gone to his own city. Thus, Great King, Puṇṇaka, because of her that was dear and well grown, tried to bring about my death, but because of me he gained a wife. After he had heard my *dhamma* teaching I was given leave by the pacified *nāga* king, and I received this jewel—belonging to a Universal Monarch and granter of all wishes—from Puṇṇaka. Take the jewel, Your Majesty.' He gave the jewel to the king. Then the king, wishing to speak to the residents of the city about the dream he had had that morning, told them, 'Oh residents of the city, hear about the dream I saw this morning!' and said:

'A tree arose in my doorway:
Its trunk was wisdom and branches were made of morality.
Full grown it stood in wealth and duty,
Its fruits that of the cow and covered in elephants, cows, and horses. (303)
While it resounded with dance and song and music,
There was a man who destroyed it,
But he returned it to our house.
You should pay honour to this tree! (304)
Whoever is joyful because of me,
They should all display it today.
Making eager offerings,
You should pay honour to this tree! (305)
Whoever in this kingdom is bound by me,
They should all be freed from their bonds.
Just as this one has been freed from his bonds
So should they be freed from theirs! (306)
[328] They should put away their ploughs for a month,
And the brahmins should feed on meat and boiled rice,
And those worthy of drink who are not drunkards should drink,
With full vessels overflowing! (307)
Let them be continually summoned to the high street,
And let them provide thorough protection in the kingdom
Such that nobody harasses anyone else.
You should pay honour to this tree!' (308)

Thus it was said:

The harem ladies and princes and merchants and brahmins
Offered lots of food and drink to the wise one. (309)
Elephant drivers, cavalry, charioteers, and infantry
Offered lots of food and drink to the wise one. (310)
[329] The assembled country folk and the citizens come together
Offered lots of food and drink to the wise one. (311)

The populace were pleased at seeing the wise one come
And waved their garments when the wise one was regained. (312)

The festival came to an end after a month, and the Great Being taught the *dhamma* to the populace and instructed the king as if performing the duties of a Buddha. Having remained there for the rest of his life he went to heaven, and having established the king and so on in his advice, all the inhabitants of the Kuru country were generous and so on and made merit, and at the end of their lives they filled the heavens.

The Teacher, having given this *dhamma* teaching, said, 'Not only now, monks, but also in the past has the Tathāgata been endowed with wisdom and skill in means.' He identified the births: 'At that time the royal family were the parents of the wise one, Rāhula's mother was the eldest wife, Rāhula was the eldest son, Sāriputta was the *nāga* king Varuṇa, Moggallāna was the king of the *supaṇṇas*, Anuruddha was Sakka, Ānanda was King Dhanañjaya, and I myself was the wise Vidhura.'[74]

74. VRI adds that Channa was Puṇṇaka and the company was the Buddha's entourage.

10

The Birth Story of Vessantara

(*Vessantara-jātaka*)

INTRODUCTION

The *Vessantara-jātaka* lies at the heart of the ritual, storytelling, and collective psyche of Southern Buddhists, an extraordinary story that has inspired festivals, recitals, dramas, poems, art, and the underlying emotional basis of those regions where it is told and retold, acted and reenacted (PGPV introduction; McGill 1997; Pannavamsa 2007a; Lefferts and Cate 2013). In its 'original' form, or in vernaculars, song, and dance, it is the single tale that defines Buddhist practice for those that listen to it and participate in its performance. It is, as Gombrich points out in his classic work on the subject, the single most popular story in South and Southeast Asian temple art (PGPV introduction). There are said to be many hundreds of *Rāmāyaṇas*; *Vessantara-jātaka*, Collins (1998: 498) notes, also has hundreds of variations. Peter Skilling's (2006b) scholarly and far-ranging study has found some interesting parallels and dissimilarities amongst them. A new volume of essays edited by Steven Collins (2015), exploring many aspects of the story's tellings, also stresses its pre-eminence throughout South and Southeast Asian cultural and religious life.[1] Festivals involving

Introduced and translated by Sarah Shaw.

1. I am very grateful to Steven Collins for discussions we had on the subject. His introduction to this important new volume, which I read just after writing this chapter, provides an excellent literary analysis of the tale and its variants, and we

its performance are happy collective gatherings for entire villages and communities, full of carefully and specially prepared ritual foods, sweets, songs, banners, funny and beautiful costumes, decorated vans, flags, ice creams, processions, water sprinklings, dance, and enjoyment (Gerini 1892; McGill 1997; Pannavamsa 2007a; Lefferts and Cate 2013). Potentially utterly tragic in its outcome, it ends in rejoicing, the affirmation of the community and family, and a celebration of generosity, an underlying ideal of regions that have been steeped in its ethos for centuries. In Northeast Thailand, the golden notes of the Isan vernacular melody of the story mingle with Pāli recitations, other *suttas*, and chants, such as the loving-kindness *sutta* (*Mettā Sutta*) that may be going on at the same time to make this story a polyphonic and harmonious song: an ongoing tale of redemption and freedom from suffering, a happy anticipation of the Buddha's final life, and his teaching of a way to liberation for everyone.

The story is completely simple and unified in its construction, with an internal logic that can lead to one, and only one, deeply shocking and near tragic crisis, but also to one, and only one, happy resolution. The utterly absurd and wonderful premise of its plot is this: that each Bodhisatta, in order to find complete awakening, must in a life shortly before the final one give absolutely everything they have away. This includes his wealth, possessions, inheritance of the kingdom, for this Bodhisatta the seven-hundredfold gift of alms to renunciates (a very important gift), carriage, and indeed his wife and children. The Bodhisatta in this story does all of these things; Gombrich has provided analysis of the function and meaning of the gifts in his introduction (PGPV xii–xvii). If the Bodhisatta were a tragic hero in a Shakespearean or ancient Greek drama, this impassioned giving away of what is most precious to him would constitute an act of terrible *hubris*, an action against the gods, produced from some fatal flaw (*hamartia*) that can lead only to *nemesis*, the terrible and often agonizingly appropriate destruction of the hero and his family. It very nearly does this: he really is like a tragic hero in his immense conviction, utterly undiverted focus, and complete commitment to his mission. And, after being banished to the forest and giving away his children, who suffer terribly at the hands of the brahmin, he does seem to be facing an end like a great tragic hero, alone and weeping over his wife who seems near death, like Othello over

---

have found many accords.

Desdemona or King Lear over his daughter Cordelia, with all worldly happiness and good fortune thrown away. But this is not a tragedy, nor even a comedy, though its outcome fulfils many classical expectations of both genres. For it is the very generosity of the Bodhisatta's initial vow, made aeons before, that ensures he is protected in his great acts of giving. The world systems themselves quake even when he first thinks of his acts of generosity. It quakes again when he makes his gifts, and again at the end. The gods, and even the *yakkhas* who speed the exiled family's journey from their own kingdom, know his aspiration and do not allow the family to come to harm. *Devas* prevent Maddī from being harmed but also ensure she does not intervene to prevent his gift. King Sakka, protecting the Bodhisatta from the possibility of being alone and unprotected, comes to ask for her, and then at what is the turning point of the story, gives her back and offers him eight wishes, ensuring their future happiness. Gods also come to the children's aid when they are in captivity, tucking them up in divine garments and bedding when their cruel captor has gone to sleep. By the end of the story, in, as Gombrich points out, exactly the reverse order that the gifts had been given and the banishment had taken place, the family return triumphantly, gifts successively returned, accompanied by the king and queen and their magnificent entourage back to their own city (PGPV xiii–xvi). The end does not only offer a simple palindrome, or chiasmus, unraveling events back to their beginning; it is a creative return. When they are welcomed home, the Bodhisatta is made king, and festivals are celebrated, with now universal acceptance of his code and way of life. So the Bodhisatta, with his great deed undertaken, immediately continues his acts of giving, now within the protected sphere of his kingdom and aided by King Sakka and his own people.

The plot is so economical, so utterly complete, that it moves with a unity and remorseless internal logic that rank it alongside some of the greatest dramas and epics in world literature. An initial vow, made aeons before, sets an apparently impossible task. That task is fulfilled and brings at first desperate grief and unhappiness. But through the purity and generosity of the initial intent of the vow itself, to find awakening for the benefit of all sentient beings, the gods and the very earth, with its earthquakes, respond to help both donor and those that he 'gives' away. It bestows immeasurable worldly benefit to the Bodhisatta, his family, and his kingdom in their continued happiness and good fortune, but it also provides assurance that finally, with perfections fulfilled, the Bodhisatta will indeed become a completely awakened Buddha. Traditional expectations of comedy, tragedy, romance, and epic are fused, with the renunciate and the family ideal both reconciled (see Collins 1998: 564, Meiland 2004: 62–8). It is both deeply intimate and touching, yet also formal and public. It shows extreme loneliness, but also the contagious social and communal effects of a willingness to give without conditions. So the happy mystery of generosity is generously celebrated, explored, and vindicated. *Vessantara-jātaka*, after the great dramas and sometimes complicated intrigues of the some of the earlier tales in the *Mahānipāta*, truly represents the perfection of plot. It requires no additional element to its own stately, glorious, and courtly, yet unremitting, momentum.

The story reads, or is heard, like a ritual, with its gracious and formal yet often poignantly personal language all expressing the leisurely pace but also the public necessity of the Bodhisatta's ordeal. Despite the extraordinary events, the rule of courtesy transforms much of its social interchange into a kind of ceremony between those participating, even when the malignantly comic brahmin encounters the ascetic and Vessantara: this of course makes his complete neglect of basic verbal and physical kindness with the children so utterly shocking. There are twenty-nine verses in the whole story devoted entirely to greeting, describing greetings, leave-taking, or enquiries about health and their responses (vv. 211, 230–2, 356–64, 436–43, 613–20, 724–8, and 734–7). This is far more than in any of the others of the *Mahānipāta*, where formal greetings are expressed in verse but are almost always brief first lines, as in verse 5 of this story or summaries made by the Teacher in the present; usually greetings and leave-takings are described in prose before the verses. In this story, courtly enquiries are central to the verses themselves (the oldest level of the text) and most of them occur, interestingly, out of the court, as if the ceremony of the great undertaking is being scrupulously maintained.

So the sense of the protective power of a great ritual permeates the story from the outset. It starts at the time of the Buddha, after the awakening, when he too has returned to his family at Kapilavatthu, and there is an auspicious shower of lotuses that brings the story to his mind. It opens in heaven—a reassuring contrast to the memories of the hells that opened the Bodhisatta's life in the *Temiya-jātaka* at the beginning of the Great Ten. The first verse is set in the realm of the Thirty-Three Gods, an auspicious setting which the story reminds us 'establishes' the great tale in the realms of the *devas* (*Eva esā Mahāvessantaradhammadesanā devaloke patiṭṭhāpitā nāma hoti*; Ja VI 482).

It describes the beautiful Phusatī, Vessantara's mother, a reminder that he is part of a larger family and *saṅgha* of followers, and an echo of the visit the Buddha himself has just made 'in the present' to teach the *Abhidhamma*, his highest teaching, to the same character, his mother, who comes down from the Tusita realm to hear him in the Heaven of the Thirty-Three Gods at the time of the Twin Miracle, a marvel only Buddhas can perform. This sense of participation in a larger plan prevails throughout the story, and we can feel it guarding the Bodhisatta and his family. While it cannot save them from the inevitable crisis, the interventions of the *devas*, and the friendly nurturing of the forest and its wild animals, are also a necessary part of the Bodhisatta's lone struggle. Although he is constantly offered support from the gods, Sakka, the Cetans, his mother, wife, and children, he is a hero alone, and part of the unbearable pathos of the story is his vulnerability and ever greater heroism, yet also, in his crisis, his exhaustion and fear as he goes willingly to make his succession of terrible gifts.

We need to be aware of this magnificent ritual aspect first, because if one hears the story out of context and takes its message literally as suggesting policies universally applicable at all times, or even reads descriptions of the Bodhisatta as he goes about his work, it sounds frankly appalling. Are we really meant to give away our family and friends? Is it really skilful to cause such suffering to those around? The Bodhisatta is described at various times in this story with powerful imagery. This is of course positive, in comparisons, for instance, to a sheltering tree and a 'river that flows at all times and never dries up' (v. 445), both, interestingly, epithets described by the brahmin or a peaceful *paccekabuddha* (Ja VI 520). It is also sometimes very surprising, as when his passion is compared to that of a drunk waiting for his drink (Ja VI 542). Can he really be seen as a noble hero? So before we go on and readers who may be completely unfamiliar with the tale put down the story in bemused alarm, some things should be said about the nature of and way of describing generosity in Buddhist texts.

Within the canon, and in Southern Buddhist life and practice, generosity is described as an essential basis of all dealings with others. It is associated with *cāga* 'letting go', a quality that is present, in *Abhidhamma* terms, at the very moment a gift is given. At such times, for one moment, consciousness is skilful, whatever may have been present before or after: this gives such acts great power. Such moments, where the giving has been skilful, are encouraged as a recollection at the end of life, to bring about a peaceful death and a happy rebirth. In daily life, it is considered a practice that ensures the mind is not fixed or closed, and which can be remembered as a recollection (*cāgānussati*).[2] Generosity should be extended at the right time, at the right place, and for the right people (AN III 172; IV 62, 236). Alms given to ascetics and monks are the highest kind of giving of material goods (AN IV 62, 238). Generosity with goods, and even one's life, is not described as the highest in *suttas*. The highest generosity is in the giving of the teaching. All others can be measured, but this is of measureless benefit. This requires the greatest *cāga*, and it is this the Buddha does in his final life. When he recollects his generosity and calls the earth to witness at the opening of the *Jātaka-nidāna*, it is the seven-hundredfold gift of alms that enables him to be free of Māra and confident of his place under the Bodhi tree. In *jātakas* the qualities that are transformed into supramundane attributes are often metaphors of those he exhibits in his final life. As a layman, he supported those who offer teaching, and so is deserving of his greatest quest: for awakening.

The point about the *Vessantara-jātaka* is that what he is doing is, for that particular life only, completely appropriate giving. It is *cāga*, manifest in acts of *dāna*, which is what the Bodhisatta is cultivating, and the ritualized acts of giving away what is most dear formalize this. The seven-hundredfold gift of alms to the ascetics provides an external symbol of his generosity in the world of renunciation that will be remembered and publicly stated by him when he calls the earth to witness on Māra's challenge of his right to sit in meditation. It does not of course mean that other people, in other situations, should make all these gifts. Although the *Vessantara-jātaka* shows us a largely happy kingdom, in contrast to some of the others of the Great Ten, and although there are references to aspects of a Universal Monarchy, such as when the Bodhisatta wishes that his son may become one, and when the elephant is described as a 'treasure', it is a very human world. The Bodhisatta's wish to give away in this lifetime is not presented as a generally applicable practice, however: it is just one for a special occasion, his last life as a human being before his long wait in the Tusita heaven preceding his final existence as a Buddha. Indeed in others of the Great Ten, generosity without appropriateness is actively discouraged. In

2. The recollection of skilful giving is Buddhaghosa's twenty-fifth object of calm meditation, which does not lead to *jhāna*, but which helps in the cultivation of *jhāna* and other practices, as well as with other practices and the keeping of *sīla*, helping to ensure confidence and cheerfulness in daily life (Vsm VII 107–14).

Nemi-jātaka for instance, we are given lists of generous heroes and kings who nonetheless did not find happy rebirths as a result of this because their *sīla* was bad (Chapter 4, vv. 7–11). This sentiment is also found in the *suttas* (AN IV 241–3). Sacrificing one's children is also not advised, as the *Candakumāra-jātaka* clearly indicates; that story, as its introduction points out, shows a kind of parody of the Bodhisatta path, based on wrong view (see Chapter 7). But as this is the last life of a Bodhisatta before his heavenly sojourn and final life, these are the right gifts for this time. Starting in a heaven where beings are reborn for rightly timed and suitable acts of generosity and *sīla*, and, we know, ending up in one (the Tusita heaven), it is a special occasion, as a life requiring one major task to be fulfilled. In this it still shows us, despite an apparent contradiction, the importance of the unstinting quality of generosity, when it is appropriate and at the right time. The last life is not dedicated to the last perfection, of equanimity, but goes back to the first.[3] The two verses asking each child to be a boat to help the Bodhisatta across to the 'farthest shore' (460–3) demonstrate that even with a strictly diachronic reading of the text, excluding all *Cariyapiṭaka* verses and all prose, this story was intended from the outset to be special in some way, in a life where such generosity is appropriate. In no other *jātaka* does the Bodhisatta make such gifts, encourage others to do so, or speak to his children in this way.[4] So the story is 'true' on many levels: as an allegory, a metaphor, a description of what it feels like to give, and, in its own context, a quite literal account of what a Bodhisatta, at that time, was expected to do in that particular life.

A parallel with Shakespearean drama seems very useful indeed here. C. L. Barber, in a then groundbreaking study of Shakespeare's comedies, described them as 'festive' dramas, particularly embedded in a day of carnival and celebration of the qualities associated and enacted within them, outside the rules of usual interchange (Barber 1972). *Twelfth Night*, on the festival of that name, when a Lord of Misrule is elected to upset the

3. It is very odd that Dhammapāla does not mention *jātaka*s once in his treatise on the perfections. He does however follow a *jātaka* pattern in that he describes how each is superior to the one before—and then goes back after that to expressing the importance of generosity in all one's dealings. It is as if the others can only be 'perfections' if they have the basis in the first, the quality that animated the initial Bodhisatta vow.

4. For some recent discussion of the gifts, see Collins 2015: introduction. For discussion of them and the accompanying earthquakes, see *Milindapañha* IV 113–19.

social order for a day, is characterized by a complete tumbling down of all hierarchy and organisation in its chaotic middle; all is happily brought back to normality and rearranged in a restoration of the health and the correct social alignment of the participants. *Midsummer Night's Dream*, about the day when spirits of the forest are, in Europe, traditionally supposed to come to the human realms, shows the interactions between these beings until again there is a comic resolution of the various problems: the beings have helped to cause them but help bring their resolution too. These plays are therapeutic dramas, designed to release particular kinds of energy and ebullience. These then meet polar opposite qualities, which allow characters and plot to get into terrible tangles. So those who are generous meet those who are mean, and those enjoying the spirit of misrule meet others with obsessive interests in hierarchy. All is then resolved, with energies integrated and celebrated in the ritual comic setting. The play most strikingly similar in mood to *Vessantara-jātaka* is *The Merchant of Venice*, which is not associated with a specific festival but nonetheless, as Barber shows, demonstrates an occasion for the comic spirit in its portrayal of a society and system of interaction whereby generosity is the 'currency' of goodwill and good fortune. Those who are generous, and are willing to hazard all in a spirit of *cāga*, find happiness and the resolution of problems. The one who is not generous or not willing to participate in the festive spirit of the day, is, in the European comic manner, ruthlessly excluded from the festival and the harmony at the end. So in *Twelfth Night*, Malvolio, who hates 'cakes and ale' and partying, cannot live and participate gladly in the world of misrule, and so has to be rejected. In *The Merchant of Venice*, Shylock cannot give. The way this 'misfit' is treated is rather like the attitude towards brahmins in *Vessantara-jātaka*, an undesirable attitude perhaps to a modern audience, but, as the children point out when being given away, not all brahmins are bad. It is both Shylock's and the brahmin's individual crimes, and unwillingness to give, that are important. Shylock's failure to participate in the ritual comedy means that according to its ancient mores, he must be kept out of a society that functions through what he denies. Everything for him is a transaction, and in his demands for the 'pound' of flesh, and in his routing, whereby Portia insists, in equally transactional manner, that he take no drop of blood, the paucity of such 'accounting' as a way of living in the world of human relationships is shown. Only the free flow of generosity, in the willing acceptance of the choice of the lead casket, whose motto says, 'Who chooseth me, must give and hazard all he hath' (*The Merchant of Venice*, Act II, scene 7, line 9), wins the hand of Portia. This casket, rather than the glittering gold or silver ones chosen by the other suitors, brings Bassanio, the suitor who will love Portia for herself, good fortune and good results. Indeed Portia's speech provides an eloquent contrast to her ruthless 'accounting' of the drop of blood that must not be taken if Shylock must keep to the letter of the law when he is cutting his pound of flesh from Antonio. It is like a paean to the mood of an underlying willingness to give that characterizes this play, filled with images of gold, wealth, and music, just as the *Vessantara-jātaka* is.

> The quality of mercy is not strain'd,
> It droppeth as the gentle rain from heaven
> Upon the place beneath: it is twice blest;
> It blesseth him that gives and him that takes:
> 'Tis mightiest in the mightiest: it becomes
> The throned monarch better than his crown;
> (*The Merchant of Venice*, Act IV, scene 1)

Disproportionate or inappropriate generosity is not sanctioned in either work: giving and receiving is simply the emotional communication system whereby that society works. In *Vessantara-jātaka*, where wealth is always flowing, and where the mercantile ethos is seen in the Bodhisatta's birthplace, Vessa Road (Commercial Road), and in the great valuings of jewels, possessions, gold, and golden ornaments, as well as the many 'possessions' that are beyond price, the origins of generosity are examined and allowed to flow within the setting that is suitable for them. Verses describing wealth, jewelry, possessions and their great value, or statements that they are 'beyond value' abound. At the end, Vessantara returns to his generosity and almshouses, and is sanctioned in this by Sakka, seen so often in the stories as a kind of embodiment of beneficent common sense.

Just as Shakespearean dramas, mediaeval Western mystery plays and ancient Greek tragedies and comedies did, *Vessantara-jātaka* has its own day, or days. Often, though not always, associated with Vesākha, the story was, it says in the 'story in the present', recounted on the day of the Buddha's return to his family, and gives us a powerful anticipation of this later event. The return of the Buddha to his family and relatives to teach them is central to his long path; it brings full circle his work and shows his acknowledgement of their work through his many lives on a path involving many friends, and, in particular, his family. The story is a *jātaka*, not a play, although often acted, but in this regard it needs to be seen both as taking place in a special time, this one lifetime of the Bodhisatta, and as being recounted on a special festive day. For both these reasons it has its own rules, embedded as it still is as a ritual affirmation of the yearly round of monastic and lay interchange in Southern Buddhist communities, and a reminder of the Buddha's willingness after the awakening to teach his friends, family, and newcomers. But before exploring this, it would be useful here to examine its sections.

The 'Chapters' of the *Vessantara-jātaka*

The 'chapters' are in 'sections' (*khaṇḍa*), 'descriptions' (*vaṇṇanā*), or 'episodes' (*pabbam*). No great significance seems to attach to the different names, and it is a method occasionally used in other long *jātakas*, such as the *Bhūridatta-jātaka*. As in that story, each section has a certain completeness and represents an important phase in the momentum of the story as a whole.

1. THE DESCRIPTION OF THE RELATING OF THE TEN WISHES

The story from the present aligns this tale with the very opening of the *jātakas* in the first line and the time immediately after the first sermon, in which the Buddha expounds the doctrine of the middle way and the eightfold path to the five ascetics who had shared his austerities before the enlightenment. After that, he moves to Kapilavatthu to visit and then teach his family. At the opening of the story, a shower of lotus blossoms has taken place. The only other time this term occurs in the *jātakas* is in the *Jātaka-nidāna*, the introduction to the stories, at the time when the Buddha tells the *Vessantara-jātaka* (J I 88). The implication is that this was actually the first *jātaka* recounted by the Buddha, immediately after the setting in motion of the wheel of *dhamma* for his followers—in another wheel-like development whereby the first *jātaka* told is the last, just as the perfection with which it is associated is seen as the first and is the last enacted. In the *Buddhavaṃsa*, *devas* shower down lotuses and other flowers when the Buddha creates a walkway, demonstrating the power of the Buddha; the commentary to that work says the *Vessantara-jātaka* was also recited by the Buddha then.

At its outset, the tale says it has a thousand verses. Gombrich and Alsdorf note that some of the early verses are indeed taken from, or at least the same as, the *Cariyapiṭaka* account of the tale (*Cariyāpiṭaka* I 9), and Cone marks them as '[Cp]' in her translation.[5] Here 'a thousand' is really a figure of speech, emphasizing the great completeness and auspicious connotations of the tale: a popular chant to this day in Southeast Asia, for instance, is termed *Sahassanaya*, to denote the many states of mind described in the *Abhidhamma*.[6] In this story there are 786 verses, along with two unnumbered verses. There is however a verse epilogue of forty lines, with a verse eulogy of another seventeen lines. Gombrich has noted that the verses for this story are all early, dating from no later than the third century BCE.[7] So while the *Cariyapiṭaka* verses raise some doubts, the story seems to have been always much as it is now. Thousands come up throughout this story: a thousand coins are given to him by his mother to give away. A thousand sticky rice balls are made in Thai/Lao festivals as part of the ceremony, as well as a thousand betel nut packages, a thousand candles, and a thousand flags. The thousand verses (*khatha phan*) are quickly recited while the balls are being rolled (Pannavamsa 2007a; Lefferts and Cate 2012: 49).

The chapter describes in the past the greatly meritorious background of the Bodhisatta's mother-to-be, Phusatī (Sprinkling). Dedicated to generosity, she has had many happy lives and is now Sakka's consort. When he realizes she is going to 'fall away' from a *deva* state, he offers her eight wishes: she asks to be married to the king of the Sivis, and for great endowments of beauty. She also wishes to keep the same name, and to

5. Verses that appear also in the *Cariyapiṭaka* are vv. 14–19, 160, 212, 218, 220–30 and 627–8. For an explanation of this problem and the contention of Alsdorf (Alsdorf 1957: 3–6) that they are later additions, with v. 20 being the real first verse of the story, see Cone/Gombrich 2011: xxii–xxiii. For further discussion of the number of verses in this story and its implications for the pre-eminence of the tale in certain regions, see Appleton 2010a: 70–5 and Skilling 2006b.

6. The chant known as *Sahassanaya* 'a thousand ways' describes the various combinations of four or five *jhānas* with the sixty states of skilful consciousness that accompany the path of stream-entry (*Dhammasaṅgani* 72 ff). (According to the *Abhidhamma* system, there are five rather than four *jhānas*, with the first in the sutta system being classified under two headings, one with initial thought [*vitakka*] and one without.) It is also sometimes known as *Lokuttarajhānapāṭha* 'the paths of transcendent *jhāna*' and for its reminder of the many routes to awakening is often chanted at funerals.

7. See Gombrich 1985: 428; see also Appleton 2010a: 53–7 for a summary on some aspects of dating of the *jātakas*; and Skilling 2006b.

bear a son, who will be very generous and not refuse alms to anyone. Sakka rejoices in her merit, and promises her what she has asked.

2. THE DESCRIPTION OF THE HIMALAYAS

Now she is born in the Kingdom of the Maddas as a very beautiful princess, who is married to the king of Sivis at sixteen. She has great pregnancy cravings to give to others, and in the manner of Indian literature, these cannot be denied. So she has almshouses made at the four gates of the city, in its middle, and at the gates of the palace. From the moment of conception, the king starts to receive all kinds of income and gifts, and the child is born on Vessa Road.[8] As soon as he is born he, like Mahosadha and Siddhattha in his final life, speaks. This time, as when Mahosadha, it is to his mother, as he asks if he can give something. She happily gives him a thousand coins, telling him to give whatever he likes, thus validating his role in this story. A magical elephant arrives, called Paccaya (Cause). Although, as Gombrich points out, the name is a scribal mistake, it is a fortunate one and it is easy to see how the tradition adopted it. As we see, it is the cause—in *Abhidhamma* terms the strong support (*upanissaya*)—from which the action of the story devolves.[9] As the child grows, he is dedicated to giving, supported by his mother. The earth quakes as he makes a wish to give any part of himself to others. Brahmins from Kaliṅga, where there is a drought, arrive and ask for the auspicious elephant to bring them rain and good luck. The Bodhisatta gives it to them to the horror of the people of Sivi. His father hears about it, and summons his royal steward to inform his son that he is banished from the kingdom. The steward does this, and the Bodhisatta tells his wife Maddī to be kind to his family, and to be generous: 'For there is no other certain foundation for all living beings than generous gifts' (v. 66). She protests that she will go willingly with him, deploying the

8. On the name Vessantara, see Alsdorf 1957; Norman 1991: II 172–3; and PGPV xxvii. Norman suggests that it means 'all-conquering', Alsdorf 'giving everything', and Gombrich 'all-saving'.

9. 'Strong support' (*upanissaya*) is an unusual condition amongst the twenty-four 'causes' of the *Paṭṭhāna,* the seventh—and considered the highest—book of the *Abhidhamma.* As the ninth of such causes, and the one that seems most apt here, it describes the event in the world that can trigger a change of state, such as contact with a particular person, food, or condition, that allows *jhāna* or a stage of a path to be realized. In its *Abhidhamma* sense it is the particular event that works for a specific individual at a given moment in their spiritual practice. Here, it is the means through which the Bodhisatta will be able to fulfil his role perfecting generosity in this lifetime.

regally splendid image that recurs throughout the story: a female elephant that follows her mate (v. 74). She says she will find no happiness without him, and will bring the children too. Reassuring him, she gives a paean to the beauties of the Himalayas, anticipating the rural idyll they find when they leave.

3. THE DESCRIPTION OF THE SECTION ABOUT GENEROSITY

The queen hears the two talk, and tries to dissuade Maddī from going. She and the women of the household make their laments. Given one day to prepare himself, the Bodhisatta formally makes the gifts of the seven hundreds: seven hundred elephants, male attendants, female attendants, and so on, and also the crucial seven-hundredfold gift of alms to ascetics; the earth quakes again. The king makes a last attempt to dissuade Maddī from going, pointing out the dangers of the forest, but she is adamant in her resolve, pointing out the terrible lot of widows. Insisting on taking the children too, the pair take their leave, and after one last look at the city, at which the earth quakes again, they continue in a carriage—until that too Vessantara gives away. They proceed on foot.

4. THE DESCRIPTION OF THE ENTRY INTO THE FOREST

Compassionate *yakkhas* speed them on their journey and even the trees bow down in sympathy to them, until they reach the city of the Cetans, where they are welcomed warmly. Vessantara is asked to stay, and offered rulership in the kingdom, which he refuses. The Cetans give directions to go on his way, again anticipating the beauties that lie ahead, and one is placed as a guard. The four follow their instructions, rest and recuperate, and find the 'single-track path' that leads to the Crooked Mountain.[10] Sakka helps them, sending Vissakamma to arrange a hermitage; when they arrive, they change to bark clothes, and live in chastity but happily, extending loving-kindness around the hermitage. On Maddī's suggestion, she goes to get fruits for them to eat and the Bodhisatta looks after the children, and they live in this way for seven months.

10. For this path, see Norman 1983: 80. He points out that *ekapadī* is not the 'path that leads only one way' (*ekāyano maggo*) of the *Satipaṭṭhāna Sutta* (DN 22), but a path that only one person at a time can walk on.

5. THE DESCRIPTION OF THE EPISODE CONCERNING JŪJAKA

We now move to some bathos and comic relief, to the brahmin Jūjaka, the villain of the piece, who lives in a dreary village with his much younger wife. Teased by other women for her marriage, she insists the brahmin go to ask Vessantara, of whose arrival she has been told, for his children as slaves. The brahmin, enslaved by his own desire for his wife, agrees, and he sets on his way. He too is guided by a *deva* to the Crooked Mountain, and meeting the Cetan he asks him the way. The brahmin persuades him that he has come to ask Vessantara to return, and the Cetan overcomes his suspicions to feed him and direct him on his way.

6. THE SHORT DESCRIPTION OF THE FOREST

The Cetan feeds the brahmin generously and, with descriptions of the beauties of the forest, sends him on a 'single-track' path that will lead him to the ascetic seer Accuta, who will help him find Vessantara.

7. THE GREAT DESCRIPTION OF THE FOREST

The brahmin finds Accuta, who, with the hospitality that characterizes people while they are in the forest, feeds him. His suspicions about the brahmin's intent are also overcome when he is reassured that the brahmin wants to meet a 'noble one'. Accuta then describes the forest to him and directs him to the single-track path, telling him that all is delight where Vessantara lives peacefully with his children (v. 431).

8. THE EPISODE CONCERNING THE CHILDREN

We now come to the most harrowing scenes of the story, as Maddī has a terrible dream and goes about her work unwillingly. The Bodhisatta, knowing what is to happen, is happy in anticipation, 'like a golden image' (Ja VI 541), with the children playing at his feet. This unusually modern idyll is disrupted as the brahmin enters and the hospitable enquiries and greetings are extended to him. Although the children, Jāli and Kaṇhajinā, recognize his evil nature and try to hide, they are called, each separately, by the Bodhisatta, who makes his request to his son:

> Come, dear son, fulfil my perfection,
> Consecrate my heart and do just as I say.
> Be a steady boat that takes me on the ocean of becoming,

For I shall cross to the farthest shore, and bring freedom to the world
and its gods.
(vv. 460–1)

He then repeats this to his daughter, addressing her (vv. 462–3). Both individually consent, knowing even as children that they are participants in a larger vow. So they are given, with the Bodhisatta setting a price on each one's head; the earth quakes, and the children are led weeping, being beaten, away. The children manage to escape and run back, asking for their mother to be there when they go. The Bodhisatta is overcome by grief, compared to an elephant caught by a lion, or the moon by an eclipse. He considers killing the brahmin—and then remembers the Bodhisatta lineage, the necessity for this gift, and that he must now accept the consequences of what he has done. Grief-stricken and struggling for his composure and equanimity, he sits motionless while the children are led crying away.

9. MADDĪ

When the earth quakes Maddī is in the forest; she feels dizzy, loses her sense of direction, and cannot work properly. *Deva*s who live in the forest disguise themselves as wild animals and block her single-track path home; eventually she pleads with them and pays them homage, and they decide to free her. She gives a long lament at the absence of her children. With her mind in 'black night', she pleads with the Bodhisatta, but after criticising her lateness as a means of dispelling her grief, he refuses to speak. Devastated and deranged, she spends the night searching the forest, until when the 'night starts to lighten' she returns to the hermitage, lamenting with increasing confusion and dismay, convinced they are dead. The forest, usually so full of cheerful noise too, has fallen silent. She collapses in grief, and the Bodhisatta revives her and reveals what has happened, explaining he had not wanted to make her suffer by telling her earlier, and saying, 'Children are the supreme gift' (v. 606). She, regaining her composure, echoes his speech and agrees: they are the greatest gift. She encourages him to 'clear his mind with faith' (v. 607), and continue giving. He encourages her, telling her of the earthquake that had happened when the great gift had been made.

10. SAKKA

King Sakka sees what is happening, and is now concerned that the

Bodhisatta would be left 'without a protector and without support' if Maddī were given away to someone unworthy, so he decides to disguise himself as a brahmin and ask for her (Ja VI 568). After the usual forest courtesies, he does so. Then, having received her, he gives her back to Vessantara in what is now the turning point of the story: from this time on, Vessantara is a recipient as well as a giver, and his gifts are returned in reverse order. Vessantara is given eight wishes: (1) that his father might welcome him home again, (2) that he abolish the death penalty, (3) that he be a support to all, (4) that he not be unfaithful to his wife, (5) that he might have a son—though this possibly means that he wishes his son to flourish—and that this son is a Universal Monarch, (6) that when the 'night starts to lighten' there will be heavenly food, (7) that he will continue to be unstintingly generous, and (8) that he will find a heavenly rebirth (vv. 640–8).[11]

11. THE GREAT KING

While the pair continue to live in tranquillity, the children are guarded by the *devas*. The brahmin sleeps in a tree, scared of wild animals, and ties up the children beneath, but they are washed, fed, nursed, and given bedclothes by *devas* every night, so they remain unharmed. But the brahmin is directed by *devas* to the court of King Sañjaya, Vessantara's father, who recognizes the 'golden coins' of his grandchildren immediately:

> Like lions emerging from their den, both these children are so alike too:
> These children look as if they are made of gold!
> (v. 652)

The children, knowing their lowly status, keep to one side. But Sañjaya, asking their price, redeems them from the brahmin with great wealth; Jūjaka then dies from overeating and the wealth returns to the crown. With the 'goods' of their children washed and dressed in beautiful clothes on their laps, they hear the story of what has happened. The children tell them how their mother is becoming thin and ill, and their grandfather admits his terrible wrong. He orders a magnificent army of the sixty thousand ministers, all born at the same time as the Bodhisatta, to go and fetch him and Maddī back, with Jāli as the guide.

11. Many of these wishes raise a number of issues pertaining to the story: these are discussed in the notes to that section.

12. THE SECTION ABOUT THE SIX NOBLE WARRIORS

As the army arrives, the Bodhisatta is afraid that they have come to kill him, and goes with Maddī up the mountain to look at his people, in an echo of the glance they both gave when they left their city. But Maddī reassures him, wishing him safety, so he returns to his hut and gathers strength. The king, Vessantara, and Maddī meet alone, and his first wish to Sakka is fulfilled. After the forest courtesies, the Bodhisatta breaks his pattern and now admits that he has struggled in his way of life and that they have missed their parents. Then, in great emotion, the earth quakes again, and the family are reconciled. Overcome, they all faint, and are revived by the lotus shower described at the beginning of the story. The people around them beg both Sañjaya and Vessantara to rule the kingdom.

13. THE DESCRIPTION OF VESSANTARA

The king, acknowledging his faults, anoints Vessantara, when he has washed and changed, as regent, and the earth shakes again. They stay in the forest for some time for a festival, and return triumphant on a road now festively decorated for them. As he returns, he sees he needs to give more gifts to suppliants, and Sakka, 'as the night starts to lighten', ensures that he has plenty with which to do so.

The Family

The story is so densely interrelated, so full of interweaving patterns of repetition, courtly greetings, descriptive epithets and rhetorical pleas, laments and rejoicing, it is like a woven song, with multiple parts echoing one another, epithets reiterated, and refrains varying slightly in different situations. It is not possible to do justice here to the way character, plot, language, imagery, and poetry all dance in and out of each other in stately measures, with the sixteen-syllable *vatta*s used throughout the verses, counting out the movement and rhythms of the characters' relationships to one another. The form lends itself to the repetition and borrowing of eight-syllable phrases, often very simple, that can occupy a half-line at the end of each verse in a lament, song of praise, or plea. This allows for a great range of emotions to be explored and expressed, as in Maddī's lament at the loss of the children, while also sustaining a stable, repetitive beat to the emotionally precise detailing of her feelings of grief and loss. Two or three such phrases are also woven together in this way in the children's lament in the forest for instance, with echoes between theirs and hers.

The method allows extensive verbal resonances between the speeches of various characters, at quite different points of the story; some of the key repetitions and images are described in the notes to this translation. Formal exchanges of greetings, ritual offerings of food and drink, and enquiries about health all resonate with one another in shared patterns of speech and interchange. The whole is a kind of symphonic enactment of the complexity of the Bodhisatta vow, and the people the Bodhisatta needs to support and be supported by, in his lengthy search for the perfections.

All the key players are here for his last lifetime as a human being before the one in which he gains complete awakening—even his charioteer and driver, Channa, appears as the Cetan guard. The sense throughout the story is of rhythm and pattern, comings together and movings apart, laments that explore with a highly nuanced emotional precision the stages of grief, despair, disorientation, and finally, hope. It is easy to see, as Gombrich points out, why so many women who had lost loved ones and children would feel this story speaks to their innermost grief, and happiness too (PGPV xiv–xvii). Celebrations of wealth are comparably nuanced and stately, weaving in with laments, and then greetings, until the final reconciliation and triumphant return, when even the cats are freed. In this story, the unusual epithet for dawn, 'when night starts to lighten', acts like a gentle pulse through the momentum of the drama, until the end, when it heralds the start of a new day, and for the Bodhisatta, yet more chances to give. All are interrelated; all tread a 'single-track path.' The story is like a final ritual dance within the world of *saṃsāra,* before the great drama of the final life.

But it is very human and personal too. As there is not space to consider all aspects of this in detail, a few features can be explored briefly here. The first is the nature of the family and the Bodhisatta's relationship to it. At the beginning of the *Mahānipāta*, the Bodhisatta is determined to refuse both kingship and his father's role and authority. Although father and son are reconciled, outside the city and kingdom, it is a happy truce between parent and child that does not offer resolution within these; here the reunion leads back to, not away from, kingship and home. Family relationships in the story are beautifully observed: the loving giving of gifts to Maddī by her mother-in-law; the father's desperate attempts to be reconciled with his son; the Bodhisatta's urgent desire, in his first wish, to find a homecoming to his parents; the children's 'charming little speeches' yet their great courage and nobility in wanting to give their toys to their mother when being led away (v. 494), and their being deferential when they are slaves back in the palace yet happily and accurately guiding their grandparents back to their parents when redeemed; the mother's terrible grief at the loss of her children, expressed in laments by Phusatī and Maddī. All of these have echoes in other stories in the *Mahānipāta*, and all are reconciled here. The story is about kingship, but it explores the fine network of relationships within families too. Every single character acts from freely expressed will. 'Children are the supreme gift' is one of the refrains of the story. It is an elliptic and intriguing statement that lingers in the mind. For the children have choice too. Within this very Buddhist story, they have inherited their own karma, like all the other characters, and in future lives they will be the heirs of what they do now. In Buddhist terms, no being is 'owned' by another, whatever their status. The arrival of children is itself a gift, perhaps subtly acknowledged by this refrain, and parents would have felt that about their own children. But whatever the Bodhisatta does, to them or to any other being, the Buddhist irony of this story is that he cannot really 'give' them away at all. They can never really be given, except by themselves, and they do this, albeit in great misery, thus taking their part in the formal ritual dance of the drama that is needed for the attainment of Buddhahood.

In this regard the relationship between the Bodhisatta and Maddī, including the 'giving away' of Maddī, is also important. Throughout the *jātakas*, in thirty-two stories in all, a number suggesting some completion and deliberation in a Buddhist context, Rāhulamātā has accompanied the Bodhisatta, only ever married to him.[12] She appears as the wife of Janaka, Mahosadha, Canda, and Vidhura as well as Vessantara. To Buddhist audiences, she too would have been felt to be following a path of her own, in adhering to a vow to accompany her spouse in their lifetimes together. In each story she acts appropriately to the world that she is in: As Janaka's wife she is proud and haughty, exhibiting the great strength that propels this tale; in the end, accepting her husband's renunciation, she herself renounces too, and attains meditative happiness. As Mahosadha's wife she is clever and ingenious, but also kind, as fitting the wise Bodhisatta of that story. In this one, she becomes, oddly enough, a necessary opposite pole

12. A number of lists in early Buddhism suggest the completion of a cycle or a world with the number thirty-two or thirty-three: the parts of the body, the marks of a Great Man, and the realms of existence. This makes her life as Yasodharā (Rāhulamāta) the thirty-third with the Bodhisatta.

to him. His quest means that in some ways he has to reject his father, his environment, and his affections in order to make his gifts. But she does not. She fights to stay with her husband, but she always acts in harmony with the environment around her, complementing her husband's passion with an equally committed intent to live within her circumstances, and not to fight them. She goes with the Bodhisatta to the forest of her own free will, understands and appreciates the forest, where she is not harmed, accepts the giving of the children despite her grief, and roars like a lion, one of the wild animals that has just protected her, when she supports him. She freely accepts her husband giving her to Sakka. But throughout, it is she who supports the family, reassures him when he is frightened at the arrival of his father, and sees him through the great crisis of his gift giving. She is not obviously a modern heroine in this regard, but her flexibility and willingness to adapt to new environments makes her an embodiment of supporting strength. She demonstrates an ideal of willing but strong acknowledgement of interdependency that balances the Bodhisatta's search for freedom, involving as it does his inevitable isolation and fear. In this regard, her courage represents an auspiciousness like that of Sītā, as Meiland (2004: 62–8) points out. Throughout South and Southeast Asia, Maddī is loved by women.

In her final life, as Yasodharā, her laments are fused with those of Maddī in South and Southeast Asian song and poetry. In Sri Lanka, great prominence is accorded to *Vessantara-jātaka* from the eighteenth century, but since the mediaeval period Maddī's later rebirth as Yasodharā has been fundamentally linked to this pre-eminence, as his partner in the culmination of the great generosity of that earlier rebirth. Laments and songs, sung at funerals and by women in the fields, all show Yasodharā as the heroine that resonates, but her life is inextricably linked to Maddi's as the culmination of her auspicious generosity of spirit in Vessantara. In the fifteenth-century version of Yasodharā's lament, reference is made to her earlier life as Maddī:

> When you lived with me in *saṃsāra* you were attached to the idea of giving; you gave away our children. When I bore you yet more children, you gave them away too to supplicants. Yet I was not distressed. [This happened] in uncountable lives, I know. (Obeyesekere 2009: 71)

In the lament, she speaks of her life as Maddī in a way that fuses the two lives, just as the last life of the Buddha is felt to be so interwoven with that of other *jātakas*, and with that of Vessantara in particular:

> As Vessantara, do you recall how we went into the forest?
> Did I not look after you then, comb the forest for fruit.
> A care never crossed your mind then, was that not the truth?
> My moon-like lord did I not constantly protect? (84)
> Like the marks on the moon was I not with you always?
> Who told you then to abandon me today?
> When I was asked to stay in Sandamaha city,
> Did I not, weeping, follow you that day? (85)
> I did not protest when you gave away our children.
> Was I not then a Vessantara that day?
> Did I not bear you the lovely prince, Rāhula?
> Why then did you leave me and walk away? (86)
> (Obeyesekere 2009: 49–50)

This heroism is acknowledged by the Bodhisatta/Buddha in the poem. In another part of the poem, the Bodhisatta, about to leave the palace, looks wistfully at his wife and says:

> You've wept more tears for me than the seas hold water,
> Does this wide world hold a woman as good as you?
> Today I leave you in order to become a Buddha
> I must destroy my desire, be firm in my resolve. (49)
> (Obeyesekere 2009: 44)

The blurring of distinctions between Yasodharā/Bimbā/Rāhulamātā (some of her names) and her earlier self as Maddī occurs throughout South and Southeast Asia; Bimbā's lament, translated by Donald Swearer, gives a Southeast Asian version (Swearer 1999). Stressing the consonance between Maddī and Bimbā, at one point it borrows from the *Vessantara-jātaka* in its use of images from this verse:

> 'The banner is the signifier of the chariot, smoke the signifier of fire;
> The king is the signifier of the kingdom; a husband is the signifier of a woman.

> Yes, it is bitter being a widow in this world. I will go, lord of
> charioteers.'
> (v. 191)

It is a very discerning play of images, for what use is the banner without the chariot, smoke without a fire, or a king without a kingdom? Maddī is a necessary helper in the Bodhisatta's work, and it is important that she is a free moral agent and willing too, a Buddhist heroine. As Sakka points out to Vessantara:

> Just as milk and a conch-shell are of the same colour,
> So you and Maddī are of the same heart and thought.
> (v. 637)

Throughout this story she lives in the world of conditions, or *paccayas*, and their interrelatedness, which she always acknowledges, as in her homage to the beasts of the forest while her children are being taken away. But she has her own path too. In her final *Apadāna*, canonical verses by *arahats*, she reveals the universe, with the four continents and the islands, to the Bodhisatta, before speaking from emptiness, just before her death (*Yasodharā-therī, Apadāna* 584–90). The universe she reveals to him in this story is a sustaining one, and she is one agent that ensures his safety.

The Forest

Another aspect of the story that should be considered is the forest. This section falls exactly in the middle of this tale, and it is core to its overall effect. While Cone judiciously puts most of this as an appendix, as it involves excessive annotation, it seems better, however, for this translation to include it within the text, with footnotes at the bottom of each page. The passage offers a beautiful and important pastoral respite of profuse and highly differentiated variegation that feels like it oxygenates the story: it allows the mind to rest and appreciate the natural world that is protecting the couple and their children before the harrowing events that follow. Indeed it is this world that helps to ensure both that the gift of children is given and that they will be reunited at the end.

Forests feature symbolically in many cultures: Shakespeare often allowed problems to unravel and resolve in his Forest of Arden, and in the *Śakuntalā*, it is where the heroine and the king have their first romantic encounter. In Thailand, it frequently features as the dark green background to mural paintings, a field in which *Rāmāyaṇa* stories, *jātaka*s, and local legends can be distinct patches of illuminated colour but share a common and darkly verdant background. In some ways the forest is also like the Miltonic paradise of the Garden of Eden, but it is Vessantara who engineers the loss of idyll, not Maddī, who lives in happy accord with all the natural world around her. Read or heard now, it feels like an ecological celebration of the diversity of the natural environment: of Orissa, at any rate, though apparently, it has been argued, not the Himalayas (see PGPV xxii). The plants, trees, and animals are highly idiosyncratic and fruitful, with the evocation of grasses, flora, and fauna allowing the mind to breathe a little before the great drama ahead. As Gombrich points out, it is very like, and indeed must have strong associations with, the forest passages in the *Rāmāyaṇa*, though as he points out it lacks the sophisticated complexity of the Sanskrit verse (Gombrich 1985).

Here is nature in restful harmony: birds repeatedly sing to their mates, a reassuring reminder of happy conjugal union after the bathetic quarrels of the brahmin and his wife, and before the dark events that are to come. This emphasis also, in what would have been a chanted text, reminds us of the aural sense of the forest as well as the visual, though other senses are evoked too, such as the softness of the peacocks' throats. In this diversity, trees and shrubs are, however, distinct—rather as in the *Sāma-jātaka* where the goddess makes an act of truth based on the single identity of each tree within the forest (Ja VI 92). In the short description of the forest the trees also have low branches (vv. 334–5) and the fruits are easy to pick and the grasses not too high and thus perfect for humans (v. 377), features discussed by Steven Collins as reminiscent of the Land of Cockayne in Western fable (Collins 1998: 497 ff.). Such features, as in the short description of the forest, are very experiential, appealing to the senses of taste and touch. It seems miraculous—but it is definitely the human realm; there is little that is otherworldly. It is noteworthy so many of the herbs and plants are used for food and flavouring as well as medicine to this day, as if each fulfils a quite separate and distinct function. Despite the king's warnings to Maddī in the second section of the wild beasts and bugs in the jungle, no mention is made of the underbelly of jungle life or the struggle to survive, even when some description of potentially dangerous wild beasts is included. The forest demonstrates the natural world at its most idyllic. It is appreciated, ordered, and named by the seer Accuta, rather as Adam names species in the Garden of Eden (Genesis 2:20).[13] The dangers of the jungle, as described by the King of the Sivis, the wary urban courtiers, and people of the more gentle country of Ceta, fail to materialise. Accuta delights in his ascetic life and classifies the plants and wildlife of the region with clear enjoyment. As we see in the ninth section, Maddī, however, is the only character in the entire story who really trusts and interacts with them, as if her own virtue finds an answering note in the natural environment she loves and respects. From an *Abhidhamma* point of view they are *kusalavipāka* (skilful resultant), a kind of birthright to those lucky enough to gain a human rebirth, and the result of fortunate actions performed in the past. By and large the creatures are natural and based on close observation rather than legend. There is no mention of gods and spirits, though some *makaras*, possibly denoting lizards, and monsters are briefly cited (vv. 405, 409). Surprisingly for this region, there is no citrus fruit, though it is possible some unidentified plant and tree names refer to members of this family.

From the point of view of the accuracy of the names, Cone's work remains unchallenged (see PGPV 89–96). The taxonomy of South and Southeast Asia was laid down by the mid-twentieth century, and in some respects there has not been the same interest in finding consonance between language in ancient texts and the modern system of classification of wildlife and botany since that time, as a look at early editions of the *Journal of the Bombay Natural History Society* will attest. Getting the 'right' species can itself be a debatable exercise, given the changeability of prevalence patterns in particular regions. Another potential factor in assessing the *Vessantara* use of terms is the possible extent to which early Sri Lankan classification, where there is a strong endemic botanical signature, may have influenced ways the text was understood in subsequent commentaries. There is a twelfth-century Sri Lankan treatise (*Sanne*) on botany in this story in Elu.[14] By that time, particularly with all the to and fro between Sinhala languages and Pāli that had gone on by then, we cannot be sure if the Sinhalese did not simply call some plants by Pāli names, or vice versa. So we can enjoy the list as it is, perhaps not recognizing all the names—as indeed, once Pāli ceased to be known generally, it would have appeared to centuries of people hearing it chanted. In this story the forest is only silent when something bad is

13. The name Accuta seems to mean 'not having died'.
14. I am grateful for discussions with Ven. Nyanatusita and Margaret Cone about this.

happening, and Maddī is bereft. So the section describes a kind of still if noisily harmonious place, as if the mind has gone to the deepest part of itself and just looked in solitude at the world around. Indeed this is clearly what the seer and ascetic Accuta must have done himself, giving us this long but restfully musical chant of Pāli names, a breathing space in the middle of the tale.

Festivals

Festivals for Vessantara recitation, songs, chant, and drama are knitted into the fabric of the yearly round in parts of South and Southeast Asia. This affects its timing. It is celebrated at the end of the rains retreat in Central Thailand, between October and November. In Northeast Thailand, it is held after the harvest and before the beginning of the hot season, so sometime from February to April; Lao Buddhists call it Bun Phawet (Tiyanavich 2003: 25–32). In Chiang Mai it is in December; in many other places, around the time of Vesākha. The whole carnival of processions, festivities, and chant makes the occasion central to the whole community. Sometimes it occurs outside a village, in the fields that need to be reached in a procession: at the culmination, the procession seems to spill out from the procession at the end of the story, with all participants dancing and singing as they return to their village. Policemen are both policeman and soldiers, vans have big sheets on the back with the ever-pervasive Vessantara elephants painted on; the monk who has chanted the last section is brought back in honour, reaffirming his status as a monk, as well as Vessantara, and welcoming him as such back into the community. Tiyanavich (2003: 30) points out that Lao villagers feel as 'if the bodhisat and his wife, Matsi, really existed in a different realm'. In Si Sa Ket, people dress up as their favourite characters. Glamorous girls tend to like being Maddī and text other Maddīs so they can meet up in the same place, and older men enjoy being the brahmin, threatening others with their sticks and making jokes to all around. In performances of the story, the favourites are also Matsi and Chuchok: 'The Matsi episodes elicit great sadness as Matsi mourns the loss of her children; the Chuchok episode elicits gales of laughter when Chuchok is shown to be a buffoon' (Tiyanavich 2003).

It is thought that if one sat through all of the thirteen sections of Vessantara one would be reborn as a human being at the time of the future Buddha, Metteyya (see Collins 2015: introduction). Monks and novices from various *wats* are invited to perform characters: it takes 'discipline and training for preachers to act their role effectively' (Tiyanavich 2003: 28). In some parts of Southeast Asia each 'chapter' of the Vessantara has a particular association, and is sponsored by specific parts of the community; certain sections are set pieces for boy novices, to recite to their parents when they come to visit. Thai royalty has always been associated with the story, and historically many Thai kings have participated and chanted in Vessantara ceremonies. A unique form of the story, in Tai-Khün, a dialect closely linked to Thai, Laotian, and Lanna, is used alongside the Pāli in Kengtung, Shan State, Myanmar; different sections are chanted for varied purposes. In Kengtung, this ceremony is held during the rains retreat, from the middle of July to October (Pannavamsa 2007a). In banners, temple murals, and commemorative pamphlets, the thirteen scenes have come to each be routinely depicted by one easily recognizable incident. So some temples simply show the *Vessantara-jātaka* around the walls, in thirteen murals; in Northeast Thailand a special banner depicting the thirteen is paraded and draped in the *ubosot* hall (Lefferts and Cate 2013).

Art

'There is hardly a major Buddhist site in India which has no representation of Vessantara', notes Gombrich (PGPV xxix). In Sri Lankan art, *Vessantara* has preeminence: it is often shown alone, or in a place of honour amongst others, such as at the Madavela Temple, where it is placed by the seven weeks of reflection after enlightenment (Holt 1996: 56). In other temples, it is frequently one amongst a very few stories given special treatment (see Holt 1996: plates 30–4 and 50; Coomaraswamy 1979: plate 1). The first edition of Richard Gombrich's introduction to Margaret Cone's 1977 translation of the story contains extensive Kandyan examples too. We cannot assess quite the specific effect of this tale in early times: it does appear to have been some prominence, with murals from it in Caves 16 and 17 at Ajanta, for instance. In early Myanmar it also appeared on *sīmā* or ordination stones, perhaps more prominently than other *jātakas* (Murphy 2010: 249–54). There is a cave in Nakhon Phanom called Vessantara Cave (Tham Phawet). In South and Southeast Asia, the story has become by far the most influential of all of the *Mahānipāta*. Just as the ten perfections and the associated images from the tales animate the walls of temples throughout Southeast Asia from the eighteenth century onwards, so in the twentieth century the *Vessantara-jātaka* has superseded even these. Many temples have all or most of their mural art devoted to *jātakas*; if the ten last stories are shown, this one is often given extra precedence, and perhaps twice the space of each of the others, frequently in a more central position in the shrine hall. The thirteen sections, depicted on banners and murals, are known by thirteen stock scenes, which as a sequence immediately evoke the auspiciousness of the tale and demonstrate the events seen as key in this flowering of popularity of a tale already regarded as central to Buddhist narrative.

From a literary point of view the story has been so influential in Asia it would be impossible to explore all aspects of this here. It has inspired many variations (Skilling 2006b; PGPV). In Thailand and Myanmar it has inspired drama, poetry, songs, and all kinds of literary expression.[15] Rajadhon's comments on the Thai understanding of the story would be shared in many other regions:

> His life the people like to hear recited, for the supreme sacrifice of Prince Wetsandon touches their hearts deeply. . . . It greatly influences the life of the mass of the people. The story also serves as an inspiration to Thai poets and artists of old classical art, for the reason that the story contains noble sentiments, pathos, humour and beautiful descriptive scenes which give free play to their power of imagination and artistic expression. (Rajadhon 2009: 56)

Song composition, as has been indicated, is also strong; Collins explores some of these traditionally associated with the story in various regions (Collins 1998: 541 ff.).

Conclusion

Utterly simple in plot, poignant in its expression of the deepest fears of those that listen to it, and redeeming in its course and conclusion, the *Vessantara-jātaka* is a profoundly ritual text, one that effects a true *catharsis* (purification of emotion), arousing the 'pity and fear' Aristotle describes as involved in all tragedy. It also introduces the resolution of traditional

15. I am particularly grateful to extensive discussions with Venerable Dr Pannavamsa, whose unpublished Ph.D. dissertation for Peradeniya University, Kandy, 'A Critical Study of the *Vessantara-jātaka* and its Influence on Kengtung Buddhism, Eastern Shan State, Burma,' (2007b) includes a great deal of material pertaining to court drama and literature, in Myanmar in particular.

comedy in the happy reconciliation of family and state, in a stately yet friendly manner that arouses rejoicing and calm. Acted and performed, it is just very funny at times, with the brahmin's villainy so cruel, yet so hilarious, that he becomes like a villain in a pantomime, booed, jeered, and hissed and laughed at by all around. It is indeed a truly Buddhist drama, with a brahminic sacrifice (*yañña*) that is not brahminic in the sense understood then, because it does not cause harm but instead promotes the underlying Buddhist ethos of *dāna*, where gifts can only be given freely. Each character that participates in its festive ethos is completely enmeshed with others through complex causes (*paccayas*) yet is also independent, on a 'single-track path' that only he or she can tread, with his or her own free will and choice. Those that practise generosity, with right intention (*cetanā*) at the right time and place, and accept their interrelatedness to others, thereby free themselves within their world and bring happiness to others too. The Bodhisatta's job is so frightening and awesome precisely because its isolating demands go so against his deepest nature; his terrible task is only possible through the support of wife, children, family, and gods, who protect him by their commitment to their own paths and the way of liberation for all. This dedication to awakening makes the communal ritual that protects him and those around him, and brings delight to all involved. Recognised since the earliest days of Buddhist practice, this last *jātaka* should take its place, along with others in this magnificent collection, amongst the greatest narratives of the world. Like the teaching of the Buddha, it seems to me beautiful in its beginning, in its middle, and in its end. It has some imperfections—some imported verses, some commentarial material that does not quite flow, and an occasional oddity of logic—but perhaps even because of these defects, the product of its being loved and retold, evolving over centuries, it is the perfect way to end the *Mahānipāta*.

'PHUSATĪ, EXCELLENT AND SHINING...'

1. THE DESCRIPTION OF THE RELATING OF THE TEN WISHES (*DASAVARAKATHĀVAṆṆANĀ*)

[479] The Teacher told this story while he was staying in the Banyan Grove near Kapilavatthu, about a shower of lotus blossoms. When the Teacher had set in motion the Excellent Wheel of the Dhamma, he went to Rājagaha, where he spent the winter. With the elder Udāyi showing the

way, and surrounded by twenty thousand of those who had exhausted the corruptions, he went on his first journey and entered Kapilavatthu.[16]

At that time the Sākyan chiefs were assembled together, and thought, 'Let's go and see the greatest member of our family.'[17] They examined the place where he was staying and exclaimed, 'What a delightful place is this Banyan Grove; it is worthy of Sakka!' They then gave careful directions for its upkeep. They sent, first, adorned in every way, with perfumes and flowers in their hands, the city boys and girls, then the young girls and boys, and then the royal princes and princesses, then they in the same way, with perfumes, flowers, and powders and suchlike in their hands, also went and paid homage to the Blessed One right there in the Banyan Grove. There the Blessed One, with his retinue of twenty thousand of those who had exhausted the corruptions, sat on the excellent seat specially arranged for the Buddha.

Now the Sākyans are proud in their birth and stubborn in pride, and they thought, 'This Prince Siddhattha is younger than we are; he is our younger brother, our nephew, our son, and our grandson.' So they said to the chief's sons, 'You pay homage to him, and we'll sit behind you.' When they sat down without paying homage to him, the Blessed One saw their thoughts, and deliberated, 'These kinsmen of mine are not paying homage, so now I shall pay homage to them.' So he entered into the *jhāna* that provides the basis for the higher knowledges, and, emerging, he rose up into the sky and as if shaking the dust off his feet on their heads, he performed the Twin Miracle, as he had done at the foot of the Knotted Mango Tree.[18]

16. Udāyi was the son of a brahmin of Kapilavatthu and became a monk after seeing the Buddha, after which he became an *arahat*. In one *sutta* he describes the factors of awakening which helped him to do this (DPPN and SN V 89 ff.).

17. This is when the Buddha goes to Kapilavatthu after the awakening. The Buddha recounts this story after returning to see his family: at that time a large rain cloud sent a lotus shower and streams of copper-coloured water. Again those who wished to get wet did, but those who did not wish to did not (Ja I 88–9). The commentary to the *Buddhavaṃsa* says that it is related at the end of a recital of that work at the time. See also Ja I 31 for another reference to Vessantara. The almsgiving in *Vessantara* is recollected at the time of the awakening (Ja I 44).

18. The twin miracle (*yamaka pārihāraya*) is supposedly only possible for fully awakened Buddhas, and involves issuing the antithetical elements fire and water from the body at the same time. After this, the Buddha is supposed to have visited the Tāvatiṃsa heaven to teach the *Abhidhamma* to his mother, who had come down from the Tusita heaven to listen to him. This scene is one of the most popular of Southeast Asian temple art, usually depicted behind the shrine at the front of the hall. The

When the king saw this miracle, he said, 'Sir, on the day of your birth, when you were brought to pay homage to Kāḷadevala, I saw your feet turned and placed on the brahmin's head, and I paid homage to you: this was my first paying of respects. Then, on the day of the ploughing festival, I saw you when you sat on the auspicious couch under the shade of the rose-apple tree, and the shadow of the rose-apple tree did not move around, and then I paid homage to you.[19] This was my second paying of respects. And now, a miracle that has never been seen before has been seen by me. I pay homage to you, and this is my third paying of respects.' And when the king had paid his respects, there was no Sākyan who could not do so too, and they all paid homage. Then, the Blessed One, after the relatives had been made to pay respects, came down from the sky and sat on the appointed seat. The gathering of the family, having entered into the training, all sat with a unified mind, and then a great rain cloud arose and rained a shower of lotus blossoms. Copper-coloured water poured down with a great gushing noise, and whoever wished to get wet got wet, and not even a drop of water [480] fell on the body of anyone who did not want to get wet. Seeing all these, their minds were filled with amazement and wonder: 'This is amazing! This is a wonder! Oh, the great power of Buddhas, that such a lotus shower rains upon the assembly of his relatives!' And they became involved in animated conversation about it.

When he heard this the Teacher said, 'It is not the first time, monks, that a great shower of lotus blossoms has rained upon my relatives.' Saying this, when asked, he told to them this story of long ago.

In times past, in the kingdom of Sivi, in the city of Jetuttara, ruled a great king of the Sivis, who had a son named Sañjaya. When he came of age the king had a princess brought called Phusatī (Sprinkling), the daughter of the king of the Maddas, and he made Phusatī his chief wife. Here is a summary of her previous lives.

placing of this, next to a tale that gives such prominence to his mother as the earlier rebirth of Phusatī at the outset, is significant.

19. According to the *Jātaka-nidāna*, this was the time when, at the age of seven, the Bodhisatta attained the first *jhāna* spontaneously under the shade of the rose-apple tree (Ja I 58).

Once, ninety-one aeons ago, a Teacher named Vipassī[20] arose in the world. And while he was living in the Khema deer park attached to the city of Bandhumatī, a certain king sent King Bandhuma a garland of gold, worth a hundred thousand coins, together with choice sandalwood beyond price. But the king had two daughters; he wished to give a special present to them. He gave the elder the choice sandalwood and gave the younger the garland of gold. They thought, 'We will not wear these on our selves: let's pay homage to the Teacher.' They both said to the king, 'Dear one, we are going to pay homage to the Ten-Powered One with the choice sandalwood and the garland of gold.' When he heard this the king agreed to this and said, 'Very well.' The elder had the sandalwood powdered and had it placed so that it filled a golden casket. The younger sister had a breast ornament made from the garland of gold and had it placed in a golden casket. They then both went to the monastery in the deer park and the elder sister paid homage to the golden body of the Ten-Powered One with the powdered sandalwood, and the rest she scattered in the perfumed hut where he lived. And she made a resolve: 'Bhante, may I in the future become the mother of a Buddha like you.' The younger paid homage to the golden body of the Tathāgata with the golden garland, made into a breast ornament, and made her resolve, 'Bhante, may this ornament not leave my body, until I attain arahatship.' And the teacher rejoiced in the merit of their wishes.

The girls lived out [481] their lifespans and took rebirth in a *deva* world. The elder travelled in *saṃsāra*, from the *deva* world to the world of men, and from the world of men to the *deva* world, until, after ninety-one aeons, she became Queen Māyā, the mother of the Buddha. The younger sister travelled in *saṃsāra* in the same way, until, at the time of the Ten-Powered Kassapa, she took rebirth as the daughter of King Kiki. At her birth it was as if her breast was adorned with a golden ornament, painted in a picture, and she was named Uracchadā (an Ornament on the Breast). When she was a girl of sixteen, she heard the Teacher giving a blessing after a meal,[21] and on that very day attained to the first fruit of the path. Subsequently, on the

20. Vipassī was the nineteenth of the twenty-four Buddhas; his awakening is described in the *suttas* (SN II 5 and *Mahāpadāna Sutta*, DN 14).

21. It is customary for Buddhist monks, after a *dāna*, a meal offered by the laity, to give a short *dhamma* talk and a blessing, the *anumodana*, transferring the merit of the occasion to all beings around.

day her father too attained this state, she attained arahatship. She then took the going forth and eventually attained *nibbāna*.[22]

King Kiki had seven other daughters named

> Samaṇī, Samaṇā, Guttā, the nun Bhikkhudāsikā,
> Dhammā, Sudhammā, and Saṇghadāsī, the seventh.

In the time of the Buddha they were

> Khemā, Uppalavaṇṇā, Paṭācārā, Gotamā,
> Dhammadinnā, Mahāmāyā, and Visākhā, the seventh.[23]

Amongst these Phusatī was the one called Sudhammā, and she practised generosity and many other auspicious things. She travelled through *saṃsāra*, amongst gods and men, with a body that looked as if red sandalwood essence had been sprinkled onto it, the result of the homage she had paid to the Buddha named Vipassī with powdered sandalwood, and in due course she took rebirth as the chief wife of Sakka, king of the gods. She remained there for the duration of her life, but King Sakka recognized that when five signs appeared[24] her lifespan was due to end. He went with her with great splendour to the Nandana Grove, and, as she lay down on the ornamented couch, he sat beside her. 'Dear Phusatī, I grant you ten wishes: please accept them.' Saying this, he spoke the first verse of the *Great Vessantara-jātaka*, which is adorned with a thousand verses:[25]

22. This is *parinibbāna*, the entrance into *nibbāna* at death.

23. These are the most distinguished of the Buddha's female disciples in his final life: Khemā is the nun pre-eminent in wisdom, Uppalavaṇṇā in psychic powers. Paṭācārā lost her children, and in distress turned to the Buddha, and became awakened; she became a highly revered teacher. Gotamā is Mahāpajāpatī Gotamī, the younger sister of Queen Māyā, who becomes his chief queen after Mahāmāyā's death, and leads those requesting the Buddha to set up an order of nuns. Dhammadinnā was a married woman who left domesticity to become a nun and was described by the Buddha as foremost in teaching amongst the nuns. Visākhā was a rich, generous, and beautiful laywoman, with ten sons and ten daughters, described as foremost of those who tend to the monastic orders. She too became a nun at the end of her life (for all of these, see DPPN and the list of 'foremost' nuns found in AN I 25–6; Bodhi 2012: 111).

24. Technically there is no bodily death in *deva* worlds but a 'falling away' (*cavana*). *Devas* often know their life in a heaven realm is due to end when five signs appear: their garlands wither, their clothes become dirty, they start to sweat under the arms, they lose their radiance, and they take no delight in their seat. As they leave, the other *devas* invite them to return soon (*Itivuttaka* 76–8).

25. The self-referential comment within the narrative prose, to the story itself, indicates the status accorded to the first verse in this case by the tradition: the first words of each verse are given at the outset of each story in the manuscripts by what

'Phusatī, excellent and shining, on whose limbs sits beauty,
Choose ten gifts on earth, amongst the things which are dear to your heart.' (1)

[482] In this way the teaching of the *Great Vessantara-jātaka* was established in the *deva* world.

She, not realizing that she was about to fall away from that realm, was disturbed, and said the second verse:

'O king of the gods, I pay my respects to you. What evil deed have I done,
That you make me fall away from this delightful place, as the wind topples a tree?' (2)

And Sakka, seeing that she had become disturbed, spoke these two verses:

'You have done nothing bad, and you are not out of favour with me.
I speak to you in this way as your merit is now finished. (3)
You are near death, and there will be a separation.
So please accept what I am offering you.' (4)

When she heard Sakka's words she realised that her own death was certain. Making her choice, she said:

'Greetings to you, Sakka, the lord of all beings. If you have granted me a wish,
Then please may I have the good fortune to live in the home of King Sivi. (5)
O giver of gifts in the past,[26] may my eyes be dark and my eyebrows dark,
Just like a doe, and may I have the name Phusatī there too. (6)
May I obtain a son[27] who is generous, and not mean in responding to requests for alms,

---

is presumably the memory tag for each narrative. That this first verse, and hence the whole of this auspicious story, starts with the name Phusatī, an earlier incarnation of Māhāmāyā, the Buddha's mother, rather than the two verse lists of names of daughters, which are not included in the verse numbering, indicates that she is being selected for particular prominence. As this story is supposed to have been given at the time of the teaching of *Abhidhamma* to Mahāmāyā in the Heaven of the Thirty-Three Gods, the link with her earlier life is particularly touching. For discussion about the possibly doubtful status of some of the first verses in this story, see the introduction above.

26. Although really meaning 'breaker of fortresses', commentarial convention took *purindada* to mean 'one who has given gifts in the past.' (See PED 469).

27. The verb in the phrase *puttaṃ labetha* is in the third person in all three manuscripts cited in F, but I have taken it in the first person, *puttaṃ labheyyaṃ*, as suggested by F in a note. Cone puts 'may the king obtain a son.' (PGPV 5).

Who is famous and of a good reputation, honoured by hostile kings. (7)
When the baby is in the womb may my waist not become swollen,
Or my stomach, but like an even, polished bow. (8)
[483] May my breasts not sag, O Vāsava,[28] and may I not go grey.
May dust not stick to my body.[29] May those that are condemned be freed. (9)
The home of King Sivi is filled with the cries of peacocks and herons,
Is filled with the most lovely women, with hunchbacks and maidservants crowded around,[30] (10)
Ringing with the brightly coloured door bolts, made of the seven jewels,[31]
And calls to meat and drink. I would dearly love to be the chief queen there.' (11)

Sakka replied:

'Through my gift, whatever ten things that you wish, O lady whose every limb is loveliness,
You will obtain, in the kingdom of the king of the Sivis.' (12)

[484] Saying this, the king of the *devas*, Vāsava Sujampati, the bountiful,[32] rejoiced in her merit, and granted her wish. (13)

The description of the relating of the ten wishes is finished.

2. THE DESCRIPTION OF THE HIMALAYAS (*HIMĀLAYAVAṆṆANĀ*)

When she had made her wish, she fell from that state and took rebirth in the womb of the king of the Maddas' chief queen. As her body when she was born looked as if she had been sprinkled with powdered sandalwood, on her name-giving day she was given the name Phusatī, and she grew up with a great retinue. When she reached sixteen years of age, she had the most excellent beauty of form, and then the great king of the Sivis had her brought for his son, Sañjaya, over whom he raised the royal parasol.

28. An alternative name for Sakka.

29. Fausbøll (483 n. 2) notes that Cks gives *raje*, amended to *rajo* 'dust' rather than the text *rāgo* 'desire'. This feature is considered auspicious: the eleventh of the thirty-two marks of the Great Man is that dust does not stick to his body (see DN 30, *Lakkhaṇa Sutta*).

30. Cone amends *khujjatecalākkhakākiṇṇe* (F) to *khujjacelāpakākiṇṇe*, as found in Be and Ce (DP I 770). For the Rouse translation, see J VI 249 n. 4, which rejects this interpretation, suggesting it means 'shawls waving in the air', with a word such as *celaṃ* 'cloth' or *celakkhepa* 'the waving of cloths'. Cone revises her translation slightly in the new PTS imprint (PGPV 5).

31. This interpretation is suggested by the commentary and in part by PGPV 5.

32. See SED 772.

Making her the most senior of sixteen thousand women, he established her as the chief queen. So it is said:

> Falling from there, this Phusatī was reborn amongst warriors,
> And in the city of Jetuttara she was married to Sañjaya. (14)

She was dearly loved by Sañjaya and pleasing to him, and Sakka, noticing this, thought, 'Nine of the wishes given by me to Phusatī have been successful.' Then he saw, 'But one wish, for a son, has not been fulfilled. I will fulfil it for her.' Now at that time the Great Being was living in the Heaven of the Thirty-Three and had reached the end of his lifespan. Sakka, realizing this, went up to him. 'Sir, it is time for you to go to the world of men. There, it would be suitable for you to take rebirth in the womb of Phusatī, chief queen of the king of the Sivis.' When Sakka had received his permission, and that of the sixty thousand other gods who were about to fall away from that state, he went back to his own abode. The Great Being fell from that state, and was born there, and the remaining sixty thousand gods were reborn in the homes of sixty thousand ministers. When the Great Being had been conceived in her womb, Phusatī had a pregnancy craving[33] for six halls for giving to be constructed: at the four gates of the city, in the middle of the city and at the gate of the palace. She had a great wish to be generous, and each day gave away six hundred thousand coins. The king heard about her pregnancy craving and consulted the soothsayers. 'Great King, the queen carries in her womb a being who will delight in giving, and he will never be satisfied with his giving!' When he heard this, the king was delighted in his heart, and he organized liberality in the way that has been explained. [485]

And from the time the Bodhisatta had taken conception there was no limit to the king's income, and because of the power of his merit, kings from all over Jambudīpa (India) sent him special presents. And the queen, in the tenth lunar month, carrying the child and accompanied by a large retinue of attendants, wished to look at the city, and informed the king of this. The king had the city decorated as if it were the city of the *devas* and, placing the queen in the best carriage, arranged for her to tour in

33. The craving (*dohaḷini*), which must be satisfied for the well-being of the woman who feels it, is usually associated with pregnancy and is very important as an agency of the plot in Indian literature, as well as in *jātakas*. In the *Vidhura-jātaka*, the craving of the queen for the Bodhisatta's heart is described in this way, though we are not told she is pregnant (Chapter 9: 464).

a circle around the city, keeping it to her right.[34] In the middle of Vessa Road (Commercial Road)[35] labour pains started to grip her as her time had come. They informed the king, and right there in Vessa Road he had a confinement chamber set up, and she gave birth to her son. So it is said:

> 'She carried me for ten lunar months, and then while touring around
> the city, keeping it to her right,
> In the middle of Vessa Road, my mother Phusatī gave birth to me.' (15)

The Great Being was quite clean when he left his mother's womb, and he emerged with his eyes open. Even as he was being born he stretched out his hand to his mother, saying, 'I wish to make a gift, dear one: is there anything I can give?' She said, 'Dear one, you can give gifts as much as you like.' And she placed a purse of a thousand coins in his outstretched hand. The Great Being spoke at birth on three occasions: in the *Ummagga-jātaka*, in this *jātaka*, and in his last birth.[36] And on his naming day they gave him the name Vessantara, as he had been born in Vessa Road. So it is said:

> 'My name does not come from my mother, nor from my father;
> I was born in Vessa Road, and because of this I am Vessantara.' (16)

On the very day of his birth a certain female flying elephant brought for him an utterly white elephant, considered very auspicious, and, after placing it in the stable for auspicious elephants, departed. Because the elephant had come through the cause of the Bodhisatta, they gave it the name Paccaya (Cause).[37]

34. People often encircle an honoured person in *jātaka* stories. Her actions here both pay respects and demonstrate an important commitment to the city and her future son's kingdom.

35. This is an interesting aspect of the *Vessantara-jātaka*: the Vessas are the third caste, the merchants, traders, or in modern terms, businessmen. That the child should be of a royal *khattiya* caste but aligned with the merchants gives a kind of approbation to this class: the first *jātaka* also involves a trader, in the caravan trader who takes his entourage to safety (see Shaw 2006a: 9). In his final birth, the Bodhisatta is also born unexpectedly, halfway between his father's palace and his mother's own home. For Gombrich's discussion of the name see PGPV xxvii.

36. Mahosadha's first words are to ask his mother to heal others with the herb Sakka has given him (see Chapter 5: 206). The Buddha is said to have walked seven steps in each of the four directions, and said: 'In heaven above and on earth below I am the most honoured one. I will dispel the suffering that fills the world.'

37. Gombrich notes that this is a curious name for an elephant, and explains it in terms of a line later in the story in which the adjective *paccaya* (proper, suitable) is used for the elephant, and then mistaken for its name (v. 751). He notes that verses 754–6, which use the word *paccaya* in its usual meaning of cause, are then translated

The king arranged for the Great Being to have sixty-four wet nurses with sweet milk, avoiding those with defects, such as being too tall, and had nurses given to the sixty thousand boys born at the same time.[38] He grew up with the sixty thousand boys and a great entourage, and the king had made for him a piece of jewellery fit for a prince, worth ten thousand coins. By that time he was four or five years old, [486] but he took the jewellery off and gave it to his nurses, and would not take it when they tried to give it back. They told the king what had happened, and the king said, 'What is given by my son is given well, a gift of Brahmā.' And he had another piece of jewelry made. While still a little boy the prince gave the jewelry nine times to his nurses. When he was eight years old, while sitting on his bed, he thought to himself, 'I make external gifts, but this does not satisfy me. I'd like to give a gift from inside me. If anyone should ask me for my heart, I would split open my chest and pull my heart out and give it, and if anyone requested my eyes I would pull them out and give them, and if anyone asked for the flesh from my body I would cut the flesh from my entire body and give that to them.' And as he reflected on his essential nature and mind in this way the great earth, four myriads wide and two thousand *yojanas* deep, shook, trumpeting like an elephant maddened in must. Sineru, the great king of the mountains, bowed down like a wet bamboo shoot, as if he were a dancer, and stood facing the city of Jetuttara. At the rumbling of the earth, the god rained down a great shower and flashes of lightning, lightning flashes issued out, the ocean was whipped up, and Sakka, the king of the gods, clapped his hands, Great Brahmā cried 'Well done!' and as far as the Brahmā realm there was one big commotion. As it is said:

> 'When I was just a little boy, eight years of age,
> Sitting in the palace I reflected upon the giving of gifts.[39] (17)

---

by some storytellers to refer to the elephant again. See the introduction to this story for more discussion of this. The giving of the elephant is one of the most popularly depicted scenes in South and Southeast Asian temple and manuscript art, from as early as Ajanta Cave 17 (see also PGPV xiiff; and, for instance, Roveda and Yem 2009: 58, 113; Ginsburg 1989: 68).

38. For the defects of wet nurses, see *Temiya-jātaka* (Chapter 1: 57-8).

39. This is an interjection from the Buddha in the present. Interventions of this kind are frequent in *jātakas*, reminding the reader/listener of the omniscient perspective of the narrator who is recounting the tale, though usually prefaced by a statement that it is the 'Teacher', or sometimes the 'Buddha' speaking. The occurrence of the Buddha speaking, as is the case here, in first-person recollection is less frequent.

I would give my heart, my eye, my flesh, and my blood; I would give my
body, being made to hear that anyone would ask me for them. (18)
As I reflected upon my nature, which is unwavering and steady,
The earth, wrapped with woods on Mount Sineru, quaked.' (19)

Even by the time he was sixteen, the Bodhisatta had attained to mastery in all skills and crafts. His father wanted to hand over the kingdom to him, and after consulting his mother, he had brought a daughter from the same mother in the family of the king of the Maddas, called Maddī. He made her the chief queen, the senior of sixteen thousand women, and anointed the Great Being in the kingship. From the time he was appointed to the kingship, the Great Being established a great donation, whereby he handed out six hundred thousand gold coins on each day. In the course of time Queen Maddī [487] gave birth to a son, and they received him in a golden net, and because of that they gave him the name Jāli (Having a Net). By the time he was walking she gave birth to a daughter, and they received her in a black hide, and because of this they gave her the name Kaṇhājinā (Lady of the Black Hide). Each month the Bodhisatta, mounted on the back of his richly adorned elephant, inspected the six *dāna* halls.

Now at that time in the kingdom of Kaliṅga, there was a drought. The crops did not ripen and a great famine prevailed.[40] People could not survive, so took to thieving. Gripped by famine, the people met together in the royal courtyard and shouted their anger. The king heard this, and asked, 'What is going on?' They explained the problem to him and the king responded. 'Very well, dear ones. I shall make it rain.' So, letting them go, he kept the *uposatha* and took up the five precepts, but still he could not make it rain. So he had a meeting called in the city, and asked them, 'I have lived according to the five precepts for seven days, and I cannot get it to rain. What should be done?' They replied, 'If sire, you cannot get the god to rain, in the city of Jetuttara there is a prince of King Sañjaya, Vessantara, who delights in giving. He has an auspicious, utterly white elephant. Wherever the elephant goes, there it rains. Tell the brahmins to ask for the elephant and bring it here.' The king agreed. He called together the brahmins and

40. Drought appears to be a recurrent problem for the people of Kaliṅga. In the *Kurudhamma-jātaka* their brahmins ask the people of Kuru for their auspicious elephant, in the hope of attracting rain. It is freely given, but rain only comes to Kaliṅga in that story when the people adopt the five precepts, the real 'gift' from the people of Kuru (J 276).

selecting eight from them gave them their expenses and ordered them, 'Go and ask Vessantara for the elephant and bring it back.'

The brahmins in due course arrived at Jetuttara and enjoyed a free meal at the donation hall. They scattered dust and smeared mud on their body, wanting to ask the king for the elephant on the full moon day. They went to the east gate at a time when the king was going to be coming to the donation hall. When the king arrived, he thought, 'I'll go and look over the donation hall.' Washing in sixteen bowls of perfumed water, he ate, and adorned himself, and, mounted on the richly adorned elephant, he arrived at the eastern gate. The brahmins had not been able to find space there, so they went to the southern gate, stood on raised ground, and watched the king making donations at the eastern gate.[41] When the king reached the southern gate, they stretched out their hands and said, 'Victory to lord Vessantara!' The Great Being saw them, steered his elephant to where they were standing, and, seated on the elephant's back, spoke this first verse:

> [488] 'Brahmins who have long nails and hair, dirty teeth, and dusty heads
> Are stretching out their right hands, and making entreaties to me—what are they asking for?'[42] (20)

Hearing this the brahmins said:

> 'We ask, sire, prosperity of the kingdom, for a treasure,[43]
> The great big animal with tusks like the poles of a carriage.' (21)

When he heard this the Great Being thought, 'Really, I wish to give

41. The south is considered less lucky than the most auspicious direction, the east, as it associated with death, and charnel grounds. Could this be the reason why they cannot make their request at the eastern gate? See also *Temiya-jātaka* (Chapter 1), when the driver takes Temiya by the eastern, not the western, gate.

42. This is the verse that Alsdorf argues begins the story (Alsfdorf 1957: 3–6). For discussion of this, and the relationship of early verses with the *Cariyapiṭaka*, see Gombrich 1985 and Appleton 2010a: 99 ff.

43. The elephant is the second treasure (*ratana*) of the Universal Monarch (see DN 17, *Mahāsudassana Sutta*, where he is also white). In this *jātaka* the elephant is seen as key to the kingdom. While the monarchs of some of the other *Mahānipāta* stories have extended lifespans and features associated with Universal Monarchs (e.g. J 95), this story interestingly does not. Like most others of the *Mahānipāta* it is a very 'human' kingship. Indeed in none of the Great Ten is the kingship described explicitly associated as involving a Universal Monarch. The elephant is not termed a 'treasure' again until the end, when Vessantara assumes the kingship, when it is called the 'elephant treasure' in the prose narrative: an example of the way vocabulary as well as events recur as the events unravel in reverse order (Ja VI 588).

something from inside me, like my head. They are just asking for something external; I will fulfil their wish.' Thinking this, while still mounted on the elephant, he said:

> 'I give what the brahmins ask me, and I do not waver:
> The tusked trumpeting elephant in rut, fit for riding, the best of elephants.' (22)

And he consented.

> The king, the bringer of prosperity to the kingdom of the Sivis, with his heart freed by letting go (*cāgādhimānaso*),
> Got down from the back of the elephant and gave it as a gift to the brahmins. (23)

The ornamentation on its four feet was worth four hundred thousand coins. The ornamentation on its flanks two hundred thousand; the woollen cloth under its belly a hundred thousand; the three nets on its back, one of pearls, one of gold, and one of jewels, three hundred thousand; the bells on its ears two hundred thousand; and the woollen rug on its back a hundred thousand; the jewel on its frontal globe[44] one hundred thousand; its three head ornaments[45] three hundred thousand; the adornment at the root of the ears two hundred thousand; the adornment around its two tusks two hundred thousand; the auspicious jewel[46] on its trunk two hundred thousand; the adornment for its tail one hundred thousand. So, not taking into account priceless items, the decorations on the body were worth two million, two hundred thousand coins.[47] The ladder for mounting was worth a hundred thousand; its feeding pot a hundred thousand; [489] So that makes two million, four hundred thousand, so far. But there was also a jewel on the parasol on its back, the jewelled crest, the jewel in the string of pearls, the jewel in its goad, the jewel in the pearls on the wrapping round the elephant's throat, and a jewel in the frontal globe. These six items

44. See PED 221.

45. PED 594 says 'a kind of head ornament, perhaps ear-ring or garland, worn around the forehead.'

46. PED 726 suggests an auspicious mark, but I am taking Cone's 'lucky jewel' as being more likely (PGPV 10–11).

47. The maths make it 2,400,000 coins, and then with the other two hundred thousand, 2,600,000 coins. Could something have been added on at some point? Whereas some numbers such as a 'thousand,' as in the number of verses attributed to this story at its outset, can be generic, the maths in *jātaka* stories for specific numbers where items have been listed usually works out correctly, so this anomaly is puzzling.

were priceless, so with the priceless elephant there were seven priceless items, and he gave them all to the brahmins. In addition, there were the elephant's attendants, five hundred families altogether, with mahouts and keepers. And when he made this gift, there were tremors in the earth, of the kind that have just been described.

Explaining the matter the Teacher said:

Then there was this awe-inspiring event;
Then there was something to make the hair stand on end:
When the great elephant was given away, the very earth[48] trembled. (24)
Then there was this awe-inspiring event;
Then there was something to make the hair stand on end:
When the great elephant was given away, the city shook. (25)
Then the city was thronged with people, and there was a great deal of shouting,
When the great elephant was given away,
The bringer of prosperity to the kingdom of the Sivis.[49] (26)

Now they say that the brahmins received the elephant at the southern gate[50] and, sitting on the back of the elephant, with the people all around, they went to the middle of the city. And when the people saw them they shouted out, 'Hoy, brahmins! Where are you going, sitting on the back of our elephant? Where are you taking it?'

'It was given to us by the great king Vessantara,' they replied. 'And who are you?' And, insulting the crowd with rude hand gestures, they went into the middle of the city and left by the northern gate. People were furious, but turned back by a god, they met at the gate of the royal palace and shouted out their reproaches.

Explaining the matter the Teacher said:

Then a great noise arose, a horrifying tumult:
When the great elephant was given away, the very earth trembled. (27)
Then a great noise arose, a horrifying tumult:
When the great elephant was given away, the city shook. (28)
Then a great noise arose, a horrifying tumult,
When the great elephant was given away,

48. The word for 'earth' used is the Vedic *medinī* 'the friendly one'.

49. This earthquake is one discussed in the questions of King Milinda, as vindication and encouragement that the Bodhisatta is acting correctly (for discussion of this and related references, see Appleton 2010a: 69 and *Milindapañha* IV 113–19).

50. Cone translates this section, in small type in F, as part of the main body of the story, a decision supported here.

The bringer of prosperity to the kingdom of the Sivis. (29)

[490] Then, with their tempers stirred because of his gift, the citizens informed the king, and this is what was said:

Mighty lords and princes, merchants and brahmins,
Mahouts and guards, charioteers and foot soldiers; (30)
The Sivis and all the people from country towns[51] met together;
When they saw the elephant being led away, they made this known to the king. (31)
'Lord, your son would destroy your kingdom, sire.[52]
How could he give away our elephant, a lord of elephants, honoured in the kingdom? (32)
How could he give our elephant, with tusks like carriage poles, able to carry great burdens,
Experienced in the terrain of all battles, utterly white, the most precious of elephants? (33)
Covered with its white blanket, devastating, enemy crushing,
Tusked, with its tail fanning, snow-white, like Mount Kelāsa; (34)
With its white parasol, its cushion, and its doctor, skilled in elephant lore;
A noble vehicle, a carrier of kings: he gave that great wealth to brahmins!' (35)

Having said this, they continued:

'If you had just given food and drink, clothes or somewhere to stay,
This would have been a suitable gift, worthy of brahmins. (36)
You are the bringer of prosperity to the lineage of the Sivis,
Sañjaya, how could your son Vessantara just dole out the elephant as a handout?[53] (37)
If you do not act in accordance with what the Sivis say,
Just think—the Sivis will deal with you as they deal with your son.' (38)

[491] When he heard this, the king realized, 'They want to kill Vessantara!' and said:

'Let my country cease to exist, and my kingdom be ruined—
I could not send my son, who is blameless, away from his own kingdom,
Just because the Sivis say so:
For he is my son, the child of my heart. (39)
Let my country cease to exist, and my kingdom be ruined—
I could not send my son, who is blameless, away from his own kingdom,

51. *Kevalo cāpi nigamo.*
52. Norman suggests some form of the optative for *vidhamaṃ.*
53. *Bhājeti* is 'to divide, distribute, deal out'.

Just because the Sivis say so:
For he is my son, born from myself. (40)
I would not cause him harm, for he is nobly good.
It would be disreputable of me, and would cause great evil.
How could I kill with a sword Vessantara, my son?' (41)

The Sivis said:

'Do not use a sword or a stick; he does not deserve to be imprisoned;
Send him away from the kingdom, and let him live on the Crooked Mountain.'(42)

The king said:

'If this is indeed the wish of the Sivis, I shall not oppose their wish.
But let him stay one night and enjoy all pleasures of the senses. (43)
Then, as the night starts to lighten, and the sunrise is near,
Let the Sivis assemble, and let them banish him from the kingdom.' (44)

They agreed to the king's suggestion, and said, 'He can stay one night.' He sent them on their way. To impart the message to his son, he told a royal steward[54] to send the news to him. He agreed, and went to Vessantara's palace and informed him about what had happened.

[492] These verses have been given explaining the matter:
'Get going, my steward; go quickly and tell Vessantara:
"The Sivis, sire, and people from all the market towns, are angry with you and have assembled together. (45)
Mighty lords and princes, merchants and brahmins,
Mahouts and guards, charioteers and foot soldiers;
All the Sivis and people from all the market towns have gathered together. (46)
And as the night starts to lighten, and the sunrise is near,
The Sivis have assembled, and will banish you from the kingdom."' (47)
The royal steward, quickly acting on the king of Sivi's command,
Adorned with bracelets on his arms, in fresh clothes, sprinkled with sandalwood powder, (48)
His head bathed, with water still on it, and wearing jewelled earrings,
Reached the delightful palace of Vessantara. (49)
There he saw the prince, enjoying his own pleasures,
Sitting surrounded by his ministers like Vāsava amongst the Thirty-Three Gods. (50)
The royal steward quickly delivered his message to Vessantara and said,

54. *Kattar* or steward; DP I 624–5. He comes up again towards the end of the story and is addressed with the same first three words, another example of chiasmus in the story (see v. 672).

'I am going to tell you something terrible. Please do not be angry
With me, lord of charioteers.' (51)

Crying as he greeted him, the royal steward spoke to the king:

'Great King, who looks after our every wish, you are my supporter.
I am going to tell you something terrible. May they let me breathe easy! (52)
The Sivis, sire, and people from the country towns, are angry with
You and have met together. Mighty lords and princes, merchants and brahmins, (53)
Mahouts and guards, charioteers and foot soldiers;
All the Sivis and people from the country towns have gathered together. (54)
And as the night starts to lighten, and the sunrise is near,
The Sivis are assembled, and will banish you from the kingdom.' (55)

The Great Being replied:

'But why are the Sivis angry with me? I do not see any wrongdoing.
Tell me, royal steward, on what grounds are they banishing me?' (56)

[493] The steward said:

'Lords and princes, merchants and brahmins,
Mahouts and guards, charioteers and foot soldiers,
They are appalled at the gift of the elephant.
Because of this they are banishing you.' (57)

Hearing this, the Great Being was delighted, and said:

'I'd give my heart, or an eye!
What is external wealth to me—gold, money, pearls, a jewel of lapis lazuli?[55] (58)
If I saw anyone who came and asked me, I would give my arm!
I would give, and I would not hesitate: my mind delights in giving. (59)
Let all the Sivis expel me and even kill me!
I will not give up giving, even if they cut me in seven pieces.' (60)

Hearing this, the steward delivered another message—not one given by the king, nor one given by the people of the city, but one that came from his own mind:[56]

'The Sivis and the people of all the country towns have met together and speak in this way:

55. *Veḷuriya* is either beryl or lapis lazuli.

56. The word is *mati.* Creative suggestions are often the result of a *deva*'s intervention, as we see here, and perhaps in the case in the water-spirit question coming to Bherī too, at the end of *Mahosadha-jātaka.*

"Let the lord who keeps good vows go to the Mount Ārañjara, by the
shore of the Kontimārā River."'[57] (61)

Now they say that he spoke in this way as he was under the sway of a *devatā*.

Hearing this the Bodhisatta said, 'Very well, I will go on a journey taken by criminals, but they banish me for no other fault than my giving the elephant. In that case, I shall make the great gift, of the seven hundreds.[58] Let them give me the space in the city on one day so that I can make this gift. When I have made the gift myself, on the third day I shall leave.' And he said:

[494] 'I will go on the road that those who do wrong go,
Just please allow me a night and a day, until I have made my gift.' (62)

The steward said, 'Certainly, sire, and I shall inform the citizens,' and left.

The Great Being summoned an army guard and addressed him. 'Tomorrow I am going to give a donation of the seven hundreds—seven hundred elephants, seven hundred horses, seven hundred chariots, seven hundred women, seven hundred cows, seven hundred female slaves, seven hundred male slaves—and supply various kinds of food and drink and suchlike, including even spirits. Please make the arrangements, of all things of a quality suitable to be given.' So, having considered carefully the seven hundredfold gift, he dismissed his ministers and alone went to Maddī's living quarters, and sitting on the royal couch, he started to have discussions with her.

Explaining the matter the Teacher said:

The king spoke to Maddī, she whose every limb is lovely, and said,
'Whatever I have given you that is to be found—wealth and grain, (63)
Money or gold or pearls, plentiful beryls—all of this, store away,
Including the wealth given to you by your father.' (64)
The princess Maddī, whose every limb was loveliness, enquired of him,
'Sire, where should I store this? Answer me this.' (65)

Vessantara said:

'Maddī, be generous to those who are good, and who deserve it.

57. Ārañjara is in Majjhimanidesa, and is said to be where beautiful women bathe (DPPN).

58. This gift assumes particular importance in the final life (Ja I 74) as it is through the recollection of this, and its recollection by the Earth, that the Bodhisatta vanquishes Māra and then attains awakening.

For there is no other certain foundation for all living beings than
generous gifts.' (66)

[495] She said, 'Very well,' and concurred with his words. And then he gave her the following advice:

'Maddī, be kind to your children, and to your parents-in-law.
Whoever wishes to come forward as your husband, wait on him
courteously. (67)
And if no one wishes to come forward as your husband when I am
living away,
Then you search out for one, and do not waste away without me.' (68)

And then Maddī thought to herself, 'Why on earth is Vessantara making these speeches?' And she asked him, 'Why, sire, do you speak in such a bizarre way?' The Great Being replied, 'Dear one, the Sivis are furious at my giving away of the elephant, and banish me from the kingdom. Tomorrow I'll make a great gift, of the seven hundreds, and on the third day I am going to leave the city.' And he said this:

'I go to the forest, beset with wild, ferocious animals,
My life is in doubt, all alone, in the great forest.' (69)
Maddī, whose every limb was loveliness, addressed him:
'What! What are you saying?[59] That is a terrible thing to say! (70)
It just is not right, Great King, that you go all alone.
O warrior, wherever you go, there I go too. (71)
If it is death with you or life without you,
Then that death is a much better choice than life without you. (72)
Death on a blazing fire, as one unified flame,
Is better than life without you. (73)
[496] Just as the female elephant follows her noble tusked elephant of
the jungle,
As he moves over difficult terrain and mountain passes, rough and
smooth. (74)
In this way, I am going to follow you, and bring our children.
I will be a light burden, and I will not cause trouble for you.' (75)

Then she described the Himalayan region, as if she had seen it before:

'Seeing these children, with their sweet voices and dear little speeches,
Sitting amongst the bushes in the forest, you will not remember the
throne.[60] (76)

59. Amended to *abbhu me, kathan nu bhaṇasi* with Cone from *abhumme kathaṃ bhaṇasi* (F). *Abbhu* is an expression of horror; see DP I 186.

60. The phrase at the end of this line, 'you will not remember the throne' is

Seeing these children, with their sweet voices and dear little speeches,[61]
Playing amongst the bushes in the forest, you will not remember the throne. (77)
Seeing these children, with their sweet voices and dear little speeches,
In a delightful hermitage, you will not remember the throne. (78)
Seeing these children, with their sweet voices and dear little speeches,
Playing in a hermitage, you will not remember the throne. (79)
Seeing these children, adorned and wearing garlands,
In a delightful hermitage, you will not remember the throne. (80)
Seeing these children, adorned and wearing garlands,
Playing in a delightful hermitage, you will not remember the throne. (81)
Whenever you look at the children dancing and wearing garlands
In a delightful hermitage, you will not remember the throne. (82)
Whenever you look at the children dancing and wearing garlands,
Playing in a delightful hermitage, you will not remember the throne. (83)
Whenever you look at an elephant, the noblest beast, of sixty years of age,
Prowling alone in the forest, you will not remember the throne. (84)
Whenever you look at an elephant, the noblest beast, of sixty years of age,
Prowling in the evening and in the morning, you will not remember the throne. (85)
[497] Whenever you look at a male elephant in front of a herd of young elephants,
All keeping together, and the noble elephant will be trumpeting, of sixty years of age.
Hearing him roar, you will not remember the throne. (86)
Whenever you look at forest blossoms, and forests thronged with animals of prey and deer,
And whatever is wished on both sides, you will not remember the throne. (87)
Seeing the *pañcamāli* deer, as they come in the evening,
And the *kinnaras*[62] dancing, you will not remember the throne. (88)
Whenever you hear the rush of the river flowing
And the song of the *kinnaras*, you will not remember the throne. (89)
Whenever you hear the screech of the owl, flying through mountain caves,

---

repeated twenty-two times: the multi-sibilants of *na rajjassa sarissasi* effectively suggest persuasiveness.

61. *Piyabhāṇine* is amended to *piyabhāṇino*, the usual accusative plural form, here and in vv. 78 and 79, in line with v. 76 (Bd).

62. *Kiṃpurisa*: a mythical being, perhaps a *kinnara* (DP I 603).

You will not remember the throne. (90)
Whenever you hear in the forest the animals of prey, the lion,
The tiger, the rhinoceros, and the buffalo, you will not remember the throne. (91)
Whenever you look at the peacock perched on the top of the mountain,
Dancing, surrounded by peahens, you will not remember the throne. (92)
Whenever you look at the peacock, with its richly coloured tail, dancing,
Surrounded with peahens, born from an egg, you will not remember the throne. (93)
Whenever you look at the crested peacock, with its deep blue throat,
Dancing, surrounded by peahens, you will not remember the throne. (94)
Whenever you look at the trees that bear flowers in winter,
Spreading their perfume, you will not remember the throne. (95)
Whenever you look at the earth, green in a winter month,
Covered with red cochineal beetles, you will not remember the throne. (96)
Whenever you look at the trees that bear flowers in winter,
The *kuṭaja*, the flowering *bimba* tree, and the filamented lotus,[63]
You will not remember the throne. (97)
Whenever you look at the forest, flowering in a winter month,
And the falling petals of the lotus, you will not remember the throne.' (98)

[498] In this way Maddī, in just that many verses, extolled praises of the Himalayas, as if she had lived there.

The description of the Himlayas is finished.

3. THE DESCRIPTION OF THE SECTION ABOUT GENEROSITY (*DĀNAKHAṆḌAVAṆṆANĀ*)

Now Queen Phusatī thought, 'My son has been given a very harsh edict. What is he going to do? I'll go and find out.' And she went in a covered carriage and, standing outside the royal door, she heard their conversation, and grieved piteously.

Explaining the matter, the Teacher said:

Hearing the conversation between her son and daughter-in-law,
The queen grieved in sympathy.[64] (99)
'It would be better for me to die from poison, or throw myself off a precipice,
Or throttle myself with a rope. Why do they banish Vessantara,

63. The word is *lomapadmakaṃ* (PED 589 suggests a kind of plant).

64. In *jātakas* the word *karuṇā*, which is used here, in practice always translates well as compassion, its canonical meaning.

Who has done nothing wrong? (100)
Why do they banish my son, Vessantara, who is learned in the texts,
A lord in generosity, open-handed with requests, not at all stingy,
Honoured by hostile kings, and of great renown and reputation,
When he has done nothing wrong? (101)
Why do they banish my son, Vessantara, who supports his parents,
And who pays due respects to people in his family, and to his elders,
When he has done nothing wrong? (102)
Why do they banish my son, Vessantara, who is so considerate of his king and queen,
So considerate of his friends and relatives, indeed of the whole kingdom,
When he has done no wrong?' (103)

[499] In this way she grieved in sympathy, and when she had comforted her son and daughter-in-law, she went into the presence of the king, and spoke:

'Like honeycombs that have been cast away, like mangoes left fallen on the ground,
This will be how your kingdom is, when they banish someone who has done no wrong. (104)
Like a goose with damaged wings in a pond that has dried up,
You will be left alone, sire, rejected by your ministers. (105)
I am saying this to you, Great King: do not overlook your own welfare.
Do not, because of a request from the Sivis, banish someone who has done no wrong.' (106)

When he had listened to her, the king said this:

'I act in honour of what is right, disciplining the symbol of the Sivis.
I banish my own son, dearer to me than life itself.' (107)

When the queen heard this, she lamented:

'The one who in days gone by, banners followed in procession,
Like yellow *kaṇikāra* blossoms, today he will go, alone.[65] (108)
The one who in days gone by, banners followed in procession,
Like a forest of yellow *kaṇikāra* blossoms, today he will go, alone. (109)
The one who in days gone by, armies followed in procession,
Like yellow *kaṇikāra* blossoms, today he will go, alone. (110)
The one who in days gone by, armies followed in procession,
Like a forest of yellow *kaṇikāra* blossoms, today he will go, alone. (111)
[500] Gandhārans, wearing white woollen blankets, who shine like the cochineal beetle,

65. The emendation taken here is suggested here by Norman (1991: II 176), of *yaṃsa* for *yassa*, and is also taken by Cone (PGPV 98).

Used to follow him, in procession. Today he will go alone. (112)
The one who in days gone by used to travel on an elephant,
In a palanquin, on a carriage, how will he go today by foot? (113)
How will the one who, with limbs anointed in sandalwood, is awakened by singing and dancing,
Bear the ascetic's rough antelope hide, the pole for carrying his measure of provisions,[66] and the axe? (114)
Why do they bring[67] yellow ascetic robes and black antelope skins?
Why do they bind the bark onto him, as he goes into the great jungle? (115)
And how can these people, banished by the king, wear these?
What will Maddī do, wearing a dress of bark? (116)
Maddī is used to wearing clothes of fine linen, and Koṭumbara cloth, worth a thousand coins.
What will she do, wearing a dress of bark and *kusa* grass? (117)
She is used to travelling in litters, on a palanquin, on a carriage.
How will she, with her perfect limbs, travel the path today by foot? (118)
She, who has soft-palmed hands, and whose feet always stand on a pleasant footing,
How will this timid one, with her perfect limbs, walk in the forest? (119)
She, who has soft-palmed hands, and whose feet always stand on a pleasant footing,
Who feels constricted even when she walks in golden slippers,[68]
How can she, with her perfect limbs, travel the path today by foot? (120)
She is used to walking garlanded, attended by a thousand women:
How can she, with her perfect limbs, walk in the forest all alone? (121)
When she heard the howl of a jackal, even inside her home, she was immediately frightened.
How shall this timid one, with her perfect limbs, walk in the forest? (122)
When she heard the screech of the owl, that kinsman of Indra,
She used to be terrified at the noise as if possessed by a god.[69]
How shall this timid one, with her perfect limbs, walk in the forest? (123)
Like a bird whose chicks have been killed, seeing an empty nest,

66. *Khārikājaṃ*: the pole for carrying the container for a measure of grain, traditional for an ascetic (DP I 762).

67. Cone notes that this verse is obscure and probably corrupt (PGPV 98).

68. Cone suggests, with K. R. Norman, *pīḷiyamānā* for *pīḷamānā* (PGPV 98 and see also PED 462).

69. The verse refers to gods who are followers of Varuṇa, the lord of the ocean: they are present at the great meeting of deities on the occasion of the *Mahāsamaya Sutta* (DN 20, PTS edn II 259), for instance. Presumably there was some belief that such a deity could take possession of humans: the commentary suggests that Maddī is like a servant girl possessed.

So I shall be worn away by a long sorrow when I come to this empty home.[70] (124)
[501] Like a bird whose chicks have been killed, seeing an empty nest,
My hair will grow grey through not seeing my dear children. (125)
Like a bird whose chicks have been killed, seeing an empty nest,
I'll run here, there, and everywhere, through not seeing my dear children. (126)
Like an osprey whose chicks have been killed, seeing an empty nest,
So I shall be worn away by a long sorrow when I come to this empty home. (127)
Like an osprey whose chicks have been killed, seeing an empty nest,
My hair will grow grey through not seeing my dear children. (128)
Like an osprey whose chicks have been killed, seeing an empty nest,
I'll run here, there, and everywhere, through not seeing my dear children. (129)
Just like a ruddy goose in a pond that has been dried up,
So I shall be worn away by a long sorrow when I come to this empty home. (130)
Just like a ruddy goose in a pond that has been dried up,
My hair will grow grey through not seeing my dear children. (131)
Just like a ruddy goose in a pond that has been dried up,
I'll run here, there, and everywhere, through not seeing my dear children! (132)
In this way, you banish someone who has done no wrong from the kingdom to the forest,
Even though I grieve so badly—I will die, just think about that!' (133)

[502] Explaining the matter the Teacher said:

When they heard her lament, all the ladies of the household
Stretched out their arms and cried aloud. (134)
Like *sāl* trees hurled and crushed by the wind,
Children and wives lie prostrate in the home of Vessantara.[71] (135)
And, as the night starts to lighten, and the sunrise is near,[72]

70. Lament for the real, apparent, or potential loss of children is a recurrent theme, primarily in the poetry and sometimes the prose, of the *Mahānipāta*. It is usually, but not always, expressed by women: see Chapters 1, 3 (on the part of Sāma's parents), 6, and 7. In Chapter 9, it is on the part of a father, and in this story, both parents grieve, as Maddī does at the thought of leaving her children.

71. The same image is used in the *Bhūridatta-jātaka*, when the Bodhisatta, as a *nāga*, goes missing and the wives find out (Chapter 6, v. 80). The wording is identical, except for the name of the hero. The verse is also found in *Vidhura-jātaka* (Chapter 9, v. 181).

72. The first line is identical to the first lines in vv. 47 and 55, and, except for the first word, to that of v. 44. This rather unusual description of dawn is frequent in the

Then Vessantara the king embarked on his giving of gifts. (136)
'Give clothes to those that want clothes, and drink to the drinkers!
Give food to those that need food, and give completely! (137)
Let no one cause trouble to any beggars who have come here,
Give them food and drink to their satisfaction, so that they may go away fully honoured.' (138)
So the beggars, and those who were afflicted[73] and exhausted, gathered together
At the departure of the great king of the Sivis, bringer of prosperity to the kingdom.[74] (139)
'They cut down a robust tree that bears various kinds of fruits,
When they banished Vessantara from the kingdom, one who has done no wrong. (140)
They cut down a stout tree, which granted all wishes,
When they banished Vessantara from the kingdom, one who has done no wrong. (141)
They cut down a tree, which brought all the things one could wish for,
When they banished Vessantara from the kingdom, one who has done no wrong!' (142)
Old and young, and those in middle age, stretched out their arms
And cried aloud at the departure of the great king. (143)
Overseers, eunuchs, and the women of the royal harem
Stretched out their arms and cried aloud
At the departure of the great king, the bringer of prosperity to the Sivis. (144)
All the women who were there, in that city,
Stretched out their arms and cried aloud
At the departure of the great king, the bringer of prosperity to the Sivis. (145)
Whatever brahmins and ascetics there were, and even beggars,
Stretched out their arms and cried, 'It is not right (146)
That Vessantara the king, making a sacrifice in his own home, is sent away from the kingdom at the say so of the Sivis! (147)
[503] He gives seven hundred elephants, adorned in every way,

story, returning at the end of Maddī's long night searching for her children (Ja VI 565), when Sakka comes to ask for her (v. 612), and in the sixth wish of Vessantara (v. 645), when he asks, sensibly, for Sakka to arrange some heavenly food in the morning, after his wife has been returned. At the very end, Vessantara knows that when the night starts to lighten supplicants will come, and Sakka comes to his aid again.

73. Amended to *Te su m'attā* instead of *Te su mattā* in F.

74. Cone moves this section, vv. 138–60, to after the description of the seven-hundredfold gift (Ja VI 504; see PGPV 21–3).

Decked with golden ribbons, elephants with perfumed golden
harnesses,[75]
Mounted with village chiefs with *kusa* grass spears in their hands:
This king, Vessantara, is driven out of his own kingdom! (148–9)
He gives seven hundred horses, adorned in every way,
Noble, thoroughbred Sindhs with swift chariots,
Mounted with village chiefs who carry short-swords and bows:
This king, Vessantara, is driven out of his own kingdom! (150–1)
He gives seven hundred chariots, fully equipped, with banners flying,
Covered in tiger skins and adorned in every way,
Mounted with village chiefs clad in armour, with bows in their hands:
This king, Vessantara, is driven out of his own kingdom! (152–3)
He gives seven hundred women, each standing in her own chariot:
They are clothed completely in gold, with golden ornamented strands,
With golden-coloured adornments, golden-coloured dresses, and
golden-coloured embellishments,
With beautiful hips and slender waists, with curly eyelashes and
charming smiles:[76]
This king, Vessantara, is driven out of his own kingdom! (154–5)
He gives seven hundred cows, each with its own bronze milking pail:
This king, Vessantara, is driven out of his own kingdom! (156)
He gives seven hundred women slaves and seven hundred men slaves:
This king, Vessantara, is driven out of his own kingdom! (157)
He gives seven hundred each of elephants, horses, chariots, and
women, all adorned:
This king, Vessantara, is driven out of his own kingdom!' (158)
Then there was such an awe-inspiring thing, enough to make your hair
stand on end:
When the great gift had been given, the whole earth quaked. (159)
Then there was such an awe-inspiring thing, enough to make your hair
stand on end:
That was when the king was expelled from his own kingdom, and held
his hands in a humble gesture of respect. (160)

[504] And so it was that he gave the great gift of the seven hundreds:[77] the

75. The description of the elephants in these two verses (148–9) appears in the *Janaka-jātaka* when Janaka is leaving the city behind (Chapter 2, vv. 48–9). The same epithets are also used for the horses and chariots as in the Janaka series (Chapter 2, vv. 50–3).

76. For *hasula* and its possible meanings, see PED 731, which suggests some possible association with 'smiling', or being 'charming'.

77. All of this page is assigned commentarial status in F, but like Cone I have translated one section as being likely to be the story itself (Ja VI 504, lines 1–18).

seven hundred elephants, adorned with gold, with golden banners flying, and covered in golden nets; seven hundred horses, adorned in the same way; seven hundred chariots covered with the hides of lions and other animals, and adorned with various jewels of all colours, with golden banners flying, resplendent with all kinds of embellishments; seven hundred noble women of the warrior class, and of others too, of supreme beauty of form; seven hundred women slaves and seven hundred men slaves, well trained and well taught; seven hundred cows, each giving a pailful of milk, and mated with seven hundred bulls; and endless supplies of food and drink. And as he made his act of generosity in this way, the inhabitants of the city of Jetuttara, brahmins, warriors, tradesmen, and labourers all grieved: 'Lord Vessantara, the inhabitants of the kingdom of the Sivis are expelling you as one who gives gifts, and yet you give more!' As it is said:

> Then there arose such a tumultuous noise and uproar:
> 'They banish you because of your generosity, and still you give more!'

And when those that had been given gifts received them, they thought, 'Now, they say, King Vessantara will go into the jungle, leaving us helpless.[78] Whom shall we go to from now on?' And falling hither and thither as if their feet had been cut off, they wailed their grief with a great noise.

Explaining the matter the Teacher said:

> So the beggars, and those who were afflicted[79] and exhausted, gathered together
> At the departure of the great king of the Sivis, bringer of prosperity to the kingdom.[80]

[505] And the *devatās* let it be known over the entire continent of Jambudīpa (India), 'Vessantara is giving a great *dāna*, of noble ladies and other things.' So, through this divine power, warrior noblemen came by carriage and took a noble lady, or some other gift.[81] In this way, warriors,

78. See DP I 102 for discussion of various possibilities in translating *anātha*. There are a number of possible meanings, ranging from 'not begging', 'not being in control', not having a protector and so 'being helpless', to acting like a Jain. I have favoured 'being helpless'.

79. Amended to *Te su m'attā* instead of *Te su mattā* in F.

80. This is the same verse as v. 139.

81. The stress on the noble warriors here perhaps suggests that the noblewomen go to them, rather than to those of other castes. Respect for caste is in fact a common feature of the Bodhisatta's behaviour, as in the *Mataṅga-jātaka*, where the Bodhisatta respects his wife's caste, and does not touch her; their child is conceived through

brahmins, merchants, and labourers derived benefit from the donation, and left. By the evening he was still giving. Then he went back to his own home and thought, 'I shall pay my respects to my mother and father, and then I'll go tomorrow.' He went in a richly decorated carriage. Maddī said, 'I should go with him too, to get permission from my father- and mother-in-law.' And she went with him. When the Great Being had paid his respects to his father, he told him he was leaving.

Explaining the matter the Teacher said:

He addressed king Sañjaya, the most excellent of those who are good:
'You expel me, sire, and I go to the Crooked Mountain. (161)
Whatever beings there are, Great King, of whatsoever kind,
They all go to the realm of Yama[82] dissatisfied with the sense world. (162)
I have offended my own, making the sacrifice in my own city,
And because the Sivis have demanded it, I am expelled from the kingdom.[83] (163)
I will become used to this misfortune in the forest, thronged with animals and deer, rhinoceros, and leopard.
I will do good things; you will sink into the mud.'[84] (164)

Then the Great Being, with these four verses, had words with his father, and then he went up to his mother, asking her for permission to leave his home, and said:

'Give me leave, my dear mother, it pleases me to leave my home.
I have offended my own, making the sacrifice in my own city,
And because the Sivis have demanded it, I am expelled from the kingdom. (165)
[506] I will become used to this misfortune in the forest, thronged with animals and deer, rhinoceros, and leopard.
I will do good things; you will sink into the mud.' (166)

When she heard this Phusatī said:

'I give you leave, my son. May the going forth be successful for you.

Sakka (J 497).

82. The commentary notes that all beings, past and future, encounter this. Yama is the lord of death. The four marks of birth, sickness, old age, and death are regarded as his messengers as warnings to men (DPPN): Yama questions all those that die as to whether they have seen them and taken heed of them. Does this mean that at that moment all beings see that the sense sphere is inherently unsatisfactory?

83. This verse occurs again as the second and third lines of v. 165. For *abhisasiṃ* see DP I 218.

84. This verse is repeated as v. 166.

But let this lovely Maddī, whose hips[85] are beautiful and whose waist is slim,
Stay here with the children, for what will she do in the jungle?' (167)

Vessantara replied:

'I would not undertake to guide her, or indeed even a slave girl, into the forest against her wishes.
Let her follow me if she wishes, and if she does not, let her stay here.' (168)

And then the great king started to make his entreaties. Explaining the matter, the Teacher said:

Then the great king began his pleas to his daughter-in-law:
'You are used to sandalwood. Do not cover your body with dirt and mud. (169)
You wear finest linen. Do not put on a *kusa* grass and bark dress.
It is tough-going living in the forest—do not go, with your auspicious marks!'[86] (170)

The princess Maddī, whose every limb is loveliness, spoke:

'I would not wish for this kind of comfort without Vessantara.' (171)
Then the great king, increaser of prosperity for the Sivis, spoke.
'Now look here, Maddī, listen to the terrible things that are there in the forest. (172)
There are many insects, winged creatures, mosquitoes, and bees. They might
Sting or bite you and it will be even tougher for you. (173)
[507] Think about the other torments which stay by the river:[87]
Snakes, called "goat eaters", that are not poisonous but are very strong. (174)
They wrap their coils around any human or deer that comes near,
In attack, and so bring them under their power. (175)
There are others: animals with black hides—valuable animals, known as "bears".
Any human seen by them does not get away, even by climbing a tree! (176)
Going at loggerheads with one another, horns clashing and striking,
Buffaloes wander down there, towards the river Sotumbara. (177)
When you see herds of deer, wandering in the forest,

85. See PED 715; this is probably *sosaññā*, of beautiful hips, rather than the F *susaññā*, of good understanding.

86. The marks (*lakkhaṇā*) of a great man are the thirty-two marks with which Buddhas and those destined to be Universal Monarchs have at birth. Maddī too, it seems, has such features.

87. Cone amends *ūpa nisevite* to *ūpanisevano* (PGPV 99).

Like a cow longing for her errant calf, what will you do, Maddī? (178)
When you see monkeys gathering together in the treetops,
Making squawking sounds,[88] you will be terrified. (179)
Whenever you hear the screech of the jackal in the city, you tremble
in fear,
What will you do, Maddī, when you have reached the Crooked
Mountain? (180)
Even in the middle of the day, when the birds have gathered together,
The great jungle is filled with noises. Why do you want to go there?' (181)

Then the princess Maddī, whose every limb is lovely, spoke:

'Whatever scary things in the forest you tell me about, all of these I will
be able to bear.
Despite this, I will go, lord of charioteers. (182)
[508] I will stand against *kāsa* reeds, *kusa* and *poṭalika* grass, *usira* roots,
Muñja and *babbaja* grass with my chest.[89] I will not be a burden
to him. (183)
There are many kinds of practices through which a young girl keeps a
husband:
By concealing imperfections through corset bone wrappings that
constrict her hips,[90] (184)
By tending the sacred flame, by sweeping out with water.
Yes, it is bitter being a widow in this world. I will go, lord of
charioteers. (185)
Even if he has not obtained leftovers for her to eat,
A man can seize her hands and seduce her, against her will.
Yes, it is bitter being a widow in this world. I will go, lord of
charioteers. (186)
Grabbing her by the hair and pulling her to the ground,
A man can give great and terrible suffering, and not go away;
Yes, it is bitter being a widow in this world. I will go, lord of
charioteers. (187)
White-skinned sons of widows, grand in their good fortune, give her

88. Reading *dummaggesu plavaṃgame* for *dumagge suplavaṃgame* (PGPV 99). *Plavaṅgama* can be a frog too (SED 715), but the context and commentary suggest a monkey.

89. Reading *muñjababbajaṃ* for *muṇjapabbajaṃ* (ce). See, for *padahessāmi*, *padahati* in PED 409.

90. This is a very odd passage: *udarass' uparodhena gohanubbeṭhanena ca.* We could take it as something to do with dung, as Rouse does, in the woman's readiness to roll up dung balls and fast (see *avidyagohana* [SED 99] + *ubbeṭhāna* 'envelope, wrap'). Cone goes by the commentary *gohanunā kaṭithālakaṃ koṭṭhāpetvā veṭhena* (DP II 69), suggesting some sort of wrapping around the hips with 'cow's jawbone'. I have followed this.

only a pittance, and then drag her around like crows dealing with an owl.
Yes, it is bitter being a widow in this world. I will go, lord of charioteers. (188)
Even if she lives with her family and relatives, rich in bronze,
She doesn't get away from reproach from her brothers and women in the family.
Yes, it is bitter being a widow in this world. I will go, lord of charioteers. (189)
A river with no water is stripped bare, a kingdom without a king is stripped bare:
Women who are widows are stripped bare, even if they have ten brothers.
Yes, it is bitter being a widow in this world. I will go, lord of charioteers. (190)
The banner is the signifier[91] of the chariot, smoke the signifier of fire;
The king is the signifier of the kingdom; a husband is the signifier of a woman.
Yes, it is bitter being a widow in this world. I will go, lord of charioteers. (191)
The woman who is content[92] as a beggar when he is a beggar and rich when he is rich,
The gods praise her, for she does something that is very tough. (192)
I will follow my husband continually, wearing the yellow robes:
I would not wish even to be queen[93] of the earth, without Vessantara.
Yes, it is bitter being a widow in this world. I will go, lord of charioteers. (193)
I would not want even the earth, the bearer of wealth,
Bounded by the ocean and filled with jewels of every kind, without Vessantara. (194)
What kind of a heart do women have—surely it is very hard—
Who wish only for their own happiness when their husband is suffering? (195)
As the great king of the Sivis, the bringer of prosperity, has been banished,
I will follow him, for he is the granter of all my wishes.' (196)

91. The word is *paññāṇaṃ*, which can mean (1) intelligence and (2) a sign, token, emblem (PED 390). For discussion of this, see the introduction to this story.

92. *Kittimā*, meaning 'clever' here, is regarded as a misspelling for *tittimā* 'satisfied, contented' (see PED 215).

93. J VI 263 n. 2 notes that it is a first occurrence here of *icche*, which means 'to rule'.

[509] Then the great king spoke to Maddī, whose every limb was loveliness:

'Leave these young children, Jāli and Kaṇhājinā both,
Go auspiciously beautiful lady, but I will care for them.' (197)

Then the royal princess Maddī, whose every limb was lovely, replied:

'The young children, Jāli and Kaṇhājinā, both of them, are so dear to me.
They will bring joy to our sorrowful life in the forest.' (198)

[510] The great king, bringer of prosperity to the Sivis, spoke:

'They are used to fine and pure rice and well-cooked meat, with fine sauces;
When they are eating the roots of the trees, how will they manage then?[94] (199)
They are used to well-made dishes of gold and silver;
When they are eating the roots of the trees, how will they manage then? (200)
They are used to wearing fine cloth, and the best linen from Koṭumbara;
When they are wearing *kusa* grass clothes, how will they manage then? (201)
They are used to travelling in carriages and palanquins;
When they are running around on foot, how will they manage then? (202)
They are used to sleeping in good roofed houses, with fastened doors;
When they are sleeping at the roots of trees, how will they manage then? (203)
They are used to lying on cushions and couches spread with woollen throws and brightly coloured rugs;
When they are lying down on a rug of grass, how will they manage then? (204)
They are used to being anointed with perfumes, and light sandalwood;
Wearing dirty old rags, how will they manage then? (205)
They are used to resting happily, being fanned with peacock fans.
Bitten and stung by bugs and mosquitoes, how will they manage then?' (206)

As they conversed in this way, the night started to lighten, and when the night sky had become light, the sun rose. The Great Being's adorned carriage, yoked with four Sindh horses, was brought and stopped at the gate of the palace. Maddī paid respects to her parents-in-law, and taking leave

94. Again songlike repetitions of a simple phrase are repeated throughout this sequence of verses.

of the other women and saying goodbye to them, she took the children and climbed into the carriage before Vessantara.

Explaining the matter the Teacher said:

The princess Maddī, whose every limb was lovely, spoke:
'Do not grieve, sire, do not be distracted.
The children will get by just as we will.' (207)
Saying this, princess Maddī, whose every limb was lovely, left.
The lady endowed with auspicious beauty took her children and
followed on the road of the Sivis. (208)
[511] Then the noble warrior, Vessantara the king,
Made his farewells to his mother and father,
And circumambulated them, keeping them to his right. (209)
Then he quickly climbed onto the swift carriage yoked with four horses,
And started on his way to the Crooked Mountain, escorting his wife and
children too. (210)
And then, where there was a large crowd of people, Vessantara the
king made an address:
'We bid you farewell, and go. May our families have good health!'[95] (211)

In this way the Great Being addressed the populace at large. 'Be generous, and create good fortune for yourself.'[96] He gave instructions to them, and, as he was going, the Bodhisatta's mother thought, 'My son, who is so rich in his generosity, should make a gift.' So she had sent to him, on both sides, wagons filled with seven kinds of jewels, and other ornaments. Vessantara took off the jewellery he was wearing on his own body too, and eighteen times he gave valuables to those that asked him, so that there was nothing left over. He left the city, but wished to say goodbye and take a last look, and because of that wish the part of the earth which had his carriage on split off and turned around, so that the carriage was pointed towards the city. He could now see his parents' dwelling. Because of this, there was an earthquake, and other such events:

As he left the city he turned around to have a look:
And the very earth, turbaned with the woods of Sineru, quaked. (212)

When he had looked, he got Maddī to look too, and spoke this verse:

'Come Maddī! Look at this delightful sight, and take it all in:

95. See Norman 1991: II 179 on *āmanta*, which he says is an absolutive used as a stock phrase.

96. This is a loose translation for the word *puñña*—but making merit can sound a bit dull. The word has associations with both the auspicious effect and the action that brings it.

The home of the Sivis, and the abode of my parents.'[97] (213)

[512] Then the Great Being contemplated the sixty thousand ministers who had been born at the same time as him, and the remaining people. Then he turned the carriage back and set it on its way. He spoke to Maddī, 'Dear one, if any suppliants come, watch out for them.' And so she sat looking out. Then four brahmins came to the city who had not been able to get to the great gift of the seven hundreds. 'Where has the king gone?' they asked, and when they were told, 'He has gone after giving his donation,' they asked, 'Did he take anything when he left?'

'He went in his carriage,' was the reply. When they heard this, they followed him, saying, 'Let's ask for his horses.' Maddī saw them coming, and informed him, 'Sire, there are suppliants.' The Great Being stopped the carriage and when they arrived they asked him for his horses. The Great Being gave him his four horses.

Explaining the matter the Teacher said:

Brahmins followed him, and they asked him for his horses.
Asked by them, he gave the four horses to them. (214)

With the horses given away, the carriage poles stood in mid air, and then when the brahmins had gone on their way, four *devas* came, in the guise of red deer, and took up the yoke. The Great Being recognized them as *devas*, and said this verse:

'Come now, sit down, Maddī. This is a great wonder to see.
Our ceremonially honoured horses drive us in the guise of red deer!'[98] (215)

But then another brahmin arrived and came up to them and asked for the carriage. The Great Being lifted his wife and children down and gave

97. This backward glance is paralleled by Vessantara telling Maddī to view his parents' wealth on the mountain of their retreat, the first time they see their approach to bring them back (vv. 717–8)—a last look, and a first, another example of chiasmus.

98. Alsdorf noted that this verse probably elicited the commentarial story about the horses being exchanged for red deer, through a misunderstanding of the word *migarohiccavaṇṇena*, which those that told the story thought meant that the four horses were exchanged for red deer. So they inserted the incident with the gods changing into deer, when it really meant that the horses had the appearance of red deer. This mistake then affects Āryaśūra's version (Khoroche 1989: 48). This sounds likely, for as Gombrich notes in his introduction (PGPV xxv–xxvi), it is a very minor supernatural event for a tale where divine interventions tend to be a little more spectacular.

him the carriage. And, when the carriage had been given, the *devas* simply disappeared.

The Teacher, explaining how the gift of the carriage came to be, said this:

And then a fifth came there, and asked for this carriage.
Asked by him, he gave it, and his mind was not at all perturbed. (216)
Then King Vessantara lifted down his own,
And gave satisfaction to this wealth-seeking brahmin. (217)

[513] And so it was that from that time they all went by foot, and the Great Being said to Maddī:

'You carry Kaṇhājinā, Maddī, for she is light and the younger.
And I'll take Jāli, for he is the older, and heavier too.'[99] (218)

So when he had said this, they each took one of the children and went on their way.

Explaining the matter the Teacher said:

The king took the son and the queen the daughter;
And so they travelled in companionship, chatting affectionately to one another. (219)

The description of the section about generosity is finished.

4. THE DESCRIPTION OF THE ENTRY INTO THE FOREST (*VANAPAVESANAKHAṆḌAVAṆṆANĀ*)

They went on their way and saw some people. 'Where is the Crooked Mountain?' they asked. 'Far away,' was the reply, and so it was said:

'Whenever anyone comes on the road coming from the opposite direction,
We ask, "Where is the Crooked Mountain?" (220)
They see us and grieve, in sympathy, and declare the bad news:
"The Crooked Mountain is far away!"' (221)

The children cried out when they saw trees bearing all kinds of fruit on the road, and through the power of the Great Being, the fruit-bearing trees bent down[100] so that he could reach them, and he picked the fully ripe

99. By the nineteenth century this scene, of Vessantara carrying their son and Maddī their daughter, had become an evocation of domestic happiness; see for instance the Vessantara depiction at Wat Saket in Bangkok (Fig. 10.21).

100. We are now entering a kind of pastoral idyll, like, as Steven Collins has pointed out, the legendary Land of Cockayne. For Collins's analysis of the tale and its many Buddhist 'felicities', see Collins 1998: 497 ff.

fruits and gave them to them. Seeing this, Maddī declared it a miracle, and so it is said:

Whenever the children see the fruitful trees on the mountain sides,
The children cry with wishes for these fruits. (222)
Seeing the children in tears, the abundant trees were alarmed
And bent down to reach out to the children. (223)
Seeing this wonderful thing, which would make your hair stand on end,
Maddī, whose every limb was loveliness, exclaimed her appreciation. (224)
'Surely this is a wonderful thing in the world, which would make your hair stand on end,
By the shining power (*tejena*) of Vessantara, the very trees bow down!' (225)

[514] Now from the city of Jetuttara to the Golden Mountain top it was five *yojanas*, and from there to the river Kontimārā it was another five, and from there to the Arañhara Mountain it was another five, and from there to the brahmin village of Dunivitṭha (Bad Dwelling)[101] yet another five. And from there it was ten *yojanas* to his uncle's city: so the distance from Jetuttara was thirty *yojanas*. But *devas* made the road short, and in one day they had reached his uncle's city. So it is said:

Yakkhas, out of compassion for the children, made the road short,
And in one day they reached the kingdom of Ceta. (226)

So although they set out from the city of Jetuttara only at breakfast time, they reached the kingdom of Ceta, his uncle's city, by the evening.

Explaining the matter the Teacher said:

They travel on the long road to the kingdom of Ceta,
A wealthy, prosperous city, abundant in meat, drink, and rice. (227)

At that time, at his uncle's city, there lived sixty thousand noble warriors, and the Great Being did not enter the centre of the city but sat in a lodging at the gates of the city. Here Maddī washed dust from the Great Being's feet and massaged them. 'I'll let them know that Vessantara has arrived,' she thought, and left the lodging and stood on the road within sight of him. The women going in and out of the city saw her and gathered around.

Explaining the matter the Teacher said:

The Cetan women surrounded the auspiciously marked one when they saw her, saying:[102]

101. Cone has a wonderful translation of Dunnivitṭha in 'Foulstead' (PGPV 30).
102. Preferring *parivāriṃsu* (Bd) here for *parikirimsu* (F).

'This is a lady indeed, delicately nurtured, yet travelling by foot! (228)
Surely this noble lady is used to travelling in carriages and palanquins,
But today Maddī goes in the jungle by foot.' (229)

[515] The general populace saw that Maddī and Vessantara and their children had arrived without a protector, and went to inform the king. The sixty thousand nobles, weeping in grief, came up to him.

Explaining the matter the Teacher said:

Seeing him the Cetan leaders approached him, crying,
'Are you in good health, sire? Are you alright?
Is your father well, and the people of Sivi healthy? (230)
Where is your power, Great King? Where is your circle of chariots?
You have come such a long way without horses and carriages!
Perhaps you came to this region because you were defeated by your enemies?' (231)

And then the Great Being explained to these leaders the reason for his coming there:

'Yes, I am in good health. I am perfectly alright.
My father is well, and the people of Sivi are healthy. (232)
I gave an elephant with tusks like carriage poles, able to carry great burdens,
Experienced in the terrain of all battles, utterly white, the most precious of elephants.[103] (233)
Covered with its white blanket, devastating, enemy-crushing,
Tusked, with its tail fanning, snow-white, like Mount Kelāsa. (234)
With its white parasol, its cushion, and its doctor, skilled in elephant lore;
A noble vehicle, a carrier of kings: I gave that to brahmins. (235)
On this account the people of Sivi were angry with me, and my father distraught in his mind.
The king banished me and I am going to the Crooked Mountain.
Do you know, my friend, a place in the forest where we might stay?' (236)

They replied to the king:

[516] 'You are most welcome, Great King!
It is no misfortune that you have come here.
You have arrived as the lord of whatever you see. (237)
Eat, Great King: vegetables, lotus sprouts, honey, meat,
White rice, raw and cooked; you are here as our guest.' (238)

103. The same epithets are used for verses 233–5 as for verses 33–5, though instead of the third-person *adā dhananti* at the end of v. 35, there is *adās' ham* 'I gave'.

Vessantara replied:

'I accept the hospitable offerings of everything you give to me.
The king has banished me, and I go to the Crooked Mountain.
Do you know, my friend, a place in the forest where we might stay?' (239)

They replied to the king:

'Stay right here, in the kingdom of the Cetans, lord of charioteers,
Until such time as the Cetans go into the presence of the king, the great king of the Sivis,
Who brings prosperity to the kingdom, to plead with him and bring him round. (240)
At whatever time this is, the Cetans will be delighted to serve you,
Taking supplies, and will go as your entourage.' (241)

The Great Being said:

'Please do not set your mind on going to the king to plead with him,
To bring him round. The king is not in charge there. (242)
Haughty are the people of Sivi, both army and citizens.
They wish to destroy the king on my account.' (243)

[517] They said to the king:

'And if, bringer of prosperity of the kingdom, you come into our kingdom,
Exercise monarchy with an entourage of Cetans. (244)
This kingdom is wealthy and prosperous; the countryside is magnificent and fertile;
Set your mind on ruling this kingdom, sire.' (245)

Vessantara answered:

'There is no willingness or thought in me for ruling this kingdom,
Since I have been exiled from my own. (246)
The people of Sivi, both the army and the citizens, would be unhappy
If the people of Ceta were to anoint me king, since I have been banished from that kingdom. (247)
There would be discord between them because of me, and there would surely be
Conflict with the people of Sivi, and a great many people would be harmed. (248)
I accept the hospitable offerings of everything you give to me.
The king has banished me, and I go to the Crooked Mountain.
Do you know, my friend, a place in the forest where we might stay?'[104] (249)

104. This verse repeats verse 239, which itself ends with the question about

In this manner, although asked in various ways, the Great Being did not express a wish for the throne. And then they paid respects with great honour to the king, for even though he did not wish to enter the city, they arranged his lodging for him, made him a curtain of hemp, and had prepared a big bed. They all surrounded it to set up a guard, and he stayed in the lodging one day and one night, under their protection. The next day he ate various kinds of choicely flavoured foods and, surrounded by the leaders, left the lodging. And the sixty thousand nobles accompanied him on the road for fifteen *yojanas*, [518] and, staying at the entrance to the forest, described to him the fifteen *yojanas* that led ahead on the road:

'Truly we will declare to you those skilful ascetics,
Who make the fire sacrifice and have concentrated minds. (251)
Over there there is a rocky mountain, Great King, known as
Gandhamādana,
Where you can stay with your wife and children.' (252)
The people of Ceta, with crying faces and eyes filled with tears, gave
instructions to him.
'So, go there, Great King, facing straight towards it. (253)
Then you will see, dear friend, the delightful mountain known as
Vipula (Abundant),
Crowded with various kinds of trees that provide a cooling shade. (254)
When you have passed that, dear friend, you will see a river known as
the Ketumatī,
A deep river, coming out from a cleft in the mountain. (255)
Between beautiful banks, its waters are in full flood, swarming with flat
fish.[105]
Bathe, drink, and restore yourself there, with your children. (256)
Then you will see, dear friend, a banyan tree with honeyed fruit,
Growing on a delightful peak, and providing a cooling shade. (257)
Then you will see, dear friend, the rocky mountain Nālika,
Its sides thronged with flocks of birds, of many different species,
frequented by *kinnaras* too. (258)
To the north-east of that is the lake, Mucalinda,
With its carpeting of lotuses and white water lilies. (259)
The forest, which always appears like a misty cloud, grassy green,
Strewn with flowers and trees, and trees laden with fruit: (260)
The lion, prowling for meat, plunges into a forest thicket.

---

somewhere to stay that Vessantara has put before, reinforcing the peculiarly interwoven language of the verses in this story.

105. This is possibly the barb fish, the *puntius* or *pethiya* (Rajith Dissanayake).

There, flocks of birds of many colours, in trees filled with seasonal flowers,
Call out to each other's call, with melodious, full-rounded voices. (261)
Going past the difficult mountain terrain and the sources of the rivers,
You will see a lotus pond, surrounded by Indian beech and *arjuna* trees.[106] (262)
Between beautiful banks, its waters are in full flood, swarming with flat fish.[107]
It has even waters, four sides, and is sweetly perfumed. (263)
Build a leaf hut in the eastern part, and when you have it built,
Get busy gathering food from the wild.' (264)

[519] In this way they described to the king a journey of fifteen *yojanas*, and took their leave. But in order to avert fear of danger or harm, they considered the possibility that an enemy might take the chance of hurting him. So, for protection at the entrance of the forest, they appointed a certain experienced and well-disciplined Cetan, saying to him, 'You stop anyone coming or going.' Then they went back to their own city. Vessantara and his wife and children went to the Gandhamādana mountain and stayed there for a day. Then, heading for the north, they passed by the foot of the Vipula mountain and sat down on the banks of the Ketumatī river. There they ate honey and meat given to them by a forester, and they gave him a golden needle. They bathed, drank, and, becoming tranquil, they put aside their cares. They then crossed the river and remained at the roots of a banyan tree, on the ridge of a mountain, sitting down for a while. They ate the fruits of the banyan and reached from there the mountain known as Nāḷika, encircled it, and then came to its north-eastern edge, by the banks of Lake Mucalinda. They entered into the dense forest on a single-track path, and when they had crossed through that, they arrived at the four-sided lotus pond, with the difficult mountainous territory in front of them.

At that moment the king of the gods, Sakka, turned his attention to what was going on, realised what was happening, and thought, 'The Great Being has entered the Himalayas and it is important to get him somewhere to stay.' [520] So he gave instructions to Vissakamma: 'Go, sir, to a valley within the Crooked Mountain, and when you are in a delightful spot, have a hermitage built there.' Vissakamma did so, and going there had constructed

106. See DP I 643 and 605. *Karañja* is the tree *Pongamia pinnata; kakudha* is the tree *Terminalia arjuna*, or myrobalam.

107. The first line of this verse is the same as the first line of v. 256.

two leaf huts, two walking areas, and areas suitable for the night-time and the daytime. At the ends of the covered walking areas he arranged here and there for there to be various flowers and shrubs, and an orchard of banana trees, and made ready everything needed for a hermitage for those who had taken the going forth. Then he wrote the words:

Let anyone wishing to take the going forth have this.[108]

After that, he sent away any non-human spirits, as well as any wild animals and birds who had frightening calls, and went to his own abode.

The Great Being saw the path where only one person could go at a time, and thought, 'This will be somewhere to stay for those taking the going forth.' He left Maddī and the children at the gate of the hermitage and entered it and saw the writing. 'Sakka has seen me,' he realised. Opening the door of the leaf hut, he entered it and laid down his sword and bow and took off his outer clothes; he put on the clothes of an ascetic and picking up the ascetic's staff, he left the leaf hut.[109] He stepped into the walkway and walked backwards and forwards, with the peacefulness of a *paccekabuddha*, who has found awakening for himself, before going up to his wife and children. Maddī wept and threw herself at the Great Being's feet and then accompanied him into the hermitage, and then went into her own leaf hut and put on her ascetic's dress, and then they dressed the children as ascetic's children. And so these four noble people lived in a valley in the Crooked Mountain.

Then Maddī asked the Great Being for a favour. 'Sire, so that we can find different kinds of fruit, you stay here with the children and I will go and bring a variety of fruits back.' From that time, she used to go into the forest for wild fruits, and cared for all three of them. Then the Bodhisatta asked her for a favour. 'Maddī, from now on we should be true ascetics. A woman

108. The *Mahosadha-jātaka* has many written notes (see Chapter 5), but this is the only other of the *Mahānipāta* that describes writing.

109. The adoption of ascetic garb is also seen as symbolically significant in the *Mahānipāta*. It is through doing this, and shaving his head, that Janaka is enabled to leave his kingdom: his wife, Sīvalī, an earlier rebirth of Maddī, salutes him as an ascetic when she passes him on the stairs and thus symbolically releases him from their marriage (Chapter 2: 107). He marks the territory when he has left the city with his ascetic's staff.

is a stain on the renunciate life.[110] So from this time on, do not approach me at an unsuitable time.' She agreed to this. Through the power of the loving-kindness of the Bodhisatta, all the animals around, for three *yojana*s in each direction, also felt loving-kindness for one another.[111]

Every day, when it was sunrise, Maddī rose early and provided food and drink for them, bringing water for rinsing out the mouth, providing a toothpick and sweeping out the hermitage. Then she left the two children with their father and, carrying a basket, a spade, and a scythe in her hands, entered into the jungle. [521] Picking various kinds of woodland roots and fruits, she filled her basket and returned in the evening, left the various fruits in the leaf hut, and then she told the children to go and bathe. And then the four noble people used to sit at the door of the leaf hut and eat various kinds of fruit. After that, Maddī, taking her truly royal children,[112] went to her own leaf hut. Following this routine they spent seven months in the mountain valley.

The description of the entry into the forest is finished.

5. THE DESCRIPTION OF THE EPISODE CONCERNING JŪJAKA (*JŪJAKAPABBAVAṆṆANĀ*)

Now at that time in the kingdom of Kaliṅga, in the brahmin village of Duniviṭṭha (Bad Dwelling), there was a brahmin called Jūjaka, who had earned by begging a hundred *kahāpaṇa*s, which he deposited with a certain brahmin family and then went off in search of more wealth. As he was away for a long time, the brahmin family spent the *kahāpaṇa*s and when he came back, urged for the money, they could not repay him and instead gave him their daughter, Amittatāpanā (Lady Who Is a Scourge to Her Enemies). He married her and went to live in the village of Duniviṭṭha. Amittatāpanā looked after him perfectly. But some other young brahmins saw her happily successful achievement and reproached their wives. 'This

110. Literally 'the brahma-faring life'; that is, life where extra precepts are taken and there is no sexual intercourse. The usual five lay precepts permit and encourage sexual activity with one's spouse. It should not be seen in this context as an unkind negation, rather the active embracing of the 'Brahmā mind', associated, as we see in the next line, with the *brahma-vihāra* of loving-kindness.

111. This sympathetic 'catching' of loving-kindness occurs in *Sāma*, when the forest creatures also feel the loving-kindness of the small family (Chapter 3: 127).

112. The word *devaputte* suggests godlike children. The Rouse translation amends *deva* to *dva*, two, but Cone's choice of 'royal' for this is preferred here.

lady really cares for her old brahmin. Why are you negligent with us?' and the women gathered together by the sides of the river, and in other places, to revile her.

Explaining the matter the Teacher said:

There was a brahmin, called Jūjaka, who lived amongst the people of Kaliṅga.
And his wife was called Amittatāpanā. (265)
Women collecting water from the river went and discussed it,
And, ganging together, they taunted her with great vehemence. (266)
'You certainly have an enemy in your mother! And certainly an enemy in your father!
Who gave you to an old man when you are so young.[113] (267)
Your family conspired to bring harm against you in secret,
Who gave you to an old man when you are so young. (268)
Your family conspired to bring unhappiness for you in secret,
Who gave you to an old man when you are so young. (269)
Your family conspired to bring evil to you in secret,
Who gave you to an old man when you are so young. (270)
Your family conspired to bring unpleasantness for you in secret,
Who gave you to a clapped-out old man when you are so young! (271)
You live an unpleasant life, living with an old man when you are so young.
Death would be better for you than your life. (272)
Even though you are lovely and pretty, your father and mother just could not get you a husband
And gave you to an old man, when you are so young. (273)
You must have done a sacrifice wrong on the ninth day,[114] and not done the fire offering,
So they gave you to an old man, when you are so young. (274)
You must have offended those keeping precepts, who are of great learning,
Ascetics, brahmins, and those following the brahma-faring life,
For you live with an old man, even though you are young. (275)
There is no suffering in being bitten by a snake, no suffering in being harmed by a sword,[115]

113. The second line of this verse is repeated in each verse of vv. 268–71 to reinforce the taunt; repetition also reinforces the mockery in subsequent lines, of the young woman living with the old man. *Dahariyaṃ sati* has been amended to *dahariyā satī* (Ce, A, and PGPV 99).

114. This refers to the offering made on the ninth day of the lunar month (DP II 516). *Aggihuttakaṃ ye* has been amended to *aghihuttakaṃ yā* (PGPV 99).

115. Here *daḍḍham* 'burnt' has been amended to *daṭṭham* 'bitten' (Be, Ce, Vds, PGPV 99).

But looking at an old husband—now that really is fierce suffering! (276)
There is no fun, no sex life[116] and no interesting chat with an old husband.
Even his laughter is not attractive. (277)
Whenever a young man and a young woman meet in private,
Whatever sorrows there are rooted in her heart completely dissolve. (278)
You are a beautiful young woman, desired by men.
Go back to your family—what kind of a good time can an old man give you?' (279)

At their unkind laughter she took her water pot and went home in tears. When the brahmin asked, 'Why are you crying?' she explained what had happened, and spoke this verse:

[523] 'Brahmin, I cannot go to bring back water in the river,
The women mock me at being married to an old husband.' (280)

Jūjaka said:

'Do not do this chore for me. Do not fetch water.
I will bring the water, and they won't be angry with me.' (281)

The brahmin's wife replied:

'But I was not born into the sort of family where you would bring water—
Know this, brahmin: I cannot stay in your house. (282)
If you do not bring me a slave or a slave girl, brahmin—
Know this, brahmin: I cannot stay in your house.' (283)

Jūjaka responded:

'I have no useful skill, no wealth nor grain, brahmin lady,
From where would I bring you a slave or a slave girl, for my honoured lady?
I will wait on my honoured lady, do not be angry with me.' (284)

The brahmin's wife replied:

'Go. I will tell you something that I have heard:
That king Vessantara lives in the Crooked Mountain. (285)
You go to him, and ask him, brahmin, for a slave and a slave girl.

116. The word *rati*, from the root *ram*, 'delight', usually suggests sexual pleasure too. The theme of the old brahmin, incapable of satisfying his wife in bed, is popular in *jātakas* (see for instance *Sattabhastu-jātaka*, J 402). See also v. 279. In fairness to the unfortunately named Amittatāpanā, whose name permits her teasers to dwell on its 'enemy' part, her behaviour until now has been exemplary in comparison with the brahmin's wife in the *Sattubhastu-jātaka* for instance.

When he is asked, this noble man will give you a slave and a slave girl.' (286)

Jūjaka said:

'But I am old and weak. The road is long and difficult to travel!
Do not grieve, honoured lady, do not be out of sorts.
I will wait on my honoured lady. Do not be angry with me.' (287)

The brahmin's wife replied:

[524] 'You are like someone who admits defeat even when they have not engaged in a fight.
That is you, brahmin, defeated without a fight! (288)
If you do not bring me a slave or a slave girl, brahmin—
Know this, brahmin: I cannot stay in your house.[117]
I will resort to unpleasant behaviour. Oh yes, there will be trouble for you. (289)
Whenever you see me adorned for festivals and holidays,
And having fun with other men, O yes, there will be trouble for you. (290)
Through not seeing me, old man, out of grief,
Your hair will become whiter than the Crooked Mountain!' (291)

Explaining the matter the Teacher said:

And so the brahmin, terrified and dominated by his wife,
Worn down by the passion of his desire for her, said this to his wife: (292)
'Make preparations for the journey, brahmin lady, cakes and sugary cakes![118]
Honey balls, well baked, and barley meal, brahmin lady. (293)
I will bring back both of the children as slaves,
And they will wait on you, night and day, tirelessly.' (294)

She quickly prepared his provisions and gave all sorts of orders. So he made a weak spot in the house sound, mended the door, brought firewood from the forest, fetched water in a jug, filled all the bowls, and then he took his ascetic's clothes. He instructed her, 'Dear one, from this time, do not go out at night, and take particular care until my return.' Then, putting on his sandals, he slung his bag of provisions over his shoulder. Ceremonially circling Amittatāpanā, keeping her to his right, he left, with his eyes brimming with tears.

[525] Explaining the matter the Teacher said:

117. These lines are the same as v. 283, with the addition of another line.

118. The brahmin's chosen menu for his journey foreshadows the reason for his demise.

Doing this, the 'kinsman of lord Brahmā'[119] put on his sandals,
After having private discussions with his wife, he circled his farewell, keeping her to the right. (295)
With tears streaming down his face the brahmin, true to his word, left.
Searching for slaves, he travelled to the wealthy city of the Sivis. (296)

He went to the city and asked the people assembled there, 'Where has Vessantara gone?' Explaining the matter the Teacher said:

He went there and spoke to the assembled people.
'Where has Vessantara gone? How might I see the noble warrior?' (297)
The people who were gathered there told him:
'The noble warrior was too generous by nature to your sort, and it was his downfall, brahmin.
He has gone forth from his own kingdom, and lives on the Crooked Mountain. (298)
The noble warrior was too generous by nature to your sort, brahmin.
He took his children and lives in the Crooked Mountain.' (299)

'In this way our king was destroyed, and yet you come back! Just stay right there!' And they pursued the brahmin with sticks and clods of earth in their hands. But he was helped by a *devatā*, and found the road to the Crooked Mountain.

Explaining the matter the Teacher said:

This brahmin, goaded by his wife and greedy with sense desire,
Experienced hard living in the forest, the home of wild animals and rhinoceros, and haunt of the panther. (300)
Taking his *vilva* wood staff, his sacred fire and water pot,
He entered the great jungle where he heard the granter of wishes was. (301)
When he entered the jungle wolves surrounded him,
He cried out, and strayed far from his path. (302)
Then the brahmin, profligate in desire, went on his way unthinking:
Becoming lost and sidetracked by the Crooked Mountain, he uttered these verses. (303)

[526] Surrounded by dogs, he sits in a tree and sings these verses:[120]

'Who knows about the prince, a bull amongst men, victorious,
Unconquered, who is the giver of protection from fear? (304)

119. Brahmins claimed their descent from the god Brahmā; here, as in, for example, v. 433, the term is surely being applied sarcastically, and so this epithet is always placed in inverted commas.

120. This line is in small type in F. The brahmin also does this when he has taken the children.

Is there anyone who knows of the one who is the support of suppliant beings,
The great earth, for he is one who is just like the great earth,
A great king—who can tell me of Vessantara? (305)
Is there anyone who knows of the one who people go to,
Like flowing rivers to the sea, for he is like the ocean,
A great king—who can tell me of Vessantara? (306)
He is like a beautifully banked lake, with clear water, delightful cool water,
Covered with lotus blossoms, where lotus filaments shed their pollen,
A great king—who can tell me of Vessantara? (307)
Like a fig tree by the road, a celestial tree[121] providing shelter,
A cool delightful shade, and a resting place for those who are exhausted,
Such a one is the great king—who can tell me of Vessantara? (308)
Like a banyan tree by the road, a celestial tree providing shelter,
A cool delightful shade, and a resting place for those who are exhausted,
Such a one is the great king—who can tell me of Vessantara? (309)
Like a mango tree by the road, a celestial tree providing shelter,
A cool delightful shade, and a resting place for those who are exhausted,
Such a one is the great king—who can tell me of Vessantara? (310)
Like a *sāl* tree on the road, a celestial tree providing shelter,
A cool delightful shade, and a resting place for those who are exhausted,
Such a one is the great king—who can tell me of Vessantara? (311)
Like a tree on the road, a celestial tree providing shelter,
A cool delightful shade, and a resting place for those who are exhausted,
Such a one is the great king—who can tell me of Vessantara? (312)
I am lamenting in this way as I have come into the great jungle:
If anyone can let me know, saying, "I know!" I would be so happy! (313)
So if anyone can answer my lament and can let me know, saying, "I know!"
With just one statement, he would generate great merit!' (314)

[527] Now the Cetan who had been positioned for protection was wandering in the jungle, as he delighted in hunting. He heard the sound of his wailing and thought, 'This brahmin is wailing in order to find the dwelling place of Vessantara. He has not come here to do any good, and will ask for Maddī and the children. I'll kill him right here.' Going up to him he said, 'Brahmin, I am not going to let you go alive.' And he drew up his bow.

Explaining the matter the Teacher said:

121. *Santāna* is one of the five celestial trees (PED 676): the fact that there are five verses on trees suggests the five in Indra's garden, mentioned in the *Nārada-jātaka* (Chapter 8, v. 128 and n. 52; Ja VI 239).

The Cetan hunter wandering in the jungle heard him.
'The noble warrior was too generous to your sort, brahmin.
He has gone forth from his own kingdom, and lives on the Crooked Mountain.[122] (315)
The noble warrior was too generous to your sort, brahmin,
He has taken his wife and children and is staying on the Crooked Mountain. (316)
A good-for-nothing dunderhead you are who leaves to hunt out the prince,
Like a heron a fish in water. (317)
Because of this I will let not let you go alive, brahmin,
And my arrow, when shot by me, will drink your blood. (318)
I'm going to cut off your head, tear out your heart,
And then make a sacrifice with your flesh to the birds in the road. (319)
And, brahmin, when I have torn out your heart,
I shall make an offering of you with your flesh, fat, and head. (320)
Yes, I'll make a nice sacrifice and a well-arranged one, with your flesh, brahmin,
And you will not lead away the wife and children of a royal prince.' (321)

[528] When he had heard what he said, terrified of dying, the brahmin spoke a lie:

'But listen to me, son of the Cetans, I am a brahmin messenger, and so cannot be touched,
Because they do not kill the messenger: this is an ancient doctrine. (322)
All the people of Sivi are appeased, his father wishes to see him,
And his mother is now weak, and her eyes will soon fail. (323)
I have been sent as a messenger. Listen to me, son of the Cetans.
I am going to take the royal prince home. If you know where he is, tell me.' (324)

Then the Cetan thought, 'It sounds like he comes to bring Vessantara back.' And, delighted at this, he tied up his dogs and making the brahmin come down, he sat him down in some branches and, spoke this verse:

'A messenger that is dear is dear to me too. I will give you a full meal, brahmin,
And this water vessel filled with honey, and a venison thigh.
I will show you the area where the granter of wishes lives at peace.' (325)

The description of the episode concerning Jūjaka is finished.

122. This verse is the same as v. 298, and echoes the citizens of Sivi's rejection of the brahmin.

6. THE SHORT DESCRIPTION OF THE FOREST (*CŪḶAVANAVAṆṆANĀ*)

The Cetan fed the brahmin, gave him a gourd of honey and a side of venison as provisions for the journey and, raising his right hand, he pointed him on his way and described the place where the Great Being lived:

That crag there, great brahmin, is the Gandhamādana mountain,
In the place where the king, Vessantara, lives peacefully with his children. (326)
Adopting the brahmin's guise and manners, he has matted hair, a hook and a ladle for sacrifices,[123]
He wears animal hide, sleeps on the ground, and pays homage to the sacred fire. (327)
There dark trees that bear many different kinds of fruit can be seen.
Their peaks are high and look like jet-black mountains in dark storm clouds. (328)
Trumpeting *dhava* shrubs, acacia,[124] *sāl* trees, and creepers that tremble
Sway in the wind like young men drunk for the first time. (329)
Above and encircling the trees can be heard a chorus of singing,
As *najjuha* birds and cuckoos meet in flocks and fly from tree to tree. (330)
[529] Calling to the traveller, they throng the branches and greenery,
Delighting the new arrival, they give pleasure to those who live around,
In the place where the king, Vessantara, lives peacefully with his children. (331)
Adopting the brahmin's guise and manners, he has matted hair, a hook and a ladle for sacrifices;
He wears animal hide, sleeps on the ground, and pays homage to the sacred fire.' (332)

Then he described the hermitage further:

'Mango, wood apple, and breadfruit trees, and *sāl* trees, rose apple,
Beleric, yellow *myrobalan* and Indian gooseberry, fig trees and jujubes.[125] (333)
Beautiful is the movement of the gaub trees, banyans, and Portia trees;[126]

123. See PED 525, which combines the *ca* just before in the line to make the word *camasañ* 'a ladle for sacrificing' rather than *masañ*.

124. *Khadira* is *Acacia catechu*, often known as *Mimosa catechu*.

125. *Harītaka* is *Terminalia chebula*, or Chebulic myrobalan; in Sri Lanka it is known as *aralu* and in India as *harad* or *haritaki*. It is used in ayurvedic medicine for a number of ailments, particularly digestive disorders. *Āmalaka* is *Philanthus emblica*, and is known as *āmla* or Indian gooseberry. It is used in ayurvedic medicine as a tonic and source of vitamin C.

126. *Timbarukkha* is possibly *Diospyros embryopteris* or *malabarica* (DP II 328), the pale-moon ebony tree or gaub. Perhaps the *kapitthana* is *kapītana*, the Pārsipal tree (*Thespesia populnea*; cited in DP II 633), commonly known as the Portia tree?

The honey trees drip with honey, and the fig trees have low branches. (334)
Persimmon and starfruit, grapes and pure honey:
In that place you can pick them for yourself and eat.[127] (335)
There, there are blossoming mango trees, and some with nascent fruit,
Some that are not yet ripe, and some that are. Both are the colour of frogs. (336)
And there a man can pick ripe mangoes with his hands, and even the fruit that is not yet ripe, as well as the ripe, is of the best colour, taste, and perfume. (337)
Oh yes! It seems to me that it is a quite wonderful place,
It just looks so beautiful, like the Nandana Grove, the dwelling place of the gods![128] (338)
Palmyras, coconut trees, and date palms stand like woven garlands in the immense forest,
Like the tops of standards, and are heaped with many kinds of flowers, like stars in the sky.[129] (339)
[530] Kuṭaja trees, crape ginger trees, and *tagara* shrubs,
Trumpet flowers in blossom, laurels and mountain laurels, and mountain ebony.[130] (340)
Pudding-pipe trees, *soma* trees, and plentiful aloe trees,[131]
Puttajīvas and *arjuna* trees and Indian laurel trees in flower. (341)
There are *kuṭaja* trees, *salaḷas*, Indian oak, *kosamba* and *dhava* shrubs,

127. *Pārevata* seems to be another species of *Diospyros embryopteris*, so it is translated here as persimmon, as the fruits of this one can be eaten (PED 455). *Bhaveyya* is possibly *Averrhoa carambola* (PED 500), known usually as starfruit, because when it is cut sideways it makes a five-pointed star.

128. The Nandana grove of the gods is so named because it awakens delight in all who see it; it is where the gods of the Tāvatiṃsa go for their pleasure. See also vv. 343 and 379. This short description of the forest is very 'hands on', with the seer describing with an expression of wonder (*hiṃkāro*) the experience of the fruits as they appear to all the senses first-hand.

129. *Vebhedika* is palmyra palm (PED 630), one of the most prevalent and multi-purpose trees in Southeast Asia. It was often used for making paper in India. *Khajjura/khajjurī* is *Phoenix sylvestris* (DP I 743), a kind of date palm. All the items in this verse are palm trees. Coconuts are maritime trees, so perhaps this element was added in Sri Lanka.

130. *Kuṭṭha* is *Costus speciosus*, or crape or wild ginger. Search 'costus speciosus' at ntbg.org/search.php. *Koviḷāra* is *Bauhinia variegata* (DP I 739), or mountain ebony. Search 'mountain ebony' at pfaf.org.

131. *Uddālaka* is probably *Cassia fistula* (DP I 426); *agaru/agaḷu* is the fragrant wood or resin of *Aquilaria agallocha*, aloe. *Arjuna* is *Terminalia arjuna*, which is used in traditional medicine for heart conditions. *Asana* is *Terminalia tomentosa*, or Indian laurel: the wood is used for furniture and the bark is used for stomach complaints.

And *sāl* trees, strewn with flowers like a threshing floor with straw.[132] (342)
Nearby it, in a delightful piece of ground, there is a lotus pond,
Covered with lotus blossoms, like the Nandana Grove of the gods.[133] (343)
And there cuckoos, in the trees that flower in their season,
Are intoxicated with the juice of the flowers, and calling, fill the mountain with their song. (344)
And the nectar of the flowers drips down, with drops of its goodness, lotus by lotus,
And in that place breezes blow from the south and from the west,
And the hermitage is sprinkled with pollen from the filaments of the lotus. (345)
Tough four-sided trees are there,[134] and both rough and fine rice,
And plenty of fish and turtles swim around, and crabs,
And from the lotus fibres drips nectar, and from the stalks, the lotus milk and its ghee. (346)
A sweet perfumed breeze blows through the forest, filled with many smells,
The forest is steeped in the perfume of the flowers and their foliage. (347)
Bees buzz around in the perfume of the flowers.[135]
At that place there are birds of many colours, so many birds.
They sing to one another and rejoice with their mates! (348)
"Halloo, halloo, happy children! Dearest children! Happy children!
Dearest children!" call the birds who live by the lotus pond.[136] (349)
Woven garlands are there, like the tops of flying banners,
Sweet smelling, with healthy and variegated flowers,[137]
In the place where the king, Vessantara, lives peacefully with his children.

132. *Nīpa* is *Anthocephalus chinensis*, Indian oak (DP II 631). For *kosamba* see DP I 740. The shrub *dhava* is *Grislea tomentosa*, native to India, parts of China and Southeast Asia.

133. This verse also appears as v. 379.

134. *Siṃghāṭaka* means a crossroads, or a square. The commentary suggests that there are big types of this variety, but assumes that the reader would know what it is.

135. The bees line is found in vv. 383 and 397. The next two lines are the same as v. 425; the second line of this couplet is also repeated at vv. 418 and 427: the interleaving of the 'bees' image in these lines skilfully suggests a moving, buzzing effect.

136. Cone suggests the onomatopoeia of this verse well with 'Cheery children, deary children! Deary children! Cheer up dearie!' (PGPV 43).

137. 'Healthy' is not the usual translation for *kusala*, except when enquiring about someone's health, but the word has connotations of both physical and mental health, so it seems suitable here. From an *Abhidhamma* point of view the perception of all the beauties of the forest, and their appreciation with all the senses, would be seen as *kusala vipāka*, the result of former *kusala*, or skilful, 'healthy' past action (see *Atthasālinī* 270).

Adopting the brahmin's guise and manners, he has matted hair, a hook and a ladle for sacrifices,
He wears animal hide, sleeps on the ground, and pays homage to the sacred fire.'[138] (350)

[531] In this way Jūjaka was told about the dwelling place of Vessantara by the Cetan and, delighted, Jūjaka spoke his appreciation and uttered this verse:

'This barley meal steeped in honey, please accept from me.
I give you honey balls and well-cooked barley meal.' (351)

When the Cetan heard this he said:

'Let them be your provisions—take them, I have no need of them.
Now you get going brahmin, at your own pace. (352)
[532] This is the single-track path. It goes straight to the hermitage.
The seer Accuta, with blackened teeth and head grey with dust, lives there. (353)
Adopting the brahmin's guise and manners, he has matted hair and a hook and a ladle for sacrifices.
He wears animal hide, sleeps on the ground, and pays homage to the sacred fire.
You should go there and ask him, and he will point out the path.' (354)
When he heard this the 'kinsman of Brahmā' ceremonially circled his farewell to the Cetan, keeping him to his right,
And then left in high spirits toward the seer Accuta. (355)

The short description of the forest is finished.

7. THE GREAT DESCRIPTION OF THE FOREST (*MAHĀVANAVAṆṆANĀ*)

So the descendant of Bharadvāja[139] went off to see the seer Accuta,
And when he met with him, Bharadvāja's descendant greeted him. (356)
'Are you well sir? Are you in good health sir?
I hope you are keeping yourself going on good gleanings, and many roots and fruit.[140] (357)

138. See vv. 327, 354, 371, and 432, which all repeat the same wording. The use of the same lines and description align the two figures of Accuta and Vessantara in their espousal of true brahminic practices and their spiritual intent.

139. This refers to Jūjaka. Gombrich points out that this name used here is important: in the *Mahābharata*, Bharadvāja is a great seer; the irony is undoubtedly intentional (Gombrich 1985).

140. Verses 357 and 358 are in archaic language, perhaps suggestive of older layers of the text. The greeting is found also in Ja V 323 and Ja V 377. The verses are repeated by the brahmin in vv. 436–7, by Sakka, pretending to be a brahmin, in vv.

I hope there are not many bugs and mosquitoes and creepy-crawlies,
And that the wild animals and deer of the forest are not harming you. (358)

The ascetic replied:

'Yes, I am quite well, brahmin, and I am in good health.
I am keeping myself going on good gleanings, and many roots and fruit.[141] (359)
There are not too many bugs and mosquitoes and creepy-crawlies,
And the wild animals and deer of the forest do not harm me. (360)
I have stayed many rains in my hermitage,
And I do not think that any illness or unpleasant malady has come up for me. (361)
Welcome, great brahmin, you are most welcome.
Come in, dear friend, and let me massage your feet. (362)
Eat, the choice of the most choice fruits: persimmons,[142] almondettes,
Butter-tree flowers,[143] and kashmir fruits,[144] sweet as honey. (363)
This water is cool and has been brought down from a mountain stream,
Drink it, great brahmin, if you are longing for some.' (364)

Jūjaka said:

[533] 'I accept all of your kind offerings, and the water for the guest,
I have come to see the son of Sañjaya, who has been banished.
If you know, would you tell me where he is?' (365)

The ascetic said:

'It is not for any good reason that this honourable sir comes to see the king of the Sivis.

613–4, and, with slightly different wording for his son, by the king in vv. 726–7. See the introduction to this story for the pervasiveness of such courtesies in *Vessantara*.

141. At last the brahmin has found a character who shares his speech patterns, and does not reject him. The ascetic echoes all of his phrases, and is the first character to treat him with immediate kindness. While at this point he is not hoodwinked by the brahmin, however, he soon is.

142. *Tiṇḍuka/tinduka* (PED 303) is *Diospyros embryopteris*, or persimmon.

143. Almondette (*Buchanania lanzan*) is the usual name for *piyāla*. Search 'almondette' at flowersofindia.net; for more detailed info, see giftingtrees.blogspot.com/2011/04/almondette-tree.html. SED 628 gives *piyāla* as *Buchanania latifolia*, which is now called *Buchanania lanzan*. Latin names regularly change in taxonomical descriptions, and in some cases are not the same as in SED (Ven. Nyanatusita has provided this information). Butter tree is the usual name for *madhuka*, which is *Bassia latifolia*; the flowers are eaten and sometimes fermented for alcoholic drinks. See curis.ku.dk/ws/files/36089871/Madhuca_longifolia.pdf.

144. *Kāsumārī* is *Gmelina arborea*, the Kashmir or *gamhar* tree. Its fruit is used for medicinal purposes in ayurvedic medicine.

I think this honourable sir wishes to have the king's devoted wife. (366)
I think you wish to take Kaṇhājinā as a slave girl and Jāli as a slave,
And you have come to lead away these three, mother and children, from the jungle.
The king has no luxuries here—not grain, nor wealth, brahmin.' (367)

When he heard this Jūjaka replied:

'I am someone without anger for you, I do not come to beg.
It is just very good to see a noble one. It is always happy just staying nearby. (368)
I have not seen the king of the Sivis, who was banished by the Sivis, before.
I have come to see him. Would you be able to let me know where he is?' (369)

The ascetic then trusted him: 'Good, I will tell you then. Just stay with me here today.' And he entertained him with various kinds of fruits, and on the next day he showed him his path by raising his hand:

'That crag there, great brahmin, is the Gandhamādana mountain,
In the place where the king, Vessantara, lives peacefully with his children.[145] (370)
Adopting the brahmin's guise and manners, he has matted hair, a hook and ladle for sacrifices,
He wears animal hide, sleeps on the ground, and pays homage to the sacred fire. (371)
There dark trees that bear many different kinds of fruit can be seen.
Their peaks are high, and look like jet-black mountains in dark storm clouds. (372)
[534] Trumpeting *dhava* shrubs, acacia, *sāl* trees, and creepers that tremble
Sway in the wind like young men drunk for the first time. (373)
Above and encircling the trees can be heard a chorus of singing,
As *najjuha* birds and cuckoos meet in flocks and fly from tree to tree. (374)
Calling to the traveller, they throng the branches and foliage,
Delighting the new arrival, they give pleasure to those who live around,
In the place where the king, Vessantara, lives peacefully with his children! (375)
Garlands of musk rose[146] cascade on the delightful part of the ground,

145. These seven verses (370–5) are exactly the same as verses 326–32, given when the Cetan sets the brahmin on his path.

146. Cone says *kareri* is a kind of tree (DP I 646); her 'musk rose' is used here (PGPV 46); the idea is that some sort of flower in clumps drops its petals on the ground. There is a Kareri Lake north-west of Dharamsala.

The green and grassy earth, and there no dust rises. (376)
Like a peacocks' throat, soft to the touch like a tuft of cotton,
Grasses grow all around, not exceeding four fingers length in height.
Mangoes, rose apples, wood apples, and ripe figs grow low;
That forest is a bringer of delight, with trees rich in fruit. (377)
Resembling the colour of a beryl, crowded with schools of fish,
The flowing river water courses there, pure and sweet smelling. (378)
Nearby it, in a delightful piece of ground, there is a lotus pond,
Covered with lotus blossoms, like the Nandana Grove of the gods. (379)
There are three species of lotus in that pond, brahmin,
In varied colours of dark blue, white, and red.' (380)

When he had praised the four-sided lotus pond, he spoke of the Mucalinda lake:

'The lotuses are like linen, white and sweet scented;
The lake Mucalinda is covered with plants of the water. (381)
And at that place unbounded lotuses in flower can be seen, in the summer
And in the winter, covering it with a carpet and surely reaching up to the knee! (382)
The many-coloured perfumed blossoms are always in flower and spread their fragrance,
While bees buzz around in the perfume of the flowers. (383)
[535] And at that place, at the edge of the water, trees stand, brahmin:
Kadamba trees, trumpet-flower trees in blossom, and mountain ebony in flower,[147] (384)

147. *Kadamba* is *Anthocephalus chinensis; pāṭalī* is *Stereospermum suaveolens,* the trumpet-flower tree and *kovilāra* is *Bauhinia purpurea* (Sanskrit *kovidāra*). Cone sensibly puts the following section, from vv. 384–432, as an appendix in her translation. The passage is full of technical terms referring to birds and trees that may be unfamiliar: her meticulous and extensive research is recorded in her notes (for her sources and her translation of this passage, see PGPV, appendix II, 89–96). I am indebted to her for this work. For this translation, the intention has been to focus on narrative flow and to bring the section back into the middle of the story. So notes on the technical terms used in each verse are given together in one note at the end of that verse for easier reading. Latin terms traced by Rhys Davids (PED) and, in particular, Cone, either in her translation or her dictionaries, are given there too; many terms not in her original translation have been found in her dictionaries. English names are used, however, when they can be. Also, for the sake of readability, suggested translations, some of which were posited with a question mark by Cone, have been used, or literal translations of words used where a species is unknown: these are noted too. Pictures of many species can be found on websites pertaining to herbal medicine, ayurvedic medicine, and Himalayan flora and wildlife, which are too numerous to list: a few that seem reliable are cited. I am very grateful to Dr Rajith Dissanayake, Ven. Nyanatusita,

Sage-leaved alangium, redwood, flowering *parichattaka*,
Three-leaved caper and ironwood trees, around Lake Mucalinda.[148] (385)
Black siris, white tulip trees, and Himalayan wild-cherry trees suffuse their perfume,
And there are chaste trees, lucky chaste trees, and flowering Indian laurel trees there.[149] (386)
Paṅguras, medlar trees, *sāl* and horseradish trees in flower,
Screw pine, silk-cotton trees, and oleander in blossom.[150] (387)
Arjuna trees, *ajjukaṇṇas*, and sugar-cane trees stand,
And flame-of-the-forest trees, their tips blazing in full bloom.[151] (388)
The white-leaf tree, the seven-leafed scholar tree, banana, safflower,
The pea tree in flower, the sissoo and caper.[152] (389)
Moringa and *sibala* trees, incense trees in blossom, setageru trees,
Tagara shrubs, Indian valerian herbs, wild ginger plants, and *kulāvara* trees.[153] (390)
Trees young and mature, straight and flowering,
Surround the hermitage on both sides, all around the hut and its fire. (391)
[536] And at that place, at the edge of the waters, there is marjoram in abundance,
And kidney beans, *karati* beans, slithery green algae, and plants of the water.[154] (392)

---

and Ven. Dhammika for help on terms and their modern taxonomy. Many of the trees and flowers mentioned in this section have historically been used for medicinal, as well as many other, purposes. Some implications of this, and the literary function of this passage, are explored further in the introduction to this story.

148. There is a coral *parichattaka* tree in Sakka's heaven. This seems to undergo seasonal stages like its worldly counterpart, as Bhikkhu Bodhi's precisely differentiated translation of these changes demonstrates (See AN IV 117–20; Bodhi 2012: 1083–5).

149. *Padmaka* is *Prunus cerasoides*, the Himalayan wild cherry or chokecherry (ayurvedicmedicinalplants.in). *Sāl* is *Shorea robusta*. *Nigguṇdi* and *siriniggunḍi* are 'chaste trees' and 'lucky chaste trees', respectively (PGPV 90 nn. 9–10); chaste trees have traditionally been used for gynaecological problems.

150. *Paṅgura* cannot be identified. *Sobhañjanaka* is *Moringa oleifera*, the horseradish tree. *Ketaka* is *Pandanus odoratissimus*, the screw-pine tree. *Karṇikāra* is *Pterospermum acerifolium*, the silk-cotton tree.

151. *Ajjukaṇṇa* is *Pentaptera tomentosa*, or possibly *Terminalia tomentosa* (PGPV 91 n. 4).

152. For these see PGPV 91 nn. 5–10.

153. The *tagara*, or valerian, is used for sleeping problems in some medicinal systems. *Maṃsi* is *Valeriana jatamansi*, or Indian valerian, used in traditional medicine for eyes, blood, and liver (www.flowersofindia.net/catalog/slides/Jatamansi.html). For *kuṭṭha* see v. 340.

154. In Sri Lanka, *sevāla* is the current term for green algae found in ponds (Rajith Dissanayake).

Above the natural swaying assafoetida buds, there are flying insects:
And there are *dāsima* and low water plants, and an abundance of low swamp cabbage.[155] (393)
The trees stand covered with flowering creepers, brahmin:
For seven days their blossoms can be worn, and their perfume is not lost. (394)
On both sides of lake Mucalinda, carpeted with blue water lilies, stand flowers that irradiate the forest:
For a fortnight their blossoms can be worn, and their perfume is not lost. (395)
Dark blue butterfly-pea flowers, flowers that seem sprinkled with colour, clusters of mountain flowers in blossom:[156]
The forest is carpeted with *kaṭeruka* and creepers and basil. (396)
Indeed the whole forest is pervaded with the perfume of the flowers and foliage,
While bees buzz around in the perfume of the flowers.[157] (397)
There are three species of gourd by the lake, brahmin,[158]
The fruit of one is the size of pots, of the other two the size of a small drum. (398)
And in that place there is plentiful mustard seed, growing in the water, green in shade,
*Asī*s stand like palm fans, and there are many blue water lilies to be picked.[159] (399)
Jasmine and sun-creeper, dark and smelling of honey, the *aśoka* and *mudayanti*,
The gourd with tiny flowers. (400)
Yellow amaranth and flowering *anoja* and betel creepers grow there,
And flowering flame-of-the-forest creepers climb up the tree. (401)
Kaṭeruhas, hiptage, white-flowered jasmine, smelling like honey, indigo plants,

155. Attributions here are as in PGPV 92. *Hiṅgu* is *Assafoetida ferula*; *dāsima* is unidentified; *nīcekalambaka* is a kind of low *kalambaka* plant (DP I 653; DP II 631); *kalambaka* is *Ipomoea aquatica*.

156. *Nīlapupphi* is *Clitoria ternatea*. This species of *Clitoria* is widely used for medicinal purposes in ayurvedic medicine, and the flowers can be eaten. *Sekadhārī* is not identified; could it be something to do with the flower wearing a 'sprinkle' of colours? *Girikaṇṇika* is *Clitoria ternatea*. As the word means 'mountain clusters' an English term has been used to suggest this too.

157. This last phrase is found also in v. 383.

158. This phrasing echoes v. 380. Gourd is a more likely translation for *kakkaru* than pumpkin here (see DP I 606): Dr Rajith Dissanayake suggests that the first category mentioned could be the gourd still hollowed out and used for pots in Sri Lanka today.

159. *Asī* cannot be identified (PGPV 93 n. 2).

The great-flowered jasmine, shoe flower and safflower.[160] (402)
Trumpet flowers and sea-cotton trees and flowering silk-cotton trees
That look like nets of gold seem as brilliant as the tips of a flame. (403)
Whatever flowers there are, on water or on land,
All of them can be seen there, and that great expanse of water is in this way delightful. (404)
And in that lotus pond, there are all kinds of creatures of the water:
Red fish, *naḷapins*, *siṅgu* fish, crocodiles, *makaras*, and alligators.[161] (405)
There is honey, and licorice plants, and Indian plum, long-stalk plants,
Himalayan wild-cherry plants, fragrant *unnaka*, big nut grasses, dill, and *lolupa*.[162] (406)
Perfumed *tagara* trees abound and, with long stalks,
Crape ginger, Indian spikenard, other kinds of wild ginger and plants, and pea plants.[163] (407)
Turmeric, fragrant plants, beard grass, and guggul, palmyra palms,
Perfume plants, wild ginger, camphor, and fork-tailed shrike.[164] (408)
And in that place there are lions and tigers, and monsters and elephants,
Eṇi deer, antelopes, spotted chital deer, and red deer.[165] (409)
Jackals and dogs, small deer, flying foxes the colour of reeds,[166]
Yaks, the roaming antelope and the leaping antelope, monkeys, *jhāpita* and *picu* monkeys. (410)

160. *Kaṭeruha* has not been identified. *Vāsanti* is *Hiptage benghalensis*.

161. *Makaras* are mythical sea beings; it is possible that water monitor lizards are meant either by, or as well as, these (Rajith Dissanayake). PED 721 suggests 'alligator' for *susu*.

162. *Taḷisa* is *Flacourtia cataphracta*, or Indian plum tree. *Tuṅgavaṇṭaka* is unidentified; it means 'having a long stalk'. As Cone indicates, smell is particularly important here, as the commentary indicates that all are perfumed, in an appeal to the nose as well as the visual and the sweet-tasting.

163. *Padmaka* is *Costos speciosus*, or crape ginger. *Narada* is *Nardostachys jatamansi*, or Indian spikenard, an ayurvedic medicinal herb used for insomnia. *Kuṭṭha* is also *Costos speciosus*, presumably another variety. *Jhāmaka* is unidentified.

164. *Gandhasīla* is unidentified, and so is translated, for its name, as 'fragrant plant'. *Hirivera* (PED 732), a kind of andropogon, is translated here by its common name, 'beard grass'. *Guggula* (DP II 55) is guggul, or *Commiphora mukul Engl.*, a tree native to India whose balsamic gum is particularly fragrant. Though its once high status as a perfume seems to have diminished now in South Asia it would be seen then as offering a very refined appeal to the sense of smell (see McHugh 2012: 285 n. 85). It is also used in ayurvedic medicine (see gugulipid.com/commip.htm). *Coraka* is a plant used for making perfume (PED 273). *Kappura* is camphor (DP I 637). *Kaliṅgara* is fork-tailed shrike.

165. PED 445 gives spotted antelope for *pasata* (*pasada*). There are very few spotted antelopes, however; it is more likely to be a spotted chital deer (Rajith Dissanayake).

166. PED 347 gives *nalasannibha* 'reed-coloured'. PED 467 suggests a monster for *purisālu*, a monstrous being living in the wilderness (Ja V 416).

[538] Large roaming animals and antelopes, bears and many wild oxen,
Rhinoceros, boars, and black mongooses in large numbers.[167] (411)
Buffaloes, dogs, jackals, and apes all around;
Iguanas, chameleons, spotted deer, and panthers.[168] (412)
Hares and birds, lions, wolf-slayers, and octopods;
Peacocks, white geese, and junglefowl.[169] (413)
Greek partridges, cocks, and great eagles, singing out to one another,
Herons, cranes, gallinules, and blue jays, cranes and calling herons.[170] (414)
Hawks, red-backed birds, wild birds, pheasants,
Partridges and francolin partridges, nesting birds and *paṭikuttaka* birds.[171] (415)
Maddālaka, *cetakedus*, the bald-headed birds, partridges, and *nāmakas*;
Celāvakas and *piñgula* owls, *godhakas* and *añgahetukas*.[172] (416)
Indian songbirds and *saggās*, flying high above, owls and junglefowl.
So many different varieties and flocks of birds; so many different kinds of calls! (417)
[539] And in that place there are birds, dark in colour and with beguiling voices,[173]
Singing to one another and rejoicing with their mates. (418)
And in that place there are birds, birds with beguiling voices,

167. *Kakkaṭa* and *katamāya*: the commentary says they are large deer or wild animals (PGPV 95 nn. 1 and 2), so the translation 'antelope' is conjectural.

168. PED 417 suggests ape or a kind of bird for *pampaka*. Given the context, 'ape' is used here and 'wild bird' in v. 415.

169. *Bhassara*: the commentary says this is a white goose; *kakuttha* birds: Cone suggests a wild cock (Sanskrit *kukkutaka*; PGPV 95 n. 6).

170. Cone suggests 'elephant birds' for *nāga* here; as these are native to Madagascar, perhaps great eagles are meant (Rajith Dissanayake). *Dindibha* is the blue jay (DP II 393). *Koñcavādika* appears to refer to two species of heron, but to break the list *vādika* has been translated with reference to its other meaning, of speaking or uttering.

171. DP II 239 gives a pheasant or partridge for *jīvajīvaka*. The unidentified *kulāva* is so like the word *kulāvaka* (DP I 718), a nest, that the translation 'nesting bird' has been made. *Patikuttaka* is not identified.

172. These all seem to be species of birds. Ingenuity admits defeat; no satisfactory name can be found for these unknown species described in a region famous as the heartland of highly varied pheasant, wild fowl, and partridge life. All names in the verse remain unidentified, as in Cone's note (PGPV 95 n. 10).

173. The word *mañju* is derived from a term describing persuasive market traders selling their wares (PED 515). This section is again marked by a kind of woven repetition of lines describing the many-coloured nature of the birds, and accounts of the variety of their calls to one another, a repeated appeal both to the visual and the aural sense of the listener/reader that skilfully suggests birds and their song. Despite mentioning other, sometimes dangerous kinds of wildlife, these harmonious interchanges are the only interactions between the various species delineated here.

White above their fortunate eyes, egg born, with many coloured wings.[174] (419)
And in that place there are birds, birds with beguiling voices, white,
With dark throats and crests, singing out to one another. (420)
There are jungle fowl, crab birds, *koṭṭha* birds and cranes,
Kāḷāmeyya birds and *baḷīyakkha birds*, black geese, parrots, and *saṃka* birds.[175] (421)
Turmeric coloured, red, white, and black:
The vultures, *assafoetida* birds, black geese, parrots, and cuckoos.[176] (422)
Ospreys, geese, spoonbills, *parivedantikā* birds, *pāka* geese,
Birds of great strength, gallinules, and *jīvajīvaka* pheasants.[177] (423)
Doves and sun geese, ruddy geese that roam the river,
Varaṇa birds whose beautiful song resounds at two times, day and night. (424)
At that place there are birds of many colours, so many birds:
They sing to one another and rejoice with their mates! (425)
At that place there are birds of many colours, so many birds:
They all sing beguilingly around the lake Mucalinda. (426)
At that place there are birds known as Indian songbirds; these birds,
They sing to one another and rejoice with their mates. (427)
And at that place there are birds known as Indian songbirds; these birds,
They all sing beguilingly around the lake Mucalinda.[178] (428)
The forest, crowded with *eṇi* deer, the roaming ground of the elephant,
Is covered with variegated creepers and frequented by *kadali* deer. (429)
And in that place there is an abundance of mustard seed, wild rice, and plentiful beans.
The rice has ripened in uncultivated earth, and there is no lack of sugar cane too. (430)
Here is the single-track path, which goes straight up to the hermitage;

174. Many otherwise highly-coloured birds of this region have either a white rim around the eyes (white-eyes) or a kind of soft white eyebrow (white-browed bulbuls or white-browed pinions; Rajith Dissanayake).

175. It has been suggested that *kukutthaka* is the Sanskirt *kukkuṭaka* or *phasianus gallus*, both kinds of jungle fowl and cocks. See dictionary.buddhistdoor.com/word/90224/kukutthaka. The possibility of a 'crab bird' is tentatively suggested by Cone for *kuḷīraka* (PGPV 96). 'Grey-black geese' is given by Cone for *kadamba* (DP I 628).

176. Cone suggests 'vulture' for *vāraṇa* (PGPV 96). *Hiṅgu* is *assafoetida* (PGPV 92 n 5): perhaps the bird *hiṅgurāja* in this verse was named in part after this.

177. The commentary says of *āṭa* that it is a bird with a beak like a ladle; the aptly named spoonbill must surely be meant here (Rajith Dissanayake). Here 'birds of great strength' are the unknown *atibala* 'very strong', which could simply be descriptive.

178. *Karavī[ka]* is the Indian songbird or Indian cuckoo (DP I 645).

The one who reaches it does not know hunger, thirst, lack of good humour, there,
In the place where the king, Vessantara, lives peacefully with his children![179] (431)
Adopting the brahmin's guise and manners, he has matted hair and a hook and ladle for sacrifices.
He wears animal hide, sleeps on the ground, and pays homage to the sacred fire.' (432)
[540] Hearing this, the 'kinsman of Brahmā' circled the seer, keeping to his right.
In high spirits he left, to the place where Vessantara was. (433)

The great description of the forest is finished.

8. THE EPISODE CONCERNING THE CHILDREN (*KUMĀRAPABBAṂ*)

Jūjaka then went on the path described by Accuta and reached the four-sided lotus lake and thought, 'Now it is late in the day, Maddī will have come back to the hermitage, and womankind is obstacle-making. Tomorrow, when she has gone to the forest, I'll go to the hermitage and ask Vessantara for his children and I'll leave before she gets back.' So he climbed up into a ridge in the mountain and went to sleep in a comfortable place.

Now, during the night, Maddī had a dream and it went like this: a certain dark man, wearing two yellow robes, and with red garlands adorning both ears, came and frightened her with a weapon in his hand. He arrived and entered the leaf hut and grabbed Maddī by the hair, threw her on her back to the ground. Then, as she was screaming, he dug out her eyes, cut off her arms and split her breast and took out her heart, dripping with blood, and took it with him as he left. She woke up and was terrified, and thought, 'I have just had the most terrible dream. There is no one who is equal to Vessantara in interpreting dreams: I must ask him.' [541] She went into Vessantara's leaf hut and tapped on the door. The Great Being said, 'Who is it?' She replied, 'It is Maddī, sire.'

'Dearest one, why have you come here and broken our arrangement by coming at an unsuitable time?'

'Sire, I do not come through the power of the defilements: it is just that I have had a terrible dream.'

'Then tell me about it,' he said. When she had explained the events

179. The second line repeats the second line of vv. 331, 350, etc.

as they had happened to her, the Great Being saw the meaning of the dream. He thought to himself, 'I am going to fulfil the perfection of giving. Tomorrow a suppliant will arrive and he will ask for the children. I will comfort Maddī, and then send her away.' 'Maddī, you must have been in an uncomfortable position, or had some food that disagreed with you, and your mind was unsettled: don't be frightened.' Comforting her, he kept her in ignorance and sent her away. When the night had given way to light, she went about her business and embraced her two children, and kissed their heads. She advised them, 'Today I had a terrible dream—do take care, you two.' Entrusting the children to the Great Being with the words, 'Sire, take care of the children,' she took her basket and with tears flowing from her eyes went into the woods to look for roots and fruit.

Now Jūjaka thought, 'She will be gone by now.' Climbing down from the mountain ridge he went on the single-track path in the direction of the hermitage. The Great Being left his leaf hut and sat on a slab of rock as if he were a golden image. 'Now the suppliant will come.' And, as if he were a drunkard anxious for his drink, sat watching out for his arrival. The children were playing at his feet. He watched the path and saw the brahmin arriving, and as if assuming the yoke of generosity, which had been abandoned for seven months, said, 'Come over here, brahmin.' With great happiness he spoke this verse to the young Jāli:

> 'Get up now, Jāli, and be a support: it is as if something from the past is in view.[180]
> I might just see a brahmin, and delight overwhelms me.' (434)

[542] Hearing this the boy said:

> 'I see him too, dear one. He certainly seems to me to be a brahmin.
> Perhaps he is a suppliant, and will be our guest.' (435)

Saying this, the boy paid respects, and rising from his seat asked him if he could take his things. When the brahmin saw him, he thought, 'This will be Jāli, Vessantara's son. From now on I am going to speak to him with great harshness.'

'Clear off, clear off!' And he snapped his fingers.

180. The commentary suggests this means he is remembering the suppliants who came from all directions when he was in Jetuttara. It could of course be applied to his 'past life' contact with the brahmin, who is described at the end of the story as an earlier rebirth of the Buddha's cousin Devadatta, who plotted against him in his final life and who assumes the role of villain in many *jātakas*.

'This brahmin is really far too harsh,' the boy thought, and looking at his body, saw the eighteen human defects that denote bad character.[181] The brahmin approached the Bodhisatta and gave him a greeting:

'Are you well sir? Are you in good health sir?
I hope you are keeping yourself going on good gleanings, and many roots and fruit.[182] (436)
I hope there are not many bugs and mosquitoes and creeping creatures,
And that the wild animals and deer of the forest are not harming you.' (437)

The Bodhisatta also greeted him and said:

'Yes, I am quite well, brahmin, and I am in good health.
I am keeping myself going on good gleanings, and many roots and fruit. (438)
There are not too many bugs and mosquitoes and creeping creatures,
And the wild animals and deer of the forest do not harm me. (439)
For seven months I have lived this sorrowful life in the forest.[183]
This is the first brahmin we have seen, who seems just like a god,
Carrying his *vilva* stick, sacred fire, and water pot. (440)
Welcome, great brahmin, you are very welcome.
Come in, dear friend, and let me massage your feet. (441)
Eat, the choice of the most choice fruits: persimmons, *piyāla* fruit,
Bassia flowers, and kashmir fruits, sweet as honey. (442)
This water is cool and has been brought down from a mountain stream.
Drink it, great brahmin, if you are longing to drink.' (443)

When he had said this, the Bodhisatta thought, 'This brahmin has not come to the great jungle without a reason: I'll not waste time, and I'll ask him his reason for coming here.' And he said this verse:

[543] 'In what capacity, and for what reason, have you come to the great jungle?
Do explain to me in answer.' (444)

Jūjaka said:

'You are just as the river that flows at all times and never dries up,[184]

181. Maddī has sometimes been termed as having auspicious marks. The brahmin however appears to have their inauspicious counterparts.

182. Verses 436–7 are the same as 357–8. The Bodhisatta's response is the same as the ascetic's (vv. 359–60).

183. The Bodhisatta's statement that it is a 'sorrowful life' echoes Maddī's sentiments that the children will bring joy in their 'sorrowful life', in v. 198.

184. *Vārivāha* is literally a 'water carrier' and so a rain cloud or, more usually, a river (PED 609). The river is considered greatly auspicious and is usually used in a very positive

So I have come to make a request: at my request, give me your
children.' (445)

When he heard this the Bodhisatta was filled with joy, and, as if placing a purse of a thousand coins into an outstretched hand, he roared out, sounding throughout the mountain valley:

'I give and I do not waver, take them, brahmin, as master!
The princess left in the morning, and she will come back with her
gleanings in the evening. (446)
For one night, stay here, and then go in the morning, brahmin,
She will have washed and anointed them, and they will be wearing
garlands. (447)
For one night, stay here, and then go in the morning, brahmin,
Then when you go they will be adorned with various flowers and
anointed with various perfumes,
Carrying all kinds of roots and fruits as provisions.' (448)

But Jūjaka said:

[544] 'I do not wish to stay, I want to get going.
There might be an obstruction to me, so I will go, lord of charioteers. (449)
They are not generous, you know. Women are obstacle makers.
They know spells. They get the wrong end of the stick. (450)
Out of faith, you are making a gift, so don't make me see their mother.
She will put up obstructions, so I will go, lord of charioteers. (451)
Summon your children, and do not make me see their mother.
Out of faith you are making a gift, and in this way your auspicious
merit will grow and prosper. (452)
Summon your children, and do not make me see their mother.[185]
It is through giving to one such as me, O King, that a person will go to
heaven.' (453)

Vessantara replied:

'And if you do not wish to see my devoted wife,
Then let their grandfather see them, Jāli and Kaṇhājinā both. (454)
Seeing these children, with their charming dear little speeches,

---

sense in Pāli literature. For instance in AN II 56 and III 53 the generous man receives streams of merit described in this way, flowing to him just as the waters go down to the ocean. Water and generosity are inextricably associated in the Southern Buddhist tradition: the ancient custom was to pour water into the hands of a recipient to mark the irreversibility of a gift. Water is also poured in ceremonies for the transference of merit.

185. As so often in this *jātaka*, often songlike repetition is used to reinforce a strong sentiment.

He will be happy and pleased, and will give you a great deal of
wealth.' (455)

But Jūjaka replied:

'I am frightened of being robbed or harmed—listen to me, royal prince,
The king might have me beaten with a stick, or might sell me, or kill me.
Deprived of wealth and slaves, I will be told off by my wife, a
kinswoman of Brahmā.' (456)

[545] Vessantara said:

'But seeing these children, with their charming and dear little speeches,
The great king of the Sivis, the bringer of prosperity to the kingdom,
Who stands firm in *dhamma*, will be overtaken by joy and happiness,
And give you plenty of wealth.' (457)

Jūjaka said:

'No. I will not do as you suggest:
I will take the children as servants for my wife.' (458)

When they heard this harsh speech, the children rushed round to the back of the leaf hut and then ran taking hold of a clump of trees, but there, thinking that Jūjaka might come and get them, trembling, they ran here, there, and everywhere, unable to stay put. They went to the banks of the four-sided lotus pond and, putting on their strong bark clothes, they went into the water, immersed themselves in the water, and put a lotus leaf on their heads and stayed there.

Explaining the matter the Teacher said:

Then the children, trembling at the speech of the cruel man,
Ran here and there, Jāli and Kaṇhājinā both. (459)

Jūjaka could not see the children, and reproached the Bodhisatta: 'Lord Vessantara, you have just now given me the children, but as soon as I said that I would not go to the city of Jetuttara, but would take the children as servants for my wife, you gave a hand signal to them. This made the children run away while you sit there, as if you did not know. I don't think there is anyone in the world who is such a great liar as you!' When he heard this the Bodhisatta was shaken, and thought, 'They will have run away.'

'Do not worry, brahmin, I'll fetch the children.' And getting up he went behind the leaf hut, and realizing that they had gone into the forest thicket, [546] he followed the trail of their footprints to the banks of the lotus pond. When he saw these went into the water he realised they must be staying put under the water. And summoning them, he spoke these two verses:

'Come, dear son, fulfil my perfection,
Consecrate my heart and do just as I say.[186] (460)
Be a steady boat that takes me on the ocean of becoming,
For I shall cross to the farthest shore, and bring freedom to the world and its gods.' (461)

Then he called out, 'Jāli!' The prince, hearing his father's voice, thought, 'Let the brahmin do to me what he wants, I will not go against what my father says.' And raising his head, he removed the lotus leaves and came out of the water and fell at the Great Being's right foot, and sobbed, clutching him firm by the ankle. Then the Great Being said, 'Dear one, where is your sister?'

'Dear father, those beings in whom fear arises protect themselves.'

And the Great Being, realizing that they must have come to some mutual agreement, said, 'Come here, dear Kaṇhā!' And, summoning her, he spoke these two verses:

'Come, dear daughter, fulfil my perfection,
Consecrate my heart and do just as I say. (462)
Be a steady boat that takes me on the ocean of becoming,
For I shall cross to the farthest shore, and bring freedom to the world and its gods.' (463)

And so she then also thought, 'I will not go against what my father says.' And she came out from there and threw herself at the Great Being's left foot, and sobbed, clutching him firm by the ankle. Their tears fell on the Great Being's feet, which were the colour of the lotus in full bloom, and his tears fell on their backs, which were the colour of golden dishes. Then the Great Being raised them, and gave them words of comfort. 'Dear Jāli, do you know the great pleasure in giving that I have? Help me to attain my greatest wish.'[187] Saying this, just where he was, he placed a price upon his head, as if valuing oxen. And he gave these directions to his son: 'Dear Jāli, when you wish to be clear[188] of the brahmin, [547] you will become free if you give the brahmin one thousand coins. And, as for your sister, she is

186. The word 'consecrate', used by Cone and Rouse for this verse, is an excellent choice for a verb that refers to the sprinkling and anointing of kings. (PGPV 52; J VI 282). For discussion of this see Gombrich's introduction (PGPV xvii). Appleton notes this is the only time the word 'perfection' is used in *jātaka* verse (Appleton 2010a: 57).

187. The word *ajjhāsayaṃ* seems to mean, literally, 'hanging on' or 'leaning on' and then becomes an inclination or a wish (DP I 38; PED 11).

188. The word is *bhujissa*, associated with purification and cleansing, used when redeeming or freeing a slave (PED 506).

unusually beautiful: if anyone of low birth gave the brahmin money for her, it would be a breach of caste. No one but a king would be able to pay by the hundreds. So, if your sister wishes to be free of the brahmin, let her become free through the gift of a hundred slaves, a hundred slave girls, a hundred elephants, a hundred horses, and a hundred bullocks, and a hundred gold coins.' Setting a price on the children, he comforted them and led them to the hermitage. Then, he took some water in a jug and said, 'Now, come here, brahmin.' He made an aspiration for complete ominiscience and, while pouring the water, he declared, 'Omniscience is a hundred times, a thousand times, a hundred thousand times more dear to me than my child.' And the great earth resounded, as he gave to the brahmin the gift of his children.[189]

Explaining the matter the Teacher said:

Then, taking the children, Jāli and Kaṇhajinā both,
The bringer of prosperity to the kingdom of the Sivis gave the brahmin his gift. (464)
Then, taking the children, Jāli and Kaṇhajinā both,
He gladly gave the brahmin his children, the supreme gift of all. (465)
And then there was an awe-inspiring thing, enough to make your hair stand on end:
For the great earth quaked at the gift of the children. (466)
And then there was an awe-inspiring thing, enough to make your hair stand on end:[190]
When the king, holding his hands in a gesture of respect, gave his children, who had dwelled in happiness.
The bringer of prosperity to the kingdom of the Sivis gave the brahmin his gift. (467)

[548] When the Great Being gave his gift, great joy arose. 'Ah, I have given an excellent gift.' He stood still, considering his children. Jūjaka entered into the forest thicket and cut a creeper with his teeth. Then he bound the boy's right hand and the girl's left hand together, and went off, beating them with creepers.

Explaining the matter the Teacher said:

Then the cruel brahmin cut a creeper with his teeth,
Bound their hands with the creeper, and beat them with a creeper. (468)

189. See Appleton 2010a: 70 for discussion of the way this event is perceived as a vindication of the virtue of the act, in the questions asked by King Milinda.

190. Again, the proclamations of the Teacher acquire an almost incantatory quality through repetition of one line in the next verse.

Then taking a rope and taking a stick,
Scourging them, the brahmin led them as the king of the Sivis looked on. (469)

When he beat them, their skin broke and blood streamed out. And at the time when they were being hit they put their backs against each other's. Then, on an uneven piece of ground, the brahmin lost his footing and fell, and the tough creeper slipped off the children's hands. Weeping, they ran away and went up to the Great Being.

Explaining the matter the Teacher said:

Then the children ran away, freed from the brahmin,
And with eyes streaming with tears, the boy looked at his father. (470)
Quivering, like a leaf on a bodhi tree,[191] he paid homage at the feet of his father,
And, when he had paid homage to his father, he spoke in this way: (471)
'Dear Father, we have got away and now you can see us.
Please do not give us away, Father, until we have seen our mother. (472)
Dear Father, we have got away and now you can see us.
Please do not give us away, Father, until our mother is here.
And then let this brahmin here sell us or kill us as he please! (473)
Splay-footed, dirty-nailed, and swollen-calfed is he;[192]
He has a long underlip, bad manners, projecting teeth, and a broken nose! (474)
He is pot-bellied, crooked-backed, and his eyes are aslant.
His beard is red and his hair is greeny-yellow. He is pocked with wrinkles and blemishes. (475)
He has bloodshot eyes, and great hands, crooked and deformed; he wears a black antelope hide.
He is really not a human, but a terrifying ghoul! (476)
[549] What kind of human or *yakkha*, who feeds off flesh and blood,
Comes to the forest and asks you for your wealth, dear father?
How can you just watch as we are taken off by this monster? (477)
Surely your heart is made of iron, or bound tightly up,
If you do not react at this money-grabbing, cruel, profligate brahmin who drives us like cattle? (478)
Let Kaṇhā stay right here: she does not know anything.
She cries like a little doe separated from its herd, crazy for milk.' (479)

[550] When he had said this, the Great Being was silent. Then, the boy made this lament about his mother and father:

191. *Assatha* is *Ficus religiosa*, the *bodhi* tree (DP I 267).

192. DP I 155 suggests *andhanakha*, meaning dull, dirty nails, for *addhanakha* here.

'This is not too painful for me. This is to be expected for a man.
But that I won't see my mother, that is more painful than this.[193] (480)
This is not too painful for me. This is to be expected for a man.
But that I won't see my father, that is more painful than this. (481)
My wretched mother will weep for a very long time
When she cannot see her daughter, the lovely Kaṇhājinā. (482)
My wretched father will weep for a very long time
When he cannot see his daughter, the lovely Kaṇhājinā. (483)
My wretched mother will weep for a long time in the hermitage
When she cannot see her daughter, the lovely Kaṇhājinā. (484)
My wretched father will weep for a long time in the hermitage
When he cannot see his daughter, the lovely Kaṇhājinā. (485)
My wretched mother will weep for a very long time,
At midnight and through the night. Her tears will run dry,
like a river. (486)
My wretched father will weep for a very long time,
At midnight and through the night. His tears will run dry,
like a river. (487)
These rose-apple trees, *vedisa* trees, and chaste trees:
All these different trees we leave today![194] (488)
These fig trees and breadfruit trees, and these banyan and Portia trees,
With their different kinds of fruit: all these we leave today![195] (489)
These gardens, the cool waters of the river, where we used to play:
These we leave today! (490)
The different flowers we used to wear, which grow on the mountain:
These we leave today! (491)
The different fruits we used to eat, which grow on the mountain:
These we leave today! (492)
These little elephants and horses, and our little oxen, toys that we used
to play with:

193. In the Pāli, these lines of vv. 480 and 481 are exactly the same as vv. 19 and 20 of the *Sāma-jātaka* (Chapter 3), given when Sāma has been shot with an arrow by the cruel king. The resonance is significant: as in the *Sāma-jātaka*, the polarity between the mother and the father is established, here by alternate verses dealing with the mother, then the father, in powerful two-verse repetitions, where only the gender and agreeing adjectives differentiate the parents from one another. This is also suggested in vv. 21 and 22 of the *Sāma*, though the lament then moves on to both of them. These verses have been translated slightly differently in this work.

194. Oddly enough, *vedisa* trees and bodhi trees (*assatha*; v. 489) are not specifically mentioned amongst the trees in the forest. Could *vedisa* derive its name from *vidisa*, an intermediate point in the compass, or intermediate region? See, in SED, *sindhuvārita* 'the five-leafed chaste tree' (*Vitex negundo*).

195. Could *Kapitthana* be *kapītana*, the Pārspipal tree (*Thespesia populnea*)?

These we leave today!' (493)

[551] And, as he was lamenting like this, with his sister, Jūjaka came and, beating them, took them away. Explaining the matter the Teacher said:

The children said this to their father as they left:
'Wish our mother well, Father, and please may you be happy! (494)
These little elephants and horses and bullocks of ours,
Please give them to our mother so she can keep her grief in check. (495)
These little elephants and horses, and our little oxen,
When our mother looks at these she will be able to control her grief.' (496)

Powerful grief for the children arose for the Great Being, and the very flesh of his heart was burning. He was like an elephant seized by a hairy lion, or the moon caught by Rāhu, the god of the eclipse. Shaken right to the core, he could not bear it and, with tears flowing from his eyes he entered the leaf hut and grieved in compassion.

Explaining the matter the Teacher said:

Then Vessantara the noble warrior king made his gift,
And entered the leaf hut and grieved in compassion.
And here are verses of the Great Being's lament: (497)
'Where will the children be today, when they cry in hunger and thirst,
In the evening and when it is bedtime: who will give them food? (498)
Where will the children be today, when they cry in hunger and thirst,
In the evening and when it is bedtime: "Mother, we are hungry, give us some food!" (499)
[552] How will they travel on the road, by foot, and without their sandals,
And with swollen feet? Who will take their hands? (500)
How could he not be ashamed, beating those children who have done no wrong,
Right in front of me? That brahmin has no shame! (501)
Who, with any shame, would beat my slave girl or boy,
Or any other servant, even the most inferior? (502)
Now that I cannot see him, he consciously abuses and beats my dear children,
Like fish stuck in the mouth of a fish trap.' (503)

Then, through his deep affection for his children, this thought came to him: 'This brahmin treats my children far too cruelly.' He could not bear his grief. 'I will follow the brahmin and kill him and bring my children back,' he thought. But then he reflected. 'To feel regrets after the gift has been given, because my children are suffering too much, this is not the practice of good men.' There are two verses of his inner debates, to explain the matter:

'Surely I should take my bow, and bind my sword to my left side?

And bring back my own, my children: their suffering is a punishment for me. (504)
For sure, it is real suffering when my children are hurt,
And knowing the *dhamma* of good men, who regrets when he has made a gift?' (505)

And it is said that at that moment, he remembered the lineage of Bodhisattas, and the gifts given by all Bodhisattas: [553] of wealth, of limbs, of one's life, one's children, and one's wife.[196] He thought, 'All those in the past who become Buddhas would not have done so if they had not given up these five great gifts. I belong to their line: it is not possible for me to become a Buddha if I do not give up my son and daughter.' The perception arose, however, 'You, Vessantara, will not know the suffering of others who have given up their children into slavery, if you follow the brahmin and kill him.' He censured himself in this way. 'It is not fitting to be regretful after giving a gift. Indeed if he kills the children after they have been given, then it is not connected with me.' Setting his mind upon this strong undertaking, he left the leaf hut, and sat at the door of the hut, on a stone slab, like a golden image. [197]

Jūjaka led the children, beating them. And then the prince made this lament:

'Oh yes, it is true what some men say:
Someone who has lost his mother might as well not exist.[198] (506)
Come, Kaṇhā, we will die. There is no purpose in our living.
We have been given by the prince of men to a money-grabbing,
Cruel, profligate brahmin who drives us like cattle? (507)
These rose-apple trees, *vedisa* trees, and chaste trees:

196. This paragraph is put in small type in F, as a gloss for 'of good men.' As it contains important narrative background material for the story, it has been included. The word used here for giving, *pariccagitvā*, is associated with the word *cāga*, the act of giving, or the renunciation required to give. So in the recollection of generosity, *cāgānussati*, it is the recollection of the state of mind, and of renouncing, that is central when one remembers past acts of giving. It is this state of mind, perhaps, of renunciation, that is the key to the importance of these five 'great' acts of generosity (Vsm VII 107–14; Shaw 2006b: 125–7).

197. These are the same images used for him while he awaits the brahmin (Ja VI 541). The verb for 'setting his mind' here is *adhiṭṭhāya*, used at the moment of taking the Bodhisatta vow, and associated with resolve (*adhiṭṭhāna*).

198. Rouse, following the Burmese version, amends *sakāmatā yatthā n'atthi* to *sakā mātā, pitā n'atthi* 'who has no mother is fatherless too' (Bd).

All these different trees we leave behind, Kaṇhā![199] (508)
These fig trees and breadfruit trees, and these banyan and Portia trees,
With their different kinds of fruit: all these we leave behind, Kaṇhā! (509)
These gardens, the cool waters of the river, where we used to play:
These we leave behind, Kaṇhā! (510)
All the different flowers we used to wear, which grow on the mountain:
These we leave behind, Kaṇhā! (511)
All the different fruits we used to eat, which grow on the mountain:
These we leave behind, Kaṇhā! (512)
These little elephants and horses, and our little oxen, toys that we used to play with:
These we leave behind, Kaṇhā!' (513)

Explaining the matter the Teacher said:

As they were being led away, the children got free of the brahmin,
And ran, Jāli and Kaṇhājinā both, here and there and everywhere. (514)

[554] Jūjaka rose quickly and, spitting like the fire at the end of a world aeon,[200] he caught them, rope and stick in hand, saying, 'So you are really smart, running away!' Tying their hands he led them away.

Explaining the matter the Teacher said:

Taking a rope and taking a stick, the brahmin, beating the children,
Led them away even though the king was looking on. (515)

As they were being led away like this, Kaṇhājinā, turned back, looked at her father and called to him. Explaining the matter the Teacher said:

Then Kaṇhājinā called out to him, 'Father, this brahmin beats me with a stick,
As if I had been born a slave in his house! (516)
He is no brahmin, Father! There are good and just brahmins.
But this one is a *yakkha* in the guise of a brahmin, and leads us, father to eat us!
How can you just watch as we are led away by a demon?' (517)

Seeing his little girl going off wailing and trembling, powerful grief welled up in the Bodhisatta, and his heart became hot. His breathing through his nose became snatched, and he sighed hot breaths from his mouth; the tears from his eyes were drops of blood. Recognising that such pain had arisen through no other cause than the fault of his own affections,

199. This and the following five verses use the same phrases as verses 488–93, with the change in the final address to Kaṇhā, instead of the word 'today' (*ajja*).

200. The universe is destroyed at various times; a preponderance of one of the three elements of water, fire, and air engulf it in each world aeon. See MN 28.

he put aside his affection and through the power of his self-knowledge he pulled out the dart of grief, and knew that middleness (*majjhattā*) and equanimity should be developed. Then he sat down in his customary position. Even though they had not reached the entrance to the mountains, the little girl wailed out loud as she walked:

'We have such sore feet, and the road is long and hard-going.
The sun hangs low and the brahmin urges us on. (518)
[555] We call on the spirits of the mountains and the forests!
We prostrate with our head to the spirits of the lake and the river, with its beautiful banks. (519)
Grasses and creepers, medicinal herbs, mountains and forests:
Please tell our mother to keep well. This brahmin is leading us away. (520)
Please, venerable sirs, speak to our mummy, our mother Maddī.
If you want to follow us, then you must do it quickly! (521)
This single-track path goes straight to the hermitage:
If you follow it, you will see us easily. (522)
Oh no! Ascetic lady, when you bring roots and fruit from the forest
And see the hermitage empty, you will suffer so terribly. (523)
Surely it is because she is carrying such a great bundle of gatherings that she is so late
She does not know that we have been tied up by a money-grabbing,
Cruel, profligate brahmin, who drives us on like cattle?[201] (524)
Oh, if we could just see our mother as she comes back in the evening from her gathering.
Our mother would give the brahmin fruit, mixed with honey. (525)
Then, satisfied after enjoying the food, he would not urge us on so hard.
Our feet are swollen, the brahmin urges us on so hard.'
And in this way, pining for their mother, the children made their lament. (526)

The episode concerning the children is finished.

9. MADDĪ

[556] The earth resounded with a roar when the beloved children had been given away to the brahmin, and there was a commotion as far as the Brahmā world. The *devas* who lived in the Himalayas were frightened at heart by the brahmin leading them away, and heard their lament. 'If Maddī returns at the usual time to the hermitage and does not see the children there, she will ask and hear that they have been given to the brahmin.

201. This line is the same as the last lines of vv. 478 and 507, spoken by her brother.

Through her great love she will run and follow them and she will suffer terribly!' And then they said, 'Transform yourself into a lion, tiger, and leopard and obstruct her path until sunset, even though she pleads with you, and do not let her pass through. Then she will reach the hermitage by moonlight. In this way you will also make a guard so that she is not harmed by lions or other wild animals.'

Explaining the matter the Teacher said:

> Hearing the crying of the children, three wild animals of the forest,
> A lion, a tiger, and a leopard, made this statement:[202] (527)
> 'The princess must not return from her gathering this evening,
> But no wild animals in the forest, in our patch, must harm her. (528)
> If the lion, or the tiger, or the leopard were to harm the auspiciously beautiful one,
> Then there would be no more Jāli, and what become of Kaṇhājinā?
> The auspiciously beautiful one would lose both husband and children!' (529)

And then the gods agreed, and taking heed of the *devatā*'s words, changed into a lion, a tiger, and a leopard, and lay down obstructing the path that she was going to be taking. Maddī thought, 'Today I had such a bad dream. I will gather the roots and fruits and get back to the hermitage in good time.' [557] Deeply shaken, she looked out for roots and fruits. But her spade fell from her hand, the strap that held her basket slipped from her shoulder, her right eye throbbed. The trees that bore fruit seemed to have none, and the trees that did not bear fruit seemed to have them. None of the ten directions seemed clear. She thought, 'O what is going on today? This sort of thing just did not happen before!'

> 'My spade falls down and my right eye throbs.
> There is no fruit on the fruit trees, and all the directions seem confused to me.' (530)
> When she was going back to the hermitage in the evening,
> When the sun had set, wild animals appeared in her path.[203] (531)
> 'The sun is hanging low and the hermitage is surely far away.

202. Animals speak frequently of course in early *jātakas*, but rarely in the last ten. In *Bhūridatta* the tortoise cleverly extricates himself from death through deviously clever speech (see Chapter 5).There are a few chatty animals in the Mahosadha, such as the dog, the ram, the parrot, and the mynah bird.

203. This scene is very popular in modern temple art: see for instance Roveda and Yem 2009: 273 and this book (Fig. 10.26), showing a mural at Wat Buak Khrok Luang, Chiang Mai Province, Thailand.

I am bringing their food, the only things they have to eat. (532)
The noble warrior is sitting around in the leaf hut,
Cheering up the hungry children, as he cannot see me return. (533)
Surely my children, in the evening and at bedtime, are like babies thirsty for milk!
O how sorry and wretched am I! (534)
Surely my children, in the evening and at bedtime, are like babies thirsty for water!
O how sorry and wretched am I! (535)
Surely my children wait to rush out to me, like young calves to their mother.
O how sorry and wretched am I! (536)
Surely my children wait to rush out to me, like geese flying over a lake.
O how sorry and wretched am I! (537)
Surely my children wait to rush out to me, when I get near the hermitage.
O how sorry and wretched am I! (538)
A single-track path, the only path, with a lake on one side and a pit on the other.
I cannot not see any other route to get to the hermitage.
O how sorry and wretched am I! (539)
O wild animals of the wood, you of magnificent power, kings of the forest, I pay homage to you.
Be brothers in accordance with *dhamma*! I beseech you, give me a way through! (540)
I am the wife of the noble king who was banished,
And I shall never desert him, as Sītā never deserted Rāma.[204] (541)
You can see your children, when it is time for lying down to sleep,
And I would like to see my children, Jāli and Kaṇhājinā both. (542)
Here is a large bundle of roots and fruit to eat.
I will give you half, but I beseech you, give me a way through! (543)
[558] I am a princess and a mother; my husband is a king and a father.
Be brothers, in accordance with *dhamma*, I beseech you, give me a way through!' (544)

And then the *deva*s considered the time and realised, 'Now it is the time to give her a way through.' And then they rose and went away.

Explaining the matter the Teacher spoke this verse:

204. References to Sītā and Rāma in the *jātaka*s are not frequent, though one story, the *Dasaratha-jātaka* (J 461) specifically deals with them. Gombrich however notes the close and important parallels between the forest episodes and those in the *Rāmāyaṇa* (Gombrich 1985). Justin Meiland has explored various aspects of Maddī's affinity with Sīta in Meiland 2004.

When they heard her sorrowful words,
That were filled with such deep compassion, and were so clear,
The wild animals moved away from the path. (545)

And indeed she arrived at the hermitage after they had let her go. It was the night of the full moon, and when she reached the end of the walking area she could not see the children in the places where they usually were, and said this:

[559] 'This is the place where the children, covered with dirt,
Usually wait to rush out to me, like young calves to their mother. (546)
This is the place where the children, covered with dirt,
Usually wait to rush out to me, like geese flying over a lake. (547)
This is the place where the children, covered with dirt,
Usually wait to rush out to me: it is not far from the hermitage. (548)
Like wild animals,[205] with their ears pricked up,
They usually run around all over the place,
Having fun and joyous, quivering, as if leaping in the air!
But today I do not see my children, Jāli and Kaṇhājinā both. (549)
Like a wild she-goat and her kid, or a bird freed from a cage,
I left the children behind, like a lioness hungry for meat.
But today I do not see my children, Jāli and Kaṇhājinā both. (550)
Sprinkled with sand and covered with dirt, my children usually run around all over the place,
But today I do not see my children, Jāli and Kaṇhājinā both. (551)
They used to come out towards me, from the forest stretching far away,
But today I do not see my children, Jāli and Kaṇhājinā both. (552)
Like kids to a she-goat, they used to come out to me
When they looked out for me far from the hermitage, but I do not see my children now. (553)
Just here they have dropped a toy—a yellow *vilva* fruit.
But today I do not see my children, Jāli and Kaṇhājinā both. (555)
My breasts are full, my heart is torn apart.
Today I do not see my children, Jāli and Kaṇhājinā both. (556)
He lingers on my lap, she hangs on one breast.
But today I do not see my children, Jāli and Kaṇhājinā both. (557)

205. *Migā* perhaps suggests deer here, rather than a more general wild animal, but as it is has just been used to describe the wild animals of the forest, the choice of wording here seems to create a deliberate parallel between the children and the creatures of the forest; in this and other speeches Maddī constantly deploys imagery of wild animals and their young to describe her relationship with her children. Maddī's grief-stricken lament in the forest and on her return to the hermitage are both marked by great repetition, of full and half lines, of her distress. This verse is striking in particular for its skilled observation and a palpable sense of the children's animal delight.

Covered in dirt in the evening, the children wriggle around on my lap.
But today I do not see my children, Jāli and Kaṇhājinā both. (558)
This hermitage here used to seem to me like a festival ground,
But today, as I do not see my children, it seems to whirl around.[206] (559)
[560] Why does the hermitage seem to have so little sound today?
Even the crows do not squawk: my children must be dead! (560)
Why does the hermitage seem to have so little sound today?
Even the birds do not cry: my children must be dead!' (561)

Grieving in this way, she approached the Great Being, and set down the basket of fruit. But she saw him sitting in silence, with no children near him. She said:

'Why are you so silent? My mind is in black night.
Even the crows do not make a noise: my children must be dead. (562)
Why are you so silent? My mind is in black night.
Even the birds do not cry: my children must be dead. (563)
Have some wild animals eaten my children, noble sir?
Or have my children been taken away by someone, into the
inhospitable forest?[207] (564)
[561] Is it that you have sent the dear-voiced children on an errand
To give a message? Is it that they are asleep?
Is it that they were busy with their games and somehow went away? (565)
Their hair cannot be seen, nor their hands and feet,
Did a vulture swoop down for Jāli? Who has taken my children?'[208] (566)

206. The slight movement away from the repetition of the last line gives this verse extra force, and Maddī's disorientation prepares us for the next repetitive line, as her response to the silence, and the certainty her children must be dead.

207. *Iriṇa/īriṇa* 'barren, inhospitable' (DP I 377); this is the first time that Maddī has used a critical term for the forest.

208. The Pāli here is very odd. The commentary elaborates on the narrative in an improbable gloss to *sakuṇānañ ca opāto ti*: 'Now in the Himalayan regions there is a vulture with a bill like an elephant's trunk who swoops down from the sky. "And I ask this: have they been taken by these birds? Or has some other bird swooped down and taken them? Tell me this: who has taken my children?"' For the *hatthiliṅgasakuṇa*, see PED 728 and *Dhammapada* stories, *Dhammapada-Aṭṭhakathā* I 164: this commentarial tale (associated with *Dhammapada* vv. 137–40) describes such a bird swooping down and catching a pregnant queen, who had been too scared to move while her husband ran inside. Despite her terror, the queen kept her presence of mind, and reflecting that animals fear a human voice and might drop her, decided not to give any cry at all but wait until he had taken her somewhere, and then frighten him, so he would run away. Through this wisdom she preserved her own and her child's safety. The bird took her to a large banyan tree in the Himalayas, and she cried to divert him, but went into labour and gave birth. Saved by an ascetic, after carefully ascertaining that both were of the same warrior caste, she managed to get down from her tree. The child later

When she had said this, the Great Being still said nothing. And then she said, 'Sire, what have I done? Is there something that is my fault?' And spoke:

'This is much worse pain. This is a wound like being pierced by an arrow.
Today I do not see my children, Jāli and Kaṇhājinā both. (567)
But this second dart shakes my heart:
Today I do not see my children, and now you do not speak to me. (568)
If you do not explain this to me today, this very night,
Just remember, I will die, and you will not see me in the morning, with life all gone.' (569)

The Great Being thought, 'I will help her dispel her grief for her children by speaking harshly to her,' and he spoke this verse:

[562] 'Is it not the case that Maddī, the renowned princess, with the beautiful hips,
Went out early for her gatherings: why has she come back so late this evening?' (570)

'Maddī, you have a lovely appearance. In the Himalayas there are all sorts of foresters, ascetics, and those with knowledge of magic wandering around. Who knows what you have been up to? You left early and then came back at this time in the evening. Married women do not do that sort of thing, going off into the forest and leaving their children behind. It did not occur to you what might happen to the children, or what your husband thought, when you went off so early and came back by the light of the moon. This is the fault that has given rise to my sorry state!' And so he spoke, pretending to upbraid her. Hearing his words, she said:[209]

'But did you not hear the noise of the roaring lion and the tiger
As they put their heads down to drink at the lake? (571)
An omen came to me as I was wandering through the great forest.
My spade fell from my hand and the band for holding my basket came off my shoulder. (572)
And then I was shaking and frightened, and I paid my respects,
And I paid homage to all the directions, so that there might be safety there. (573)
"Let the prince not be slain by a lion or a leopard;
Let the children not be seized by a bear, or a wolf, or a hyena." (574)
Three wild animals, a lion, a tiger, and a leopard,
Roamed around my path, as I came back in the evening.' (575)

became king (Burlingame 1921 I 249 ff.).

209. This paragraph is in small type in F but I have followed Cone in translating it for its narrative content.

Having just said this much to her, the Great Being did not say anything more until sunrise, so from that time Maddī gave vent to her sorrow in all kinds of ways:

[563] 'Just like a young man serves his teacher, so I looked after my
husband and children,
Day and night, wearing the tangled hair of the brahma-faring ascetic. (576)
Wearing the antelope skin, carrying forest roots and fruit,
I wander, day and night, through love for you, my children. (577)
I have brought golden turmeric for you, my children, to play with,
And yellow *vilva*, and the ripe fruits of the trees.[210] (578)
This lotus bulb, and stalk, and these roots from the lily and water plants,
Mixed with honey: eat them, royal prince, with the children. (579)
Give Jāli the red lotus and the white lily to the princess,
Watch them playing, wearing garlands, Sivi, and call out
"children"![211] (580)
Then, lord of charioteers, notice how Kaṇhājinā
With her sweet and beguiling voice approaches the hermitage. (581)
We have been of accord, in happiness and suffering, since being
banished from the kingdom,
But could you not get me to see Jāli and Kaṇhājinā both? (582)
O, I must surely have reviled, in the world, ascetics or brahmins,
Those following the brahma-faring life, who are virtuous and have
heard much,
That today I cannot see my children, Jāli and Kaṇhājinā both!' (583)

[564] The Great Being still did not say anything to her as she lamented in this way. Trembling at his silence, she went by the light of the moon searching here, there, and everywhere for her children, around the rose-apple and other trees, and the places where they used to play, and when she got to them, crying, she said:

'These rose-apple trees, *vedisa* trees, and chaste trees:

210. The turmeric (*Circuma longa*) and *hāliddi* have misshapen rhizomes which would be good for pretend characters and vehicles as children's toys. Vilva, or bael (*Aegle marmelos*), sometimes known as Bengal quince (*beluva*), has wood used for ascetic staffs, described in this story. The fruit has a hard shell, and so would be suitable for games. Richard Gombrich noted this, along with many other observations recorded in this chapter, in Palī reading classes.

211. The *paduma* can be either a red or white lotus, but I follow Cone in taking it as the more common red (PED 410), with a contrast to the white water lily (*komudī*; PED 229) surely intended. There is great emotional precision of her deranged sense that the children can be called and that her daughter is arriving, akin, in Shakespearean drama, to Lady Macbeth's madness and Ophelia's laments after her rejection in *Hamlet*.

All these different trees, but no sight of the children![212] (584)
These fig trees and breadfruit trees, and these banyan and Portia trees,
With their different kinds of fruit: but no sight of the children! (585)
These gardens, the cool waters of the river, where they used to play:
But no sight of the children! (586)
The different flowers they used to wear, which grow on the mountain:
But no sight of the children! (587)
The different fruits they used to eat, which grow on the mountain:
But no sight of the chldren! (588)
These little elephants and horses, and our little oxen, toys that they used to play with:
But no sight of the children!' (589)
These brown hares and owls, and many *kadali* deer,
They used to play amongst them: but no sight of the children! (590)
These geese, herons and peacocks, with their many-coloured wings,
They used to play with these: but no sight of the children!' (591)

Unable to see her children at the hermitage, she left and entered the forest, with its flowers, and looked all over the place for them. She said:

'These forest thickets filled with flowers that blossom in all seasons,
Where they used to play: but no sight of the children! (592)
These delightful lotus ponds, filled with the sound of ruddy geese,
And covered with water plants and lotuses of blue, red, and white,[213]
Where they used to play: but no sight of the children!' (593)

As she was looking in places to find the children, the Great Being went up to her, and seeing his disconsolate face, she said:

'You have not chopped the wood, you have not brought the water;
The fire is not tended. Why are you brooding, and being lazy? (594)
A dear one meeting with a dear one, my confusion is destroyed,
But today I do not see Jāli and Kaṇhājinā both.' (595)

When she had said this the Great Being sat, still in silence. She was overcome by grief by him not speaking, and trembling, like a wounded fowl, went back to search the places she had searched before, and, when she returned, said this:

'Sire, I do not see the children, or the means by which they have been killed.

212. The next six verses precisely echo Jāli's lament as he leaves, and as he addresses his sister (vv. 488–93 and 508–13), with a change to 'they' rather than 'I' in 488–93 and 'we' in verses 508–13).

213. These two lines occur in *Janaka*, when the Bodhisatta is describing the beauties of Mithilā, which he longs to leave (Chapter 2, v. 47).

Even the crows do not make a noise—surely my children are dead! (596)
Sire, I do not see the children, or the means by which they have been killed.
Even the birds do not cry—surely my children are dead!' (597)

But when she had said this the Great Being still did not say anything. She then, reflecting on her grief for her children, went a third time and searched with the speed of the wind their various haunts. And in one night the area of her hunting for them was fifteen *yojanas*. And then the night started to lighten, and at the moment of dawn she returned, and stood there with the Great Being and grieved.

Explaining the matter the Teacher said:

She grieved in the mountains, she grieved in the woods;
She returned to the hermitage yet again, and in front of her husband wept. (598)
[566] 'Sire, I do not see the children, or the means by which they have been killed.
Even the crows are silent—surely my children are dead! (599)
Sire, I do not see the children, or the means by which they have been killed.
Even the birds do not cry—surely my children are dead! (600)
Sire, I do not see the children, or the means by which they have been killed,
Even though I have searched at the roots of trees, in the mountains, and in the caves!' (601)
So Maddī, the renowned princess, with the beautiful hips,[214]
Stretched out her arms and cried out, and right there collapsed onto the ground. (602)

The Great Being, trembling with the thought, said, 'She is dead! Maddī has died in a strange land, and if she had died in Jetuttara there would have been a great ceremony at her funeral, and two kingdoms would have been rocked. But I am alone in the forest. What shall I do?' A great grief arose in him, but, regaining his mindfulness, he said, 'I will find out how she is.' Getting up, he placed his hand on her heart, and feeling signs of warmth, he brought water in a jug, and, although he had not touched her body for seven months, his grief was so powerful that he could not think of his ascetic way of life, and with eyes filled with tears he lifted her head

214. The Bodhisatta uses the epithets to describe Maddī here in the first line of verse 570, his greeting when she returns in the evening to find the hermitage empty.

and put it against his chest. Then, sprinkling her with water, he stroked her face and her heart.

After a little time Maddī stirred to life, and regained consciousness, and with self-respect and composure (*hiri* and *ottappa*) she got up and paid homage to the Great Being.[215] 'Husband, Vessantara, where have the children gone?' she asked.

'My lady, I gave them as slaves to a brahmin,' he replied.

Explaining the matter the Teacher said:

> He sprinkled the princess, who had collapsed, with water.
> Seeing that her breathing had revived, he said this to her.[216] (603)

[567] In response to her words, 'But sire, why did you not tell me, while I spent the whole night grieving and searching?' the Great Being said this:

> 'At first, Maddī, I did not wish to make you suffer.
> An impoverished old brahmin came to our home as suppliant,
> I gave him our children. Maddī, take comfort, and do not be afraid. (604)
> Look at me, Maddī, and do not grieve too strenuously for the children.
> We will get the children, and while we are alive and in good
> health.[217] (605)
> Children, cattle, grain, and any other wealth in his house,
> A good man gives as a gift when he sees suppliants coming to him.
> Rejoice in what I have done, Maddī. Children are the supreme gift.'[218] (606)

Maddī replied:

> 'I do rejoice in what you have done, sire. Children are the supreme gift.

215. These two qualities, sometimes translated as 'shame' and 'fear of consequence', are said to the guardians of the world, and in traditional *Abhidhamma* are said to be present in all moments of skilful consciousness (*Dhammasaṅgaṇī* 14).

216. There is an occasional disjunct in *jātakas* between prose and verse, as seen here.

217. What he says is *lacchāma putte jīvantā ārogā ca bhavāmase.* Does he mean we will get our children back, or get more? Cone translates suggesting they will have more children, with *lacchāma* used for begetting (PGPV 66). *Bhavāmase* is the first person middle of *bhavati*. But is this not odd if they are living as chaste ascetics? Rouse suggests that they will get them back healthy, which cannot be the translation, as healthy (*jīvantā*) is in the nominative, whereas the children are in the accusative. Does Vessantara think Bodhisattas always get their great gifts returned? The commentary says he makes this statement as they will 'certainly' (*avassam*) see the children, and assumes that he knows that the gifts will be returned. It is not clear, and I have translated on the basis of his confidence that somehow they will see the children while he and Maddī are alive and healthy.

218. *Anumodanā* has a technical meaning in Southern Buddhist countries, as a rejoicing in the merit of anyone's actions, and as a chant involving the transference of merit to other beings.

Now you have given, clear your mind with faith;[219] be a giver of yet
more gifts. (607)
You, O King, the bringer of prosperity to the kingdom of the Sivis,
Amongst humans and beings who are miserly, gave a gift to
a brahmin.' (608)

When she had said this the Great Being said, 'Maddī, what do you say to this? If my mind had not been made tranquil through giving, these miracles would not have happened!' And he related everything, beginning with the roaring of the earth [568]. And then Maddī praised the miracles, and rejoiced in his gift.

'The earth has been made to roar. The sound has echoed to the three
heavens!
Lightning flashed all around, and the mountains resounded, as if in
accord. (609)
Both Nārada and Pabbatā[220] rejoice in this:
Indra, Brahmā, and Pajāpatī,[221]
Soma, Yama, and Vessavana the king.
All the *devas* of the Heaven of the Thirty-Three, and King Sakka,
rejoice!'[222] (610)
And then Maddī, the renowned princess, with the beautiful hips[223]
Rejoiced with Vessantara: for children are the supreme gift. (611)

In this way the Great Being described his act of generosity, and Maddī turned the matter over in her mind. 'Great King Vessantara, the gift you gave was nobly given!' And Maddī praised the act of generosity, and sat

219. The word *pasādehi* is crucial here: it is the quality of faith when it arises that it is said to clear the mind (Gombrich 1988). Acts of appropriate generosity, accompanied by the quality of *cāga,* or letting go, are thought to be the means of doing this (Vsm VII 107–14).

220. These gods are from unspecified heavens, but the latter are known for their wisdom (DPPN).

221. Pajāpatī, literally 'lord of the people' is another name for Māra, the lord of delusion, whose domain extends up to the highest sense-sphere heaven. He is routed on the night of the enlightenment by the Buddha, when Gotama calls the earth to witness of the seven-hundredfold gift of alms he makes as Vessantara. The earth quakes in agreement, remembering this gift and Māra's armies disappear. He tends to turn up to meditators when they are making progress, voicing their secret doubts, but is always routed again when recognised for what he is (see DPPN).

222. The commentary says that these two *devas* were positioned to guard the hermitage, and they delight in the merit of this action, thus validating its worth.

223. See vv. 570 and 602.

down, rejoicing in his merit. And that was when the Teacher told the verse we have just heard.[224]

End of the episode about Maddī

10. SAKKA (*SAKKAPABBAṂ*)

Sakka saw them chatting happily with one another in this way, and thought, 'The earth was made to roar by Vessantara giving his gift, but now some inferior man might approach him and ask him for the virtuous Maddī, who is endowed with all the auspicious marks of beauty, and take her away. Then he would be without a protector and without support.[225] I will approach him in the form of a brahmin, and ask for Maddi. This will get him to gain the peak of the Perfection, so that she will be unavailable for anyone else; then I'll give her back to him, and go away.' At sunrise he then went up to him.

Explaining the matter the Teacher said:

As the night started to show glimmers, and the sun to rise,
Sakka, in the guise of a brahmin, appeared to them. (612)
[569] 'Are you well sir? Are you in good health sir?
I hope you are keeping yourself going on good gleanings, and many roots and fruit. (613)
I hope there are not many bugs and mosquitoes and creeping creatures,
And that the wild animals and deer of the forest are not harming you.'[226] (614)

The Great Being replied:

'Yes, we are well, brahmin, and we are in good health.
We are keeping ourselves going on good gleanings, and many roots and fruit. (615)
There are not too many bugs and mosquitoes and creeping creatures,
And the wild animals and deer of the forest do not harm us. (616)
For seven months we have lived this sorrowful life in the forest.[227]

224. Cone moves the verse from its place within the text to the end of the section. I have kept it where it is, but worded the last statement so that it shows which verse is meant.

225. This is a particularly interesting remark: it is the Bodhisatta whom Sakka sees as needing support and protection, not Maddī.

226. The two-verse response echoing the inquiry recurs throughout the story: see verses 359–60 and the ascetic responding to the brahmin.

227. See the encounter between Jūjaka and Vessantara in v. 440, which is the same as this verse except for the word 'second' rather than 'first', and Maddī's sentiments that the children will bring joy in their 'sorrowful life', v. 198.

This is the second brahmin we have seen, who seems just like a god,
Carrying his *vilva* stick, sacred fire, and water pot. (617)
Welcome to you, brahmin, you are very welcome.
Come in, dear friend, and let me massage your feet. [228] (618)
Eat, the choice of the most choice fruits: persimmons, *piyāla* fruit,
Bassia flowers, and kashmir fruits, sweet as honey. (619)
This water is cool and has been brought down from a mountain stream.
Drink it, great brahmin, if you are longing to drink.' (620)

Then, having extended a greatly courteous welcome to him:[229]

'In what capacity, and for what reason, have you come to the great jungle?
Do explain to me in answer.' (621)

When he had asked him his reason for coming, Sakka said to him: 'Great King, I am old and have come here to ask you for your wife Maddī, give her to me.' And he uttered this verse:

'You are just as the river that flows at all times and never dries up,
So I have come to make a request: at my request, give me your wife.' (622)

When he had said this, the Great Being thought, 'Yesterday I gave the children to the brahmin. How can I exist alone if I give Maddī to you?' But he did not say this, and as if placing a purse of a thousand gold coins into an outstretched hand, free from attachment, free from ties, and free from any kind of clinging, he said this verse, making the mountain resound:

'I give her that you ask from me, and I do not waver,
I do not hold back; my mind delights in giving.' (623)

Speaking in this way he quickly, right there, took a jug of water and, pouring water on his hands, he gave his wife to the brahmin. And at that moment, all kinds of miraculous marvels occurred, of the kind that have been described before.

Explaining the matter the Teacher said:

Taking Maddī by the hand, the bringer of prosperity to the kingdom of the Sivis
Took a jug of water and made his gift to the brahmin. (624)
Then there was this awe-inspiring event, then there was something to make the hair stand on end:

228. The same three verses are in *Sāma-jātaka*, vv. 46–8, with the exception of line 2 in v. 46.

229. The Bodhisatta questions Sakka in exactly the same way as he did Jūjaka (vv. 444–5).

At the giving away of Maddī, the very earth trembled. (625)
And Maddī did not frown; she did not become resentful or weep.
But looking on she was silent, thinking, 'He knows the best thing to do.' (626)

'Brahmin, sir, a hundred times, a thousand times, a hundred thousand times dearer to me than Maddī is omniscience. May this gift be a support for my attainment of omniscience.' Making this wish, he gave the gift. So it is said: [230]

'Having given up Jāli, my daughter Kaṇhājinā, and my devoted wife, queen Maddī,
I did not think of anything other than the obtaining of awakening.[231] (627)
'Neither of my children is disagreeable to me, and Maddī the queen is not disagreeable,
But omniscience is dear, and because of this I have given even those dear to me away.' (628)

And then the Great Being thought, 'How is it with Maddī?' and asking, looked at her face. 'What, sire, are you looking at?' she said, and then she roared with the roar of a lioness:

'I was a maiden wife of my husband and lord.
Let him give me away or sell me or kill me as he wishes.' (629)

[571] And then Sakka, realizing the nobility of their resolve, spoke in praise. Explaining the matter the Teacher said:

Recognising their intention, the lord of the *devas* said this:[232]
'All obstacles, divine and human, are conquered. (630)
The earth has been made to roar. The sound has echoed to the three heavens!
Lightning flashed all around, and the mountains resounded, as if in accord.[233] (631)
Both Nārada and Pabbatā rejoice in this:
Indra, Brahmā, and Pajāpatī,

230. This paragraph is in small type in F, but is included for its narrative content, which helps to explain the background. It is comparable to the aspiration made at the time of giving away the children.

231. See Geiger 1943: 197.

232. The word is *saṃkappa*; *sammāsaṃkappa* is right intention, or right resolve, the second factor of the noble eightfold path. An intention or resolve is stated at the outset of brahminical rituals.

233. These two verses (631–2), with the exception of the last line that leads into verse 633, are the same as verse 609–10, uttered by Maddī at the gift of the children at the culmination of that section.

Soma, Yama, and Vessavana the king.
All the *devas* rejoice; he has done what is hard to do. (632)
Those who do evil[234] do not imitate those who do what is hard to do,
Those that give what is hard to give. The way of the good is hard to follow. (633)
Because of this, the good and the bad have different destinations:
The bad go to hell and the good find relief in heaven. (634)
While dwelling in the forest you have given your children and given your wife:
When you have made the journey in the vehicle of Brahmā,
May this act bring fruit for you in heaven.[235](635)

In this way Sakka delighted in the Great Being's merit. 'And now, without delaying, I should give her back to him, and get on my way.' Thinking this, he said:[236]

[572] 'Sir, I give to you your wife Maddī, whose every limb is loveliness.
It is only right for Maddī to be with you and for her to be with her husband. (636)
Just as milk and a conch shell are of the same colour,
So you and Maddī are of the same heart and thought. (637)
You are both of noble birth, endowed with great lineage,
On both your mother's and your father's sides.
You were banished to this forest, where you live peacefully in a hermitage.
Do whatever good things you can, giving yet more and yet more.' (638)

When he had said, this, he showed himself in order to grant a wish.

'I am Sakka, lord of the gods, and I have come before you.
Make a wish, O seer king, and I will give you eight wishes.' (639)

As he said this, by his divine power he stood in the sky, like the sun in the early morning. And then the Bodhisatta made his wish:

'O Sakka, lord of all beings, you have granted me a wish.
May my father take delight in having me return to my own home,
And may he call me to sit upon my seat. This is my first wish. (640)
May I not consent to the execution of any man, even if he has committed a terrible crime.

234. See SN I 19.

235. PED 494 gives 'the best vehicle' for *brahmayāna.* See also SN V 5; Bodhi 2000: 1526, where Bhikkhu Bodhi gives 'divine vehicle'; the eightfold path is termed this in comparison with a beautiful carriage.

236. This is the turning point of the story. From now on, the Bodhisatta is primarily a recipient, until the end, when he again becomes a donor.

May I free the condemned from death. This is my second wish. (641)
Those who are old and those who are young, and those you are in middle age:
May they find support in their lives from me. This is my third wish. (642)
May I not go with another man's wife; may I be true to my wife.
May I not come under the sway of women. This is my fourth wish.[237] (643)
And Sakka, may I have a son and may he have a long life:[238]
May he conquer the earth through *dhamma*. This is my fifth wish. (644)
As the night starts to lighten and the sun to rise,
May heavenly food appear. This is my sixth wish. (645)
May my generosity never be exhausted. May I never regret any gift.
May my heart become clear and tranquil through giving. This is my seventh wish. (646)
[573] When I am released from this life, may I go to heaven.
May I attain distinction, and then may I never be reborn. This is my eighth wish.'[239] (647)
When he had heard his declaration, the lord of the gods said this:
'Certainly it will not be long before your father comes to see you.' (648)

In this way Sakka gave the Great Being his advice, and then went back to his own abode. Explaining the matter the Teacher said this verse:

When the king of the gods, the Maghavā, Sujampati, had said this,
He granted Vessantara his wish and went to the people of heaven. (649)

The episode about Sakka has finished.

237. Cone translates as the 'domination' of women. I am reading it more as coming under the sexual temptation of other women, not his wife.

238. *Putto me Sakka jāyetha yo ca dīghayuko siyā.* This could mean 'may I have a son born to me' (as PGPV 71). But DP II 200 also gives 'grow' for *jāyati*: it would be nice to make it apply to the son that he already has, and I think it would be possible, to read, 'may my son grow and may he have a long life', though this does seem to be a less probable reading. Presumably auspicious marks would have already marked out the living boy as a potential Universal Monarch, if he had been meant here. As Collins notes, this is the only explicit mention of the Universal Monarch ideal in the story (Collins 1998: 516). This is one wish that does not find fulfilment in the story.

239. This verse appears to read at first sight that the Bodhisatta wishes never to be reborn after attaining a heavenly rebirth, but obtain awakening from there. This is an odd aspiration in the light of the Bodhisatta vow, which requires one more human rebirth after a heavenly one, in order that he can obtain Buddhahood. I read the 'distinction' or 'higher state' as being the attainment of a human birth and Buddhahood after this. The commentary takes the 'distinction' or 'higher state' as being a rebirth in the Tusita heaven, and then a final rebirth in which Buddhahood is attained. Cone reads: 'may I go to heaven and reach a higher state, and may I never be reborn from there.' This leaves the place from where he obtains enlightenment open, as the 'higher state' may be maintained when he takes human form (PGPV 71).

11. THE GREAT KING (*MAHĀRĀJAPABBAM*)

The Bodhisatta and Maddī lived in great happiness together and stayed in the forest hermitage, given to them by Sakka. Meanwhile, Jūjaka travelled the sixty *yojanas* with the children; and *devatās* put up a guard to protect the children. Every night at sundown he used to tie the children to a small tree and got them to sleep on the ground, while he, through fear of wild animals and beasts, climbed a tree and lay in the middle of a fork in the branches. At that moment, a god in the form of Vessantara and a goddess in the form of Maddī would come and untie the children, rub and wash their hands and feet, make them look nice, and get them to eat food. They arranged for them to sleep on a heavenly bed [574] and then at dawn they put them back as they had been, tied up, got them to lie down, and disappeared. In this way, through the kind assistance of the gods, they travelled on in good health. Jūjaka, because a god had taken him under his sway, thought that he would go to the kingdom of Kaliṅga, but managed to get to the city of Jetuttara instead, in a fortnight.

That day, before dawn, Sañjaya, the king of the Sivis, had a dream, and this is how it went: as the king was sitting in his Great Judgement Hall, a man holding two lotuses placed them in the king's hand. The king put them on his two ears, and their pollen dropped down onto his front. When he woke up the next morning he consulted the brahmins, and they explained, 'Some relatives who have been away a long time will come back.' In the morning he ate foods of various choice flavours, and sat down in the Judgement Hall. The gods then led the brahmin and set him down in the royal courtyard. At that moment the king looked around and saw the children. He exclaimed:

> 'Whose is the face that shines like gold refined in the fire,
> Like a golden coin forged in the furnace? (650)
> Both are alike in their limbs, both are alike in auspicious markings,
> One is just like Jāli; one is just like Kaṇhājinā. (651)
> Like lions emerging from their den, both these children are so alike too.
> These children look as if they are made of gold!' (652)

In this way in three verses the king praised the children, and gave an order to a certain minister: 'Go and bring this brahmin here with the children.' He brought them quickly, and the king addressed the brahmin:

> 'O descendant of Bharadvāja,
> Where have you come from bringing these children?' (653)

Jūjaka said:

'Sire, these children were given to me freely and gladly, Sañjaya.
Today it is fifteen nights since I asked, and the children were given to me.' (654)

[575] The king said:

'And at what sacrifice were you the minister for that fee? I am not confident that it was by a rightful means.
Who gave you this donation? For children are the supreme gift.'(655)

Jūjaka said:

'The one who is the support of suppliants, as the great earth supports all creatures:[240]
That one, Vessantara, gave me the children as slaves, while he was living in the forest. (656)
The one whom people go to, like flowing rivers to the ocean,
That one, Vessantara, gave me the children as slaves, while he was living in the forest.' (657)

When they heard this, the ministers spoke, berating Vessantara:

'Sir, it is a wrong thing for a king to do, out of faith, even when he is living at home.
How could he give away his children when he is banished in the forest? (658)
Sirs, listen to this, while we are met together here,
How Vessantara the king gave his children away while living in the forest. (659)
He might give a slave and a slave girl, or give a horse and donkey cart,
And a trumpeting elephant. But how could he give away his children?' (660)

When he heard this criticism of his father, the boy, as if holding out his arm while wind strikes Mount Sineru, said this verse:

'For someone who has no slave in his house, nor horse, nor donkey cart,
Nor a trumpeting noble elephant, what is there for him to give, grandfather?' (661)

The king said:

[576] 'I praise his gift, and I do not reproach him, children.
How was his heart, when he gave you to the miserable beggar?' (662)

The boy replied:

'He was suffering in his heart and, furthermore, his breath was hot.

240. As the story starts to unravel backwards, epithets used to describe Vessantara start to return too. See verses 305–6.

His eyes became red like Rohiṇī, and tears rolled down.'[241] (663)

And then he recounted the conversation:

'Well, Kaṇhājinā said, "This brahmin is beating me with a stick
As if I were a slave who had been born in his house. (664)
But this is no brahmin, Father—there are good and just brahmins—
He is a *yakkha* in the guise of a brahmin[242] and he leads us away to eat us,
How can you just watch as a demon leads us away?"' (665)

When the king saw that the brahmin was not releasing the children, the king said:

'Your mother is a royal princess and your father a royal prince.
Before you used to climb onto my lap. Why do you stand at
a distance?' (666)

The prince replied:

'Our mother is a royal princess and our father a royal prince.
But we are slaves. Because of this we stand at a distance.' (667)

The king said:

'Do not speak like that, dear ones: you burn my heart,
As if my body is on a funeral pyre, and I cannot be comfortable in my
seat. (668)
Do not speak like that, dear ones: you make my grief the greater.
We will redeem you with what will be a mere trifle,[243] and you will not
be slaves. (669)
[577] What price did your father set on you when he gave you to the
brahmin?
Tell it to me it as it really was, and let them offer it to the brahmin.' (670)

The boy answered:

'It was a price of a thousand that my father set on me when he gave me
to the brahmin.
And for the maiden Kaṇhā, a hundred elephants and so on.'[244] (671)

241. Rohiṇī has all her children killed, but then gives birth to Balarāma and Kṛṣṇa. She is associated with one of the Indian lunar mansions.

242. This is a pretty accurate account of the interchange.

243. There must be something wrong with the text here, which says 'with a punishment' or 'with a stick' (*daṇḍena*). Cone amends this to be *dabbena*, wealth (*dabba*), as does the commentary implicitly by glossing the word *danḍena* as *dhanena*, by *wealth* (*dhana*). I have taken it with Bd as *appena*, by means of a trifle, as that is what it would be to him, but none of these are satisfactory. See, for Gombrich's comments on this passage, PGPV xxvi–xxvii.

244. Reading *hatthinādi satena* with Bd, but it is problematic as there is a hanging *cā* 'and' at the end of the line.

The king ordered compensation to be given to the brahmin:

'Get going, my steward: pay off the brahmin;[245]
Give him as compensation for the children a hundred male and female slaves,
A hundred elephants, a hundred bulls, and a thousand gold coins.' (672)
And then the royal steward hastened to pay off the brahmin,
He gave him as compensation for the children a hundred male and female slaves,
A hundred elephants, a hundred bulls, and a thousand gold coins. (673)

He also gave to the brahmin a palace with seven storeys, and a large retinue. The brahmin arranged his wealth and went up into the palace, where he had an enormous banquet of food, and went to sleep on a magnificent couch. The children, meanwhile, were bathed, given food, and adorned, and their grandfather took one, and their grandmother the other, and set them on their laps.

Explaining the matter the Teacher said:

Redeeming, bathing, and feeding the children, and adorning them too,
They took their 'goods'[246]on their laps. (674)
[578] When they were washed by pouring water on the head,
Dressed in fresh clothes, and adorned in every way,
The king their grandfather took them on his lap and asked them questions. (675)
Wearing earrings that jingled, and garlands, and adorned in every way,
Their grandfather took them on his lap and said this: (676)
'Are both your mother and father in good health, Jāli?
I hope they are keeping themselves going on good gleanings, and many roots and fruit.[247] (677)
I hope there are not many bugs and mosquitoes and creeping creatures,

245. The introduction of the royal attendant or steward at this stage echoes the instruction of the king, in much the same words, in v. 45, line 1 (Ja VI 492) when this figure is told to give the terrible message to Vessantara that he is to be banished. *Kattar* as an 'attendant, steward or chamberlain' (DP I 624–5) is not terribly common but Vidhura is also a *kattar*, and is so called in the *Mahābhārata* stories about him (see introduction to Chapter 9 and Ja VI 259). The steward's recurrence here, and the same address to him reinforces the mirror image effect of this story, whereby we find again the elements in reverse that set the story going at the outset.

246. *Bhaṇḍa* refers to stock and possessions that one has bought (PED 497). A sense of this is retained in the translation as it shows the 'buying off' that has been going on in quite a different light.

247. This is a variation on the greeting seen so often in the story (e.g. vv. 357–8).

And that the wild animals and deer of the forest are not harming them.' (678)

The boy replied:

'Yes, both my mother and father are in good health, sire.
They are keeping themselves going on good gleanings, and many roots and fruit. (679)
There are not many bugs and mosquitoes and creeping creatures,
And the wild animals and deer of the forest are not harming them. (680)
Digging, gathering edible roots, and tubers and bulbous plants,
And gathering jujube, marking nuts, and *vilva* fruits, she feeds them to us.[248] (681)
Whatever she brings, bringing forest roots and fruits, that is what we all eat
At night-time, when we meet together, though not in the day. (682)
But our mother is pale and thin, through bringing us fruits from the trees
In winds and the heat: she is like a delicate lotus clenched in the hand. (683)
In her wandering in the great forest, which is crowded with wild animals,
And where the rhinoceros and other beasts go, her hair has become thin. (684)
Tying up her hair like an ascetic, and with sweat beneath her armpits,
She wears animal hide, sleeps on the ground, and pays homage to the sacred fire.'[249] (685)

And so in this way he related the tough existence endured by his mother, and he reproached his grandfather with this verse:

'In this world, children, when they come, are dear to men,
But for his children our grandfather feels no affection.' (686)

[579] And then the king, disclosing his fault, said:

'Yes, I did something very bad, my child, like killing an unborn child,
When I banished a man who had done nothing wrong, because of the people of Sivi. (687)
Let Vessantara come: let him have whatever grain and wealth there is,
And let him be king in the kingdom of the Sivis.' (688)

The boy said:

'The best person of the Sivis will not come if I say so, sire.
The king must go himself and shower his son with wealth.' (689)

248. The Pāli reads *āluka, biḷāli, takkala.* The last two are tubers. *Kola* is jujube, *bhallāṭaka* (PED 499) the *Semicarpus anacardium*, or marking nut.

249. The last line aligns her with the ascetic Accuta and her husband.

Then Sañjaya the king gave orders to his general:

'Let the army of elephants, horses, chariots, and infantry then be equipped,
And let the citizens and brahmins and priests follow me. (690)
Then let sixty thousand soldiers, handsome to behold, quickly come and assemble, fully equipped and adorned with various colours. (691)
Some wearing blue, some yellow, others with red headdresses, and some in white,
Let them quickly come and assemble together fully equipped, adorned with various colours. (692)
Just as the snowy Gandhāran mountain Gandhamādana,
Which is covered with various kinds of trees, (693)
And with various divine plants, so that it shines in all directions,
So quickly may they assemble and shine too, in all directions. (694)
And then let them harness fourteen thousand elephants, powerful,
With golden ribbons and golden girdles, (695)
Ridden by village chiefs bearing staffs and pikes; let the mahouts quickly come
And assemble, fully equipped, and dressed for action, upon the elephants' backs. (696)
Then, let them harness fourteen thousand horses, Sindhs,
Of pure pedigree, swift mounts, (697)
Ridden by village chiefs carrying short-swords and bows: let the riders quickly come and assemble,
Fully equipped and dressed for action, upon the horses' backs. (698)
[580] And then let them yoke fourteen thousand chariots,
With the rims of the wheel beautifully wrought in iron and edges covered with gold. (699)
And let them raise the standards, and put on leather and chain mail.
Let the strong-bow archers draw their bows and let the charioteers quickly assemble,
Fully equipped and in their chariots.' (700)

When the king had considered the limbs of his army in this way, he said, 'The road that will be taken by my son, from the city of Jettuttara to the Crooked Mountain, should be made evenly surfaced, for a width of eight *usabhas*. And there are various things, such as this and this, that you should do.' And he gave various orders. Then he said:

'Let puffed rice and flowers and flower garlands, perfumes and ointments, be scattered around,
Let festive columns be placed on the road that he will travel. (701)
Village by village, let a hundred jars of spirits and drinks
Be laid out by the road, on the road that he will travel. (702)

Let meat and cakes baked in a pan, cakes, and broth mixed with fish
Be laid out on the road, the road that he will travel. (703)
Let ghee, sesame oil, curds and milk, millet, rice, and plenty of drink
Be placed by the road, on the road that he will travel.[250] (704)
Let there be chefs and cooks, dancers, acrobats, and singers,
Strummers of hand instruments, jar drummers and cymbal players and kettle drummers! (705)
Let them play all kinds of lutes, drums, and kettle drums,
Let them blow conch shells, and let the one-skinned drum resound! (706)
Little drums, cymbals, conches, and stringed instruments and lutes:
Let them play them all, and many kinds of drums!' (707)

[581] In this way the king went over all the details of the decoration of the road. But as it happens, Jūjaka had eaten far too much and could not digest it, and so he died right then.[251] The king had the funeral performed and had a drum beaten to announce it. But no relative appeared, and his wealth went back to the king. And on the seventh day the entire army met together; the king, followed by a great retinue, made Jāli the expedition guide, and they departed.

Explaining the matter the Teacher said:

This was a magnificent army, ready for action, carrying the Sivis.
With Jāli as its guide for the expedition, it started its journey to the Crooked Mountain. (708)
The powerful great elephant, sixty years old, made a great trumpeting noise;
While the girdle around its middle was being put on, it trumpeted loudly. (709)
The thoroughbred horses neighed and the wheels ground noisily into action,
Dust clouds covered the sky when the army of Sivis was ready for action. (710)
This was a magnificent army, ready for action, taking everything in its wake.
With Jāli as its leader on the road, it started its journey to the Crooked Mountain. (711)
They entered into the great forest, with its massy foliage and flocks of birds,
Filled with both trees in flower and trees in fruit. (712)

250. *Kaṅgu* is *Panicus Italicus*, millet, or panic beans.

251. Lefferts and Cate (2012: 90) note that in Thailand they constantly found people who could relate a list of all the foods Jūjaka ate that brought about his end, as recounted in the Siamese versions!

There flocks of birds, of many colours, called to one another
In melodious, full-rounded voice in the trees, all flowering in their season. (713)
They travelled on the long road and after several days and nights
They reached the region where Vessantara was. (714)

The episode about the great king is finished.

12. THE SECTION ABOUT THE SIX NOBLE WARRIORS (*CHAKHATTIYAKHAṆḌA*)[252]

[582] Prince Jāli stationed a fortified camp at the beautiful banks of Lake Mucalinda, with forty thousand chariots, on the road they had just taken, and he had established guards at various points against lions, tigers, and rhinoceros and other wild animals. There was a noisy commotion from the elephants and other animals. The Great Being, when he heard it, thought, 'Clearly enemies of my father have killed him, and have come here for me too.' Fearful of death, he took Maddī up the mountain till he looked down at the army.

Explaining the matter the Teacher said:

When he heard the commotion Vessantara was afraid;
And, worried, he climbed up the mountain to look at the army.[253] (715)
'Come here, Maddī! Hear what a commotion there is in the forest.
Thoroughbred horses are whinnying, and you can just see the tops of standards. (716)
It looks like some hunters are in the forest
Who will snare herds of deer with nets, or get them to fall into a pit,
And, shouting out, will kill the best of them with their sharp weapons. (717)
We were banished into the forest, although we had done nothing wrong;
Now have a look at the slaughter of the weak, who have fallen into the power of enemies.' (718)

When she had heard what he had said, Maddī looked at the army. 'This must be our army.' And she said this verse in encouragement:

[583] 'No enemy could overcome you, as a flame cannot overcome the waters.
Just consider this, and may there be safety for you in this.' (719)

252. The six noble warriors are Vessantara, Maddī, the two children, and the parents.

253. This incident parallels their last view of their home as they leave.

And then the Great Being put aside his grief, and climbing down from the mountain sat in the leaf hut. Explaining the matter the Teacher said:

And then Vessantara the king came down from the mountain
And sat in the leaf hut, making his mind strong. (720)

At that moment Sañjaya addressed his queen: 'Dearest Phusatī, if we all go at the same time there will be great emotion, so I will go first, and when you think, "Now the emotion will have quietened down, and they will be sitting down together," then come with your great retinue. And then, after a little time, tell Jāli and Kaṇhājinā to come.' Then he had the chariot turned around to face the way they had come and, putting a guard at various points, rode on the back of his adorned elephant and went up to his son.

Explaining the matter the Teacher said:

When he had turned back the chariot and put his soldiers into position,
The father approached the son, living alone in the forest. (721)
Coming down from the elephant's back, with his robe over one shoulder, he made an *añjali*,
And, surrounded by ministers, went to anoint his son with the royal sprinkling. (722)
And there he saw his son, of beautiful appearance, sitting
With a concentrated mind, and meditating, without fear, in the leaf hut. (723)
[584] When they saw their father arriving, longing for his son,
Vessantara and Maddī went out to him and paid homage to him. (724)
Maddī paid her respects by prostrating her head on the ground at his feet,
And then she said, 'I, Maddī, your daughter-in-law, pay homage to you, O King!'
He embraced them there, and caressed them with his hand. (725)

Then the king wept and poured out his grief. When his sorrow had been quieted, he made this courteous address:

'Are you well, my son? Are you in good health, my son?
I hope you are keeping yourself going on good gleanings, and many roots and fruit. (726)
I hope there are not many bugs and mosquitoes and creeping creatures,
And that the wild animals and deer of the forest are not harming you.' (727)

When he heard his father's words the Great Being said:

'Yes, we have the means of living here, and enough for us to get by.

But our way of life is very hard, as we live just on what we have
gathered and gleaned. (728)[254]
Lack of wealth trains a poor man, just as a charioteer trains his horse,
So we, being poor, have been well trained. (729)
But our flesh has wasted away through not seeing our father and mother;
Great King, we have lived a life of sorrow, banished into the forest.' (730)

And when he had said this, he went on to ask for any news of the children:

'Those who are the best of the Sivis, your heirs, disappointed in their
hearts,
Jāli and Kaṇhajinā both, are now under the power of a brahmin,
Profligate and cruel, who drives them like cattle. (731)
[585] These royal children! If you know anything about them,
Please give us relief quickly, as a man cures a snake bite.' (732)

The king said:

'Both children are redeemed—yes, Jāli and Kaṇhājinā both.
We gave compensation to the brahmin, so do not worry, and take
comfort.' (733)

Hearing this, the Great Being was overwhelmed with relief and made this courteous inquiry:

'Are you well, dear father? Are you keeping in good health?
I hope, Father, my mother's eyes are not worn out through
weeping.'[255] (734)

The king replied:

'Yes, I am well and I am keeping in good health.
And your mother's eyes are not worn out through weeping.' (735)

The Great Being said:

'And how is your carriage—without problems? And how is your vehicle
going?[256]
I hope the country is prosperous, and that there is no drought.' (736)

The king replied:

'Yes my carriage is fine, without any problems, and my vehicle goes
fine too.

254. This is the first time this question, with its ancient greeting, gets an equivocal answer: the Bodhisatta is changing his tack.

255. The commentary adds at this point that it would be through weeping, so this has been added to the text.

256. Are we right to sense a perennial father–son bonding moment in the questions about vehicles while the wife and her attendants wait outside? Humour is very difficult to assess in an ancient text!

The country is certainly prosperous, and there is no drought at all.' (737)

As they were conversing in this way, Queen Phusatī thought to herself, 'By now they surely must have allayed their grief a little and will be sitting down.' And so, with her large retinue, she approached near her son.

[586] Explaining the matter the Teacher said:

When they were talking in this way, their mother, the royal lady,
Came into view at the entrance of the mountain, on foot and without her sandals. (738)
Seeing their mother coming, longing for her son,
Vessantara and Maddī went out to her and paid homage to her. (739)
Maddī paid her respects by prostrating her head on the ground at her feet,
And then she said, 'I, Maddī, your daughter-in-law, pay homage to you, my lady!' (740)
When the children saw Maddī, their mother, safe, from far off,
They cried out to her and ran to her like young calves to their mother. (741)
And when Maddī saw her children, safe, from far off,
Like someone possessed, shaking, she sprinkled them with streams of milk from her breasts. (742)

And it is said that she sobbed with great intensity, and shaking, fell down unconscious, lying prone on the earth, and her children also rushed up to her and fell unconscious on top of their mother. And at that moment two streams of milk poured out of her two breasts and flowed straight into their mouths, and if, they say, they had not had this comfort they would have died, as their hearts were all dried up. And when Vessantara saw his children he could not control his emotion, and fell unconscious right there. And the mother and father also fell unconscious right where they were. So did the sixty thousand ministers born at the same time as Vesssantara. Indeed no one who saw this pitiful sight could bear it and the entire hermitage was like a wood of *sāl* trees knocked down by a storm at the end of an era.[257]

And at that moment, the mountains roared and the earth shook; the great ocean heaved and Sineru, the king of the mountains, bent down, and the six sense-sphere heavens were in commotion.[258] And Sakka, the king of

257. This paragraph is in small type in F.

258. The six sense-sphere heavens are the *deva* realms, above the human but below the Brahmā realms.

the gods, thought, 'Six noble warriors are lying unconscious amongst their followers. And not one was able to get up and sprinkle water on anyone's bodies, so I had better rain a shower of lotus blossoms.' So he caused a lotus blossom shower to rain on the six noble warriors, and those who wished to become wet did, and not a single drop stuck on those who did not wish to become wet. It was like a shower falling on a cluster of lotuses, in which water just drops off the leaves. [587] And the six noble warriors found relief, and the people cried out, 'A shower of lotuses has fallen on the family! It is a miracle, and the great earth itself has quaked!'

Explaining the matter the Teacher said:

When the family was reunited there was a deep sigh,[259]
As the mountains roared and the great earth quaked. (743)
In great streams of rain, the god sent down rain,
Just at the time when Vessantara was reunited with his family. (744)
Grandchildren, daughter-in-law, son, and king:
When they were reunited there was such a thing as would make your hair stand on end.
Weeping in the terrifying forest, the people who had arrived made an *añjali* (745)
To Vessantara and Maddī. All those who had come together from the kingdom pleaded with him, crying:
'Truly you are our lord and king. May both of you rule the kingdom.' (746)

The section about the six noble warriors has finished.

13. THE DESCRIPTION OF VESSANTARA

When he heard this the Great Being talked with his father, and said this:

'Even though I ruled the kingdom in accordance with *dhamma*, you expelled me from the kingdom—
You and the country people and the citizens, all gathered together.' (747)

Then the king asked his son to forgive him:

'Yes, I did something very bad, my child, like killing an unborn child,
When I banished a man who had done nothing wrong, because of the people of Sivi.'[260] (748)

Saying this verse, he pleaded with his son to remove his great suffering:

259. The commentary said it was a sigh or a boom or noise (*ghora* can denote any of these) of sympathy, or compassion (*kāruññaghosa*).

260. This is the admission he made to his grandson in v. 637.

'Whatever suffering there is, in whatever form it is, in father, mother, sister,
It should be rooted out, even at the cost of one's life.'[261] (749)

[588] But the Bodhisatta was happy to rule the kingdom, even without these comments. 'It is not a burden,' he said to the king, and agreed, 'Very well.' Then the sixty thousand ministers who had been born at the same time realised that he had consented, and shouted out:

'It is the time for bathing, Great King, for washing off the dirt and sweat!' (750a)

And then Vessantara the king asked them to wait a little. And going into the leaf hut he took off his seer's clothes, and put them aside. Coming out of the leaf hut, he announced, 'For nine and a half months I have lived according to the way of the ascetic. It was here that the earth quaked when I attained the peak of Perfection by my giving.' And he walked three times around the leaf hut, keeping it to his right in respect, and made a fivefold prostration.[262] Then he stood. The barber and other attendants of the king cut and dressed his beard, and saw to his needs, and then, when he was adorned so that he shone like the king of the gods, they anointed him as king. As it is said:

And then Vessantara the king washed away the dirt and sweat. (750b)

After that his glory was magnificent. Wherever his gaze rested, the earth shook. Those who speak and chant auspicious blessings cried out blessings and took up all kinds of musical instruments. And there was a great noise, like thunder, in the depths of the ocean. They decorated the elephant treasure[263] and brought him on, and he bound on his jewelled sword and climbed up on him, and sixty thousand ministers of equal birth, adorned

261. The commentator's wish to explain and understand a rather cryptic verse makes him gloss it in this way: '"For a child to give up his life would be a great grief and sorrow for the mother and father. Therefore, do as I say: give up the paraphernalia of a seer, and take up the clothes of a king, my dear son!" And they say that this was his meaning here.'

262. This involves five points of the body: head, two hands, and two feet.

263. This is the first time that the elephant has been called a treasure, or a jewel, by implication the second treasure of the Universal Monarch (*cakkavattin*). The Bodhisatta has been reborn several times as such a monarch; although this is not one of those rebirths, the implication is that the elephant has now become the possession of a *cakkavattin* king, by the Bodhisatta's assumption of the monarchy. The other time in the Great Ten when the elephant assumes this role is in the *Candakumāra-jātaka*, when the horse treasure is also mentioned (Chapter 7, vv. 94–5).

and equipped in every way, made his retinue. And they bathed Maddī the queen, and adorned her and anointed her, and as they sprinkled water to consecrate her on the head, they cried, 'May Vessantara protect you!' and other blessings.

Explaining the matter the Teacher said:

Having bathed by pouring water over his head, in fresh clothes and adorned in every way,
He mounted the correct elephant and bound on his sword, the scourge of his enemies.[264] (751)
And then the sixty thousand warriors, handsome to behold, born at the same time as him,
Surrounded the lord of charioteers and cheered him. (752)
[589] And then the Sivi maidens gathered together to bathe Maddī and said:
'May Vessantara look after you, and Jāli and Kaṇhājinā,
And may the great king Sañjaya guard you well!' (753)
Because of this cause, and their own former affliction,
They rejoiced in the delightful mountain dell. (754)
Because of this cause, and their own former affliction,
The lady of auspicious beauty was joyful and happy and glad, reunited with her children. (755)
Because of this cause, and their own former affliction,
The lady of auspicious beauty was joyful and happy and delighted with her children. (756)

Delighted in this way with her children, she said:

'Before this I had just one meal a day and slept on the bare ground,
And that was the vow I undertook through my affection, children. (757)
That vow of mine is today successful as I am reunited with you, children.
May this vow taken by your mother and your father bring protection to you, children.
And may the great king Sañjaya guard you well! (758)
Whatever merit that has been made by me and your father,
By this good truth, may you be free from old age and death!' (759)

[590] Phusatī the queen said, 'From now on, may my daughter-in-law put on these clothes, and wear these ornaments!' And she had boxes filled and sent to her.

Explaining the matter the Teacher said:

264. For the word *paccayo*, see Gombrich's discussion in PGPV xxiv. See also Norman 1983: 83.

Cotton clothes and silk, and garments of fine linen:
The mother-in-law sent these to her daughter-in-law, to let Maddī's beauty shine. (760)
And then a golden armlet,[265] a bracelet, and a jewelled girdle:
The mother-in-law sent these to her daughter-in-law, to let Maddī's beauty shine. (761)
And then a golden armlet, a bracelet, and a choker made from jewels:
The mother-in-law sent these to her daughter-in-law, to let Maddī's beauty shine. (762)
An ornament that seemed to flower round her face, and many kinds of jewels and gems:
The mother-in-law sent these to her daughter-in-law, to let Maddī's beauty shine. (763)
A pearl necklace,[266] a string of gems, a girdle, and jewels for the feet:
The mother-in-law sent these to her daughter-in-law, to let Maddī's beauty shine. (764)
As that best of women, the royal princess, gazed on these jewels, threaded and unthreaded,
She shone like a heavenly maiden of the Nandana Grove. (765)
Having bathed by pouring water over her head, in fresh clothes, and adorned in every way, the princess shone like a nymph of the Tāvatiṃsa heaven. (766)
Like a plantain tree touched by the wind, in woodland of many coloured creepers,
The princess, with her perfect array of teeth,[267] let her beauty shine. (767)
Like a bird in a female form, with many coloured feathers,
With her lips as red as banyan fruit, or red amaranth,[268] the princess let her beauty shine. (768)
[591] They then led to her a strong trumpeting elephant, who had not grown too big,
A powerful animal with tusks like poles, patient against sword and patient against arrow. (769)
And Maddī alighted onto the elephant, who had not grown too big,

265. *Komañ ca* 'linen' has been amended with Bd to *hemañ ca* 'golden', as it is in the next verse.

266. A pearl necklace is suggested by DP I 394 for *uggatthana*. *Giṅgamaka* is given as a necklace (DP II 48).

267. *Dantāvaranasampannā*: I think this means that she is endowed with a rampart of teeth. Cone takes it to mean the lips, presumably as the protector of the teeth (PGPV 85), which fits well with the quivering of the plantain tree image.

268. *Bimba* is *Momordica monadelpha* (PED 487), red amaranth. Bimbā is a name often associated with Rāhulamāta, or Yasodharā, the Bodhisatta's wife in his last life, in what will also be Maddī's last rebirth.

A powerful animal with tusks like poles, patient against sword and
patient against arrow. (770)

Then they both travelled with great ceremony to the army camp. For a month, King Sañjaya organized mountain games and forest games amongst the twelve brigades. Through the power of the Great Being, no wild animal or bird harmed anyone in the forest.

Explaining the matter, the Teacher said:

In all of the forest, whatever wild animals there were there,
Through the power of Vessantara they did not cause each other
harm. (771)
In all the forest, whatever birds there were there,
Through the power of Vessantara they did not cause each other
harm. (772)
In all the forest, whatever wild animals there were there,
They gathered together in one place for the departure of Vessantara,
The bringer of prosperity to the people of Sivi. (773)
In all the forest, whatever birds there were there,
They gathered together in one place for the departure of Vessantara,
The bringer of prosperity to the people of Sivi. (774)
In all the forest, whatever wild animals there were there,
They did not make their beguiling noises for the departure of
Vessantara,
The bringer of prosperity to the people of Sivi. (775)
In all the forest, whatever birds there were there,
They did not make their beguiling noises for the departure of
Vessantara,
The bringer of prosperity to the people of Sivi. (776)

[592] When the games had been going on for a month, Sañjaya, the lord of men, summoned his army general and asked him, 'For a long time now we have stayed in the forest. Has the road for my son now been made ready and decorated?' The general said, 'Yes, sire, it is now a good time to go.' So he had Vessantara informed, and set off with the army. And so, the Great Being travelled sixty *yojana*s, the distance between the Crooked Mountain dell and the city of Jetuttara, on a fully decorated road, in the midst of a magnificent retinue.

Explaining the matter the Teacher said:

All ready was the royal road to Jetuttara, from the place where
Vessantara had been,
And strewn with flowers of many colours. (777)
And then the sixty thousand warriors, handsome to behold,

Gathered all around at the departure of Vessantara,
The bringer of prosperity to the kingdom of the Sivis. (778)
The women of the household, the princesses and merchant and brahmin women,
Gathered all around at the departure of Vessantara,
The bringer of prosperity to the kingdom of the Sivis. (779)
The mahouts and guards, the charioteers and foot soldiers,
Gathered all around at the departure of Vessantara,
The bringer of prosperity to the kingdom of the Sivis. (780)
Soldiers with skulls on their helmets,[269] leather-clad, with swords in their hands, well-armed,
Journeyed on in front, at the departure of Vessantara,
The bringer of prosperity to the kingdom of the Sivis. (781)

The king travelled the sixty *yojana*s of the road for two months before reaching the city of Jetuttara, and he entered a city that had been decorated and made ready for him, and went up into the palace. Explaining the matter the Teacher said:

They entered the delightful city, with its many archways and ramparts,
Now furnished with food and drink and filled with dancing and singing (782)
As friends, country people, and townspeople gathered together
At the arrival of the prince, the bringer of prosperity to the kingdom of the Sivis. (783)
There was a waving of cloths at the arrival of the giver of wealth,
And a drum was beaten at the release of all prisoners within the city. (784)

[593] Even the cats were included as Vessantara the king freed all living creatures. On the very day of his entry into the city, at dawn, he thought, 'When the night starts to lighten into day tomorrow, suppliants will arrive, having heard about my return. What shall I give to them?' At that moment, the seat of Lord Sakka became hot. Turning his attention to the cause of this, he realised the cause of this, and caused there to be a rain of the seven kinds of jewels, like a dense rain cloud, that came up to waist level in the areas to the west and the east of the king's palace, and in the entire city up to knee level. On the next day the Great Being gave a decree that the jewels that had fallen to the west and the east of the palace should go to the families that lived there. He had the rest gathered up, and arranged to

269. DP I 646 suggests that *karoṭiya* refers to a type of soldier who is possibly wearing a skull.

have it put it into his treasure houses with the money in his own house: and he established the practice of generosity.

Explaining the matter the Teacher said:

A shower of gold the god of rain sent on that place
At the arrival of the prince, the bringer of prosperity to the kingdom of the Sivis. (785)
And then Vessantara the king, the noble warrior, gave his gift.
And at the break-up of his body, endowed with wisdom, he was reborn in heaven. (786)

And when the Teacher had given this dhamma teaching about Vessantara, adorned with its thousand verses, he made the connections in the births: At that time, Devadatta was Jūjaka, Ciñcamānavikā was Amittatāpanā,[270] Channa was the Cetan, Sāriputta was the ascetic Accuta, Anuruddha was Sakka, the great king Suddhodana was Lord Sañjaya, Great Māyā was Queen Phusatī, Rāhulamātā was Queen Maddī, Rāhula was Prince Jāli, Uppalavaṇṇā was Kaṇhājinā, and followers of the Buddha were the other people. And I was Vessantara.[271]

The description of Vessantara is brought to an end.

270. Ciñcamānavikā was a beautiful follower of the Buddha who falsely claimed he had made her pregnant (DPPN).

271. The cast of characters includes many that have featured throughout the *Mahānipātā*, who make the Bodhisatta's family, and followers as Buddha, in his final life. Included here is Channa, Gotama's driver, as the Cetan, and Anuruddha, a disciple famous for his practice of breathing mindfulness (DPPN). It brings the whole body of the *jātaka*s to a natural conclusion, and a full circle. The story is mentioned several times in the *Jātaka-nidāna*, with the telling of the life and previous lives of the Bodhisatta/Buddha. It is mentioned as occurring in the birth immediately before the Bodhisatta's stay in the Tusita realm, waiting for the moment to take his final rebirth (see also Skilling 1998 and Appleton 2010a: 72 ff.).

Glossary

Abhidhamma One of the three 'baskets' of Pāli scriptures, the others being the discourses (*suttas*) and monastic regulations (*vinaya*); *abhidhamma* is the scholastic tradition of 'higher teaching', in which the *dhamma* is classified, systematised, and analysed.

Act of Truth (*saccakiriya*) A statement of truth powerful enough to change the course of nature or gain the attention of the gods.

adhiṭṭhāna Resolve or determination; one of the ten perfections.

añjali A respectful gesture in which hands are placed palm together and raised towards the object of respect.

arahat 'Worthy'; a human that has achieved *nibbāna*.

asura An anti-god or demon, said to be in constant opposition to the *devas*.

bhagavā 'Blessed One'.

Bhante 'Venerable'; a respectful way of addressing a monk.

Bodhisatta An 'Awakening Being', a bodhisatta is a person on the way to Buddhahood; here it is used to refer to the Buddha-to-be in his past lives.

Brahmā A god of the Brahmā realms, sometimes parallel to that of Hindu mythology.

brahma-faring (*brahma-cariya*) A way of life committed to chastity and observance of the precepts.

Brahmā realm(s)/heaven(s) A series of high heavens of varying levels of abstraction. See Table 4 in Introduction (p. 23).

brahmin A member of the priestly caste, primarily responsible for Vedic learning, carrying out sacrifices, and giving advice to kings.

Buddha, *buddha* 'Awakened One'.

cāga 'Letting go, giving'; the state of mind present when generosity takes place.

dāna Generosity or giving; one of the ten perfections.

deva A god, usually belonging to one of the six lower heavens.

devatā A god, usually one that is bound to the earth, living in a tree or other object.

dhamma 'Truth' or 'teachings', also 'duty, religion, law'.

divine abidings Four ideal Buddhist qualities: compassion, loving-kindness, sympathetic joy, and equanimity.

gandhabba A type of spirit deity, usually a celestial musician.

garuḷa, garuḍa An eagle-like spirit deity, enemy of the *nāgas*; also called *supaṇṇa*.

gāvuta A linear measure, usually reckoned one quarter of a *yojana*.

Heaven of the Thirty-Three (Tāvatiṃsa) One of the six lower heavens, ruled over by Sakka.

higher knowledges (*abhiññā*) Five of these are considered 'mundane' (they can be achieved by an advanced meditation practitioner) and a sixth characterises awakening. They are: magical bodily powers (such as flying through the air or multiplying one's body), the 'divine ear' (being able to hear sounds far away, even in the heaven realms), penetration of the thoughts of others, memory of past lives, the 'divine eye' (seeing beings passing away and being reborn according to their karma), and—the sixth—the destruction of the defilements. The Bodhisatta often achieves the five in his *jātaka* stories, but only achieves the sixth at the moment he becomes Buddha.

Indra Another name for Sakka.

Jambudīpa The 'Island of the Rose-Apple Tree'; the continent of India.

jhāna A state of meditative absorption, usually listed as either four or eight.

kahāpana A small copper coin of unknown amount.

***kamma*, karma** 'Action', referring to the idea that actions have consequences for the doer either in the current life or future lives.

kasiṇa An object of concentration used as a meditation aid; the meditation practice of this type.

khanti Forbearance or patience; one of the ten perfections.

kiṃpuruṣa A 'what-man'; a type of spirit deity associated with forest dwelling.

kinnara Another term for the above.

kinnarī A female *kinnara*.

koṭi A large number, literally the 'endpoint, summit'.

kusala skilful, wholesome, good, or healthy.

makara A sea monster.

mettā Loving-kindness; one of the ten perfections.

nāga A serpent deity.

nāgī A female *nāga*.

nekkhamma Renunciation; one of the ten perfections.

nibbāna The 'going out' of the causes of rebirth; liberation from *saṃsāra*.

paccekabuddha A 'solitary Buddha', usually understood as a person who attains *nibbāna* during a time without Buddhist teachings.

paññā Wisdom; one of the ten perfections.

paritta 'Protection'; a ritual or chant that brings protective benefits.

sacca Truth; one of the ten perfections.

Sakka King of the gods, overlord of the Heaven of the Thirty-Three.

samatha 'Calming' meditation practice.

saṃsāra The cycle of rebirth and redeath, literally 'wandering on'.

saṅgha The 'community', either referring to the community of monks and nuns or to the wider Buddhist community including lay supporters.

sīla Morality, good conduct; one of the ten perfections.

supaṇṇa An eagle-like spirit deity, enemy of the *nāgas*; also called *garuḍa*.

sutta A 'discourse' of the Buddha, as preserved in the Pāli *Nikāyas*.

Tathāgata 'Thus-gone' or 'thus-like'; an epithet of the Buddha.

Tāvatiṃsa *See* Heaven of the Thirty-Three.

Universal Monarch (*cakkavattin*) A king who rules the entire continent according to the *dhamma*. Universal Monarchs share the same special physical marks as a Buddha.

upekkhā Equanimity; one of the ten perfections.

uposatha The holy day once every lunar fortnight, on which special attention is paid to moral conduct and extra precepts may be observed.

usabha A measure of length, usually reckoned to be equivalent to 140 cubits.

Vāsava Another name for Sakka.

viriya Vigour, energy; one of the ten perfections.

Vissakamma The architect of the gods, whose main role in *jātaka* stories is to build hermitages for the Bodhisatta under the orders of Sakka.

yakkha A type of spirit deity that can be malevolent or protective.

yakkhinī A female *yakkha*.

yojana A measure of length that is the distance one can travel on a single yoke of oxen, usually reckoned to be approximately seven miles.

Bibliography

Ahir, D. C. (ed.). 2000. *The Influence of Jātakas on Art and Literature*. New Delhi: BR Publishing Company.

Alsdorf, L. 1957. 'Bemerkungen zum Vessantara-Jātaka'. *Wiener Zeitschrift für die Kunde Süd-und Ostasiens* 1: 1–70.

———. 1977. 'Das *Bhuridatta-Jātaka*. Ein antibrahmanischer Nāga-Roman', *Wiener Zeitschrift für die Kunde Süd-und Ostasiens* 21: 25–55.

Appleton, Naomi. 2007. 'A Place for the Bodhisatta: the Local and the Universal in Jātaka Stories'. *Acta Orientalia Vilnensia* 8/1: 109–22.

———. 2010a. *Jātaka Stories in Theravāda Buddhism: Narrating the Bodhisatta Path*. Farnham: Ashgate Publishing.

———. 2010b. 'Temptress on the Path: Women as Objects and Subjects in Buddhist Jātaka Stories'. In Pamela Anderson (ed.), *New Topics in Feminist Philosophy of Religion: Contestations and Transcendence Incarnate*, 103–15. Dordrecht: Springer.

———. 2011. 'In the Footsteps of the Buddha? Women and the Bodhisatta Path in Theravāda Buddhism'. *Journal of Feminist Studies in Religion* 27/1: 33–51.

———. 2014. *Narrating Karma and Rebirth: Buddhist and Jain Multi-life Stories*. Cambridge: Cambridge University Press.

———. Forthcoming. 'Indra'. In Naomi Appleton and James Hegarty (eds), *The Story of Story in Early South Asia: Narrative Across Hindu, Jain and Buddhist Traditions*.

———, Sarah Shaw, and Toshiya Unebe. 2013. *Illuminating the Life of the Buddha: An Illustrated Chanting Book from Eighteenth-Century Siam*. Oxford: Bodleian Libraries.

Aristotle. *Poetics*. 350 BCE. Trans. S. H. Butcher. The Internet Classics Archive. http://classics.mit.edu/Aristotle/poetics.1.1.html.

Baker, Chris and Pasuk Phongpaichit. 2005. *A History of Thailand*. Cambridge: Cambridge University Press.

Balbir, Nalini. 1991–2. 'Prakrit Riddle Poetry'. *Annals of the Bhandarkar Oriental Research Institute* 72/73, no. 1/4: 661–73.

Barber, C. L. 1972. *Shakespeare's Festive Comedy: A Study of Dramatic Form and Its Relation to Social Custom*. Princeton: Princeton University Press.

Basham, A. L. 1951. *History and Doctrines of the Ājīvikas: A Vanished Indian Religion.* London: Luzac.

Bautze-Picron, Claudine and Joachim Bautze (photographs). 2003. *The Buddhist Murals of Pagan: Timeless Vistas of the Cosmos.* Bangkok: Orchid Press.

Bhumibol Adulyadej, His Majesty King. 1996. *The Story of Mahājanaka.* Bangkok: Amarin Book Center Company Limited.

Bode, Mabel. 1909. *The Pali Literature of Burma.* London: Royal Asiatic Society.

Bodhi, Bhikkhu (trans.). 1978. *The All-Embracing Net of Views: The Brahmajala Sutta and its Commentaries.* Kandy: Buddhist Publication Society.

Bodhi, Bhikku (trans.). 2000. *The Connected Discourses of the Buddha: A Translation of the Saṃyutta Nikāya.* Boston: Wisdom Publications.

Bodhi, Bhikkhu (trans.). 2012. *The Numerical Discourses of the Buddha: A Translation of the Aṅguttara Nikāya.* Bristol: The Pali Text Society in association with Wisdom Publications.

Brockington, M. 2010. 'Daśaratha, Śyāma, a Brāhman Hunter, and Śrāvaṇa: The Tale of Four Tales (with Pictures)'. In Eli Franco and Monika Zin (eds), *From Turfan to Ajanta: Festschrift for Dieter Schlingloff on the Occasion of his Eightieth Birthday.* Vol. I, 89–116. Bhairahawa, Rupandehi: Lumbini International Research Institute.

Bronkhorst, Johannes. 2011. *Karma.* Honolulu: University of Hawaii Press.

Brown, Robert L. 1997. 'Narrative as Icon: The *Jātaka* Stories in Ancient Indian and Southeast Asian Architecture.' In Juliane Schober (ed.), *Sacred Biography in the Buddhist Traditions of South and Southeast Asia*, 64–109. Honolulu: University of Hawaii Press.

Buddhaghosa, Bhadantācariya. 1991. *The Path of Purification: Visuddhimagga.* 5th edn. Trans. Bhikkhu Ñāṇamoli. Kandy: Buddhist Publication Society.

Burlingame, Eugene Watson. 1990 (1921). *Buddhist Legends.* 3 vols. Cambridge, MA: Harvard University Press/Oxford: The Pali Text Society.

Carbine, Jason A. 2012. '*Sāsanasuddhi/Sīmāsammuti:* Comments on a Spatial Basis of the Buddha's Religion.' In Peter Skilling et al. (eds), *How Theravāda is Theravāda? Exploring Buddhist Identities*, 241–273. Chiang Mai: Silkworm Books.

Cate, Sandra. 2003. *Making Merit, Making Art: A Thai Temple in Wimbledon.* Honolulu: University of Hawaii Press.

Chirapravati, Pattaratorn. 2008. 'Illustrating the Lives of the Bodhisatta at Wat Si Chum'. In Peter Skilling et al. (eds), *Past Lives of the Buddha: Wat Si Chum; Art, Architecture and Inscriptions*, 13–39. Bangkok: River Books.

Cholvijarn, Jak. Forthcoming. 'Temiya and the Power of Silence in *Temiya Jātaka*'. *Mahāchulalongkorn Journal of Buddhist Studies.*

Collins, Steven 1998. *Nirvana and other Buddhist Felicities.* Cambridge: Cambridge University Press.

Collins, Steven (ed.). 2015. *The Vessantara Jātaka: Columbia Readings of Buddhist Literature.* New York: Columbia University Press.

Cone, Margaret. 2001–. *A Dictionary of Pāli*. 2 vols with more forthcoming. Bristol: The Pali Text Society.

——— and Richard F. Gombrich. 2011 (1977). *The Perfect Generosity of Prince Vessantara*. 2nd edn. Bristol: The Pali Text Society (1st edn. Oxford: Clarendon Press).

Coomaraswamy, Ananda K. 1979. *Mediaeval Sinhalese Art*. 3rd edn. New York: Pantheon.

Coulson, Michael. 1981. *Three Sanskrit Plays: Kālidāsa*. Harmondsworth, Middlesex: Penguin.

Cousins, L. S. 1983. 'Pali Oral Literature.' In P. Denwood and A. Piatigorsky (eds), *Buddhist Studies Ancient and Modern*, 1–11. London: Curzon Press.

———. 1996. 'Good or Skilful? *Kusala* in Canon and Commentary'. *Journal of Buddhist Ethics* 3: 136–64 and http://www.buddhistethics.org/3/cousins1.pdf.

———. 1999. 'Supreme Qualities: The Development of the Lists of Four, Six and Ten Pārami(tā)s'. Paper presented at the 12th Conference of the International Association of Buddhist Studies, Lausanne.

Cowell, E. B. (ed.; several translators). 1895–1907. *The Jātaka, or Stories of the Buddha's Former Births*. 6 vols. Cambridge: Cambridge University Press.

Crosby, Kate. 2014. *Theravāda Buddhism: Continuity, Diversity and Identity*. Chichester: Wiley Blackwell.

Dante Alighieri. 1805. *Divina Commedia*. Trans. H. F. Cary. Project Gutenberg. http://www.gutenberg.org/files/8800/8800-h/8800-h.htm.

Dante Alighieri. 1993. *The Divine Comedy (Divina Commedia)*. Trans. D. Higgins. Oxford: Oxford University Press.

DeCaroli, Robert. 2004. *Haunting the Buddha: Indian Popular Religions and the Formation of Buddhism*. Oxford and New York: Oxford University Press.

Dhammika, Ven. 2015. *Nature and the Environment in Early Buddhism*. Singapore: Buddha Dhamma Mandala Society.

Dutoit, Julius (trans.). 1908–21. *Jātakam: Das Buch der Erzählungen aus früheren Existenzen Buddhas*. 7 vols. Leipzig: Lotus.

Edgerton, Franklin. 1953. *Buddhist Hybrid Sanskrit Grammar and Dictionary*. 2 vols. New Haven: Yale University Press.

Ehara, N. R. M., Soma Thera, and Kheminda Thera (trans.). 1977. *The Path of Freedom by the Arahant Upatissa: Vimuttimagga*. Kandy: Buddhist Publication Society.

Eoseewong, Nidhi. 2005. *Pen and Sail: Literature and History in Early Bangkok*. Chiang Mai: Silkworm Books.

Fausbøll, V. (ed.). 1877–96. *The Jātaka Together with its Commentary, being Tales of the Anterior Births of Gotama Buddha*. 6 vols. London: Trübner and Co.

Geen, Jonathan. Forthcoming. 'Nārada, Non-Violence and False Avatāras in the Hindu and Jaina Traditions'. In Peter Flügel and Olle Qvarnström (eds), *Jaina Narratives*. SOAS Jaina Studies Series, Routledge.

Gehman, H. (trans.). 1974. *Petavatthu: Stories of the Departed. London: Pali Text Society.*

Geiger, Wilhelm. 1943. *Pāli Literature and Language*. Trans. B. Ghosh. Calcutta: Calcutta University.

Gerini, G. E. 1976 (1892). *A Retrospective View and Account of the Origin of the Thet Mahâ Ch'at Ceremony*. Bangkok: Sathirakoses-Nagapradipa Foundation.

Gethin, Rupert. 1998. *Foundations of Buddhism*. Oxford: Oxford University Press.

Ginsburg, Henry. 1989. *Thai Manuscript Painting*. London: British Library.

Gombrich, Richard F. 1985. 'The Vessantara Jātaka, the Rāmāyaṇa and the Dasaratha Jātaka'. *Journal of the American Oriental Society* 105/3: 427–37.

———. 1988. *Theravāda Buddhism: a Social History from Benares to Modern Colombo*. London: Routledge.

———. 1996. *How Buddhism Began: The Conditioned Genesis of the Early Teachings*. London and Atlantic Highlands, NJ: Athlone Press.

———. 2012. *What the Buddha Thought*. London: Equinox.

Gomez, Luis O. 1996. *The Land of Bliss: the Paradise of the Buddha of Measureless Light; Sanskrit and Chinese Versions of the Sukhāvatīvuyha Sūtras*. Honolulu: University of Hawaii Press.

Green, Alexandra. 2002. *Burma: Art and Archaeology*. London: British Museum Press.

———. Forthcoming. *Felicity, Power, and Piety: Essays on Late Burmese Wall Paintings*.

Grey, Leslie. 2000. *A Concordance of Buddhist Birth Stories*. 3rd edn. Oxford: The Pali Text Society.

Hallisey, Charles. 2010. 'Moral Creativity in Theravāda Buddhist Ethics'. In A. Pandian and D. Ali (eds), *Ethical Life in South Asia*, 141–52. Bloomington: University of Indiana Press.

Handlin, Lilian. 2010. 'The many Vidhura(s) in Myanmar's Past', *Bulletin of the Burma Studies Group* 85: 14–30.

———. 2012. 'The King and his Bhagavā: The Meanings of Pagan's Early Theravādas'. In Peter Skilling et al. (eds), *How Theravāda is Theravāda? Exploring Buddhist Identities*, 165–236. Chiang Mai: Silkworm Books.

Harischandra, D. V. J. 1998. *Psychiatric Aspects of Jātaka Stories*. Galle, Sri Lanka: Upuli Printers.

Härtel, Herbert. 1993. *Excavations at Sonkh: Two Thousand Five Hundred Years of a Town in Mathura*. Berlin: D. Reimer.

Harvey, Peter. 2000. *An Introduction to Buddhist Ethics: Foundations, Values and Issues*. Cambridge: Cambridge University Press.

———. 2013. *An Introduction to Buddhism: Teachings, History and Practice*. 2nd edn. Cambridge: Cambridge University Press.

Holt, John Clifford. 1996. *The Religious World of Kīrti Śrī: Buddhism, Art and Politics in Late Medieval Sri Lanka*. Oxford and New York: Oxford University Press.

Homer. 2004. *The Odyssey*. Trans. A. S. Kline. http://www.poetryintranslation.com/PITBR/Greek/Odhome.htm.

Horner, I. B. (trans.) 1952. *The Book of the Discipline*. Vol. 5. London: The Pali Text Society.

Horner, I. B. (trans.) 2000 (1975). *The Minor Anthologies of the Pali Canon, Part III: Chronicle of the Buddhas (Buddhavaṃsa) and Basket of Conduct (Cariyāpiṭaka)*. Oxford: The Pali Text Society.

Huang, Jo-Fan. 2006. 'A Technical Examination of 7 Thai Manuscripts in the 18th, 19th, and 20th Centuries.' Harvard University. http://cool.conservation-us.org/anagpic/2006pdf/2006ANAGPIC_Huang.pdf.

Huxley, Andrew. 1997. 'The Traditions of Mahosadha: Legal Reasoning from Northern Thailand.' *Bulletin of the School of Oriental and African Studies*. 60/2: 315–26.

Jacobi, Hermann (trans.). 1895. *Gaina Sûtras, Part II*. Oxford: Clarendon Press.

Jacobi, Hermann. 1960. *The Rāmāyaṇa*. Trans. S. N. Ghosal. Baroda: Oriental Institute.

Jaini, Padmanabh S. (ed.) 1981–3. *Paññāsajātaka*. 2 vols. London: The Pali Text Society.

Jayawickrama, N. A. (trans.). 1990. *The Story of Gotama Buddha: The Nidāna-kathā of the Jātakaṭṭhakathā*. Oxford: The Pali Text Society.

Jones, John G. 2000 (1979). *Tales and Teachings of the Buddha: The Jātaka Stories in Relation to the Pāli Canon*. 2nd edn. Christchurch, New Zealand: Cybereditions (1st edn London: George Allen & Unwin).

Jones, J. J. (trans.). 1949–56. *The Mahāvastu*. 3 vols. London: Luzac and Co.

Karunaratne, David (trans.). 1962. *Ummagga Jātaka: The Story of the Tunnel; translated from the Sinhalese*. Colombo: Gunasena and Company.

Keown, Damien. 1992. *The Nature of Buddhist Ethics*. Basingstoke: Macmillan.

Khoroche, Peter (trans.). 1989. *Once the Buddha was a Monkey: Ārya Śūra's Jātakamālā*. Chicago and London: The University of Chicago Press.

King James Bible. 1611. The Official King James Bible Online. http://www.kingjamesbibleonline.org

Lefferts, Leedom and Sandra Cate. 2012. *Buddhist Storytelling in Thailand and Laos: The Vessantara Jataka Scroll at the Asian Civilisations Museum*. Singapore: Asian Civilisations Museum.

Legge, James. (trans.). 1886. *A Record of Buddhistic Kingdoms*. Oxford: Clarendon Press.

Leksukhum, Santi and Giles Mermet (photographs). 2001. *Temples of Gold: Seven Centuries of Thai Buddhist Paintings*. London: Thames and Hudson.

Luce, G. H. 1956. 'The 550 Jātakas of Old Burma'. *Artibus Asiae* 19: 291–307.

———. 1969. *Old Burma: Early Pagan*. Locus Valley, NY: Artibus Asiae and the Institute of Fine Arts, New York University.

Machiavelli. 2006. *The Prince*. Trans. W. K. Marriott. Project Gutenberg. http://www.gutenberg.org/catalog/world/readfile?fk_files=3581155

Malalasekera, G. P. 1997 (1938, 1960). *Dictionary of Pāli Proper Names*. 2 or 3 vols. Oxford: The Pali Text Society. See also http://www.palikanon.com/english/pali_names/dic_idx.html. [References are to term rather than page number, to enable use of the different editions.]

Masefield, Peter (trans.). 1989. *Vimāna Stories (Vimānavatthu)*. Bristol: The Pali Text Society.

Maung, U Win. 2012. 'The Evolution of Stūpas in Myanmar'. *Collected Papers, the International Seminar on the Preservation and Protection of Buddhist Cultural Heritage*: 48–68. Yangon, Myanmar: Sitagu International Academy.

McGill, Forrest. 1997. 'Painting the "Great Life"'. In Juliane Schober (ed.), *Sacred Biography in the Buddhist Traditions of South and Southeast Asia*, 195–217. Honolulu: University of Hawaii Press.

McHugh, James. 2012. *Sandalwood and Carrion: Smell in Indian Religion and Culture*. Oxford: Oxford University Press.

Meiland, Justin. 2004. *Buddhist Values in the Pāli Jātakas, with Particular Reference to the Theme of Renunciation*. D.Phil. Thesis, University of Oxford.

Meiland, Justin (trans.). 2005. *Maha-bharata IX: Shalya*. Vol. 1. Clay Sanskrit Library. New York: New York University Press and the JJC Foundation.

Milton, John. 1971. *Paradise Lost*. Edited by Alastair Fowler. London: Longman Group Limited.

Moačanin, Klara Gönc. 2009. 'Epic vs. Buddhist Literature: The case of *Vidhurapaṇḍitajātaka*'. In Petteri Koskikallio (ed.), *Parallels and Comparisons: Proceedings of the Fourth Dubrovnoik International Conference on the Sanskrit Epics and Purāṇas*, 373–98. Zagreb: Croation Academy of Sciences and Arts.

Monier-Williams, Monier. 1899. *A Sanskrit-English Dictionary*. Oxford: Clarendon Press.

Moore, Elizabeth H. and Hänsjorg Mayer. 1999. *Shwedagon: Golden Pagoda of Myanmar*. London: Thames and Hudson.

Müller, F. Max and Bunyiu Nanjio. 1883. *Sukhāvatīvuyha Sūtra: Description of Sukhāvatī, the Land of Bliss*. Oxford: Clarendon Press.

Murphy, Steven A. 2010. *The Buddhist Boundary Markers of Northeast Thailand and Central Laos 7th–12th Centuries CE: Towards an Understanding of the Archaeological, Religious and Artistic Landscapes of the Khorat Plateau*. Ph.D. dissertation, School of Oriental and African Studies, London (available online on SOAS Library site).

Nabar, Vrinda and Shanta Tumkur. 1997. *The Bhagavad Gītā*. Crib Street Ware, Hertforshire: Wordsworth Classic Series.

Ñāṇamoli, Bhikkhu, and Bhikkhu Bodhi (trans.). 2009. *The Middle Length Discourses of the Buddha: A Translation of the Majjhima Nikāya*. 3rd edn. Boston: Wisdom Publications.

Norman, K. R. 1983. *Pāli Literature: Including the Canonical Literature in Prakrit and Sanskrit of All the Hīnayāna Schools of Buddhism*. Wiesbaden: Harrowitz.

———. 1991. *Selected Papers*. Vol. 2. Oxford: The Pali Text Society.

Norman, K. R. (trans.). 1995. *The Group of Discourses (Sutta-Nipāta)*. 3 vols. Oxford: The Pali Text Society.

Nyanasampanno, Maha Boowa. 1976. *The Venerable Phra Acharn Mun Bhūridatta Thera: Meditation Master*. Bangkok: Mahamakut Rajavidyalaya Press.

Oberlies, Thomas. 2002. 'A Study of the *Campeyya Jātaka*, Including Remarks on the Text of the *Saṅkhapāla Jātaka*'. *Journal of the Pali Text Society* 9: 115–46.

Obeyesekere, Ranjini. 2009. *Yasodharā, the Wife of the Bodhisattva: The Sinhala Yasodharāvata and the Sinhala Yasodharāpadānaya*. New York: State University of New York Press.

———. 2013. *The Revered Book of Five Hundred and Fifty Jātaka Stories (Translated from the 14th Century Sinhala Version)*. Colombo: Gunasena and Company.

Olivelle, Patrick. 1993. *The Āśrama System: The History and Hermeneutics of a Religious Institution*. New York: Oxford University Press.

Oxford Buddha Vihāra. c. 2010. *Morning Chanting and the Dhammacakkapavattana Sutta*. Oxford.

Pannavamsa Sengpan. 2007a. 'Recital of the Tham Vessantara-Jātaka: A Social Cultural Phenomenon in Kengtung, Eastern Shan State, Myanmar'. In K. Crosby (ed.), *The Book of Papers from Shan Buddhism and Culture Conference*. London: School of Oriental and African Studies.

———. 2007b. 'A Critical Study of the *Vessantara-Jātaka* and its Influence on Kengtung Buddhism, Eastern Shan State, Myanmar.' Doctoral Dissertation. University of Kelaniya, Sri Lanka.

Parry, Adam. 1964. 'The Language of Achilles'. In G.S. Kirk, *The Language and Background of Homer: Some Recent Studies and Controversies*. Cambridge: Heffer.

Perera, M. D. R. 1976. *The Sage of India, or the Mahā-Ummagga Jātaka*. Colombo: State Printing Corporation.

Peris, Merlin. 1978. 'The Tunnel Maker and the Labyrinth Builder.' In S. Paranavitana, L. Prematilleka, and J. Engelberta van Lohuizen-de Leeu (eds). *Senarat Paranavitana Commemoration Volume*, 145–65. Leiden: Brill.

Pollock, Sheldon I. (trans.). 1986. *The Rāmāyaṇa of Vālmīki, Volume II, Ayodhyākāṇḍa*. Princeton NJ: Princeton University Press.

Rajadhon, Phraya Anuman. 2009. *Essays on Thai Folklore*. 3rd edn. Bangkok: Institute of Thai Studies, Chulalongkorn University.

Reynolds, Craig J. 2006. *Seditious Histories: Contesting Southeast Asian Pasts*. Singapore: NUS Press.

Rhys Davids, C. A. F. (trans.). 1929. *Stories of the Buddha, Being Selections from the Jataka*. London: Chapman and Hall.

Rhys Davids, T. W. (trans.). 1925 (1880). *Buddhist Birth-Stories (Jataka Tales): The Commentarial Introduction Entitled Nidāna-kathā, The Story of the Lineage*. New and revised edn by C. A. F. Rhys Davids. London and New York: Routledge and Dutton.

Rhys Davids, T. W. and William Stede. 1921–5. *Pali-English Dictionary*. London: The Pali Text Society.

Roebuck, Valerie (trans.). 2010. *The Dhammapada.* Global Classics series. London: Penguin.

Roveda, Vittorio and Sothon Yem. 2009. *Buddhist Painting in Cambodia.* Bangkok: River Books.

Samatha Trust. 2008. *Chanting Book.* Llangunllo, Powys, UK: Samatha Trust.

Schiefner, A. 1876. 'Kandjur'. *Indische Erzahlungen (Melanges Asiatiques)* 7.

Schlingloff, Dieter. 1987. Studies in the Ajanta Paintings: Identifications and Interpretations. Delhi: Ajanta Publications.

Shakespeare, William. 1951. *The Complete Works.* Ed. Peter Alexander. London and Glasgow: Collins.

Shaw, Sarah (trans.). 2006a. *The Jātakas: Birth Stories of the Bodhisatta.* New Delhi: Penguin.

Shaw, Sarah. 2006b. *Buddhist Meditation: An Anthology of Texts from the Pāli Canon.* London: Routledge.

———. 2010. 'And That Was I: How the Buddha Himself Creates a Path between Biography and Autobiography'. In Linda Covill, Ulrike Roesler, and Sarah Shaw (eds), *Lives Lived, Lives Imagined: Biography in the Buddhist Traditions*, 15–47. Boston: Wisdom Publications.

———. 2012a. 'Picturing the *Mahājanaka Jātaka*'. *Collected Papers, the International Seminar on the Preservation and Protection of Buddhist Cultural* Heritage: 221–254. Yangon, Myanmar: Sitagu International Academy.

———. 2012b. 'Crossing to the Farthest Shore: How Pāli Jātakas Launch the Buddhist Image of the Boat onto the Open Seas'. *Journal of the Oxford Centre for Buddhist Studies* 3: 128–56.

———. 2013. 'Shipwrecks and Escapes from Drowning in Southern Buddhist Narrative and Art'. In Carl Thompson (ed.), *Shipwreck in Art and Literature: Images and Interpretations from Antiquity to the Present Day*. Abingdon, Oxon: Routledge.

———. 2014. 'Art and Narrative in Changing Conditions: Southern Buddhist Temple Art as an Accommodation of the New and Diverse'. In J. Hegewald (ed.), *In the Shadow of the Golden Age: Art and Identity from Gandhara to the Modern Age*. Berlin: EB-Verlag, Studies in Asian Art and Culture (SAAC) series: 227-56.

Shervanichkul, Arthid. 2008. 'Self-Sacrifice of the Kings in the Siṃhāsana Dvātriṃśikā and Thai Buddhist Narratives.' *Rian Thai: International Journal of Thai Studies* 1: 1–23.

Shin, Ba. 1962. *The Lokahteikpan. The Lokahteikpan.* Rangoon: Burma Historical Commission.

Silabhadra, Bhikkhu. 2000. 'The Influence of Buddhist Jātakas on Literature'. In D. C. Ahir (ed.), *The Influence of Jātakas on Art and Literature*: 73–81. New Delhi: BR Publishing Company.

Skilling, Peter. 2006a. 'Jātaka and Paññāsa-jātaka in South-East Asia'. *Journal of the Pali Text Society* 28: 113–73.

———. 2006b. 'The Antepenultimate Birth of the Śākyamuni'. Paper presented at the World Sanskrit Conference, Edinburgh.

Skilling, Peter (ed.). 2008. *Past Lives of the Buddha: Wat Si Chum; Art, Architecture and Inscriptions*. Bangkok: River Books.

Skilling, Peter. 2008 'Narrative, art and ideology: *Jātakas* from India to Sukhothai' and 'Illustrating the *Jātakas*: Wat Si Chum, Wat Khrua Wan and the Ananda temple compared'. In Peter Skilling et al. (eds), *Past Lives of the Buddha: Wat Si Chum; Art, Architecture and Inscriptions*, 59–104 and 105–10. Bangkok: River Books.

———. 2009. 'Pieces in the Puzzle: Sanskrit Literature in pre-Modern Siam.' In C. Cicuzza (ed.), *Buddhism and Buddhist Literature of South-east Asia: Selected papers*, 27–45. Materials for the study of the Tripiṭaka, Vol. 5, Lumbini International Research Institute, Bangkok and Lumbini: Fragile Palm Leaves Foundation.

———. 2012. 'King Rāma I and Wat Chetuphon: The Buddha-śāsanā in Early Bangkok.' In Peter Skilling et al. (eds), *How Theravāda is Theravāda? Exploring Buddhist Identities*, 297–352. Chiang Mai: Silkworm Books.

Söhnen, Renate. 1991. 'Indra and Women'. *Bulletin of the School of Oriental and African Studies* 54: 68–74.

Spenser, E. 1882 (1590). *Faerie Queene, The Complete Works in Verse and Prose of Edmund Spenser*. London: Grosart. Prepared by R. S. Bear 1993–6. http://darkwing.uoregon.edu/~rbear/fqintro.html.

Sponberg, Alan. 1992. 'Attitudes toward Women and the Feminine in Early Buddhism'. In José Ignacio Cabezón (ed.), *Buddhism, Sexuality and Gender*, 3–36. Albany NY: State University of New York Press.

Stadtner, Donald M. 2011. *Sacred Sites of Burma: Myth and Folklore in an Evolving Spiritual Realm*. Photography by Paisarn Piemmattawat. Bangkok: River Books.

Strachan, Paul. 1989. *Pagan: Art and Architecture of Old Burma*. Arran, Scotland: Kiscadale Publications.

Strong, John S. 1997. 'A Family Quest: The Buddha, Yaśodharā, and Rāhula in the Mūlasarvāstivāda Tradition.' In Juliane Schober (ed.), *Sacred Biography in the Buddhist Traditions of South and Southeast Asia*, 113–28. Honolulu: University of Hawaii Press.

Swearer, Donald K. 1995. 'Bimbā's Lament'. In Donald S. Lopez (ed.), *Buddhism in Practice*, 541-52. Princeton: Princeton University Press.

———. 2004. *Becoming the Buddha: The Ritual of Image Consecration in Thailand*. Princeton: Princeton University Press.

Tambiah, S. J. 1970. *Buddhism and the Spirit Cults in North-east Thailand. Cambridge:* Cambridge University Press.

Tayac, Sébastien. 2010. 'The order of Buddhist paintings in the monasteries of the province of Chiang Mai'. Unpublished doctoral dissertation. 3 vols. Paris: Sorbonne Nouvelle University.

Thompson, Stith. 1955–8. *Motif Index of Folk-Literature*. Revised and enlarged. Bloomington: University of Indiana Press. http://www.ruthenia.ru/folklore/thompson/.

Tiyavanich, Kamala. 1997. *Forest Recollections: Wandering Monks in Twentieth-Century Thailand*. Honolulu: University of Hawaii Press.

———. 2004. *The Buddha in the Jungle*. Seattle: University of Washington Press.

Trenckner, V. (ed.) 1997 (1880) *The Milindapañho*. Oxford: The Pali Text Society.

Tun, T. 1983. 'The Royal Order (Wednesday 28 January 1795) of King Badon'. *Journal of Asian and African Studies*, Institute for the Study of Languages and Cultures of Asia and Africa, Tokyo University of Foreign Studies, 26: 153–201.

van Beek, Steve and Luca Invernizzi Tettoni. 1991. *The Arts of Thailand*. Revised edn. London: Thames and Hudson.

Virgil. 2002. *The Aeneid*. Trans. A. S. Kline. http://www.poetryintranslation.com/PITBR/Latin/VirgilAeneidI.htm.

von Hinüber, Oskar. 1967. 'Pāli *ulloka-*'. *Kuhns Zeitschrift* 81: 247–53.

———. 1996. *A Handbook of Pāli Literature*. 2 vols. Berlin: Walter de Gruyter.

———. 1998. *Entstehung und Aufbau der Jātaka-Sammlung*. Akademie der Wissenschaften und der Literatur. Stuttgart: Franz Steiner Verlag.

Walshe, Maurice (trans.). 1995. *The Long Discourses of the Buddha: A Translation of the Dīgha Nikāya*. Boston: Wisdom Publications.

Warder, A. K. 1979. *Indian Buddhism*. Delhi: Motilal Banarsidas.

Williams, C. 1946. *The English Poems of John Milton*. London: Oxford University Press.

Winternitz, Moriz. 1977. *A History of Indian Literature*. Trans. Shilavati Ketkar and Helen Kohn. 2nd edn. New Delhi: Oriental Books Reprint Corporation.

Wongthet, Pranee. 1989. 'Jātaka Stories and the Laopuan Worldview'. *Asian Folklore Series* 48/1: 21–30.

Wray, Elizabeth, Clare Rosenfield, and Dorothy Bailey. 1996 (1972). *Ten Lives of the Buddha: Siamese Temple Painting and Jataka Tales*. New York and Tokyo: Weatherhill.

Yamazaki, M. and Y. Ousaka. 2003. *Index to the Jātaka*. Oxford: The Pali Text Society.

Yoe, Shway (George Scott). 1882/1989. *The Burman: His Life and Notions*. Arran, Scotland: Kiscadale Publications.

Index of Illustrations

Myanmar
- Ananda temple, Pagan 1.1–1.4, 2.1–2.3, 3.1–3.4, 4.3–4.6, 5.1–5.8, 6.1–6.8, 7.1–7.4, 8.1–8.2, 9.1–9.4, 10.1–10.8
- Hpetleik Stūpa C, 2.4
- Laung u Hmaw 2.6
- Lokamangin Temple, Monywe Town 5.20
- Minyegyi complex, Amyint Village 6.11
- Monywe complex, Salingyi 9.9
- *nāga* shrine, Yangon 6.10
- Payani temple, Pakhangyi 8.5
- Pokala temple, Shwezayan Village 3.5
- Powindaung caves 1.5, 10.11
- Shwedagon pagoda B, 1.6, 2.5, 3.6, 3.7, 4.2, 5.9–5.12, 6.9, 7.5, 8.3, 8.4, 9.5, 9.6, 10.9, 10.10
- Ywagyigone complex 4.1
- Zedidawdaik complex, Anein Village 7.9

Thailand
- *samut khoi* manuscript [Bodl. MS. Pali a. 27 (R)] 1.7, 1.8, 2.7, 2.8, 3.8, 3.9, 4.8, 4.9, 5.13, 5.14, 6.13, 6.14, 7.7, 7.8, 8.8, 8.9, 9.7, 9.8, 10.15, 10.16
- Vessantara festivals 10.29–10.33
- Wat Amphawan, Chiang Mai Province 9.13
- Wat Buak Khrok Luang, Chiang Mai Province 4.12, 5.17, 9.10, 9.11, 10.23–10.26
- Wat Chai Sathan, Chiang Mai Province 8.11
- Wat Chang Khong, Chiang Mai Province 1.11
- Wat Khrua Wan, Bangkok A
- Wat Kongkaram, Ratchaburi Province 8.6, 9.12
- Wat Makham No / Wat No Putthangkun, Suphanburi Province 2.9, 3.10, 5.15, 6.12, 7.11, 10.17, 10.18
- Wat Nak Prok, Bangkok 1.9, 1.10, 2.10, 2.11, 4.11, 5.18, 5.19, 6.15, 7.10, 8.7, 10.19
- Wat Phra Chao Lueam, Chiang Mai Province 5.21
- Wat Phra That Doi Kham, Chiang Mai Province 2.12
- Wat Ping Noi, Chiang Mai Province 10.12
- Wat Rang Si Sut Thawat, Chiang Mai Province 6.16
- Wat Rong San, Chiang Mai Province 3.14
- Wat Saen Luang, Chiang Mai Province 4.10
- Wat Saket, Bangkok 3.11, 3.12, 4.7, 4.13, 5.16, 10.13, 10.14, 10.20–10.22
- Wat Santon Mueang Nua, Chiang Mai Province 8.1

Thailand (*continued*)
Wat Si Koet, Chiang Mai Province 10.34
Wat Si Ping Mueang, Chiang Mai Province 10.28
Wat Si Soda, Chiang Mai Province 10.27
Wat Suan Dok, Chiang Mai Province 5.22
Wat Thung Yu, Chiang Mai Province 3.13, 7.6
Wat Ubosot, Chiang Mai Province 1.12
Wat Upakhut, Chiang Mai Province 4.14, 6.17

Index

Abhidhamma 147 n. 4, 156 n. 20, 159 n. 23, 188, 200–1, 337, 511, 517, 518, 530, 536 n. 18, 539 n. 25, 584 n. 137, 615 n. 215, 641
abhiññā, *see* higher knowledges
Act of Truth (*saccakiriya*) 19, 56, 86, 120, 135, 140–1, 420, 456–7, 529, 635, 641
adhiṭṭhāna, *see* resolve
Ajātasattu 396, 402, 424
Amarā 189, 191, 202, 213 n. 30, 243–51, 266, 275 n. 88, 333
Ānanda 8–10, 15, 116, 144, 162, 185, 394, 427, 453, 505
Ananda Temple, Pagan, ix, 39, 40
Aṅguttara Nikāya 15, 146 n. 3, 167 n. 40, 538 n. 23, 589 n. 148
Anuruddha 8–9, 144, 185, 505, 639

Bhaddaji 453
Bhaddakāpilānī 9, 144
Bherī 9, 10 n. 8, 21, 189, 199, 325–33, 550 n. 56
Bhūridatta-jātaka 3–5, 7, 10, 13, 24, 30, 36, 38, 44 n. 36, 46, 277 n. 90, 335–94, 427 n. 5, 516, 557 n. 71, 607 n. 202
Bimbā (Rāhulamātā, Yasodharā) 8–9, 20, 116, 333, 422, 505, 525 n. 12, 526–8, 636 n. 268, 639
Bimbisāra 396, 402, 428 n. 10
Bodhisatta
  the *bodhisatta* path 3–4, 14, 27, 30, 36, 40
  and friends and family 7–11, 18–21, 523–8
  as hero of *jātaka* stories 3–4, 28, 34–5, 188–9, 198–201, 340–1, 428
  and kingship 11–18, 53–5, 82–6, 121
  and the perfections 4–7, 38, 53, 81–3, 119, 148–53, 187–8, 338, 398–40, 423, 455–7, 507–16
  and the realms of rebirth 12, 21–4, 54–5, 153–9, 335–9, 426
Brahmā (god or gods) 15, 23, 29, 143, 159, 205, 339, 343, 383–4, 387–8, 423–4, 426–7, 429, 445, 446, 543, 579, 585, 594, 598, 616, 619, 620, 641
Brahmā realm/heavens, *see* heavens
brahma-faring (*brahmacariya*) 368, 575 n. 110, 576, 612, 641
brahmā-vihāras, *see* divine abidings
Brahminical tradition 28–30, 84–5, 338, 341, 344, 383–92, 397–8, 534
brahmins, nature and role of 10, 30, 52, 189, 338, 341–2, 344, 397–8, 510, 514, 518, 520–2, 534, 641
Buddha (Gotama) 1, 4–5, 8–11, 15, 17, 18, 27, 31, 33–5, 36, 40–1, 48, 83, 124, 146 n. 3, 201, 204 n. 16,

Buddha (Gotama) (*continued*)
335–6, 339, 345–7, 348, 395–6, 400–3, 408 n. 10, 424, 426–9, 510–11, 512, 515–6, 535–6, 641
buddhas
absence of during time of *jātakas* 165 n. 33, 378 n. 62, 394
Kassapa Buddha 176 n. 55, 435–6, 451 n. 65, 537–8
Metteya Buddha 532
as point of comparison 181, 209, 224, 230, 242, 459, 464, 481, 485, 493–4, 505
as suitable to be asked a difficult question 405, 433
Vipassī Buddha 537–8
Buddhaghosa (commentator) 17, 33 n. 28, 38, 147 n. 4, 424, 512 n. 2
buddhahood 3, 4–7, 12, 14, 16–18, 42, 55, 82, 393 n. 101, 459, 509–10, 525, 527, 604

cakkavattin, *see* Universal Monarch
Candakumāra-jātaka 3, 5, 6, 9, 11, 12–13, 20, 22, 28, 30, 35, 390 n. 93, 395–422, 457, 513, 635 n. 263
Cariyāpiṭaka 4–6, 53, 119, 149, 151, 399–400, 513, 517, 545 n. 42
Channa 505 n. 74, 524, 639
Ciñcamānavikā 639

dāna, *see* generosity
determination, *see* resolve
deva, *devatā*, *see* gods
Devadatta 3, 5, 8, 10, 277 n. 90, 333, 342 n. 4, 394, 395–7, 401, 402–4, 408 n. 10, 422, 427, 453, 595 n. 180, 639
Dhammapada 24–5, 28, 163 n. 30, 357 n. 28, 397, 610 n. 208
Dhammapāla (commentator) 17 n. 16, 38, 152 n. 16
Dīgha Nikāya xv, 17 n. 16, 32, 147, 157, 167 n. 37, 204 n. 17, 235 n. 49, 286 n. 96, 345, 346, 394 n. 103, 424, 519 n. 10, 537 n. 20, 540 n. 29, 545 n. 43, 556 n. 69
divine abidings (*brahmā-vihāras*) 7, 15, 72, 147, 156 n. 20, 163, 184, 200, 642

energy, *see* vigour
equanimity (*upekkhā*) 5, 7, 15, 18, 27, 33, 34, 147, 152, 156 n. 20, 200, 423–4, 513, 521, 606, 642, 643

forbearance, patience (*khanti*) 5, 7, 110, 395–6, 399, 463, 642
Formless realms, *see* heavens

gandhabba 462–3, 465, 642
garuḷa, *garuḍa* (or *supaṇṇa*) 24, 337, 339 n. 3, 340, 341, 345, 346 n. 13, 364–8, 372, 376, 459–63, 471, 505, 642, 643
generosity, giving (*dāna*) 5–7, 14, 19, 22, 23, 28, 29, 31, 33–4, 45, 74, 97, 123, 143, 146–52, 158–9, 160–1, 164–7, 177–81, 183–4, 194, 201 n. 10, 204 n. 17, 348, 398–9, 434, 438, 443, 447, 451–2, 460, 486, 493 n. 66, 496, 499, 508–19, 521, 524–6, 534, 538, 541, 544, 550, 554, 558, 560–1, 566–7, 595, 597, 599, 604, 616–21, 634, 639, 641, 642
gods (*devas*, *devatās*), *see* Brahmā, goddesses, heavens, Mātali, Sakka, Vissakamma
goddesses 8–9, 19, 23–4, 38, 55, 59, 79, 82–3, 90–2, 116, 118, 120–1, 135–6, 141, 143, 175, 177, 191, 196, 199, 249, 251, 253–5, 260, 324, 475, 529, 622
good conduct, *see* morality

Heaven of the Thirty-Three (Tāvatiṃsa), *see* heavens
heavens 12, 21–4, 26, 29, 38, 56, 58, 78, 101 n. 42, 118, 145–62, 163 n. 29, 164, 168–9, 175–84, 299, 338–40, 357, 360, 385, 394, 395, 404–5, 408–9, 412–13, 418, 421, 428, 440, 444, 451, 473–4, 489, 502, 505, 510–13, 522, 538 n. 24, 541, 616, 619–22, 633, 636, 639, 641–3
  Brahmā realms/heavens 15, 23, 53, 54, 78, 109, 116, 126–7, 145, 146, 148, 152, 159–60, 163–4, 166, 184, 205, 369, 446, 452, 460, 543, 606, 633 n. 258, 641
  false routes to 11, 13, 150, 384–5, 386–92, 390 n. 93, 398–9, 405, 408–9, 412–3, 418, 489, 597
  formless realms/heavens 23, 101 n. 42
  Heaven of the Thirty-Three (Tāvatiṃsa) 22, 56, 146, 150, 155, 156 n. 21, 161, 164, 168, 182, 206, 209, 218 n. 38, 269 n. 80, 338–9, 340, 343, 356, 385 n. 77, 404, 413 n. 15, 442, 444, 459, 461, 473, 473 n. 34, 510–11, 536 n. 18, 539 n. 25, 541, 550, 583 n. 128, 589 n. 148, 616, 636, 642
  kamma leading to 20, 22, 53, 72, 82, 114–5, 121, 123, 135–6, 142–3, 145–162, 164–9, 175–84, 338, 357, 360, 378, 384–5, 394, 421, 433, 444, 451, 456, 512–3, 522, 597, 620–1, 639
  lifespans in 22, 26, 86–8, 444, 537, 538, 541
  Sense-sphere 23, 38, 53–4, 78, 151, 203, 230, 299, 336, 474 n. 35, 489, 616 n. 221, 633
  Tusita 12, 18, 34, 385 n. 77, 474, 511, 512–13, 536 n. 18, 621 n. 239, 639 n. 271
hells 11, 12, 22–3, 26, 27, 38, 54–5, 56, 58–62, 69, 71–2, 101, 121, 134–5, 139, 146–7, 150, 153–7, 159–62, 164, 166, 169–75, 203, 212, 236, 239, 246, 338, 343, 360, 368, 396–7, 398, 405, 408–9, 411, 421, 426, 428, 433, 435, 440–1, 443, 448–52, 486, 491, 510, 620
higher knowledges (*abhiññā*) 53, 54–5, 72, 78, 109, 116, 143, 369, 459, 535, 642

Indapatta 457, 459, 470, 494, 501
Indra, Inda, *see* Sakka

Janaka outside the *Janaka-jātaka* 28–9, 83–6, 184
Janaka-jātaka 3, 5, 7, 11, 12–13, 17, 18–20, 22, 24, 25, 27, 28–9, 33, 36–8, 46, 54, 81–116, 120, 191, 199, 265 n. 76, 525, 559 n. 75, 574 n. 109, 613 n. 213
Jātaka-atthavaṇṇanā 1–5, 9, 18, 21, 28, 30, 47–8, 54, 120, 396, 401, 456, 461 n. 7, 468 n. 22
Jātakamālā 29, 428
Jātaka-nidāna 4–6, 53, 149, 151, 187, 370 n. 48, 399, 457, 512, 516, 536 n. 19, 639 n. 271
Jeta Grove 55, 86, 122–4, 204, 348, 458
Jetuttara 537, 541, 543, 545, 560, 569, 598, 614, 622, 637, 638
jhāna 15, 17, 23, 27, 78 n. 46, 146, 147, 149, 159, 201, 218 n. 38, 337, 424, 442 n. 51, 512 n. 2, 517 n. 6, 518 n. 9, 535, 536 n. 19, 642; *see also* meditation; *samatha*

Kapilavatthu 510, 516, 535
karma, *kamma* 20, 22, 54, 58, 110, 129, 147, 156, 160, 166, 169–77,

karma, *kamma* (*continued*)
180–1, 190, 199, 382, 393 n. 101, 423, 425–8, 435–6, 438, 440, 441, 444, 525, 642
Khaṇḍahāla-jātaka, see *Candakumāra-jātaka*
khanti, *see* forbearance
Khemā 116, 538
kingship 11–18, 22, 23, 27, 37, 40, 54–5, 82–6, 121, 148–9, 457, 524–5, 545 n. 43
kinnara, *kinnarī* 128, 130, 132, 290, 553, 572, 643
Kusināra 15

loving-kindness (*mettā*) 5, 7, 15, 16, 26, 33, 34, 117, 119–20, 127, 131 n. 26, 147, 156, 159, 161, 194, 200, 201 n. 10, 263, 445, 508, 519, 575, 642–3

Magadha 324, 424, 428, 441, 443
Mahābhārata 28–9, 84, 108 n. 53, 345 n. 12, 384 n. 72, 451 n. 65, 455, 457–8, 481 n. 46, 481 n. 47, 585 n. 139, 625 n. 245
Mahājanaka-jātaka, see *Janaka-jātaka*
Mahākassapa 9, 144, 422
Mahāmāyā 8–9, 333, 422, 537, 538, 539 n. 25, 639
Mahānāradakassapa-jātaka, see *Nārada-jātaka*
Mahāpajāpatī Gotamī 538 n. 23
Mahā-Ummagga-jātaka, see *Mahosadha-jātaka*
Mahāvastu 117–19, 128 n. 17
Mahosadha-jātaka (*Mahā-Ummagga-jātaka*) 3, 5, 7, 9, 10 n. 8, 13, 15, 16, 19, 21, 24, 27, 36, 40, 43, 46, 47, 49, 54, 187–333, 341, 342, 343, 518, 525, 542, 551 n. 56, 574 n. 108, 607 n. 202
Majjhima Nikāya xv, 32 n. 27, 145 n. 2, 153 n. 18, 185 n. 59, 205 n. 19, 347, 357 n. 30, 605 n. 200
manuscripts
of the *jātakas* xv, 3, 47–8, 203, 539 n. 25
illustrated with *jātakas* x, 44, 51, 83, 162, 277 n. 90, 326 n. 152, 543 n. 37
Mātali 8, 22, 28, 146, 155, 158, 160, 167–85
meditation 13–14, 17, 20, 23, 27, 32–3, 53–5, 78, 83, 109, 110, 116, 119, 120, 121, 122–3, 145–9, 152, 159–60, 162, 165 n. 33, 167 n. 40, 201, 337, 343, 369, 424, 442 n. 51, 512, 525, 616 n. 221, 630, 642–3; see also *jhāna*; *samatha*
mettā, *see* loving-kindness
Mithilā 6, 25, 29, 82, 84–5, 86–92, 101, 108, 112, 116, 147, 158, 162–3, 167–8, 179, 183, 184, 189, 192, 198, 202, 205, 206, 229, 230, 266–71, 281–3, 288, 293–4, 310–15, 318, 322, 429, 448
Moggallāna 8–9, 116, 394, 422, 505
morality, good conduct, virtue (*sīla*) 5, 7, 17 n. 16, 23, 31, 33–4, 56, 100, 147, 149–51, 162, 164, 167, 181, 190, 198–200, 289, 336, 338, 339 n. 3, 342–3, 364–70, 394, 451, 458, 460, 501, 504, 512 n. 2, 643
Mūgapakkha-jātaka, see *Temiya-jātaka*
Myanmar ix-x, 17, 30–1, 35–41, 45–6, 203 n. 13, 204, 345, 532–3; *see also* Ananda Temple; Shwedagon Pagoda

nāga 8, 20, 24, 38, 45, 131–2, 137, 151 n. 14, 335–94, 455–8, 459–68, 471, 489, 491, 494–505, 557 n. 71, 642–3

Nārada outside the *Nārada-jātaka* 23, 29, 85, 109–10, 116, 616, 619
Nārada-jātaka 3, 5, 7, 8, 10, 13, 15, 16, 20, 23, 29, 85, 333 n. 163, 339, 343, 423–53, 580 n. 121
nekkhamma, *see* renunciation
Nemi-jātaka 5, 6, 12, 13, 16, 22, 26, 28, 38, 46, 53, 54, 85, 86, 145–85, 199, 343, 450 n. 64, 513
Nimi-jātaka, see *Nemi-jātaka*
nibbāna 22, 60 n. 13, 81, 83, 142 n. 41, 165 n. 33, 538, 641, 643

paccekabuddha 37, 82, 85, 96, 99, 100, 107, 145 n. 1, 378 n. 62, 433, 511, 574, 643
paññā, *see* wisdom
Paññāsa Jātaka 38, 203
pāramī, *pāramitā*, *see* perfections
paritta 52, 68 n. 23, 205 n. 19 345, 346, 643
past-life memory 54–5, 58, 69, 71, 146, 335–6, 423–4, 427, 435, 438, 441–3, 642
patience, *see* forbearance
perfections (*pāramī*, *pāramitā*) 3, 4–7, 11, 16, 17 n. 16, 22, 23, 26, 27, 28, 33–5, 38, 41, 42, 45, 53, 55–6, 65 n. 17, 65 n. 19, 81, 87, 119, 120, 149, 150, 151–3, 160, 187–8, 194, 204, 338, 343, 369–70, 395, 398–9, 423, 455, 456–7, 458, 487, 509, 513, 516, 520, 524, 532, 595, 599, 617, 634; *see also individual perfections*

Rāhula 8–9, 116, 422, 505, 527, 639
Rāhulamātā, *see* Bimbā
Rājagaha 385 n. 78, 428 n. 8, 441, 469, 535
renunciation (*nekkhamma*) 1, 5, 6, 11–18, 20, 26, 29, 33–5, 36, 37, 53–4, 55, 70, 76, 81–6, 99 n. 38, 109, 111, 116, 121, 122–3, 128, 145–9, 151–2, 160, 163, 185, 348, 512, 525, 604 n. 196, 643
resolve, determination (*adhiṭṭhāna*) 4–7, 12, 33–5, 51, 53–5, 59, 70, 82–3, 100, 136, 152, 336, 340, 341, 357, 358, 369, 370, 435, 457, 487, 519, 527, 537, 604 n. 197, 641

sacca, see truth, truthfulness
saccakiriya, *see* Act of Truth
Sakka (Inda, Vāsava) 8–10, 13, 22–4, 28, 56, 66–7, 72, 77, 85 n. 6, 87–8, 98, 101, 118, 127–8, 144, 146–7, 150, 160–2, 164–8, 175, 181–5, 187, 202, 205, 206, 218–19, 221, 241, 259, 262, 276, 299, 313, 338, 339, 340, 356–7, 358, 359 n. 33, 361, 380, 385, 386, 390, 393, 401, 413 n. 15, 420, 442, 443 n. 52, 444, 460–3, 469, 473 n. 34, 480, 505, 509, 511, 515, 517–19, 521–3, 526, 528, 535, 538–41, 543, 550, 556, 558 n. 72, 561 n. 81, 573–4, 580 n. 121, 616–22, 633, 638–9, 642–4
Sāma-jātaka 3, 5, 7, 9, 11, 13–16, 19, 22–3, 26, 28, 33, 36–7, 45, 117–43, 194, 199, 208 n. 22, 340, 370 n. 49, 456, 529, 557 n. 70, 575 n. 111, 602 n. 193, 618 n. 228
samatha 17, 20, 32, 152, 643; see also *jhāna*, meditation
Saṃyutta Nikāya 18, 124 n. 8, 146 n. 3, 205 n. 19, 535 n. 16, 537 n. 20, 620 n. 234, 620 n. 235
Sāriputta 8–9, 79, 116, 333, 394, 396, 422, 427, 453, 505, 639
Sāvatthi 122–4, 181, 204 n. 16, 347
Shwedagon Pagoda x, 41
sīla, *see* morality

Sivi (king/kingdom) 288, 289, 290, 292, 451, 451 n. 65, 517–18, 530, 537, 539–41, 546–52, 555, 558–62, 565–7, 570–1, 579, 581, 586–7, 598, 600–1, 612, 616, 618, 622, 626–8, 631, 634–5, 637–9
Suddhodhana 8–9, 333, 639
Sunakkhatta 8, 10, 394, 426–7, 453
supaṇṇa, see *garuḷa*
Suvaṇṇasāma-jātaka, see *Sāma-jātaka*

Tāvatiṃsa, *see* Heaven of the Thirty-Three
Temiya-jātaka (*Mūgapakkha-jātaka*) 3, 5, 6, 9, 11, 12–15, 18–20, 22–3, 28, 36, 43, 46, 51–79, 81, 82, 86, 120, 121, 127, 144 n. 42, 148, 150, 199, 208 n. 22, 338, 510, 543 n. 38, 545 n. 41
temple illustrations of *jātakas* ix-xi, 30–1, 33, 35–47, 51, 83, 146, 160, 161–2, 197, 202, 204, 335–6, 345, 507, 532–3, 536 n. 18, 543 n. 37, 607 n. 203
ten perfections, *see* perfections
truth, truthfulness (*sacca*) 5, 16, 33–5, 74, 120, 132–3, 140–1, 177, 199, 213, 255, 320, 343, 359, 388, 393 n. 101, 401, 420, 445, 447, 455–8, 475 n. 40, 477–9, 483, 496, 498, 635, 641; *see also* Act of Truth
Tusita, *see* heavens

Universal Monarch (*cakkavattin*) 15–16, 146–9, 167 n. 37, 202, 235 n. 49, 469, 503, 504, 512, 522, 545 n. 43, 562 n. 86, 621 n. 238, 634 n. 263, 643
upekkhā, *see* equanimity
uposatha 5, 7, 24, 31, 38, 56, 78, 90, 147, 158, 160, 164, 177–80, 229, 259, 336–40, 348, 356–61, 369, 375, 394, 435, 438–9, 456, 460–1, 503, 544, 644
Uppalavaṇṇā 8–9, 10 n. 8, 116, 144, 326 n. 152, 333, 394, 422, 538, 639
Uruvela Kassapa 426, 428–9, 453

Vārāṇasī 56, 70, 78, 126, 130–1, 143, 341, 348–52, 354, 358, 365, 371, 379, 381, 384 n. 73, 394, 404, 435, 459
Vessantara-jātaka 3, 5, 7, 11, 12, 14, 16, 19, 21–3, 26, 29 n. 21, 30, 32, 36–7, 40, 42–7, 49, 150, 187, 192–5, 208 n. 22, 275 n. 88, 340, 342, 343, 382 n. 68, 398–9, 507–639
Vidhura-jātaka (*Vidhurapaṇḍita-jātaka*) 3–5, 7, 13, 20, 24, 27, 29, 36–7, 43–7, 195, 252 n. 64, 455–505, 525, 541 n. 33, 557 n. 71, 625 n. 245
vigour, energy (*viriya*) 5, 7, 18, 27, 33, 81, 83–4, 433–4, 644
vinaya 398, 402, 405 n. 6, 641
viriya, *see* vigour
Vissakamma 22, 28, 66, 72, 78, 127, 208, 275 n. 88, 519, 573, 644
Visuddhimagga 17, 27, 159 n. 23, 163 n. 30, 423 n. 1, 424 n. 2, 512 n. 2, 604 n. 196, 616 n. 219

wisdom (*paññā*) 5, 7, 13, 18–19, 21, 27, 32, 33–5, 70, 98, 146 n. 3, 164 n. 31, 187–205, 207, 218, 226–7, 238–42, 250–3, 257, 260, 267, 271, 276, 307, 316, 319–20, 327, 333, 336–7, 343, 357, 386, 388, 452, 455, 457, 458–9, 462–3, 465–6, 482, 486, 492, 494–5, 498, 500–1, 504–5, 538 n. 23, 616 n. 220, 639, 643

yakkha, *yakkhinī* 24, 63, 93 n. 22, 176, 205, 214–15, 259, 305, 351, 359, 360, 420, 435 n. 34, 455, 459, 465–80, 488–95, 502–3, 509, 519, 569, 601, 605, 624, 644
Yasodharā, *see* Bimbā